Rethinking the Value of Humanity

Rethinking the Value of Humanity

Edited by
SARAH BUSS AND L. NANDI THEUNISSEN

OXFORD
UNIVERSITY PRESS

Oxford University Press is a department of the University of Oxford. It furthers
the University's objective of excellence in research, scholarship, and education
by publishing worldwide. Oxford is a registered trade mark of Oxford University
Press in the UK and certain other countries.

Published in the United States of America by Oxford University Press
198 Madison Avenue, New York, NY 10016, United States of America.

© Oxford University Press 2023

All rights reserved. No part of this publication may be reproduced, stored in
a retrieval system, or transmitted, in any form or by any means, without the
prior permission in writing of Oxford University Press, or as expressly permitted
by law, by license, or under terms agreed with the appropriate reproduction
rights organization. Inquiries concerning reproduction outside the scope of the
above should be sent to the Rights Department, Oxford University Press, at the
address above.

You must not circulate this work in any other form
and you must impose this same condition on any acquirer.

Library of Congress Cataloging-in-Publication Data
Names: Buss, Sarah, author. | Theunissen, L. Nandi, author.
Title: Rethinking the value of humanity / edited by Sarah Buss and Nandi Theunissen.
Description: New York, NY, United States of America : Oxford University Press, 2023. |
Includes bibliographical references and index.
Identifiers: LCCN 2022027422 (print) | LCCN 2022027423 (ebook) |
ISBN 9780197539361 (hardcover) | ISBN 9780197539385 (epub)
Subjects: LCSH: Respect for persons. | Humanity.
Classification: LCC BJ1533.R42 B87 2022 (print) |
LCC BJ1533.R42 (ebook) | DDC 179/.9—dc23/eng/20220815
LC record available at https://lccn.loc.gov/2022027422
LC ebook record available at https://lccn.loc.gov/2022027423

DOI: 10.1093/oso/9780197539361.001.0001

1 3 5 7 9 8 6 4 2

Printed by Integrated Books International, United States of America

Contents

Acknowledgments	vii
List of Contributors	ix

Introduction   1
Sarah Buss

1. Decomposing Humanity   24
Jon Garthoff

2. Do the Ancients See Value in Humanity?   48
Richard Bett

3. Spinoza's Anti-Humanism: Human Value and Dignity   74
Yitzhak Y. Melamed

4. Slavery, Freedom, and Human Value in Early Modern Philosophy   97
Julia Jorati

5. Valuing Humanity in "Common Life": Grotius and Pufendorf on Equal "Sociable" Dignity   127
Stephen Darwall

6. The Dignity of Humanity   153
Ralf M. Bader

7. Great Beyond All Comparison   181
Kenneth Walden

8. Fichte on the Value of Rational Agency   202
Michelle Kosch

9. Explaining the Value of Human Beings   225
L. Nandi Theunissen

10. Are We of Equal Moral Worth?   248
Andrea Sangiovanni

11. The Normative Significance of Humanity   273
Peter Railton

12. Finding the Humean Value in Humean Humanity   291
Don Garrett

vi CONTENTS

13. Other People 314
    Kieran Setiya

14. Learning from Love: Reasoning, Respect, and the
    Value of a Person 337
    Kyla Ebels-Duggan

15. The Invention of Value and the Value of Humanity 366
    Elijah Millgram

16. The Human Foundations of Our Political Ideals: An Essay on
    Gandhi's Political Radicalism 394
    Akeel Bilgrami

Index 425

Acknowledgments

We are grateful for all the help we received as we put together this collection. It all began with a conference Nandi organized at Johns Hopkins in which historians of philosophy presented a wide range of views philosophers have held on the value of humanity. Several of these talks were developed into papers that appear in this volume. We would like to thank Sara Magrin for helping us to review one of these papers early in the editing phase, the anonymous referees who reviewed our proposal for Oxford University Press, Stephen Harrop for helping us copy-edit the references, and Julia Jorati for additional advice when questions came up at this final stage. Our editor, Peter Ohlin, has been unfailingly supportive throughout the process. We could not have asked for more. Our partners, Ben and Hank, have been good-natured consultants on all sorts of matters—from the wording of a sentence to the design of the book's cover. We value their support beyond price. Most importantly, we wish to thank the contributors to this volume. We have learned so much from reading (and rereading!) their essays. We feel privileged to have been part of the discussions with them that extended over the past few years.

Contributors

Ralf M. Bader is a professor of philosophy at the Université de Fribourg, where he holds the Chair for Ethics and Political Philosophy.

Richard Bett is a professor of philosophy and classics at Johns Hopkins University.

Akeel Bilgrami is Sidney Morgenbesser Professor of Philosophy at Columbia University.

Sarah Buss is a professor of philosophy at the University of Michigan.

Stephen Darwall is Andrew Downey Orrick Professor of Philosophy at Yale University.

Kyla Ebels-Duggan is an associate professor of philosophy at Northwestern University.

Don Garrett is Silver Professor of Philosophy at New York University.

Jon Garthoff is a professor of philosophy at the University of Tennessee.

Julia Jorati is a professor of philosophy at the University of Massachusetts, Amherst.

Michelle Kosch is a professor of philosophy at Cornell University.

Yitzhak Y. Melamed is Charlotte Bloomberg Professor of Philosophy at Johns Hopkins University.

Elijah Millgram is E.E. Ericksen Distinguished Professor of Philosophy at the University of Utah.

Peter Railton is Gregory S. Kavka Distinguished University Professor and John Stephenson Perrin Professor of Philosophy at the University of Michigan.

Andrea Sangiovanni is a professor of philosophy at Kings College London.

Kieran Setiya is a professor of philosophy at the Massachusetts Institute of Technology.

L. Nandi Theunissen is an associate professor of philosophy at the University of Pittsburgh.

Kenneth Walden is an associate professor of philosophy at Dartmouth College.

Introduction

Sarah Buss[*]

Some General Remarks

I begin the task of writing this introduction at a precarious moment in U.S. history—and, indeed, in the history of humanity. Many people are far more qualified than I am to shed light on the rise of authoritarian regimes across the globe, the increasing power of groups organized around programs of exclusion and violence, the normalization of unapologetic expressions of hatred and contempt. For insight into these matters, we must turn to historians, sociologists, political scientists, economists, and journalists. But there are other questions. Philosophical questions. On what grounds can we claim that someone is mistaken if she believes that certain human beings have no right to be treated with concern and respect (the same concern and respect as others) because they belong to a given tribe, race, ethnicity, religion, or are citizens of a certain nation, or have a certain sexual orientation or gender? To what can we appeal to justify our conviction that it is wrong to distribute power and privilege and status on the basis of such distinctions?

We have heard the answer many times: to treat some human beings as less worthy of concern and respect is to lose sight of their humanity. Surely, this is a thought we have all had ourselves. But to what are we calling attention when we express this thought? What is the connection between our "common humanity" and the fact that we are morally obligated to treat one another in certain ways? How does someone's humanity impose constraints on what other human beings have reason to do? What is the value of humanity, such that we fail to acknowledge this value if we fail to acknowledge these constraints? These are the guiding questions of the essays collected here.

Each essay approaches these questions in a different way, and each offers different, though overlapping, answers. Together they constitute an invitation to reflect on some of the challenges to our deepest moral assumptions. I will briefly single out some of the themes that recur in these essays. Before I take up this task, however, I want to place the philosophical enterprise to which they contribute in a broader context. Though the main readership of this volume is sure to be other philosophers, Professor Theunissen and I realize that the issues raised here are

---

Sarah Buss, *Introduction* In: *Rethinking the Value of Humanity.* Edited by: Sarah Buss and L. Nandi Theunissen, Oxford University Press. © Oxford University Press 2023. DOI: 10.1093/oso/9780197539361.003.0001

2 RETHINKING THE VALUE OF HUMANITY

not purely disciplinary, or even scholarly. We thus think it is important to address those who share our interest in these issues but have misgivings about the sort of inquiry to which we and all the contributors are committed.

Such misgivings are not without some justification. After all, I have just acknowledged that the beliefs, attitudes, actions, and policies we reject when we appeal to the value of humanity have a complex political, social, and economic history. Surely, this is no less true of *our own opposition* to these beliefs, attitudes, actions, and policies: if we are convinced that human beings have a value that grounds certain rights and obligations, this conviction must reflect the influence of a complex set of contingent factors. Once we concede this point, moreover, we may wonder what to make of any attempt to *justify* this conviction. Isn't the additional (higher-order) belief that there is a compelling justification also the product of a complex set of influences—including, importantly, the influence of structures of power and privilege? What, then, is the point of attempting to determine whether anything can be said in support of our appeal to "the value of humanity"? Isn't any such inquiry bound to be naïve, at best (because it mistakes mere contingent attitudes for something timeless), and morally suspect, at worse (because it obscures the special interests that underlie these attitudes and are served by them)?[1]

Even if we leave such worries to one side, the fact that our evaluative assumptions reflect a particular cultural, economic, and social reality can appear to rule out the possibility that we can fruitfully—and even intelligibly—explore whether human beings *really do* have a morally significant value.[2] In any case, we know that whatever arguments appear to provide the looked-for support will be provisional in the important sense that they will not be immune to further challenges. So, again, why should we bother probing the moral significance of our common humanity? Shouldn't we concede that, even if this is not a morally problematic exercise, there is nothing to be gained from it?

The essays in this volume reject such a counsel of despair. They reflect the conviction that in investigating the value of humanity—where this includes investigating the history of philosophical positions on the moral significance of being human—we can gain genuine insight into what is at stake for us when we appeal to our "common humanity", and what can be said for and against the evaluative assumption that underlies this appeal. As those with the concern mentioned in the previous paragraph would predict, these essays do not yield any uncontroversial conclusions. They call attention to how difficult it is to make sense of the value of humanity *in terms we ourselves can accept*. In part for this reason, they encourage us to take on the important task of deepening our own understanding of where we stand on this subject—and why. They urge us to rethink our assumptions about the moral significance of being human, where this rethinking involves everything from probing these assumptions more fully to offering alternative, revisionary, accounts.

INTRODUCTION 3

Professor Theunissen and I believe that the value of such inquiry is best appreciated by engaging with the essays themselves and reflecting on the dialogue established among them. Nonetheless, I would like to supplement their implicit response to the concerns raised above by making a few general observations. Since these concerns direct our attention to the extent to which our values are the product of various contingent power structures, it is fitting for me to begin these observations by turning to an important power struggle in the past.

In 1380 John Wycliffe completed his English translation of the Bible. This was the moment at which the English word "humanity" first appeared in print ("Humanity, n. 1" n.d.). Wycliffe's aim was to make the Gospel available to everyone. In response to this effort, representatives of the Catholic Church mounted a powerful attack. They condemned Wycliffe for turning "the jewel" of the clergy into "the playthings of laymen." The "Evangelists' pearls," the Church leaders claimed, were being "trampled by swine" (Knighton 1995, 245).[3] Thus did an appeal to our common humanity provoke the representatives of a powerful institution to acknowledge their commitment to dehumanization.

The stakes in this ideological debate were high. They still are. Together, the essays in this volume provide us with some of the conceptual tools we need if we are to understand what would have to be true in order for the Church to have been mistaken. Without these tools, we are reduced to the sort of position recently forcefully articulated by Bernard Harcourt, a law professor who has dedicated himself to helping defend prisoners on death row. "Human rights," Harcourt avows in a panel discussion on the topic (Harvard University n.d.),[4] may well be an "illusion." But, he claims, in order to argue that his clients are entitled to different treatment, he need not be "sentimentally attached" to any particular value "discourse." All that really matters is what is "useful"—whatever "stories" and "images" invoke and evoke "an internal sense of injustice."

Harcourt is surely right to avail himself of whatever legal "weapons" will enable him to defend his clients. Yet in response to his avowedly instrumental justification of the means he takes to his end, it is natural and reasonable to ask: What justifies the end? What is the "sense of injustice"? What are the values served by the appeal to "human rights"? Would the efforts to defend death row prisoners make sense if the conviction that human beings have a morally significant value were merely an illusion? These are the concerns that underlie the reflections in this volume.

All such reflections—like every movement in thought—take place under causal influences, including influences that dispose us to favor certain inferences over others. (All thought would grind to a halt if there were nothing to cause it to take one direction rather than another.) But this necessary condition of every attempt to make sense of our world and ourselves is not itself a reason to abandon such attempts. Nor, in particular, can we discover such a reason in the fact that further questions can always be raised about whatever inferences we draw.

4 RETHINKING THE VALUE OF HUMANITY

Again, it is important to keep in mind what is at stake. As Nadezhda Mandelstam (1999, 167) notes in *Hope Against Hope,* the injustices that shaped daily life in the Soviet Union under Stalin were supported by the "blithe" observation that the "ancient commandment 'Thou shalt not kill' . . . was a symptom of 'bourgeois' morality." "Since," Mandelstam continues, "art, and particularly literature, only carried out the orders of the ruling class, it followed that a writer should consciously put himself at the service of his new master" (167). The point, of course, is that this does *not* follow. (Mandelstam is deriding this inference, not endorsing it.) Even if artists are always under pressure from those in power, it is not pointless to wonder which exercises of power (and which accommodations) are more problematic morally than others. More generally, Mandelstam reminds us that it is possible to criticize certain social and legal norms by appealing to considerations whose moral significance does not depend on any contingent relations of power. Such appeals need not be instances of bad faith.

Of course, as Mandelstam herself well knows, things are complicated by the fact that the power at issue includes the power to confer status. Our moral significance is, at least in part, a function of the significance attributed to us by the social and political structures within which we live, as well as by the human beings with whom we interact within these structures. In short, these structures help determine the normative facts, as well as our *beliefs* about what these facts are. As several of the contributors to this volume note, whether one person has certain rights depends, to a considerable extent, on whether others acknowledge, or recognize, these rights. If, for example, no one recognizes someone's communicative actions as legitimate demands or as refusals to grant consent, then there is an important sense in which these actions have no such significance.

Jean Amery (1978) defends an extreme version of this point—a version that eliminates the qualifications "to a considerable extent" and "in an important sense." There is, Amery insists, nothing more to the value of our humanity than the value conferred on us by others: "Dignity can be bestowed only by society . . . and the merely individual, subjective claim ('I am a human being and as such I have my dignity, no matter what you may do or say!') is an empty academic game, or madness" (145). This is the hard lesson Amery draws from his experience as a prisoner in Auschwitz. Yet in the very next sentence, he reveals how difficult it is to make sense of this extreme position: "Still, the degraded person, threatened with death, is able . . . to convince society of his dignity by taking his fate upon himself and at the same time rising in revolt against it" (145).[5] This prompts the retort: What conviction is such a person seeking to elicit? How does insisting on one's "dignity" differ from a simple exercise of power?[6]

If "I am a human being!" is no mere rhetorical shove in response to attitudes and actions and policies we are unwilling to tolerate, then we have good reason to try to unpack the argument to which this declaration implicitly appeals. What

INTRODUCTION 5

is it about human beings in virtue of which there are moral constraints on how governments and individuals can treat these beings (even, as in the cases at issue in debates over the death penalty, when they have committed a serious crime)? If we are to take responsibility for our conviction that such treatment cannot be justified, and for the things we do under the guidance of this conviction, we cannot ignore this question.

Of course, in seeking an answer, we may conclude that some of our most basic moral beliefs are not really justified. Or that what justification there is to be had does not lie in the value of humanity. This brings me back to the essays in this volume. Some of these essays examine, and in some cases defend, the latter position. Other essays argue that in order to be justified in attributing a special moral value to human beings, we need not be able to construct a case that could convince those who do not perceive this value themselves. Still others offer arguments intended to persuade anyone who is capable of appreciating certain conceptual relations. Each of these exercises in rethinking the value of humanity forces *us* to rethink the others. In the summaries that follow I aim to point the way to some of these (overlapping) paths of thought.

* * *

The Essays

Many philosophers have explored the assumption that human beings are beings with dignity, i.e., that there is something about each of us in virtue of which we are justified in making certain claims on each other. Necessarily, the essays in this collection represent a small fraction of what can and has been said on this subject. (For example, though Yitzhak Melamed mentions Descartes, no essay is devoted to this philosopher whose observations about the distinctive human capacity for rational control influenced the conception of human moral status that is central to the work in this volume. Nor is there a discussion of the views of Augustine, or any other premodern Christian thinker.)[7] Our aim as editors is not to offer a comprehensive survey. Rather, we have chosen to highlight several important positions in the history of Western philosophy, as well as the views of several philosophers currently working in ethics.

Talk of "the value of humanity" is most closely associated with the work of Kant. The point of this collection is to consider a wide range of alternative positions. Many of these owe nothing to Kant, and others owe very little. This having been said, though only one of the essays here (Ralf Bader's) attempts to reconstruct Kant's position, and though only two others (Peter Railton's and Kenny Walden's) offer interpretations of sorts, each essay can be read as an implicit

6 RETHINKING THE VALUE OF HUMANITY

commentary on the second formulation of the Categorical Imperative: "Act in such a way that you always treat humanity, in your own person or another, never simply as a means, but always at the same time as an end" (4: 429). In what remains of this introduction, I will try to say just enough about these essays to give the prospective reader some clues as to what is distinctive about each one. In so doing, I will also call attention to some of the common themes that emerge, despite the significant differences in content and approach.

* * *

In "Decomposing Humanity" Jon Garthoff presents the widely shared Kantian view that, as Garthoff puts it, "the capacity to represent reasons as such, and so to form thoughts about reasons and justifications" is a morally significant capacity. According to Garthoff, it is this capacity that makes sense of the assumption that rational beings cannot be treated in certain ways without their consent, that they are "entitled to the space to develop their own conceptions of what is good and right, and to realize these in their own lives within reasonable bounds" and that they can be held morally accountable for the choices they make in living their lives. Garthoff also shares the popular view that even beings who lack the rational capacities characteristic of human beings have a claim to moral consideration insofar as they are sentient. On this view, because they have the capacity for conscious awareness, nonrational animals have a right to be treated with concern about how our actions will affect them, where this right requires us to treat their feelings as constraints on what we have reason to do.

Having presented the view that differences in moral status are grounded in differences in basic natural capacities, Garthoff calls attention to attitudes and actions that suggest we are also committed to a third, distinct, intermediate moral status. He notes that our relationships to many nonhuman animals presuppose that though these animals are not proper objects of *respect*, they have a claim to something more than our *concern*. We typically treat dogs, horses, apes, dolphins, and many other animals as worthy of our *recognition*. Though they lack the capacity to apply the concept 'reason,' we take ourselves to be obligated to try to make our interactions with them intelligible *to them* and to help them improve their responsiveness to the sort of reasons they are capable of appreciating. This, Garthoff suggests, is because we rightly regard them as capable of forming judgments about how we treat them and of developing their cognitive capacities in response to our reactive attitudes.

Other contributors to this volume discuss the moral significance of the capacity to respond "intelligently" to one's circumstances, and they explain how being rational relates to being accountable and to having a claim to recognition. Garthoff, in effect, asks us to consider whether some of these discussions overlook certain morally relevant distinctions—e.g., between the capacity for

INTRODUCTION 7

judgment and the capacity to reason critically and reflectively, and between different types of accountability. In so doing, he also prompts familiar questions—explicitly raised by Railton and Andrea Sangiovanni, but also addressed by those who seek to vindicate the special moral significance of the capacity to reason (Walden and Bader)—about the possibility of justifying a hierarchy of discrete moral statuses.

To the concern that is raised by an appeal to hierarchy we can add the related worry about what this alleged hierarchy implies about the moral status of human beings who lack the rational capacity often taken to ground the claim to respect. Do these human beings have the same moral status as many *nonhuman* animals? If not, is this despite the fact that their rights do not have the same basis as ours? If the answer to either question is yes, what follows? Clearly, this is a question about how we are justified in treating certain human beings. But it is also a question about the theory that underwrites such affirmative answers. In particular: Do the problems associated with the sort of approach Garthoff endorses force us to jettison this approach? Is it a mistake to try to ground the moral significance of humanity in the (characteristic) capacities of (most) human beings? Might there not be a better way to understand why it matters how we treat one another? Precisely because Garthoff's essay does not address these questions—precisely because it presents us with a clear sketch of a widely endorsed conceptual scheme without saying much about the considerations that might be offered for and against this way of understanding the moral significance of human beings—it highlights the need to investigate further. This is the task of rethinking the value of humanity that the other essays help us take up.

* * *

Several of these essays explore the answers offered by some of the most influential philosophers in the Western tradition. Richard Bett begins his survey of ancient Greek thought on the value of humanity ("Do the Ancients See Value in Humanity?") by noting that the Greeks did not typically regard human beings as the sort of thing that has value. (They reserved the application of the concept 'value' to mere things and states of affairs.) For this reason, anything we can say about their position on the subject of this volume must rely on piecing together various suggestive comments. When we do so, we discover many different opinions. Though none of these opinions implies that human beings have a special moral value in virtue of their humanity alone, Bett shows that several do "get close" to this position in certain important respects.

The Greeks champion a sort of "fellow feeling" among human beings, which we might characterize as an expression of "humanity." They do not generally take this form of sociability to be *justified* by any distinctive human capacity. Nonetheless, they do stress that "[h]umans are distinctively rational beings," and

8 RETHINKING THE VALUE OF HUMANITY

that this *explains* why we are disposed to enter into various ethically significant social and political relations with each other, and why other animals are excluded from these relations.

According to Plato, the Stoics, and many others, our rationality not only "makes us special" in this respect; it is also the "capacity to achieve kinship with the divine." Yet the value these philosophers associate with this capacity is the value of *manifesting* it, and they stress that very few human beings have what it takes to do so. Similarly, though in at least one place in the *Nicomachean Ethics* Aristotle suggests that slaves and women have a morally relevant value *as human beings,* he also insists that all women and some slaves are naturally subordinate to others because they lack some of the qualities that set human beings apart from the other animals. As Bett puts it, on Aristotle's view, "human nature itself comes in degrees," with some human beings "completely lack[ing] the delibera-tive element" by nature and others (women) being naturally incapable of being governed by it. It is interesting to compare this view with that of the Sophists, at least one of whom "seems to have argued explicitly in favor of the [natural] equality of Greeks and non-Greeks."

As this brief summary indicates, though we can find no explicit defense of the moral value of humanity as such in ancient Greek thought, there is wide-spread agreement that whether someone has a special moral status is not en-tirely a matter of contingent laws and practices. To the extent that ancient Greek philosophers are committed to defending inegalitarian, hierarchical political and social arrangements, they find it necessary to appeal to alleged distinctions among human capacities.

* * *

When we turn our attention to the early modern philosophers, we find a range of positions at least as varied as those defended by the philosophers of ancient Greece. Some early moderns deny that to be human is to have a special moral status. Among those who defend this position, some insist that moral constraints are grounded in actual or rational human decisions, while others claim that all such constraints are imposed by (and ultimately owed to) God. Well before Kant defends his influential brand of moral rationalism, some natural rights theorists anticipate his view that the authority of reason is a special source of moral claims. Some of these philosophers also stress the essentially reciprocal nature of these claims, suggesting that the capacity to reason is the source, not only of human "sociability," but also of the obligation to maintain the reciprocal authority rela-tions that constitute this sociability.

As Yitzhak Melamed explains in "Spinoza's Anti-Humanism: Human Value and Dignity," Spinoza holds the first of these positions. He explicitly denies that there is anything about human beings in virtue of which they have a special god-like value. To be sure, he believes that our very being is inseparable from God's. But this does not set us apart from anything else in creation: our "being-in-God" is a characteristic "we share with everything that is (sea waves and porcupines included)." According to Spinoza, human beings are worthy of admiration insofar as they employ their rational capacities to enhance their self-understanding and their understanding of other aspects of reality. But this value varies from human being to human being, and it is not the basis of moral status.

Like the ancient Greeks, Spinoza acknowledges that human beings have a special feeling of solidarity with others of their own kind. He argues, moreover, that it is rational, as well as natural, for us to act on this feeling, which involves privileging the interests and needs of other human beings over those of all other animals. "Apart from men," he writes, "we know no singular thing in nature whose Mind we can enjoy [*gaudere*], *and which we can join to ourselves in friendship, or some kind of association. And so whatever there is in nature apart from men, the principle of seeking our own advantage does not demand that we preserve it"* (italics original).

Hobbes endorses many elements of this view. There is, he insists, nothing about human beings in the state of nature in virtue of which they have rights to be treated in certain ways. Human beings outside a system of conventional laws are justified in doing whatever it takes to promote their own interests. It is the natural right to self-preservation that gives each human being good reason to grant all the others whatever claim rights are necessary to maintain the peace among them.

What do these claim rights amount to? In particular, do they include (or ground) a right not to be enslaved or "completely dominated" by others? As Julia Jorati notes in "Slavery, Freedom, and Human Value in Early Modern Philosophy," Hobbes believes that treating another human being as one's property is perfectly compatible with the value of humanity. On his view, the value of any given human being is "his price, that is to say, so much as would be given for the use of his power." He famously claims that the self-interested rationale for agreeing to abide by certain "natural laws" is also a rationale for granting governments unrestricted rights over their citizens. So, too, he believes that human beings can be justifiably enslaved if they choose to subordinate themselves in exchange for food and shelter.

Like Hobbes, Locke believes that it is permissible to enslave human beings if they deserve to be punished by death, and that enslaving a combatant in a just war can be a legitimate way of continuing to wage war against him. But, unlike Hobbes, he insists that the rights of masters over slaves are not absolute. This, he argues, is because every human being is the property of God, and because it is not permissible to damage or destroy someone else's property against his will. For the same reason, parental power is limited by the natural obligation to "preserve,

10 RETHINKING THE VALUE OF HUMANITY

nourish, and educate" the young human beings under one's control, and there are moral constraints on what husbands can do in exercising their (legitimate) power over their wives.

Jorati warns against exaggerating the differences between Hobbes and Locke. On Locke's view, she stresses, "[i]f there were no god who owns what he has created, it would not be morally wrong for rational creatures to kill, enslave, or harm each other." What's more, despite insisting that human beings in the state of nature have a natural right to freedom, and thus ought not to "harm [one] another in [their Lives], Health, . . . or Possessions," Locke supported the slave trade. Indeed, some of his words and deeds imply that, like Aristotle, he thought some human beings were naturally suited to be owned by others.

It is only when Jorati turns her attention to Leibniz that she comes to a philosopher who, at least later in his life, insisted that human beings and other rational creatures have a special intrinsic value the acknowledgment of which is incompatible with the institution of chattel slavery. According to Leibniz, in order to do justice to the value of humanity, we must (as Jorati puts it) "love each other in a disinterested way." This means that each of us is obligated to treat the well-being of all others as an end in itself. Though Leibniz is not opposed to all relations of domination and control among mature human beings, he insists that even in these cases, the one with the greater power owes it to the others to promote their happiness and virtue.

Whereas Hobbes links our basic rights and obligations to our rationality by appealing to the benefits to be gained by creating and abiding by a moral regime, Leibniz suggests that it is the unconditional value of rationality itself that grounds our most basic rights and obligations. This is an idea we have come to associate with Kant. As Stephen Darwall notes, according to Kant, rational beings have a value "that can be adequately appreciated only within a conception of moral right and not through concepts of the good of any kind alone." In "Valuing Humanity in 'Common Life': Grotius and Pufendorf on Equal 'Sociable' Dignity" Darwall explains how key aspects of this Kantian "doctrine of the dignity of persons" can be found in the philosophy of Grotius and Pufendorf. In particular, these philosophers call our attention to the reciprocal authority relations that are constitutive of human "sociability." They argue that social relations among human beings "are grounded in the capacity of rational persons to recognize their common competence and authority to make reasoned claims and demands against one another and hold one another accountable for conducting themselves on terms that respect this common standing."

Apparently, Grotius and Pufendorf do not address the possibility that, as Garthoff suggests, some social relations involving the "standing to make claims and demands" may not require the capacity to apply the concept 'reason.' In any case, like many (though certainly not all) of the other philosophers in this collection, their focus is on the moral relations among those who do have this capacity. According to Grotius and Pufendorf, these relations of mutual respect reflect a commitment on the part of each party to acting in ways they can justify to the others. Pufendorf claims that this is an obligation imposed on us by God. But he also suggests that God's commands have no authority over us unless we can appreciate their legitimacy. As Darwall points out, this means that, on his own account, human beings have obligations to each other because and only because their capacity to reason disposes them to "hold themselves accountable through their own internal acceptance" of moral demands.

* * *

This volume contains one more essay on the thought of an early modern philosopher. But this essay, Don Garrett's discussion of Hume, comes later in our lineup. This is because it highlights views that contrast more significantly with Kant's, and because some of the distinctively un-Kantian elements of Hume's approach can be found in the positions defended by the contemporary moral philosophers in whose company we have placed him. (Of course, this does not mean that these positions are not also—and in some cases avowedly—heavily indebted to Kant.)

The intervening essays include two on Kant and one on an early German idealist (Fichte) who puts a distinctive spin on some basic Kantian theses. According to one of the most basic of these theses, human beings have a unique dignity in virtue of their capacity for self-governed choice. "Everything in nature works in accordance with laws," Kant observes. But "only a rational being has the power to act *in accordance with his idea of laws—that is, in accordance with principles*" (4: 412). As Darwall indicates, this idea is inseparable from the idea that there is an essential connection between the value of humanity and the capacity to appreciate the authority of moral commands. The essays by Bader and Walden help us to understand this connection by helping us to understand what Kant has in mind in claiming that such beings have a value "above all price" (4: 434).

If, as Kant claims, the value of humanity is not the sort of value something has when it is good of a kind (if, e.g., it is not the sort of value attributable to a Stoic sage), and if it is not the value of some state of affairs (if, e.g., it is not the value of developing and exercising one's rational capacities and/or putting these capacities to use in promoting one's interests), then what is it, exactly? As Darwall notes, it must be a value of a "singular kind," which "conceptually implicates the right." In "The Dignity of Humanity" Bader argues that we can best understand this value if we read Kant as arguing that the capacity to reason grounds a special *status*. According to Bader, it is misleading, at best, to identify this status as a sort of value. More important, it is a mistake to think that our rationality grounds this status because it has a special value itself.

Kant does not make these mistakes, Bader argues. In defense of this conclusion, he marshals an impressive array of textual evidence. This evidence includes, among other things, (1) Kant's claim that, as Bader puts it, "something is morally good because it is to be brought about, rather than to be brought about because it is good"; (2) Kant's identification of the "good will" as the only thing that is unconditionally good; and (3) Kant's conception of the necessary conditions for being a bearer of value. Bader also argues that we cannot make sense of *imperfect* duties on the assumption that the inviolability of persons is a function of their value.

How, then, are we to understand Kant's claim that humanity is an end-in-itself? Bader's proposal, in a nutshell, is that this is a claim about the scope of the rational requirement that we act only on action-guiding principles ("maxims") we can will to be universal laws. To whom must these universal laws apply in addition to us? Kant's answer is: all and only those other agents who are capable of forming the intention to comply with a law because it is capable of being a law—i.e., because it is universalizable. This is why requirements govern our relations with other *rational* agents only—and not just *any* rational agents, but only those who can "unconditionally determine the faculty of choice by means of the mere representation of its maxims as qualifying for universal law-giving and thereby be practical by itself." In short, on Bader's reading of Kant, to say that human beings have a special, unconditional, value is to say that they can be motivated by noninstrumental concerns, and that only beings who satisfy this condition fall within the scope of the principles whose universalizability is a necessary condition of rational choice.

In offering this distinctive interpretation of what Kant has in mind in declaring that "humanity" has a "dignity" "beyond price," Bader suggests, more generally, that no axiological account could do justice to the fact that humanity "is inviolable and does not admit of trade-offs." In response to this challenge, Walden argues that we can make sense of the judgment that rational beings have an "infinite" value. In defending this conceptual possibility, he also shows how to justify the evaluative assumption that presupposes it.

Walden begins his account in "Great Beyond All Comparison" with the observation that when we evaluate things—when we consider what might be said for or against a given attitude, action, or state of affairs—we necessarily do so from some perspective. There is, he then points out, an important difference between (1) whatever has value only insofar as it is valued from one or another evaluative perspective and (2) the value of those who take up these perspectives. If we call everything in the first category a "thing," then all things are valuable insofar and only insofar as they are valued. Valuers differ from things in being the condition of the values of things. And nothing can be more valuable than that on whose value its value depends.

Walden identifies another feature of valuers that is at least as important as their distinction from things of value. Because nothing imposes any limits on the additional perspectives a valuer can take (where this includes, importantly, perspectives on her perspectives), there is no perspective with which we can identify any such valuers. Given, moreover, that valuers are the condition on there being such a limitless, open-ended "framework for representing value," their value must itself be infinite. Indeed, it must have the sort of "absolute infinity" Cantor attributes to incomplete totalities like the set of all sets. In short, according to Walden, we are right to think that we have a value "beyond all comparison" for the simple reason that the value of the capacity to reason does not satisfy the necessary preconditions for comparing the significance of one value with another.

* * *

With Michelle Kosch's essay on Fichte ("Fichte on the Value of Rational Agency"), we turn from Kant and philosophers who anticipate important aspects of his position on the value of humanity to a philosopher whose account owes much to Kant, even as it is also distinctive in many respects (including some respects that are interestingly similar to the appeals to instrumental rationality we find in Spinoza and Hobbes). Like Kant, Fichte argues that whether, as Kosch puts it, someone has a claim to "moral consideration" does not depend on this person's "socioeconomic class or caste, [her] degree of moral virtue, or other differences." And like Kant, he takes this moral equality to follow from the conceptual connection between moral obligations and the constitutive end of rationality. Fichte's account diverges from Kant's, however, insofar as he argues that our fundamental end as rational beings is self-sufficiency. This leads him to defend the very un-Kantian view that the fundamental principle of practical rationality enjoins us to regard rationality as a good to be maximized. He also differs from Kant in stressing the extent to which a person's moral claims on us depend on her willingness to abide by the norms of social cooperation that enable us to live together while maintaining a significant measure of independence.

One of the interesting features of Fichte's account is the epistemic role of this social cooperation: one person is obligated to acknowledge the moral standing of another only if together they "engage in free reciprocal activity," and it is only if one person "summons" another to engage in this activity that they are in a position to know whether such mutual recognition is possible. On Fichte's account, if a human being cannot relate to others on terms of social cooperation, or if she chooses not to, then she lacks the basic rights of a rational being. However, as long as there is some reason to believe that such a "rightless" individual can one day (re)join the cooperative community, efforts must be made to "(re)integrate" her, and/or—as in the case of children—to cultivate her rational capacities.

14 RETHINKING THE VALUE OF HUMANITY

Though Kosch does not address the possibility that certain nonrational animals have a distinct moral status, she does note that, for all Fichte says, the obligation to cultivate the rational capacities in others could include an obligation to improve the rational capacities of nonhuman animals. She also observes that, on Fichte's account, human agents have no greater claim on us than do agents whose intelligence is "artificial." She provocatively adds that if Fichte is mistaken about the tight connection between being rational and being disposed to cooperate with other rational agents, then he has no case against AI agents doing what they can to replace us—at least if the result is not a blow to rationality, more generally.

* * *

As Walden's talk of perspectives indicates, the Kantian story about the value of humanity offers a way of making sense of the intuition that to respect another human being is to respect her point of view, where this involves being open to altering one's own point of view in response. In relating to another human being in this way, one is, in effect, treating her judgments as relevant to what one has reason to do. But what about those *human* beings who will never acquire the capacity to reason with other human beings? Even if we were satisfied with Kant's (or Fichte's) account of the special moral significance of this capacity, we would still be left with the worry I raised earlier: Can this account of the "value of humanity" be reconciled with the assumption that we have special obligations to all human beings *as such*? Can we defend this assumption in a way that goes beyond Spinoza's observation that we have a natural disposition to identify with others of our own kind—that we (most of us) have feelings of fellowship which *dispose* us to *grant* all human beings the same basic rights, even though we are *rationally required* to treat only some of these beings as ends in themselves? What, if anything, can be said in defense of these dispositions?

Many of the essays I have discussed thus far offer interesting remarks on this issue. (These include remarks by Kosch and Jorati on the related question of how we *know* whether someone has the relevant capacity to reason.) In focusing less exclusively on the moral significance of rationality, the remaining essays suggest additional responses, some more explicitly than others. Three of these essays— those by Theunissen, Sangiovanni, and Railton—start from the assumption that no values are unconditional, or infinite. In different ways, each author focuses on the extent to which the value of humanity is the value that human beings and human lives have *for us*. In exploring this relational aspect of the value of humanity, they help us to consider whether any such value can provide a sufficiently solid basis for moral imperatives.

The relational aspect of the value of humanity is the central focus of Theunissen's "Explaining the Value of Human Beings." Her essay begins with a general proposition about value. In her view, nothing is good *simplicter*, i.e., good independent of a capacity to be *good for* something or someone. "The good," she says, "is essentially such as to change or alter something or someone in a positive way." Of course, this means that "positive" changes, "benefits," and "improvements" cannot themselves be understood in terms of a more basic notion of value. According to Theunissen, to benefit a human being is to help this being to flourish, where this condition consists, at least in part, in the exercise of the human capacity to value.

Like many others, Theunissen argues that this capacity is the key to the value of humanity. But she eschews familiar ways of justifying this assumption—including, importantly, Kantian approaches that appeal to norms of reasoning whose significance has nothing to do with the benefit of complying with them. On Theunissen's account, because the activity of valuing is a constituent of living a good human life, by valuing things, human beings benefit themselves. As she succinctly puts it, "the capacity to value is of value because its exercise is valuable, where its exercise is valuable because it constitutes [our] flourishing."

Theunissen anticipates questions about the normative implications of her account of the value of humanity. Why should we think that human beings cannot live well without complying with basic moral constraints? Why should we think that acknowledging the value of someone's capacity to flourish requires treating this human being with concern and respect? Without trying to offer conclusive arguments in response to these questions, she urges us to grant the plausibility of two claims. First, it is very difficult for human beings to thrive if they lack the attitudes and feelings that are constitutive of ethical virtue. Second, to appreciate that something has value is to recognize that we have reason to protect this value. This means that in order to acknowledge the value of humanity, we must avoid destroying human beings. We also have reason to help one another lead good lives, where this includes helping one another develop the ability to do so. This story about the value of humanity has striking similarities to the story Garrett tells in his essay on Hume, even as it offers an interesting alternative to the stories Bader and Walden tell in their discussions of Kant.

Sangiovanni shares Theunissen's conviction that we cannot make sense of our moral obligations to each other without appealing to the fundamental conditions of a good human life. As he explains in "Are We of Equal Moral Worth?," his shift in focus from the value of human beings to the value of human flourishing is motivated by his skepticism about the prospects of attempts to ground the moral value of humanity in one or more (allegedly) distinct human capacities. "We should," he says, "abandon the search for absolute-unconditional-intrinsic-good-making natural properties possessed to an equal extent by each one of us."

Sangiovanni also identifies a more positive motivation for his approach. As I noted at the beginning of this introduction, "They, too, are human beings!" is often offered as a compressed argument against oppressive hierarchies.

16 RETHINKING THE VALUE OF HUMANITY

Sangiovanni lists the familiar targets: "stigmatization, infantilization, objectification, instrumentalization, marginalization, and dehumanization." What, he asks, is our objection to the attitudes and actions that constitute these power and authority relations? Why is Hobbes mistaken to think there may be *nothing* wrong? Sangiovanni's answer is that oppressive hierarchies involve the infliction of grave harms. Most fundamentally, they involve an attack on an essential condition of human flourishing: "the sense that one's projects, commitments, and pursuits ought to matter to others." This is a serious harm because without "social recognition," few human beings can "maintain an integral sense of self." (It is interesting to compare this line of argument with Fichte's appeal to the connection between social recognition and self-sufficiency.)

Toward the end of his essay Sangiovanni addresses an important challenge to his account: Why does it matter whether human beings are harmed? Don't *our interests* matter only if *we* matter *ourselves*? Doesn't this bring us back to the value of humanity? Don't we need a story about this value in order to explain why the interest that each of us takes in *our own* projects, commitments, and pursuits imposes a constraint on what *others* have reason to do? Sangiovanni offers two responses to this challenge. First, he suggests that the moral value of human flourishing is no less mysterious than the moral value of any human capacity. The essays by Bader and Walden help us to assess this claim. Second, he suggests that we might be able to defend the value of humanity itself in terms of its relation to human flourishing—along the lines Theunissen proposes. Here, too, his essay points us to other discussions in the volume.

Railton's essay ("The Normative Significance of Humanity") also helps us to consider how we might defend the normative significance of humanity without tracing this significance to something about human beings that has either "infinite" or nonrelational value. Railton encourages us to focus on the differences between humanity as such and rational nature as such, and to consider how these differences might affect the distinctive character of human sociality and the normative standing of humanity. Interestingly, in exploring the relational value of humanity and the psychological conditions that enable us to appreciate and be moved by this value, he explicitly borrows key elements from Kant. Human beings, Kant argues, must exercise self-constraint in response to their inclinations, and they cannot rely exclusively upon their empirical or rational nature to do this. This gives every human life the form of a struggle. And the capacity to engage in this struggle is a source of dignity that every human being can recognize in every other.

Railton highlights the capacities for universal sympathy and personal communication as key features of a distinctively human sociability, regulated by moral norms. These capacities enable us to regard one another as ends, and thereby to be, as Kant puts it, "receptive to the concept of duty." In particular, universal sympathy enables us to matter to each other, regardless of our personal relations. Our communicative nature also enables us to establish relations of mutual respect, where these relations reflect our appreciation of the fact that whatever grounds we have for granting authority to our own ends are also grounds for granting authority to the ends of others.

In stressing the moral significance of the human dispositions to sociality, as well as the dependence of values on valuers, Railton implicitly calls our attention to Humean elements in Kant's developed moral theory. He thus directs us back to this early modern thinker. In "Finding the Humean Value in Humean Humanity" Garrett examines the role that sentiments and passions play in Hume's account of our moral stance toward one another. As Garrett explains, Hume does not believe that humanity, in the sense of being human, is itself one of the qualities or relations that engender love or admiration, and thereby determine a passion-based value. Nonetheless, he acknowledges that there are many human qualities that are proper sources of love, admiration, and respect. In offering a positive evaluation of such qualities, we implicitly endorse the feelings in light of which we value them.

According to Hume, we naturally approve of those who are useful and agreeable to themselves and others. We thus value the capacity to reason insofar as it helps us to discern the facts that dispose us to behave in useful and agreeable ways. Reasoning is also a valuable means to drawing conclusions about the attitudes of others and thereby ascertaining whether these attitudes are the sort we associate with virtue.

Valuable though the capacity to reason clearly is, Hume suggests that the capacity to feel (sentience, or what Hume calls "sensibility") is even more important to our moral sentiments. For one thing, he believes that "only beings capable of feeling passions can be motivated to act . . . and only beings capable of being motivated to act can have virtues." For another, only sentient beings are possible objects of sympathy, and, on Hume's account, moral sentiment generally requires sympathy.

Garrett surveys these and other aspects of the fellow feeling that connects human beings to each other on Hume's account. According to Hume, these feelings of humanity are, as Garrett puts it, the "basis" of the value of humanity. It is by experiencing these feelings that we "bestow value on one another." In short, we are justified in expecting others to treat us with concern and respect because we are justified in expecting them to acknowledge the value we have for anyone who shares our humanity.

* * *

For all their differences, Hume shares Aristotle's conception of the virtuous human being as someone who *sees* other human beings *as ethically significant*.

18 RETHINKING THE VALUE OF HUMANITY

Without directly addressing the vexed questions about the metaphysics of value that are provoked by the metaphor of "sight," Kieran Setiya and Kyla Ebels-Duggan argue that (1) the experience of another human being as having a value beyond price has a role to play in justifying our moral judgments, and that (2) this experience cannot itself be vindicated by an appeal to considerations whose moral significance can be established independent of this experience. In defending these claims, they also ally themselves with others I have discussed by stressing the moral elements of love.

In "Other People" Setiya calls our attention to the ethical significance of directly confronting another human being. Not only, he argues, is personal acquaintance a sufficient basis for love; it also plays a key role in our moral concern for other human beings *as individuals*. This role is evident in both (1) contractualist accounts of the conditions under which it is possible to justify a policy to those who will be affected by it and (2) discussions of the conditions under which benevolent concern supports the decision to kill a smaller number of people in order to save a larger number of lives. In both cases, it appears to be morally relevant how we "pick out" the people who will be harmed by our decisions. In the typical trolley problem case, for example, it matters whether you know who is on the bridge or simply know that there are six people, and you can save the five on the track by pushing a button that will cause the one on the bridge to fall to his death. As Setiya explains, "if personal [benevolent] concern is what determines how one ought to act, one ought to push the button" in the second case, but not in the first.[8]

Setiya concludes that "concern mediated by personal acquaintance has an ethical significance that is not shared by concern for the person, whoever it is, that meets a given description." But this prompts the question: What is personal acquaintance such that it matters morally? For help in answering this question, Setiya turns to Levinas and the ethical significance Levinas attributes to our face-to-face confrontation with another human being. According to Levinas, to be thus directly acquainted with someone is to discover that she merits one's personal concern. One need not look for any other basis for this ethical response.

Can it really be so simple? Surely, it is reasonable to wonder *what* one sees in seeing another human being as an object of personal concern—what one sees that *justifies* the conviction that this person has a special moral status. Setiya acknowledges the force of this challenge. His main point is that we must confront it, given the irreducible role personal acquaintance plays in our moral judgments. To this admonition, he adds a tentative proposal. Perhaps, he suggests, the personal concern that is prompted by our personal acquaintance with another human being is justified because "human nature, and the facts of human life, play a constitutive role in ethics." The idea, very roughly, is that the "natural history of human life" provides the standards of right and wrong.

INTRODUCTION   19

In making this suggestion, Setiya evokes Aristotle. And, as Garrett's essay makes clear, Aristotle's appeal to the constitutive role of natural human functioning has affinities with Hume. As a form of "constitutivism," the suggestion is also in the spirit of Kant. There is, however, an important respect in which it is strikingly un-Kantian. As Setiya notes, personal acquaintance is not an essentially *reciprocal* relation of mutual recognition, of the sort highlighted in the essays by Darwall and Kosch. We can relate to another human being in the way Levinas describes even if this being lacks the capacities necessary for being a moral agent. This is the point of saying that the object of personal acquaintance is a particular human being as such.

In "Learning from Love: Reasoning, Respect, and the Value of a Person" Ebels-Duggan also highlights this aspect of directly experiencing the value of humanity. And there are additional points of agreement between her essay and Setiya's. Just as Setiya notes that personal acquaintance can justify love as well as personal concern, so Ebels-Duggan notes that love and respect are two ways of directly apprehending someone's value as a human being. Most important, she endorses Setiya's suggestion that there are moral insights we cannot gain via reasoning. Indeed, she takes this to be a very general point about our moral life. If, she claims, someone has never been "*struck by* the value of someone's humanity," then there is nothing we can say to convince her that things really are as they appear to those of us who have had this experience.

Whereas Setiya appeals to human nature to explain why we are justified in seeing other human beings as ethically significant, Ebels-Duggan claims that it is a mistake to think that human beings would lack ethical significance if we could offer no such explanation. She illustrates this point with the case of parental love. Seeking a justification for loving one's child is incompatible with really loving him. So, too, she argues, "seeking arguments back to an affirmation [of someone's dignity] is itself incompatible with moral respect."[9] Again, the lesson Ebels-Duggan draws from these observations is that respect and love are distinct sources of knowledge. To apprehend one's child as worthy of love is, she says, to recognize that this human being has "an infinite and irreplaceable" value. One discovers the same fact when one apprehends someone as worthy of one's respect—whether directly or by witnessing another person's loving response to this human being.

* * *

In "The Invention of Value and the Value of Humanity" Elijah Millgram discusses Nietzsche's rejection of the possibility of such knowledge. Nietzsche sides with those who deny that human beings have "infinite" value, and that this—or any other value—is the sort of thing one can discover in the way one discovers something whose existence is independent of one's cares and concerns. More important, Nietzsche parts ways with all those who assume that there is something about human beings (something at least most of them have in common) in virtue of which they have a special moral status, or something about human nature in virtue of which granting this status is essential to human flourishing. He accepts a central point of Walden's essay: that a thing's value is its value *from a perspective*. But he does not grant that valuers themselves have a different sort of value. What's more, in insisting that each human being is responsible for her own value, he not only downplays the role of mutual recognition in valuing humanity; he also claims, far more radically, that in order to make ourselves valuable, we must invent the values in terms of which we evaluate ourselves.

How do we determine which values to invent if we cannot appeal to already existing standards? Millgram argues that, according to Nietzsche, we have no choice but to use trial and error to discover what answers our needs, even as these needs are shaped by our evolving evaluative expectations. Millgram explores the theoretical difficulties involved in trying to make sense of this conception of the value of humanity, as well as the practical impediments we face in trying to live up to the metavalue of value innovation. (He argues that Nietzsche's Overman is intended to represent this metavalue in a way that illustrates the problems that arise whenever we confer on our values the "legibility" they must have if they are to serve as "effective guide[s] to assessment.")

Millgram offers several examples of value invention. The last essay in this volume can be fruitfully read as supplementing these examples by offering a case study of sorts. In "The Human Foundations of Our Political Ideals: An Essay on Gandhi's Political Radicalism" Akeel Bilgrami shows us that Gandhi's critique of certain widely shared liberal values is, in effect, a call to reinvent these values so that they better suit our needs. Gandhi takes these needs to be essentially social, and as Bilgrami stresses, he is much more sympathetic than Nietzsche with Ebels-Duggan's appeal to the possibility of direct moral perception. Nonetheless, at the heart of his critique is a plea to abandon old values that are not serving us well.

More particularly, according to Bilgrami's reconstruction of Gandhi's argument, the familiar liberal conceptions of "liberty" and "equality" cannot do justice to the value of humanity. This is evident, Bilgrami argues, in the widely acknowledged difficulty of reconciling these two values with each other. This problem can be traced to the moment, early in the development of liberal thought, when respect for individual choice was interpreted in such a way as to underwrite property rights that supported extreme inequalities of power. On Bilgrami's account, Gandhi offers us a compelling alternative. He shows us how to reconceive the value of self-determination so that we can respect the value of individual liberty without abandoning the commitment to realizing a kingdom of ends. The key to this reevaluation of old values is to reinterpret liberty and equality as expressions of a third value: nonalienation. This requires adopting a radically different conception of ourselves that involves identifying some of our own most fundamental interests with the interests of others.

* * *

Like many other contributors to this collection, Bilgrami evokes a substantive conception of human flourishing in explaining what we must do if we are to do justice to the value of humanity. This suggests that we can contrast his (and Gandhi's) approach to the topic of this volume with the Kantian appeal to "pure" reason. Alternatively, we can regard him as exemplifying what Kantians themselves have in mind when they talk of respect for the value of humanity: he is offering the sort of proposal that human beings make to one another when they are committed to living together in ways that each of them can rationally endorse.

Respect for the value of humanity requires taking Gandhi's proposal seriously, as it requires being open to the proposals offered in each of the other essays in this volume (including Ebels-Duggan's proposal that we should not take certain proposals seriously). I began this introduction by defending the value of such reflective engagement. Here I am suggesting that reflecting on the value of humanity is not only an important way of taking responsibility for our moral assumptions. It is also an important measure of respect. One way to respect the value of humanity is to consider what other human beings have to say about it. The essays in this volume are a good place to start.

Notes

*. I am grateful to Nandi for her extremely helpful comments on an early draft of this introduction. I also wish to thank the contributors to this volume for reviewing and, in several cases, helping me to improve my summaries of their essays.

1. Perhaps no philosopher has pressed this point more powerfully than Nietzsche, whose views Elijah Millgram discusses in his contribution to this volume. As Alasdair MacIntyre (1981, 111) puts it, "the power of Nietzsche's position depends upon the truth of one central thesis: that all rational vindications of morality manifestly fail and that *therefore* belief in the tenets of morality needs to be explained in terms of a set of rationalizations which conceal the fundamentally nonrational phenomena of the will."

2. Some avowedly liberal philosophers who stress the contingency of social norms reject all appeals to "the value of humanity" as naïve and fruitless. Thus, Richard Rorty (1998, 178) declares, "To get whites to be nicer to blacks, males to females, Serbs to Muslims, or straights to gays, to help our species link up into what [Eduardo] Rabossi calls a 'planetary community' dominated by a culture of human rights, it is of no use whatever to say, with Kant: notice that what you have in common, your humanity, is more important than these trivial differences." Interestingly, many philosophers who support a generally conservative approach to politics also criticize talk of universal human rights

22 RETHINKING THE VALUE OF HUMANITY

as involving a naïve (and potentially dangerous) failure to appreciate the role that cultural traditions necessarily play in human relations. (For the seminal elaboration of this position, see Burke 1987.)

3. For three slightly different translations of the relevant passage, see Dove 2007, 6; Christian History Institute n.d.; Spartacus Educational n.d.

4. Harcourt is, in effect, endorsing the sort of approach Rorty defends in the essay cited in note 2.

5. It is interesting to compare Amery's position with the observation of another thinker whose views Bilgrami addresses in his essay. In his *Theses on Feuerbach*, Marx (1978, 145) claims that "the human essence is no abstraction inherent in each single individual. In its reality it is the ensemble of the social relations."

6. It is perhaps worth stressing that I do not mean to be here rejecting the Hegelian insight that "self-consciousness exists in itself and for itself in that and by the fact that it exists for another self-consciousness; that is to say, it exists only in being acknowledged" (Hegel 1967, 229). The point of the previous two paragraphs is to caution against drawing hasty conclusions about the contingency of any human being's moral value from the fact that there is an important respect in which our identity—and the significance of this identity—depends on our relation to others.

7. For illuminating reflections on how these thinkers contributed to the development of the modern (and postmodern) conception of the human "self," see Taylor 1989.

8. It is perhaps worth noting that Setiya rejects the antecedent of this conditional.

9. It is interesting to compare her position to the position Bernard Williams (2006) defends in "The Human Prejudice" and the position Cora Diamond (1978) defends in "Eating Meat and Eating People." In particular, though Ebels-Duggan shares Williams's skepticism about the possibility of a reasoned defense of our most basic moral commitments to one another, she endorses a moral epistemology according to which we should not conclude that these commitments are best understood as a form of prejudice. In so doing, she also seems to reject Diamond's (1978, 470) claim that apprehending human beings as having a certain moral significance is "not justified by what human beings are" but is "one of the things which go to build our notion of human beings." The other essays in the volume can also be read as more or less sympathetic responses to the challenges posed by Williams and Diamond.

References

Amery, Jean. 1978. "On the Necessity and Impossibility of Being a Jew." In *At the Mind's Limits: Contemplations by a Survivor on Auschwitz and Its Realities*, translated by Sidney Rosenfeld and Stella P. Rosenfeld, 82–101. Bloomington: Indiana University Press.

Burke, Edmund. 1987. *Reflections on the Revolution in France*. Edited by J. G. A. Pocock. Cambridge, MA: Hackett.

Christian History Institute. n.d. "Why Wycliffe Translated the Bible." Accessed January 2021. https://christianhistoryinstitute.org/magazine/article/archives-why-wycliffe-tra nslated.

Diamond, Cora. 1978. "Eating Meat and Eating People." *Philosophy* 53 (206): 465–479.

Dove, Mary. 2007. *The First English Bible: The Text and Context of the Wycliffite Versions*. Cambridge: Cambridge University Press.

Harvard University. n.d. "History and Human Rights: A Panel Discussion." Accessed January 2021. https://www.youtube.com/watch?v=LozSSje2tpc&t.

Hegel, G. W. F. 1967. *The Phenomenology of Mind*. Translated by James B. Ballie, with an introduction by George Lichtheim. New York: Harper Torchbooks.

"Humanity, n. 1." n.d. *OED Online*. Oxford University Press. Accessed July 2021.

Kant, Immanuel. 1900–. *Kants gesammelte Schriften*. 24 vols. Edited by Königlich Preussische Akademie der Wissenschaften zu Berlin, Deutschen Akademie der Wissenschaften zu Berlin, and Akademie der Wissenschaften zu Göttingen. Berlin: De Gruyter.

Kant, Immanuel. 1964. *Groundwork of the Metaphysics of Morals*. Translated by Herbert J. Paton. New York: Harper & Row. [Cited by volume and page of the Akademie edition]

Knighton, Henry. 1995. *Knighton's Chronicle 1337–1396*. Edited and translated by Geoffrey H. Martin. Oxford: Clarendon Press.

MacIntyre, Alasdair. 1981. *After Virtue*. Notre Dame, IN: University of Notre Dame Press.

Mandelstam, Nadezhda. 1999. *Hope Against Hope*. Translated by Max Hayward. New York: Modern Library Paperback Editions.

Marx, Karl. 1978. *Theses on Feuerbach*. In *The Marx-Engels Reader*, edited by Robert C. Tucker, 2nd ed., 143–145. New York: W. W. Norton.

Rorty, Richard. 1998. "Human Rights, Rationality, and Sentimentality." In *Truth and Progress*, 167–185. Cambridge: Cambridge University Press.

Spartacus Educational. n.d. "John Wycliffe." Accessed January 2021. https://spartacus-educational.com/NORwycliffe.htm.

Taylor, Charles. 1989. *Sources of the Self: The Making of the Modern Identity*. Cambridge, MA: Harvard University Press.

Williams, Bernard. 2006. "The Human Prejudice." In *Philosophy as a Humanistic Discipline*, 135–152. Princeton, NJ: Princeton University Press.

1

Decomposing Humanity

Jon Garthoff

Introduction: At Least Three Types of Moral Status

It is an arresting feature of the world that some individuals within it, including but not limited to human persons, *matter*. It is significant whether things go well or poorly for these individuals, and it is also significant whether they are excellent or defective members of their kinds. We should not be indifferent to the well-being and excellence of these individuals, moreover, *because* they matter. To think otherwise fetishizes well-being or excellence, treating these things as of worth independent from those who bear them. Against this, some individuals are appropriate, and indeed often obligatory, objects of our concern. Following a common usage, I will say that any individuals who matter in this way possess *moral status*.

There are presently two philosophical literatures primarily concerned with moral status, this entitlement to practical concern. The first is that into which most of the essays in this volume fall. This literature involves articulations of and disputes about both the moral status of human persons and what grounds this status. Writers in this literature often take Immanuel Kant's conception of *humanity*, and of *dignity* as the moral status characteristic of humanity instantiated in persons, as their point of departure.[1] This literature typically follows Kant—in my view correctly—by claiming the distinctive respectworthiness of human persons is grounded in their capacities for reflective and critical reasoning.

The second philosophical literature addresses whether, and if so in virtue of what, any nonhuman organisms possess moral status.[2] The focus is often on a putative criterion of moral status. Views commonly propounded or criticized in this literature include that all and only living organisms possess moral status and that all and only sensate organisms possess moral status.[3] While both of these views are plausible, my working hypothesis is closer to the second: as I explain briefly below, I maintain that possession of the most minimal type of moral status is grounded in the capacity of consciousness.

Not all differences in how we do or should treat different types of animals are explained by differences among their moral statuses. Whether an animal is domesticated or wild, and more generally whether we stand in a special relationship

Jon Garthoff, *Decomposing Humanity* In: *Rethinking the Value of Humanity*. Edited by: Sarah Buss and L. Nandi Theunissen, Oxford University Press. © Oxford University Press 2023. DOI: 10.1093/oso/9780197539361.003.0002 to the animal, bears on how we should treat it. Different animals also obviously have needs that differ in both kind and extent: a relatively asocial animal able to procure its own food calls for different treatment than a relatively social animal dependent on others for its survival.

But some differences in treatment are plausibly grounded in differences in moral status. One important example is that our fellow human persons must be treated as social equals, while nonpersons need not be. What to do in circumstances of triage is also often informed by the moral status of recipients of scarce necessary resources.

These days it is commonly believed, especially among those with sympathy for Kant's ethical theory, that there are at least two types of moral status.[4] These two types correspond to the literatures mentioned; indeed each may be understood as exploring a particular status in part by investigating its lower boundary. I share in the growing consensus that there are two types of moral status, but I am further convinced that there is at least one additional type. A primary aim of this essay is to articulate and defend that view.

Achieving this aim has two parts.[5] First is to motivate that there are in fact important differences in how we should treat different types of nonhuman animals. Fortunately this can be accomplished readily, for it is reflected in pretheoretical common sense. We concern ourselves with being understood by some animals, for example, but not with being understood by others. This is especially true of cats, dogs, horses, and other commonly domesticated animals. It is not true in virtue of their domestication, however, as is witnessed by the relationships zookeepers form with animals of comparable psychological capacities. Cases of triage also reveal a need to differentiate animals. The last lifeboat seat, or more plausibly the last dose of life-saving medicine, should be given to an ape in preference to a lizard; this is true even though both possess moral status and neither possesses the moral status of a human person. If there is a moral status intermediate between mere concernworthiness and the respectworthiness of a human person, that would explain these differences in how we ought to treat different types of animals.

The second part of defending the existence and importance of this intermediate status is to explain why we should account for our pretheoretical convictions in terms of such a status. An alternative explanation would hold that there is a continuum of different treatments of different types of animals. A proponent of this alternative might even agree that differences in treatment are mainly explained by differences in animal psychology; their proposal would deny, however, that it is fruitful to understanding these differences in terms of tiers of status.[6]

Most of the remainder of this paper is an effort to explain, as against this proposal, why we should think there are at least three tiers of moral status. More

26 RETHINKING THE VALUE OF HUMANITY

specifically it is an attempt to elaborate a type of moral status intermediate between that of human persons and that shared by all beings with any moral status at all. I aim to show that there is a constellation of moral concerns that hang together and are jointly explained by the psychological capacities possessed by those animals who possess this intermediate status.[7]

In the paper I thus attempt to make progress in explaining the moral status of higher animals, as distinct from both that of human persons and that of lower animals. This distinction between "higher" and "lower" is partly intuitive, reflecting differences in how we both do and should relate to different types of animals. But as I describe below, this distinction can be made more precise, since it tracks a distinction made by philosophers of mind and cognitive scientists between those animals that possess a capacity for belief or inference and those that do not. On the proposal developed here, the capacity for judgment—which helps to constitute capacities for belief and inference—underlies possession of the moral status above mere concernworthiness but below the respectworthiness owed to human persons.

1. Concernworthiness

In this section I briefly summarize the type of moral status typically regarded to be at stake in discussions of nonhuman organisms. I label this type of status *concernworthiness*, since the best summary statement of what it entitles individuals to is at least some form of concern, a non-disregard for the individual and its welfare. As was indicated in the opening paragraph of this essay, I think that what is at stake in adjudicating questions about the lower boundary of status is who *matters*. All and only beings with genuine moral status matter as such, and consequently are in some way entitled to our concern.

One crude entry point into thinking about this kind of status is to ask what objects or individuals a person might, in ordinary circumstances, permissibly vent their frustration on with physical force. It is normally permissible to kick the ground, but not to kick a dog. This is of course no criterion of standing, as there are many reasons other than its possession of moral status why it may be impermissible to kick something. An object may belong to someone else, or may in some other way be valued by or valuable for a being who matters. But having moral standing is close to a sufficient condition for being entitled against this treatment, at least for beings that can be harmed, damaged, or perturbed by physical assault. Any kicking of concernworthy animals demands special justification. This point generalizes in a complicated way, so that the harm or perturbation of morally considerable beings raises a yellow flag in conscientious persons.[8] We must be attuned to when our actions involve or cause such harms

DECOMPOSING HUMANITY 27

or perturbations, or are likely to do so, and we must be disposed to refrain from such actions except when circumstances provide special justification.[9]

Similarly, an individual's being concernworthy entails that we may have obligations to aid it or to interfere on its behalf if it is suffering or maltreated, and where this is impossible or inappropriate, we may have obligations to advocate for such aid or interference. I do not mean with these brief comments to enter interesting and vexing disputes about how individuals should respond to these concerns when they can respond to each but cannot respond to all.[10] The point is only to articulate some of the most minimal, and hence most secure, claims about our obligations with respect to concernworthy beings.

To summarize the discussion of this section thus far: if an individual has moral status, then it is worthy of our concern. This concern must consist at least in having some minimal regard for the individual; we cannot disregard the individual without fault. So stated, the moral obligations flowing from bare concernworthiness may sound minimal, but this need not be the case. The sheer number of concernworthy animals in a condition of suffering or maltreatment may make these obligations accumulate in a way that is demanding. There may be moral obligations that flow from mere concernworthiness, moreover, beyond obligations of non-disregard. I make no attempt here to characterize these obligations comprehensively, since my primary purpose is not to provide a detailed elaboration of what flows from each type of moral status I discuss, beyond what is needed to differentiate them as types.

While there have been disputes about whether the class of concernworthy individuals on Earth extends beyond the human species, I regard those disputes as resolved in the affirmative. Thus the distinctive capacity of persons—critical and reflective reason, which I describe in the next section—is not necessary for concernworthiness. These days the most commonly proposed criterion for the lower boundary of moral status is *sensation*, the capacity for feeling or affect.[11] The motivation for this view is typically that (morally speaking) we cannot but attend to sensate beings because they experience pleasure and pain. Though for present purposes the difference is not greatly significant, I would note that I favor the slightly broader criterion of *consciousness*. Consciousness is in principle a broader criterion than sensation because it is possible to be aware without experiencing feelings.[12] To my mind it suffices for an individual to matter that there is something—anything—it is like to be them.[13] Whether they care about anything, or experience pleasures or pains, is another issue. It seems to me that if an individual is the subject of any conscious experience, sensate or otherwise, then on pain of moral failure we must be concerned with the nature and quality of its experiences. This is in part because not everything that matters in a life need be such that the individual can be pleased or pained by it. But more fundamentally I am moved by the idea that the "lights being on"—subjective conscious

28   RETHINKING THE VALUE OF HUMANITY

mental states are presented to the being from the inside—constitutes what is special about the type of being it is.

Another popular candidate criterion of moral status, which is at least not implausible, is life.[14] This is a much broader criterion than consciousness or sensation, since many animals lack consciousness; plants, fungi, and single-celled organisms are also alive but not conscious. A living being is more separate from the remainder of nature than is (say) a rock or a river, since living beings function to maintain themselves. This functional self-maintenance entails that events can go well or poorly for living things as such, depending on whether the events promote or detract from the being's functioning. This separation and this possession of interests—which is reflected in the fact that we ordinarily speak of things as good or bad for living beings as such, without reference to other individuals—may be taken as an indication that living beings matter in their own right.

I doubt that life alone supports moral status, however, mainly because I have difficulty isolating circumstances where putative reasons to be concerned for a nonconscious living being for its sake fail to be overwhelmed by reasons to be concerned for it for the sake of conscious beings.[15] In any case it is likely best for the purposes of this essay to operate with consciousness or sensation as the criterion of concernworthiness, since advocates of life agree that conscious living things possess moral status. Indeed I suggest more specifically that we view an amphibian such as a frog or a salamander as a paradigm of a merely sensate being who possesses only the most minimal type of moral status.[16]

2. Respectworthiness

The minimal moral status discussed in the previous section is of course a far cry from the moral status of human persons. What we owe to persons includes the obligations articulated in the previous section—human persons are conscious—but extends beyond this in important respects. In my view it is a great virtue of the work of Kant and his followers that they treat the moral status of persons as distinctive, a feature they mark with the label "dignity."

Kantian theories plausibly propose *humanity* as that in virtue of which a person possesses this status.[17] In this use, "humanity" does not refer to membership in the human species, nor to sympathetic or sensitive dispositions. It is instead a technical term that refers to the embodied rationality characteristic of human beings which might also be instantiated in members of other Earthly species or in alien beings with whom we share no phylogeny. Kant notoriously provides several variant glosses of the term, and I do not here weigh in on interpretive disputes about the details of his understanding of it. Instead I note that all have in common an emphasis on what, following Tyler Burge, I call *critical reason.*[18] This includes the capacity to represent reasons as such, and so to form thoughts about reasons and justifications.[19] Critical reason is thus required for the formulation and assessment of theories. It is also required to formulate basic questions of ethics, such as "Is this action justified?," "How should a human person live?," and "What sort of a person should I (or another) become?" Persons can formulate these questions, and can guide their actions by their working answers to them. They can also make a lifelong project of revisiting these and related questions, improving their answers to them.

The moral significance of critical reason is importantly reflected in the presumption that in normal circumstances we must secure the consent of other persons in our relations with them.[20] Full-blown consent entails that the individual giving consent judges their treatment acceptable, which in turn requires that they have the capacity to represent reasons and justifications. It also requires that they can understand themselves as in relationships with others that are partly defined by shared understandings about justification. And if they can understand themselves in this way, then—as Kantian theorists often note—it is a morally problematic use or manipulation of them to treat them in a way that bypasses their understanding.

It is only a short step from this emphasis on consent to the thought that coercing persons is morally hazardous. There is a similarly short step, as Kantians often point out, from emphasis on consent to the thought that deceiving persons is morally hazardous. In each of these types of morally problematic action, an attempt is made to influence how a person acts without securing full consent in the process. Thus human persons are entitled, in ordinary circumstances, not to be coerced or deceived. Just as conscientious agents flag actions that harm a conscious being, so too do they develop sensitivities that disallow nonconsensual treatment in normal circumstances and flag such treatment as potentially problematic in all circumstances.

Dignity not only grounds the need for consensual relationships among persons; it also grounds the need for fundamental social *equality* among persons. Fundamental stratification of persons, as occurs in aristocratic or caste systems, is morally unacceptable. Similarly, beings with dignity are entitled to not be subjected to slavery or other forms of social domination. Entitlement against unjust discrimination or subordination, the social realization of which is pursued in civil rights and other liberation movements, also flows from possession of human dignity.

Furthermore, the need for fundamental equality among conscious persons helps explain both the moral danger of self-aggrandizement and the need to treat others as capable of self-direction. If I act as though my interests are systematically more important than other people's, or as though the status of other people depends on their relationship to me or to my projects, this reflects a failure on my part to treat other people as social equals.

30 RETHINKING THE VALUE OF HUMANITY

Similarly, if I act as though I am entitled to make decisions for another person, or as though I have a veto over decisions they make about how to live, this reflects a failure to recognize the fundamental social equality of persons.

Beings with critical reason are thus entitled to autonomy, though it is difficult to specify precisely what this entitlement consists in.[21] At a minimum conscious persons are entitled to the space to develop their own conceptions of what is good and right, and to realize these in their own lives within reasonable bounds.

Persons also possess entitlements grounded in the fact that, in virtue of their possession of critical reason, they are morally responsible and are plausibly understood to have a capacity for moral conscience.[22] One important example is that human persons are entitled to the education needed to meaningfully exercise their critical capacities. This includes entitlement to specifically moral education, especially when we are children. Such education is the point of practices of moral responsibility.

One way to capture what consensuality and equality have in common, such that they are grounded in the same distinctive type of moral status, is to note that conscious persons are both entitled to receive and obligated to provide *reasonable* treatment. This supports the importance, manifest in the lived experience of morally sensitive persons, of checking in with each other and where appropriate securing consent in our treatment of each other. It also supports the appealing ideas that we should more generally be open to critical feedback from each other—especially in the context of ongoing relationships—and to involve all parties in the shaping and guiding of these relationships.[23] Reasonableness involves checking in with ourselves, moreover, and with our working conceptions of what is right and good, to attempt sincerely to hold ourselves to the standard of justifiable treatment of (ourselves and) others. In relationships with other persons, among the most important ideas we must use to ensure they are justified is that of fundamental equality of status. One aspect of being reasonable is not losing sight of this fundamental equality in the bustle of life and inattention to others into which we inevitably sometimes fall.[24]

Another apt term for the status often called the dignity of persons is *respectworthiness*.[25] This is because "respect" is often understood to be owed to equals or superiors, whereas "concern" is often understood to be owed to equals or inferiors. In Section 4, I motivate a moral status that is intermediate between respectworthiness and concernworthiness. But first, in Section 3, I make a few important observations about these two more familiar types of moral status.

3. Comments on Concernworthiness and Respectworthiness

The first observation is that each moral status supports a *tier* of related moral phenomena. I have laid out only the barest sketch of how the phenomena relate to one another in each case, but I hope to have illuminated their deep interrelation. The way these underlying psychological capacities support their correlated statuses, moreover, makes these statuses differ not only in magnitude but also in kind. As I explain more fully below, on the account developed in this essay the moral status of human persons is superior to that of merely concernworthy animals.[26] The marks of this status mentioned above—consensuality, equality, and mutual justifiability—define appropriate relations among persons, moreover, so that these differ essentially from appropriate relations between persons and frogs. In any plausible scale of status this constitutes punctuation, and not a mere point on a continuum.

Second, the role of the capacities that underlie each tier of status is not merely to be a necessary, or even a constitutive, condition of a possible morally significant action.

The role of consciousness in explaining why conscious beings are entitled not to be caused pain for the sake of amusement is not merely that we can be amused only by the pain of conscious beings, since only conscious beings are capable of experiencing pain. Rather, the consciousness of the being helps to explain *why* being amused by a conscious being's pain is morally suspect.[27] There is something it is like to be a conscious being, and that is plausibly why we should not disregard, much less enjoy, its pain. It is typically bad to *feel* pain; it is not merely bad to be in a state, namely pain, that is such that it is constitutively felt. Similarly, lying to a conscious person is morally suspect not merely because only persons are linguistic and so possible recipients of lies. Rather, the critical capacities of a person are manipulated or circumvented by a lie, and this helps to explain not only the lie's existence but also its morally suspect nature.

Third, respectworthiness presupposes concernworthiness, but the converse does not hold. Persons are worthy of respect only if they are also worthy of concern.[28] I return to this theme after discussing the moral status intermediate between respectworthiness and concernworthiness. I hypothesize that these types of status constitute not only a hierarchy but also a developmental sequence.

4. Recognitionworthiness

In this section I describe another type of moral status, one intermediate between the two already articulated. This type of moral status has not previously been isolated from others. This is not to say, of course, that people have overlooked the moral phenomena I associate with this tier of moral status. It is to say, rather, that these phenomena are normally accounted for in terms of one of the other two moral statuses, most usually the dignity of human persons. According to my proposal, by contrast, the obligations and entitlements I discuss in this section

32　RETHINKING THE VALUE OF HUMANITY

indicate the need for (at least) an additional tier of status which I distinguish from both respectworthiness and bare concernworthiness. These phenomena are not grounded in respectworthiness, for they are present in our relationships with higher animals who lack specifically critical reason. They are not grounded in concernworthiness, for they are not present in our relationships with lower animals that lack beliefs and other reason-responsive mental states.

I begin this section by explaining the marks of this mode of status, in the same manner as I explained the more familiar types of status in Sections 1 and 2. Again following the pattern of those sections, I proceed to explain the appropriateness of a label for the status—in this case it is *recognitionworthiness*—as well as the capacity that I hypothesize underlies its existence. Since this type of status is less familiar than the two discussed previously, I more clearly distinguish it in this section from concernworthiness. Following that, in Section 5, I distinguish it at greater length from respectworthiness.

The first mark of the intermediate moral status is what I will call a capacity for mutual *intelligibility*. This involves the ability to interpret what others do, and to be interpreted by them in turn. In interactions with persons, this includes an entitlement that they address themselves *to* beings who possesses this status. This is a required feature of our relationships with at least some nonhuman animals. If one has contact with any of the more sophisticated animals, it is morally problematic never to acknowledge the animal as an individual with its own point of view.[29] We often do this by talking to the animal, even if it is nonlinguistic, indeed even if it has little or no understanding of what our words refer to. This makes sense because language is our usual mode of making ourselves understood by others.

A second, related mark of the intermediate moral status is *accountability*. We can, and sometimes should, hold certain nonhuman animals responsible for how they behave. Philosophers may initially balk at this claim, since nonhuman animals are rarely discussed in philosophical conversations about responsibility. But responsibility-entailing ideas are clearly present in our ordinary practices, including punishment of pets and young children, and many of these practices survive reflective scrutiny.[30] Domesticity is neither necessary nor sufficient, moreover, for an animal to be accountable. It is not sufficient because some domesticated animals, such as guppies, lack the cognitive capacities to be held responsible. It is not necessary because these practices already extend to many wild animals held in captivity, such as elephants and lions. To the extent that we enter into relationships with wild animals in their natural habitats—and we will at least sometimes be obligated to do so—these ideas will have appropriate application there too. Social relations are needed for certain kinds of responsibility, perhaps including punishability. Even where this is true, however, psychological capacities underlie and make possible social relations of the relevant kind.

DECOMPOSING HUMANITY 33

I think *judgment* is the psychological capacity underlying possession of the moral status of recognitionworthiness. By "judgment" I mean the ability to respond functionally to rational or logical relations. This contrasts with functional capacities such as perception and memory, which pertain to accuracy and to the preservation of accuracy, but not to relations of rational or logical support. It also of course contrasts with those functional capacities, such as digestion, which are not psychological and do not pertain even to accuracy.

Belief is a paradigmatic mental state involving judgment. If a mental state is not formed or maintained in response to reasons—is not formed or maintained in response to considerations bearing on truth or truth-preservation—it is not a judgment, and hence not a belief. Preference is another judgment-involving mental state. Propositional attitudes in general presuppose a capacity for judgment, as I use the term here, since even when they are not themselves assessable in terms of truth they involve constituents that are.[31] A propositional desire *that I now exercise* is not the sort of thing that can be true or false, nor is this attitude made fitting or appropriate by the truth of the proposition it is an attitude toward. Still, the fittingness of the desire depends on the relations between the truth of its propositional content and the truth of other propositions, such as *that I become more healthy* or *that I promised I would exercise now*.

Though not all judgments are formed on the basis of inference, it is likely that a capacity to judge entails a capacity to infer.[32] It is difficult to see how a mental state could qualify as a belief if its bearer had no capacity to draw an inference from it. This point about the connection between judgment and inference generalizes to all propositional attitudes.

It is important to observe that judgment, as it is understood here, does not entail critical capacities to represent or reflect on reasons as such. Responding to reasons is one thing; representing them or reflecting on them is another.[33] Though arguments have been attempted to show the former entails the latter, it is doubtful such arguments succeed.[34] Investigations into which nonhuman animals have beliefs and other judgment-involving attitudes are conducted in large measure by assessing whether these animals infer. If an animal solves a problem where it is implausible the animal could have learned to solve it by means of conditioned associations, and it is also implausible that they are genetically disposed to solve in virtue of experiences of their ancestors, then there may be good reason to attribute a capacity for inference to the animal. In attributing this capacity to the animal, one need not commit to its having any capacities to reflect or to criticize, nor need these capacities be tested for in the relevant experiments.[35]

As with the other two types of moral status, the capacities in virtue of which the status is held help explain the nature of the status itself. I have hypothesized that judgment, the capacity to respond to rational or logical relations, underlies recognitionworthiness. This helps explain both the nature of the status and

34 RETHINKING THE VALUE OF HUMANITY

what possessing it entitles a being to, for judgment may be the least sophisticated psychological capacity involving understanding or appreciation.[36] The capacity for understanding enables beings to be satisfied or dissatisfied with the way the world is, as opposed to merely attracted or averse to things in the world. Satisfaction and dissatisfaction involve a greater degree of remove from their objects than do mere attraction and aversion. An individual is satisfied *in* things, and is satisfied *because of* things, in a rational rather than merely causal sense of "because." An individual is not merely satisfied *by* things.[37]

The remove of understanding-mediated satisfaction contrasts with the immediacy of deriving (brute) pleasure from a meal or an orgasm.[38] It also contrasts with the immediacy of perception, a representational capacity unmediated by understanding. In accurate perception the object perceived must be immediately present (even if it is a distant galaxy), in the sense that it must in fact be the cause of the perceptual state. A true belief, since it is mediated by a capacity for understanding, need not be caused by its object.

The capacity for judgment also enables a being to have some understanding of how it is treated. This connects the mark of intelligibility with that of accountability: both require that a being have a capacity to appreciate its treatment.[39] As is illustrated in actual social practices with higher animals, this in turn enables the appropriate deployment of reactive attitudes toward—and indeed even among—animals with this status. In particular, those who express reactive attitudes need not have mental states about the mental states of others.[40]

It is sometimes said reactive attitudes are appropriate only when their target is a moral agent, where this is a being with moral obligations or other specifically moral responsibilities.[41] But this is not correct. Just as there are nonmoral responsibilities, so too are there nonmoral reactive attitudes that are made appropriate by failures to discharge responsibilities. To illustrate: anger-involving responses to failures of pets or very young children to act as they should are not limited to mere anger on the one hand and (unjustified) moralized resentment on another. An intermediate category—resentment in general—is sometimes appropriate to their failures. This attitude is nonmoral because it is not a response to a failure to discharge a moral obligation or otherwise fulfill a moral responsibility. Some nonhuman animals are appropriate objects of such nonmoral reactive attitudes; others are not.[42] On my suggestion, all and only those individuals who are appropriate objects of such attitudes have capacities for judgment.[43] These capacities involve the ability to understand, which is presupposed by directing reactive attitudes at another. They also involve the ability to respond to reasons, and so they enable these practices to function to instruct their participants about how to act and thereby to improve their response to reasons.

As with dignity, possession of the status explicated in this section presupposes possession of concernworthiness. If an individual is not concernworthy, it has no moral status as such, hence is not recognitionworthy. Recognitionworthiness is in turn presupposed by respectworthiness: consent is impossible without intelligibility; social equality is impossible without accountability. Reasonableness, we might say to summarize this section, is impossible without responsibility.[44] But as I describe more fully in the next section, the converse of each of the above claims is false. Concernworthiness does *not* presuppose recognitionworthiness, which in turn does *not* presuppose respectworthiness. These three types of moral status accordingly constitute an ordered sequence, where each member of the sequence constitutively presupposes those earlier in the sequence, but not the other way around.

5. Distinguishing Recognitionworthiness from Respectworthiness

I expect that most readers accept that recognitionworthiness (as expounded here) is a status distinct from concernworthiness. More likely to elicit resistance, or at least call for further elaboration, is the claim that recognitionworthiness is a status distinct from respectworthiness. It is common to express the claim that human persons are victims of disrespect or discrimination by appealing to their entitlements to recognition. As I noted, some philosophers argue either directly that these statuses must accompany one another or indirectly that the psychological capacities most plausibly thought to underlie each status must also underlie the other.[45]

I now turn to explain why I reject these claims. I proceed by building on contrasts stated briefly at the end of the preceding section. According to the framework developed in this essay, the phenomena of responsibility (namely, intelligibility and accountability) are characteristic of recognitionworthiness, while the phenomena of reasonableness (consensuality and equality) are characteristic of respectworthiness. More specifically intelligibility required by responsibility contrasts with the more stringent consensuality required by reasonableness, and accountability required by responsibility contrasts with the more stringent social equality required by reasonableness. I now explain each of these contrasts in turn.

Let us first consider intelligibility. In saying that recognitionworthy beings are entitled to intelligible treatment, I mean that since they possess a capacity for understanding we have some obligation to enable them to understand what we do to them. This, I suspect, underlies the most fundamental demand of recognitionworthiness, addressing ourselves *to* recognitionworthy beings. We must sometimes check that what we do has appropriate uptake or appreciation. While this is an obligation of communication, it demands more than the mere transmission of information. It demands that our actions be intelligible to the being in that its functional capacities to understand are appropriately engaged, including in the guidance of its actions, in its relations with us. When an animal is frightened we may talk to it soothingly or establish gentle physical contact with it, for example, in recognition of what it is experiencing. Similarly, we may speak to an animal or direct its attention toward familiar playthings, to express concern for the discomfort it is suffering due to its lack of understanding that the family has moved into a new home.

There are of course limits to this. Merely recognitionworthy animals have no capacity for linguistic communication, nor for scientific or philosophical understanding. Our relations with the most sophisticated nonhuman animals and very young children illustrate and illuminate, however, the importance of acting intelligibly.[46] In particular these contrast with our relations with animals that lack capacities for understanding.

Recall that many sensate beings lack understanding; I suspect this is true, for example, of most or all actual amphibians. Nothing is intelligible to such animals, so we have no obligation to make ourselves intelligible to them. Any communication we share with them is highly attenuated, and any efforts we make to alter their behavior consist in mere conditioning. I propose that this is why we are not required to address ourselves to them, nor to act with their understanding of our behavior in mind. They cannot understand our behavior. But other animals can and do, for the capacity to understand is part and parcel of the capacity to respond to reasons.

Note that the obligation to be intelligible to another creature is, as such, easier to satisfy than an obligation to secure their consent. I assume nonpersons, even those with a capacity for understanding, are not capable of consent.[47] This is in part because most or all of these animals lack most or all psychological concepts. But more fundamentally, since they lack the specific concept *reason*, they cannot assess their treatment by another in terms of its justifiability. Consent involves giving permission, but permission is intelligible only in the space of justifications.

There is an analog to consent, beyond mere intelligibility, that has important application in our relations with recognitionworthy animals. There is a difference between a dog getting into a car willingly and getting in unwillingly, and the dog's willingness is mediated in part by what it understands. This phenomenon is worthy of fuller investigation, as are its moral implications. But whatever that investigation reveals, it is crucial to remember that this analog to consent is not the same thing as consent. This helps to explain why there is a much broader range of circumstances in which it is permissible to coerce a recognitionworthy animal than in which it is permissible to coerce a respectworthy person. In taking a frightened dog to the veterinarian, I must attend to its fear, doing what I can to allay its concerns on terms the animal understands. But I need not defer to the dog's judgment about whether to go. Nor (of course) need I defer to its judgment whether it ought to go; as a non-critically-rational being, it makes no such judgments. In taking a frightened person to the doctor, I must similarly attend to their fear, doing what I can to allay their concerns on terms the person understands. But I also must defer to the person's judgment about whether to go, if the person is mature, not experiencing duress, and not incapable of critical reflection. In the typical case this is due to the need to defer to the person's judgment about whether they ought to go, including in many circumstances where I think the person judges erroneously.

This in turn means that straightforward arguments against the permissibility of deceiving or coercing an animal, in parallel with Kant's arguments in *Groundwork* II against deceiving or coercing persons (in normal circumstances for normal reasons), are not available.[48] I do not doubt that there are analogs to wrongful deception and wrongful coercion that can arise with the more sophisticated animals.[49] But since they lack reflective thought and theoretical understanding, their capacity to understand our treatment of them is severely attenuated. Accordingly it does not have the same moral moment to bypass these systems as it does to bypass critical reason in a human person. This is especially true if the bypassing is done for the sake of promoting or realizing the animal's welfare or excellence.[50]

The potential for intelligibility in interactions with sophisticated nonhuman animals in turn supports the possibility of *mutuality* in our relations with them. The way we should take their point of view into account when deciding what to do involves crucial elements not present in the case of merely concernworthy beings. In particular we must sometimes take account of what they find intelligible, including their understandings of how we treat them.

It also entails openness to being held responsible by them, in the attenuated sense that they are capable of doing this. We should be open to improving our responsiveness to reasons in light of their attitudes toward us and their social interactions with us, including acts of quasi-punishment such as the temporary withholding of their attention. This is true even though these interactions do not involvement judgments on their part that we have done wrong and need not even involve judgments about our mental states. It is also true even though these interactions are not discursive and do not involve the articulation or exchange of reasons. Such exchanges of reasons are partly constitutive of instances and practices of holding others morally responsible. But as was noted in Section 4, instances and practices of holding others nonmorally responsible, including by means of nonmoral reactive attitudes, do not require this, even though they involve relationships of mutual understanding and accountability.

Being obligated to act in a way intelligible to others and mutual with them does not as such entail obligations to treat oneself as *equal* with these others.

38 RETHINKING THE VALUE OF HUMANITY

We moderns are accustomed to thinking moral concern for another consists in treating them relevantly as an equal; the unfair discrimination of racism and sexism are our central paradigms of violated moral status. That is appropriate so far as it goes, but proper treatment is not always marked by equal status. We need merely think about animals and very young children to remind ourselves of this. As common sense and common practice attest, the early animal rights slogan "All animals are equal" is false.[51]

Conclusion: More Than Three Types of Moral Status?

In this essay I have explicated three types of moral status possessed by actual animals. Concernworthiness entails that an individual matters, and so is the base type of moral status that explains reasons to care about an individual's interests or excellence. Recognitionworthiness presupposes concernworthiness, and it grounds reasons to relate to others with intelligibility and accountability. This intermediate type of moral status thus brings with it the applicability of the family of ideas associated with responsibility. As Hegel claimed, punishment is the right of the transgressor.[52] Liability to punishment, and more generally to reactive attitudes, indicates a moral status of great moment.

As I argue here, however, recognition and responsibility do not presuppose specifically moral responsibility. They do not presuppose the capacity for wrongdoing or justifiable action. They presuppose judgment, understood as the capacity to respond to reasons, but not critical reason, the capacity to evaluate the force of reasons. Thus they do not presuppose the phenomena of consent, moral equality, moral educability, or mutual respect.

Education constitutively involves critical reasoning and coming to appreciate justifications. Instruction, and more generally animal training, does not; a horse or dog can be instructed about how to navigate an obstacle or agility course, for example, but cannot be educated about how to do so.[53]

This opens space for responsibility, intelligibility, accountability, and mutuality to define the contours of our relationships with the higher animals, as distinct both from our relationships with merely concernworthy animals and our relationships with conscious persons. It also opens space for a better understanding of how the phenomena of this tier figure in human relationships. Respectworthiness is the status characteristic of conscious persons. This status involves moral responsibility, entitlements to consent and equality, and more generally entitlements to mutually reasonable and justifiable relations with other persons.

The three kinds of moral status discussed here constitute a developmental sequence as well as a status hierarchy. This sequence occurs both in the evolutionary history of organisms and in the development of each organism. There was a time when each respectworthy individual was merely recognitionworthy, and there was a time when each recognitionworthy individual was merely concernworthy. This is significant, since it opens new possibilities for understanding the moral status of fetuses, very young children, and the most psychologically sophisticated animals. Some actual animals are recognitionworthy but not respectworthy. Debates about the moral status of apes and dolphins do not concern only whether they are persons. Similarly, debates about abortion do not concern only when humans come to possess the dignity of mature persons.[54]

The claim of status hierarchy is also significant in the context of triage. When distributing scarce and necessary life-saving resources, respectworthy animals should enjoy priority over merely recognitionworthy animals, which in turn should enjoy priority over merely concernworthy animals. In these contexts humans should have priority over apes, for example, and apes should have priority over frogs. I do not here argue explicitly for these conclusions; as was indicated in the introduction, I take them instead to be part of enlightened pretheoretical judgment.[55] But my hope is the status tiers delineated and explicated here both make sense of these judgments and reinforce our confidence in them.

Supposing that this essay's claims about developmental sequence and status hierarchy are correct, are they exhaustive? Or are there further, as yet unexplained tiers of moral status distinct from those discussed here? Additional types of status cannot lie beneath concernworthiness, as I have explicated that idea. If we have no reason to concern ourselves with a being, then that being lacks moral status altogether. So if life supports moral status, contrary to my working hypotheses, then this status is concernworthiness. A distinct status would then likely need to be articulated for conscious or sensate beings.

What about a status above respectworthiness? We do not know whether beings such as angels or gods can exist. Even supposing they do exist, we have little understanding of their nature. Hence we have little understanding of any purportedly appropriate higher kinds of moral status, such as aweworthiness or worshipworthiness, these beings may be thought to possess.

To my mind the most interesting questions of statuses distinct from those discussed here concern the interstices. Is there a type of moral status intermediate between concernworthiness and recognitionworthiness, or between recognitionworthiness and respectworthiness? I do not think we now know, but I am skeptical that any capacity for sociality or communication grounds such an interstitial status. Different types of social relationships help define each tier of moral phenomena, and of course more specific social relationships are crucial in ethics. But my working hypothesis is that psychological capacities, not social capacities or relationships, fundamentally ground each type of moral status.

40 RETHINKING THE VALUE OF HUMANITY

It is also important to ask whether the status of recognitionworthiness should be subdivided. I have argued that moral phenomena often believed to hang together—recognition and respect—must be pulled apart to be properly understood. It may emerge that some phenomena I associate here with recognition must themselves be pulled apart. Perhaps there are capacities for imagistic cognition or for emotional engagement, say, of a type more sophisticated than conscious representation yet less sophisticated than inferential judgment. If so, then animals with those capacities may have a moral status above frogs but below apes, and so may have a proper subset of the entitlements I here associate with recognitionworthiness. That issue awaits future research. Meanwhile it is vital to recognize that there are at least three types of animal moral status, but few if any beyond.

Notes

1. Kant articulates and elaborates his distinctive notions of humanity and dignity in the *Groundwork* (4: 426–437). These notions are developed further in *Religion within the Boundaries of Mere Reason* (6: 26–27) and throughout *The Metaphysics of Morals*.
2. See Section 1 below for references.
3. These literatures overlap in at least two respects. First, expounders of Kant's ethical theory have taken up the question of nonhuman moral status, arguing that a relatively orthodox Kantianism can accommodate such status; see Wood 1998 and Korsgaard 2005, 2018. Second, there is a topic at the boundary of these literatures that encompasses elements of each, namely the moral status of so-called marginal cases of human beings. These include humans at early stages of development and humans suffering from profound mental disabilities. Addressing this topic requires discussing both the status of paradigmatic human persons and how those who are not paradigmatic persons might share this status, including comparing and contrasting their moral status with that of nonhumans. This is a large and diverse literature, but some representative publications are Warren 1997; Hacker-Wright 2007; McMahan 2008; Jaworska and Tannenbaum 2015.
4. See, for example, Anderson 1993; Darwall 2002; Garthoff 2010b.
5. I thank Sarah Buss and Nandi Theunissen for emphasizing the need to differentiate the two parts of what this paper aims to achieve.
6. Most theorists in animal ethics today adopt this alternative approach. Varner (2012) is an exception, but his intermediate proposal, "near-personhood," differs from mine. Another line, pursued by Korsgaard (2018), denies that types of moral status are comparable.
7. This approach is currently unfashionable in part because the correlated understanding of psychology in terms of tiers of sophistication is currently unfashionable. In composing this essay I express my conviction that the old fashion should, and likely will, again become new. I would note, however, that in emphasizing the

explanatory significance of tiers of psychological sophistication I do not thereby endorse the view that these tiers must be separated by sharp boundaries.

8. Another, related feature of concernworthiness is entitlement against being harmed for entertainment. It matters when individuals who matter are harmed, and so in normal circumstances we are obligated not to engage in activities whose point consists in part in inflicting such harm, and we are obligated further to develop a sensibility that does not relish inflicting such harm.

9. For more on such attunement, see the account of "rules of moral salience" in Herman (1993) and the account of "v-rules" in Hursthouse (1999); for further development, see Garthoff 2015b.

10. For more about this topic, see Garthoff 2004a, 2004b; for an excellent earlier discussion see O'Neill 1996, esp. chap. 5.

11. This view enjoys support from theorists as distinct as Singer (1975) and Korsgaard (2005, 2018). The capacity for sensation is sometimes labeled "sentience."

12. Some phenomenological qualities, such as *appearing red*, may not be well understood as feelings. Indeed in more sophisticated beings some conscious states, such as thinking *that 2 + 2 = 4*, may have no associated phenomenology whatsoever. For more on these distinctions, see Block 1995, 2005; Burge 1997, 2006. I say "in principle" because all conscious earthly organisms are probably sensate.

13. The phrase "what it is like" was popularized in Nagel (1974), a justifiably famous account of the difficulty of understanding conscious phenomenology in scientific terms.

14. See Kraut (2007, esp. chap. 2) for an example of this sort of view.

15. These conscious beings importantly include, but are also importantly not limited to, myself. For a fuller development of this criticism, see Garthoff 2010b.

16. In the conclusion I return briefly to the lower and upper boundaries of moral status, during the course of a brief discussion about whether there are types of moral status distinct from those I focus on here. In this essay I take no stand on that question.

17. Some doubt that humanity, rather than rational nature, is the locus of respect in Kant's view; see Timmermann 2006, for example, especially sec. 2. I suspect humanity is the locus of respect, and that this helps explain Kant's otherwise cumbersome formulation "humanity, whether in your own person or that of any other" in his canonical statement of the formula of humanity. In this I concur with Wood 1998. Whether this view is correct is not crucial, however, for this essay.

18. For a sophisticated account of critical reason, see Burge 2011, and for a related view see also Kitcher 2005.

19. Critical reason has additional constitutive conditions, such as a long memory and a robust conception of self. Korsgaard (1996, 2005, 2018) also emphasizes this capacity when distinguishing human persons from nonhuman animals.

20. For an exemplary treatment of consent, see O'Neill 1985. For criticism of this account and the development of a broadly allied rival account, see Pallikkathayil 2011.

21. I would note in passing that I suspect the relevant notion is generic self-government, not the specifically Kantian notion of self-legislation. For relevant criticism of Kant's notion of self-legislation, see Larmore 2008a, 2008b; Garthoff 2015a.

42 RETHINKING THE VALUE OF HUMANITY

22. I will not discuss here the possibility raised by Kant in *Religion* of a being with humanity but not personality, his generic term for moral capacities.

23. I am grateful to Yannig Luthra for discussion of these issues.

24. Where law exists, it can serve as a crucial vehicle for enabling and maintaining reasonable relationships. Accordingly we must encourage and sustain the rule of law, while also encouraging and sustaining healthy suspicion of laws when they enable or retrench domination. For discussion of how to frame that balance of attitudes, see Garthoff 2010a.

25. I make no distinction between dignity and respectworthiness, but for two reasons I henceforth use the latter as my standard term for the moral status of conscious persons. First, though I believe there is much to learn from Kant's account of dignity, I do not think our confidence in the significance of this idea derives mainly from its role in Kantian ethics; this significance principally derives, rather, from reflection on its role in actual social practice (in both ordinary life and more technical domains, such as human rights law). Second, I mean to emphasize the connection between possessing each type of status and the best umbrella term for what that status entitles a being to. Thus there is a parallel among the three types of status I discuss: they each in turn support an entitlement to concern, to recognition, and to respect.

26. In this I oppose the view of Korsgaard 2018.

27. This undergirds the intuitive concern that hedonistic total utilitarianism mistakenly treats individuals as mere "vessels of pleasure." It also suggests extending Rawls's famous idea of the "separateness of persons" to a more general "separateness" of all beings with moral status; see Rawls 1971, 190–191. It is similar in spirit, though again more general in content, to the following comment from David Velleman (1999, 611): "[W]hat's good for a person is worth caring about only out of concern for the person, and hence only insofar as he is worth caring about." I think these (Kantian) ideas of Rawls and Velleman are extremely important. They help to define the subject matter of this essay—moral status—and any ethical theory that fails to do these ideas justice is for that reason doubtful.

28. This is why group rational agents and intelligent nonconscious machines have no moral status of their own but instead derive whatever status they possess from concernworthy individuals. For a defense of this view, see Garthoff 2019.

29. Thus in my view contractualists like T. M. Scanlon (1998, 2008) and Stephen Darwall (2006) are correct to focus attention on mutuality and recognition, but mistaken to associate these moral phenomena with specifically critical reason.

30. For much fuller development of this point, see Garthoff 2020c.

31. If there are nonpropositional judgments, they likely are constituted by a sophisticated form of imagistic cognition. For discussion of the boundary between propositional thought and less sophisticated capacities of representation, see Camp 2007; Burge 2010, 537–551.

32. It may even entail a capacity for free action; for defense of that hypothesis, see Garthoff 2020a.

DECOMPOSING HUMANITY   43

33. For further elaboration of this point in the context of animal ethics, see Garthoff 2020a, 2020b, 2020c.

34. For a compelling defense of this claim, see Burge 2010, 154–210. Burge here opposes arguments of Strawson (1959) 1990, Evans 1982, and Davidson 1982.

35. For evidence of inference in nonhuman animals, see Allen 2006.

36. Note the notion of understanding I work with here is that of comprehension, in particular comprehending the concepts that figure in judgments and other thoughts. It is not the notion of scientific or other theoretical understanding; that sort of understanding is possible only for beings with critical reason.

37. Judgment, as the most primitive locus of reasons-response, is thus also the most primitive psychological capacity that supports rational *incentives*.

38. It is also possible to derive satisfaction from a meal or an orgasm, but that only underscores the point in the text. This satisfaction is not identical to the brute pleasure of the event. In these cases the satisfaction is more readily divorced in time from its object; one can be readily satisfied by remembering something, but one cannot readily reexperience a brute pleasure.

39. Mutual accountability requires further that each party to the relationship have teleological concepts; this is required for each to represent the other as an agent, and so is required for them to represent themselves as acting together. Note that the relevant notions of agency and teleology are not psychological notions, and also that possession of concepts—let alone teleological concepts, or mutual accountability—is not necessary for joint action. For more on the primitiveness of agency, see Burge 2010, 326–338.

40. This claim is developed and defended in Garthoff 2020c.

41. For a classic example of this view, see Strawson 1962.

42. There are also nonmoralized third-personal reactive attitudes that are analogs to moralized indignation, and there are nonmoralized first-personal reactive attitudes that are analogs to moralized guilt. (Against both Strawson [1962] and Darwall [2006], I believe that third-personal reactive attitudes are prior in the order of normative explanation to first- and second-personal reactive attitudes.) Animals may experience nonmoralized attitudes even if they lack specifically critical reason. It is worth dwelling briefly on how this is possible. For such an attitude to be appropriate, not only must its target have failed to exercise good judgment, but the attitude's bearer must also direct the attitude toward themselves; this may seem impossible in a being that lacks the robust representation of self that is made possible by critical reason. But such a robust conception of self is not necessary to direct guilt (say) at oneself. Conscious animals in general, hence also recognitionworthy animals in particular, are immediately and nonrepresentationally aware of themselves in virtue of their consciousness. Conscious states in general are the subjective presentation of the inside of the mind of those who have them. Conscious states thus need not involve *representation* of self to involve *presentation* of self. Since reactive emotions like guilt are constitutively conscious, it is possible for them to involve the self even when they do not represent the self. Note the claim that emotions are constitutively conscious states does not entail that every occurrent emotional state is conscious. The claim is rather

44   RETHINKING THE VALUE OF HUMANITY

that emotions in general, and so the reactive emotions in particular, are typed in part by their phenomenology. A state typed by its phenomenology can occur even in the absence of that phenomenology; and this is true not only for emotions but also for nonrepresentational feelings. Pains are what they are because of how they feel, but this does not entail I must be presently feeling a pain in order to be presently in a state of pain. For discussion of these points I thank Yannig Luthra, and for relevant background, see Burge 1997, 2006.

43. Judgment (reasons-response) is also plausibly the least sophisticated psychological capacity that involves freedom. But even if so, since judgment does not entail critical reason, it does not as such involve the full freedom that comes with the ability to represent, and thereby explicitly criticize, one's own grounds for action. There is a more basic capacity for freedom, however, which consists in having a nonalgorithmic psychology and a capacity for understanding. For elaboration and defense of these claims, see Garthoff 2020b.

44. My use of "reasonableness" and "responsibility" is not identical to that found in Rawls 1999. There are interesting parallels between his uses of these terms and mine, however, which I will not explore here.

45. As was noted previously, Strawson ([1959] 1990) and Evans (1982) attempt such arguments in the philosophy of mind. Korsgaard (2008a, 2008b, 2008c) attempts such arguments in ethical theory.

46. This claim is developed further in Garthoff 2020c.

47. Thus simple, direct arguments for veganism fail. I make no commitment here about whether veganism is obligatory, or would become so if more urgent mistreatments of animals were first corrected. But I doubt it. And more important for present purposes: an argument for veganism must show either (1) that intelligibility and mutuality alone, without a need for consent or social equality, prohibits any use of animals, or (2) that veganism is the only permissible means to advocate for the reform of terrible existing practices of animal exploitation. I take (2) to be more plausible than (1) as a route to obligatory veganism in the current context, but I am skeptical of both. None of this is of course any argument against the *advisability* of veganism or of near-veganism, nor is it any objection to simple, direct arguments for (near-) vegetarianism.

48. See Section II of the *Groundwork*.

49. In our relationships with merely concernworthy animals, by contrast, I doubt there is even an analogous wrong. One could violate a frog or salamander by misleading it or by forcing it to do things, but I doubt that the fact that one manipulates its representations or constrains its guidance of its behaviors by means of those representations as such constitutes a major moral consideration. Interfering with normal functioning of conscious animals may in general be morally problematic, but that is no analog to deception or coercion.

50. The way in which a human life is tragic thus differs from the way in which a merely recognitionworthy animal's life is tragic. Our lot is tragic because (among other reasons) we are aware of realistic possibilities that we inevitably fall short of, because we are aware of the great goods we must forgo in order to enjoy others, and because

our profoundly social nature makes us dependent on others, some of whom we expect to act unjustly. The fundamental tragedy of a recognitionworthy animal's life may be instead that they have capacities for understanding but lack the ability to develop these except in an extremely partial way.

51. Singer (1975) popularized this phrase, and Regan (1983) also holds that morally considerable animals are equal in moral status. Korsgaard (2018) enigmatically denies the question is a meaningful one. I depart from all of the above, as I think the slogan is straightforwardly (and fairly obviously) false.

52. For attribution of this line to Hegel, see Skorupski 2000, 160. Skorupski does not indicate where in Hegel's corpus this statement appears, and I have been unable to locate it. Presumably the source text is either the *Philosophy of Right* or the *Philosophical Propadeutic*.

53. For much fuller development of the contrast between human education and the instruction and training of animals, see Garthoff 2020c.

54. In my view apes are almost certainly not persons; there is perhaps more of a question regarding certain cetaceans. They are both more difficult to study and more difficult to interpret than apes, since their form of life differs more radically from our own. For a defense of the view that humans are the only natural persons on Earth, see Burge 1999.

55. What I take to be among the starting points for ethical theory—relatively fixed points of judgment—is not the particular tiers and psychological groundings articulated here. It is the thought that, absent special justifications or circumstances, a human being can rightly object if scarce life-saving medicine is provided to a horse in preference to them, and similarly that any of us can rightly object on behalf of a horse if the medicine is given to a lizard in preference to it.

References

Allen, Colin. 2006. "Transitive Inference in Animals: Reasoning or Conditioned Associations?" In *Rational Animals?*, edited by Susan Hurley and Matthew Nudds, 175–186. Oxford: Oxford University Press.

Anderson, Elizabeth. 1993. *Value in Ethics and Economics*. Cambridge, MA: Harvard University Press.

Block, Ned. 1995. "On a Confusion about a Function of Consciousness." *Behavioral and Brain Sciences* 18(2): 227–247.

Block, Ned. 2005. "Two Neural Correlates of Consciousness." *Trends in Cognitive Sciences* 9(2): 46–52.

Burge, Tyler, 1997. "Two Kinds of Consciousness." In *Foundations of Mind*, 383–391. Oxford: Oxford University Press, 2007.

Burge, Tyler. 1999. "A Century of Deflation and a Moment about Self-Knowledge." *Proceedings and Addresses of the American Philosophical Association* 73(2): 25–46.

Burge, Tyler. 2006. "Reflections on Two Kinds of Consciousness." In *Foundations of Mind*, 392–419. Oxford: Oxford University Press, 2007.

Burge, Tyler. 2010. *Origins of Objectivity*. Oxford: Clarendon Press,.

46   RETHINKING THE VALUE OF HUMANITY

Burge, Tyler. 2011. "Self and Self-Understanding." In *Cognition through Understanding*, 140–226. Oxford: Oxford University Press.

Camp, Elisabeth. 2007. "Thinking with Maps." *Philosophical Perspectives* 21(1): 145–182.

Darwall, Stephen. 2002. *Welfare and Rational Care.* Princeton, NJ: Princeton University Press.

Darwall, Stephen. 2006. *The Second-Person Standpoint.* Cambridge, MA: Harvard University Press.

Davidson, Donald. 1982. "Rational Animals." *Dialectica* 36(4): 317–328.

Evans, Gareth. 1982. *The Varieties of Reference.* Edited by John McDowell. Oxford: Clarendon Press.

Garthoff, Jon. 2004a. "The Embodiment Thesis." *Ethical Theory and Moral Practice* 7(1): 15–29.

Garthoff, Jon. 2004b. "Zarathustra's Dilemma and the Embodiment of Morality." *Philosophical Studies* 117(2): 259–274.

Garthoff, Jon. 2010a. "Legitimacy Is Not Authority." *Law and Philosophy* 29(6): 669–694.

Garthoff, Jon. 2010b. "Meriting Concern and Meriting Respect." *Journal of Ethics and Social Philosophy* 5(2): 1–29.

Garthoff, Jon. 2015a. "The Priority and Posteriority of Right." *Theoria* 81(3): 222–248.

Garthoff, Jon. 2015b. "The Salience of Moral Character." *Southern Journal of Philosophy* 53(2): 178–195.

Garthoff, Jon. 2019. "Decomposing Legal Personhood." *Journal of Business Ethics* 154(4): 967–974.

Garthoff, Jon. 2020a. "Against the Construction of Animal Ethical Standing." In *Kant and Animals*, edited by John Callanan and Lucy Allais, 191–212. Oxford: Oxford University Press.

Garthoff, Jon. 2020b. "Animal Psychology and Free Agency." "Humans and Other Animals," edited by Noel Kavanaugh. Special Issue of *Yearbook of the Irish Philosophical Society* 2017/18: 73–95.

Garthoff, Jon 2020c. "Animal Punishment and the Conditions of Responsibility." *Philosophical Papers* 49 (1): 69–105.

Hacker-Wright, John. 2007. "Moral Status in Virtue Ethics." *Philosophy* 82(3): 449–473.

Herman, Barbara. 1993. *The Practice of Moral Judgment.* Cambridge, MA: Harvard University Press.

Hursthouse, Rosalind. 1999. *On Virtue Ethics.* Oxford: Oxford University Press.

Jaworska, Agnieszka, and Julie Tannenbaum. 2015. "Who Has the Capacity to Participate as a Rearee in a Person-Rearing Relationship?" *Ethics* 125(4): 1096–1113.

Kant, Immanuel. 1900–. *Kants gesammelte Schriften.* 24 vols. Edited by Königlich Preussische Akademie der Wissenschaften zu Berlin, Deutschen Akademie der Wissenschaften zu Berlin, and Akademie der Wissenschaften zu Göttingen. Berlin: De Gruyter.

Kant, Immanuel. 1996. *Religion within the Boundaries of Mere Reason.* In *Religion and Rational Theology*, 39–216. Edited and translated by Allen W. Wood and Georgi Di Giovanni. Cambridge: Cambridge University Press. [Cited by volume and page of the Akademie edition]

Kant, Immanuel. 1997. *Groundwork of the Metaphysics of Morals.* Edited and translated by Mary Gregor. Cambridge: Cambridge University Press. [Cited by volume and page of the Akademie edition]

Kitcher, Patricia. 2005. "Two Normative Roles for Self-Consciousness." In *The Missing Link in Cognition*, edited by Herbert S. Terrace and Janet Metcalfe, 174–187. Oxford: Oxford University Press.

Korsgaard, Christine M. 1996. *The Sources of Normativity*. Edited by Onora O'Neill. Cambridge: Cambridge University Press.

Korsgaard, Christine M. 2005. "Fellow Creatures." In *The Tanner Lectures on Human Values*, edited by Grethe B. Peterson, vol. 25, 79–110. Salt Lake City: University of Utah Press.

Korsgaard, Christine M. 2008a. "Acting for a Reason." In *The Constitution of Agency*, 207–229. Oxford: Oxford University Press.

Korsgaard, Christine M. 2008b. "The Myth of Egoism." In *The Constitution of Agency*, 69–99. Oxford: Oxford University Press.

Korsgaard, Christine M. 2008c. "The Normativity of Instrumental Reason." In *The Constitution of Agency*, 27–68. Oxford: Oxford University Press.

Korsgaard, Christine M. 2018. *Fellow Creatures: Our Obligations to the Other Animals*. Oxford: Oxford University Press.

Kraut, Richard. 2007. *What Is Good and Why*. Cambridge, MA: Harvard University Press.

Larmore, Charles, 2008a. "The Autonomy of Morality." In *The Autonomy of Morality*, 87–136. Cambridge: Cambridge University Press.

Larmore, Charles 2008b. "Back to Kant? No Way." In *The Autonomy of Morality*, 33–46. Cambridge: Cambridge University Press.

McMahan, Jeff. 2008. "Challenges to Human Equality." *Journal of Ethics* 12(1): 81–104.

Nagel, Thomas. 1974. "What Is It Like to Be a Bat?" *Philosophical Review* 83(4): 435–450.

O'Neill, Onora. 1985. "Between Consenting Adults." *Philosophy and Public Affairs* 14(3): 252–277.

O'Neill, Onora. 1996. *Towards Justice and Virtue*. Cambridge: Cambridge University Press.

Pallikkathayil, Japa. 2011. "The Possibility of Choice; Three Accounts of the Problem with Coercion." *Philosophers' Imprint* 11(16): 1–20.

Rawls, John. 1971. *A Theory of Justice*. Cambridge, MA: Harvard University Press.

Rawls, John. 1999. *The Law of Peoples*. Cambridge, MA: Harvard University Press.

Regan, Tom. 1983. *The Case for Animal Rights*. Oakland: University of California Press.

Scanlon, Thomas M. 1998. *What We Owe to Each Other*. Cambridge, MA: Harvard University Press.

Scanlon, Thomas M. 2008. *Moral Dimensions*. Cambridge, MA: Harvard University Press.

Singer, Peter. 1975. *Animal Liberation*. New York: Random House.

Skorupski, John. 2000. *Ethical Explorations*. Oxford: Oxford University Press.

Strawson, Peter. (1959) 1990. *Individuals*. London: Routledge.

Strawson, Peter. 1962. "Freedom and Resentment." *Proceedings of the British Academy* 4848: 1–25.

Timmerman, Jens. 2006. "Value without Regress." *European Journal of Philosophy* 14(1): 69–93.

Varner, Gary. 2012. *Personhood, Ethics, and Animal Cognition*. Oxford: Oxford University Press.

Velleman, J. David. 1999. "A Right of Self-Termination?" *Ethics* 109(3): 606–628.

Warren, Mary Anne. 1997. *Moral Status: Obligations to Persons and Other Living Things*. Oxford: Clarendon Press.

Wood, Allen 1998. "Kant on Duties regarding Nonrational Nature I." *Proceedings of the Aristotelian Society* supplementary volume 72(1): 211–228.

2
Do the Ancients See Value in Humanity?

Richard Bett

Numerous essays in this volume take off from what seems like a basic thought: that we are subjects of ethical concern. This then leads to the question why this should be so, and one very appealing answer is that there must be something about us that makes us valuable, and hence deserving of such concern. That leads, in turn, to what this value-creating feature or features might be, and *why* this feature or these features make us valuable. At this point one might go in a Kantian direction and appeal to a notion of absolute value, or one might appeal to the ancient notion of the good as beneficial and develop an account of the value of humanity on that basis.[1] But either way (and there may be other options as well), the goal is to provide an explanation for what seems a very intuitive starting point in moral thinking: that there are certain ways people ought to be treated, and certain other ways they ought not to be treated.

I agree that the starting point of these reflections is a basic thought. But it is not the thought with which ancient Greek ethics typically begins. As has often been noted (e.g., Williams 1985; Annas 1993), the most common basic thought for ancient Greek ethics is an interrogative thought: How should I live my life? This does not mean that Greek ethics is egoistic, as it has sometimes been accused of being—at least, not in any objectionable sense; for one thing, the question can equally well be posed in the third person (How should *one* live . . . ?). But it does mean that the focus is typically on what the *agent* should ideally be like rather than on what the people *affected* by the agent's actions or inactions actually are like, such that they warrant certain kinds of treatment and not others. A specification of what the agent should be like will of course have to include an account of what sorts of things the ideal agent will do or not do, and a central aspect of this account will no doubt be the nature of the agent's interactions with other people. But this does not suffice to shift the focus away from the agent and toward the agent's beneficiaries or victims and their status. A striking case is this: when Socrates argues in several of Plato's dialogues—most explicitly in the *Gorgias*, but also in, for example, the *Republic* and the *Crito*—that it is worse to do injustice than to suffer it, the central point is always the bad effect of committing injustice on the agent (specifically, on the state of the agent's soul) rather than the

---

Richard Bett, *Do the Ancients See Value in Humanity?* In: *Rethinking the Value of Humanity.*
Edited by: Sarah Buss and L. Nandi Theunissen, Oxford University Press. © Oxford University Press 2023.
DOI: 10.1093/oso/9780197539361.003.0003

bad effect on those unjustly treated, let alone the fundamental wrongness of such treatment given that the victims are human beings.

So if there is something to be said about ancient conceptions of the value of humanity—and I think there is—it will have to be approached somewhat indirectly, and the ideas that emerge from the inquiry may turn out to be implicit rather than explicit. In what follows, I shall pursue several lines of thought that seem to bear upon the issue. In the first section I focus on ancient Greek philosophers' notions of value, and in the second, on their notions of humanity. In both cases, we can find what look like promising starting points for a conception of the value of humanity, but these never seem to get fully developed, in part because of powerful countervailing ideas held by the same philosophers. In the third and final section, I consider egalitarian currents of thought that look as if they might have gone further toward articulating a picture of the value of humanity; however, the evidence is not sufficient for us to conclude with confidence that they did so. In the end, then, this inquiry will not reveal anything approaching an ancient *theory* of the value of humanity.

1.

A natural place to start might seem to be a Greek word that can often be appropriately translated as "value," namely *axia*; "worth" and "desert" are other possible renderings in many contexts. Yet, in the philosophical context in which the word comes closest to being a technical term—that is, in Stoic ethics—it is of very little help for the present project; this is perhaps illustrative of the difficulties we are up against. The Stoics divide things into good, bad, and indifferent, with only virtue and certain things necessarily connected with virtue (such as virtuous actions, virtuous persons, etc.) counting as good, only vice (with the same supplement, *mutatis mutandis*) counting as bad, and everything else indifferent. However, within the very large category of the indifferent, they notoriously distinguished among (1) indifferents that are "according to nature," the more important of which are called "preferred" indifferents; (2) indifferents that are "against nature," the more important of which are called "dispreferred" indifferents; and (3) indifferents that are neither. For something to be "according to nature" or "preferred" is for it to be such as to contribute, generally speaking and most of the time, to the preservation or enhancement of a desirable natural condition and/ or social position; health, wealth, and good reputation are standard examples. And it is the things "according to nature" that are said to have *axia*, "value," while those "against nature," which are the negative counterparts of these, are said to have *apaxia*, "disvalue."

50   RETHINKING THE VALUE OF HUMANITY

Now, it is clear that "value" in this sense is not going to be of any help in guiding us to an ancient conception of the value of humanity. For, first, "value," so understood, is something like conduciveness to our well-being, and it is states or commodities that qualify as having "value." Human beings characteristically *pursue* (or seek to retain) the things that have value, and it is generally worth their while to do so;[2] however, it would be a category mistake to think of human beings as themselves having value, in this sense.[3] But second—and this is why I said "*something like* conduciveness to our well-being"—the point of calling all of the things having value "indifferent" is that they are not in any sense components, however small, of one's true well-being or "happiness" (*eudaimonia*)—that is, the fulfilment of one's natural end.[4] It is only the virtuous who attain that pinnacle of achievement, and only things that are essential components of this achievement that qualify as genuinely beneficial or good. While the correct *attitude toward* the indifferents, including those that have "value," is an absolutely crucial element in virtue, no amount of "value" is itself equivalent to having virtue, and no amount of "disvalue" is equivalent to lacking or losing it; we are dealing with two quite different and incommensurable levels. Since the modern notion of the value of humanity is a distinctively ethical one, it would seem that any ancient analogue would have to be connected to virtue and the good, not with anything on the level of the indifferent, where the Stoic notion of "value" belongs.[5]

Do the Stoics allow another sort of value that applies specifically to virtuous actions and virtuous persons? It looks as if they do. But, first, this leaves only a small trace in the surviving sources; the default sense of "value" in both Diogenes Laertius and Stobaeus, where our two main summaries of Stoic ethics appear, seems to be the one I have just been discussing. And second, this higher value opens up a new problem: rather than pointing us toward a picture in which human beings as such have value, it restricts value to a vanishingly small, perhaps even nonexistent class of human beings. On the first point, both Diogenes Laertius (7.105) and Stobaeus (2.84,4–17) report three senses of *axia* in Stoicism. There is the one we have already considered; there is monetary value (also irrelevant for our purposes); and there is what Diogenes calls "a contribution to the life in agreement,[6] which applies to every good."[7] Similarly, Stobaeus refers to a sense of "value" "according to which we say that certain things have worthiness (*axiôma*) and value, which does not apply to indifferent things, but only to those that are good" (2.84,11–13).[8] While these formulations are hardly self-explanatory—and explaining them fully would take us too far afield—they give us a notion of value in which *good* things, and not merely indifferent things, can possess value, and since persons are among the items that can qualify as virtuous or good, this allows us a way of saying, in Stoic terminology, that human beings have value. The thought is never developed—this higher notion of value is just barely mentioned—but it is at least clearly available. However (and this leads us to the second point), it is certainly not human beings in general who possess value in this higher sense. Indeed, the Stoics notoriously hold that only a very few people in history (not including themselves) have actually achieved virtue; the wise or virtuous person is said to be rarer than the Phoenix, and while possible exemplars are occasionally mentioned (Socrates, Cato), there is no agreed-upon list of people who did attain the end. All the rest of us are fools and sinners, whose condition is one of vice. So the higher type of value spoken of here is not the value of humanity but the value of one or two utterly exceptional human beings.

I will return to the Stoics. For now I want to switch to Aristotle, who is rather more explicit than the Stoics about the possibility of human beings having value, but where, again, value is generally conceived very much in an aristocratic fashion rather than as common to human beings as such. While Aristotle is not as systematic in his use of the term *axia* as the Stoics, he does use it in numerous different contexts in the *Nicomachean Ethics*. In one of these it again refers to monetary value, which we can dismiss (1119b26, 1133b24). But several others are more relevant to our concerns.

The first of these is the discussion of the "magnanimous" or "great-souled" (*megalopsuchos*) person, in the course of his treatment of all the different virtues of character. Modern readers have not always found much to admire in the virtue of "great-souledness"; while attempts have been made in recent years to rehabilitate the "great-souled" person in relation to contemporary sensibilities (e.g., Pakaluk 2004; Crisp 2006; Sarch 2008), I must admit that he (and it is definitely a "he") still comes across to me primarily as a pompous, self-important jerk. But Aristotle thinks very highly of him, even being disposed to regard "great-souledness" as the pinnacle of the virtues of character, carrying with it all the other virtues of character and somehow enhancing them (1123b29–1124a4). The defining mark of this virtue is being such as to deserve great honors and other accolades, knowing this, expecting others to recognize this appropriately, and when this happens, taking it as no more than his due (1123b1–2, 1124a4–7). Aristotle even admits at one point that this attitude may come across as disdainful (1124a20), but he clearly considers this a misguided reaction, since the person does in fact warrant the encomia he receives. Throughout the chapter on this virtue (4.3), Aristotle characterizes the "great-souled" person's superior status by saying that he has a great deal of *axia*, value, and is therefore worthy (*axios*) of this admiration. Here, then, we have an implied hierarchy of comparative amounts of value.[9] It is not ruled out that everyone might have some degree of value. But it is not stated, either; another possibility, at least as consistent with the general tenor of Aristotle's view, is that some people might have positive value and others negative value. In any case, we certainly do not have the notion of a basic and ethically significant kind of value attaching to all humans qua humans. On the contrary, the kind of value Aristotle is talking about is a kind of which

52   RETHINKING THE VALUE OF HUMANITY

some people have much more than others, with corresponding differences in the levels of respect due to each, and of which some people quite possibly have none.

The same conception is evident in Aristotle's discussion of friendship in books 8 and 9. The account of friendship generally involves a rough equality between the parties. But at book 8, chapter 7 he introduces a different kind of friendship, one that can exist between unequals, where the inequality is integral to the character of the friendship. The examples he lists are the friendship between a father and a son, an older and a younger person, a man and a woman, and in general anyone in a role of ruler and someone in the correlative role of ruled (1158b12–14). Aristotle actually says "for a father *toward* a son," etc., but it is clear from the ensuing discussion that the friendship is supposed to go both ways. However, because of the inequality, the expectations on each party are not the same (unlike in the paradigmatic cases of friendship). In particular, the loving must be unequal just as the friendship is, and the better and more beneficial party must be loved more than he or she loves;[10] so, apparently, the parent is supposed to be loved by the child more than vice versa (etc.), because the parent is the better and more beneficial party (1158b23–26). Whether or not this would be either realistic or desirable by our lights, it is then glossed by another remark about comparative value: Aristotle says that "when the loving occurs according to value, then in a way equality occurs, which in fact seems to be characteristic of friendship" (1158b27–28). The inequality is, as it were, canceled out by the superior degree of love accorded to the superior party. Hence we get a kind of equality, which allows this kind of relationship to be assimilated to regular friendship. But of course, this is possible only given that the inequality in the value of the two parties is recognized and, in a sense, compensated for (cf. 1159a33–b2 for the same point). Again, we have a comparative scale of value in human beings, and again, while this does not exclude the possibility of everyone having a certain baseline level of value, it does not require it, and it certainly does not draw attention to any such idea—quite the reverse.

But perhaps friendship is not a context in which we should expect to find ideas about a value shared by everyone equally. Justice might seem more promising in this respect. Yet even here, one is hard-pressed to find Aristotle giving any attention to ideas of this sort. Earlier in the *Nicomachean Ethics*, in his discussion of justice in book 5, Aristotle makes another allusion to the value of human beings. Everyone agrees, he says, that justice in distributions must be in terms of value, but they do not think of value in the same way; democrats think of it as the status of a free citizen, oligarchs as the possession of wealth, others as good birth, and aristocrats as virtue (1131a25–29). He is thinking here in particular of the distribution of political power, and the idea is that different people have different conceptions of what makes someone deserve this power, because they have different conceptions of what makes someone a person of value. Here, even

DO THE ANCIENTS SEE VALUE IN HUMANITY? 53

the most capacious conception, the democratic one, will exclude a great many people from having value; women were not citizens in this full sense, and neither, of course, were slaves. So it looks as if the relations of justice, based on actual political arrangements, that Aristotle and his contemporaries were able to conceive were simply not capable of supporting the idea that human beings as such have value.

Aristotle's remarks on slavery deserve further attention. Given his notorious approval of the practice, one might expect his comments on this subject to do nothing but reinforce the picture we have seen so far. In some respects they certainly do so. In one of the chapters on friendship (8.11), he associates the prospects for friendship in various kinds of political community with the extent to which justice is present in each of them. He points out that relations both of friendship and of justice require at least something in common between the ruler and the ruled. Hence in a tyranny, where the gulf between ruler and ruled is at its most extreme, there is only a minimal degree of either—at least, between the tyrant and his subjects. As examples of relations where both friendship and justice are impossible, he mentions the relations of craftspeople to their tools and of soul to body. But the same is true in some cases where both relata are animate (body being conceived as, all by itself and not including the soul, inanimate), and here the examples Aristotle gives are a person's relation to a horse or cow or to a slave—"for there is nothing in common" (1161b3). Presumably, although this is not specified, he has especially in mind the relation between the slaveholder and his own slave, since he refers to the slave, using the term also employed in the *Politics*, as an "animate tool." Now, the language of value is not present in this chapter, but if we put this discussion together with the discussions of friendship and justice in which the language of value does occur, it is hard to see how Aristotle can regard the slave as having any value at all.

At this point, then, any notion of the value of humanity as such in Aristotle may seem to be decisively ruled out. Yet immediately afterward in the same chapter, we find a surprising twist. For Aristotle says that one cannot have friendship toward a slave "insofar as he is a slave" (1161b3, 5). However, insofar as he is a human being, friendship with him is possible (5–6). And we then find the following remarkable passage, which seems to open up the possibility of something much closer to a modern conception of the value of humanity: "for there seems to be some justice for every human being toward everyone who is capable of community in law and agreement;[11] friendship too, then, in so far as he is a human being" (1161b6–8). As often in Aristotle, the thought is quite compressed, and the second part, in particular, is generally expanded by translators at least into a complete sentence, often with additional elements to fill out the idea.[12] But whether or not one puts extra elements into the translation (something I prefer to avoid whenever possible), the underlying thought is tolerably

54 RETHINKING THE VALUE OF HUMANITY

clear. There is some level of both justice and friendship that applies between every human being and every other, at least if they are both "capable of community in law and agreement," and this includes even slaves. What these relations of justice and friendship involve deserves considerable elaboration, but in line with Aristotle's own discussions of both topics, I take it there is some level of both obligation and entitlement on both sides. It must be a very low level in the present case, given that it apparently leaves the institution of slavery intact. But still, we can draw a distinction between a slaveholder's relatively humane treatment of slaves and an absolutely oppressive treatment of them,[13] and this is perhaps the kind of thing Aristotle has in mind. It is also not quite clear what he means by the phrase "capable of community in law and agreement"; who, if anyone, is this supposed to exclude: the mentally ill, those with Down syndrome or similar disorders, or perhaps (if this is distinct from the mentally ill) the "bestial" person whom he introduces at the beginning of book 7 as occupying a level below regular human vice? Whatever the answer, we are clearly dealing with cases that Aristotle regards as quite exceptional. And even modern ideas of the value of humanity need not exclude the possibility that in certain exceptional cases people might either forfeit their value as human beings or lack a sufficient degree of the distinctively human capacities that underpin this value in the first place.[14]

So at this place in Aristotle we have at least a glimmer of the idea that human beings as such are valuable. But it is not developed, and it is not easily assimilable to the much more hierarchical picture we find in most of his thinking, where some people have more value and others less. Perhaps we can imagine a composite picture in which everyone (except perhaps for the special cases just mentioned) has a minimal level of value, and then there is room for higher levels of value for some. But, first, while this does not, as far as I can see, contradict anything in the text, it is not something Aristotle chooses to say anything about. And second, the dominant conception in which people's value is unequal, and some people's at best pretty small, seems to cut against the usual aspiration of those who have advocated notions of the value of humanity—namely, that these notions should have real ethical import, significantly affecting how we view and treat one another. To return to Aristotle's distinction between considering one's slave as a human being and as a slave: if in the latter respect the slave lacks value (except monetary value), which seemed to be an implication of various things he said, then the value the slave possesses in the former respect, along with everyone else, really cannot amount to much.

So far, then, we have not found much to encourage the idea that the ancients had a conception of the value of human beings as such. In Stoicism it looks as if almost no one has the kind of value that could be useful for this conception, while in Aristotle it looks as if some people have a lot of value, others much less, and some quite possibly none at all. One passage in the *Nicomachean Ethics* seems to point in a more promising direction, but the promise is not remotely realized. In the remainder of the paper, I will explore whether there are other ideas in ancient Greek thought akin to that of the value of humanity. In the end, this exploration will not take us much further, but there are several points that may mitigate the generally rather dispiriting picture we have encountered up to now.[15]

2.

So far we have concentrated on the term "value." What do we learn if we shift our focus to the conception of "humanity"? Of course, the word "humanity" derives from the Latin *humanitas*, and there was at least some tendency among Roman thinkers to associate *humanitas* specifically with the pursuit or attainment of education and learning. The second-century CE essayist Aulus Gellius, whose interests sometimes extend to philosophy, says that those who use the word correctly mean by it *eruditionem institutionemque in bonas artes*, "education and training in the good arts [generally translated 'liberal arts']" (13.17.1). Gellius goes on to say that this kind of learning is unique to human beings, and that is why it is called *humanitas*; he refers to Cicero and Varro as authors who use the word in this sense, quoting a passage of Varro and arguing plausibly that this is what he must mean in context (namely, any person of *humanitas* will know about the sculptor Praxiteles). He does not quote Cicero, but it is easy enough to find passages of Cicero to support the claim, where *humanus* is either used alongside *doctus*, "learned," as a more or less synonymous variant (*De divinatione* 1.2), or *humanitas* appears alone in the sense of "learning" or "culture" (*De oratore* 1.71, 2.72). Obviously there is still a remnant of this usage in our own term "humanities," as applied to a set of long-standing academic fields that are both cherished and yet frequently under threat for their supposed impracticality.[16]

Now, this usage of *humanus* and *humanitas* may seem to lead us right back to the kind of exclusivity that we found earlier. For clearly the relevant kind of learning is never going to be shared by all human beings, even all adult human beings. However, if we ask more generally what distinguishes human beings from other animals or other parts of the universe, a range of ancient authors, both Greek and Roman, give an answer that is more accommodating to humans in general yet not unrelated to the usage of the word *humanitas* that we have been discussing. Returning to Aristotle and the Stoics, our main sources in the first part of the paper, we find a clear and consistent answer expressed in terms of a crucial difference between the souls of humans and those of other animals (or, in the case of Aristotle, plants):[17] unlike that of any other regular natural organism, the human soul has thought, reason or intellect. In his work *On the Soul*, Aristotle simply says that humans differ[18] in having *to dianoêtikon te kai nous* (414b18),

56 RETHINKING THE VALUE OF HUMANITY

"the thinking capacity and intellect"; and his account of the workings of intellect in the same work (3.4–5) is among the most cryptic portions of his entire corpus. But the Stoics clearly associate the rational soul with the occurrence of rational impressions, which have linguistically expressible content (Sextus Empiricus, *Adversus Mathematicos* 8.275–276; Diogenes Laertius 7.49; Aetius 4.21.1). Here, then, is an outward distinguishing mark of the human being: the power of language. And this point is noted, as obvious and needing no support, by numerous ancient authors, including Aristotle in another context (*Politics* 1253a9–10), and also authors concerned with the theory and practice of rhetoric, for whom it has a special relevance (Isocrates, *Nicocles* 5–6; Cicero, *De oratore* 1.32).

Plato, in his dialogue *Protagoras*, has the Sophist of that name express a slightly broader view. In the myth that Protagoras tells here about early human history and the origins of human society, it is *technê*—regularly translated as "craft," "skill," "expertise," or "art"—that is given to humans and them alone (321d). Fire is mentioned as necessary for the effectiveness of the *technai* in general, and its production is identified just below (321e) as itself a *technê*, but it is the technical wisdom of both Hephaestus (fire) and Athena (the *technai* in general) that is the gods' special gift to humans. Once they start using their *technê*, language is one of their first products, along with houses, clothes, shoes, bedding, and crops (322a). Interestingly, while Protagoras mentions all of these as on a par, language simply being the first on the list, one of the authors cited in the previous paragraph, Isocrates (*Nicocles* 5–6), identifies language as the *source* of the *technai* and of "just about all the things devised by us," in addition to cities and laws. The *technê* of politics also occurs in Protagoras's speech, but at a subsequent stage (322b–d), brought in by the gods because the *technai* distributed so far were not sufficient to keep people safe from the ravages of the natural world; for that, it was necessary for them to come together into communities. An essential feature of this *politikê technê* is that everyone has some minimal sense of justice, this too being singled out as indispensable for being human (323c). And this too recalls one of the texts cited just above in which language is assumed to be definitive of humanity. When Aristotle alludes to this in the *Politics*, he adds that language is "for[19] showing the beneficial and the harmful, hence also the just and the unjust; for this is peculiar to humans in comparison to other animals—alone having a sense of good and bad, just and unjust, and the rest—and it is community in these things that makes a household and a city" (1253a14–18).

Not everyone I have mentioned in the previous few paragraphs proposes exactly the same ideas. But there is a great deal of overlap, and we might sum up a kind of composite view, much of which any one of them would assent to, as follows. Humans are distinctively rational beings. A central facet of their rationality is language, and language in turn is the basis for both the technical achievements of civilization and the ability to form societies, with the ability to grasp ethical and political concepts that this entails. This cluster of related abilities is what makes us special, as compared with the rest of the natural world, and the ethical and political dimension of these abilities is what ensures that we will treat each other differently from the way we treat the other creatures and objects we encounter. Humanity in its highest manifestations may involve a more refined cultivation of the rational and linguistic capacity than most people have either the time or the ability to pursue. But this capacity itself is shared by humans in general, and that is a very significant fact.

Does this amount to a recognition of the *value* of humanity? Not in so many words, but we are perhaps not far from that point. In the passage where Aulus Gellius explains the elevated notion of *humanitas* that he considers correct, he contrasts this with a generally accepted (but in his view bogus) sense of the term in which it is equivalent to the Greek *philanthrôpia*, that is, "a certain indiscriminate willingness and benevolence toward all human beings" (13.17.1). Gellius may scorn this usage, but he acknowledges that it is widespread, and it may remind us of Aristotle's mention of the friendship and justice connecting every human being with every other. Now, neither text indicates that this fellow-feeling reflects an appreciation of the rationality, linguistic capacity, etc. of all humans. But if we made that link, we might be getting close to an ancient conception of the value of humanity. We would need to connect the dots in a way that the ancients themselves do not seem to do explicitly. But the resources seem to be there, and it is arguably not much of a stretch.

Another thing that Plato's Protagoras says, in the speech we have already drawn on, is that humans were the only animals to worship the gods (322a); this is said to be "because of their kinship with god." And this points to another, related way in which we might perhaps be able to identify an ancient vision of the value of humanity. Since we have independent evidence that Protagoras was an agnostic, it is not clear, in his case, what the cashed-out value of "kinship with god" would be. But others took the notion of kinship with god, and the accompanying aspiration to become as much like god as possible, very seriously (and literally).

In the remainder of this section, I shall explore this theme in Plato, Aristotle, and the Stoics. As we shall see, each of these philosophers has ideas that seem to chime with and reinforce the picture derived from the various reflections on which we were just focusing—reflections concerning what it is to be human— where we seemed to be getting relatively close to a conception of the value of humans as such. Yet in this context too, we never quite reach a fully realized version of that conception, and in this case it is for a familiar reason: namely, that these ideas always appear alongside other ideas pointing to the dominant picture that emerged from our reflections on value, a picture in which value is distributed very unevenly among human beings, and most people's value is insignificant.

58 RETHINKING THE VALUE OF HUMANITY

The ideal of becoming like god is explicit, and held out as possible to a considerable degree, in a famous passage of Plato's *Theaetetus*. Socrates has been examining Theaetetus's proposal that knowledge is perception, a view that he assimilates to the Protagorean thesis that "a human being is measure of all things." Examining this thesis has led him to consider the idea that what counts as just and unjust varies from one community to another. In the midst of this long discussion, there is a digression in which Socrates draws attention to the character of the philosopher, as opposed to the person concerned with day-to-day affairs (172c–177c).[20] The philosopher has the leisure to think beyond these immediate concerns and contemplate eternal verities—including the true nature of justice and injustice, as opposed to what passes for just and unjust in the law courts and elsewhere. The philosopher may well seem ridiculous if forced to engage in conventional legal proceedings, but it is the philosopher who is in touch with the things that really matter. As has often been noticed, the passage has much in common with the cave image in the *Republic*, although there is no explicit reference to Platonic Forms as the realities the philosopher grasps. In any case, escape from the everyday world into the realm of pure truth is described as "becoming like god." This is, we are told, a state of justice as well as wisdom (176b1–3). And, to return to our main theme, the fact that this is a human possibility suggests that humanity has a special status in the order of things.

We might draw a similar lesson from a related theme that occurs in several Platonic dialogues, the idea that "learning is recollection." According to this view, humans possess all knowledge from before birth, and what we call learning is merely recollection of the knowledge that one already has. The idea is put to different purposes in different dialogues. But in both the *Phaedo* and the *Phaedrus*, the souls in this out-of-body state are clearly described as akin to the divine, if they maintain their pure state, and in the *Phaedrus*, indeed, in the presence of the divine (*Ph.* 80a–81a, *Phdr.* 246d–e248a–c, 249c), while in the *Meno*, at least the insight into the soul's immortality and its possession of all knowledge is described as divine (81a10–b2).

The problem, of course, is in the qualification "if they maintain their pure state." For although the soul's immortality and prebirth possession of knowledge is quite general, which suggests that we all have the capacity to achieve kinship with the divine, both the *Phaedo* and the *Phaedrus*, where (unlike in the *Meno*) the soul's fate is explored in some detail, make clear that the chances of success are not particularly high. Contamination by the body in the *Phaedo*, and distraction by the nonrational parts of the soul in the *Phaedrus*, are ever-present dangers to which most souls succumb. So actual kinship with the divine is limited to a few; just as in the *Theaetetus* passage with which we began discussing this theme, it is only the philosopher of whom it can be said that he "becomes like god." In the *Republic*, again, only the philosophers commune with the Forms,

DO THE ANCIENTS SEE VALUE IN HUMANITY? 59

while the rest, to switch to the figurative mode, never leave the cave. This is not merely due to lack of opportunity or failure to exercise one's capacities; in the *Republic* everyone's place in society is set by their nature (however that is supposed to be determined),[21] and only a select few are of a nature to philosophize and rule. If we take this last point seriously, the idea that "learning is recollection" and, more generally, that human beings can assimilate to the divine does not after all appear to support the supposition that human beings as such have value.

Aristotle is a similar case. He too sees the highest human good as philosophizing, and he too regards this as an activity that expresses something divine in us. This is most fully and clearly discussed at the end of the *Nicomachean Ethics* (10.7–8), where philosophical contemplation emerges as the most fitting candidate for the highest good for human beings. It is also at least implicit in his remarks about the unmoved mover in *Metaphysics* Λ; this divine being is eternally engaged in intellectual contemplation, and we can to a limited extent imitate this activity (1072b14–15). This ability of course sets us apart from other terrestrial beings. Or perhaps it is better to say that, given our capacity for contemplation, Aristotle is genuinely conflicted as to whether we humans should be considered purely terrestrial beings. This comes out in his struggles with how to accommodate thinking within his generally very biological conception of the soul. Despite having defined the soul as the form of an organic body (412a19–21), he insists that thinking is a nonbodily process because thought's ability to direct itself to any object whatever (and hence take on any form whatever) means that it cannot have any inherent or antecedent nature of its own, which involvement with the body would give it (429a18–27). The tension is also apparent in the chapter where the definition of the soul appears. As a consequence of the definition, he says that the soul is not separable from the body (since in Aristotle, unlike Plato, forms are not separable from the things of which they are forms). But even in saying this, he immediately wants to limit it to just some parts of the soul, intellect being clearly the exception he has in mind (413a3–9). Scholars have come to Aristotle's rescue, arguing that the contradiction is only apparent (e.g., Irwin 1991, 72–73; Caston 2006, esp. 336–341; Shields 2007, chap. 7). But it is at least clear that he regards thinking as something quite distinct in kind from the various other functions of the soul; and even those who take Aristotle to be consistent tend to give up when it comes to the active, rather than the passive, aspect of the intellect, which is said to be not only separable from the body but also immortal (430a23).

So again, thought, and especially philosophical thought, gives us a special status, and a kinship with the divine; and in the *Ethics* Aristotle insists, against the usual Greek horror of *hubris* (thinking oneself on a level with the gods), that we should cultivate this ability of ours as much as possible (1177b31–34).[22] Of course, a life of *nothing but* philosophical thinking would be superhuman

60 RETHINKING THE VALUE OF HUMANITY

(1177b25–26), but our own limited engagement in this activity far surpasses in its "power and dignity" (*dunamei kai timiotêti*—the latter rendered "value" in Irwin 1999) anything else of which we are capable. But as with Plato, there is a real question as to whether we can consider this an endorsement of the value of humanity as such. For even though the *Ethics* is presented as an account of the human good, with no qualifications attached, it is clear, first of all, that given any realistic social arrangements, only a very few will in fact be able to engage in this activity. Of course, one might think that the mere possession of a *capacity* to do so could confer value, whether or not conditions allowed for this capacity to be exercised. But second, it turns out in the *Politics* that human nature itself comes in degrees; in other words, by no means everyone has even the needed capacity. In the final chapter of book 1 Aristotle raises the question whether the virtues are the same for free people as for slaves and for men as for women (and children)—or whether those other than free men have virtues at all (1259b21–30). The answer (and what is especially appalling about this, from a contemporary perspective, is the matter-of-fact tone in which Aristotle lays it all out) is that they do have virtues, but given differences in the grade of soul belonging to each group, the virtues are different from those of free men. All have rational elements to their souls, but of different levels, so to speak. Those who are by nature slaves completely lack the deliberative element; women have the deliberative element, but it is without authority (*akuron*), whatever that means; in children (that is, I assume, children who are going to grow up to be free men) it is undeveloped (1260a10–15). While philosophic ability is not relevant here, we can hardly doubt that those who do not have fully functioning deliberative abilities also lack any philosophical ability. So Aristotle, like Plato, leaves us in a position where only some humans are even in the running for the human good—and this is a product of nature, not just of social arrangements.[23] Again, what looked like a basis for attributing a special value to humanity turns out not to be adequate for that purpose.

The Stoics go further than any other ancient Greek philosophical school in articulating what looks like an account of the value of humanity, though their story ultimately follows a similar trajectory. As far as we can tell, this story begins with the second-century BCE Stoic Panaetius of Rhodes. Cicero's *De Officiis*, usually translated as *On Duties*, gives us a good idea of Panaetius's view.[24] Cicero tells us that we have two *personae* or "roles" (1.107): one is common to all of us and is based on our human nature, while the other is specific to each of us and is based on our individual nature.[25] The universal role reflects the fact that "we are all participants in reason and in that superiority by which we excel over the beasts, from which everything honorable and fitting is derived, and out of which a method of finding our duty is discovered." Similar sentiments are expressed rather more fully by Epictetus in a chapter of the *Discourses* revealingly called

"How is it possible to find out what is incumbent on us (*ta kathêkonta*) from our titles (*onomatôn*)," which again distinguishes a variety of roles or "titles," beginning with the role of human being. It is worth quoting from this chapter at some length:

> Examine who you are. First, a human being—that is, you have nothing more authoritative than the power of decision,[26] but you hold other things subordinate to this, whereas it is not enslaved or subordinated. Consider then, from what are you separated in virtue of your reason. You are separated from wild animals, you are separated from sheep. In addition to this you are a citizen of the world and a part of it—not one of the menial parts but one of the principal parts; for you are capable of tracing the divine administration and calculating what comes next. (*Diss.* 2.10.1–3)

Both passages emphasize our rationality, both cite this as placing us above the beasts, and both connect this with our ability to think ethically. The Epictetus passage goes rather further in introducing the theme of cosmopolitanism and in ranking us one of the "principal" (*proêgoumena*) parts of the world in virtue of our grasp of the world's divine organization. This is not quite equivalent to calling us akin to the divine, but since rationality is one of the defining characteristics of the divine (e.g., Diogenes Laertius 7.147), calling attention to our rationality, our status as a "principal" part of the cosmos, and our awareness of divinity makes that inference so easy as to be hardly an inference at all. The preeminence of rationality in the Stoics' understanding of god also means that all of this follows very naturally from the more limited Cicero/Panaetius picture, even though nothing about divinity is actually mentioned there. It is no doubt passages such as these that led the influential French scholar Pierre Hadot (1992, 331) to conclude that "le Stoïcien croit en la valeur absolue de la personne humaine."

However, I think this is too quick. For although we may all be rational beings, we still have to contend with the radical difference of level between the sage and everyone else, to which I drew attention near the beginning. With a truly minute number of exceptions, we are all failures; we may *have* rationality, but its condition is severely defective. The sage is the one who really does understand the divinely providential nature of the world and is therefore fully in harmony with it. And the Stoics do not hesitate to put the sage on the same level as god (Plutarch, *On Common Conceptions* 1076a–b). In contrast, though the rest of us—that is, for practical purposes, all of us—are "*capable* of tracing the divine administration,"[27] we do not actually succeed in doing so, and we remain fools and sinners. Again, as with Aristotle, one might wish to appeal to the capacity itself as a bearer of value. But again, on further examination, it is far from clear whether the claim that we even have this capacity can really be borne out. In the Stoic case, this is

62 RETHINKING THE VALUE OF HUMANITY

because our lack of success is itself part of that same providence with which the sage alone is in tune; the defectiveness of our rationality is not a product of accidental circumstance but is built into the nature of things.

I think that this is in fact a major tension in Stoicism. How can we take seriously the providential nature of the world, and our kinship with the divine, when the ideal state that is teleologically ordained for us as part of the divine plan is almost never realized—especially when that too is part of the divine plan? Or, to put it slightly differently, how can we take seriously that humanity is as valuable a part of the world as the Epictetus passage proclaims, when the end that the world itself sets for us is an end that we are also, with almost no exceptions, divinely determined not to achieve? One may object that the later Stoicism of Epictetus, Seneca, and others—going back perhaps as far as Panaetius—was not as rigorous as the Stoicism of Zeno and Chrysippus. It is true that there is a lot more emphasis in later Stoic texts on practical guidance for ordinary mortals, and a lot less emphasis on the character of the sage. But, first, this may be in part an artifact of the evidence that has survived; many other Stoics besides Panaetius wrote books *Peri tou Kathêkontos*,[28] and if these had survived, we might have rather less sense of a shift over time. And second, unless the distinctions between the sage and the fool, virtue and vice, wisdom and folly, etc., are abandoned or substantially rewritten—which the later Stoics show no sign of doing—the tension does not go away.[29]

3.

What we have found, then, is a number of ideas that look as if they could easily be developed into a robust conception of the value of humanity, with the Stoics, or some Stoics, coming closest to spelling out such a conception. But we have also seen a recurring pattern: these ideas keep coming up against a variety of other ideas that push powerfully in a much more hierarchical—some might say, elitist—direction, where value is shared very unequally, some humans having a great deal of value and others much less, if any. Now, at this point one might reasonably wonder: Is there any evidence from antiquity of this hierarchical tendency being actively resisted in favor of a more egalitarian or universalizing conception of human value? We have seen several facets of the hierarchical tendency in Aristotle and the Stoics; we have also seen it in the Platonic conception of humanity's relation to the divine. The one place where we have not seen it, among the thinkers we have considered so far, is in Protagoras as depicted in Plato. And this will serve as the starting point for the final element in my story.

Recall that Plato depicts Protagoras as offering an account of human prehistory and the origins of human society. Though couched in mythical terms, it appears to suggest an optimistic picture of human progress over time, in contrast to the common Greek picture, from Hesiod onward, of a prehistoric Golden Age from which current human life is a depressing decline. Most important for my purposes, it makes no mention of a hierarchy among humans, where a select few make all the inventions and discoveries and the rest are passive beneficiaries; the growth of human competencies and of civilization looks like a collective exercise, with everyone on an equal footing. By the same token, as mentioned earlier, Protagoras stresses that everyone has a share of justice—otherwise they would not be human (323c). The importance of this element is emphasized by the fact that Zeus makes an explicit choice about it; Hermes asks whether justice should be allocated selectively (like the other forms of expertise) or to everyone alike, and Zeus responds that it should be the latter (322c–d). As we saw in the previous section, all of this seems like fertile ground for the idea that there is a value to all human beings as such; and unlike the comparable ideas that we found in other thinkers, there are no countervailing considerations that place some people on a very different level from others.

Concerning this last point, the same might be said of Protagoras's most famous saying, "[A] human being is measure of all things: of the things that are, that they are, and of the things that are not, that they are not," which is quoted and discussed, as I mentioned, by Plato in the *Theaetetus*, but which also appears in Sextus Empiricus (*Adversus Mathematicos* 7.60–64) and several other authors. We have only the one sentence from Protagoras himself, and a great deal about the view is obscure.[30] But one thing that is clear from Plato's treatment of the view is that he reads it as implying a fundamental equality in human perspectives; however things appear to a person, things *are* that way for that person—whatever specifically that may amount to. The view clearly drives Aristotle crazy and provokes a sarcastic response: for Aristotle the "measure" of things, including of good and bad, is not any arbitrary human being, but the person who is mentally and physically adjusted to see things as they really are—a state achieved by only a few (*Nicomachean Ethics* 1113a31–33, 1176a17–19). And already in the *Theaetetus*, a major problem for the view is how it can allow for the existence of various types of expertise that Protagoras himself would surely have wanted to accept. There is no clear indication that Protagoras developed his "measure" doctrine in such a way as to spell out a conception of universal human value, but one can see how it looks much more accommodating to such a conception than the hierarchical ideas of the other thinkers we have examined,[31] and the account of human prehistory that Plato puts in his mouth in the *Protagoras* perhaps gives us a taste of how he might have begun to develop it.

It appears that Protagoras was not alone in this respect. Another fifth-century BCE Sophist, Antiphon, seems to have argued explicitly in favor of the equality of Greeks and non-Greeks. We may draw distinctions of value between the laws

64   RETHINKING THE VALUE OF HUMANITY

and practices of different societies, but these distinctions have no basis in nature; all of us, he argues, have a common basic nature, and whether we live in Greek or non-Greek societies is, as far as that nature is concerned, purely accidental.[32] This is one of several themes explored by the Sophists that build upon the distinction between *phusis*, "nature," and *nomos*, "law" or "convention"; here the suggestion is that *nomos* is a barrier to recognition of our basic equality. What this equality was taken to imply in practical terms is impossible to say from the evidence we have. Plato puts a similar sentiment—that *nomos* stands in the way of our recognizing natural equals—in the mouth of another Sophist, Hippias of Elis, in the *Protagoras* (337c–d). But here the equality seems to be among the distinguished wise company to whom he is speaking; there is no indication that it applies to human beings in general. Still, the idea of natural equality at least seems to open up the possibility that all of us are of value simply as humans.

The presence of such egalitarian ideas in this period (roughly, a few decades before and after 400 BCE) is also indicated by the suspicions cast on them by those who did not share them. Perhaps the most obvious case is Aristotle's defense of slavery. While, as we noted in the first section, Aristotle argues that slavery—at least, when the right people are enslaved—is both natural and just, he clearly has in mind a set of opponents who believed the opposite. He does not name these opponents of slavery, but he takes it as a question worth discussing whether there are people of such a nature as to be appropriately enslaved; his own answer is that there certainly are, but he acknowledges that some have thought otherwise, and he admits that they are right to the limited extent that sometimes those who are in fact enslaved are not natural slaves (*Politics* I.4–6).

Another interesting case is the famous choral ode in Sophocles's *Antigone* (332–375), beginning *polla ta deina*, "many are the wonders," which elaborates on human powers and achievements. The text speaks of seafaring, agriculture, hunting, language, laws, and society; much of this is reminiscent of Protagoras's account of early human history, and this is surely not accidental. In summary, humanity is described (I translate some difficult poetic language as literally as possible) as "possessing, in the ingeniousness of expertise, something wise beyond expectation" (*sophon ti to machanoen technas huper elpid' echôn*, 365–366). This is often read as a celebration of humanity, and in that spirit it might be taken as a central representative of the egalitarian line of thinking I have been pointing to in the previous few paragraphs. But in fact I think it expresses a sharp sense of danger in that line of thinking. For one thing, *deina*, which I initially translated as "wonders"—of which humanity is singled out as the supreme example—has multiple connotations, by no means all of them positive. It can mean "wonderful" in a positive sense, also "clever,"[33] but it can also mean "terrible" or "awful." In addition, the phrase I quoted just above, about human beings' astonishing ingenuity, is immediately followed by "[humanity] proceeds sometimes toward bad,

DO THE ANCIENTS SEE VALUE IN HUMANITY? 65

sometimes toward good" (367). Certainly the dramatic context in which this ode is embedded does not inspire great confidence about what human ingenuity may achieve in the political or social realm; the central conflict of the play, between Antigone and the ruler Creon, leads to the death of most of the main characters, and to Creon's being led away a broken man. Finally, one of the prime human achievements, agriculture, is described as "wearing away ... Earth, oldest of the gods" (337–339)—an activity that (at least under that description) seems to carry with it a whiff of hubris.[34]

Nonetheless, whatever attitude Sophocles wishes the chorus to project in this ode,[35] it at least suggests awareness of the existence at this time of an optimistic mindset in which human beings as such were regarded as admirable for their abilities and achievements. This attitude, as I said, seems to have a good deal in common with the ideas expressed by Protagoras in the speech Plato gives him in the dialogue named after him. And if we take all the points considered in this section together, we seem to have a cluster of views that point in an egalitarian direction, and that can easily be imagined as the starting point for a conception of the value of humanity not hobbled by the kind of hierarchical tendencies that we have found in the Stoics, Aristotle, and Plato. How far those who held these views progressed in this direction, or how widely such views were held in the first place, is impossible to say with any confidence. These egalitarian and perhaps more broadly pro-democratic views are now largely lost to us; indeed, they are often available to us only via the works of those who opposed them. One point that may well give us pause is that in the same papyrus in which Antiphon speaks of the equality of Greeks and non-Greeks, he also speaks of justice as a set of rules (*nomoi*) created by society, rules that prevent us from meeting our natural needs; the most advantageous course of action, he says, is therefore to ignore justice except when the authorities are watching.[36] As before, *nomos* is conceived as an obstacle to nature, but here the natural state of affairs is identified as one in which one looks out for one's own interests—more specifically, one's own pleasure and avoidance of pain—at others' expense, if necessary. These two lines of thinking are not incompatible; after all, the natural prerogative to ignore *nomos* and pursue one's self-interest (so understood) apparently applies equally to everyone. But if one was hoping for the first (that is, the reflections on the equality of Greeks and non-Greeks) to serve as the basis for a conception of human beings as intrinsically valuable, and hence deserving certain kinds of respectful treatment simply as humans, the appeal to naked self-interest embodied in the second hardly looks encouraging.[37]

And so, while we can find hints of a nonhierarchical view of humanity, perhaps associated especially with the Sophists, we simply lack the evidence to be able to see with any specificity whether this view was ever developed in such a way as to accord a distinctive kind of value to human beings as such. In the end,

66 RETHINKING THE VALUE OF HUMANITY

then, the search for an alternative to the Stoic, Aristotelian, and Platonic pictures in which, despite a number of promising suggestions, value turns out to be very unevenly distributed among human beings, has not led to any determinate result. Nor do other ancient Greek thinkers seem to offer anything more helpful in this regard. I have not touched on the Epicureans because their focus on pleasure as the highest good, and their generally instrumentalist approach to questions of value, seem to put them in a different universe of discourse from those who would concern themselves with the value of humans as such. Though they may in practice have been more egalitarian in their treatment of others than the figures on whom I have mostly concentrated—for example, Epicurus is supposed to have included his slaves in his philosophical discussions (Diogenes Laertius 10.3, 10)—they do not seem to have had an interest in the kind of theorizing that might have been helpful for current purposes. The skeptics are clearly hopeless: though Sextus Empiricus does at one point describe the skeptics as "philanthropic" (*Outlines of Pyrrhonism* 3.280), this can only be a matter of what they happen to feel, unconnected with any articulated views concerning the value of humanity. They would have been more interested in undermining such views— supposing there had been some available to consider—than in developing them. And while the late Platonist tradition stemming from Plotinus is certainly far from skeptical—they believe a great many extraordinary things—it is not obvious why they would be any more likely to endorse "the value of humanity" than Plato himself.

This survey has of course not been exhaustive, and so my answer to the question posed in the title—Do the ancients see value in humanity?—is bound to be tentative. But the evidence considered here seems to favor the answer "To a limited degree, but not in any sustained or systematic way." In our own era, an editorial following one of the recent and all-too-frequent terrorist attacks (London, June 3, 2017) can reflexively say, "Each single human life is infinitely precious in a way that its random destruction only serves to amplify" (Williams 2017). While the ancient Greeks and Romans of course honored and mourned their dead, I doubt they would ever have expressed themselves in quite the same way. Indeed, the funeral speech put in Pericles's mouth by Thucydides, which is one of the most famous ancient Greek encomia to the dead, includes, in a passage explicitly flagged as consolation to the dead soldiers' parents, the advice to have more children (if they are still young enough to do so) so as to forget those who are gone (2.44). To those of us familiar with the "infinitely precious" conception, this cannot but sound jarring in the extreme.[38] This does not mean that ancient thought can never be seen as inspiration for ideas bearing on the value of humanity; for example, it is not hard to see how the Stoics could have made some contribution to modern notions of human rights. I would simply guard against the suggestion that such conceptions already had a full-fledged presence in ancient thought.[39]

Notes

1. This is the approach of Theunissen 2020.
2. Sarah Buss raised the question whether the term "pursue" might be too narrow; might one not *admire* or *appreciate* things of value—works of art, for example—without having any inclination to make them one's own? But in the ancient sources, things with value are classified in a way that tracks a standard classification of goods: of the soul, of the body, and external (e.g., good memory, health, and wealth, respectively; see Diogenes Laertius 7.106–7; Stobaeus 2.79,18–81,10). Both goods and things with value are thus conceived in close relation to persons; they are all things that might in some sense belong to one. Even the external category is comprised of various kinds of possessions—either material ones, such as wealth, or such things as one's social standing. And so, while it would not be simply mistaken to think of works of art as indifferents that have value, I think the Stoics would find it a more accurate formulation to speak of *art appreciation* as what has value (presumably in the category "of the soul"). And if so, pursuit—not of (ownership of) the artworks themselves but of the conditions in which one can appreciate them—would indeed be an appropriate attitude.
3. One more qualification: among the examples of external things that have value are parents and children. But here, of course, the value is value *to* the person whose parents or children they are, and they have value to this person because of their particular relation to him or her. Human beings as such could not possibly have value in this sense.
4. It is of course possible that one's possession of certain valuable indifferents, such as mental agility or physical health, could affect one's chances of achieving well-being or happiness, in the sense of creating the conditions in which one is best placed to make the moral progress necessary for the transition to true wisdom and virtue. But nothing indifferent figures as an *element in* well-being. Thanks to Sarah Buss for pushing me to make this clarification.
5. Nandi Theunissen pointed out that not everyone makes a sharp distinction between ethical and nonethical values; on some views, there is simply a continuum of valuable things—from a glass of water, for example, to a work of art, to a person. But I take it that any view (or at least, any nontheological view) dealing with the value of humanity would place this value at the top end of the scale. Hence, if we are looking for hints of such a view in the Stoics, we would expect to find them at the top end of their evaluative hierarchy—in other words, in connection with their notions of virtue and the good, not the indifferent.
6. "The life in agreement" is one of many Stoic characterizations of our natural end. This is a complicated topic. A good account is Brennan 2005, chap.10; in partial disagreement is Bett 2006.

68 RETHINKING THE VALUE OF HUMANITY

7. Translations of Greek and Latin texts are my own, unless otherwise noted. I refer to the original Greek and Roman works using the standard titles (which are sometimes in Latin) and the standard numbering systems for each author.

8. This threefold classification in Stobaeus is attributed to Diogenes of Babylon (2.84,4). Another threefold classification, attributed at least in part to Antipater, appears just before in Stobaeus (2.83,11–84,3); the order is different, but the sense of *axia* apparently marking out something higher is *tên dosin kai timen kath'hauto* (2.83,12). This is very difficult to translate, but some attempts are "a thing's contribution and merit per se" (Long and Sedley 1987, passage 58D), "the estimation and honor [for something] in itself" (Inwood and Gerson 1997, passage II-95, 7f.), and "its contribution and esteem in itself" (Pomeroy 1999, 49); whether this too applies only to good things and not to indifferents is not entirely clear, but it at least seems possible.

9. Talk of comparative *amounts* of value possessed by different people (as opposed to one person being in some way qualitatively superior to another) may sound odd to modern ears. But for Aristotle the quantitative assessment is just as natural for human value as it would be for monetary value. He describes the great-souled person as being worthy of great things—specifically, of great amounts of honor—and as having a correct assessment of this; the latter point is expressed by saying that "he values himself according to his value" (1123b14–15), whereas (following the usual threefold pattern for Aristotle's virtues of character) the corresponding vices of vanity and "small-souledness" (*mikropsuchia*) consist in claiming *too much* and *too little* honor, respectively, and therefore being excessive and deficient, respectively, in the self-assignment of value (1123b15). The actual honor merited comes in different amounts for different people— amounts that one might or might not judge correctly in one's own case—and this is a function of equivalent differences of amount in these people's value. Taylor's commentary on this chapter is very helpful; see Taylor 2006, 217–226.

10. I say "he or she" this time because although Aristotle does not mention them, one could see a friendship between an older and a younger woman, and perhaps between a mother and a daughter, as instances of this type.

11. "Capable of community in law and agreement" is borrowed verbatim from the translations of both Terence Irwin (1999) and Roger Crisp (2000); I cannot see a better way to put it. This idea of a human capacity to form a "community in law and agreement" is shared by the Stoics (Arius Didymus in Eusebius, *Praeparatio evangelica* 15.15.3–5; passage 67L in Long and Sedley 1987), who stress that it *distinguishes* humans from other animals; I return to this theme in my treatment of the Stoics in the next section. The Epicureans also restrict justice to those capable of making agreements, but it is not clear that this even includes all humans; see Epicurus, *Kuriai Doxai* 32–33.

12. Irwin (1999) surely takes the cake here, as often—though, to be fair, he does include brackets to make clear what is in the actual text and what is added: "hence [every human being seems] also [to have] friendship [with every human being], to the extent that [every human being] is a human being."

13. Frederick Douglass, for example (2001), has no trouble distinguishing markedly different levels of ill-treatment among the various slaveholders or their subordinates to

whom he was subject, even while abhorring the immorality of slavery as a whole and the dehumanizing effect it has on slaveholders as well as slaves.

14. Such cases may admittedly be a source of discomfort among those concerned to defend the value of humanity as such; they can also be a motivation for skepticism about the whole idea. John Rawls identifies "the capacity for moral personality" as the basis for humans' entitlement to just treatment—which is surely not so different from being "capable of community in law and agreement," the feature identified by Aristotle. But Rawls admits that those who permanently lack moral personality (such as the severely mentally defective, or psychopaths) "may present a difficulty"—one that he does not attempt to resolve; see Rawls 1999, section 77 (p. 446 for the words just quoted). Still, if Rawls allows, however uneasily, that some humans may fall outside the scope of justice, we need not be too hard on Aristotle for suggesting something similar. A classic case of skepticism is Peter Singer, who, in part because of the difficulty posed by such cases, rejects any attempt to rest our status as subjects of ethical concern on distinctively human capacities, and for this reason refuses to make a sharp divide between the ethical concern owed to humans and to other animals; see Singer 1979 (and later editions), chaps. 2 and 3.

15. My language here and elsewhere may seem to presuppose that finding a notion of the value of humanity in ancient Greek ethics would be a good thing. In part this is a function of the way I have posed the central question: Can we find such a notion in ancient thought? In these terms, "yes" naturally sounds like success and "no" like failure. Now, I do not in fact mean to take a decisive stand on this matter; there may be respectable ethical theories that deny that people are bearers of value (and the title of this volume, *Rethinking the Value of Humanity*, is meant to leave open that possibility). However, to the extent that the ancients' lack of any fully developed conception of the value of humanity shows up precisely in their acceptance of slavery and of other forms of elitism that few would tolerate today—and there will be more to say about this as we continue—I think it is hard for us not to regard this as a deficiency in their ethical thinking. (Of course, if they had had such a conception, ancient Greek ethics would have been quite different, and features that are often now admired about it might have been absent. You cannot have everything.)

16. Thanks to Christopher Celenza for the reference to Aulus Gellius, for several of the other references in this paragraph and the next, and for drawing my attention to this theme. For a fascinating history of broadly this conception of humanity, from the ancient world to the present, see Celenza 2008.

17. Aristotle ascribes to plants a rudimentary kind of soul, which regulates their life functions (nutrition and reproduction). The Stoics, on the other hand, give plants a lower capacity than soul, which they call *phusis*, "nature." But since soul and "nature" are different grades of the same divine "breath" (*pneuma*) that holds things together and endows them with their qualities (with a still lower grade, *hexis* or "holding," being responsible for the same function in inanimate objects like rocks), it is not clear that much turns on this terminological difference.

18. Aristotle says that this faculty of soul is possessed by humans and "anything else of this kind or more honorable" (414b18–19); presumably this is designed to accommodate

70 RETHINKING THE VALUE OF HUMANITY

divine beings (although these, at least in Aristotle's conception of the divine, will not have the lower parts we humans share with animals and plants).

19. The Greek preposition is *epi* with the dative. This can have a variety of different nuances, but "for the purpose of" seems the most suitable here. At any rate, *epi* indicates some kind of correlation between the possession of language and the grasp of ethical and political notions.

20. The purpose and function of the digression has often been regarded as puzzling. A reading of the passage that neatly integrates it in the dialogue as a whole is Sedley 2004, 65–81.

21. One important consideration here is how the "noble lie" passage at the end of book III (414b–415d) is to be interpreted. An excellent recent treatment of this is Rowett 2016.

22. A good account of Aristotle's views on this subject is Burnyeat 2008.

23. It looks as if the position of the craftsmen is different; their status in society is apparently not naturally ordained. The brief glossary entry "Vulgar Craftsmen" in C. D. C. Reeve's (1998) translation of the *Politics* puts it very well.

24. He tells us he is closely following Panaetius (3.7), and in a letter to Atticus (16.11.4) he makes clear that the work of Panaetius was *Peri tou Kathêkontos, On What Is Incumbent,* of which his own title *De Officiis* is a translation (cf. *De Officiis* 1.8). Virtually every Stoic back to the school's founder, Zeno of Citium, wrote works of this title, although very little is known about their contents; see Sedley 1999, esp. 137.

25. Later (1.115) a third and fourth role are added: that deriving from chance circumstances and that deriving from our own decisions.

26. "Power of decision" is my rendering of *prohairesis*; on the importance of this term in Epictetus, see Long 2002, 210–220. (Long's favored translation is "volition.")

27. The Greek is *parakolouthêtikos . . . têi theiai dioikêsei.* Adjectives ending in *-ikos* mark an ability or tendency to do something, without commitment as to whether or not this is in fact fulfilled, on any given occasion or indeed ever.

28. See again n.24.

29. Since the Stoics are often thought of as the most Kantian of ancient Greek philosophers, it is interesting that a comparable tension can be found in Kant. On this, see Darwall 2008.

30. For detailed discussion, see Lee 2005.

31. I say "accommodating"; I do not say that it gets us all the way. Hierarchy could of course be introduced by people's judgments; what if some humans were generally judged more valuable than others—just as other things are judged more or less valuable in various respects? On the other hand, judgments of this kind would have no monopoly on the truth; those who made opposite comparative valuations, or who explicitly proposed that everyone was equally valuable, would have just as much claim to be considered correct. And none of the evidence on Protagoras himself suggests that he was interested in making hierarchical rankings among human beings.

32. The text is a fragmentary papyrus. It can be found with facing English translation in Laks and Most 2016, vol. 9, passage 37 D38b.

33. And note that "clever" itself need not always be positive. The "clever" (*deinos*) person is contrasted in Aristotle's ethics with the person who has ethical insight (the *phronimos*)

DO THE ANCIENTS SEE VALUE IN HUMANITY? 71

(*Nicomachean Ethics* VI.12–13); whereas the latter by definition is oriented toward what is genuinely good, the "clever" person is simply effective in achieving goals, be they good or bad.

34. The cautionary spirit projected by Sophocles may reflect another strand of thinking about humanity in Greek culture, very different from the one on which I have concentrated in this section and the last. Here humanity is thought of as feeble and limited, in sharp contrast with the immortal gods; a good example in philosophy is Socrates's claim in Plato's *Apology* to possess a characteristically human form of wisdom (20d), a wisdom that turns out to consist precisely in the understanding that he *lacks* knowledge of anything truly worthwhile or valuable. On this view the "wonders" that this ode starts by celebrating would turn out to be largely illusory. I have not focused on this conception of humanity because it seems much less helpful to notions of the value of humanity than the one introduced in the previous section. (Indeed, as we saw, Aristotle explicitly rejects it in his account of philosophical thought as bringing us close to the divine.) However, it is undeniably an important aspect of popular Greek thought. Thanks to Eckart Förster and Nandi Theunissen for reminding me of this.

35. Sophocles is of course not writing a philosophical treatise, but this ode might invite reflection on whether capacities themselves may be worthy of respect. (Compare the remarks in the previous section on capacities in Aristotle and the Stoics.) Is Sophocles suggesting that we need to be very careful to use well the powers that we have—and that there is a serious risk of our not doing so—or is he suggesting that the powers themselves have an inherently self-destructive aspect? The line of thought mentioned in the previous note would suggest the latter, but I am not sure; while there would be a cautionary message either way, in the former case there would be room for a measure of optimism. Thanks to Sarah Buss for pressing this whole issue of capacities as possible bearers of value.

36. This line of thinking appears in passage 37 D38a in Laks and Most 2016, vol. 9.

37. This is true even if (contrary to initial appearances) one does not think that Antiphon means to *advocate* the pursuit of self-interest, regardless of *nomos*, whenever one can get away with it; for an example of this kind of interpretation, see Gagarin 2002, chap. 3. Whatever Antiphon is doing with the *phusis/nomos* contrast in this section, it seems to be contributing to a very different project from that of explaining a conception of the value of humanity. However, his distance from that project seems especially stark if the pursuit of self-interest is in fact something he is recommending; I have argued for this reading (and against some alternatives, although Gagarin's was not yet published at the time) in Bett 2002, sec. II.

38. For the notion of children as replaceable, see also Sophocles, *Antigone* 909–910.

39. I have discussed this with respect to human rights in Bett 2012. Fred D. Miller (1995) has also made the case that Aristotle's political theory can be understood in terms of human rights. A complete issue of the journal *Review of Metaphysics* was devoted to discussion of this book. Of particular relevance to the theme of this paper, the essay by John Cooper (1996) argues that there can very well be room for talk of rights—even natural or human rights, rather than merely legal rights—in interpreting Aristotle's political theory, but not if human rights are conceived in the modern way, represented

72 RETHINKING THE VALUE OF HUMANITY

paradigmatically by Hegel. To quote Cooper: "This thing that Aristotle according to Hegel cannot envisage is what Hegel calls the 'principle of subjective freedom'—the idea that in possessing this power of arbitrary self-determination we have something of infinite worth in each of us individually that must be honored and respected in any acceptable political regime" (863). In other words, an idea of the value of humanity as such. Cooper endorses Hegel's historical claim that the principle of subjective freedom is postclassical. I find Cooper's reading sufficiently plausible that I decided not to include a discussion of human rights in the main body of the paper, despite having originally planned to do so. Another paper pointing in a similar direction is Burnyeat 1994.

In addition to the original Johns Hopkins workshop in April 2016, I discussed this paper at the History of Philosophy Roundtable at UC San Diego. I would like to thank the participants on both occasions for valuable feedback that has improved the final result, especially Yitzhak Melamed at Hopkins and Monte Johnson and Casey Perin at UCSD. I also thank Sarah Buss and Nandi Theunissen for comments that prompted a great many improvements at several different stages—including, but by no means only, in the places where they are mentioned in footnotes, and Sara Magrin for some helpful comments at the final stage.

References

Annas, Julia. 1993. *The Morality of Happiness*. New York: Oxford University Press.

Bett, Richard. 2002. "Is There a Sophistic Ethics?" *Ancient Philosophy* 22: 235–262.

Bett, Richard. 2006. "Stoic Ethics." In *A Companion to Ancient Philosophy*, edited by Mary Louise Gill and Pierre Pellegrin, 530–548. Malden, MA: Blackwell.

Bett, Richard. 2012. "Did the Stoics Invent Human Rights?" *Oxford Studies in Ancient Philosophy*, Supplementary Volume 2012: 149–169.

Brennan, Tad. 2005. *The Stoic Life: Emotions, Duties, and Fate*. Oxford: Clarendon Press.

Burnyeat, Myles. 1994. "Did the Ancient Greeks Have the Concept of Human Rights?" *Polis* 13: 1–11.

Burnyeat, Myles. 2008. *Aristotle's Divine Intellect*. Milwaukee, WI: Marquette University Press.

Caston, Victor. 2006. "Aristotle's Psychology." In *A Companion to Ancient Philosophy*, edited by Mary Louise Gill and Pierre Pellegrin, 316–346. Malden, MA: Blackwell.

Celenza, Christopher. 2008. "Humanism and the Classical Tradition." *Annali d'italianistica* 26: 25–49.

Cooper, John. 1996. "Justice and Rights in Aristotle's *Politics*." *Review of Metaphysics* 49(4): 859–872.

Crisp, Roger, ed. and trans. 2000. Aristotle, *Nicomachean Ethics*. Cambridge: Cambridge University Press.

Crisp, Roger. 2006. "Aristotle on Greatness of Soul." In *The Blackwell Guide to Aristotle's Nicomachean Ethics*, edited by Richard Kraut, 158–178. Malden, MA: Blackwell.

Darwall, Stephen. 2008. "Kant on Respect, Dignity and the Duty to Respect." In *Kant's Ethics of Virtue*, edited by Monica Betzler, 175–200. Berlin: DeGruyter.

Douglass, Frederick. 2001. *Narrative of the Life of Frederick Douglass, an American Slave, Written by Himself.* Edited by John W. Blassingame, John R. McKivigan, and Peter P. Hinks. Textual editor Gerald Fulkerson. New Haven, CT: Yale University Press.

Gagarin, Michael. 2002. *Antiphon the Athenian: Oratory, Law, and Justice in the Age of the Sophists.* Austin: University of Texas Press.

Hadot, Pierre. 1992. *La Citadelle intérieure: Introduction aux Pensées de Marc Aurèle.* Paris: Fayard.

Inwood, Brad, and L. P. Gerson, eds. 1997. *Hellenistic Philosophy: Introductory Readings,* 3rd ed. Indianapolis, IN: Hackett.

Irwin, Terence. 1991. "Aristotle's Philosophy of Mind." In *Psychology: Companions to Ancient Thought 2,* edited by Stephen Everson, 56–83. Cambridge: Cambridge University Press.

Irwin, Terence, ed. and trans. 1999. Aristotle, *Nicomachean Ethics,* 2nd ed. With introduction, notes, and glossary by Terence Irwin. Indianapolis, IN: Hackett.

Laks, André, and Glenn Most, eds. 2016. *Early Greek Philosophy.* Cambridge, MA: Harvard University Press.

Lee, Mi-Kyoung. 2005. *Epistemology after Protagoras: Responses to Relativism in Plato, Aristotle, and Democritus.* Oxford: Clarendon Press.

Long, A. A. 2002. *Epictetus: A Stoic and Socratic Guide to Life.* Oxford: Clarendon Press.

Long A. A., and D. N. Sedley. 1987. *The Hellenistic Philosophers.* Cambridge: Cambridge University Press.

Miller, Fred D. 1995. *Nature, Justice, and Human Rights in Aristotle's Politics.* Oxford: Clarendon Press.

Pakaluk, Michael. 2004. "The Meaning of Aristotelian Magnanimity." *Oxford Studies in Ancient Philosophy* 26: 241–275.

Pomeroy, Arthur J., ed. and trans. 1999. Arius Didymus, *Epitome of Stoic Ethics.* Atlanta, GA: Society of Biblical Literature.

Rawls, John. 1999. *A Theory of Justice.* Revised ed. Cambridge, MA: Harvard University Press.

Reeve, C. D. C., trans. 1998. Aristotle, *Politics.* With introduction and notes by C. D. C. Reeve. Indianapolis, IN: Hackett.

Rowett, Catherine. 2016. "Why the Philosopher Kings Will Believe the Noble Lie." *Oxford Studies in Ancient Philosophy* 50: 67–100.

Sarch, Alexander. 2008. "What's Wrong with *Megalopsuchia?*" *Philosophy* 83: 231–253.

Sedley, David. 1999. "The Stoic-Platonist Debate on *Kathêkonta.*" In *Topics in Stoic Philosophy,* edited by Katerina Ierodiakonou, 128–152. Oxford: Clarendon Press.

Sedley, David. 2004. *The Midwife of Platonism: Text and Subtext in Plato's Theaetetus.* Oxford: Clarendon Press.

Shields, Christopher. 2007. *Aristotle.* London: Routledge.

Singer, Peter. 1979. *Practical Ethics.* Cambridge: Cambridge University Press.

Taylor, C. C. W., trans. 2006. Aristotle, *Nicomachean Ethics,* Books II–IV. With a commentary by C. C. W. Taylor. Oxford: Clarendon Press.

Theunissen, L. Nandi. 2020. *The Value of Humanity.* Oxford: Oxford University Press.

Williams, Bernard. 1985. *Ethics and the Limits of Philosophy.* Cambridge, MA: Harvard University Press.

Williams, Zoe. 2017. "Defy the London Bridge Terrorists, but Know Too That It's OK to Admit Our Fear." *The Guardian,* June 5. https://www.theguardian.com/commentisfree/2017/jun/05/london-bridge-terrorists.

3
Spinoza's Anti-Humanism: Human Value and Dignity

Yitzhak Y. Melamed

You were not intended
to be unique. You were
my embodiment, all diversity.
—Louise Glück, "Midsummer" (1992)

Introduction

Kant's *Anthropology from a Pragmatic Point of View* opens with a celebration of the uniqueness and *dignity* (*Würde*) of humanity:

> The fact that the human being can have the "I" in his representations raises him infinitely above all other living beings on earth. Because of this he is a *person* [*Person*], and by virtue of the unity of consciousness through all changes that happen to him, one and the same person—i.e., through rank and dignity [*Rang und Würde*] and entirely different being from *things* [*Sachen*], such as irrational animals, with which one can do as one likes. This holds even when he cannot say "I," because he still has it in thoughts, just as all languages must *think* it when they speak in the first person, even if they do not have a special word to express the concept of "I." (7: 127; italics in original)[1]

Unlike animals, which are mere *things*, human beings are *persons* (cf. 4:428). This clear-cut bifurcation of entities in Kant's moral universe seems to be grounded in the unique qualities that bestow human beings with *dignity*.[2] Self-consciousness, rationality, and the capacity to act freely, a capacity Kant stresses in other contexts (cf. 28: 255), create a gulf between human beings and the rest of nature (the distinctive capacity of a human being "raises him infinitely above all other living beings on earth"). Kant was not alone among modern philosophers in asserting a deep and unbridgeable divide between humanity and the rest of nature. Arguably, *humanism*—in a sense to be spelled out shortly—constituted the mainstream of

Yitzhak Y. Melamed, *Spinoza's Anti-Humanism: Human Value and Dignity* In: *Rethinking the Value of Humanity.*
Edited by: Sarah Buss and L. Nandi Theunissen, Oxford University Press. © Oxford University Press 2023.
DOI: 10.1093/oso/9780197539361.003.0004

modern philosophy. For Descartes, human beings are endowed with free will, reason, mental life, and substantial mind, all of which are absent in the lower animals.[3] By virtue of these capacities, claims Descartes, human beings have been properly described in the Hebrew Bible as being created "in God's Image" (Gen. 1:26–27).[4] Descartes's veneration of humanity is documented already in one of his earliest writings, a set of notes written in his twenties. One of these fragments reads, "The Lord has made three marvels [*mirabilia*]: something out of nothing; free will; and God in Man [*Hominem Deum*]" (AT X 218 / CSM I 5). Two out of God's three great *mirabilia*, per Descartes, are instantiated by humanity.

Unlike Descartes, Leibniz was willing to acknowledge not only that animals have souls (*âmes*), but even that animal souls are unperishable (cf. "Discourse on Metaphysics" §34 / AG 65). Still, Leibniz stresses—in his 1686 *Discours de métaphysique*—that rationality and self-consciousness are distinctive human capacities on account of which "all other creatures must serve" humanity (§§12 and 36 / AG 44, 67). For Leibniz, these distinctive human capacities not only elevate them above other animals, or souls, but also place them in community with God, even making them God-like:

> Only spirits[5] are made *in God's image* and are, as it were, of his race [*quasi de sa race*], or like children of his household, since they alone can serve him *freely* and act with knowledge in imitation of the divine nature. . . . And this nature of spirits is so noble that it brings them as near to divinity as it is possible for simple creatures. . . . It is because of this that God humanizes itself [*qu'il s'humanise*], that he is willing to allow anthropomorphism, and that he enters into society with us, as a prince with his subjects. ("Discourse on Metaphysics" §36 / AG 67; italics added)

The religious undertones of Leibniz's view of humanity as "God's race" are quite salient in his invocation of both the Hebrew Bible (Gen. 1: 26–27), and the New Testament ("God's humanizing itself," i.e., God's choice to incarnate itself in a *human* body). The view of humanity as being in a middle rank between the divine and nature is quite common in Western religious thought. Following the catastrophes of World War II and with the advent of a more reflective and critical perspective on modern secularism, the question of the *justification* of humanism—and particularly whether it is not a mere uncritical residue of traditional, anthropomorphic, religions—came to the forefront. In the decades following the Second World War, the notions of *humanism* and *anti-humanism* have been discussed extensively (mainly among continental philosophers).[6] Because these notions carry a variety of historical and ideological meanings, it is important to provide at the outset at least a rudimentary clarification of *my* use of these two terms. By humanism I mean a view which (1) assigns a *unique value* or *rank* to human beings among other things in nature; (2) stresses the primacy—or even the constitutive role—of the human *perspective* in understanding the nature of things; and (3) attempts to point out an essential property of humanity which *justifies* its elevated and unique status. Prima facie, claims (1) and (2) do not entail each other, though one can point out tacit and nonextravagant premises that would allow the inference of the one from the other.[7] Claim (3) rules out arbitrary and speciesist versions of humanism. Historically, claims (1)–(3) have been frequently asserted together as elements of a cohesive worldview.[8]

By ascribing a unique value to human beings, humanism assumes a certain gulf between humanity and nature which does not allow us to treat human beings like any other things in nature.[9] For many humanists the nature vs. humanity gulf does not even allow the application of the methods of natural sciences to the disciplines of the humanities.[10]

Philosophical humanism does not commence with modernity, and it can perhaps be traced back to Protagoras's celebrated dictum "Man is the measure of all things, of things that are, that they are, and of things that are not, that they are not"[11] and to Sophocles's "Ode to Man."

In an earlier work, I argued that Spinoza is the great enemy of the school of humanism (see Melamed 2010b). In contrast to the humanist philosophers, Spinoza considered human beings as marginal and limited beings in nature, beings whose claims and presumptions far exceed their abilities. "What do the common people not foolishly claim for themselves . . . they confuse God's decrees with men's decisions and posit a nature so limited that *they believe man to be its chief part!*" (TTP, chap. 6 / G III/82/7–10).

The critique of anthropocentric and anthropomorphic thinking is a persistent and central theme in Spinoza's thought from early on,[12] and it only becomes stronger and more extensive in his later works.[13] One of the most figurative statements of this critique appears in a letter that recasts the famous saying of Xenophanes. Here Spinoza responds to Hugo Boxel's criticism that Spinoza went much too far in rejecting the attribution of *any* human perfections to God:

> When you say that you do not see what sort of God I have if I deny in him the actions of seeing, hearing, attending, willing etc., and that he possesses those faculties in an eminent degree, I suspect that you believe there is no greater perfection than can be explicated by the aforementioned attributes. I am not surprised, for I believe that *a triangle, if it could speak, would likewise say that God is eminently triangular, and a circle that God's nature is eminently circular.* In this way each would ascribe to God its own attributes, assuming itself to be like God and regarding all else as ill-formed. (Ep. 56 / G IV/260/1–10; italics added)

SPINOZA'S ANTI-HUMANISM   77

Alongside his critique of anthropomorphism, Spinoza frequently attacks the view of humanity as either the most important part of nature[14] or as transcending nature. Both in the *Ethics* and in the *Political Treatise* Spinoza scolds those who uphold the common perception of humanity as a "dominion within a dominion [*imperium in imperio*],"[15] i.e., as constituting an autonomous realm of beings that disturb rather than strictly follow the laws of nature by virtue of their unique endowment with free will.[16] In an earlier work (see Melamed 2010b), I argued that whatever exclusive qualities the humanists claim bestow humanity with a unique status, elevated above the rest of nature, Spinoza would either argue that the belief that humans have this quality is a cozy fairy tale (as in the case of free will), or he would deny that human beings are *unique* in having these qualities (as in the cases of self-consciousness, love, or the ability to act morally). Spinoza's strict naturalism about human beings—i.e., his insistence that human beings play according to the very same rules as the rest of nature—elicited a strong repulsive reaction among his contemporaries and successors,[17] though, in the case of Nietzsche, it also earned him an admirer.[18]

Spinoza's clear-headed view of human beings, their limited rationality, their desires, ambitions, and delusions, does not, however, lead him to misanthropy. As he writes:

> Let the Satirists laugh as much as they like at human affairs, let the Theologians curse them, let Melancholics praise as much as they can a life that is uncultivated and wild, let them disdain men and admire the lower animals. Men still find from experience that by helping one another they can provide themselves much more easily with the things they require, and that only by joining forces can they avoid the dangers that threaten on all sides. (E4p35s)[19]

Indeed, Spinoza's *Ethics* is a book whose aim is to lead us toward *human* blessedness and freedom.[20] The *Ethics* is a book about human beings not because humanity is elevated above the rest of nature, but for the simple reason that its author, being a human being, desperately wished to know the conditions required for *his* pursuit of blessed life.

Instead of reiterating my overview of Spinoza's systematic and multilayered attack on humanism (see Melamed 2010b), I would like to concentrate in this chapter on *one* question: whether in spite of Spinoza's deep critique of humanism, we can rescue from his thought any notion of human value, rank, or even dignity. Given my claims so far, one can easily see that this is not a trivial task. Still, because the main aim of the *Ethics* is charting the paths toward human flourishing and blessedness, and because Spinoza believed we should *equally* strive to promote the flourishing of other human beings,[21] one might wonder whether this striving toward shared blessedness is grounded or motivated by a unique

78 RETHINKING THE VALUE OF HUMANITY

value or rank shared by human beings. The two most promising venues which could lead Spinoza to ascribe substantial value to human beings are human friendship (recall the end of the last quote) and human (partial) rationality. I will begin by examining the value of human friendship. Then, in the second part of the chapter, I will consider the question of whether Spinoza's modest view of humanity's status within nature allows for any notion of human *dignity*. In the third and final part, I will examine the value Spinoza ascribes to *rationality*, and the implications of this issue for his understanding of the value of humanity.

1. The Value of Human Friendship

To begin our discussion of the value of human friendship we will turn first to Spinoza's critique of vegetarianism (the reasons for this choice will become clear before long). As we shall shortly see, Spinoza has a view quite distinct from, if not fully opposed to, that of Kant about the metaphysical or ontological differences between human beings and the lower animals. Still, ironically, both end up with virtually the same conclusion: we may use animals "at our pleasure, and treat them as is most convenient for us."[22] Spinoza writes:

> The law against killing animals is based more on empty superstitions and un-manly compassion [*muliebri misericordia*] than sound reason. The rational principle of seeking our own advantage teaches us the necessity of joining with men, but not with the lower animals [*brutis*], or with things whose nature is different from human nature. We have the same right against them as they have against us. Indeed, because the right of each other is defined by his virtue, or [*seu*] power, men have a greater right against the lower animals than they have against men. Not that I deny that the lower animals have sensations [*Nec tamen nego bruta sentire*]. But I do deny that we are therefore not permitted to con-sider our own advantage, use them at our pleasure, and treat them as is most convenient for us. For they do not agree [*conveniunt*] in nature with us, and their affects are different in nature from human affects. (E4p37s1 / G II/236/ 34–237/10)

In this passage Spinoza openly asserts that in many respects the lower animals are very much like us: they have sensations ("not that I deny that the lower an-imals have sensations"), and they even have rights ("we have the same right against them as they have against us"). In other passages in the *Ethics* Spinoza affirms that animals have minds and mental lives,[23] and in one passage he even refers to the "animals that are *called* irrational [*quae irrationalia dicuntur*],"[24] thus insinuating that at least to some degree all nonhuman animals *are* rational.

Still, attempting to explain briefly "the excellence of the human mind over" the minds of other things, Spinoza writes:

> I say this in general, that in proportion as a Body is more capable than others of doing many things at once, or being acted on in many ways at once, *so its Mind is more capable than others of perceiving many things at once.* And in proportion as the actions of a body depend more on itself alone, and as other bodies concur with it less in acting, *so its mind is more capable of understanding distinctly.* And from these [truths] we can know *the excellence of one mind over the others.* (E2p13s / G II/97/8–14; italics added. Cf. E2p14 / G II/103/8–9)

I cannot elaborate here on the intricate features of Spinoza's epistemology which account for the relative excellence of minds, since such a discussion would take us far afield from our main topic.[25] For our purposes it suffices to note that, generally speaking, Spinoza considers the human mind more capable—and more powerful—than the minds of other animals, though this difference seems to be one of degree.[26] I stress that it is only generally speaking that the human mind is superior to the minds of all other animals, since in the context of another discussion in the *Ethics*, Spinoza asserts that in some cases the capacities of the lower animals exceed those of humans: "Many things are observed in the lower animals that surpass human ingenuity [*quae humanam sagacitatem longe superant*]" (E3p2s / G II/142/10).

Let us return to the issue of vegetarianism and look closely at Spinoza's argument against vegetarianism. Spinoza's argument in E4p37s1 relies on two major premises. The first is his principal claim that the right of each thing is coextensive (if not strictly identical) with its power.[27] We will not study this crucial and intriguing claim here. The other major premise is that insofar as we do not share the same nature with the lower animals, we cannot "join them," i.e., *we cannot "use" them as friends.* Spinoza elaborates on this last point in the Appendix to Part 4 of the *Ethics*:

> Apart from men we know no singular thing in nature whose Mind we can enjoy [*gaudere*], *and which we can join to ourselves in friendship, or some kind of association.* And so whatever there is in nature apart from men, the principle of seeking our own advantage does not demand that we preserve it. Instead, *it teaches us to preserve or destroy it according to its use, or to adapt it to our use in any way whatever.* (E4app26 G II/273/16–24; italics added)

Spinoza repeatedly claims that nothing is more *useful* to men than other human beings.[28] Thus, for the sake of our own advantage, we better strive to preserve them and use them most advantageously. The best use we can have of another

80 RETHINKING THE VALUE OF HUMANITY

human being is through friendship. Friendship with a human being who is guided to reason is especially useful and empowering. Thus, in the same appendix, Spinoza writes:

> Nothing can agree more with the nature of any thing than other individuals of the same species. And so (by VII) nothing is more *useful* to man in preserving his being and enjoying a rational life than a man who is guided by reason. (E4app9 / G II/268–269/20–23; italics added. Cf. E4p35c1 / G II/233/16–17)

Spinoza's reasoning in rejecting vegetarianism is quite simple. We do not share the same nature with other animals. Since the affects (emotions) of animals are grounded in their natures, our affects are also significantly different from the affects of other animals.[29] The fact that we do not share the nature and affects of other animals prevents us from joining them to ourselves in friendship (E4app26 / G II/273/16).[30] *Friendship is the most valuable thing we can find in other creatures insofar as it empowers us significantly* (E4p18s / G II/223/8). Since we cannot use animals as friends, we are allowed to use, preserve, and destroy them according to our other interests (E4app26 / G II/273/16).[31]

There are quite a few problems with this argument. Spinoza's categorical assertion that two entities that do not share the same nature and affects cannot join in friendship can be attacked from various angles. First, consider the relationship between a blind person and her guide dog. No doubt the nature and affects of the two entities are significantly different. Still, it seems that frequently there is a close emotional bond between a blind person and her guide dog, a bond that is closer than the one the blind person has with many (human) friends. Spinoza obviously might reply that such a bond might be exceptional in some other respects but does not constitute genuine friendship. Nevertheless, given the fact that for Spinoza at least part of the value of friendship is mutual[32] empowerment,[33] it would seem that such genuine relations of mutual empowerment between animals belonging to different species are at least possible.

From a different angle, we might raise doubts about Spinoza's commitment to the claim that "all men share the same common nature" (TP chap. 7 / G III/319).[34] In the *Theological Political Treatise*, Spinoza mocks the view that there are different species of men—presciently denouncing the basis of various forms of modern racism (TTP chap. 3 / G III/47/2), yet in the *Ethics*, immediately following his explanation of the difference in affects between humans and lower animals, Spinoza notes, "Finally, from P57 it follows that there is no small difference between the gladness by which a drunk is led and the gladness a Philosopher possesses. I wished to mention this in passing" (E3p57s / G II/187/18–20). E3p57, to which the last quote refers, states, "Each affect of each individual differs from the affect of another as much as the essence of the one differs from the essence of the other." Spinoza's appeal to E3p57 in order to explain the difference between the gladness of the drunk and that of the philosopher clearly implies that he considers the essence, or nature, of the two types of people to be distinct as well. Obviously, the difference in nature between the philosopher and the drunk may well be more modest than the difference in nature between the drunk person and his dog. Yet these differences seem to be a matter of degree rather than a clear-cut dichotomy between human and nonhuman animals.[35]

Before we conclude our discussion of the value of human friendship for Spinoza, let me stress three important points. First, the fact that we share the same nature with other human beings is important for Spinoza as a condition for cultivating *friendship*. Issues of procreation—which is presumably restricted to members of the same species—seem to be of little, if any, concern for Spinoza.

Second, the importance of friendship is confined to the perspective of the entity which seeks friendship. We cannot *use a wolf as our friend*, and hence we may use it in whatever way we see fit. Along the same lines, the wolf cannot use us as friends, and therefore she may use us "as she pleases." The perspective of the wolf is just as good and important as ours.

Now we can address our third and final point. For Spinoza, not all perspectives are equal, since beyond the perspectives of the myriad creatures of Spinoza's universe there is one objective perspective. That is *God's* perspective on the world.[36] Our nature and God's nature are utterly different,[37] and thus we have different affects[38] and cannot join in friendship with God. Moreover, God's existence, omnipotence, and omniscience are strictly guaranteed by his essence,[39] and he does not seem to need my friendship. Thus, from the ultimate objective perspective, human friendship is not valuable, or at most it is valuable among certain entities as they are perceived from God's point of view,[40] but it is not valuable *for* God himself.[41]

One might perhaps be tempted to challenge this conclusion by pointing out that Spinoza allows God to love human beings.[42] Thus, in E5p36, Spinoza writes:

> From this[43] it follows that insofar as God loves himself, he loves men, and consequently that God's love of men and the Mind's intellectual Love of God are one and the same [*Hinc sequitur, quod Deus, quatenus seipsum amat, homines amat, et consequenter quod amor Dei erga homines et mentis erga Deum amor intellectualis unum et idem sit*].

Spinoza's God may perhaps love human beings,[44] but given Spinoza's scathing critique of those who think that human beings are more important, or closer to, God than any other creatures,[45] it would seem that if God loves any finite beings, he should love them all:[46] porcupines, rhinos, and humans included. In the *Theological Political Treatise*, Spinoza pointedly criticizes the Hebrews' view

82 RETHINKING THE VALUE OF HUMANITY

of themselves as God's beloved, chosen people.[47] Similarly, in his discussion of miracles, Spinoza criticizes those who take humanity to be the chief part of nature, and the end toward which the whole of nature works.[48] Thus, if we are to avoid the claim that human beings are God's *chosen species*,[49] we must admit that *if God loves anyone*, God loves donkeys and porcupines just as much as he loves humans.

2. Human Dignity?

We have seen in Section 1 that human beings *are valuable* to each other by virtue of their ability to join together in friendship, that human beings do not seem to be valuable to God (nor God to human beings) qua friends, and that if God loves anyone, human beings are not the preferred object of his love.[50] Let us turn now to the question of human *dignity*.

Spinoza begins his early work, the *Treatise on the Emendation of the Intellect*, with the simple confession that experience taught him "that all the things which regularly occur in ordinary life are empty and futile [*vana, & futilia esse*]" (TIE §1 / G II/5/8–9). He then turns to examining the things that people normally seek in life:

> For most things which present themselves in life, and which, to judge from their actions, men think to be the highest good, may be reduced to these three: wealth, honor [*honor*], and sensual pleasure. The mind is so distracted by these three that it cannot give the slightest thought to any other good. (TIE §3 / G II/5/26–6/3)[51]

After noting the vanity of sensual pleasure, Spinoza scrutinizes two other apparent "highest goods":

> The mind is also distracted not a little by the pursuit of honors [*honores*] and wealth, particularly when the latter is sought only for its own sake, because it is assumed to be the highest good. [5] *But the mind is far more distracted by honor. For this is always assumed to be good through itself* [*bonum esse per se*] *and the ultimate end* [*finis ultimus*] *toward which everything is directed.* Nor do honor and wealth have, as sensual pleasure does, repentance as a natural consequence. The more each of these is possessed, the more joy is increased, and hence the more we are spurred on to increase them. But if our hopes should chance to be frustrated, we experience the greatest sadness. And finally, honor has this great disadvantage: to pursue it, we must direct our lives according to other men's

powers of understanding—fleeing what they commonly flee and seeking what they commonly seek. (TIE §§4–5 / G II/6/2–20; italics added)

These considerations—the distraction of the mind, the insatiable urge to pursue more honor, and the dependence on the recognition of others—lead Spinoza to *reject* honor—along with wealth and sensual pleasure—as the ultimate goods he should seek in life. We may use all three as limited means for achieving our true good,[52] but this is the only positive use we may make of them, and we should be constantly alerted to the danger of pursuing these means as ends in themselves (cf. TIE §11 / G II/7/31).

Whatever is true about the honor of individual human beings should also be true about collectives of human beings. The concept of national honor might be a useful political device, and for the most part, Spinoza accepts the use of deception in politics. Thus, for example, he praises Alexander the Great for presenting himself as the son of Jupiter. Having the sovereign considered as being of divine origin yields sweeping political benefits, and Spinoza praises Alexander for his shrewdness (TTP chap. 19 / G III/258–259; cf. Melamed 2013c, 180–181). Accordingly, the use of the notion of national honor as a political tool for a worthy aim[53] might be accepted by Spinoza, especially if all the required precautions are taken to avoid turning this nationalist cult into an end in itself. (A more prudent Spinozist may well object that no such precautions can ever assure us that the cult of national honor would not turn into an end in itself, and that therefore we should avoid the cult of national honor by any means.)

If the Spinozist allows for the prudent political use of the (rather vain) notion of *national honor* for worthy aims, she should just as well allow for a similar use of the notion of *human honor* for worthy aims. But would it make sense for Spinoza to genuinely recognize (rather than merely employ as a political tool) the notion of humanity as having *dignity* and noninstrumental worthiness?[54]

The notion of dignity (*dignitas*) does not appear in the *Ethics*. The closest Latin terms in the *Ethics* are *honor* and *gloria*. Can we retrieve from Spinoza's text any notion of honor or glory that is unique to humanity as a species?

One interesting text which may help us address the question is E3p55s2:

So when we said above (in P52S)[55] that we venerate [*venerari*] a man because we wonder at his prudence, strength of character, etc., that happens (as is evident from the proposition itself) because we *imagine* these virtues to be peculiarly in him, and not as common to our nature. Therefore, we shall not envy him these virtues any more than we envy trees their height, or lions their strength. (G II/184/9–14; italics added)

84 RETHINKING THE VALUE OF HUMANITY

Spinoza seems to state here that we venerate excellent individuals, but not qualities which are typical of an *entire species* such as humanity. Still, insofar as this veneration of individuals is the result of the activity of our *imagination* (the lowest kind of cognition and the only source of error in Spinoza's epistemology), rather than the *intellect* (Spinoza's second kind of cognition which is immune from error),[56] we have no reason to assume that this psychological mechanism (i.e., our tendency to venerate individuals rather than species) is a *reliable* source for value judgments, and to that extent cannot prove that Spinoza would avoid ascribing dignity to the human species.[57] Perhaps a Spinozist could defend a notion of human dignity that is grounded in the activity of reason and the intellect? Let us consider another possible path for retrieving human dignity from Spinoza's claims.

In a recent compelling article on Spinoza's key notion of *acquiescentia* (self-esteem), Clare Carlisle (2017) has argued that Spinoza distinguishes between three kinds of *acquiescentia,* each grounded in one of Spinoza's three kinds of cognition: imagination, intellect/reason, and *scientia intuitiva.* As one can expect, *acquiescentia* (or self-esteem) resulting from the activity of the imagination (Spinoza's lowest and least reliable kind of cognition) is much less valuable than *acquiescentia* resulting from the activity of reason (the second kind of cognition) and *scientia intuitiva* (the third kind of cognition). For Spinoza, both the second and third kinds of cognition provide us with adequate and true ideas. The emotions resulting from these two higher kinds of cognition are stable and not self-centered:

> When *acquiescentia* is based on imagination, it is a hollow, volatile, egotistical satisfaction; when it is rooted in the second, rational kind of cognition, it becomes a stable joy that can be shared with others; within the third kind of cognition, *acquiescentia* signifies the feeling-quality of participation in God's eternity. (Carlisle 2017, 218)

As Carlisle points out, in E3p35s1 Spinoza defines self-love or self-esteem (*Philautia, vel Acquiescentia in se ipso*) as "Joy arising from considering ourselves." He then elaborates:

> And since this [self-esteem] is renewed as often as a man considers his virtues, *or* his power of acting, it also happens that everyone is anxious to tell his own deeds, and show off his powers, both of body and of mind—and that men, for this reason, are troublesome to one another.
>
> . . . For whenever anyone imagines his own actions, he is affected with Joy (by P53), and with a greater Joy, the more his actions express perfection, and the more distinctly he imagines them, i.e. (by IIP40S1), the more he can distinguish

them from others, and consider them as singular things. . . . *But if he relates what he affirms of himself to the universal idea of man or animal, he will not be so greatly gladdened.* (E3p55s1 / G II/183/1–18; italics added)

In the very last sentence of the passage, Spinoza notes that our recognition of human (or animal) worthiness is not as powerful an affect (i.e., does not elicit as much joy) as the (imaginary) recognition of our unique capabilities as individuals. On the other hand, our imaginary self-esteem as unique individuals is heavily dependent on the recognition of others ("everyone is anxious to tell his own deeds, and show off his powers") and is subject to the great vicissitudes and instability Spinoza associates with the imagination. As a result, it would seem that neither individual nor group pride provides us with powerful and stable self-esteem and joy.

In contrast to our individual or human pride, the *acquiescentia* that is grounded in *scientia intuitiva*—Spinoza's third and highest kind of cognition—is stable and equanimous. This kind of *acquiescentia* is "constituted by our consciousness of Being-in-God" (Carlisle 2017, 226), which is stable and permanent:

Whatever we understand by the third kind of cognition we take pleasure in, and our pleasure is accompanied by the idea of God as cause.

Demonstration: From this kind of cognition there *arises the greatest satisfaction of Mind* [*Mentis acquiescentia*] there can be (by P27), i.e. (by Def. Aff. XXV), Joy; this Joy is accompanied by the idea of oneself, and consequently (by P30) it is also accompanied by the idea of God, as its cause, q.e.d. (E5p32; italics added. Cf. Carlisle 2017, 226–231)

Scientia intuitiva, Spinoza's third kind of cognition, is a cognition which proceeds from the adequate idea of one of God's attributes to the adequate cognition of the essence of things (such as your essence, my essence, or the essence of a certain porcupine).[58] In a sense, when we think through the third kind of cognition, we think like God. I cannot elaborate here on many of the details of Spinoza's demonstration of E5p32 since they assume much of his theory of the affects in Parts 3 and 5 of the *Ethics*. Still, in a nutshell, Spinoza's main point here is that when we are able to think through *scientia intuitiva* we rejoice and are greatly satisfied by the activity and advancement of our mind.[59]

The *acquiescentia* resulting from the third kind of cognition is not related to my belonging to any group or species *unless* one holds that only humans are capable of such cognition, and that human beings should be respected by virtue of their unique capacity to achieve the third kind of cognition. For all I can tell, Spinoza does not consider the ability to conceive things through *scientia intuitiva* as unique to human minds. The porcupine's mind takes part in *scientia intuitiva* at least to a rudimentary degree.[60]

86 RETHINKING THE VALUE OF HUMANITY

So far, our attempts to rescue a notion of a unique human dignity in Spinoza were not crowned with success. He does not seem to have much appreciation for the cults of honor and dignity, and even less so for individuals and species claiming to be chosen or elevated above the rest of nature. Yet, in order to properly address the question of humanity's alleged intellectual uniqueness (as affirmed within the humanist tradition) we must also examine Spinoza's take on the value of reason, rationality, and specifically human rationality.

3. Reason and Knowledge

Unlike his older contemporary Thomas Hobbes, who rejected the very notion of the Highest Good,[61] Spinoza employed this notion habitually in almost all of his writings,[62] and it plays a central role in his ethical theory. In spite of some slight variances of stress from one text to another, the core of Spinoza's account identifies the human *summum bonum* with *understanding* (*intelligere*) and *knowledge*.[63] Understanding, or knowledge,[64] should be the ultimate aim of all our actions, and they should be sought for their own sake. A typical statement of this view appears at the end of Part 4 of the *Ethics*:

[B]lessedness is nothing but that satisfaction of mind that stems from the intuitive cognition of God. But perfecting the intellect is nothing but understanding God, his attributes, and his actions, which follow from the necessity of his nature. *So the ultimate end of the man who is led by reason, i.e., his highest Desire, by which he strives to moderate all the others, is that by which he is led to conceive adequately both himself and all things that can fall under his understanding.* (E4app4 / G II/267/5–14; italics added)

Given Spinoza's limitless appreciation for understanding and knowledge, one might be tempted to think that on his view the inherent rationality of human beings grants them a unique value above all other things.

Spinoza, however, could hardly accept this argument, at least not without some significant amendments. In spite of his appreciation for the excellence of the human mind,[65] Spinoza is deeply aware of the very limited nature of human rationality. Thus, on one occasion Spinoza reminds his readers that "nature is not constrained by the laws of *human* reason" (TTP chap. 16 / III/190/35; italics added) and that therefore it would be just wishful thinking to "want everything to be directed according to the usage of *our* reason" (TTP chap. 16 / III/191/8; italics added).

Next to his sober recognition of the very restricted nature of human reason, Spinoza also rejects any claim about the exclusivity of human beings as rational agents. As we have seen before, Spinoza ascribes rationality to other animals as well.[66] In another study, I argued that Spinoza ascribes knowledge of God—in a rudimentary or infinitesimal degree—not only to animals, such as fish, but even to the waves of the sea (cf. Melamed, n.d).

For Spinoza, there is nothing we should value more than understanding and reason. To the extent that various individuals—drunkards, philosophers, porcupines, and worms—instantiate reason, they are valuable.[67] Thus, for Spinoza, human beings are not devoid of value, but their value is limited and proportional to their exhibition of understanding.[68] This moderate assessment of human value is indeed a far cry from the grandiose appraisal of human dignity one may find in some other modern philosophers, but such a sober evaluation of things is Spinoza's trademark.

Conclusion

Sarah Buss (2012, 343) has convincingly argued that the value of humanity cannot be posited as a brute fact. No doubt, given Spinoza's commitment to thoroughgoing explicability,[69] he would be averse to such a brute fact. In the current paper, we have considered several attempts to provide Spinozistic grounds to human value.[70] Our study showed that Spinoza assigns a limited value to human beings, primarily because he values friendship (which—Spinoza believed—we can have only with humans) and by virtue of humans' (limited) instantiation of rationality. Human rank, dignity and honor, just like most other forms of honor, seem to be vain for Spinoza. The genuine self-esteem Spinoza believed we should have is grounded in our being-in-God, a characteristic we share with everything that is (sea waves and porcupines included).

In his discussion of Spinoza in the *Lectures on the History of Philosophy*, Hegel scolds Spinoza for "utterly blotting out the principle of subjectivity, individuality, and personality" (Vol. III, 287). Earlier, in the same lectures, Hegel criticizes the suggestion that Spinoza was an atheist, arguing that Spinoza's view is the precise *opposite* of atheism, since in Spinoza's philosophy *only God* truly exists while finite things (such as human beings) are mere evanescent appearances (Vol. III, 280–281; cf. Melamed 2010a). At this point, Hegel cynically notes, "Those who speak against Spinoza do so as if it were on God's account that they were interested; *but what these opponents are really concerned about is not God, but the finite—themselves*" (Vol. III, 280; italics added). Hegel's quip notwithstanding, Spinoza is not in the business of eliminating human beings, as most of the *Ethics* is dedicated to a painstaking study of the human mind, its emotions, its frequent illusions, and its path toward a blessed life. Still, Hegel is right that Spinoza is striving to undermine our common myths about the nature and value

88 RETHINKING THE VALUE OF HUMANITY

of humanity, and this critique is arguably as deep and devastating as Spinoza's better-known critique of traditional religion.[71]

Notes

1. All references to Kant's works are to the volume and page of the Akademie edition. Unless otherwise marked, all references to Spinoza's works and letters are to Curley's translation (Spinoza 1985–2016). I rely on Gebhardt's critical edition (Spinoza 1925) for the Latin text of Spinoza and cite the texts in this edition by "G" followed by volume/page/line number. Hence III/82/7–10 refers to lines 7–10 of page 82 of volume III of Gebhardt. I use the following standard abbreviations for Spinoza's works: TIE—*Treatise on the Emendation of the Intellect* [*Tractatus de Intellectus Emendatione*], CM—*Metaphysical Thoughts* [*Cogitata Metaphysica*], TTP—*Theological-Political Treatise* [*Tractatus Theologico-Politicus*], TP—*Political Treatise* [*Tractatus Politicus*], Ep.—*Letters*. Passages in the *Ethics* will be referred to by means of the following abbreviations: a(-xiom), c(-orollary), p(-roposition), s(-cholium), and app(-endix); "d" stands for either "definition" (when it appears immediately to the right of the part of the book) or "demonstration" (in all other cases). Hence, E1d3 is the third definition of part 1, and E1p16d is the demonstration of proposition 16 of part 1. Unless otherwise marked, all references to Descartes are to Descartes 1985 (CSM, cited by volume and page number, thus: CSM II 231). I rely on Adam's and Tannery's critical edition (Descartes 1964–1976) for the original language text of Descartes and cite the texts in this edition by "AT" followed by volume and page. Thus "AT VII 23" stands for page 23 of volume 7 of this edition. This essay has benefited greatly from discussions with, and comments by Arash Abazari, Eckart Förster, Don Garrett, Zach Gartenberg, Sarah Buss, and Nandi Theunissen.
2. For more on Kant's unambiguous bifurcation between persons and things, see Bader 2022, §§ 2.3, 3.2, 3.3.
3. See, for example, Descartes's Second Set of Replies (AT VII 134 / CSM II 96); *Discourse on Method* (AT VI 2; 57–58 / CSM I 112; 140); French preface to the *Principles of Philosophy* (AT IXB 4 / CSM I 192), and *Principles of Philosophy*, I 37 (AT VIII 19–20 / CSM I 205); and Descartes's June 11, 1640, letter to Mersenne (AT III 85 / CSM 148).
4. See Descartes's Third (AT VII 51 / CSM II 35) and Fourth (AT VII 57 / CSM II 40) Meditations.
5. I have amended here Ariew and Garber's translation, rendering *espirits* as "sprits" rather than "minds." For Leibniz, animals have souls (*âmes*), but not *espirits*.
6. Heidegger, Althusser, and Foucault are probably the most prominent figures associated with anti-humanism, though at least in the case of Heidegger, the appropriateness of this association is, to my mind, highly questionable. In his "Letter on Humanism" (1947)—itself a critical response to Sartre's 1946 *L'existentialisme est un humanisme*—Heidegger criticizes the traditional understanding of the essence of man as *animal rationale*. According to Heidegger, this definition fails to recognize man's *unique* relationship with language and Being. "Only man is admitted to the destiny of ek-sistence.

Therefore ek-sistence can also never be thought of as a specific kind of creature among others" ("Letter on Humanism," in Heidegger 1977, 204). Given the working definition I will shortly suggest, Heidegger should be considered an *arch*-humanist.

7. For example, by adding the premise that a subject is bestowed with unique value by virtue of having the right, constitutive, perspective on the world, we can infer (1) from (2). Protagoras's dictum which I shall discuss shortly seems to follow this path.

8. It is easy to detect the Kantian undertones of my characterization of humanism, though a similar view is expressed by Max Black (1983, 99): "[I]n calling human beings *persons*, we are rightfully ascribing to them important properties that cannot, even in principle, apply to other animals or to inanimate material beings." According to Black, self-consciousness is one such distinctive characteristic of human beings (104). *Philosophical* humanism—as characterized above—has only little in common with the *historical* notion of Renaissance humanism. The Renaissance humanism of Lorenzo Valla, Erasmus, and Reuchlin has much more to do with the revival of the *studia humanitatis* than with the veneration of humanity (though admittedly, these were not completely separate). Giovanni Pico Della Mirandola (see his *De hominis dignitate*) is almost the only figure of Renaissance humanism who is clearly a champion of the philosophical humanism I characterize above. Let me also note that my characterization of philosophical humanism matches quite well common understandings of the notion suggested by philosophical dictionaries and encyclopedias. See, for example, "humanism" in Robert Audi 1995.

9. In the case of Kant this gulf is expressed most sharply in the bifurcation of humanity into the *homo noumenon* and *homo phaenomenon* (6:335). The former is free but not part of nature; the latter is part of nature, but not free.

10. Some famous proponents of the latter view were Wilhelm Dilthey and the Neo-Kantian philosophers Wilhelm Windelband and Heinrich Rickert. Here again, Max Black (1983, 99) provides a clear statement of this position: "I believe that there are features of human personality that are outside the purview of any of the natural or social sciences, and that there is something therefore conceptually—or, if you like, ontologically—special about human beings." As we are about to see shortly, on this issue, too, Spinoza provides a sharp contrast to the humanist stand. In the preface to the third part of the *Ethics*, Spinoza makes an assertion that is the *precise* opposite of the Dilthey, Windelband, and Rickert view: "[In this part] I shall treat the nature and powers of the Affects, and the power of the Mind over them, by the same Method by which, in the preceding parts, I treated God and the Mind, and *I shall consider human actions and appetites just as if it were a Question of lines, planes, and bodies*" (EIIIpref / G II/138/24–27).

11. Plato, *Theaetetus* 152a. For the "Ode to Man," see Sophocles's *Antigone* (lines 332–375). For a somewhat different assessment of the presence of humanism (in the sense spelled out above) in Ancient Greek culture, see Richard Bett's contribution to this volume. Cf. Vogt 2017, 92–94.

12. See CM II / G I/249/20 and CM II, 3 / G I/254/35.

13. In the *Cogitata Metaphysica*, the appendix to Spinoza's earliest work in which he presented Descartes's *Principles of Philosophy* in geometrical order, Spinoza accepts

90 RETHINKING THE VALUE OF HUMANITY

the Cartesian claim that only human minds are thinking substances (CM II, 12 / G I/275/12, though see CM II, 4 (G I/260/11), where Spinoza suggests that *perhaps* animals too are constituted by a union of a soul and a body). In his late philosophy, Spinoza will explicitly criticize the view of the human mind as a substance (see E2p10 and E2p11) and fully reject the Cartesian (and humanist) notion that only human beings are endowed with mental capacities (see E2p13s / G II/96/23–32).

14. TTP, chap. 6 / G III/82. Cf. TTP chap. 16 / G III/190–191.

15. See E3pref (G II/137/11), and TP chap. 2 (G III/277). For Leibniz's critical response to this claim of Spinoza, see AG 280.

16. See E3pref / G II/137/14, and TP chap. 2 / G III/277–278.

17. See, for example, Blijenbegh's protest to Spinoza that his claims "make man dependent on God in the *way the elements, stones, and plants are*" (Ep. 20| / G IV/103/15; italics added), and that according to Spinoza's views "we men would be made like beasts" (Ep. 20 / G IV/109/15). Leibniz's *Discours de métaphysique* is, in part, a response to Spinoza's vehement and notorious attack on anthropocentric and anthropomorphic thinking in the appendix to part 1 of the *Ethics*.

18. See Nietzsche's July 30, 1881, letter to Franz Overbeck in Nietzsche 1977, 92. Cf. Yonover 2021.

19. Cf. E4app15; G II/269/26–270/3: "[M]any, from too great an impatience of mind, and a false zeal for religion, have preferred to live among the lower animals rather than among men. They are like boys or young men who cannot bear calmly the scolding of their parents, and take refuge in the army."

20. Following the first part of the *Ethics* (*De Deo*) in which Spinoza presents the foundation of his metaphysics, the preface to the second part of the book tells the readers that the rest of the book will zoom in on the issues "that can lead us, by the hand, as it were, to the *knowledge of the human mind and its highest blessedness*" (E2pref / G II/84/11–12; italics added).

21. "E4p37 / G II/235/12–14: The good which everyone who seeks virtue wants for himself, he also desires for other men; and this Desire is greater as his knowledge of God is greater."

22. Compare this claim with Kant's assertion in the opening paragraph of the *Anthropology* that "with the irrational animals one can do as one likes" (7:127).

23. See E2p13s / G II/96/26–97/16. In Ep. 32 / G IV/171/11–12 Spinoza ascribes reasoning to a worm.

24. E3p57s / G II/187/5; italics added.

25. For a helpful explanation of this part of Spinoza's epistemology, see Della Rocca 1996, 20–22.

26. Notice Spinoza's formulation: "In proportion as a Body is more capable than others of doing many things at once, or being acted on in many ways at once, so its Mind is more capable than others of perceiving many things at once" (E2p13s / G II/97/7–10). The last sentence presents the capabilities of both minds and bodies as coming in *degrees*.

27. See, for example, TTP chap. 16 / G III/189/24 and Ep. 50 / G IV/240/20–24. This view of rights as socially and legally recognized privileges, or as mere social

institutionalization of one's political powers is the historical—medieval and early modern—source of the notion of rights. The much more recent inventions of the notions of civil and human rights should be seen as attempts to annul the exclusivity that was originally built into the notion of rights.

28. "To man, then, there is nothing more useful than man. Man, I say, can wish for nothing more helpful to the preservation of his being than that all should so agree in all things that the Minds and Bodies of all would compose, as it were, one Mind and one Body; that all should strive together, as far as they can, to preserve their being; and that all, together, should seek for themselves the common advantage of all" (E4p18s / G II/223/8–14).

29. "Both the horse and the man are driven by a Lust to procreate; but the one is driven by an equine Lust, the other by a human Lust. So also the Lusts and Appetites of insects, fish, and birds must vary. Therefore, though each individual lives content with his own nature, by which he is constituted, and is glad of it, nevertheless that life with which each one is content, and that gladness, are nothing but the idea, or soul, of the individual. And so the gladness of the one differs in nature from the gladness of the other as much as the essence of the one differs from the essence of the other" (E3p57s / G II/187/9–18).

30. It is noteworthy that Spinoza's interpretation of the primordial sin (in E4p68s / G II/262/1–5) ascribes great importance to Adam's ignorance about the difference between him and the lower animals: "But that after he believed the lower animals to be like himself, he immediately began to imitate their affects (see IIIp27) and to lose his freedom." For Spinoza, we only imitate the affects of beings we deem to be like us (E3p27 / G II/160/5–6).

31. Notice that, unlike the views of Kant and other humanists, Spinoza's argument for the impossibility of friendship with animals due to our heterogenic nature need not assume that our nature is in any sense *better* than other animals. I am not useful as a friend for my spider, just as she is not useful as a friend to me.

32. Friendship between rational (or even mostly rational) people should be *mutual*, since (1) the basic condition for the possibility of friendship (sharing the same nature) is symmetric, and (2) the same (or at least, roughly the same) considerations which lead one rational person to pursue the friendship of another rational person should obtain also in the case of the other.

33. "There are, therefore, many things outside us which are useful to us, and on that account to be sought. Of these, we can think of none more excellent than those that agree entirely with our nature. For if, for example, two individuals *of entirely the same nature* are joined to one another, they compose an individual twice as powerful as each one" (E4p18s / G II/223/3–8; italics added).

34. It is not at all clear whether Spinoza's understanding of essence—as stated in E2d2—allows for distinct things to share fully the same essence.

35. Who, then, would be most useful to the drunk person? If usefulness is determined merely by having very similar essence, it would seem that another drunk person would be more useful to the original drunkard than a philosopher. On the other hand,

in several other passages Spinoza asserts that no one is more useful to a human being than a *rational* human being (E4app9 / G II/268–269/20–23).

36. This is the perspective partly developed in part 5 of the *Ethics* when we strive to understand things—at least to some extent—"*sub specie aeternitatis.*"

37. See E1p17s / G II/63/1–2; E2p10 / G II/92/28–29; and Ep. 54 / G IV/253/10–11: "[T]he difference between the greatest, most excellent creature and God is the same as that between the least creature and God."

38. God has no passions (E5p17 / G II/291/5–6), but he has active affects.

39. See E1p20 / G II/64/29; E1p34 / G II/76/35; and E2p3 / G II/87/5–6, respectively.

40. Namely, from God's objective perspective, human beings are valuable to each other.

41. In a reciprocal manner, God cannot be valuable for a human being qua friend. As we shall see in Section 3, *knowledge of* God (or, what is the same for Spinoza, knowledge *simpliciter*) is humanity's *summum bonum*.

42. If God indeed loves human beings, he should also value them qua object of his love. So might the argument go.

43. The reference here is to E5p36 / G II/302/13–17: "The Mind's intellectual Love of God is the very Love of God by which God loves himself, not insofar as he is infinite, but insofar as he can be explained by the human Mind's essence, considered under a species of eternity; i.e., the Mind's intellectual Love of God is part of the infinite Love by which God loves himself." The same considerations which lead Spinoza to ascribe intellectual love of God to human beings apply, though in a more rudimentary manner, to the minds of all other beings.

44. For the reasons for my doubtful tone, see E5p17c / G II/291/15 ("Strictly speaking, God loves no one, and hates no one") and Melamed 2020.

45. See E1app / G II/77/20.

46. Because the differences among creatures are negligible in comparison to God's absolute infinity: "[T]he difference between the greatest, most excellent creature and God is the same as that between the least creature and God" (Ep. 54 / G IV/253/10–11).

47. TTP chap. 3 / G III/44/1.

48. TTP chap. 6 / G III/82/4–6; III/88/10. Cf. the appendix to the first part of the *Ethics*.

49. Cf. Leibniz's claim in the *Discourse on Metaphysics* that human beings "are, as it were, of [God's] race [*quasi de sa race*]" (§36 / AG 67).

50. Spinoza's understanding of love goes through several important transformations through his writings. I detect those in Melamed 2020. In the current chapter I have attempted to stick to the features of Spinoza's understanding of love that are more or less stable throughout his philosophical development.

51. Compare with the *Nichomachean Ethics* (1095b16–1096a8). Cf. Manzini 2009, 56–57.

52. Thus, if honor could be conducive for either physical survival or for the acquisition of knowledge, we should use it at need (while making sure not to become addicted).

53. For example, if one were to invoke the national sentiment of, say, the citizens of Utopia, by claiming that it is unbefitting of "the great moral heritage of Utopians" to treat foreigners in a discriminatory manner, such use of group honor would be a legitimate political instrument in spite of the vanity of group honor.

SPINOZA'S ANTI-HUMANISM 93

54. On the alleged ambiguity of the notion of human dignity—or its being a "multifaceted term"—see Waldron 2015, 15–19. I am using 'dignity' as equivalent to 'noninstrumental worth' following Kant (4:435) and in agreement with much of the current literature.

55. E3p52 (G II/179/31–33): "If we have previously seen an object together with others, or we imagine it has nothing but what is common to many things, we shall not consider it so long as one which we imagine to have something singular [*aliquid singulare*]."

56. For Spinoza's taxonomy of the three kinds of cognition—imagination (*imaginatio*), intellect/reason (*ratio*), and *scientia intuitiva*—see E2p40s2 / G II/122/1. For Spinoza's demonstration that cognitions of the second and third kind must be true, see E2p41 / G II/122/33. For an overview of this taxonomy, its central role in Spinoza's epistemology, and its development in Spinoza's writing, see Melamed 2013a.

57. In E3DA27e / G II/197/10, Spinoza also stresses the cultural relativity of what one deems honorable.

58. See E2p40s2 / G II/122/18.

59. For more on *scientia intuitiva*, see Melamed 2013a.

60. Two crucial features of *scientia intuitiva* are its (1) being free from reliance on universals (unlike cognitions of the first and second kind, which employ universals), and (2) its conception of the essential features of things as grounded in God's essence. I am not aware of any text of Spinoza that shows he believed animals must think only through universals. As to (2), in E2p47s / G II/128/13–14, Spinoza argues that "God's . . . essence . . . is *known to all*," and the considerations he employs there seem to be perfectly applicable to the case of nonhuman minds (see Melamed, n.d.). I assume that for Spinoza animal minds would have some rudimentary variant of *scientia intuitiva* by grasping the most trivial causal trajectory between God's essence and the simplest things.

61. Thus, Hobbes writes, "There is no such *Finis ultimus* nor *Summum Bonum* as is spoken of in the old books of the old moral philosophers. . . . Felicity is a continual progress of the desire, from one object to another" (I 11 1).

62. See, for example, TIE §13 / G II/8/18; CM I 6 / G I/247/31; TTP chap. 4 / G III/60; E4p28d / G II/228/10; E4app4 / G II/267/1; E5p25 / G II/296/23–24; Ep. 21 / IV/127/34; and Ep. 43 / IV/220/31–221/21.

63. Sometimes Spinoza refers specifically to "knowledge of God," but since for Spinoza everything is in God, a fortiori every knowledge is knowledge of God. See TTP Ch. 4 / G III/59/60. 'Reason' (*ratio*) is used by Spinoza in more than one sense (see LeBuffe 2018, xii). In one of these uses, 'reason' is virtually equivalent to 'understanding' and 'knowledge.'

64. For Spinoza, understanding and knowledge are intimately related. Genuine understanding cannot result in false belief. His bar for genuine understating is quite high and requires adequate knowledge of the cause of the thing understood.

65. "We ought to reckon human power not so much by the strength of the Body as by the strength of the Mind" (TP chap. 2 / G III/280/19).

66. See Section 1.

94 RETHINKING THE VALUE OF HUMANITY

67. In passing, let me note that for Spinoza the function of reason is *not* merely (or even primarily) *instrumental*. Reason and understanding not only allow us to find the proper means for a given end but also tell us what are the proper goals we should pursue in life. For example, by unmasking the irrational elements in our fear and conception of human death, understanding helps us realize that while we should try to avoid danger, we should not fear death (see E4p67; 4p69d / G II/261/1; II/262/14). More important than the length of our lives is the kind of lives we pursue. Understanding the nature of human beings, the nature of God, and the natures of eternity and temporality allows us to scrutinize and revise our common beliefs (and emotions) and set the right goals for our conduct. Ridding ourselves from the various myths of humanism is a crucial step in this process, at the end of which we may realize that there is a continuity between the death of a human being and the death of a tree.

68. Is understanding valuable *for God*? Spinoza defines the good as "what we certainly know to be useful for us" (E4d1 / G II/209/12–13), and shortly afterward he spells out the last definition: "[W]e call good . . . what is useful to . . . preserving our being . . . i.e. . . . what increases . . . our power of acting" (E4p8d / G II/215/23–25). God needs no assistance in preserving its being since God's being is secured by its very essence (in fact, God's essence just is existence; E1p20 / G II/64/29). For this reason, it seems that for Spinoza's God nothing is good or evil (cf. E4p68 / G II/261/13). Still, there is one thread Spinoza develops toward the very conclusion of the *Ethics* which opens the possibility that not only is progress *toward* perfection good, but that even being (permanently) in a state of perfection is good (E5p33d / G II/301/1). In this sense, God's intellectual perfection, i.e., his permanent and infinite understanding, would be valued as good. I am indebted to Sarah Buss for posing this question.

69. For Spinoza's assertion that everything must be explainable, see E1a2 / G II/47/22–23. Cf. Melamed and Lin 2020, §2.

70. Of course, one could entertain alternative grounds for human value and then consider to what extent the Spinozist is likely to accept them. Thus, we may, for example, consider Theunissen's (2018, 369) insightful suggestion that valuers are of value because they are good for themselves. The Spinozist is not likely to follow that path as well, however, since for her everything is "good for itself" insofar as any thing "posits the thing's essence and does not take it away" (E3p4d / G II/145/25). In other words, it belongs to the nature of every thing to strive to persevere in its existence (as having the specific essence, or nature, it has). For an insightful discussion of this doctrine, see Garrett 2003. Notably, Theunissen (2020, 109) would allow for many animals "to be valuers in the sense that they are able to respond to practically relevant features of the world."

71. For a preliminary overview of Spinoza's critique of our humanistic myths, see Melamed 2010b.

References

Aristotle. 1984. *The Complete Works of Aristotle*. Edited by Jonathan Barnes. 2 vols. Princeton, NJ: Princeton University Press. [Cited by Bekker number]

SPINOZA'S ANTI-HUMANISM 95

Audi, Robert, ed. 1995. *The Cambridge Dictionary of Philosophy*. Cambridge: Cambridge University Press.

Bader, Ralf M. 2022. "The Dignity of Humanity." In *Rethinking the Value of Humanity*, edited by Sarah Buss and Nandi Theunissen. Oxford: Oxford University Press.

Black, Max. 1983. "Humaneness." In *The Prevalence of Humbug and Other Essays*, 97–114. Ithaca, NY: Cornell University Press.

Buss, Sarah. 2012. "Value of Humanity." *Journal of Philosophy* 109: 341–377.

Carlisle, Clare. 2017. "Spinoza's *Acquiescentia*." *Journal of the History of Philosophy* 55: 209–236.

Della Rocca, Michael. 1996. *Representation and the Mind-Body Problem in Spinoza*. Oxford: Oxford University Press.

Descartes, René. 1964–1976. *Oeuvres de Descartes*. Edited by Charles Adam and Paul Tannery. 12 vols. Paris: J. Vrin.

Descartes, René. 1985. *The Philosophical Writings of Descartes*. Translated by John Cottingham, Robert Stoothoff, Dugald Murdoch, and Athony Kenny. 3 vols. Cambridge: Cambridge University Press.

Garrett, Don. 2003. "Spinoza's Conatus Argument." In *Spinoza: Metaphysical Themes*, edited by Olli Koistinen and John Biro, 127–158. Oxford: Oxford University Press.

Glück, Louise. 1992. *The Wild Iris*. New York: Harper Collins.

Hegel, G. W. F. 1995. *Lectures on the History of Philosophy*. Translated by Elizabeth S. Haldane and Frances H. Simson. 3 vols. London: University of Nebraska Press. [Cited by volume and page]

Heidegger, Martin. 1977. *Basic Writings*. Edited by David Farrell Krell. New York: Harper & Row.

Hobbes, Thomas. 1994. *Leviathan*. Edited by Edwin Curley. Indianapolis, IN: Hackett. [Cited by part, chapter, and section]

Kant, Immanuel. 1900– . *Gesammelte Schriften*. Edited by the Königlichen Preußischen (later Deutschen) Akademie der Wissenschaften. Berlin: Georg Reimer/Walter De Gruyter.

Kant, Immanuel. 1996. *Practical Philosophy*. Edited and translated by Mary G. Gregor. Introduction by Allen Wood. Cambridge: Cambridge University Press.

Kant, Immanuel. 2001. *Lectures on Metaphysics*. Edited and translated by Karl Ameriks and Steve Naragon. Cambridge: Cambridge University Press.

Kant, Immanuel. 2007. *Anthropology, History, and Education*. Edited by Günter Zöller and Robert B. Louden. Translated by Mary Gregor, Paul Guyer, Robert B. Louden, Holly Wilson, Allen W. Wood, Günter Zöller, and Arnulf Zweig. Cambridge: Cambridge University Press.

LeBuffe, Michael. 2018. *Spinoza on Reason*. Oxford: Oxford University Press.

Leibniz, G. W. 1989. *Philosophical Essays*. Edited and translated by Roger Ariew and Daniel Garber. Indianapolis, IN: Hackett. [Cited as AG, followed by page]

Manzini, Frédéric. 2009. *Spinoza: Une Lecture d'Aristote*. Paris: Presses Universitaires de France.

Melamed, Yitzhak Y. 2010a. "Acosmism or Weak Individuals? Hegel, Spinoza, and the Reality of the Finite." *Journal of the History of Philosophy* 48: 77–92.

Melamed, Yitzhak Y. 2010b. "Spinoza's Anti-Humanism: An Outline." In *The Rationalists*, edited by Carlos Fraenkel, Dario Perinetti, and Justin E. H. Smith, 147–166. Dordrecht: Springer.

Melamed, Yitzhak Y. 2013a. "'*Scientia Intuitiva*': Spinoza's Third Kind of Cognition." In *Übergänge—diskursiv oder intuitiv? Essays zu Eckart Försters "Die 25 Jahre der Philosophie*," edited by Johannes Haag and Markus Wild, 99–116. Klostermann: Frankfurt a.M.

Melamed, Yitzhak Y. 2013b. *Spinoza's Metaphysics: Substance and Thought.* Oxford: Oxford University Press.

Melamed, Yitzhak Y. 2013c. "Spinoza's *Respublica divina.*" In *Baruch de Spinozas Tractatus theologico-politicus*, edited by Otfried Höffe, 177–192. Berlin: Akademie Verlag.

Melamed, Yitzhak Y. 2020. "The Enigma of Spinoza's *Amor Dei Intellectualis.*" In *Freedom, Action and Motivation in Spinoza's Ethics*, edited by Noa Naaman-Zaudrer, 222–238. London: Routledge.

Melamed, Yitzhak Y. 2021. "Spinoza and Some of His Medieval Predecessors on the *summum bonum.*" In *The Pursuit of Happiness in Medieval Jewish and Islamic Thought*, edited by Yehuda Halper. Turnhout: Brepols Press, 377–392.

Melamed, Yitzhak Y. n.d. "On the Fish's Knowledge of God's Essence, or Why Spinoza Was Not a Skeptic." Unpublished manuscript.

Melamed, Yitzhak Y., and Martin Lin. 2020. "Principle of Sufficient Reason." In *The Stanford Encyclopedia of Philosophy* (Spring 2020 Edition), edited by Edward N. Zalta. <https://plato.stanford.edu/archives/spr2020/entries/sufficient-reason/>.

Nietzsche, Friedrich. 1977. *The Portable Nietzsche.* Edited by Walter Kaufmann. New York: Penguin.

Spinoza, Baruch. 1925. *Opera.* Edited by Carl Gebhardt. 4 vols. Heidelberg: Carl Winter.

Spinoza, Baruch. 1985–2016. *The Collected Works of Spinoza.* Edited and translated by Edwin Curley. 2 vols. Princeton, NJ: Princeton University Press.

Theunissen, L. Nandi. 2018. "Must We Be Just Plain Good? On Regress Arguments for the Value of Humanity." *Ethics* 128: 346–372.

Theunissen, L. Nandi. 2020. *The Value of Humanity.* Oxford: Oxford University Press.

Vogt, Katja M. 2017. *Desiring the Good: Ancient Proposals and Contemporary Theory.* Oxford: Oxford University Press.

Waldron, Jeremy. 2015. *Dignity, Rank, and Rights.* Oxford: Oxford University Press.

Yonover, Jason M. 2021. "Nietzsche, Spinoza and Etiology." *European Journal of Philosophy* 29(2): 1–16.

4
Slavery, Freedom, and Human Value in Early Modern Philosophy

Julia Jorati

Introduction

According to a widely endorsed conception of morality, human beings possess a special status that distinguishes them from brute animals and entitles them to certain moral rights, for example, the right to freedom. While it may be morally permissible to keep nonhuman animals in cages or force them to work, it is not generally permissible to do these things to human beings because of their special status. On one attractive theory, this special status derives from an objective, intrinsic value that human beings possess and that nonhuman animals lack. On this theory, the reason it is wrong for us to treat our fellow human beings like brute animals is that it is objectively true that human beings are entitled to, or deserving of, special treatment because of something intrinsic to their nature. On other theories, the obligation to treat human beings better than animals derives from something extrinsic to them, such as our special attitudes toward them, or a command by the government or a deity, or the fact that it is prudent for us to treat them better.

This chapter focuses on the question of what, if anything, early modern philosophers have to say about the special status of human beings and its implications for the right to freedom. As we will see, they have quite a lot to say about it. I will concentrate on the question of whether, for these early modern authors, the special status of human beings makes it illegitimate for one human being to dominate other human beings completely, or to literally and fully own them. In other words, I focus on whether, according to at least some early modern thinkers, human beings can possess the same rights over other human beings as one was thought to have over the brute animals and inanimate objects that one fully owns.

Many early modern philosophers believe that the special status of human beings includes, or bestows, natural rights to freedom and equality. For some of them, these natural rights are incompatible with the absolute domination of one human being by another. That would, for instance, make chattel slavery—a form of slavery in which slaveholders possess full ownership rights over slaves—impermissible.[1] Yet, others hold that the natural right to freedom and equality

---

Julia Jorati, *Slavery, Freedom, and Human Value in Early Modern Philosophy* In: *Rethinking the Value of Humanity.*
Edited by: Sarah Buss and L. Nandi Theunissen, Oxford University Press. © Oxford University Press 2023.
DOI: 10.1093/oso/9780197539361.003.0005

98 RETHINKING THE VALUE OF HUMANITY

is compatible with some forms of absolute domination. It is indeed common in the early modern period—even among authors who defend the natural rights to freedom and equality—to argue that there are legitimate instances of chattel slavery. A few such authors also hold that parents literally own their children and can do with them whatever they want. For some, another instance of justified complete domination is the power of husbands over their wives.

This chapter will start in Section 1 with some background information about the early modern debate concerning the full ownership of human beings, slavery, and the right to freedom. After that, because I cannot do justice to the enormous complexity of this debate, I will focus on the views of three philosophers who were active in the seventeenth and very early eighteenth century: Thomas Hobbes, John Locke, and Gottfried Wilhelm Leibniz. I have chosen these three authors because they work within similar frameworks but nevertheless have quite different views about human value and its implications for freedom and the ownership of human beings. For each author, I will address the following questions: Do human beings have a special moral status because of an intrinsic value? Do they have a natural right to freedom? If so, under what circumstances (if any) can they lose this right? Under what circumstances (if any) can a human being become a slave? Are any human beings naturally slaves, as Aristotle claims? Do slaveholders have full property rights, or absolute power, over slaves? Is slavery hereditary? And are children the property of their parents?

I will argue that Leibniz attributes an intrinsic value to human beings, at least in his late writings. According to him, all rational creatures possess a special moral status because of their rationality and not just because of their relation to God. This special status makes it illegitimate for one rational creature to claim full ownership rights over other rational creatures. In contrast, Hobbes and Locke do not acknowledge such an intrinsic value and view the full ownership of human beings as legitimate in certain circumstances. For Hobbes, human beings are not generally entitled to freedom and equality. He holds that it is perfectly legitimate for one human being to have full ownership rights over another. Locke argues for more robust natural rights and liberties than Hobbes, but he derives them from God's rights over human beings rather than from an intrinsic human value. Rationality is a necessary condition for these rights, but not a sufficient condition. Like Hobbes, Locke holds that there are legitimate forms of slavery in which the slaveholder has absolute power over the slave.

1. Background

There was a lively debate about slavery, domination, and the right to freedom and equality in early modern Europe. It appears that this debate was prompted partially by political events such as the English Civil War (1642–1651), which led some early modern Europeans to reevaluate the legitimacy of various types of absolute domination (see, e.g., Skinner 2008, xiii). Additional kindling for this debate was, presumably, the growth of the transatlantic slave trade, especially starting toward the end of the seventeenth century, when this trade became much more extensive and had been encoded in positive law.[2] This confronted Europeans with a form of slavery whose cruelty disturbed at least some philosophers in that period.[3] The debate over slavery in early modern Europe often had an explicit or implicit racial dimension, especially in authors who had the transatlantic slave trade in mind when discussing slavery. But slavery was also well entrenched in many other parts of the world (see, e.g., Guasco 2014, 41ff.; Baumgold 2010), and many early modern Europeans regarded at least some instances of slavery as morally justified. Another aspect of the debate about domination were discussions about the subjection of women and children.

Some early modern authors defend chattel slavery. That is, they hold that slaveholders can have full ownership rights over slaves: it is morally permissible for slaveholders to do whatever they want with their slaves, even to kill them.[4] For instance, English theologian William Nicholls argues in his 1701 *The Duty of Inferiours towards Their Superiours* that a slaveholder "has Power of Life and Death over [the slave], and has him Absolutely as much at Command and Disposal, as he has his Ox or his Ass" (59, discourse 3). Likewise, the Dutch jurist and philosopher Ulrik Huber claims in his late seventeenth century book *De jure civitatis* that at least some slaveholders have the right to abuse and destroy their slaves (2.1.6.4, 1698, 334). These claims are in line with some Ancient views about slavery. For instance, Aristotle categorizes a slave as "a living possession" and claims that a slave "wholly belongs" to the master (*Politics* 1.4).[5] He also argues that some human beings are natural slaves, or that it is proper for some humans to be enslaved because they naturally lack the capacity for rational decision-making (*Politics* 1.4–5, 1.13).[6]

Other early modern authors argue that it is never permissible to treat human beings as mere property. That is, human beings cannot have full ownership rights over other human beings. Samuel von Pufendorf, for instance, cautions in 1673 that "since humanity bids us never to forget that a slave is in any case a man, we should by no means treat him like other property, which we may use, abuse and destroy at our pleasure" (*Duty of Man* 2.4.5; see also *De jure naturae* 6.3.7).[7] This means that even if slaves are property in some sense, slaveholders do not have full ownership rights over them and are not morally permitted to kill or abuse them. Hugo Grotius (*Rights of War and Peace* 2.5.28) and Christian Thomasius (*Divine Jurisprudence* 3.5.22–24) agree: a human being never has a moral right to destroy another human being, except when the latter has committed a capital crime. Likewise, Gershom Carmichael argues in his 1718 commentary on

100 RETHINKING THE VALUE OF HUMANITY

Pufendorf that slaves should not be viewed as having "fallen from the class of persons into the class of things" and that one human being cannot in the strict sense own another human being (*Supplements and Observations* chap. 16, 140; see also 142–143). A slaveholder can merely be a creditor, to whom a certain type of service is owed, and never literally an owner (chap. 16, 141). Similarly, James Tyrrell argues in his 1681 book *Patriarcha non Monarcha* that the "Primitive Equality and rationality of human beings entails that slaveholders cannot have the same ownership rights over slaves that they can have over horses or inanimate objects" (62–63).

Some authors also attack the Aristotelian doctrine that some human beings are natural slaves, for instance Thomasius (*Divine Jurisprudence* 2.3.17) and Pufendorf (*De jure naturae* 6.3.2, 6.3.11). Carmichael finds this doctrine so horrible that he is reluctant to attribute it to Aristotle, speculating that perhaps Aristotle was merely "flattering the vanity of his fellow countrymen, who imagined that nature had given them the right to rule barbarians" (*Supplements and Observations* chap. 8, 74). As we will see later, Hobbes and Leibniz also criticize this Aristotelian doctrine, and Locke appears to reject it as well.

Interestingly, natural law theorists, who typically claim that human beings are naturally free and naturally equal, ordinarily view several types of slavery as permissible. This is important for our purposes because Hobbes, Locke, and Leibniz can all be classified as members of the natural law tradition. For many natural law philosophers, saying that humans are naturally free and equal means that they possess freedom and equality in the state of nature, that is, in a state without a civil government. Yet, for these writers, saying that nobody is a slave by nature is compatible with multiple forms of slavery; they hold that the subordination of human beings can result from human actions. Grotius writes in 1625, for instance, "There is no Man by Nature Slave to another, that is, in his primitive State considered, independently of any human Fact . . . but it is not repugnant to natural Justice, that Men should become Slaves by a human Fact, that is, by Vertue of some Agreement, or in Consequence of some Crime" (*Rights of War and Peace* 3.7.1–3; see also Suárez, *On Laws and God* 2.14.18).

One type of slavery that natural law theorists typically acknowledge is voluntary slavery: one can voluntarily subject oneself to a master in exchange for food and shelter (e.g., Grotius, *Rights of War and Peace* 2.5.26–27; Pufendorf, *Duty of Man* 2.4.3). This type of slavery can be either permanent or temporary, and because the person voluntarily gives up her freedom, it is compatible with the natural freedom and equality of human beings. Moreover, natural law philosophers typically contend that it is permissible to enslave an enemy soldier captured in a just war. After all, the argument goes, if it is permissible to kill enemy combatants in a just war, it must *a fortiori* be permissible to enslave them. By fighting for an unjust cause, these combatants have forfeited their right to life and liberty;

enslaving them and postponing their death is a merciful alternative to killing them immediately.[8] Some natural law theories additionally make room for penal slavery, that is, slavery imposed as a punishment for a crime.[9] Moreover, a few natural law theorists argue that children born into slavery should be considered slaves at least temporarily. The justification is typically that the slaveholder in whose household these children grow up has a right to be compensated for the expense of raising them.[10]

A few early modern authors hold that parents have absolute rights over their children. Robert Filmer argues in his 1652 "Observations upon Aristotles Politiques," for instance, "Every man . . . is so far from being free-born that by his very birth he becomes a subject to him that begets him" (1991, 282). Likewise, Nicholls argues that "'tis impossible, that any one can have a firmer Right to any thing more, than they have to their Children" (*Duty of Inferiours*, discourse 2, 1701, 46–47). As we will see later, Locke and Leibniz disagree with Filmer and Nicholls in this respect: even though parents have some rights over their children, these rights are quite limited and do not amount to full ownership. Hobbes's views, in contrast, are very close to Filmer's and Nicholls's.

A final type of domination that is often discussed side by side with slavery and the subjection of children is that of husbands over their wives. It was common to view husbands as possessing extensive rights. One interesting source for such views is Margaret Cavendish's "Orations" (1662). In Oration 49—a fictional court case in which a woman petitions for a divorce because her husband is physically abusive—the defendant expresses a common attitude concerning the rights of husbands: "[I]t is as lawful for an husband to govern, rule, and correct his wife, as for parents to rule, govern, and correct their children, or for masters to rule, govern, and correct their servants or slaves" (2003, 179).[11] Indeed, several early modern authors argue that the status of women in their societies is tantamount to slavery. For instance, Sarah Fyge writes in a poem from 1703, "From the first dawn of Life, unto the Grave, / Poor Womankind's in every State, a Slave"; a few lines later, she describes marriage as "the last, the fatal Slavery" ("Emulation," 108). Likewise, one of the characters in Madame de Maintenon's dialogue "On the Drawbacks of Marriage" claims, "A woman commits herself to death and slavery when she marries" (2004, 65).

2. Thomas Hobbes

Thomas Hobbes (1588–1679) notoriously defends a social contract theory that justifies the absolute power of governments over their citizens. Moreover, and perhaps most famously, he describes life in the state of nature as "nasty, brutish, and short" (*Leviathan* 13.9). Even though he views human beings as naturally

102 RETHINKING THE VALUE OF HUMANITY

equal and free, he argues that the only way to live together peacefully and avoid the horrors of the state of nature is to give up some of this liberty and subordinate oneself to a civil government with absolute power. Thus, it is best for human beings to live under absolute domination. Such an absolute domination exists between Hobbesian governments and their citizens; it can also exist between slaveholders and slaves, as well as between parents and children. For Hobbes, as we will see, these kinds of domination grant the dominating party full ownership rights over the dominated.

In what follows, I will outline Hobbes's theory of human equality, liberty, and legitimate types of domination. I will argue that Hobbes's doctrine of the natural equality of human beings is extremely thin and not based on an intrinsic human value. In my discussion, I will draw on three of his works that provide very similar, though not identical, accounts: *Elements of Law* (1640), *De cive* (1642), and *Leviathan* (1651).

Hobbes's doctrine that human beings are naturally equal plays a central role in his argument for absolutism. Yet, to a large extent, this doctrine is descriptive rather than normative: it asserts that adult human beings are so similar in their physical and mental powers that in the state of nature, everybody has good reasons to fear everybody else. Nobody is so strong or so intelligent that they are completely safe; "the weakest has strength enough to kill the strongest, either by secret machination, or by confederacy with others" (*Leviathan* 13.1; see also *De cive* 1.3; *Elements* 14.2). This descriptive claim about the relative equality of human beings entails that by nature, no human being can dominate other adult human beings completely. Indeed, Hobbes invokes this equality to reject the Aristotelian doctrine that there are natural slaves: natural slavery "is not only against reason, but contrary to experience." This is because, Hobbes continues, practically no adult human being is mentally so inferior that they prefer being ruled to ruling themselves.[12] Conversely, being mentally superior to others is not usually sufficient for overpowering them, since those who are mentally inferior might possess significant physical strength. Thus, Hobbes insists, domination arises not from nature but from the consent of human beings (*De cive* 3.13; see also *Leviathan* 15.21; *Elements* 17.1). Human beings are not only naturally equal; they are also naturally free from domination.

Hobbes argues further that because human beings are naturally equal, each person naturally has a right to everything. Or, more specifically, each person naturally has the right to do whatever they judge useful for preserving their own life. This includes the right to kill other human beings (*De cive* 1.7-10, 2.18; *Leviathan* 14.1, 14.4). Hobbes defines this natural right as the liberty to use one's own power to do whatever one thinks is beneficial (*De cive* 1.7; *Leviathan* 14.1; *Elements* 14.6-10). Yet, because everyone has this liberty, it is quite useless: the fact that I have the right to whatever I think is beneficial does not mean that others have an obligation to let me have those things. Thus, "the effect of this right is almost the same as if there were no right at all" (*De cive* 1.11). Having a right to all things and being naturally equal is therefore not nearly as good as it may initially sound. Because of their natural equality, people in the state of nature will inevitably compete for resources and power, which results in constant fear, persistent danger, and thus a "war of every man against every man" (*Leviathan* 13.8–9; similarly in *De cive* 1.12; *Elements* 14.11). The only alternative to this state of war is subjecting oneself to the absolute power of a government and thereby giving up some portion of one's liberty, or right to all things (*Leviathan* 14.5).

When Hobbes describes the way out of the state of war, it becomes clear that there is a normative dimension to human equality, in addition to the descriptive dimension already discussed. In order to end the war of all against all, one must recognize that it is rational—that is, prudent—for everyone to obey a set of laws of nature, or "articles of peace" (*Leviathan* 13.14). One of these is the law "that every man acknowledge other [men] for his equal by nature." This is necessary for peace because even men who are naturally inferior would agree to end the state of war only on equal terms (*Leviathan* 15.21, italics removed; similarly in *De cive* 3.13; *Elements* 17.1). Acknowledging others to be equal entails additional natural laws relating to equality, for instance, that when entering into a social contract, one should not claim more rights for oneself than one is willing to grant to others (*Leviathan* 15.22; *De cive* 3.14; *Elements* 17.2).[13]

Yet, this normative dimension of human equality is clearly very thin, and it is at least primarily a prudential normativity. Hobbes is not saying that human beings naturally possess a special status that entitles them to equal treatment. Rather, he is merely arguing that in order to live together peacefully, we must enter into a social contract and, in doing so, treat others as equals. Hobbes's reason for treating others as equals is not that they have an intrinsic value or a right to be treated in that way. Rather, the reason is merely that equal treatment is a necessary means to peace and hence to self-preservation. If there is no hope for attaining peace, we do not have to act in accordance with this natural law.[14]

From what we have already seen, it is clear that the natural liberty and equality of human beings is compatible with the absolute power of governments over their citizens. Through a social contract, these citizens transfer their right to govern themselves to the civil government, which thereby acquires a supreme power over them (*Leviathan* 17.13, 18.4ff.; *De cive* 6.13). Because the social contract is among the citizens only and does not include the government—except as a beneficiary (*Leviathan* 18.4)—the rights of the government are completely unrestricted: the sovereign or council retains the right to all things. Whatever they do is rightful (*De cive* 6.18; *Leviathan* 18.6).

104 RETHINKING THE VALUE OF HUMANITY

Social contracts, through which individuals subject themselves to a government for the sake of peace, are not the only Hobbesian ways of establishing absolute domination relations. It is also possible for someone to gain absolute power over others by what Hobbes sometimes calls "natural force" (*Leviathan* 17.15). These are cases in which one person has the power to force another person to agree to enter into a domination relation.[15] This, in turn, can take two forms. One form occurs when adults—typically parents[16]—raise children and thereby gain an absolute power over these children (*Leviathan* 20.4; *De cive* 9.3; *Elements* 23.3–4). In the state of nature, this absolute power belongs, by default, to the mother (*Leviathan* 20.5; *De cive* 9.2; *Elements* 23.3). Because Hobbes holds that domination relations always arise from consent, he claims—rather implausibly—that children consent to be ruled by the parent (*Leviathan* 20.4). The other form of absolute domination through natural force occurs when one person is so afraid of another that the former submits to the latter in order to stay alive; this results in a master-slave relationship. For instance, the victor in a war can compel the vanquished to become the victor's slaves, in exchange for their lives (*Leviathan* 17.15, 20.1, 20.10; *De cive* 8.1; *Elements* 22.2).

Hobbes distinguishes two types of slaves: those who promise obedience to their master in exchange for their life and physical liberty, on the one hand, and those who are kept in chains and have not promised anything to their master, on the other hand. Even though Hobbes reserves the term "slave" for the latter and calls the former "servant" (*Leviathan* 20.10; *Elements* 23.3),[17] I will keep referring to both types as "slaves." Slaves of the former type, who have entered into a covenant with their master, owe complete obedience to the master. In contrast, slaves of the latter type do not owe their captors anything because they have not entered into a covenant; they can flee, or kill their master, without violating any obligations (*Leviathan* 20.10; *De cive* 8.4). Yet, both types of masters have supreme power over their slaves; they have the right to do to them whatever they want (*De cive* 8.5–7; *Elements* 22.4). This means that the distinction is not ultimately important for the question of whether one human being is entitled to exercise absolute power over another.

The rights of parents over children are the same as the rights of slaveholders over slaves; both parents and slaveholders have absolute power. Hobbes says about slaves taken in war and the children of such slaves that their bodies "are not in their own power, their lives depending on the will of their masters in such manner as to forfeit them upon the least disobedience," adding that they can be "bought and sold as beasts" (*Leviathan* 45.13). A slaveholder, in other words, has complete control over the bodies and lives of slaves and can do with them whatever he or she pleases. This also means that slaveholders have rights to whatever belongs to the slave, including any children that the slaves already have or to whom they give birth while in slavery (*Elements* 23.4; *Leviathan* 20.8, 20.13). Slaves, for Hobbes, are literally the property of slaveholders: a slaveholder "may say of his slave no less than of any other thing, animate and inanimate, This is mine" (*De cive* 8.5; see also *Elements* 22.1, 22.4).[18] In fact, the slaveholder can do them no wrong, not even by killing them (*De cive* 8.7; *Leviathan* 20.13, 45.13).[19] Parents have the same rights over their children: "*children* are no less subject to those who look after them and bring them up than *slaves* are to *Masters*" (*De cive* 9.7; see also *Leviathan* 20.14). Hence parents may do with their children whatever they want, and can even sell their children into slavery or "pawn them for hostages, kill them for rebellion, or sacrifice them for peace" (*Elements* 23.8).

It should already be clear that Hobbes does not view human beings as possessing any special intrinsic value that gives them genuine moral rights.[20] This is also obvious in chapter 10 of *Leviathan*, which is titled "Of Power, Worth, Dignity, Honour, and Worthiness." In this chapter, Hobbes defines "the *value* or WORTH of a man" as "his price, that is to say, so much as would be given for the use of his power" (*Leviathan* 10.16). He illustrates this with the value of a soldier, which is high during a war and low in peace. Hobbes defines 'dignity' in a similar way: it is simply "the public worth of a man, which is the value set on him by the commonwealth" (*Leviathan* 10.18).[21] Here, human value and dignity are defined as purely extrinsic and instrumental: people have value or dignity only to the extent that they are useful to others.

3. John Locke

John Locke (1632–1704) is sometimes called the "father of liberalism" because his political philosophy emphasizes the importance of the right to liberty. For this reason, one might expect him categorically to reject chattel slavery and other forms of absolute domination over human beings. The very first sentence of his 1689 work *Two Treatises of Government* meets this expectation: slavery, Locke tells us, is "so vile and miserable an Estate of Man . . . that 'tis hardly to be conceived, that an *Englishman*, much less a *Gentleman*, should plead for't" (1.1). The gentleman in question is Robert Filmer, one of Locke's main targets in the *Two Treatises* and an infamous defender of the absolute right of kings, slaveholders, and parents. Nevertheless, Locke's attitude toward slavery and the right to liberty is far more complicated than it initially seems. In what follows, I will sketch the main contours of Locke's views.

In chapter 2 of his *Second Treatise of Government*, Locke describes the state of nature as a state of perfect freedom and equality among human beings (*Two Treatises* 2.4). Indeed, he holds that each human being has an "*equal Right . . . to his Natural Freedom*," which means not being "subjected to the Will

106 RETHINKING THE VALUE OF HUMANITY

or Authority of any other Man" (2.54; see also 2.190). For Locke, then, human beings are free insofar as they have the power to "order their Actions, and dispose of their Possessions, and Persons as they think fit, within the bounds of the Law of Nature" (2.4; see also 2.57). Human beings also have obligations toward each other, even in the state of nature. Reason teaches us that "being all equal and independent, no one ought to harm another in his Life, Health, Liberty, or Possessions" (2.6). This is at least in part because, for Locke, we are the servants and even the property of God, our omnipotent and perfectly wise creator (2.6). Since human beings are God's property, we ought not to harm or destroy any human being, not even ourselves. After all, it is impermissible to damage or destroy someone else's property against the owner's will. Locke further claims that, for the same reason, we have a natural obligation to preserve ourselves and our fellow human beings (2.6).

Regarding the natural equality of human beings, Locke states that "being furnished with like Faculties, sharing all in one Community of Nature, there cannot be supposed any such *Subordination* among us, that may Authorize us to destroy one another, as if we were made for one anothers uses, as the inferior ranks of Creatures are for ours" (*Two Treatises* 2.6; see also 2.172). In other words, the fact that human beings possess similar natural capacities indicates that there are no natural domination relations among them—or at least no absolute domination that would give one human being the right to kill another. Even though Locke does not explicitly say so, this is presumably his way of rejecting the Aristotelian doctrine that there are natural slaves.

Children, according to Locke, are not born in a state of perfect equality (*Two Treatises* 2.55). Even though human beings are born free and rational—which presumably means that they have the potential for freedom and rationality from birth—they cannot actualize this potential until they reach a certain age (2.57, 2.61). Until they reach the age of reason, children are subjects of their parents. Yet, because children are God's property rather than the property of their parents, this subjection cannot be absolute: parents have a natural obligation to "preserve, nourish, and educate" their children (2.56; see also 2.58), and they do not have a power over the lives, or even liberty, of their children (2.189).[22] Moreover, parents lose the right to govern their children as soon as the children become rational and hence acquire the power to govern themselves (2.58, 2.170). Locke notes that some individuals may never acquire this power; developmental disabilities and mental illnesses can permanently prevent someone from reaching a degree of rationality that is sufficient for understanding the natural law and being able to obey it (2.60). In such cases, Locke claims, the person should always be governed by others (2.60). The permanence of their condition does not, however, eliminate the obligation of their parents (or other guardians) to preserve them and to seek their good (2.60).

Let us now turn to Locke's discussion of slavery. Here, it is important to note that Locke is presupposing a very narrow definition of slavery: he understands it as a condition in which the slaveholder has "Absolute, Arbitrary, Despotical Power" (*Two Treatises* 2.24), which means that slaveholders have, among other things, the power to take away the slaves' lives whenever they please (2.172). For him, other types of domination that involve a more limited power are not properly called "slavery" but merely "*Drudgery*" (2.24). In *Two Treatises* 2.85, he calls the subjects of drudgery "servants" and the subjects of slavery "slaves."

Locke insists that the freedom from slavery, that is, from an absolute, arbitrary power, is necessary for our preservation (*Two Treatises* 2.17, 2.23). Because, as already seen, we have an obligation to preserve ourselves, this means that we are not allowed to give up this freedom voluntarily, for instance by selling ourselves into slavery. Moreover, giving up this freedom would mean giving other human beings an absolute power over our lives, which is a power that we cannot give away since we do not possess it in the first place (2.23; see also 2.135). As we saw earlier, Locke claims that our lives are the property of God, not of ourselves (2.6). This entails that we lack not only the right to destroy our own lives but also the right to give someone else the power to destroy our lives.[23] Thus, for Locke, voluntary slavery is illegitimate.

Yet, Locke acknowledges one legitimate way of becoming a slave, in the strong Lockean sense of being "subjected to the absolute dominion and arbitrary power of . . . masters" (*Two Treatises* 2.85). While he argues, as already noted, that we cannot simply give another human being an absolute right over our lives through a voluntary agreement, he contends that it is possible for us to forfeit our own lives.[24] This occurs when we perform an action that deserves to be punished with death.[25] Those who have the right to kill us in these situations may delay our execution and instead make us their slaves (2.23). Locke mainly applies this to captives in a just war (2.85, 2.172, 2.178), though the same line of reasoning appears to apply to those who commit capital crimes, which in the state of nature any individual has the right to punish (2.11). The resulting domination is a continuation of the state of war, and these masters retain the right to kill their slaves whenever they please (2.24).[26] In short, Locke thinks that some forms of chattel slavery are morally legitimate. Unlike Hobbes, however, he denies that the power of masters over slaves extends to the property, land, or children of these captives (2.178, 2.180). Children of slaves are "Free-men," and the parents' master has no right to dominate them (2.189, 2.182–183.).

What Locke says about slavery and human value in his philosophical writings is not the only source of evidence for his attitude on these issues. As several interpreters have pointed out, it is also important to consider that, starting in the 1660s, Locke was intimately involved, in several capacities, in New World slavery.[27] He invested money in the slave trade and made a profit. He also worked

108 RETHINKING THE VALUE OF HUMANITY

as a personal secretary and counselor to Sir Antony Ashley Cooper, who was a lord proprietor of Carolina. Moreover, Locke was a member of the Council of Trade and Foreign Plantations and the secretary to the lords proprietors of Carolina. In this latter role, Locke helped shape the legal framework for slavery in Carolina. While the exact extent of his role is controversial, it has been shown that he at least edited, and possibly helped to draft, an influential document called *The Fundamental Constitutions of Carolina* (Armitage 2004, 607ff.; Farr 2008, 499). This document legitimizes race-based chattel slavery in Carolina, stating, for instance, "Every freeman of Carolina shall have absolute power and authority over his Negro slaves" (§110, 2003, 230). Interpreters disagree about whether Locke believed that the type of slavery practiced in the New World was compatible with his political philosophy (Bernasconi and Mann 2005, 95–101; Farr 2008, 508–509; Uzgalis 1998). One plausible possibility is that Locke held (proto-) racist views that made the large-scale enslavement of Africans—who were not prisoners taken in a just war and who had not committed capital crimes—seem less problematic to him than the enslavement of Europeans.[28]

Where does this leave us? Locke clearly places more restrictions on the full ownership of human beings than Hobbes does. According to the *Two Treatises*, we cannot voluntarily become slaves, that is, subject ourselves absolutely to another human being. While Locke justifies the enslavement of prisoners in a just war, he denies that one can take their property and that one can enslave noncombatants. Moreover, he writes that nobody can be a slave by birth: children who are born to slaves are free.[29] By the same token, Locke denies that children are the property of their parents, or that parents can do with their children whatever they please. Nevertheless, Locke's opposition to human ownership is not as far-reaching as one might have expected. First, he defends the moral permissibility of enslaving captives in a just war. In fact, he does not place any restrictions whatsoever on how such slaves may be treated. Hence, the general-sounding condemnation of slavery from the beginning of the *Two Treatises* is in fact quite limited. Second, Locke does not seem to view moral rights as grounded in an intrinsic human value. Even though he invokes rationality as important for human natural rights (*Two Treatises* 2.63), his ultimate reasons for worrying about the absolute subjection of human beings to other human beings are God's rights over us. Rationality merely appears to be a necessary and not a sufficient condition for having special rights. If there were no God who owns what he has created, it would not be morally wrong for rational creatures to kill, enslave, or harm each other. Our rights and obligations depend on something extrinsic, namely God's relation to us, rather than solely on something intrinsic. Finally, Locke's involvement in, and apparent endorsement of, the transatlantic slave trade may indicate that he did not view his arguments as applying to all human beings, regardless of their race.

SLAVERY, FREEDOM, AND HUMAN VALUE   109

4. Gottfried Wilhelm Leibniz

Unlike Hobbes and Locke, Gottfried Wilhelm Leibniz (1646–1716) is not widely known for his work on ethics. Yet, he discussed various ethical questions in many of his writings throughout his long career. Three themes within moral philosophy to which Leibniz keeps returning are justice, the special status of rational creatures, and disinterested love. These themes are closely connected: the special status of rational creatures entails that they are subject to the principles of justice, which in turn require them to love each other in a disinterested way. More generally, being subject to the principles of justice means having specific moral obligations and rights. Leibniz claims in a text from the early 1700s which editors have titled "On the Common Notion of Justice" that these rights and obligations make it illegitimate for one rational creature to be the property of another. On the basis of this text and some others from the same period, I will argue that according to Leibniz, human beings and other rational creatures possess a special intrinsic value that rules out chattel slavery and other forms of full ownership. Perhaps somewhat surprisingly,[30] there is evidence that the late-period Leibniz acknowledges a much more robust type of human value than does Locke.

Before examining passages from "On the Common Notion of Justice" and other texts in which Leibniz appears to describe chattel slavery as impermissible, I should note that in his early juridical writings, he discusses slavery without mentioning its moral impermissibility. For instance, he sometimes says that, legally speaking, slaves are things (*res*) rather than persons (e.g., *Nova Methodus Discendae Docendaeque Jurisprudentiae* 2.15, 1667, A 6.1.301). In a marginal note to another early legal text, Leibniz says, "A slave is not part of the family but an instrument, like a horse" (*Definitionum Juris Specimen*, 1676, A 6.3.593n9).[31] Moreover, Leibniz states in the same text, "A slave is a person who is under the authority of another [*in alterius dominio*]. Indeed, I do not see what would keep a republic from allowing the ownership [*proprietatem*] of people just as of a horse" (A 6.3.606). Leibniz mentions both voluntary and hereditary slavery in these legal writings. For instance, he states that a freeman is someone who is "neither a slave, or someone who has given himself completely to another, nor born to a slave" (preparatory work for *Elementa Juris Civilis*, 1667–1670, A 6.2.37). He also mentions the enslavement of prisoners of war in some texts (e.g., *Definitionum Juris Specimen*, A 6.3.606n44).

To the best of my knowledge, Leibniz never criticizes or questions the institution of slavery in his early legal writings. Does that mean that he does not have moral qualms about it? One possibility is that Leibniz is merely concerned with the legal status of slavery in these texts, that is, the status of slaves in the framework of Roman law. In other words, Leibniz might merely be describing the legal *status quo* rather than endorsing the moral permissibility of slavery. After all, the

110 RETHINKING THE VALUE OF HUMANITY

claims he makes about slavery in these texts are taken almost verbatim from the Roman legal tradition. Another possibility is that Leibniz considered slavery to be morally permissible when he was young, but changed his mind later in life.

One reason for thinking that Leibniz changed his mind about slavery is that he also composed a policy proposal for Louis XIV in the early 1670s advocating the abduction of boys from "Africa, Arabia, America, New Guinea, etc." in order to turn them into warrior slaves and use them to conquer the entire earth (*Modus instituendi militam novam invictam*, A 4.1.408).[32] This text has clear racist or proto-racist overtones: Leibniz not only uses the term "barbarian" to describe the geographic areas from which he proposes to kidnap warriors; he then specifies that he means "without distinction Ethiopians, Negroes, Angolians, Caribbeans, Canadians, Hurons," and goes on to describe people from these groups as "semi-beasts" (A 4.1.408). This proposal and its racial justifications[33] are clearly appalling. Even though this text does not explicitly address the moral status of slavery, one may wonder why Leibniz would make such a proposal unless he views slavery as permissible. Thus, this text is evidence that the early Leibniz is not generally opposed to slavery.

Let us now turn to Leibniz's views about human value in his late period, which starts in the mid-1690s. In many of his philosophical writings from this period, Leibniz claims that rational creatures have a very special status in the world: their rational capacities set them apart from nonrational creatures and give them moral rights and obligations. Typically, Leibniz describes this special status in theological terms: God has special concern for rational creatures and relates to them like a prince to subjects or like a father to children. In contrast, God's relationship to nonrational animals is merely like that of an engineer to machines ("New System of Nature," G 4:479–480/AG 140).

All rational creatures are part of what Leibniz calls the "City of God," a moral kingdom within the natural world. God is the sovereign of this city and governs its citizens with perfect justice: every good action will eventually get rewarded and every bad action punished ("Principles of Nature and Grace" §15, G 6:605/AG 212). Citizens in turn have moral rights and obligations with respect to each other. Brute animals are not part of this kingdom because they are not rational, and hence not capable of moral agency.[34] Leibniz sometimes cites his doctrine of the City of God as one reason why there cannot be absolute subordination among rational creatures. As he says in "On the Common Notion of Justice," even if slavery were in accordance with natural reason, masters would be "the fellow-citizens of their slaves, since the latter have the right of citizenship in the kingdom of God as well as their masters" (NCJ 177/Riley 62).[35] As we will see later, this status of co-citizenship does not rule out all forms of subordination among rational creatures. Yet, Leibniz takes it to rule out full ownership.

SLAVERY, FREEDOM, AND HUMAN VALUE   111

Even though Leibniz often discusses the special moral status of human beings in theological terms, it is clear that he views moral rights and obligations as independent of God, at least to a large extent. After all, human beings and other rational creatures play a special role in God's plan because of their rationality and their status as moral agents; their moral status is explanatorily prior to God's special treatment, not the other way around.[36] In fact, there are strong reasons to interpret Leibniz as a natural law theorist: human nature—or, more accurately, the nature of rational souls—grounds a set of moral rights and obligations that are naturally knowable by all rational beings and have a natural authority over them.[37]

One important aspect of Leibniz's ethics is that being morally good means doing what is natural for a perfectly good person (preface to *Codex Juris Gentium Diplomaticus* A 4.5.61/L 421). Because the principles of moral goodness, or justice, are the same for God as for rational creatures (NBJ 151/Riley 48), being morally good means imitating God's perfect justice. Leibniz defines 'justice,' in turn, as the "charity of the wise," that is, a wisely distributed universal benevolence or universal disinterested love.[38] In other words, a perfectly just agent promotes the happiness of all rational beings insofar as it is possible, out of love. Of course, human beings can imitate divine justice only in an imperfect way; we are not wise enough and do not love our fellow human beings enough to be perfectly just in all situations. Yet, human beings have a moral obligation to imitate divine justice to the best of their abilities (A 4.5.62–63/L 422–423; NCJ 173/Riley 60). As he puts it in his commentary on Pufendorf, "we owe it not only to ourselves, but also to society . . . that we have . . . a will which tends constantly toward the just" (Dutens 4.3.278/Riley 69).

Leibniz calls the obligation to imitate God's universal disinterested love "universal justice" or "piety" (A 4.5.62–63/L 422–423; NCJ 173/Riley 60). It is the highest degree of natural right and of justice. There are also two lower degrees. Strict right, or commutative justice, is the lowest degree, and it requires that we do not injure others. Equity, or distributive justice, is the middle degree; it requires us to give each person their due, that is, to advance the good of others insofar as it is fitting, or insofar as they deserve it (A 4.5.62/L 422; NCJ 167/Riley 56). Sometimes Leibniz identifies the Golden Rule as the principle of equity: we ought to treat others in the way that we would demand to be treated if we were in their situation (NCJ 167–168/Riley 56).

Leibniz's emphasis on disinterested love as a moral obligation points to one way in which we are morally required to respect the value of other rational agents: as Leibniz stresses in several texts, loving someone in a disinterested way means making their happiness, or their good, the end of one's own actions. In those cases, "the good of this object [of our love] is immediately, finally and in itself our aim, our pleasure and our good . . . these are ends and not means" (letter to Nicaise, August 19, 1697, A 2.3.369/LGR 159). Leibniz contrasts this with self-interested love, in which one pursues the happiness of others merely as a means to one's own happiness (A 2.3.369/LGR 159; see also letter to Electress Sophie, August 1697, A 1.14.56/SLT 162).[39] In short, Leibniz holds that we are morally obligated to make the happiness of others our end, which I take to be a way of respecting their intrinsic value.

The moral obligation to pursue the good of other rational agents has direct implications for the question of whether one human being can fully own another human being.[40] After all, having full ownership rights over something means that one can do with it whatever one pleases or whatever serves one's own ends.[41] Yet, with respect to rational agents, it is not permissible to do whatever serves our own ends; we are always required to take their good into consideration and promote it as much as we can, or insofar as it is reasonable (NCJ 168/Riley 57). This means that we cannot have full ownership rights over another human being, at least insofar as this other human being is—or has the potential to be—rational and hence a moral agent.[42]

Leibniz argues that this rules out forms of slavery in which slaveholders have unlimited rights over slaves: the rights of a slaveholder "cannot go to the point of making a slave vicious or unhappy" (NCJ 177/Riley 63, translation altered). Likewise, he says that even if slavery were in accordance with natural law, the rights of slaveholders would be limited, among other things, by "charity, which ordains that one work for the happiness of others" (NCJ 177/Riley 63). Leibniz uses the same line of reasoning to argue that parents do not have full ownership rights over their children: "when one can make men happy and virtuous, one should never leave virtue out," and therefore, it is impermissible to rule one's children despotically, without pursuing their happiness and virtue (NCJ 178/Riley 63).

Interestingly, Leibniz provides another argument against the legitimacy of full ownership of another person in "On the Common Notion of Justice": rational souls are "naturally and inalienably free" (NCJ 177/Riley 62). This inalienable freedom entails, among other things, that rational souls cannot be "acquired," that is, that they cannot become the property of someone else (NCJ 177/Riley 62).[43] Since Leibniz furthermore holds that one cannot acquire someone's body without acquiring their soul, this means that it is also impossible to have full ownership rights over someone else's body (NCJ 177/Riley 62). As a result, Leibniz explains, one human being can at most have much more limited rights over another, namely so-called usufruct rights (NCJ 177/Riley 62–63). A usufruct right is a right to enjoy the thing possessed and derive profit from it, but without altering, damaging, or destroying it.[44] For example, if you have a usufruct right in a house, you may be allowed to live in it or rent it out, but you are not permitted to demolish any walls or burn it down. Applied to slavery, this means that a slaveholder may be entitled to benefit from the slave's labor, but not to kill or maim the slave. In fact, Leibniz appears to view anything that would undermine the slave's virtue and happiness as being beyond the scope of usufruct rights (NCJ 177/Riley 63). Thus, having usufruct rights over someone is compatible with respecting their value as a rational being: it is impermissible for the holder of such rights to undermine the other person's virtue and happiness. And, as already seen, the holder of these rights has a moral obligation to promote the other person's virtue and happiness insofar as they can.

From what we have seen so far, it should be clear that, at least in "On the Common Notion of Justice," Leibniz ascribes very robust rights to rational beings—rights that, among other things, make it illegitimate for one rational creature to fully own another rational creature. Yet, there is a potential worry about this theory, given the role that rationality plays in Leibniz's discussion. If some people are not rational in the relevant sense, then Leibniz's arguments might provide no reason to object to full ownership rights over these individuals. It would be consistent for Leibniz to hold that these individuals lack the right to freedom, and possibly even that they are Aristotelian natural slaves—or in other words, that it is both permissible and appropriate for them to be slaves. In fact, in the early 1670s, Leibniz appears to use this line of reasoning to justify his proposal that Louis XIV should invade Egypt: Leibniz argues that the war is justifiable in part because it is a war "not against human beings but against animals (that is, barbarians)" (A 4.1.379).[45]

Leibniz's views in the late period concerning Aristotelian natural slavery are complicated.[46] There are strong hints in a few texts that, for him, we should afford all human beings the same robust rights. Yet, there are also hints in other texts that he sympathizes at least to some extent with Aristotle. After examining both types of evidence, I will conclude that, for Leibniz, individuals who are permanently and completely incapable of rationality—that is, who lack rational souls altogether—do not have moral rights and are not strictly speaking human beings. Yet, in almost all cases in which an individual has a human body, we should assume that they possess a rational soul and moral rights, even if they do not currently exhibit any signs of rationality. Leibniz does hold that it is appropriate for human beings who are more intelligent to rule over human beings who are less intelligent. Yet, this rule needs to be paternal rule, in which the ruler aims at the virtue and happiness of the ruled. It cannot be despotic rule, which would turn the ruled into mere instruments of the ruler.

One piece of evidence that Leibniz partially agrees with Aristotle comes from a letter to Thomas Burnett of Kemney from 1700, in which Leibniz claims that some passages in Locke's *Two Treatises* "demand a more ample discussion." Locke's observations about "the State of Nature, and . . . the equality of rights of men" are, Leibniz explains, incomplete:

114 RETHINKING THE VALUE OF HUMANITY

This equality would be certain, if all men had the same [natural] advantages, but this not being so at all, it seems that Aristotle is more correct there than Mr Hobbes. If several men found themselves in a single ship on the open sea, it would not be in the least conformable either to reason or nature, that those who understand nothing of sea-going claim to be pilots; such that, following natural reason, government belongs to the wisest. (February 12, 1700, A 1.18.380/ Riley 192)

Here, Leibniz seems to argue that there are people who are natural rulers and people who are natural subordinates. In fact, he seems to claim that there are natural differences among human beings that ground differences in their rights—at least, perhaps, in the right to rule others, or the right not to be ruled by anyone. Along quite similar lines, Leibniz writes to Friedrich Wilhelm Bierling in 1712 that those who lack wisdom "must be forced [*cogi*] by some authority [*imperio*]; and this is what Aristotle meant when he said that some are slaves by nature. I add that the less wisdom someone has, the more need he has of being forced by an authority" (October 20, 1712, G 7:508).

What should we make of these two letters? One thing to note is that Leibniz is not necessarily suggesting in these texts that less intelligent individuals have no rights whatsoever and can be owned like cattle. He may merely be suggesting that it is appropriate for them to be governed by the wise. This type of rule may be an instance of paternal rule rather than despotic rule. In other words, Leibniz might merely be saying that adults who lack wisdom have the same status as children, who need to be subordinated but whose moral status is different from that of brute animals and rules out absolute domination. This is supported by what Leibniz says in a text from 1680: after explaining that parents govern their children in order to improve them, he notes that "unintelligent people are adult children" (A 4.3.911).

What Leibniz says elsewhere about the rights of all rational beings confirms this reading. As we already saw, Leibniz holds that all rational souls are members of the City of God, which means that they possess certain basic rights and obligations. There is evidence, moreover, that for Leibniz a mere *potential* for becoming rational is sufficient for the special status and rights of rational beings. In order for a human being to have moral rights, it is not necessary that this human being currently exhibits rationality. This becomes quite clear when Leibniz discusses the status of children: even though young children are not rational, he argues that we should assume that they will eventually become as rational and as virtuous as their parents (NCJ 178/Riley 63). For this reason, parents should rule their children in a way that aims at their virtue and happiness (NCJ 178/Riley 63). As we have seen, this is an instance of a more general principle: "[W]hen one can make men happy and virtuous, one should never leave virtue out" (NCJ

178/Riley 63).[47] Because Leibniz holds that the capacities for virtue, happiness, and reasoning are coextensive, this means that being temporarily incapable of reasoning—as children are, before they reach the age of reason—is insufficient for being an Aristotelian natural slave in the full sense, that is, for having the same status as a brute animal. The individual would need to be generally, or permanently, incapable of reasoning.

Additional evidence that the mere potential to become rational is sufficient for the special status of human beings can be found in a German text from 1680 titled "Diviso Societatum." Leibniz wrote this text quite some time before the late period, on which we are currently focusing. Yet, it is valuable for present purposes because of the way it discusses natural slavery. It appears to be a commentary on Johann von Felden's 1664 book *Elementa juris universi*, which defends the Aristotelian doctrine of natural slavery. Leibniz criticizes Felden's arguments for natural slavery in a number of ways. Among other things, he says that natural slaves would have to lack even the mere capacity for rationality. Natural slavery would be permissible only "if there were no hope of bringing the slave himself to understanding; otherwise the master would be obligated to advance his slave's freedom through education, at least as far as this is necessary for the happiness of the slave" (A 4.3.909/L 428, translation altered). In other words, if there is any hope that someone might gain the capacity to reason when given the right kind of education, it is wrong to use their labor without promoting their freedom and happiness.

In this text, Leibniz acknowledges that if there were human beings "almost as dumb as cattle," then, were it not for theological considerations, it would be permissible to treat these human beings as slaves (A 4.3.909–910/L 428–429). Yet, he also expresses doubt that there are genuine examples of natural slaves as Felden describes them. In fact, he states that theological reasons settle this question: Christianity teaches us that all human beings possess immortal souls and are capable of beatitude in an afterlife. This means that they are capable of becoming rational (A 4.3.909–910/L 428). It follows, he argues, that "even if a man were born entirely brutish and incapable of any instruction, we should still not have the right to martyr, kill, or sell him to barbarians for our own good" (A 4.3.910/L 428). Insofar as this man is a human being with an immortal soul, and hence the capacity for becoming rational, he must not be treated like cattle; we must treat him in a way that respects his special status.[48]

The *New Essays on Human Understanding*—a text from 1704 in which Leibniz engages with Locke's *Essay Concerning Human Understanding*—contains further evidence that for Leibniz, human beings who do not currently manifest rational capacities nevertheless have the same special status as those who do. In the context of responding to Locke's discussion of the essence of human beings and of the boundaries of the human species, Leibniz discusses epistemic difficulties with determining whether a given creature possesses the capacity for reasoning. Typically, he claims, reason "declares its presence" (NE 313). Yet, in cases where it does not, we can merely try to infer the creature's capacities on the basis of its exterior and of facts about its birth. That is, for instance, why we assume that infants born to human parents will eventually become rational (NE 314). Leibniz applies the same line of thought to what he calls "imbeciles," that is, adults who do not exhibit signs of rationality: he points out that "we know from experience that reason is often held back so that it cannot be manifested, even in people who have exhibited it and will do so again" (NE 313; see also NE 395). Hence, we should assume that these adults are capable of rationality.

Leibniz also discusses cases in which human parents give birth to infants with severe physical abnormalities. While he acknowledges that "sometimes children who have some gross abnormality eventually reach a stage at which they manifest reason" (NE 311), he also seems to think that in extreme cases there might be sufficient evidence that the infant lacks the capacity to reason. "The presumption created by birth is erased if the shape is extremely different from the human one," he says (NE 395). For instance, if an infant is born with the head of a dog, we can know that its lack of rationality is permanent (NE 395). Because for Leibniz rationality is a necessary condition for being human, this means that such a child is not strictly speaking human. In such cases, Leibniz seems to hold that the parents do not have an obligation to raise the child (NE 315). Yet, he also points out that if we knew of cases in which a child born with, for instance, the head of a calf became rational, "we would become more circumspect about getting rid of monsters" (NE 320). Importantly, Leibniz appears to think that when in doubt, we should err on the side of caution: "[I]f this human-shaped animal is not a man, no great harm will come from caring for it while we are uncertain about its fate" (NE 395).

Considering all of this evidence, there is strong reason to believe that in his late writings, Leibniz holds that the special status of anyone with a rational soul rules out full ownership relations among humans. In fact, because they are actually or potentially rational, human beings have an inalienable right to freedom and to treatment in accordance with the principles of justice. These principles, in turn, oblige every moral agent to pursue the perfection, or happiness and virtue, of every rational being, insofar as they can. More specifically, Leibniz's ethics requires us to pursue the good of all rational agents as an end, and not merely as a means to our own happiness. Thus, it is impermissible for human beings to be ruled despotically, without regard for their perfection as rational beings. Not only does no human being have the right to exercise power over the life and death of another human being;[49] nobody even has the right to use the labor of others without pursuing their good for its own sake. This is one way in which human beings are categorically different from domesticated animals, which can be owned and used as mere instruments. As seen, some of Leibniz's reasons for viewing the full ownership of human beings as impermissible are based on theological doctrines. Yet, other reasons are not, and these latter reasons are quite powerful on their own.

If my interpretation is correct, Leibniz is committed to a robust intrinsic human value and takes a strong stance against the ownership of human beings. His restrictions on human ownership are much stronger than those of Locke and Hobbes. We must of course be somewhat cautious in drawing general conclusions about Leibniz's considered views because we do not know how committed he was to the arguments he puts forward in "On the Common Notion of Justice." It is an unpublished piece written for an unknown purpose and contains only some short passages about human ownership. Some of the claims about the impermissibility of absolute domination from this text do not seem to appear elsewhere in Leibniz's corpus. Indeed, as mentioned earlier, he seems utterly unconcerned about the morality of slavery in some earlier texts. Nevertheless, the arguments from "On the Common Notion of Justice" are clearly noteworthy and they do fit extremely well with what Leibniz says elsewhere about the special status of all rational creatures and about the moral obligations we have to other human beings.

Conclusion

The preceding sections have, I hope, shed some light on the early modern debate about human value, freedom, and slavery. I have argued that the late-period Leibniz comes closest to the attractive conception of human value and the right to freedom with which I started. For him, all rational agents possess an intrinsic value. Their rational capacities alone, and not just their relationship to God, give them a special moral status. This status includes a right to freedom that Leibniz appears to view as genuinely inalienable. As a result of this status, one rational creature can never fully own another rational creature. In fact, it is never permissible to rule rational creatures despotically, without aiming to promote their virtue and happiness. This applies even to creatures who merely have an unactualized potential for rationality, as long as they can eventually come to manifest it. In contrast, Hobbes does not view human beings as intrinsically valuable in a morally relevant sense. For him, human beings in the state of nature can rightfully treat others in whatever way they see fit. Moreover, it can be perfectly legitimate for one human being to have absolute power over another human being. Locke argues for much more extensive and universal rights, but he does not appear to ground them in an intrinsic human value. For him, rights such as the right to life and liberty derive from God's rights over us. Moreover,

118   RETHINKING THE VALUE OF HUMANITY

like Hobbes, Locke holds that there are morally permissible forms of slavery in which the slaveholder has absolute power over the slave.[50]

Notes

1. The main authors I am discussing in this chapter appear to equate full ownership of a thing with having absolute or near-absolute power over it. That is how I will be understanding it for present purposes. Yet, it is worth noting that the power over things that one fully owns can be restricted. For instance, you might fully own a piece of land but are not allowed to build on it without a permit, or you might own a pet but are not allowed to abuse it. Likewise, some slaveholding societies had laws against abusing or killing slaves, but that does not mean that slaveholders do not own their slaves fully.
2. For a helpful overview, see Guasco 2014, particularly 155ff.
3. For instance, Gershom Carmichael, a professor of moral philosophy at the University of Glasgow, writes in 1718 that "men who profess to be Christians" are, at the time when Carmichael is writing, practicing slavery "with a greater tyranny perhaps than it was by the ancient pagans" (*Supplements and Observations* chap. 16, 144). Carmichael calls this practice a "great shame" and "*a sure sign of the death of sociability*" (chap. 16, 144–145). Importantly, Locke—who was more informed about New World slavery than almost any of his contemporaries in Europe (Farr 2008, 497–500)—does not appear to be nearly as disturbed by it, as we will see.
4. That this is a consequence of giving masters full ownership rights over slaves is pointed out, for instance, by Pufendorf. He says that if I literally own a thing, I have "a Right of using, spoiling, and consuming it, to procure my Advantage, or to satisfy my Pleasure; so that what way soever I dispose of it, to say it was my own, shall be a sufficient excuse" (*De jure naturae* 6.3.7). As we will see, and as Pufendorf points out in the same passage, he does not think that one can legitimately own human beings in this literal sense.
5. In Roman law—especially in late Roman law—there were some restrictions on the rights of slaveholders over slaves (see, e.g., Gaius, in *Digest* 1.6.1; see also Honoré 2012), but these restrictions were minimal.
6. Some early modern authors defend the Aristotelian doctrine of natural slavery; see, e.g., Felden 1664, 2–3.
7. Pufendorf is enormously important for the history of the concept of human dignity (Darwall 2017). Yet, while he argues that we must regard all human beings as possessing a special dignity and equal rights, this is grounded not in the intrinsic value of human beings but rather in God's command to regard other humans in that way (Darwall 2013, 211–212).
8. See, e.g., Suárez, *On Laws and God* 2.18.8; Thomasius, *Divine Jurisprudence* 3.5.20, 3.5.29. The custom of enslaving prisoners of war goes back to Antiquity; see Plato, *Republic* V, 468a–b, 1095; Aristotle, *Politics* 1.6.
9. One example is Grotius, *Rights of War and Peace* 2.5.32 and 3.7.1.

10. See, e.g., Grotius, *Rights of War and Peace* 2.5.29; Pufendorf, *Duty of Man* 2.4.6; Pufendorf, *De jure naturae* 6.3.9; Thomasius, *Divine Jurisprudence* 3.5.25–28.

11. It is not entirely clear whether Cavendish shares the views expressed by the defendant. Yet her "Preface to the Reader" in *World's Olio* suggests that she views the subordination of women to men in at least certain domains as justified (1655, n.p.).

12. The relevance of this preference is not entirely clear to me. Hobbes appears to assume that if someone had such a preference, then others would be entitled to rule over this person.

13. For Hobbes, the social contract is among co-citizens; the sovereign is merely a beneficiary (*Leviathan* 17.13, 18.4). Hence, the lack of equality between the sovereign and the citizens is not a violation of the laws of nature (see Olsthoorn 2013). In fact, this inequality is required by the laws of nature.

14. This is also clear from Hobbes's definition of 'law of nature': it is a precept commanding things that aid our self-preservation and forbidding things that undermine self-preservation (*Leviathan* 14.3; *De cive* 2.1). Indeed, the very first law of nature tells us to seek peace insofar as we have hope of attaining it, and to otherwise "seek and use all helps and advantages of war" (*Leviathan* 14.4, italics removed; see also *De cive* 2.2).

15. Hobbes presumably calls this "natural" because the power of the dominant person is real or natural—in contrast to the power of a government, which is in some sense artificial since it is a result of the citizens' contracting away their rights.

16. In cases where a child's biological parents abandon it, this power belongs to any adult who raises the child (Hobbes, *Leviathan* 20.5; *De cive* 9.4; *Elements* 23.3).

17. See also *De cive* 8.2, where he uses the Latin term *servus* for the former and *ergastulum* for the latter. For a helpful discussion of why Hobbes may have considered imprisoned slaves as paradigmatic, see Baumgold 2010.

18. See Apeldoorn (2020) for a helpful discussion of Hobbes's views on property and the full ownership of human beings. For other treatments of Hobbes's theory of slavery, see Lott 1998; Nyquist 2013, 293ff.; Harpham 2019, 15ff.; Luban 2018.

19. If a slaveholder tries to kill a slave, the slave has the right to resist, according to Hobbes, just as a prisoner who has been sentenced to death can rightfully resist their executioner (e.g., *Leviathan* 14.8, 14.29, 21.12). This does not mean, however, that the slaveholder and the executioner are acting unjustly, or that they lack the right to kill the slave and the prisoner. For a fuller discussion of the slave's right to resist, see Luban 2018.

20. As seen, human beings naturally have a right to all things, but that is not a moral right in the relevant sense because it is not a claim right; that is, it does not place corresponding obligations on other people. I should note that Hobbes might take human beings to possess some kind of intrinsic value—for instance, he might hold that possessing physical or mental powers is intrinsically valuable—but he does not take them to possess a value entailing genuine moral rights. I thank Ken Winkler for asking me to clarify this.

120 RETHINKING THE VALUE OF HUMANITY

21. This is the prevalent meaning of the term 'dignity' at the time (see Debes 2017, 207; Darwall 2017, 187–188). Pufendorf appears to be among the first to use 'dignity' in a moral sense, as connected to rights (see Darwall 2013, 204; Darwall 2017, 200).

22. Presumably, Locke holds that God could grant parents this power through an explicit command, as in the biblical story of Abraham and Isaac. But in the absence of an explicit command, parents do not have this power.

23. Locke does sometimes talk about human beings as having self-ownership (*Two Treatises* 2.27, 2.123), but that arguably does not mean that they fully own their lives. Rather, human beings merely have use-rights (that is, limited property rights) to their lives, conceded to them by God (see Olsthoorn 2019; Welchman 1995, 75–76).

24. For Locke's distinction between voluntarily giving something away and forfeiting it, see *Two Treatises* 1.100.

25. For Locke's justification for the right to punish and kill other human beings, see *Two Treatises* 2.7–12.

26. If at any point the master and slave enter into a contract, the state of slavery ceases (*Two Treatises* 2.24).

27. For more information on Locke's involvement in the slave trade, see Farr 2008, 497; Bernasconi and Mann 2005, 89; Armitage 2004, 603; Welchman 1995, 71–74.

28. For a persuasive argument, see Bernasconi and Mann 2005. For a counterargument, see Uzgalis 1998, 56ff.

29. This is somewhat controversial; Welchman (1995, 79–80) argues that only children who are born before their parents' enslavement are free, whereas children born to parents who are already slaves are not free.

30. This might be surprising because interpreters often portray Locke as the father of liberalism, and Leibniz as far less progressive in his political views (see, e.g., Jolley 1975).

31. Unfortunately, it is unclear when Leibniz composed this marginal note.

32. For helpful discussions of this text, see Harfouch 2017; Smith 2015, 160ff.; Fenves 2005; Cook 2018.

33. Even though Leibniz apparently understands 'race' in linguistic terms (see Fenves 2005; Smith 2015, 160ff.; Harfouch 2017), it is clear that this text presents the groups it enumerates as inferior to European Christians and as similar to animals. This inferiority may not be due to any essential differences, but that does not make these claims significantly less problematic. Interestingly, Leibniz's model for the slavery he is proposing in this text appears to be that of Ottoman janissaries—elite infantrymen who were kidnapped and enslaved as children (Smith 2015, 173–174)—rather than that of transatlantic slavery. Yet, this is not directly relevant for present purposes.

34. If animals were rational, as Leibniz suggests in a text from the middle period, God's justice would require him to include them in his city (letter to Arnauld, October 19, 1687, A 2.2.259/LAr 265). For more on the City of God and the status of human beings as moral agents, see Jorati 2017, 181ff.; Adams 2014.

35. For these reasons, I interpret Leibniz's views about human rights and equality as less harsh than Wilson (2017, 46–47) presents them. This is in part because the texts on which Wilson bases her interpretation are predominantly from the early period. She

SLAVERY, FREEDOM, AND HUMAN VALUE 121

places a lot of emphasis on Leibniz's "Ermahnung an die Teutsche" (1679, A 4.3.805–806), in which Leibniz talks quite dismissively about the common man, drawing comparisons to cattle.

36. This becomes clear, for instance, in the letter to Arnauld that I already mentioned, where Leibniz says that if nonhuman animals were rational, God would have to observe the laws of justice with respect to them as well (A 2.2.259/LAr 265).

37. For a helpful discussion of the natural law tradition in ethics, see Murphy 2019. For good overviews of Leibniz's ethics, see Youpa 2016; Brown 1995.

38. Leibniz provides this definition in many places; see, e.g., NCJ 165/Riley 54; preface to the *Codex Juris Gentium Diplomaticus*, A 4.5.61/L 421; letter to Electress Sophie, August 1697, A 1.14.58/SLT 163; letter to Nicaise, August 19, 1697, A 2.3.368–369/ LGR 158–159.

39. For more on Leibniz's theory of disinterested love and his argument that it is compatible with psychological egoism, see Brown 2011.

40. Interestingly, Leibniz sometimes says that God owns, or is the master of, human beings. For instance, he writes in 1686 that "God is naturally the master of all things, and we are his slaves" (A 6.4.2382). He also claims in "On the Common Notion of Justice" that God is "the sovereign master of [human] bodies and of souls" and that this is one reason why human masters cannot possess absolute rights over slaves (NCJ 177/Riley 62). Elsewhere he uses the same reasoning to restrict the power of princes (letter to Ernst of Hesse-Rheinfels, August 14, 1683, A 1.3.314/Riley 187). In *New Method* (1667), he asserts that we belong to God and as a result are not allowed to abuse ourselves (2.75, p. 171). In a text from 1697 about the death penalty he writes that "the life of a man is a thing of such great value to God that the power over it which we obtain in this life can only be excused by a certain necessity" (A 4.6.10/SLT 154). Finally, in the preface to *Codex Juris Gentium Diplomaticus* (1693), Leibniz says about universal justice that it requires us not to abuse our bodies since "we owe ourselves and our all to God" (A 4.5.63/L 423). This suggests that Leibniz partially agrees with Locke that God owns human beings and that this explains some of our obligations. Yet, unlike Locke, Leibniz does not rely solely on this doctrine to argue against the ownership of humans by other humans. He holds that there are reasons independent of God's rights over us that rule out this kind of ownership.

41. See, e.g., Leibniz's definition of 'ownership' (*dominium*) in *Definitionum Juris Specimen* from 1676: "ownership is a right in the substance of the thing" (A 6.3.609; see also a letter to Lambert van Velthuysen, May 5, 1671, A 2.1.164). He contrasts this with more limited rights over a thing that extend only to its qualities rather than its substance, and which prohibit destroying or altering the thing (A 6.3.609; for a fuller discussion, see below and Jorati 2019, 10).

42. I will say more about the importance of the potential for rationality below.

43. We should note that Leibniz seems to have changed his mind about the possibility of acquiring rational souls; in a marginal note to *Definitionum Juris Specimen*, he suggests that if you capture someone in a war, and this person surrenders, you thereby acquire that person as your slave (A 6.3.608–609). This would mean that one can

acquire souls, though not against their wills. It is unclear when Leibniz composed this marginal note; the Akademie editors say that at least some of Leibniz's marginal notes in this text must have been composed after 1696 (A 6.3.591).

44. For more on usufruct rights in Roman law, see, e.g., Colognesi 2016, 529.

45. For an extended discussion of Leibniz's usage of the term 'barbarians,' see Cook 2018.

46. For a helpful discussion, see Wilson 2017, 46ff.

47. Leibniz qualifies this statement by saying that "virtue has its degrees, and the same virtues are not necessary to [men in] all conditions, to make a man happy" (NCJ 178/ Riley 63). It is not entirely clear what this means, but his overall claim appears to be that with respect to beings who are capable of virtue and happiness, we must always help them, insofar as it is possible, to attain (some degree of) virtue and happiness.

48. It is not entirely clear what role theology plays in this argument. At the very least, Leibniz uses theology as a source of evidence that all human beings will eventually attain rationality. Yet, he might be saying something stronger: it would be permissible to keep human beings in a state of ignorance and slavery if one could keep them ignorant during their entire existence, which would perhaps be possible if human souls were mortal. See Jorati (2019, 14) for more on this.

49. In at least one text from the late period, Leibniz discusses the death penalty and argues that extremely high standards of evidence must be used in such cases (A 4.6.10/SLT 154). Yet, he does not generally argue against the death penalty, which suggests that for him there are circumstances in which it is permissible to kill a human being.

50. I presented an earlier version of this chapter at a meeting of the Society for Early Modern Philosophy at Yale, and I thank all participants for their many excellent suggestions and comments. I also thank Johan Olsthoorn, Nandi Theunissen, Sarah Buss, and John Harpham for extensive feedback on earlier drafts.

References

Primary Literature

Aristotle. 1984. *Politics*. In *The Complete Works of Aristotle*, vol. 2, edited and translated by Jonathan Barnes, 1986–2129. Princeton, NJ: Princeton University Press. [Cited as *Politics*, followed by book and chapter]

Carmichael, Gershom. 2002. *Supplements and Observations upon Samuel Pufendorf's On the Duty of Man and Citizen* (Edinburgh, 1724). In *Natural Rights on the Threshold of the Scottish Enlightenment: The Writings of Gershom Carmichael*, edited and translated by James Moore and Michael Silverthorne, 9–217. Indianapolis, IN: Liberty Fund. [Cited as *Supplements and Observations*, followed by chapter and page]

Cavendish, Margaret. 1655. *The World's Olio*. London: Martin and Allestrye.

Cavendish, Margaret. 2003. *Orations of Divers Sorts, Accommodated to Divers Places* (London, 1662). In *Political Writings*, edited by Susan James, 111–292. Cambridge: Cambridge University Press.

The Digest of Justinian. 2009. Edited by Alan Watson. Vol. 1. Philadelphia: University of Pennsylvania Press. Project MUSE muse.jhu.edu/book/6233. [Cited as *Digest*, followed by book, title, and fragment]

SLAVERY, FREEDOM, AND HUMAN VALUE   123

Felden, Johann von. 1664. *Elementa juris universi & in specie Publici Justinianæi.* Frankfurt: Gerlach und Beckenstein.

Filmer, Robert. 1991. *Patriarcha and Other Writings.* Edited by Johann P. Sommerville. Cambridge: Cambridge University Press.

Fyge, Sarah. 1703. *Poems on Several Occasions.* London: Nutt.

Grotius, Hugo. 2005. *The Rights of War and Peace.* Edited by Richard Tuck. 3 vols. Indianapolis, IN: Liberty Fund. [Cited as *Rights of War and Peace*, followed by book, chapter, and section]

Hobbes, Thomas. 1994a. *The Elements of Law Natural and Politic.* Edited by John C. A. Gaskin. Oxford: Oxford University Press. [Cited as *Elements*, followed by chapter and section]

Hobbes, Thomas. 1994b. *Leviathan.* Edited by Edwin Curley. Indianapolis, IN: Hackett. [Cited as *Leviathan*, followed by chapter and section]

Hobbes, Thomas. 1998. *On the Citizen [De cive].* Edited and translated by Richard Tuck and Michael Silverthorne. Cambridge: Cambridge University Press. [Cited as *De cive*, followed by chapter and section]

Huber, Ulrik. 1698. *De jure civitatis, libri tres. Novam juris publici universalis disciplinam continentes. Insertis aliquot de jure sacrorum & ecclesiæ, capitibus.* 3rd ed. Franeker: Leonardi Strickii.

Leibniz, Gottfried Wilhelm. 1768. *Opera Omnia.* Edited by Ludwig Dutens. 6 vols. Geneva: Fratres de Tournes. [Cited as Dutens, followed by volume, part, and page]

Leibniz, Gottfried Wilhelm. (1875–1890) 1978. *Die philosophischen Schriften von Gottfried Wilhelm Leibniz.* Edited by Carl I. Gerhardt. 7 vols. Berlin: Weidmann. Reprint, Hildesheim: Georg Olms. [Cited as G, followed by volume and page]

Leibniz, Gottfried Wilhelm. 1923–. *Sämtliche Schriften und Briefe.* Edited by Deutsche Akademie der Wissenschaften. Darmstadt: Akademie Verlag and De Gruyter. [Cited as A, followed by series, volume, and page]

Leibniz, Gottfried Wilhelm. 1969. *Philosophical Papers and Letters.* Edited and translated by Leroy Loemker. Dordrecht: Reidel. [Cited as L]

Leibniz, Gottfried Wilhelm. 1988. *Political Writings.* Edited and translated by Patrick Riley. 2nd ed. Cambridge: Cambridge University Press. [Cited as Riley]

Leibniz, Gottfried Wilhelm. 1989. *Philosophical Essays.* Edited and translated by Roger Ariew and Daniel Garber. Indianapolis, IN: Hackett, 1989. [Cited as AG]

Leibniz, Gottfried Wilhelm. 1996. *New Essays on Human Understanding.* Edited and translated by Peter Remnant and Jonathan Bennett. New York: Cambridge University Press. [Cited as NE, followed by page number from A 6.6]

Leibniz, Gottfried Wilhelm. 2006. *The Shorter Leibniz Texts: A Collection of New Translations.* Edited and translated by Lloyd. Strickland. New York: Continuum. [Cited as SLT]

Leibniz, Gottfried Wilhelm. 2015a. "Sur la nature de la bonté et de la justice." Edited by Stefan Luckscheiter. In *"Das Recht kann nicht ungerecht sein . . .": Beiträge zu Leibniz' Philosophie der Gerechtigkeit*, edited by Wenchao Li, 143–163. Stuttgart: Steiner. [Cited as NBJ]

Leibniz, Gottfried Wilhelm. 2015b. "Sur la notion commune de la justice." Edited by Stefan Luckscheiter. In *"Das Recht kann nicht ungerecht sein . . .": Beiträge zu Leibniz' Philosophie der Gerechtigkeit*, edited by Wenchao Li, 164–179. Stuttgart: Steiner. [Cited as NCJ]

Leibniz, Gottfried Wilhelm. 2016a. *The Leibniz-Arnauld Correspondence.* Edited and translated by Stephen Voss. New Haven, CT: Yale University Press. [Cited as LAr]

124 RETHINKING THE VALUE OF HUMANITY

Leibniz, Gottfried Wilhelm. 2016b. *Leibniz on God and Religion: A Reader*. Edited and translated by Lloyd Strickland. London: Bloomsbury. [Cited as LGR]

Locke, John 1960. *Two Treatises of Government*. Edited by Peter Laslett. Cambridge: Cambridge University Press. [Cited as *Two Treatises*, followed by book/ treatise and section]

Locke, John. 2003. *Political Writings*. Edited by David Wootton. Indianapolis, IN: Hackett.

Maintenon, Madame de. 2004. *Dialogues and Addresses*. Edited by John J. Conley. Chicago: University of Chicago Press.

Nicholls, William. 1701. *The Duty of Inferiours towards Their Superiours: In Five Practical Discourses . . .* London: Evets and Bennet.

Plato. 1997. *Republic*. In *Plato: Complete Works*, edited by John M. Cooper, 971–1223. Indianapolis, IN: Hackett. [Cited as *Republic*, followed by book, Stephanus number, and page number]

Pufendorf, Samuel von. 1991. *On the Duty of Man and Citizen*. Edited by James Tully. Cambridge: Cambridge University Press. [Cited as *Duty of Man*, followed by book, chapter, and section]

Pufendorf, Samuel von. 1998. *De jure naturae et et gentium*. In *Samuel von Pufendorf: Gesammelte Werke*, vol. 4, edited by Frank Böhling. Berlin: Akademie Verlag. [Cited as *De jure naturae*, followed by book, chapter, and section]

Suárez, Francisco. 2015. *On Laws and God the Lawgiver* (1612). In *Selections from Three Works*, edited by Thomas Pink and translated by Gwladys Williams et al., 1–754. Indianapolis, IN: Liberty Fund. [Cited as *On Laws and God*, followed by book, chapter, and section]

Thomasius, Christian. 2011. *Institutes of Divine Jurisprudence*. Edited and translated by Thomas Ahnert. Indianapolis, IN: Liberty Fund. [Cited as *Divine Jurisprudence*, followed by book, chapter, and section]

Tyrrell, James. 1681. *Patriarcha non Monarcha: The Patriarch Unmonarch'd . . .* London: Janeway.

Secondary Literature

Adams, Robert Merrihew. 2014. "Justice, Happiness, and Perfection in Leibniz's City of God." In *New Essays on Leibniz's Theodicy*, edited by Larry Jorgensen and Samuel Newlands, 197–217. Oxford: Oxford University Press.

Apeldoorn, Laurens van. 2020. "Property and Despotic Sovereignty." In *Hobbes's On the Citizen: A Critical Guide*, edited by Robin Douglass and Johan Olsthoorn, 108–125. Cambridge: Cambridge University Press.

Armitage, David. 2004. "John Locke, Carolina, and the Two Treatises of Government." *Political Theory* 32: 602–627.

Baumgold, Deborah. 2010. "Slavery Discourse before the Restoration: The Barbary Coast, Justinian's Digest, and Hobbes's Political Theory." *History of European Ideas* 36: 412–418.

Bernasconi, Robert, and Anika Maaza Mann. 2005. "The Contradictions of Racism: Locke, Slavery, and the Two Treatises." In *Race and Racism in Modern Philosophy*, edited by Andrew Valls, 89–107. Ithaca, NY: Cornell University Press.

Brown, Gregory. 1995. "Leibniz's Moral Philosophy." In *The Cambridge Companion to Leibniz*, edited by Nicholas Jolley, 411–441. Cambridge: Cambridge University Press.

Brown, Gregory. 2011. "Disinterested Love: Understanding Leibniz's Reconciliation of Self- and Other-Regarding Motives." *British Journal for the History of Philosophy* 19(2): 265–303.

Colognesi, Luigi Capogrossi. 2016. "Ownership and Power in Roman Law." In *The Oxford Handbook of Roman Law and Society*, edited by Paul J. du Plessis, Clifford Ando, and Kaius Tuori, 524–536. Oxford: Oxford University Press.

Cook, Daniel. 2018. "Leibniz on 'Advancing toward Greater Culture.'" *Studia Leibnitiana* 50(2): 163–179.

Darwall, Stephen. 2013. "Pufendorf on Morality, Sociability, and Moral Powers." In *Honor, History, and Relationship: Essays in Second-Personal Ethics II*, 189–221. Oxford: Oxford University Press.

Darwall, Stephen. 2017. "Equal Dignity and Rights." In *Dignity: A History*, edited by Remy Debes, 181–201. Oxford: Oxford University Press.

Debes, Remy. 2017. "Human Dignity before Kant: Denis Diderot's Passionate Person." In *Dignity: A History*, edited by Remy Debes, 203–235. Oxford: Oxford University Press.

Farr, James. 2008. "Locke, Natural Law, and New World Slavery." *Political Theory* 36(4): 495–522.

Fenves, Peter. 2005. "Imagining an Inundation of Australians; or, Leibniz on the Principles of Grace and Race." In *Race and Modern Philosophy*, edited by Andrew Valls, 88–96. Ithaca, NY: Cornell University Press.

Guasco, Michael. 2014. *Slaves and Englishmen: Human Bondage in the Early Modern Atlantic World*. Philadelphia: University of Pennsylvania Press.

Harfouch, John. 2017. "Does Leibniz Have Any Place in a History of Racism?" *Philosophy Today* 61(3): 737–755.

Harpham, John S. 2019. "The Intellectual Origins of American Slavery." PhD dissertation, Harvard University.

Honoré, Antony. 2012. "The Nature of Slavery." In *The Legal Understanding of Slavery: From the Historical to the Contemporary*, edited by Jean Allain, 9–16. Oxford: Oxford University Press.

Jolley, Nicholas. 1975. "Leibniz on Hobbes, Locke's *Two Treatises*, and Sherlock's *Case of Allegiance*." *Historical Journal* 18(1): 21–35.

Jorati, Julia. 2017. *Leibniz on Causation and Agency*. Cambridge: Cambridge University Press.

Jorati, Julia. 2019. "Leibniz on Slavery and the Ownership of Human Beings," *Journal of Modern Philosophy* 1(10): 1–18.

Lott, Tommy L. 1998. "Early Enlightenment Conceptions of the Rights of Slaves." In *Subjugation and Bondage*, edited by Tommy L. Lott, 99–129. Lanham, MD: Rowman & Littlefield.

Luban, Daniel. 2018. "Hobbesian Slavery." *Political Theory* 46(5): 726–748.

Murphy, Mark. 2019. "The Natural Law Tradition in Ethics." In *The Stanford Encyclopedia of Philosophy* (Summer 2019 Edition), edited by Edward N. Zalta. https://plato.stanf ord.edu/archives/sum2019/entries/natural-law-ethics/.

Nyquist, Mary. 2013. *Arbitrary Rule: Slavery, Tyranny, and the Power of Life and Death*. Chicago: University of Chicago Press.

Olsthoorn, Johan. 2013. "Hobbes's Account of Distributive Justice as Equity." *British Journal for the History of Philosophy* 21(1): 13–33.

Olsthoorn, Johan. 2019. "Self-Ownership and Despotism: Locke on Property in the Person, Divine Dominium of Human Life, and Rights-Forfeiture." *Social Philosophy and Policy* 36(2): 242–263.

Skinner, Quentin. 2008. *Hobbes and Republican Liberty*. Cambridge: Cambridge University Press.

126 RETHINKING THE VALUE OF HUMANITY

Smith, Justin. 2015. *Nature, Human Nature, and Human Difference: Race in Early Modern Philosophy*. Princeton, NJ: Princeton University Press.

Uzgalis, William. 1998. "'. . . The Same Tyrannical Principle': Locke's Legacy on Slavery." In *Subjugation and Bondage*, edited by Tommy L. Lott, 49–77. Lanham, MD: Rowman & Littlefield.

Welchman, Jennifer. 1995. "Locke on Slavery and Inalienable Rights." *Canadian Journal of Philosophy* 25(1): 67–81.

Wilson, Catherine. 2017. "Leibniz on War and Peace and the Common Good." In *'Für unser Glück oder das Glück anderer': Vorträge des X. Internationalen Leibniz-Kongresses: Hannover, 18.–23. Juli 2016*, edited by Wenchao Li, vol. 6, 33–62. Hildesheim: Olms.

Youpa, Andrew. 2016. "Leibniz's Ethics." In *The Stanford Encyclopedia of Philosophy* (Winter 2016 Edition), edited by Edward N. Zalta. https://plato.stanford.edu/archives/win2016/entries/leibniz-ethics/.

5

Valuing Humanity in "Common Life": Grotius and Pufendorf on Equal "Sociable" Dignity

Stephen Darwall

Historians of ethics often contrast modern ethical philosophy, beginning roughly with Grotius, with ancient Greek ethics and the traditions that derive from it, including the classical natural law of Aquinas and his followers.[1] According to Jean Barbeyrac (1749, 67, 66), it was Grotius who first "broke the ice" of "the Scholastic Philosophy; which [had] spread itself all over Europe." Under Grotius's influence, philosophical ethics became "modern *moral* philosophy," as Anscombe (1958) put it in her famous critique. Although not exclusively, modern ethical philosophers concerned themselves with what they called "morality." Indeed, Barbeyrac (1749) titled the work in which he proclaimed Grotius's founding influence "An Historical and Critical Account of the Science of Morality." For the moderns, 'morality' expressed what Anscombe (1958, 5, 1) called a "law conception of ethics"; it essentially included the "concepts of obligation and duty . . . and of what is morally right and wrong." To put it crudely, although the ancients focused on questions of the good, in its various forms, the moderns added a focus on the *right*, conceived as moral *obligation*.

Sidgwick (1964, 198) put this contrast in terms of fundamental normative notions and faculties (forms of practical reason):

> [I]n Platonism and Stoicism, and in Greek moral philosophy generally, but one regulative and governing faculty is recognised under the name of Reason— however the regulation of Reason may be understood; in the modern ethical view, when it has worked itself clear, there are found to be two—Universal Reason and Egoistic Reason, or Conscience and Self-love.

Sidgwick understands the Greeks as *eudaimonists*, therefore, as identifying practical reason with "egoistic reason" or "self-love." By contrast, as he sees it, "the modern view, when it had worked itself clear," holds that there are two fundamentally distinct forms of practical reason, "egoistic reason" or "self-love," on the one hand, and "universal reason" or "conscience," on the other (1964: 198).

Stephen Darwall, *Valuing Humanity in "Common Life": Grotius and Pufendorf on Equal "Sociable" Dignity* In: *Rethinking the Value of Humanity.* Edited by: Sarah Buss and L. Nandi Theunissen, Oxford University Press. © Oxford University Press 2023. DOI: 10.1093/oso/9780197539361.003.0006

128   RETHINKING THE VALUE OF HUMANITY

Since Sidgwick (1967, 381) interprets "universal reason" through the principle of rational benevolence, this may seem to yield a distinction wholly within the good, between prudential and impartial good. Sidgwick stresses, however, that "conscience" in the modern view is conceived with "quasi-jural notions" of obligation, "duty," and right (106). To be sure, the notion of impartial good is also distinctive of one important strain of modern ethics. But even the utilitarian or consequentialist theories in which this notion most prominently figures are generally put forward as theories of the *right* and not just of the good, whether prudential or impartial. As generally understood, act utilitarianism is not simply the doctrine that actions that produce the greatest overall utility or happiness are impartially good or best (in what Parfit [2011, 1: 41] calls the "impartial reason-involving sense"). It is the *deontic* thesis that actions are morally right, and so not morally wrong, if, and only if, they produce no less overall utility than would any other action that is available to the agent.

Another mark of modern moral philosophy, I would argue, is the idea that there is a distinctive way of *valuing human beings*, namely, *respect* for what Kant calls their "*dignity*" as rational moral agents, that can be adequately appreciated only within a conception of moral right and not through concepts of the good of any kind alone (4: 435).[2] Both dignity and the form of respect (moral recognition respect) that recognizes this singular kind of value conceptually implicate the right (Darwall 1977). Neither the concept of prudential good nor that of impartial good (or impersonal good in Moore's [1993, preface] sense of what "ought to exist for its own sake") nor even the ancient Greek notion of *kalon* (the intrinsically good or fine) can capture what modern philosophers like Kant mean by "dignity."

This characteristically modern idea is not that the existence of persons is intrinsically desirable, nor that persons deserve, even in their most excellent instances, greater admiration or esteem than do creatures of other kinds. It is the claim rather that there are ways of mistreating human beings that violate claims of right that are grounded in their dignity, that such mistreatment is morally wrong, and that it wrongs the mistreated persons themselves. It is, I believe, the claim that Rawls (1980, 546) expresses toward the end of the twentieth century with his formulation that persons are "self-originating sources of valid claims." We respect the dignity of persons by respecting the deontic constraints it places on us in our treatment of persons.

It is no coincidence, consequently, that when early modern natural law theorists like Grotius first thought through the foundations of moral right (or, as they called it, "natural law"), they began to express versions of this distinctive way of valuing humanity. In what follows, we shall examine how the doctrine of the dignity of persons emerges in Grotius's, and in Pufendorf's, thought.[3] What is most remarkable, I think, is the way both place it within a conception of what they call "sociability," this is, of human beings relating *to* one another in what Pufendorf (1934, 1229) calls "common life." This gives Grotius and Pufendorf an account of what I call the "second-personal" nature both of the dignity of persons *and* of the distinctive attitude through which we recognize this value and so value humanity in this distinctive way (second-personal moral recognition respect) (Darwall 2006, 2013a, 2013b, 2015).[4]

Equal Dignity in Pufendorf

The claim of equal human dignity is most explicit in Pufendorf. A particularly clear instance occurs in a passage from *On the Duty of Man and Citizen* in which, as so often, Pufendorf (1991) contrasts his thought with Hobbes's. The passage occurs at the beginning of Chapter 7: "On Recognizing Man's Natural Equality." "Man is an animal," Pufendorf writes, "which is not only interested in its own preservation but also possesses a native and delicate sense of its own value" (61). Like Kant, Pufendorf calls this natural value of humanity "dignity": "in the very name of man a certain dignity is felt to lie" (61).

Now, for Hobbes (1994), there is no such thing as natural dignity. "Dignity" is the "public worth of a man," "the value set on him by the commonwealth" (X.17). Outside a commonwealth, dignity cannot exist, so it is impossible for any such fundamental value of humanity to ground rights that human beings could claim against one another in a state of nature. According to Hobbes, human beings in their natural state have no standing to claim or demand anything from one another. Any natural human rights are, in Hohfeld's (1923) terms, "liberties" rather than "claim rights." Hobbes's (1994, XIV.1) "right of nature" is a "liberty each man hath to use his own power, as he will himself, for the preservation of his own nature, that is to say, of his own life."

Pufendorf (1934) rejects this Hobbesian picture. "It is absurd to try to designate as a right," he says, something "which all other men have an equal right to prevent one from exercising" (391). Mostly, this is a rhetorical point. Once we have Hohfeld's (1923) distinction between "liberties" and "claims," we can say that Hobbes's "right of nature" is a liberty right rather than a claim right. It is, as Hobbes (1999, I.14.6) says, a "blameless liberty." It really does not matter whether we call this a natural right or not. The real question is whether any such natural liberty exists. Pufendorf denies that it does. He holds that human beings have natural claims rights that are grounded in their natural dignity. This is the "natural equality" that every person must recognize. Pufendorf broadly agrees with Hobbes that it takes covenants to establish the state, but he denies that violating human dignity in a state of nature would be blameless, even were this judged necessary for self-preservation.

130   RETHINKING THE VALUE OF HUMANITY

Pufendorf (1991, 61) notes that human beings are no less disturbed by attempts to "detract from" their fundamental worth as human beings than they are by "harm to body or goods":

> In the very name of man a certain dignity is felt to lie, so that the ultimate and most effective rebuttal of insolence and insults from others is "Look, I am not a dog, but a man as well as yourself." Human nature therefore belongs equally to all and no one would or could gladly associate with anyone who does not value him as a man as himself and a partner in the same nature. (61)

Because human beings equally have the same fundamental worth or dignity, they all can claim "equality of right" (Pufendorf 1934, 333).

Grounding the Fundamental Law of Sociability in God's Moral Power

But what does Pufendorf thinks *justifies* the claim that human or rational moral agents have dignity and with it the "equality of right" that grounds it?[5] The fundamental notion in Pufendorf's moral philosophy is that of "moral power," which is a direct ancestor of our contemporary idea of "normative power," as invoked, for example, in accounts of the obligating character of promising (Raz 1972; Watson 2010). When we promise, we exercise a normative power we take ourselves to have to place ourselves under obligation. Through the power's exercise, new obligations and rights are created: the promisor acquires an obligation and the promisee, a right. As Pufendorf (1991, 70) puts it, when I make a "perfect promise," "I not only intend in fact to be obligated, but also confer a right upon another to demand what I promise as quite simply owed to him." Similarly, when someone has the normative power to order someone else to do something, exercising this power creates new obligations and rights.

According to Pufendorf, *all* obligations and rights are grounded in moral powers. Pufendorf (1934, 18, emphasis added) defines a moral power as "that by which a man is able to do something legally and *with a moral effect.*" "Moral effects" are simply the newly created rights and obligations together with the accountability and legitimate sanctions these entail. They are part of a moral order or "space," as Pufendorf calls it, which he contrasts with natural or physical space (6–7). This reflects a fundamental distinction between what Pufendorf calls "moral entities," on the one hand, and natural or physical entities, on the other.

Physical things, their attributes, and their modes occupy space and time and are related to one another through causal laws. The physical causal order, brought into existence by God's creative act, is "physically complete" (Pufendorf

1934, 5–6). Moral entities and their various modes are "superadded," Pufendorf says, "by intelligent agency to physical things and modes" (5). Whereas "the original way of producing physical entities is creation, the way in which moral entities are produced" is by "*imposition*" (5). Pufendorf holds that imposition occurs through God's creation, but it is only by God's manifesting his will for human beings *to* them that moral entities and modes are produced. It is essential for Pufendorf, and crucially important to the points I want to make here, that genuine imposition can occur only within a reciprocally recognitional social space, that is, within a "common life."

Unlike any physical "active force" consisting in an "ability to produce any physical motion or change," the distinctive "active force" of moral entities "consist[s] only in this, that it is made clear to men along what line they *should* govern their liberty of action" (Pufendorf 1934, 6). Moral entities are inherently *directive* rather than explanatory, and their laws are intrinsically *normative* in a way that the causal laws of physical nature are not. They entail, moreover, accountability and legitimate sanction: "[I]n a special way men are made capable of receiving some good or evil and of directing certain actions towards others with a particular effect" (6). The "particular effect" is not physical or natural, but a "moral effect."

Moral effects can occur only through the exercise of moral powers and consist in "an obligation [being] laid upon" someone (Pufendorf 1934, 18). "Perfect" obligations, like those created by legitimate orders and promises, entail the standing to "demand" compliance (19; Pufendorf 2009, 92). The exercise of moral powers thus brings about obligations, making those subject to them "capable of receiving some good or evil" in a distinctively *legal* way, that is, as justly deserved or legitimate benefits or sanctions (1934, 6). The obligations that are created by exercising a moral power entail a standing to hold those obligated to one *accountable.*

Now Pufendorf's view is that all moral powers derive from a fundamental moral power that God exercises in the creation through "imposition," that is, through manifesting his will *to* his creatures, thereby creating "natural laws" with which we are obligated to comply and legitimately held to account if we do not. By addressing his will to human beings, God makes us "moral causes," that is, agents to whom actions and their effects can be *imputed* and for which we are thereby accountable. The formal nature of a moral action, Pufendorf (1934, 68) says, "consists of its 'imputativity,'" "whereby the effect of a voluntary action can be imputed to an agent." Whether the effects be "good or evil," "he must be responsible for both" (68). Pufendorf's (1672, 61) Latin makes clearer that he means "accountable": what can be imputed to us as a "moral cause" is what we must answer for or provide some account of (*ratione rederre*).[6] The "primary axiom in morals," Pufendorf (1934, 70) says, is that "a man can be asked for a reckoning" for anything in his power.[7] Or, equivalently, "any action controllable according to a moral law, the accomplishment or avoidance of which is within the power of a man, may be imputed to him" (70).

Later we shall see how Pufendorf believes that God's fundamental moral power is itself grounded. It is crucial to Pufendorf's distinction between physical and moral entities that he distinguish God's moral from his physical power. Because of the conceptual connection between moral power and accountability, to which Pufendorf is well attuned, any grounding of God's moral power must also ground the requisite accountability relations. At this point, however, we should focus on the way Pufendorf derives equal human dignity and the "equality of right" from God's fundamental moral power. "It is a fundamental law of nature," Pufendorf (1934, 208) says, "that 'Every man, so far as in him lies, should cultivate a sociable attitude.'" "By a sociable attitude," he adds, "we mean an attitude of each man towards every other man, by which each is understood to be bound to the other by kindness, peace, and love, and therefore by a mutual obligation" (208).

As Pufendorf (1934, 333) sees it, therefore, a "sociable attitude" already includes acceptance of "mutual obligation" and "an *equality of right*, which has its origin in the fact that an obligation to cultivate a social life is equally binding on all men, since it is an integral part of human nature as such." Because "human nature belongs equally to all men, and no one can live a social life with a person by whom he is not rated as a fellow man," it follows, as a precept of natural law, that "every man should esteem and treat another man as his equal by nature, or as much a man as he is himself" (330). This is a corollary of the fundamental natural law. A sociable attitude, as Pufendorf understands it, therefore itself includes mutual respect for one another's equal dignity. It is a "precept of natural law," therefore, that everyone should "permit others to enjoy the same right that he himself does" (336).

Pufendorf (2009) calls the recognition that all persons are entitled to "esteem." "Esteem of persons in communal life . . . outside of states consists in this, that [the other] is regarded as the kind of person with whom . . . it may be possible to have intercourse" (94). 'Intercourse,' like 'sociable,' is a normatively loaded term for Pufendorf. Just as taking a "sociable attitude" toward someone is already to view them as entitled to certain forms of treatment for which they can hold others accountable, so likewise, to relate to someone as apt for "intercourse" is to recognize them as having this same fundamental dignity and thereby to respect ("esteem") them, as an equal to whom one is accountable for complying with "mutual" obligations and so their correlative rights.

"Esteem" is Pufendorf's (1934, 1229) term for the attitude that values persons and their dignity: "the value of persons in common life." "In common life," Pufendorf says, persons are "valued by" esteem and things are valued by their "price," anticipating Kant's later distinction between dignity and price (4: 435), but in a way that understands, more explicitly than Kant, esteem or respect for human dignity to be a form of "sociability" or interpersonal *relating* (Darwall 2006). To esteem or respect others in this sense is to regard them as having the standing for "intercourse" as equals, along with whatever moral powers that involves (including the powers to promise and enter into pacts).

Although it is central to a sociable attitude that all human persons are obligated to one another by virtue of their common human dignity and thereby mutually accountable for respectful treatment, the obligation to view one another with this attitude is ultimately owed, not to one another, but to God. On Pufendorf's view, it is only because God has exercised his fundamental moral power in addressing his will that we have a sociable attitude to one another that we are obligated so to view each other. Our obligation is fundamentally to God and only derivatively to one another.

The Instability of Grounding Human Dignity in God's Moral Power

There are several reasons why this is an unstable view. The first involves a "wrong kind of reasons" problem. Adopting a sociable attitude is similar to adopting a belief. We are not just to act as though all human beings have equal dignity and equality of right, but to accept this internally and believe it ourselves.[8] It seems quite impossible, however, to come to accept or believe something *for the reason that* one has been ordered to, however legitimate such an order might be were it possible to be obeyed. For genuine obedience, it is necessary, not just that one fulfill an order, but that one do so for the reason that one has been legitimately so ordered. If what is ordered is the having of a belief, that just seems to be impossible.

Like pragmatic considerations, deontic considerations of God's legitimate authority seem to be "reasons of the wrong kind" to support a belief or internal acceptance in their own terms (Kelly 2002). And that is the second reason the view is unstable. Because it is impossible to adopt a sociable attitude, including belief in equal human dignity, for the reason that one is obligated to by God's command, the latter cannot be a normative reason *to* adopt that attitude.

The third reason this view is unstable is because, as I shall now argue, it is internal to the idea of a moral power that it can be exercised only with respect to beings who already have a moral authority or standing independently of the power's exercise. If that is so, it will turn out to be conceptually impossible for all moral obligations to result from the exercise of moral powers, even God's. The problem is that, properly understood, and as Pufendorf seems to understand it, the idea of a moral power presupposes that those who exercise it and those with respect to whom it is exercised (those for whom the "moral effects" of correlative

134 RETHINKING THE VALUE OF HUMANITY

obligations and rights are created) must already have a moral relationship that entails obligations to and rights against one another.

To see this, begin with the human power to obligate through what Pufendorf (1934) calls "pacts." By virtue of agreements or "conventions," individuals obligate themselves to one another to comply and give each other the right to expect their compliance. This is how Pufendorf holds that political sovereignty is created by "consent." But note how sovereignty, consent, and agreement function in this line of thought. The natural human condition is an "equality of right" in which everyone is his own "governor" and where, therefore, it takes individuals' consent to justify directing and using force against them as a putative authority would do (333, 1161). It is part of the very idea of a moral power of consent, however, that consenting legitimates direction and force that *without consent would have been wrong*, indeed that *would have wronged the person had they not consented*. The same is true of the ideas of agreement, convention, or pact. It is part of the very idea that one can create an obligation, say, to give someone something, as a part of an agreement, that it would have been wrong for the person simply to take the thing from one if one had not agreed, and, indeed, that one would have been wronged by such an unjustified taking. Parties to an agreement must presuppose this to understand what they are doing as making an agreement.

The general point is that the exercise of a moral power can legitimate direction and the use of force only if it is true and assumed by the reciprocally recognizing parties to its exercise that the thereby legitimated coercive action would wrong its recipient were the directive agent to lack the relevant power or somehow to exercise it improperly. The very existence of moral powers to create new obligations and rights must therefore presuppose *already* existing moral relationships, with already existing mutual rights and obligations, between those who have the power and those with respect to whom it can legitimately be exercised. Since this is a point about moral powers in general, moreover, the same would seem to apply to God's authority over his human subjects.

There are places where Pufendorf seems implicitly to accept this conceptual point. So that a man may not be able to complain that wrong has been done him when he is compelled to adapt himself to the free choice of a second person, it is necessary that the authority in question also be legitimate (2009, 296). But if this is implicit in the moral power of authority, it would be implicit as much in God's as in any human authority. Although Pufendorf believes that God has an authority over human beings that can legitimate whatever directive treatment of them he pleases, it seems that he is committed by an aspect of the idea of moral power that he himself accepts to thinking that the created beings with respect to whom God exercises his moral power must have moral standing independently of his superior authority. (Of course, they would not have had that power unless God had created them, but that is another matter.) Indeed, it seems to follow that

God could not have the superior authority that he distinctively has unless it were already the case that human beings had theirs, that is, a standing that makes unauthorized forceful treatment of them wrong, indeed, makes it *wrong them*.

God's authority, therefore, indeed any authority over us whatsoever, must be something we are able to accept just by virtue of our being in a position to be obligated. Either, therefore, this authority must be self-evident to any rational human being or it must be something any such being can appreciate good reasons for accepting. And Pufendorf holds that there are such reasons. Mere power is insufficient to "lay an obligation."[9] What is needed in addition, he says, is either that the putative authority "have done me some special service" or "that I should of my own accord consent to his direction" (1934, 101). Whatever force the former condition has in general, "it is all the more true I am indebted to [God] for my very being" (101). God's authority is thus grounded in the greatest debt of gratitude that a person could possibly have. For this to be true, however, there must be obligations and rights that exist independently of God's command.

Accountability, Conscience, and Human Dignity

It seems impossible, therefore, to ground human dignity and the "equality of right" in God's exercise of his superior moral power in commanding human beings to have a sociable attitude. How, then, might these be grounded? Pufendorf provides a rich, sophisticated account of what accountable moral agency itself involves. I believe that resources for grounding the dignity of persons can be found in an extension of Pufendorf's ideas about accountable moral agency and its inescapable commitments (Darwall 2006, 2013a, 2013b).

We can begin with an insightful distinction Pufendorf makes between shame and conscience, which highlights the latter's tie to accountable agency. Pufendorf (1934, 31–32) allows that we can feel shame in response to moral wrongs and defects of moral character, but he denies that shame is especially tuned to the moral: "Shame arises not merely because of some base action, but also from anything, even though not morally base, which is thought to diminish our reputation," like "shortness of stature, lameness, baldness," and so on. Shame responds, not, like guilt, to moral violations per se, but to (perhaps imagined) failures of self-presentation; it is the feeling of being justifiably seen in ways we would not wish to present ourselves (Velleman 2001). Pufendorf contrasts shame with conscience. Conscience, he says, is a "judgment passed on moral actions by the understanding, in so far as it can take cognizance of laws, and so is responsible to the lawgiver for their execution and observance" (1934, 41).

Although conscience involves the "understanding," Pufendorf characterizes it in affective terms. Conscience's judgment when contemplating actions

136 RETHINKING THE VALUE OF HUMANITY

already taken ("consequent conscience") involves the agent's "approving" or "condemning" in a way that is emotionally charged, "attended by peace of mind or agitation" (1934, 41; see also 2009, 266). Similarly, when it comes to conscience's role in deliberation ("antecedent conscience"), Pufendorf contrasts intrapersonally between "compulsion" and action from obligation in a way that echoes the interpersonal distinction between brute coercion and legitimate direction we noted in the previous section:

> This forms the main difference between obligation and compulsion, since in the latter the mind is forced to something by merely external violence contrary to its intrinsic inclination, while whatever we do from obligation is understood to come from an intrinsic impulse of the mind, and with the full approbation of its own judgment. (1934, 386)

And again:

> An obligation differs in a special way from coercion . . . the latter only shakes the will with an external force, and impels it to choose . . . only by the sense of an impending evil. (91)

An obligation "affects the will" not "by some natural weight," but "morally." It "fills [the agent's or will's] very being with such a particular sense, that it is forced of itself to weigh its own actions, and to judge itself worthy of some censure, unless it conforms to a prescribed rule" (91).

Nothing could seem clearer than the contrast these passages draw between the will's autonomous motivation ("intrinsic impulse of the mind") to comply with obligation and "external," "violent," and "coercive" avoidance of negative "natural" consequences of someone's displeasure with the agent's conduct, even God's displeasure, perhaps even the agent's own. Things are not so neat, however. When we view what is left out of the passage quoted toward the beginning of the previous paragraph, we see that Pufendorf (1934, 41) says that the "peace of mind and agitation" of consequent conscience come from an expectation "of the blessing or the wrath of the lawgiver, as well as the goodwill or anger of other men," not just within the agent's own approval or censure. Moreover, we find Pufendorf also saying that "nothing can constrain the human mind, as it deliberates on the future to do or avoid anything, except reflections on the good and evil which will befall others and ourselves from what we do" (91). This suggests that, contrary to what we might have expected when Pufendorf says that action from obligation involves an "intrinsic impulse of the mind," the only thing that can move an agent is the desire to have or to avoid (naturally) good and evil consequences. If this is right, what can the real difference be between the

VALUING HUMANITY IN "COMMON LIFE"   137

will's complying with obligation "of its own accord" and its doing so to avoid evil consequences?

It seems likely that Pufendorf's thought is in some tension here. On the one hand, the elements of his thought that I have been emphasizing push in the direction of a firm distinction between motivation by sanctions and conscientious motivation. On the other, Pufendorf (1934, 56) apparently lacks a theory of the will that is fully adequate to capturing this distinction: "[I]t belongs to the nature of the will always to seek what is inherently [naturally] good, and to avoid what is inherently evil." Pufendorf tries to maintain the distinction, but in a way that his theory of the will can accommodate. He says that while both avoidance of natural evils and obligation involve fear of an evil or "some object of terror," in the case of obligation a man is forced "to acknowledge of himself that the evil . . . falls upon him justly" (91).[10]

In *The Second-Person Standpoint* (*SPS*), I call "Pufendorf's Point" the thesis that an agent can be subject to obligation, say, by God's authoritative commands, only if the agent has the capacity to *accept* the legitimacy of the demands that bind them and be moved by them in their own conscience (Darwall 2006, 22–24, 111–115). In other words, accountable moral agency requires having a conscience with which agents can hold themselves accountable through their own internal acceptance of moral demands' legitimacy. Only with this capacity can we distinguish, as Pufendorf thinks is crucial, between being moved by fear of some natural evil (even if that evil is itself the fact of disapproval, even indeed, one's own) and by the sense that disapproval or blame is *justified*, that an action is blameworthy.

I argue that "Pufendorf's Point" fits with a Strawsonian analysis of the nature of moral responsibility (conceived as accountability) (Strawson 1968; Watson 1996; Darwall 2006, 2013a, 2013b). Accountability and blame are second-personal in their nature. This is the fundamental point that drives Strawson's (1968) argument in "Freedom and Resentment." When we have "reactive attitudes" like blame, we take up a distinctive "participant" (second-personal) standpoint, one of participation in a relationship with the blamed, even if only the relationship of a fellow person, and implicitly relate *to* them (second-personally). We do not see them from a third-personal or "objective" point of view from which issues of causation and determinism loom large. We presuppose a "common life" with them.

It is the second-personal character of reactive attitudes like moral blame that necessitates the Strawsonian presuppositions of competency and will. Blame, at least the kind Miranda Fricker (2016) calls "communicative blame," is simply unintelligible except on the assumptions that its object can understand and accept the legitimacy of the demand it implicitly makes *and* that they can hold themselves accountable from the same standpoint of a fellow person or member of the moral community that we take up in blaming them (Watson 1987; Darwall 2006,

2013a, 2013b; McKenna 2012). To be subject to moral obligations, therefore, an agent must have a *conscience*, that is, the capacity to take up the "moral point of view" and make demands of themselves from this perspective.

Now, given what we noted about the role of sanctions in Pufendorf's thought, this goes beyond anything he himself says, but it does seem implicit in the fundamental distinction he makes between motivation by fear of sanctions and the kind of conscientious motivation he holds to be necessary for accountable moral agency. I argue in *SPS* and more recent work that it is possible to ground the dignity of persons and what Pufendorf calls the "equality of right" within the presuppositions we are committed to when we take up a second-person standpoint and make any putatively legitimate demands, whether of others or ourselves, at all (Darwall 2006, 2013a, 2013b). The basic idea relies on "Pufendorf's Point" that an agent, whether God or anyone else, can make a putatively legitimate demand of someone (and hold them accountable for compliance) only if they take it that their addressee has the capacity to accept the legitimacy of their demand and be moved by that in their own conscience.

If this is right, the very possibility of moral obligation depends upon there being demands that can be justified from a standpoint that one shares with anyone who is capable of being bound by them—in Pufendorf's (2009, 94) words, any "person with whom . . . it may be possible to have intercourse." For moral obligations to exist at all, consequently, there must be fundamental demands that anyone can see to be warranted from anyone, as a representative person, to any potentially sociable person, from an impartial perspective we can share in "common life."

When we hold ourselves accountable through the exercise of our own conscience and capacity for intercourse, therefore, we are committed thereby to valuing others' exercise of this capacity as well. And when we hold others accountable, we are committed to this also. Accountability is always a reciprocal, second-personal affair. It is impossible justifiably to hold others answerable without allowing them the interpersonal, "common" space to take responsibility for themselves by making their own autonomous choices. One cannot coherently hold someone responsible for freely choosing to do something while simultaneously undermining their capacity to make the choice themselves or otherwise usurping their agency.[11] We are thus committed by presuppositions of accountable moral agency to human dignity and the "equality of right."

Grotius and Equal Sociability as "the Fountain of Right"

Grotius does not assert respect for equal human dignity as explicitly as Pufendorf. But the idea, and the equality of right it grounds, are implicit in his

VALUING HUMANITY IN "COMMON LIFE" 139

thought nonetheless. Moreover, whereas "sociable" mutual obligation and equal dignity in Pufendorf derive from God's exercise of his superior moral power, Grotius (2005, I.37), in a radical move that does not really get picked up in the early modern natural law tradition, proclaims that "sociability ... is the fountain of right." This brings the second-personal aspects of legitimate demand and mutual accountability into the very foundations of right.

Three Senses of *Ius* and *Sociable Relations*

We can begin with a three-way distinction Grotius (2005) draws at the outset of *The Rights of War and Peace* between things correctly termed *ius*, which translators translate alternately as "law" or "right."[12] First, Grotius says, *ius* can "signif[y] merely *that which is just*," where "that is unjust which is repugnant to the Nature of a Society of Reasonable Creatures" (I, 136). Grotius then quotes Florentinus's remark that "*Nature has founded a kind of* Relation between us" (I, 136). We shall see the kind of "relation" Grotius has in mind presently. But note first a distinction Grotius makes next between two different kinds of "relations" that are found in societies. Some are between "unequals," like those of "Parents and Children, Masters and Servants, King and Subject," where someone has the authority to govern another. Others are relations of "equal[s]," such as "Brothers, Citizens, Friends and Allies," where each party is conceived to be self-governing in relation to the other (I, 136). In the former instance, superiors have a "Right of Superiority"; in the latter, each has a "Right of Equality." Grotius summarizes: "So that which is *just* takes place either among Equals, or amongst People whereof some are Governors and others governed, considered as such" (I, 136).

Grotius thus defines these more specific relations in terms of relative *authority*, which he explicitly characterizes through respective claim "rights" (which, as we shall see presently, is his second category of *ius*). So understood, a relationship essentially includes the authority or standing of those within it to make claims and demands of one another. This means that the relations are already conceived as inherently involving rights (*ius*) of what will be Grotius's second kind. Since relations of these sorts are essentially conceived in terms of *ius*, it will follow straight away that anything that is contrary to the nature of people who are related *in these defined ways* will also be contrary to *ius*.

Moreover, if as Florentinus says, there is an even more fundamental relation between any and all members of a "Society of Reasonable Creatures" than either the unequal relations between superiors and inferiors *or* the equal relations between "Brothers, Citizens, Friends, and Allies," then it would seem that this more fundamental relation of equality must somehow ground the more specific relations of unequals and equals Grotius mentions. I shall be arguing that this is

140   RETHINKING THE VALUE OF HUMANITY

indeed the way we should understand Grotius's claim that "sociability . . . is the fountain of right."

Grotius's second meaning of *ius* brings out the idea of authoritative standing even more clearly. Grotius says that this second sense is different from the first, "yet aris[es] from it." In the second sense, "*Right* is a *moral Quality* annexed to the Person, *enabling him to have, or do, something justly*" (I, 138). Here Grotius introduces his famous distinction between perfect and imperfect rights, generating the modern distinction between perfect and imperfect duties or obligations.[13] A "perfect right" is a "*Faculty*" of the person, which includes the standing or authority to "*demand what is due*" to him, including, Grotius says, "*Liberty*," or "power over ourselves" (or over others who are under his authority) and property (I, 138–139). Grotius adds that such a faculty "*answers the Obligation of rendering what is owing*" (I, 139). There can be natural rights, therefore, only if there are natural obligations, that is, only if natural law includes genuine obligations to respect the rights. Moreover, among the natural perfect rights that natural law must enshrine, Grotius holds, is autonomy or "power over ourselves." Autonomy or authority over ourselves will thus be part of an "equality of right," as Pufendorf would call it, of which sociability, the fundamental relation of equality, is the "fountain."[14]

Grotius's final sense of *ius*

> signifies the same Thing as *Law* when taken in its largest Extent, as being *a Rule of Moral Actions, obliging us*. . . . I say *obliging*: for Counsels, and such other Precepts, which however honest and reasonable they be, lay us under no Obligation, come not under this Notion of *Law*, or Right. (I, 147–148)

In distinguishing between law and "counsel," Grotius follows Francisco Suarez in holding that unlike reasons for acting of other kinds ("counsel"), genuine law entails obligation, together with its conceptual connections to accountability and culpability (Schneewind 1990, I: 74–75; Darwall 2012b, 302–303).

Grotius then gives his definition of the "law" or "right" of nature:

> Natural Right *is the Rule and Dictate of Right, Reason, shewing the Moral Deformity or Moral Necessity there is in any Act, according to its Suitableness or to a reasonable Nature.* (I, 150–151)

Barbeyrac notes that other editions interpolated "*and Sociable*" between "*reasonable*" and "*Nature*" and says there is some reason to believe that these have been simply left out by a printer or transcriber (I, 151n2).[15] As Barbeyrac points out, when Grotius distinguishes between a priori and a posteriori proofs of laws of nature, he brings in sociability explicitly. A posteriori proofs appeal to a *consentium gentium*, that is, to something being "generally believed to be" natural law "by all, or at least, the most civilized Nations" (I, 159). An a priori proof, by contrast, proceeds by "shewing the necessary Fitness or Unfitness of any Thing, with a reasonable and sociable Nature" (I, 159).

We shall presently return to how Grotius might hope to ground laws of nature in reasonable sociability. Already, however, we can glimpse how norms that can be justified in this way might be genuinely obligating. If Grotius conceives of sociability as itself involving a fundamental standing to make claims and demands of one another, then being contrary to our *reasonable and sociable* character would mean being at odds with our standing to make *reasoned or reasonable claims and demands* of each other, not simply being contrary to standards of rational thought and action in general, even standards rooted in our rational nature, however social that might itself be. Only if it can be justified in some such way, indeed, would a "law of nature" be a genuine *ius*. Only if it can be grounded in an authority to issue demands would it be able to "lay us under" a genuine obligation.

Equality of Right

Richard Tuck (2001) plausibly claims that the moral/political conceptual framework we inherit from the early moderns, one that models the dignity and sovereignty of individuals on that of states, begins with Grotius.[16] Part of Grotius's purpose in writing both *The Rights of War and Peace* and the earlier *On the Law of Prize and Booty*, indeed, was to argue that organized groups of individuals, like the Dutch trading companies with which he and his family were involved, were like states in having a right to *punish* wrongs that did not violate their own rights but where the perpetrators might not otherwise be held responsible. Implicit throughout is a conception of individual persons as having the authority to rule themselves as well as the standing to hold one another responsible for respecting natural rights and law.

Consider, first, the following from *The Rights of War and Peace*, which brings out both the theme of individual autonomy as well as the analogy between the personal and the political to which Tuck refers:

> But as there are several Ways of Living . . . and every one may chuse which he pleases of all those Sorts; so a People may chuse what Form of Government they please: Neither is the Right which the Sovereign has over his Subjects to be measured . . . but by the Extent of the Will of those who conferred it upon Him. (Grotius 2005, I, 262)

142 RETHINKING THE VALUE OF HUMANITY

Or the following, often cited by Tuck, from *On the Law of Prize and Booty*:

> God created man *autexousion*, "free and *sui iuris*," so that the actions of each individual and the use of his possessions were made subject not to another's will but to his own. Moreover, this view is sanctioned by the common consent of all nations. For what is that well-known concept, 'natural liberty,' other than the power of the individual to act in accordance with his own will? And liberty in regard to actions is equivalent to ownership in regard to property. Hence the saying: "every man is the governor and arbiter of affairs relative to his own property." (Grotius [1604] 1950, 18)

The "well-known concept" of "natural liberty" is a reference to Gabriel Vasquez, but however well established the idea of self-rule was in some form, it seems clear that Grotius took the idea of a natural *right* to govern oneself significantly farther. In Vasquez's hands, for example, 'natural liberty' seems to refer alternately to a psychological faculty for free choice shared by rational agents and to a Hohfeldian liberty, that is, to a range of permitted choices that violate no law or obligation.[17] With Grotius, however, the right to rule oneself evidently includes a Hohfeldian *claim* right and therefore entails a consequent obligation of others to allow one to do so.[18]

"Right properly and strictly so called," Grotius (2005) says, "consists in leaving others in quiet Possession of what is already their own [including the "Power . . . over ourselves, which is term'd *Liberty*" (I, 138)], or in doing for them what in Strictness they may demand" (I, 89). When we fail to abstain from what belongs to others (including, again, by interfering with their liberty), their right gives them standing to demand "Restitution" of what we have taken, insofar as this is possible, and "Reparation" of any "Damage done through our own Default" (I, 86). These are all "due" to others not just in the sense that it is fitting that they have it or even that they deserve it, but also that these others have "the Faculty of demanding what is due," and that we consequently have "the Obligation of rendering what is owing" (I, 139). As Barbeyrac remarks in a footnote to the passage quoted at the beginning of this paragraph, "When we Repair the Damage he has sustained in his Person, Goods, or Reputation, whether designedly or through Inadvertency, we restore what we had taken from him, and what was his own, *which he had a strict Right to demand*" (I, 88n).

It follows that natural right, as Grotius understands it, includes obligation-entailing claim rights of individuals to demand that others conduct themselves toward them in various ways: "the Abstaining from that which is another's, the Restitution of what we have of another's, or of the Profit we have made by it, the Obligation of fulfilling Promises, [and] the Reparation of a Damage done through our own Default" (I, 86). This shapes how the law of nature must itself be understood; it must include respect for these claim rights.

VALUING HUMANITY IN "COMMON LIFE" 143

In addition, Grotius holds a view about the standing of individuals to punish violations of natural law that connects the law of nature to the dignity of individuals in yet another way. This, again, is a point that Tuck (2001, 82) has stressed, pointing to the following passage from *On the Law of Prize and Booty* (see also Tuck's introduction to Grotius 2005, I, xx):

> Is the power to punish essentially a power that pertains to the state [*respublica*]? Not at all? On the contrary, just as every right of the magistrate comes to him from the state, so has the right come to the state from private individuals; and similarly, the power of the state is the result of collective agreement. . . . Therefore, since no one is able to transfer a thing that he never possessed, it is evident that the right of chastisement was held by private persons before it was held by the state. (Grotius [1604] 1950, 91)[19]

Grotius is not so explicit about individuals' right to punish in *The Rights of War and Peace*. There he says that the "Person to whom the Right of Punishing belongs, is not determined by the Law of Nature" (2005, II, 955). All "natural Reason" tells us for sure is that "a Malefactor may be punished, but not who ought to punish him" (II, 955). Though it "suggests . . . it is fittest to be done by a Superior," it does not show that "to be absolutely necessary" (II, 955). Even if this seems weaker, there is no reason to think that Grotius has gone back on his earlier view. Indeed, in the passage where he proclaims "Sociability . . . is the Fountain of Right," Grotius adds that this Right includes not just "Abstaining from that which is another's," "Restitution," "Reparation," and "the Obligation of fulfilling promises," as I mentioned before, but also "the Merit of Punishment among Men" (I, 86).

The thrust of these remarks is that individual persons not only have the authority to demand compliance with *their own* rights and demand restitution and reparation when these are violated; they also have the standing to demand that the moral law be complied with in respect of others. In effect, they have an authority of membership in an assumed moral community of mutually accountable equals.

This adds a distinctive element to the moral law. Since the law requires respect for each person's rights, it involves obligations that are, in the first instance at least, *to patients*, that is, those whom we affect by our actions. But patients are not the only ones having the standing to demand compliance with these rights, and hence the law; all others do as well, since they have the standing to punish and not just to secure restitution or reparation on behalf of the victim. And since that is so, moral obligations involve, in the second instance, responsibilities *to* all persons and not just to patients. Here we have at least a strong suggestion, perhaps the first, of a conception of *moral community as mutual accountability*. Morality

144 RETHINKING THE VALUE OF HUMANITY

imposes genuine obligations that we are accountable for complying with, where this accountability involves being answerable to one another.[20]

"Sociability . . . Is the Fountain of Right"

We can now explore more fully Grotius's (2005, I, 85–86, 159) claims that "Sociability . . . is the Fountain of Right" and that what makes something in accordance with or contrary to natural law is its "Fitness or Unfitness . . . with a reasonable and sociable Nature." The first statement of these ideas comes in an important passage in which Grotius considers a skeptical challenge to morality or natural law. It is a passage that will be echoed by Hobbes's (1994, XV.§4) "foole," Hume's (1985, 256) "sensible knave," and Kant's worry that morality might be a "chimerical idea without any truth" (4: 445).[21] Who better to pose this challenge, Grotius says, than the ancient skeptic Carneades, who held that "*Laws . . . were instituted by Men for the sake of Interest*" (2005, I, 79):

> As to that which is called Natural Right, *it is a mere Chimera. Nature prompts all Men . . . to seek their own particular Advantage: So that either there is no Justice at all, or if there is any it is extreme Folly, because it engages us to procure the Good of others, to our own Prejudice.* (I, 79)[22]

Grotius's response to Carneades's challenge is that human beings have a "Desire of Society" in addition to self-regarding motives (I, 79). But what can our "sociable" nature be, if it is to ground natural law, as Grotius understands it, that is, something that creates genuine obligations to act, even what is against our interest?

It seems clear, first, that sociability cannot be anything like benevolence, the desire for the good of others or even of all, for at least two reasons. First, even if such a desire were universal in the species, it would be unable, by itself, to ground the idea that we are under an *obligation* to promote human welfare, that is, that we are responsible or accountable for doing so, self-interest to the contrary notwithstanding. In being benevolent, we see the flourishing of human beings as good. The notion that we are obligated to promote human flourishing, that it is wrong not to do so, is a further thought for which benevolence itself provides no foundation.

Second, the very same kind of collective action problem that can make it beneficial for an agent not to do their part in a mutually advantageous cooperative scheme can arise regarding a benevolent desire for the general good. There can be cases where an agent can produce more overall good by doing something unjust or unfair, as, for example, in Hume's famous case of deploying stolen property for

VALUING HUMANITY IN "COMMON LIFE"   145

the general good rather than returning it to a seditious, bigoted owner.[23] Neither can a desire to live among or in agreement with other human beings, or for what is necessary for a flourishing society, ground obligations for similar reasons.

Grotius is actually quite specific about the kind of "Desire of Society" he has in mind:

> *That is a certain Inclination to live with others of his own Kind, not in any Manner whatsoever, but peaceably, and in a Community regulated according to the best of His Understanding.* (I, 80–81)

To this he adds that mature human beings develop a *"peculiar Instrument"* that is necessary for such a "Community," namely, *"the Use of Speech"* (I, 85), and humans have also the related *"Faculty of knowing and acting, according to some General Principles"* (I, 85). Other animals certainly live together, and many seem capable of acting out of something like affection or concern for at least some others of their kind. What is distinctive about human beings is their capacity for and disposition toward a particular kind of social order, namely, mutually accountable community mediated by the common acceptance of "General Principles." Human beings have a capacity for and drive toward a distinctive *kind* of society, "A Society of reasonable Creatures" that hold themselves accountable to one another (I, 136).[24]

Just as it is intrinsic to the very idea of law that those who are subject to it can be held accountable for compliance only if legal standards are publicly accessible, so also is it essential to morality as mutual accountability that deontic moral standards be "General Principles" of right (Darwall 2013c). Analogous also is the role of the "Use of Speech" in the accountability practices that structure law and morality, respectively.

Recall now Grotius's reference to Florentinus's remark that *"Nature has founded a kind of* Relation between us" (I, 136). The examples that Grotius gives of social relations, again, are all relations of authority, involving standings to make claims and demands and hold accountable, whether the relation is reciprocal (*"Right of Equality"*) or not (*"Right of Superiority"*) (I, 136–137). But whereas Grotius's examples of rights "of Equality" and "of Superiority" are all *specific*—e.g., "Brothers, Citizens, Friends and Allies" being examples of equals—the relation Grotius seems to have in mind with Florentinus's remark is quite general. It would seem to hold with respect to any person who, to use Pufendorf's formulations, is capable of "intercourse" and "common life." The suggestion seems to be that we share a more fundamental relation of equal or fellow person to everyone, regardless of our more specific relations to them.

If we put these passages together with those quoted in the last paragraph concerning the "Social Faculty" (I, 87), what we get is a conception of sociability

146 RETHINKING THE VALUE OF HUMANITY

as the human capacity for and disposition toward a distinctive *kind* of social order, namely, the very kind of order that Grotius is himself trying to found in *The Rights of War and Peace*. So understood, sociability is the fountain of a mutually accountable order involving all persons that is mediated by universal "General Principles" that enshrine rights with which individual members have the standing to demand compliance. We best interpret Grotius, therefore, as holding that the law and rights of nature are grounded in the capacity of rational persons to recognize their common competence and authority to make reasoned claims and demands against one another and hold one another accountable for conducting themselves on terms that respect this common standing.

Conclusion

Respect for the equal dignity of human persons is a distinctively deontic way of valuing humanity. Dignity is no form of good, which might be appreciated through desire or esteem, but a form of value that calls for, indeed demands, respect (what Pufendorf calls "esteem"), where respect is an attitude we manifest in the formation of our wills by governing our deliberations by the constraints of right (Pufendorf's "rights of equality") that the dignity of persons places on us, and hold ourselves accountable to one another for compliance with these. It is no coincidence, I have suggested, that some of the first defenses of the dignity of persons, implicitly, in Grotius, and explicitly, in Pufendorf, arise in these first attempts to work out theories of natural law and right.

I have argued that what is most remarkable in Grotius's and Pufendorf's defense of equal dignity and right is the way both make their arguments within the context of "sociability" and "common life." This enables them to appreciate and theorize the fundamentally second-personal nature of dignity and right. We have noted that Grotius makes sociability fundamental to his theory of right in a way it is not to Pufendorf's. Pufendorf derives equal dignity and the "equality of right" from God's exercise of superior (and more fundamental) moral power. Despite this, Pufendorf's sophisticated account of accountable agency may in the end provide richer resources for grounding sociable equal dignity (in "common life") than simply positing sociability as an assumed equal authority to make claims and demands of another, and hold each other accountable, as I have presented Grotius as doing.

Once we have "Pufendorf's Point," that we can intelligibly hold someone accountable for complying with any putatively legitimate claim or demand we might wish to make them, only if we assume that they have the capacity to accept and be moved by the legitimacy of our claim, we can appreciate resources to ground equal dignity and the equality of right in a more fundamental way.

VALUING HUMANITY IN "COMMON LIFE"   147

We can argue that equal dignity and mutual accountability are grounded in assumptions that are inescapable for us whenever we make any claims of right at all (Darwall 2006, 2013a, 2013b).

Notes

1. The most prominent exception is Irwin 2007, 2008. Writers who draw this contrast include Sidgwick 1964, 198; Sidgwick 1967, 106; Anscombe 1958; MacIntyre 1981; Williams 1985, 1–6; Schneewind 1998, 67–73; Rawls 2000, 1–2; Darwall 2012b.
2. Normal mature human beings, at least, who have the basic capacities of moral agency necessary to be subject to moral obligations. I prescind here from the difficult questions both of precisely what these capacities involve (although I discuss some important relevant ideas of Pufendorf's) and of whether other human and non-human beings can have dignity in the present sense.
3. I draw here from Darwall 2012b, 2012c.
4. This aspect is arguably largely missing from Kant's account, though in *The Metaphysics of Morals*, Kant says that "a human being regarded as a *person* . . . possesses a *dignity* (absolute inner worth) by which he exacts *respect* for himself from all other rational beings in the world" (6: 434–435). Presumably, "exacting respect" requires second-personal relating. I discuss Kant's complex views on respect in Darwall 2008.
5. In what follows, I draw closely on Darwall 2012c.
6. I am indebted here to Knud Haakonssen.
7. Compare a parallel passage from *De Officio*: "The primary axiom in moral disciplines which look at the subject from the point of view of the human court is held to be: a man may be held accountable for those actions which it is in his power whether they are done or not" (Pufendorf 1991, 23).
8. Using 'belief' in a sufficiently general sense that does not require a stand on debates about metaethical expressivism versus realism.
9. Although Pufendorf does hold that the ability to create negative consequences or sanctions is necessary.
10. Pufendorf (1934, 95; cf. 1991, 28) consistently maintains that there must be actual sanctions in order for a person genuinely to be obligated: "An obligation is properly laid on the mind of man by a superior, that is, by one who has both the strength to threaten some evil against those who resist him, and just reasons why he can demand that the liberty of will be limited at his pleasure." The threat of actual sanctions is thus necessary for obligation. But Pufendorf emphasizes that his view differs from Hobbes's, at least as he understands Hobbes, since he holds that sanctions are not sufficient to obligate. It is also necessary that there be "just reasons" for the sanction, hence, that it falls on one justly. The moral motive, again, is "fear mingled with reverence" (1934, 95).

   It is a sign of the tension in Pufendorf's thought that it is unclear how to understand the desire to avoid *justified sanctions* when, as Pufendorf seems to be supposing, it

148 RETHINKING THE VALUE OF HUMANITY

involves no desire to avoid what *would justify* sanctions. To hold that the threat of actual sanctions is necessary for obligation and moral motivation, Pufendorf must think that the agent's own judgment that his action would be worthy of censure and sanction can do no independent motivational work. It is as if conscience involves being "forced of itself to weigh its own actions," but also as if judging that an action would make one "worthy of some censure" leaves one unaffected until one judges that some sanction (or censure) would actually take place. But what motivational work is conscience then doing? It is as if the judgment that one is worthy of censure is utterly external and without affect, in other words, that it involves no implicit censure or blame *of oneself.*

Motivationally, it is hard to see the difference between a desire to avoid justified sanctions that involves no desire to avoid what would justify sanction, whether or not the sanction will occur, and the desire to avoid sanctions period. But Pufendorf is at pains to distinguish these. Of course, if someone were to lack a *general* desire to avoid sanctions and desired to avoid them *only* on the condition they were justified, then the desire to avoid justified sanctions would clearly be motivationally distinct from it. But Pufendorf of course thinks we do have a general desire to avoid sanctions, whether they are justified or not. Someone who wants to avoid sanctions on the condition they are justified is most plausibly seen as someone who wants to avoid what would justify sanctions, whether or not the sanction will actually be applied.

11. I draw here on Darwall 2010.
12. I draw in what follows on Darwall 2012b.
13. First, in Pufendorf (e.g., 1934, 90). On the significance of Grotius's distinction, see Schneewind 1998, esp. 78–79, 133–134; Stewart 1854, 175–177.
14. By contrast, an imperfect right is not a "*Faculty*" but an "*Aptitude*." Under this heading, Grotius includes considerations of "*Worth*" and "*Merit*" that can recommend actions as more or less worthy or meritorious, but that no one has standing to *demand* (I, 141). "Prudent management in the gratuitous Distribution of Things" to which no individuals or society has a valid claim may nonetheless recommend giving preference to "one of greater before one of less Merit, a Relation before a Stranger, a poor Man before one that is rich" (I, 88). However, Grotius insists that "Ancients" like Aristotle, and even "Moderns" who follow him, though they may take considerations of the latter kind to be included within what they call "justice" and so "right" (it is what Aristotle and his followers include under "distributive justice"), nonetheless "Right, properly speaking, has a quite different Nature," namely, "doing for [others] what in Strictness they may demand" (I, 88–89).
15. But see Irwin 2008, 91n.
16. "We take for granted that the language in which we still describe this autonomous, right-bearing individual is in fact a language to describe states or rulers. When Hart in his famous 1955 essay 'Are There Any Natural Rights' said about promising that 'the promisee has a temporary authority or sovereignty in relation to some specific matter over another's will,' he was drawing on precisely this tradition which we find articulated for the first time in [Grotius's] *De Indis* especially" (Tuck 2001, 1–9, 83–89)

VALUING HUMANITY IN "COMMON LIFE" 149

17. For an excellent discussion of Vasquez on natural liberty, see Brett 1997, 165–204. Brett argues that Hobbes uses 'natural liberty' to refer to these two things also (205–235). See Hohfeld's (1923) classification of rights.

18. Or, at least, it was taken to include such a claim right, as is shown by Barbeyrac's remarks quoted in the next paragraph.

19. As further evidence, Grotius adds an argument that will later be picked up by Locke ([1689] 1988, 272) in *The Second Treatise of Government* to support his view that individuals in the state nature have a right to punish that is additional to their right to seek reparation for violation of their own rights, namely, that states normally claim the right to punish wrongs not only to their own citizens but also to foreigners, "yet it derives no power over the latter from civil law, which is binding upon citizens only because they have given their own consent" (Grotius [1604] 1950, 91–92).

20. In Darwall (2012a), I argue that there are two different forms of accountability. With moral obligations, whether they are owed to particular others in a way that entails correlative claim rights, all persons have a representative authority to hold accountable (as members of the moral community). But with relational or bipolar obligations the entailed claim right-holders have an individual authority to hold those obligated to them accountable as the very individuals to whom the obligations are owed.

21. I discuss this passage at some length in Darwall 2012b, 309–315.

22. Cf. Hobbes (1994a, XV.§4): "The fool hath said in his heart, there is no such thing as justice; and sometimes also with his tongue; seriously alleging, that every man's conservation, and contentment, being committed to his own care, there could be no reason, why every man might not do what he thought conduced thereunto: and therefore also to make, or not make; keep, or not keep covenants, was not against reason, when it conduced to one's benefit." And Hume (1985, 256): "[T]hough it is allowed, that, without a regard to property, no society could subsist; yet, according to the imperfect way in which human affairs are conducted, a sensible knave, in particular incidents, may think, that an act of iniquity or infidelity will make a considerable addition to his fortune, without causing any considerable breach in the social union and confederacy. That *honesty is the best policy,* may be a good general rule; but is liable to many exceptions: And he, it may, perhaps, be thought, conducts himself with most wisdom, who observes the general rule, and takes advantage of all the exceptions."

23. "When a man of merit, of a beneficent disposition, restores a great fortune to a miser, or a seditious bigot, he has acted justly and laudably; but the public is a real sufferer" (Hume 1978, 497).

24. This turns out to have been prescient. See Tomasello (2016) for a corresponding theory of the evolutionary origins of morality.

References

Anscombe, G. E. M. 1958. "Modern Moral Philosophy." *Philosophy* 33: 1–19.
Barbeyrac, Jean. 1749. "An Historical and Critical Account of the Science of Morality." In Samuel Pufendorf, *The Law of Nature and Nations,* 5th ed., edited by Jean Barbeyrac and translated by Basil Kennett, 1–88. London: J. and P. Knapton.

150 RETHINKING THE VALUE OF HUMANITY

Brett, Annabel S. 1997. *Liberty, Right and Nature: Individual Rights in Later Scholastic Thought*. Cambridge: Cambridge University Press.

Darwall, Stephen. 1977. "Two Kinds of Respect." *Ethics* 88: 36–49.

Darwall, Stephen. 2006. *The Second-Person Standpoint: Morality, Respect, and Accountability*. Cambridge, MA: Harvard University Press.

Darwall, Stephen. 2008. "Kant on Respect, Dignity, and the Duty of Respect." In *Kant's Ethics of Virtue*, edited by Monika Betzler, 175–200. Berlin: Walter de Gruyter.

Darwall, Stephen. 2010. "Moral Obligation: Form and Substance." *Proceedings of the Aristotelian Society* 110: 31–46.

Darwall, Stephen. 2012a. "Bipolar Obligation." In *Oxford Studies in Metaethics*, edited by Russ Shafer-Landau, vol. 7, 333–357. Oxford: Oxford University Press.

Darwall, Stephen. 2012b. "Grotius at the Creation of Modern Moral Philosophy." *Archiv für Geschichte der Philosophie* 94: 296–325.

Darwall, Stephen. 2012c. "Pufendorf on Morality, Sociability, and Moral Powers." *Journal of the History of Philosophy* 50: 213–238.

Darwall, Stephen. 2013a. *Honor, History, and Relationship: Essays in Second-Personal Ethics II*. Oxford: Oxford University Press.

Darwall, Stephen. 2013b. *Morality, Authority, and Law: Essays in Second-Personal Ethics I*. Oxford: Oxford University Press.

Darwall, Stephen. 2015. "Respect as Honor and as Accountability." In *Reason, Value, and Respect: Kantian Themes from the Philosophy of Thomas E. Hill Jr.*, edited by Robert Johnson and Mark Timmons, 70–86. Oxford: Oxford University Press.

Fricker, Miranda. 2016. "What Is the Point of Blame? A Paradigm Based Explanation." *Nous* 50: 165–183.

Grotius, Hugo. (1604) 1950. *De Iure Praedae Commentarius; Commentary on the Law of Prize and Booty*. Translated by Gwladys L. Williams and Walter H. Zeydel. Oxford: Clarendon Press.

Grotius, Hugo. 2005. *The Rights of War and Peace*. Edited by Richard Tuck. 3 vols. Indianapolis, IN: Liberty Fund. [References are to volume and page numbers]

Hobbes, Thomas. 1994. *Leviathan*. Edited by Edwin Curley. Indianapolis, IN: Hackett. [References are to chapter and paragraph numbers]

Hobbes, Thomas. 1999. *Human Nature and De Corpore Politico*. Edited by John C. A. Gaskin. Oxford: Oxford University Press.

Hohfeld, Wesley Newcomb. 1923. *Fundamental Legal Conceptions as Applied in Judicial Reasoning and Other Legal Essays*. New Haven, CT: Yale University Press.

Hume, David. 1978. *A Treatise of Human Nature*, 2nd ed. Edited and with an analytical index by Lewis A. Selby-Bigge. Text revised and variant readings by Peter H. Nidditch. Oxford: Oxford University Press.

Hume David. 1985. *An Enquiry concerning the Principles of Morals*. In *Enquiries concerning Human Understanding and concerning the Principles of Morals*, 3rd ed., edited by Lewis A. Selby-Bigge, text revised and notes by Peter H. Nidditch, 455–591. Oxford: Oxford University Press.

Irwin, Terence. 2007. *The Development of Ethics: A Historical and Critical Study*. Vol. 1: *From Socrates to the Reformation*. Oxford: Oxford University Press.

Irwin, Terence. 2008. *The Development of Ethics: A Historical and Critical Study*. Vol. 2: *From Suarez to Rousseau*. Oxford: Oxford University Press.

Kant, Immanuel. 1900–. *Kants gesammelte Schriften*. 24 vols. Edited by Königlich Preussische Akademie der Wissenschaften zu Berlin, Deutschen Akademie der

VALUING HUMANITY IN "COMMON LIFE" 151

Wissenschaften zu Berlin, and Akademie der Wissenschaften zu Göttingen. Berlin: De Gruyter.

Kant, Immanuel. 1996a. *Groundwork of the Metaphysics of Morals*. In *Practical Philosophy*, translated and edited by Mary J. Gregor, 38–108. Cambridge: Cambridge University Press. [References are to page numbers of the Preussische Akademie edition]

Kant, Immanuel. 1996b. *The Metaphysics of Morals*. In Kant, *Practical Philosophy*. Translated and edited by Mary J. Gregor, 354–605. Cambridge: Cambridge University Press. [References are to page numbers of the Preussische Akademie edition]

Kelly, Thomas. 2002. "The Rationality of Belief and Other Propositional Attitudes." *Philosophical Studies* 110: 163–196.

Locke, John. (1689) 1988. *Two Treatises of Government*. Edited by Peter Laslett. Cambridge: Cambridge University Press.

MacIntyre, Alasdair. 1981. *After Virtue: A Study in Moral Theory*. South Bend, IN: University of Notre Dame Press.

McKenna, Michael. 2012. *Conversation and Responsibility*. Oxford: Oxford University Press.

Moore, G. E. 1993. *Principia Ethica*. Revised ed. with the preface to the (projected) 2nd ed. and other papers. Edited and with an introduction by Thomas Baldwin. Cambridge: Cambridge University Press.

Parfit, Derek. 2011. *Agreement Matters*. 2 vols. Oxford: Oxford University Press.

Pufendorf, Samuel. 1672. *De Jure Naturae et Gentium*. Lund: Adam Junghans.

Pufendorf, Samuel. 1934. *On the Law of Nature and Nations*. Translated by Charles H. Oldfather and Willam. A. Oldfather. Oxford: Clarendon Press.

Pufendorf, Samuel. 1991. *On the Duty of Man and Citizen According to Natural Law*. Edited by James Tulley. Translated by Michael Silverthorne. Cambridge: Cambridge University Press.

Pufendorf, Samuel. 2009. *Two Books of the Elements of Universal Jurisprudence*. Edited by Thomas Behne. Translated by W. A. Oldfather, with revisions by Thomas Behne. Indianapolis, IN: Liberty Fund.

Rawls, John. 1980. "Kantian Constructivism in Moral Theory." *Journal of Philosophy* 77: 515–572.

Rawls, John. 2000. *Lectures on the History of Moral Philosophy*. Cambridge, MA: Harvard University Press.

Raz, Joseph. 1972. "Voluntary Obligations and Normative Powers, II." *Proceedings of the Aristotelian Society*, suppl. vol. 47: 79–102.

Schneewind, J. B. 1998. *The Invention of Autonomy*. Cambridge: Cambridge University Press.

Sidgwick, Henry. 1964. *Outlines of the History of Ethics for English Readers*. With an additional chapter by Alban G. Widgery. Boston: Beacon Press.

Sidgwick, Henry. 1967. *The Methods of Ethics*, 7th ed. London: Macmillan.

Strawson, P. F. 1968. "Freedom and Resentment." In *Studies in the Philosophy of Thought and Action*. London: Oxford University Press.

Stewart, Dugald. 1854. *Dissertation Exhibiting the Progress of Metaphysical, Ethical, and Political Philosophy since the Revival of Letters in Europe*. In *Collected Works*, edited by William Hamilton. Edinburgh: Thomas Constable.

Tomasello, Michael. 2016. *A Natural History of Human Morality*. Cambridge, MA: Harvard University Press.

152 RETHINKING THE VALUE OF HUMANITY

Tuck, Richard. 2001. *The Rights of War and Peace: Political Thought and the International Order from Grotius to Kant.* Oxford: Oxford University Press.

Velleman, J. David. 2001. "The Genesis of Shame." *Philosophy & Public Affairs* 30: 27–52.

Watson, Gary. 1987. "Responsibility and the Limits of Evil: Variations on a Strawsonian Theme." In *Responsibility, Character, and the Emotions: New Essays in Moral Psychology*, edited by Ferdinand D. Schoeman, 256–286. Cambridge: Cambridge University Press.

Watson, Gary. 1996. "Two Faces of Responsibility." *Philosophical Topics* 24: 227–248.

Watson, Gary. 2010. "Promises, Reasons, and Normative Powers." In *Reasons for Action*, edited by David Sobel and Steven Wall, 155–178. Cambridge: Cambridge University Press.

Williams, Bernard. 1985. *Ethics and the Limits of Philosophy.* Cambridge, MA: Harvard University Press.

6

The Dignity of Humanity

Ralf M. Bader

Introduction

Kant argues in *Groundwork II* that humanity is an end-in-itself (4:428), that it has absolute worth (4:428), that it has dignity (4:435), that it is beyond price (4:434), that it is never to be used merely as a means (4:429), and that it functions as the ground of the categorical imperative (4:428).[1] While there is much debate about how these arguments are to be interpreted and while it is unclear how exactly these various claims relate to one another, it is abundantly clear that humanity occupies a central place in Kant's ethical thought. This becomes especially apparent when one considers the second variant of the categorical imperative, namely the formula of humanity:

> *[S]o act that you use humanity, whether in your own person or that of any other, always at the same time as an end, never merely as a means.* (4:429)[2]

Kant's discussion of humanity has led many people (both Kant scholars as well as moral philosophers) to speak of the value of humanity.[3] They construe dignity as a type of value that functions as the ground of the categorical imperative and that explains why humanity is to be respected.

The first part of this paper argues that the normative significance of humanity is not to be understood in axiological terms (and that it is hence somewhat misleading to speak of the 'value of humanity'). It argues (1) that there is no room for dignity within Kant's axiological theory, since the good will is meant to be the only thing that is unconditionally good, thereby precluding humanity from likewise being unconditionally good; (2) that value bearers are ends to be effected, yet that humanity is a self-standing end; (3) that the categorical imperative cannot be grounded in a value, since this would conflict with the priority of the right over the good; (4) that a unified axiological construal cannot simultaneously explain both perfect and imperfect duties, since any attempt to explain the inviolability of persons on axiological grounds will preclude the possibility of accounting for imperfect duties, and vice versa; and (5) that construing dignity as a value conflicts with Kant's argument for humanity at 4:428.

Ralf M. Bader, *The Dignity of Humanity* In: *Rethinking the Value of Humanity.* Edited by: Sarah Buss and L. Nandi Theunissen, Oxford University Press. © Oxford University Press 2023.
DOI: 10.1093/oso/9780197539361.003.0007

154 RETHINKING THE VALUE OF HUMANITY

The second part argues that the significance of humanity is to be construed in distinctly deontological terms (and that it is accordingly preferable to speak of the 'status of humanity'). Whereas other critics of axiological approaches have advocated a deflationary reading of the role of dignity,[4] this paper puts forward a deontological reading and argues that dignity does play an important role. Dignity is construed as a deontological status that consists in humanity being a self-standing end that is to be respected. In particular, dignity turns out to play a crucial role in Kant's ethics by determining the domain over which maxims have to be universalizable.

1. Dignity as Value

Is the dignity of humanity to be construed as a type of value? Moreover, should we think of this value as being the ground of the categorical imperative? Do we have to respect humanity because it has value?

This section argues that axiological readings, which answer these questions in the affirmative, run into difficulties and are to be rejected. The next section develops an alternative deontological reading, according to which dignity is not a type of value but a deontological status.

1.1 Humanity and the Good Will

For Kant, the good will is the only thing that is unconditionally good (4:393). In fact, the good will is the supreme good: it is the condition of everything that is good (5:110). This precludes humanity from likewise being unconditionally good, which means that the absolute worth (or dignity) of humanity cannot be a type of unconditional goodness.

1. The good will is the only thing that is unconditionally good.
2. Humanity has absolute worth.
3. Good will ≠ humanity.

These three claims are inconsistent on an axiological reading. If the absolute worth of humanity is a type of unconditional goodness,[5] then a contradiction arises unless one rejects claim 3 and identifies humanity with the good will.[6] This, however, would be misguided. After all, they have different extensions. Although all rational beings have humanity, it is not the case that all rational beings have a good will.[7]

The inconsistency can be avoided by a deontological reading of humanity that distinguishes the axiological property of something that is unconditionally good

THE DIGNITY OF HUMANITY   155

from the deontological status that something has that possesses dignity. On such a reading, claim 1 attributes an axiological property to the good will, whereas claim 2 asserts of (bearers of) humanity that they have a distinctive deontological status. (What exactly this status consists in will be discussed in Section 2.) This does not involve a contradiction, since these two attributions belong to different domains that do not conflict. The status vs. value distinction, in this way, allows us to resolve this seeming conflict.

1.2 The Objects of Practical Reason

Relatedly, there is no room for humanity construed as something that is good within Kant's theory of value, which he puts forward in the second chapter of the analytic of pure practical reason in the *Critique of Practical Reason*. To be intrinsically good is to be an (immediate) object of practical reason. Given Kant's dualistic theory, there are two such objects. Happiness, or more precisely the state of affairs consisting in the agent being happy, is the object of empirical practical reason and is, as such, the natural good. The good will, or more precisely the state of affairs consisting in the agent having a good will, is the object of pure practical reason and is the moral good. Happiness and the good will, accordingly, turn out to be the only possible intrinsic goods.[8] Since these two objects of practical reason exhaust what is intrinsically good, one can find a place for dignity (which is meant to be of intrinsic significance) only by construing it in deontological rather than axiological terms.

Kant's theory of value, moreover, implies that it is a category mistake to consider humanity to be good. Since being good amounts to being an object of practical reason and since the objects of practical reason are states of affairs that are to be brought about, it follows that value bearers are states of affairs. As Kant makes clear at 5:57, these objects are possible effects that can be brought about by means of the causality of freedom. While the immediate objects of practical reason are intrinsically good and are ends that are to be effected ("*bewirkenden* Zwecke" [4:437]),[9] the mediate objects are extrinsically good and are means to be taken. Humanity, however, is not a state of affairs that is to be brought about but a self-standing end ("*selbstständiger* Zweck" [4:437]). Such ends are prior to action. Instead of being brought about by the causality of our actions, they precede our actions. The problem is thus that value applies only to ends that are to be effected (as well as the means that are to be taken to effect these ends), since only they are objects of practical reason, and not to self-standing ends. Since humanity is a self-standing end, it does not have a place in the realm of value.[10]

Furthermore, the objects of practical reason are not shared. Although all of us have the same objects when considered as types, the tokens differ from person

156 RETHINKING THE VALUE OF HUMANITY

to person. In the case of both empirical and pure practical reason, the object is an end for me, i.e. an end that I am to bring about. My being happy is the object of my empirical practical reason, whereas my having a good will is the object of my pure practical reason. These are the objects of my will, the objects that I can bring about by means of my freedom. This is particularly clear in the case of the good will. My having a good will is something that only I can bring about, since an agent's disposition (*Gesinnung*) is the result of a free choice on the part of the agent. Accordingly, it is not something that can be the object of another's will (but at most the object of another's wish; cf. 6:213). Even the highest good is to be understood as an object of each person's will. It is only the highest good of the world (as opposed to the highest good in a person) that is not restricted in this way. Yet, the highest good of the world is not an object of any finite rational creature's will, but only the object of God's will (cf. Bader 2015b, sec. 5). Humanity, however, is not an end for a particular agent that is to be brought about by him or her. It is a shared end, in particular an objective end that is to be respected by everyone (4:431). Instead of being an end for someone, it is an end-in-itself.

1.3 The Priority of the Right over the Good

Kant argues in the second chapter of the analytic of pure practical reason that the law has to come first and that value comes second in the case of morality. Unlike in the case of prudence, where value comes first and determines the principle, the law has priority when it comes to moral value (cf. the paradox of method 5:62–63).[11] Something is morally good because it is to be brought about, rather than to be brought about because it is good. Value thus cannot play a foundational role in morality.[12] Accordingly, it is not possible for the 'value of humanity' to function as the ground of morality. Morality is grounded in pure practical reason, not in values.

1.4 Perfect and Imperfect Duties

The categorical imperative is a single principle that generates both perfect and imperfect duties. If one is to ground the categorical imperative in a value, then one needs to provide a unified explanation of both perfect and imperfect duties in terms of this value. Axiological accounts, however, have difficulties in explaining these two types of duties and are unable to provide a unified explanation that underwrites both of them.

On the one hand, problems arise in the case of imperfect duties, when it comes to explaining both their strength and their content. First, value-based

THE DIGNITY OF HUMANITY   157

explanations of imperfect duties, such as the duty of beneficence, render this kind of duty too rigorous and demanding. The pursuit of self-love will no longer merely be limited by considerations of duty but will be ruled out altogether, since one will then be required to always act from duty and never on the basis of self-love whenever beneficent actions are possible.[13] This conflicts with its being a wide duty that allows for latitude. Second, they will have difficulty in explaining why the duty of beneficence is restricted to helping those who are in need rather than being an unrestricted duty to help others in general. Imperfect duties, when explained axiologically, thus risk being both too demanding and not suitably restricted.

On the other hand, axiological accounts of perfect duties also face difficulties. Since values allow for commensurability, an axiological reading conflicts with the idea that dignity is inviolable and does not admit of trade-offs. To preclude trade-offs one can try to bring in infinite or incomparable values.[14] Either way, one can at best ensure that humanity is not to be traded off against mere things, i.e. against what merely has price and lacks dignity. However, one cannot rule out trade-offs at the level of humanity, given that dignity would seem to be commensurable with itself. Accordingly, one ends up with a 'utilitarianism of rights.' As Nozick (1974, 32) notes, "Had Kant held [an axiological, or end-state, view], he would have given the second formula of the categorical imperative as, 'So act as to minimize the use of humanity simply as a means,' rather than the one he actually used." As a result, one ends up with an account of perfect duties that is too permissive and does not underwrite inviolability.[15]

It might be objected that an axiological approach can avoid these difficulties as long as it recognizes that there are different ways in which one can respond to value. If one holds that not all values are to be promoted, in the sense that one is to bring about the greatest possible instantiation of these values, but that some values are to be honored or respected, then one can underwrite inviolability by claiming that dignity is a value that is to be respected rather than promoted and hence does not allow for trade-offs.

Even if one grants that there are both values that are to be promoted and values that are to be respected,[16] it is not possible to simultaneously generate both perfect and imperfect duties on the basis of a single value. They cannot both be grounded in the value of humanity, since it is not possible for one and the same value to require both promotion and respect. For Kant, what is to be respected and what is to be promoted belong to different ontological categories. Whereas respect can be required in the case of existing objects, promoting can only be an appropriate way of responding to states of affairs that are to be brought about. Objects and states of affairs are distinct ontological categories, making it impossible for anything to belong to both of them. Since nothing can simultaneously be both an existing object and a state of affairs that is to be brought about, it is not

158 RETHINKING THE VALUE OF HUMANITY

possible for one and the same thing to be such that it is both to be respected and to be promoted. It can be only one or the other, but not both.

Since perfect duties would have to be explained in terms of a value that is to be respected, whereas imperfect duties would have to be explained in terms of a value that is to be promoted, it follows that a single value cannot underwrite both of these types of duties. Either the value of humanity is a value that is to be respected, in which case, one can account for perfect duties, yet imperfect duties fall by the wayside, or it is a value that is to be promoted, in which case one might be able to account for imperfect duties (though, as we have seen, difficulties arise regarding both the strength and the content of imperfect duties) but is unable to explain perfect duties. When proponents of the 'value of humanity' interpretation indiscriminately refer to 'respecting,' 'preserving,' 'enhancing,' 'furthering,' and 'promoting' humanity, they are grouping together radically different responses that cannot be required with respect to one and the same thing. It is, accordingly, not possible to ground both perfect duties (duties of respect) and imperfect duties (duties of promotion) in one and the same value.

1.5 The Argument for Humanity

Kant argues that there must be an end-in-itself if there is to be a categorical imperative. He considers various candidates and argues by elimination that only persons can be ends-in-themselves.[17] A puzzling feature of this argument is that Kant considers neither happiness nor the good will.[18] Their absence is rather conspicuous, especially so if one construes the idea of an end-in-itself axiologically, i.e. as something that is valuable. After all, the good will is unconditionally good, and happiness, though being only conditionally good, is nevertheless good in itself; i.e., it has conditional intrinsic value.[19] The two things that are good in themselves are both absent. This should be rather puzzling if an end-in-itself is something that is good in itself.[20]

(The absence of the good will and of happiness is puzzling not only on the elimination reading but also on the regress reading. A regress argument that starts with something valuable and then regresses to either the source or the condition of value, should consider the two prime candidates for intrinsic goods. Depending on whether the regress is to the source or the condition of value, one would end up either with happiness or with the good will. On the one hand, a regress from derivatively valuable things to the source of their value, i.e. from extrinsic value to intrinsic value, ends up with happiness. This is because things that are extrinsically good, in particular instrumentally good, derive their value from the intrinsically good things that they bring about, namely happiness.[21] On the other hand, a regress from something the value of which is conditioned to

THE DIGNITY OF HUMANITY 159

the condition of this value and ultimately to that the value of which is unconditioned, ends up with the good will, which is the supremum bonum, the unconditioned condition of everything that is conditionally valuable [cf. 5:110]. In
neither case does one end up with humanity.)

The fact that neither happiness nor the good will is considered in the argument for humanity can be explained on a deontological reading. This argument
is not concerned with what is good in itself. Instead, it is concerned with what has
dignity, construed as a deontological status. Whereas something that has value is
to be brought about and is an end that is to be effected, something that has dignity is a self-standing end that needs to be respected. Since Kant is concerned
not with what is valuable but with what has the status of an end-in-itself, all the
candidates that he is considering are existing objects. Only existing objects can
be candidates for being preexisting ends (i.e. something that "*exists* as an end in
itself" [4:428]) that can precede and hence constrain the action (which allows
them to function as the ground of the categorical imperative; see Section 2.5). It
is for this reason that happiness and the good will are excluded. They belong to
the wrong ontological category. My being happy as well as my having a good will
are not preexisting objects but states of affairs that are to be brought about by my
actions. Accordingly, they cannot be self-standing ends, but only ends that are to
be effected.

This reading needs to overcome two difficulties. First, the claim that Kant
considers only existing objects in this argument might be thought to conflict
with the first option, namely objects of inclinations (*Gegenstände der Neigungen*).
Many have construed this option as referring to ends that are to be effected (e.g.,
Allison 2011, 220–221; Timmermann 2006, 74–75). However, when Kant speaks
of 'objects of inclinations' he is concerned only with existing things, not with
states of affairs that an agent desires and intends to bring about. What he is considering are objects that we can use as means in fulfilling our desires, where a
means is an object that constitutes the ground of the possibility of acting in such
a way as to bring about an end; i.e., the means is a thing that can be used and
thereby makes possible an action that has as its effect the realization of an end.[22]
"That, by contrast, which contains merely the ground of the possibility of the action, the effect of which is the end, is called the *means*" (4:427). In the introduction to the Feyerabend lectures, Kant gives the moon as an example of such an
object that has worth (as a means) insofar as it illuminates the earth.

The second problem is to make sense of inclinations (*Neigungen*), which come
up in the second sentence of the argument:

[1] All objects of inclination have a merely conditional worth; since if the
inclinations and the needs that are based thereon were not to exist, then their
object would be without worth. [2] Inclinations themselves, however, as sources

160 RETHINKING THE VALUE OF HUMANITY

of needs, are so far from having an absolute worth, such that one would wish them themselves, that being wholly free of them has to rather be the universal wish of every rational being. [3] Thus the worth of all objects *to be acquired* through our actions is always conditioned. (4:428)

It is usually thought that Kant considers four candidates: (1) objects of inclinations, (2) inclinations themselves, (3) nonrational beings, and (4) rational beings.[23] By eliminating the first three options, we end up with persons/rational beings as the only suitable candidate. This traditional reading conflicts with the proposed interpretation. The second candidate does not fit. Inclinations are not existing objects—they are not substances but attributes. Accordingly, they are not plausible candidates for being self-standing ends. The traditional interpretation, however, is misguided in treating inclinations as one of the candidates that needs to be eliminated. Kant considers only three candidates, not four. Inclinations are not meant to be an alternative in their own right.[24]

Rather than being put forward as a possible candidate for being ends-in-themselves, inclinations are brought in only to explain why inanimate objects are not ends-in-themselves. It is for this reason that the third sentence of the argument reads, "Thus the worth of all objects *to be acquired* through our actions is always conditioned." This sentence is expressed as a conclusion (*Also*) that is meant to follow from the previous two sentences. What is concluded in this sentence corresponds pretty much directly to what is asserted in the first part of the first sentence. This causes difficulties for the standard interpretation, which takes the claim that objects of inclinations are eliminated due to having only conditional worth to be already established by the first sentence. The third sentence would then be out of place. It would be nothing but a reassertion of what was meant to have been established two sentences earlier. What reason would Kant have for eliminating options 1 and 2 in the first two sentences, respectively, and then restating in the form of a conclusion the rejection of option 1 in the third sentence?

We can avoid this problematic reading and instead treat the third sentence as stating a conclusion that does follow from the prior two sentences. The first part of the first sentence states what is to be established (objects have *bedingten Wert*). Kant then starts his argument (*denn*) for this claim in the second part of the sentence. Objects of inclinations derive their worth from inclinations and would be without any worth were it not for the inclinations. The second sentence argues that the things which condition the worth of these objects, namely the inclinations, do not have absolute worth. The conclusion stated in the third sentence then follows. Since inclinations do not have absolute worth, their objects cannot derive absolute worth from them. Accordingly, objects that can be acquired can have only conditional worth.

THE DIGNITY OF HUMANITY 161

The Feyerabend lecture notes (which were taken during the winter semester 1784, i.e. around the time Kant submitted the manuscript of the *Groundwork* to his publisher) provide further support for the two claims that (i) objects of inclinations are existing things and not ends to be effected and that (ii) Kant is concerned with only three rather than four candidates. In the opening paragraph of his lecture course, Kant puts forward an analogous elimination argument in which he only considers (1) inanimate things, (2) animals, and (3) humans. Objects of inclinations are identified with inanimate things, and inclinations themselves do not come up at all.[25]

This interpretation, moreover, allows us to establish the exhaustiveness of the candidates under consideration. An argument by elimination succeeds only when the set of candidates is exhaustive. Exhaustiveness, however, has been called into doubt: "[M]ight not Kant have overlooked some other candidate for absolute goodness?" (Kerstein 2006, 204). Kerstein puts forward the state of affairs in which all rational beings are happy as an alternative candidate. This state of affairs, however, can be excluded on the grounds that it is an end that is to be effected. Since Kant is concerned with self-standing/preexisting ends rather than with ends that are to be effected, the range of possible candidates is drastically reduced.

Not only is the range of candidates reduced but also their heterogeneity. The more heterogeneous the candidates under consideration, the more difficult it is to show that they result from a number of exhaustive divisions and consequently exhaust the set of possible candidates. If the set of candidates were to include objects of inclinations, where these are construed as ends to be effected, as well as inclinations themselves, then the candidates would form a rather heterogeneous bunch. It would then be unlikely that the entire set of possibilities could be exhausted by four candidates. This problem of heterogeneity is avoided if (i) objects of inclinations are construed as existing things rather than as states of affairs that are to be brought about and (ii) inclinations themselves are not a candidate in their own right but are brought in only to rule out objects of inclinations.

By excluding states of affairs that are to be brought about, as well as inclinations themselves, and thereby restricting the candidates for self-standing ends to existing things, i.e. substances, one ends up with a suitably homogeneous set of candidates that can be generated by two exhaustive divisions. The set of existing things can be exhaustively and exclusively divided: things are either inanimate (= option 1) or animate, and if animate then either nonrational (= option 2) or rational (= option 3). The exhaustiveness of this division ensures that by eliminating options 1 and 2, one can establish that option 3 is the correct option, i.e. that rational beings are ends-in-themselves.[26] Construed in this way, the contrast between *Sachen*, which lack dignity, and *Personen*, which have dignity, constitutes a sharp dichotomy among existing things.

162 RETHINKING THE VALUE OF HUMANITY

2. Dignity as Status

Humanity is not an end that is to be brought about, but a self-standing end that is to be respected. This means that dignity is to be construed not axiologically but deontologically. It is not a value but, as we will see shortly, a status. Speaking of the 'value of humanity' is, accordingly, misleading and to be replaced by the 'status of humanity.' Being an end-in-itself is a distinctly deontic phenomenon. The key question then is: What is the role of self-standing ends? The answer is that they determine the domain of universalization.

2.1 The Domain of Universalization

The categorical imperative requires our maxims to have universal validity. It must be possible for them to become laws. Although it is clear that our maxims have to be universalizable, it is not so clear with respect to whom they have to be universalizable. For whom is the maxim meant to be valid? For whom is it meant to become a law? These questions might seem to have an easy answer: something is universally valid if it is valid for everyone. A law is something that governs everyone without exception. "Everyone," however, is a universal quantifier over a given domain. This means that we need to be given a domain. Without a domain, the requirement of universalizability does not make sense.

There needs to be something that determines which entities are members of the domain of universalization. The members of the domain need to share certain features with the agent. There needs to be something that they share in common that makes all of them members of the domain. What is the condition that they must satisfy? What are the features that something needs to share with me such that I need to act toward that thing in ways that are universalizable?

There is an important sense in which maxims by themselves do not suffice. One needs both maxims and status. Whether X's maxim needs to be universalizable with respect to Y depends on the status of both X and Y. Both X and Y have to have dignity for this requirement to be applicable. The status of the agent together with the status of the patient explains the normative relation between them. Both of them have to belong to the domain of universalization in order for the categorical imperative to apply to their interactions. The categorical imperative governs interactions among members of the domain and does not concern relations to things that are outside of the domain. No restrictions are imposed on how mere things are to be used, nor are there restrictions on how mere things are to act toward us. The normative significance of dignity is thus restricted to others who likewise have this status, i.e. to other agents with whom one can stand in relations of reciprocity.

In order for the categorical imperative to be applicable to the actions of the agent X, he has to be capable of acting morally.[27] This means that he has to have pure practical reason, which tells him how to act, namely on maxims that are universalizable, and which provides him with an incentive, namely respect for the law, to act accordingly. Since, as we will see in Section 2.2, the capacity to act morally, i.e. act on the basis of the categorical imperative, is the ground of dignity, i.e. it is that in virtue of which someone has dignity, it follows that an agent to whom the categorical imperative applies is someone who has dignity.

The patient Y likewise has to have dignity. It is Y's status that determines whether Y, who is affected by X's action, needs to be able to act on the very same maxim as X. If Y has dignity, then Y is included in the domain of universalization, such that X's action toward Y needs to be reciprocally implementable. Otherwise, Y is a mere thing that is excluded from the domain. It is for this reason that it is possible for an action to be permissible when done to a mere thing, yet to be impermissible when done to a person. The same kind of action, involving the same maxim, is permissible in one situation but impermissible in the other.[28] The difference between these cases is due to the status of the thing being acted upon. The maxim needs to be universalizable in the case of a person but not in the case of a mere thing. How X ought to treat Y thus depends on Y's status.

Mere things are not members of the domain of universalization. They have an inferior status, in that they are subordinated to ends-in-themselves and do not have to be respected by them. Either they lack wishes, desires, and volitions (= inanimate objects), or they have them but they can be ignored (= nonrational animals). As a result, they can be treated as mere means. Ends-in-themselves, by contrast, are elevated above things that merely have a price. They have to be respected and cannot be treated as mere means. Instead of the asymmetric relationship between an end-in-itself and a mere thing, the relationship among ends-in-themselves is symmetric. Here we are dealing not with subordination but with coordination.

The domain of universalization is fixed by dignity. Something that has dignity is included in the domain of universalization rather than in the domain of things (which can be ignored when universalizing maxims). Since rational beings have dignity, they have to respect each other. The categorical imperative requires them to act on maxims that have universality over the domain of universalization. They have to treat humanity (whether in their own person or in that of others) as an end-in-itself, where an end-in-itself is something that belongs to the domain over which maxims have to be univerzalisable. They are required to not elevate themselves above other rational beings by treating them as being subordinate and on par with a mere thing. Instead, they have to respect that they all have the same status and belong to the same domain and hence are to relate to each other reciprocally. Accordingly, they are not allowed to make exceptions for themselves

164 RETHINKING THE VALUE OF HUMANITY

(/for this once), but have to act in ways that are reciprocally implementable, i.e. universalizable.

Dignity thus plays a crucial role by fixing the domain over which maxims have to be universalizable. It specifies with respect to which entities I need to coordinate my actions, as well as which entities are such that I can subordinate them to my purposes and use as mere means.

2.2 The Capacity to Act on Maxims

It might be objected that the appeal to dignity in fixing the domain of universalization is redundant since one can simply consider this domain to consist of all agents. The reciprocal implementability of maxims does not apply when an agent acts toward a nonagent. Something that cannot act on maxims is by its very nature excluded from considerations of reciprocity. It makes no sense to ask whether something that is incapable of acting on maxims can reciprocally act on the same maxim. Things that are incapable of acting on maxims are, accordingly, excluded from universalization. This restriction follows from the very idea of universalizing a maxim. The logic of universalization excludes mere things and restricts the domain to agents, i.e. to beings that can act on maxims.

Something that is not capable of acting on maxims is not something with respect to which the universalizability of maxims can be assessed. This, however, leaves it open that there could be additional restrictions on the domain. That is, there could be restrictions that are imposed by pure practical reason rather than by the very idea of acting on maxims. To address this issue we have to supplement our account of what dignity consists in, i.e. what it is to have dignity and what role this status plays in Kant's theory. We have to investigate what the ground of dignity is, i.e. in virtue of which features something has dignity. This amounts to giving an account of what humanity, i.e. the ground of dignity, consists in.

The crucial question for our purposes is whether the ability to act on maxims is the ground of being an end-in-itself (in which case the domain consists of all agents and the only things that are excluded are things with respect to which it makes no sense to universalize), or whether a more demanding condition such as having pure practical reason has to be met (leading to a more restricted domain, the specification of which does not follow from the very idea of universalizing maxims). Put differently, the question is whether the capacity to act on maxims is too thin as a ground of dignity.

Some interpreters have thought that the capacity for end-setting suffices (most notably Wood 1999 and Korsgaard 1996). However, there is a great deal of textual evidence that Kant thought otherwise. In the *Metaphysics of Morals*, Kant notes, "Even the fact that he has the advantage over them [= the other animals]

THE DIGNITY OF HUMANITY   165

that he has understanding and can set himself ends does not give him anything but an *outer* value due to his usefulness (*pretium usus*), namely of one man over another, i.e. a price" (6:434). Having understanding and being capable of setting ends does not suffice for dignity. What is needed instead is pure practical reason (*moralisch-praktischen Vernunft* [6:434]). Humanity has dignity because it is capable of acting morally (cf. 4:435, 5:87). This is because agents who are capable of acting morally partake in the dignity of morality.[29]

Dignity is not grounded in the capacity to set ends and act on maxims, but rather in the capacity to be moral. We have to distinguish between a *Vernunftwesen* and a *blos vernünftiges Wesen* (6:418; also see 6:456).[30] The latter, though being a rational being, lacks pure practical reason and hence does not have dignity (cf. 6:28). Dignity requires not only that one can engage in instrumental reasoning but that reason by itself can be practical.[31] Reason has to provide its own incentive and thereby enable us to act out of respect for the law. The capacity to be moral requires not only empirical but also pure practical reason, since this involves an entirely different source of incentives from that which is operative in the instrumental case.[32] "It does not at all follow from the fact that a being has reason that it [i.e. reason] contains the capacity to unconditionally determine the faculty of choice by means of the mere representation of its maxims as qualifying for universal law-giving and thereby be practical by itself: at least as far as we can see" (6:26n).

If there are beings that can engage in instrumental reasoning, yet that lack pure practical reason, then there are beings that can set ends and act on maxims yet nevertheless are not owed respect and are not members of the domain of universalization.[33] This means that we have to universalize across all those rational beings who are capable of acting morally. Rather than having to act only on maxims that one can will at the same time to become a law for everyone who can act on maxims, one has to act only on maxims that one can will at the same time to become a law for everyone who is capable of acting morally.

It might be suggested that this domain restriction follows from the very idea of universalizability, insofar as one is required to act reciprocally with respect to all those who are likewise required to act reciprocally. However, there is an important distinction between those who can act on maxims that are universalizable and those who can act on universalizable maxims because they are universalizable (i.e. those who can act according to duty vs. those who can act out of duty). The former merely presupposes the capacity to act on maxims. The latter, in addition, requires pure practical reason. It is not clear whether the very idea of universalizability can decide between these two possibilities and privilege the latter over the former, which suggests that the specification of the domain is imposed by pure practical reason.

166   RETHINKING THE VALUE OF HUMANITY

2.3 Dignity and the Good Will

We have seen that dignity is possessed by all those who have the capacity to act morally. It might be wondered why dignity is not only had by those who do in fact act morally, i.e. those who have a good will.[34] Kerstein (2006, 218), for instance, asks, "What justification does Kant have for holding that it is beings with rational nature who constitute the ground of a categorical imperative, rather than maintaining that it is merely beings with a good will who do so? What, for example, permits Kant to reject the view that it is not all of us, but rather only those of us with a good will, who never ought to be treated merely as means?"

The proposed interpretation allows us to answer this question. Something can be treated as a mere means if it belongs to the domain of things. The question then becomes: Why do people who have a bad will not belong to the domain of things? The answer is that those who have a bad will are equally subject to the categorical imperative and must hence likewise be members of the domain of universalization. The categorical imperative addresses itself to the members of this domain, requiring them to treat each other in ways that are universalizable. If one were to exclude those who have a bad will from the domain of universalization, then one would not only get the problematic result that those who have a good will do not need to respect them, but also that they do not need to respect those who have a good will. This is because morality is reciprocal. The requirement of universalization applies only to members of the domain vis-à-vis other members of the domain. Both the agent and the patient need to belong to this domain.

Agents who are subject to the categorical imperative need to be members of the domain, independently of how they choose. Acting in a nonuniversalizable manner would, otherwise, ensure that one would not be a member of the domain and hence not be subject to the requirement. As a result, a good will cannot be the relevant feature that makes someone a member of the domain. An agent does not have a good will prior to choice but as a result of the choice. Having a good will consists in giving priority to duty over self-love. This is something that the agent does by making a choice. The agent determines whether he has a good will or a bad will by freely ordering the sources of incentives. Since a good will does not precede the choice of maxim, the agent does not have a good will at the stage of evaluation, which ensures that this cannot be a feature that is required for belonging to the domain of universalization.

The problem is particularly pressing when it comes to duties to the self. In that case the agent is also the patient. If the good will were to be a requirement on being a member of the domain of universalization, then one would end up with contradictions. By treating oneself as a mere means and violating a duty toward oneself, one makes it the case that one has a bad will. This, then, would ensure that one is not a member of this domain. As a result, it would not be necessary that one treat oneself as an end, which contradicts the assumption that one violated a duty to oneself.

We, consequently, need to appeal to features that the agent has independently of how he chooses. Unlike in the case of the hypothetical imperative, where the imperative is grounded in an end that is to be effected and that does not precede the choice but is only brought about by the choice, self-standing ends that precede the choice are required in the case of the categorical imperative. Whereas ends guide choice in the case of hypothetical imperatives, ends constrain the agent's choice in the case of the categorical imperative. In order to constrain the choice, we need something that precedes it. It is for this reason that the domain of universalization cannot be fixed by the property of having a good will. Instead, it is fixed by humanity, i.e. the capacity of acting morally.

2.4 Dignity and Price

Like dignity, price applies to objects. It applies to preexisting things rather than to states of affairs that can be brought about. Unlike dignity, it is not restricted to objects that have a distinctive deontic status, but applies to all objects. Everything has a price. Price applies to things insofar as they can be used as means in bringing about various states of affairs. A means is something that is useful, something that can be used to bring about various effects. The price of a thing is a function of its usefulness. It is determined by the potential effects that can be brought about by means of this thing. Things that can bring about the same effect are equally useful and are hence equivalent qua means (cf. 7:292). Accordingly, it does not matter which one is used. One gets the same result either way. Accordingly, they have the same price, no matter how heterogeneous they might otherwise be. "Things that are heterogeneous can have the same worth as long as they are homogeneous in their usefulness" (*Feyerabend*, Vol. 2, 75).

Things that lack dignity merely have price. Something that is merely a means is not of significance in its own right but matters only insofar as it is useful. Things that matter only because of the effects that they can bring about are exchangeable when having the same price. Given their equivalence, they can be replaced by each other (cf. 4:434). As long as they have the same effects, they can be treated interchangeably.

Something that has dignity, by contrast, matters not merely because of how useful it is. Things that have dignity matter in their own right and not merely because of what they can effect. They are beyond price in the sense that they matter beyond their usefulness and thus, unlike mere means, cannot simply be replaced by something that is equally useful, which means that they do not have

168 RETHINKING THE VALUE OF HUMANITY

equivalents. Humanity is thus above things that merely have price, not in the sense of having a greater worth but in the sense of being elevated above them. Humanity belongs to a different sphere, namely to the domain of ends rather than the domain of mere means whose significance is exhausted by their usefulness.

The distinction between mere price and dignity is one among existing things and aligns with the distinction between things and persons. The relevant contrast is not between those things that have price and those that have dignity, but between those that merely have price and those that, in addition, also have dignity. Existing things are either mere means (that have only price) or ends-in-themselves (that have dignity in addition to price). Both things and persons can be used as means and hence have price. Yet, whereas objects that merely have price can be treated as mere means, persons have dignity and are to be respected. It is for this reason that one can treat the former as mere means, while having to treat the latter as ends-in-themselves. Persons are useful and can be treated as means, but not as mere means, since, in addition to having price, they also have dignity (cf. 6:434, R8066, R1517–1518).

The fact that human beings have both price and dignity, i.e. they are useful yet are also to be respected, shows particularly clearly that the distinction between price and dignity does not correspond to that between ends that are to be effected (= what is to be promoted) and self-standing ends (= what is to be respected). These different types of ends belong to different ontological categories (namely, valuable states of affairs that can be brought about vs. existing objects that have dignity) and hence cannot apply to one and the same thing. This means that we should not identify, as some have done (e.g., Velleman 2006, 99, 101), dignity with what is to be respected and price with what is to be promoted. Like dignity, price is not concerned with what is to be effected.[35] Things have price, yet things are not to be promoted. Instead, it is valuable states of affairs that are to be promoted. What has price is something that is useful in promoting those things that are to be promoted (namely states of affairs that have intrinsic value).[36] Instead of being an end that is to be effected, something that has price is a means that can be used in bringing about various ends.

2.5 The Ground of the Categorical Imperative

At 4:428 Kant claims that something that is an end-in-itself is the ground of the categorical imperative. Ends that are to be effected function as grounds of hypothetical imperatives, insofar as the having of the end explains why the means are to be taken. The categorical imperative, however, cannot be grounded in an analogous way, since it is not based on a means-end relationship. Accordingly, an altogether different explanation is required when explaining how a self-standing end can function as a ground of an imperative.

THE DIGNITY OF HUMANITY 169

Such an explanation can be provided by considering dignity as what fixes the domain of universalization. This is because moral laws would be inapplicable if there were no ends-in-themselves, in the same way that the laws of motion would be inapplicable if there were no matter. There must be ends-in-themselves for morality to be objectively real, in the sense of there being anything that is good or right. Otherwise, the domain would be empty and the moral law would not apply to anything. This means that we need something existent to ensure a nonempty domain. Something must exist to which the moral law applies (both qua subject/agent and qua object/patient), namely rational beings that have dignity and are ends-in-themselves.[37]

The fact that the moral law would be empty is in fact even clearer than in the case of the laws of motion, since what is needed in the case of morality is not merely something to which the law applies, i.e. something that can be subsumed under and be governed by the law, but, given that the moral law is self-imposed, someone who applies the law to himself. As Kant argues, we are not authors of the law, but are only authors of the obligation (cf. 6:227). Accordingly, the law could still be said to exist if there were no one who had dignity. Yet there would be no obligations, since there would not be anyone who would impose the law upon himself. There would not be anyone from whose pure practical reason the obligation could issue. Morality would then not be binding for anyone.

On this account, dignity is not invoked to justify moral principles. We do not derive the requirement of universalization from the idea of dignity. Dignity does not explain why maxims need to have universal validity. Instead, it explains why X's maxims need to be universalizable with respect to Y. By fixing the domain of universalization and determining across which agents maxims have to be universalizable, dignity provides objective reality to morality. Since the objective reality of morality requires not only the moral law but also a nonempty domain, it is the dignity of humanity that ensures that morality is applicable and not empty.

We can now better appreciate why *Groundwork III* is needed. Sections I and II are concerned with identifying (*Aufsuchung*) the supreme principle of morality. They analyze common moral cognition and proceed on the assumption that morality is objectively real. Section III, by contrast, proceeds synthetically and is meant to substantiate (*Festsetzung*) the supreme principle. This latter task amounts to establishing that morality is in fact objectively real, in particular that it is "something" (cf. 4:445) rather than nothing (the type of nothing at issue here is that of an *ens rationis*; cf. A290–291/B347). The concern that Kant raises at the end of Section II and addresses in Section III is not that there might be some mistake in the derivation of the categorical imperative, i.e. that he might have misidentified the supreme principle. Instead, the problem is that morality could, for all we know, be empty. It would then be a mere thought entity to which nothing corresponds in reality, a figment of the imagination that lacks any basis in reality.

170 RETHINKING THE VALUE OF HUMANITY

Groundwork III addresses this worry by establishing that we are free and that pure reason can be practical. This amounts to showing that there are beings that have dignity, that are bound by the categorical imperative and that need to be treated in accordance with it. That there are rational beings to whom morality is applicable shows that morality is not empty. Whereas in Section II we can assert the existence of ends-in-themselves only as a postulate, Section III identifies the grounds for this assertion (cf. 4:429n). Morality then turns out to be not only logically but also really possible. The dignity of humanity, accordingly, gives objective reality to the categorical imperative and hence classifies as its ground.[38]

2.6 Form and Matter

The three variants of the categorical imperative are meant to be extensionally equivalent (cf. 4:436). On the face of it, it is difficult to make sense of this equivalence, since the formula of humanity does not seem to be concerned with universalization (cf. Timmons 2017, 51) and does not, unlike the other formulas, make explicit reference to maxims. However, by construing what it is to treat someone not as a mere means but as an end-in-itself in terms of respecting that person's status as a member of the domain across which maxims have to be universalizable, i.e. as a person with whom one has to interact in ways that are reciprocally implementable, we can explain both how this formula implicitly involves maxims and how it is ultimately concerned with universalization.

Whereas the formula of the law of nature requires our maxims to be universalizable, i.e. they have to have the form of a law of nature, the formula of humanity tells us that humanity is to be included in the domain of universalization, i.e. that we are to respect the dignity of humanity by interacting with rational beings on reciprocal terms. The two variants thus differ insofar as the former focuses on the universal validity and hence law-like form that maxims are required to have, while the latter focuses on the members of the domain with respect to which maxims have to be universalizable.[39]

While being extensionally equivalent, the variants differ insofar as they emphasize different aspects of the way in which the categorical imperative relates to our maxims. By highlighting what the moral law requires with respect to the different aspects of our maxims, they help us to better appreciate its significance and bring morality closer to intuition. They thereby make it easier for the moral law to gain access (cf. 4:437). In particular, they emphasize the way in which the moral law relates to the form and matter of particular maxims taken by themselves, as well as to the complete determination of all maxims taken collectively.

THE DIGNITY OF HUMANITY 171

1. Every maxim has a form. The categorical imperative requires maxims to have a certain form, namely universality as opposed to mere generality. This means that they have to be alike to laws of nature, which have universal validity.

2. Every maxim has a matter, namely an end. The categorical imperative does not provide the matter to our maxims. Nor does humanity constitute the relevant matter.[40] The ends of the maxims that are assessed for universalizability are given not by morality but by inclinations. Our inclinations put forward ends, and instrumental reasoning identifies the practical rules that best realize these ends. It is these rules that are assessed as to whether or not they are universalizable. The ends in question are, accordingly, the various relative ends that agents have. These are ends to be effected, and it is their realization that the maxims aim at.

   Ends-in-themselves are not the ends of our maxims. Instead, they are the restricting condition of all our maxims ("restricting condition of all merely relative and arbitrary ends" [4:436]). The second variant assigns priority to self-standing ends over ends to be effected. The relative ends that we pursue are subordinated to and hence constrained by the self-standing ends that have dignity. The pursuit of our ends is in this way limited by self-standing ends. Unlike things, these self-standing ends, i.e. persons, cannot be used as mere means when pursuing our relative ends. Instead, they need to be respected. They need to be treated in a way that is fitting for members of the domain of universalization. Respecting ends-in-themselves is thus prioritized over effecting relative ends, which is why Kant speaks of the "*end prioritization* [*Zwecksvorzuges*] of rational beings in themselves" (4:431) when referring back to the second variant.

3. The third variant, the formula of the realm of ends, combines the prior two ("unites the other two by itself within it" [4:436]). It is a synthetic unity that results from their combination, analogous to the way in which the third category under each heading in the table of categories is a (nonderivative) combination of the prior two (cf. B110). Kant models the relation of the three variants on that of the categories of quantity. We have a progression from unity to plurality to totality. In the theoretical case a totality is nothing other than a plurality considered as a unity. Similarly, a realm of ends is a systematic unity that results from considering a plurality of relative ends ("*plurality* of the matter [of the objects, i.e. the ends]" [4:436]) as being unified by the form of the will, which consists in universality. The relative ends had by the ends-in-themselves are systematized and unified by the form of universality. The realm of ends, in this way, involves the law-governed pursuit of each individual's relative ends. The maxims taken together, accordingly, form a completely determined system.

172 RETHINKING THE VALUE OF HUMANITY

A number of commentators have thought that the relevant plurality that is being unified concerns ends-in-themselves rather than the relative ends that various agents are pursuing (e.g., Paton 1947, 185; Timmermann 2007, 111). This, however, is mistaken. Although ends-in-themselves are members of the realm of ends, what is being determined and unified are relative ends. As Kant notes in the *Amphiboly*, matter is the determinable, i.e. that which can be determined, whereas form is the determination thereof (cf. A266/B322). The ends-in-themselves are not being determined. They are not the determinable. Instead, it is their maxims, in particular the matter of their maxims, that is being determined. Their relative ends are coordinated, subordinated, and limited in such a way as to avoid conflicts and ensure universalizability. This is why the realm of ends is concerned with the complete determination of all maxims.

2.7 Relative Ends and Ends-in-Themselves

Relative ends and ends-in-themselves are radically different. The former are states of affairs that are to be brought about. The latter are existing objects that are to be respected. Given how much they differ, it is somewhat unclear in what sense both of them are ends. Since humanity does not constitute but instead only restricts the matter of our maxims, we cannot consider both of them to be ends on the basis that they provide the matter for our maxims. The question is thus: What unifies relative ends and ends-in-themselves, such that it is appropriate to classify both of them as 'ends'?

Although the matter of a maxim is an end, it is not the case that all ends constitute the matter of maxims. In particular, ends-in-themselves stand in a different relation to the matter of maxims. Ends are not to be understood in terms of the matter of maxims, but more abstractly. The relevant definition of what it is to be an end is provided by Kant at 4:427: "Now, that which serves the will as its objective ground of self-determination is an *end*, and it, when it is given through pure reason, must hold equally for all rational beings." An end is an objective ground of the self-determination of the will. It is something that determines how the will should determine itself, i.e. how it should act. Unlike the subjective grounds on which the agent does in fact act, objective grounds determine how an agent ought to act.[41]

There are two sources of ends. On the one hand, ends are set by inclinations. These are the various relative ends that are to be brought about and that together determine what the agent's happiness consists in. They are not ends by their nature but only as a result of being desired by this or that individual. This means that they are not ends for everyone but only relative ends for the persons having

THE DIGNITY OF HUMANITY   173

the relevant inclinations. Only those who have these inclinations have prudential reasons to bring about these ends. Such ends specify goals that are to be achieved and thereby provide positive guidance. Since the inclinations that set these ends include both desires and aversions, they provide guidance both with respect to what is to be pursued and what is to be avoided.

On the other hand, ends-in-themselves are set by pure reason. Something that is an end-in-itself is an end by its very nature (cf. "as an end according to its nature, and hence as an end-in-itself" [4:436]). It is, by its very nature, such as to constitute an objective ground of the self-determination of the will. Ends-in-themselves are, accordingly, objective ends, and the moral reasons to which they give rise apply to all agents who are capable of acting morally, independently of what desires they happen to have. Ends-in-themselves are to be respected. They constitute constraints and impose limits on what we are permitted to do in pursuing our relative ends. The guidance that they provide is entirely negative: ends-in-themselves are to be thought "only negatively, i.e. as that against which one must never contravene" (4:437).

The will determines itself negatively by imposing limits on how ends are to be pursued. The negative nature of ends-in-themselves is not to be understood in terms of their requiring omissions.[42] We should not think of relative ends as requiring us to perform certain actions, whereas ends-in-themselves require us to omit certain actions. Instead, relative ends include those set by aversions, which give rise to rules of omission, alongside those set by desires, which give rise to rules of commission. Ends-in-themselves, by contrast, require us to make exceptions to nonuniversalizable maxims. This involves negating the content of the rules proposed by instrumental reasoning when these are not universalizable. Put differently, humanity is not concerned with the copula (i.e., with the contrast between commissions and omissions) but with the content of the maxims (i.e., with what one is required to commit or omit) and thus operates in a way that is analogous to an infinitizing negation (where negation applies to the predicate: 'non-P' rather than to the copula: 'is not'). This content is limited by humanity in such a way as to ensure universalizability.[43]

Everything that one does, where this includes one's inactions just as much as one's actions, has to be respectful of humanity. None of the practical rules that one is permitted to act upon (which includes rules of omission alongside rules of commission) is to contravene against humanity. If a proposed rule does not conform to this condition, then one has to make an exception to this rule. This amounts to prioritizing ends-in-themselves over relative ends; i.e., one subordinates the pursuit of relative ends and makes respecting humanity a condition of their pursuit (= *Zwecksvorzug* [cf. 4:431]). It is for this reason that moral rules are characterized as practical rules of exception in the table of the categories of freedom that have the same place as limitation and infinite judgments in the

174 RETHINKING THE VALUE OF HUMANITY

other tables (cf. 5:65–67; Bader 2009, 809–811). Since this restricting condition applies equally to both actions and inactions, one ends up with negative as well as positive duties. By requiring an exception to a rule of commission one ends up with a negative duty, whereas one ends up with a positive duty by requiring an exception to a rule of omission.

Accordingly, there is no conflict between the claims that ends-in-themselves are to be conceived only negatively and that they can give rise to positive duties (contra Hill 1980, 89). This means that, unlike in the case of axiological accounts (cf. Section 1.4), there is no difficulty in explaining both perfect (negative) and imperfect (positive) duties on the basis of a unified deontic foundation. Correspondingly, we can see that the suggestion that there are two aspects to the formula of humanity, namely that it requires us to (1) treat humanity not merely as a means and (2) treat humanity as an end-in-itself, such that negative duties correspond to the former and positive duties to the latter, is misguided. Treating something not merely as a means is the very same thing as treating it as an end-in-itself, where this amounts to treating it as a member of the domain of universalization. There is only one requirement, not two. Negative and positive duties both follow from this single requirement.

Conclusion

Dignity is not to be construed axiologically. Instead, it is a deontic status that fixes the domain of universalization. Ends-in-themselves have dignity and are members of this domain. Rational beings have to respect such self-standing ends, which means that they are permitted to treat them only in accordance with universalizable principles. Since the domain of universalization would be empty if there should not be anything having dignity, humanity classifies as the ground of the categorical imperative.[44]

Notes

1. These arguments are conditional. At this stage of the *Groundwork*, it is still an epistemic possibility that morality is nothing but a chimera, a figment of the imagination. Ruling out this possibility and establishing the objective reality of morality is the task of *Groundwork III* (cf. Section 2.5).
2. Kant's works are cited in terms of volume and page numbers of the Akademie-Ausgabe (Kant 1900), with the exception of the Feyerabend lecture notes, which refer to the transcription in Delfosse et al. 2010, 2014. Translations are my own.
3. Most notably, Korsgaard 1996, Wood 1999, and Guyer 2000.

THE DIGNITY OF HUMANITY 175

4. Deflationary readings of dignity treat it as being derivative and not capable of doing justificatory work: "'dignity' is not itself a concept that carries any justificatory weight" (Sensen 2009, 331).

5. Something that is absolute "holds without restrictions" (A326/B382) and is contrasted with that which is restricted to certain conditions.

6. Dean (2006) endorses this approach.

7. A good will is not to be confused with a pure will (= *Wille*), which every human being has. A good will is a good disposition (*Gesinnung*), which is only had contingently when self-love is subordinated to duty and which is contrasted with a bad will, which someone has when they are self-conceited and prioritize self-love over duty.

8. Strictly speaking, happiness and the good will are not good but are good-makers. They are not value bearers but properties that are such that their instantiation is good; i.e., the state of affairs in which someone is happy or in which someone has a good will is something that is good.

9. In the case of the good will, it is good because it is to be brought about. In the case of happiness, it is to be brought about because it is good (cf. Section 1.3).

10. Section 2.7 explains in what sense both ends to be effected (relative ends) and self-standing ends (ends-in-themselves) classify as 'ends.'

11. The case of prudence shows that there is no problem as such with grounding a principle in a value, but only with grounding a principle of morality in a value. While hypothetical imperatives can be grounded in the value of happiness, the categorical imperative cannot be grounded in the (supposed) value of humanity. The (natural) good is prior to prudence, yet the right is prior to the (moral) good.

12. Although the unconditional goodness of the good will occupies a prominent role at the beginning of the *Groundwork*, the order of exposition in the *Groundwork* is the inverse of the order of justification, since Kant proceeds analytically in sections I and II of the *Groundwork*, beginning with an analysis of common rational cognition (4:392).

13. Cf. Bader 2017.

14. Incomparability approaches run into difficulties since the incomparable values cannot be integrated into an overall evaluation (cf. Bader 2015a).

15. This approach might underwrite something in the vicinity of what Cummiskey (1996) calls Kantian consequentialism but cannot constitute a foundation of Kant's deontological ethics.

    Inviolability can be generated by appealing to agent- and time-relative values. This, however, involves assigning value, not to humanity, but to the agent's actions. Moreover, one is no longer dealing with objective ends that are shared by everyone, but with agent-relative orderings that vary across agents. Instead of being based on the agent-neutral value of humanity, the resulting theory would be based on the agent- and time-relative disvalue of disrespecting humanity.

16. While it is crucial to distinguish between promoting and respecting, this distinction should not be construed as a distinction within the axiological realm. Instead of there being two ways of responding to value, there are two different things to which one is to respond. Whereas value is to be promoted, status is to be respected. The contrast is not to be found in the axiological realm but rather separates the axiological from the deontological.

17. While agreeing with Timmermann (2006), Kerstein (2006), and Allison (2011) in rejecting the regress readings put forward by Korsgaard and Wood and opting instead for the traditional elimination reading, I disagree with them on how the elimination reading is to be construed.

18. Nor does he consider one's own perfection as well as the happiness of others, which are the two ends that are duties, i.e. the ends that are set by morality.

19. Cf. Bader 2013.

20. Those who think that happiness is extrinsically valuable (due to being conditionally valuable) will nevertheless consider it to be finally valuable (cf. Korsgaard 1996, chap. 9). Since, according to the axiological proposal, ends-in-themselves are those things that are finally valuable, the absence of happiness will likewise be puzzling on this interpretation.

21. While the good will is intrinsically good, it cannot be caused but issues from an uncaused cause, namely freedom, and hence cannot be the end of a regress that proceeds from what is instrumentally valuable to the intrinsic value from which it derives its goodness.

22. Things that can be used have a price, where price is distinct from value; cf. Section 2.4.

23. On rational nature = rational being, see Timmermann 2006, 71–72.

24. For a similar reading, see Stern 2015, 98 (thanks to Nandi Theunissen for this reference).

25. Additionally, considering inclinations as potential candidates for being ends-in-themselves is rather strange (as Allison 2011, 220 recognizes).

    August Friedrich Müller, who is an important precursor of Kant in this context (see Hruschka 1990), develops a similar position. He argues that persons are ends-in-themselves and that both inanimate objects and animate yet nonrational objects are mere means: "Other substances, both living and non-living . . . that do not exist for their own sake and do not have their own ends, but are destined to be only means for the service of the first type of substances, namely persons" (Müller 1733, vol. II 401). Here, it is particularly clear that what is being considered are only substances, i.e. pre-existing objects.

26. Even when exhaustiveness is guaranteed, there is still the question whether all members of the class of rational beings are ends-in-themselves; see Sections 2.2 and 2.3. As it stands, the elimination argument does not suffice for establishing that the class of ends-in-themselves is to be identified with the class of rational beings. Yet, it does establish that the former are among the latter, i.e. that they constitute a proper or improper subclass.

    As noted earlier, the arguments in *Groundwork II* are conditional, insofar as the objective reality of morality is taken for granted. This means that the elimination argument establishes that rational beings are ends-in-themselves only on condition that the categorical imperative has objective reality.

27. It is for this reason that, for instance, the killing of a person by an animal does not amount to an infringement of dignity. (By contrast, from an axiological point of view this would seem to be equally problematic as the killing by a person, at least when considered from the perspective of the person being killed, since the value of

THE DIGNITY OF HUMANITY   177

humanity would be undermined in each case. Although one can argue that animals cannot wrong anyone, as far as the person being killed is concerned, the value of humanity is nevertheless compromised.)

28. Maxims are proposed by instrumental reasoning, which is not sensitive to distinctions in moral status but operates at the descriptive level of causal connections, where human beings and mere things can be similarly causally implicated in our actions. Accordingly, the relevant differences are not at the level of maxims.

29. It is for this reason that respect for persons is really respect for the law (4:401n).

This interpretation might seem to conflict with 4:437, where Kant claims that "rational nature is set apart from the others by this, that it sets itself an end." This passage has often been cited in support of taking the capacity to set ends as the ground of dignity, e.g., by Wood 1999, 118–119. Allison (2011, 210) goes so far as to claim that "[t]his view receives its most direct support from Kant's statement [at 4:437]." However, this involves a twofold misreading of this passage. First, it is not concerned with a general capacity to set ends, but instead with a particular end, namely an end of morality that rational nature sets for us. This is why Kant speaks of 'an end' in the singular and not 'ends' in the plural. Second, the end in question is not even an end to be effected, i.e. an end that is chosen and that we can pursue insofar as it constitutes the matter of our maxims, but a self-standing end that functions as the limiting condition of our actions. In short, whereas the ends that we set ourselves are ends to be promoted, the end that rational nature sets for us is one that we have to respect.

30. This corresponds to Kant's distinction between the different predispositions in the *Religion*, in particular the contrast between the predisposition to humanity vs. to personality (see 6:26, esp. the footnote). Also see R7308, where being an end-in-itself is explained in terms of personality. ('Humanity' in the formula of humanity is not to be understood in the narrow, technical sense given to this term in the *Religion* but as encompassing personality.)

31. Since there is a good case to be made to the effect that the normativity of hypothetical imperatives presupposes being subject to the categorical imperative, the type of instrumental reasoning of which beings who lack pure practical reason are capable may well be of a purely theoretical nature and be devoid of normativity, which would ensure that such beings would not be capable of practical (ir)rationality but only of theoretical (ir)rationality (cf. Bader 2014, sec. 3.4).

32. Asserting that reason can be practical in this way is in fact a highly troublesome commitment, given that it is impossible for us to explain how one can act without presupposing a prior interest. As Kant notes at the very end of the *Groundwork*, this is incomprehensible and goes beyond the boundaries of human reason (4:463).

33. Even if these notions should only come apart in principle and should be coextensive in practice (such that all beings capable of acting on maxims have dignity), the classification, though being extensionally adequate, would nevertheless not achieve the right result for the right reason (i.e., they would not have dignity because of having this capacity). Similarly, while the claim that "[t]hings cannot act, so can have no maxims" (O'Neill 1989, 138) would be false if there should be such beings, since they would be able to act on maxims yet nevertheless not be persons having dignity but mere things

178   RETHINKING THE VALUE OF HUMANITY

that have only price, even if these notions should be coextensive in practice the truth of the claim could not be established by analyzing the concept of a thing or by analyzing what it is to act on maxims.

34. Kant suggests this in the *Metaphysik Mrongovius*: "man has dignity only insofar as he is morally good" (29:846).

35. Accordingly, the good will and happiness neither have dignity nor price (but instead have value). They are neither self-standing ends, nor are they means. They belong to the wrong ontological category for price and dignity to be applicable.

36. Usefulness is not a type of value (cf. "[The p]rice of a thing is something other than value" [29:846]). Useful things are neither intrinsically valuable nor extrinsically valuable. Something can be useful in the absence of anything that has intrinsic value, which means that it cannot be a derivatively valuable thing that derives its value from the intrinsically valuable things to which it is related. Nevertheless, usefulness is related to value insofar as useful things are things that can be used for bringing about valuable states of affairs and thus have the potential for bringing about value.

37. Kerstein (2006, 202) asks, "But why could not a principle be unconditionally binding on us if nothing was unconditionally good?" This is a genuine problem for axiological approaches, since an unconditionally binding principle does not presuppose the existence of anything that is unconditionally good. The deontological reading, by contrast, can explain why something having dignity must exist for a principle to unconditionally bind something, since nothing would be bound if the domain were empty.

38. Freedom is thus the *ratio essendi* of the moral law (cf. 5:4n). Unlike a *ratio fiendi*, which is the ground of existence/becoming, a *ratio essendi* is the ground of the (real) possibility of a thing (cf. 29:809 and R5182).

39. Contra Rawls (2000, 183) and O'Neill (1989, chap. 7), the contrast between the formula of the law of nature and the formula of humanity does not correspond to the difference between the agent's point of view and the point of view of the person who is being affected, but the difference between the law and the domain that it governs.

40. Contra, e.g., Guyer 2000, 175 ("FHE specifies their '*matter*—that is, an end' to be achieved through the adoption of moral maxims"), O'Neill 1989, 127 ("FEI as determining the *matter* or end that they must have"), Korsgaard 1996, 106 ("rational nature or humanity as an end in itself gives us the material of the law"), also Rawls 2000, 194; Timmermann 2007, 111.

41. This means that ends are things that give rise to reasons. They are not necessarily things for the sake of which we act, contra, e.g., Wood 1999, 116.

42. For example, Korsgaard (1996, 108) misconstrues the negative role of ends in this way, illustrating it with an example of an omission which is to be explained in terms of aversions.

43. Humanity is a restricting condition that imposes limits. It does not generate content by itself but presupposes content that is independently given and that can then be limited. It is for this reason that morality is reactive and inclination always has the first word (cf. 5:146). Explanations in terms of exceptions are, accordingly, always contrastive. They explain why one ought not follow the rule of omission/commission put forward by instrumental reasoning, i.e. why the relative ends are not to be realized.

THE DIGNITY OF HUMANITY   179

By reference to the dignity of humanity we can explain why certain actions (whether commissions or omissions) ought not take place, which then plays a role in explaining why certain alternative actions ought to take place.

44. For helpful comments, I am grateful to Roger Crisp, Hyunseop Kim, Susan Shell, Maya Krishnan, Christopher Benzenberg, and audiences at Oxford, Keele, Southampton, Seoul National University, and the UK Kant Society conference at St Andrews. Special thanks to Sarah Buss, Nandi Theunissen, Ryan Davis, and Lucas Thorpe for very detailed and helpful comments.

References

Allison, Henry E. 2011. *Kant's Groundwork for the Metaphysics of Morals—A Commentary*. Oxford: Oxford University Press.

Bader, Ralf M. 2009. "Kant and the Categories of Freedom." *British Journal for the History of Philosophy* 17 (4): 799–820.

Bader, Ralf M. 2015a. "Kantian Axiology and the Dualism of Practical Reason." In *The Oxford Handbook of Value Theory*, edited by I. Hirose and J. Olson, 175–201. Oxford: Oxford University Press.

Bader, Ralf M. 2015b. "Kant's Theory of the Highest Good." In *The Highest Good in Aristotle and Kant*, edited by J. Aufderheide and R. M. Bader, 183–213. Oxford: Oxford University Press.

Bader, Ralf M. 2013. "Kant and the Conditional Intrinsic Value of Happiness." Unpublished manuscript.

Bader, Ralf M. 2017. "Kantian Beneficence: Material or Formal." Unpublished manuscript.

Bader, Ralf M. 2014. "Pragmatic Imperatives and the Value of Happiness." Unpublished manuscript.

Cummiskey, David. 1996. *Kantian Consequentialism*. Oxford: Oxford University Press.

Dean, Richard. 2006. *The Value of Humanity in Kant's Moral Theory*. Oxford: Oxford University Press.

Delfosse, Heinrich, Norbert Hinske, and Gianluca Bordoni, eds. 2010. *Stellenindex und Konkordanz zum Naturrecht Feyerabend*. Vol. 1. Stuttgart: Frommann-Holzboog.

Delfosse, Heinrich, Norbert Hinske, and Gianluca Bordoni, eds. 2014. *Stellenindex und Konkordanz zum Naturrecht Feyerabend*. Vol. 2. Stuttgart: Frommann-Holzboog.

Guyer, Paul. 2000. *Kant on Freedom, Law, and Happiness*. Cambridge: Cambridge University Press.

Hill, Thomas. 1980. "Humanity as an End in Itself." *Ethics* 91 (1): 84–99.

Hruschka, Joachim. 1990. "Die Person als ein Zweck an sich selbst." *Juristen Zeitung* 45 (1):1–15.

Kant, Immanuel. 1900. *Kants gesammelte Schriften*. Berlin: Reimer/de Gruyter.

Kerstein, Samuel. 2006. "Deriving the Formula of Humanity." In *Kant's Groundwork of the Metaphysics of Morals: New Interpretations*, edited by Christoph Horn and Dieter Schönecker, 200–221. Berlin: de Gruyter.

Korsgaard, Christine. 1996. *Creating the Kingdom of Ends*. Cambridge: Cambridge University Press.

Müller, August F. 1733. *Einleitung in die Philosophischen Wissenschaften*. Leipzig; Breitkopf.

180 RETHINKING THE VALUE OF HUMANITY

Nozick, R. 1974. *Anarchy, State, and Utopia*. New York: Basic Books.

O'Neill, Onora. 1989. *Constructions of Reason—Explorations of Kant's Practical Philosophy*. Cambridge: Cambridge University Press.

Paton, Herbert J. 1947. *The Categorical Imperative: A Study in Kant's Moral Philosophy*. London: Hutchinson.

Rawls, John. 2000. *Lectures on the History of Moral Philosophy*. Cambridge, MA: Harvard University Press.

Sensen, Oliver. 2009. "Kant's Conception of Human Dignity." *Kant-Studien* 100: 309–331.

Stern, Robert. 2015. *Kantian Ethics: Value, Agency, and Obligation*. Oxford: Oxford University Press.

Timmermann, Jens. 2006. "Value without Regress: Kant's 'Formula of Humanity' Revisited." *European Journal of Philosophy* 14 (1): 69–93.

Timmermann, Jens. 2007. *Kant's Groundwork of the Metaphysics of Morals—A Commentary*. Cambridge: Cambridge University Press.

Timmons, Mark. 2017. *Significance and System—Essays on Kant's Ethics*. Oxford: Oxford University Press.

Velleman, J. David. 2006. *Self to Self*. Cambridge: Cambridge University Press.

Wood, Allen. 1999. *Kant's Ethical Thought*. Cambridge: Cambridge University Press.

7

Great Beyond All Comparison

Kenneth Walden

In the climax of the 1990s action flick *On Deadly Danger* our hero Stump Chunkman confronts a group of villains planning to shoot cobras into an elementary school so they can rob the cafeteria. Enraged, Stump hoists the Top Villain over his head. "You were going to kill those kids—all for three hundred measly bucks? You have a grossly distorted conception of the value of humanity [*Wert der Menschlichkeit*]." Stump then defenestrates Top Villain into a volcano. The filmgoer is thrilled by this triumph of muscles over evil, but, as with many great works of cinema, she is also left with a problem. Top Villain's mistake is not just one of wronging the children by shooting cobras at them. It is also, as Stump says, doing it for such paltry gains—"for three hundred measly bucks." Top Villain's error is one of misvaluing these persons.

But what would it mean to correctly value them? Would these villains have behaved better if they held out for more money—if they had valued these children at not less than a thousand dollars a head? Most would deny that there is a dollar figure that would assuage the feeling of misvaluation. It's not that a person is worth many dollars more than three hundred. The value of humanity lies on a different level of value, one that cannot be reconciled with things valued in dollars and cents. As Stump explains in the film's coda, the world contains both "things," whose value consists in their "price," and persons, who have a completely different value. This second kind of value—"dignity"—merits a completely different kind of "estimation" than things with price, an estimation he calls "respect." Most important, Stump continues, the worth found in dignity is "*incomparable*." This means that it is a mistake not only to set the value of a person at three hundred dollars, but to set any price at all. The misvaluation is not a matter of setting the price of persons too low but talking about it as something that can *be* low or high—as something that admits of comparisons.[1]

This is stirring rhetoric, but is it sound philosophy? I think there are basically two kinds of argument for the claim that the value of persons is incomparable. The first tries to establish that comparisons of value involving persons are inapt. David Velleman's (2015, 48) position is representative:

Kenneth Walden, *Great beyond All Comparison* In: *Rethinking the Value of Humanity*. Edited by: Sarah Buss and L. Nandi Theunissen, Oxford University Press. © Oxford University Press 2023.
DOI: 10.1093/oso/9780197539361.003.0008

What makes a person special is not a value that sets him apart from others; it's a value that calls for appreciating him by setting him apart, a mode of appreciation that considers him alone. The key to this solution is that values are normative, in the first instance, not for actions or choices but rather for appreciative attitudes. To be valuable is to be worthy of being valued in some way—that is, worthy of being the object of some appreciative response. This conception allows us to understand a kind of value that is not merely incommensurable but constitutively incomparable, because it is properly appreciated by a response that essentially involves a refusal to make comparisons, an insistence on cherishing its object in isolation from others.[2]

Velleman's suggestion is that value comparisons involving persons may be possible but are prohibited, inappropriate, or unfitting because those comparisons violate a requirement inherent in the special nature of the value of humanity.

The second style of argument aims to show that value comparisons involving persons are impossible. As far as I know, this kind of argument has received no attention, save for some vague remarks by Kant. Dignity, Kant says, is "infinitely far above all price," and this means that "it cannot at all be brought into computation or comparison [with price] without, as it were, mistaking and assailing its holiness" (4:435).[3] Now we could read these remarks as falling within the first genre of argument, as suggesting that comparing the value of persons is inappropriate because it "mistakes and assails" a comparison-prohibiting kind of value. But this reading is at odds with the fact that Kant himself is making a sort of comparison when he says that dignity is "infinitely far above" price. This suggests that the reason dignity cannot be "brought into computation or comparison" is not the inaptness of personal value comparisons per se but *this* feature: dignity's being "infinitely far above" price. What Kant might mean here is that things of infinite size are, for some reason, *too big* to figure in any comparisons, and so the infinitude of dignity makes value comparisons not just inapt but impossible. This conjectural reading is reinforced by the fact that elsewhere Kant makes exactly this claim about the incomparability of the infinite. "The infinite," he says in the third *Critique*, "is absolutely (not merely comparatively) great" (5:254), and by "absolutely great" he means "great beyond all comparison" (5:248).

Putting these thoughts together suggests one argument Kant may have had in mind:

1. Persons have infinite value.
2. The size of infinite quantities and magnitudes cannot be compared to the size of other quantities or magnitudes.
3. Therefore, the value of persons is incomparable.

GREAT BEYOND ALL COMPARISON   183

This argument is obviously different from Velleman's. It does not say that we are doing something inappropriate if we compare the value of persons. It says that such a comparison cannot be made.

My goal in this chapter is to explain and defend this argument.

1. The Value of Persons Is Infinite: Brute Force

I will first offer something of a brute force argument for the first premise. To do this, I will take value to be function v from an item x to a cardinal number $v(x)$. This gives us a simple understanding of finite and infinite value. If $v(x)$ is finite, then x has finite value; if $v(x)$ is infinite, then x has infinite value.

The argument goes like this. If there is a type of object—call them "things"— that satisfies the following two principles, then we can guarantee that persons have infinite value:

Transcendence of dignity. For all persons y and possible things x, $v(y) \geq v(x)$.
Open-endedness of price. For all finite cardinals κ, there could exist a thing x such that $v(x) > \kappa$.

The inference from these principles to premise 1 is simple. Suppose, toward a contradiction, that the value of a person is a finite cardinal. Then Open-endedness would entail that there could be a thing whose value is greater. But Transcendence entails that this is impossible. So our supposition is false and the value of a person cannot be finite. Importantly, it does not matter what exactly these "things" are. All that matters is that there are some entities or other that satisfy these two conditions. It is natural to think that any entity is either a thing or a person, but this is not an assumption of the argument; there could be a third class of valuable entities.

All that said, I will try to defend these two principles by relying on a particular conception of things. Stipulate that *things* are those items whose value is entirely conditioned on their relationship to one or more persons—on their being valued by persons, desired by persons, instrumentally useful to persons, etc. If we make this stipulation, what can be said for our two principles?

Transcendence is close to conventional wisdom. Every person, no matter his warts, is worth more than all things, no matter their splendors. But it'll be useful to have an argument for the proposition, lest it turn out to be an empty piety. So let's examine the conditioning relationship that defines the relationship between things and persons. Suppose that a muffin is valuable to me. If I ask why the muffin is valuable, I am apt to receive an answer listing two kinds of considerations: a list of things that are valuable (like gustatory pleasure and

184 RETHINKING THE VALUE OF HUMANITY

nutrition) and a set of nonnormative claims about how the muffin is suitably related to those things so as to inherit their value. Call the first set of items the thing's *value conditions*; a thing is valuable because it constitutes, causes, realizes, or otherwise secures these things. It would be very surprising to hear that a thing is *more valuable* than the aggregate of its value conditions—more valuable than the mereological union of all its value conditions. It would be very odd to think, for example, that the muffin is *more* valuable than the gustatory pleasure and nutrition that it provides, since these attractions are all the muffin has going for it. Likewise, it would be surprising if three hundred dollars tuned out to be more valuable than any of the classes of commodities that can be bought with that sum, or if a memento turned out to have more value than the memory it arouses. This is most clear in the case where the relationship is instrumental. If someone told us that b is valuable only because it is a means to a but that $v(b) > v(a)$, we would want to know where the excess value comes from.

The general principle suggested by these examples relates the value of the aggregate of value conditions—which we can think of as a mereological union—to the value on which they are conditions:

> *Superiority of value conditions.* If y is the aggregate of the value conditions of x, then $v(x) \leq v(y)$.

If we adopt the conception of *things* suggested above—entities whose value is ultimately and entirely conditioned on their relationship with persons—then Superiority entails Transcendence. Persons must be at least as valuable as things so understood because the only reason that things are valuable in the first place is their bearing the right relationship to persons.[4]

Open-endedness is more controversial, since we might reasonably think that the value of things is bounded. Think of some very valuable things: cures for horrible illnesses, transformative works of art, comfortable shoes. Why not think that one of these treasures represents an upper bound on the value of things—that there is nothing whose value is greater than that of, for example, a cure for the Red Death? The simple answer is that even very valuable things can be improved. If this tube contains a serum that cures the Red Death, then it is very valuable. But if it also cures the Blue Death, then it is more valuable. If it cures both with no side effects, then it is more valuable still. And if instead of a single dose, it contains a dozen, then it is yet more valuable. In general, these imagined improvements—multiplication, recombination, and purification—can enhance things that are already quite valuable. And if these sorts of improvements can be iterated indefinitely—granted, a big "if"—then the value of things will be open-ended.

GREAT BEYOND ALL COMPARISON 185

Against this possibility, a skeptic might insist that even these iterated improvements will be bound by the needs and wants of humanity. Suppose we have a serum that cures all diseases, extends our lifespan indefinitely, teaches us Esperanto, acquaints us with the poetry of Alexander Pushkin, and is sufficiently concentrated to do these things for every human being who will ever exist. Is anything more valuable than this? Maybe not. It may be that such a thing cannot be improved upon given the actual needs and wants of humanity. But this is why it is important that Open-endedness is formulated in terms of "possible" things. The claim is not that the value of things forms an actually open-ended hierarchy but that for any finite cardinal, there *could* be something more valuable than it. This is the appropriate way to formulate a claim like Open-endedness. That humanity has a certain value is a necessary proposition and so should not depend on contingent facts like whether there are a hundred persons or a trillion, or whether human appetites are quite modest or utterly boundless. The way to respect this fact is to say that the value of a person exceeds the value of all things for any possible configuration of the universe.

This clarification opens the door to some simple arguments for Open-endedness. Adopting the definition set out above once more, we can say that the value of things is open-ended because the possible number of valuers in the world is open-ended. For any finite cardinal κ, we can imagine an experience of modest finite value t—seeing a nice painting, say—and a possible number of people n such that the value of n people having that experience will equal $nt > \kappa$. A similar argument can be premised on the idea that our valuing activities are open-ended. Suppose Veronica is the only person in the world. Now consider those things whose value is determined entirely by Veronica's evaluative attitude toward them. Veronica doesn't like mud, so mud is valueless, but she does like crackers, so crackers are valuable. Now suppose that Veronica is a bit of zealot about the value of tea. Every time she considers a challenge to her valuing tea—by imagining someone asking her "But is tea *really* valuable?"—she not only affirms her valuing but increases the amount she values tea by ¼. Further imagine that Veronica is a bit of a frenetic reasoner and so she accelerates the rate at which she entertains these challenges. She starts by taking $v(\text{tea}) = 1$ at time $t = 0$. But then she entertains a challenge at $t = ½$ and in doing so takes $v(\text{tea}) = 1¼$. Then she does this again at time = ¾ and sets $v(\text{tea}) = \frac{25}{16}$. And then again at time = ⅞. And so on. (What does it mean, we might wonder, to say that the value Veronica assigns tea increases like this? The natural thought is to say that they reflect Veronica's preferences of exchange. Maybe crackers are plentiful in Veronica's world and so make a good unit value. At $t = 0$, Veronica would exchange one cracker for a cup of tea, but at $t = ¾$ she would be willing to exchange $\frac{25}{16}$ crackers for a cup of tea.) The sequence of values that Veronica assigns to tea is divergent: it will get bigger and bigger without bound before we arrive at $t = 1$. This means that for

186 RETHINKING THE VALUE OF HUMANITY

any arbitrarily large finite cardinal κ, we can point to a moment in Veronica's world—an instant before $t = 1$—where a cup of tea is valued at a level greater than κ, which means the tea will have value $> \kappa$. Veronica may have capacities that no actual valuer does, and her valuing activity is certainly eccentric, perhaps even irrational. But I see no reason to believe her case is in any way incompatible with the demands of valuing. I see no reason to think, that is, that she is not a real valuer. Therefore, as far as valuing *as such* is concerned, there could be someone like Veronica, and that is enough to make price open-ended.

2. The Value of Persons Is Infinite: A More Philosophical Explanation

The foregoing arguments for my first premise are not very philosophically nourishing. They rely on coarse mathematical devices to produce the desired conclusion, but they don't reveal much about why these conclusions are true. For that reason, a more programmatic, if also more speculative argument may serve as a useful supplement.

Offering this argument requires me to say some general things about the infinite and Kant's conception of it. A. W. Moore (1988, 206) observes that philosophical debates about the infinite have seesawed back and forth between two different clusters of concepts:

> Within the first cluster we find: boundlessness; endlessness; unlimitedness; unsurveyability; immeasurability; eternity; that which is such that, given any determinate part of it, there is always more to come. Within the second cluster we find: completeness; wholeness; absoluteness; perfection; universality; self-sufficiency; autonomy; creativity; freedom. The concepts in the first cluster are more negative, they convey a sense of potentiality and they suggest an infinite that lies without. The concepts in the second cluster are more positive, they convey a sense of actuality and they suggest an infinite that lies within. We can label the concepts 'mathematical' and 'metaphysical' respectively.[5]

Moore suggests that Kant brooks both conceptions of the infinite, but he does so in a very special way. Metaphysically infinite things *appear* mathematically infinite when cognized by finite creatures like ourselves. For example, *the world* understood as a self-sufficient and unconditioned whole is metaphysically infinite. But we can only come to know the world by interacting with it through our finite cognitive faculties—in particular, through a bounded sensory field and a limited store of concepts—which means that what we are given must be an aspect of the world, something incomplete, partial, and distinct from us, impinging from without. But Kant argues that reception of this kind must be self-conscious, so that what we receive we must at the same time be able to recognize as conditioned.

It follows that,

> given any particular object of our knowledge, we must be able to step back, see it in a suitable context and come to know more. Only in this way are we able to see it as a feature of what is out there, independent of us, with its own conditions of existence. But coming to know more in this way simply means receiving more; and what we receive will itself, along with what was originally received, form a conditioned aspect of the world. This sets up a regress. And the regress clearly proceeds indefinitely, in the way that is the hallmark of the mathematically infinite. Here we have an argument, in very Kantian terms, for the necessity of something that Kant takes to be more or less a raw datum, namely the infinitude of space and time, in the mathematical sense. Space and time, for Kant, are not only intuitions but forms of intuition. Roughly what this means is that they constitute the framework within which our reception takes place. But that framework has to be infinite if there is to be any guarantee, as there must be, that we can receive the condition of anything that we can receive. We need, as it were, infinite elbow-room. More particularly we need elbow-room that is infinite in the mathematical sense. The mathematically infinite is a natural concomitant of a finite being's coming to know an infinite world, in the truer, metaphysical sense. More succinctly, what is metaphysically infinite must appear to a finite being under a mathematically infinite aspect. (210–211)[6]

Because our idea of *the world* is infinite in the *metaphysical* sense—complete, unconditioned, total, absolute—and because cognition demands us to seek the conditions for everything we represent, the representation of that world by finite creatures like ourselves must be "open-ended" in a way that makes the framework in which we represent that world—the manifold of space and time—*mathematically* infinite. This is the sense in which the world is mathematically infinite "in appearance."

I want to venture an analogous explanation for the infinite value of persons. Persons are metaphysically infinite. More precisely, the capacity for valuing that is grounded in our rational nature is metaphysically infinite. One of Kant's most quoted passages, from the *Critique of Practical Reason*, expresses just this idea:

> Two things fill the mind with ever new and increasing admiration and reverence the more often and more steadily one reflects on them: the starry heavens

above me and the moral law within me. . . . The first begins from the place I occupy in the external world of sense and extends the connection in which I stand into an unbounded magnitude with worlds upon worlds and systems of systems, and moreover into the unbounded times of their periodic motion, their beginning and their duration. The second begins from my invisible self, my personality, and presents me in a world which has true infinity. (5:162)

Here Kant compares the "unbounded magnitude" of the outer world to the inner world of the "invisible self," which, he says, has "true infinity."[7]

What would it mean to say that my capacity for valuing is metaphysically infinite? The world as a whole is metaphysically infinite because it possesses properties associated with that notion. It is complete (there is nothing it doesn't contain), self-sufficient (it does not depend on anything outside of itself), and absolute (it makes no sense to say that some notion is relative *to the world* as it might make sense to say that it is *relative to a community* or *a believer*). Our capacity to value is metaphysically infinite for the same reason: because it is autonomous (I am responsible for my valuing), absolute (it is the last court of appeal on questions of value), and, most important, unconstrained (there are no principled limits on the forms my valuing can take).[8]

Moore understands the claim that space and time are infinite in extension as reflecting how a metaphysically infinite world must appear to cognitively limited beings such as ourselves. I want to say something similar about our capacity for valuing. The claim that persons have infinite value is ultimately about how a metaphysically infinite humanity must appear to those same creatures. Suppose we are engaged in a systematic survey of value. How much is this bucket of treacle worth? How much is this box of nails worth? How much is this used handkerchief worth? How much is this person worth? As with our cognition of objects in space and time, answering these questions seems to require us to orient the objects of evaluation in a larger system that represents the relevant relationships between the items we value. The nails are valuable because they can be used to hold these boards together, and holding boards together is valuable because then I can stand on them to reach the top shelf, and reaching the top shelf is valuable because that's where the treacle is. And so on.

We can ask several questions about the basic shape of this network of value relations. Are there any limits on how many things can have value? On the density of relations between values? And most important, are there limits on how valuable something can be? If we take seriously the idea that our capacity to value is metaphysically infinite, then we should think the answer to each of these questions is no. We can brook no limitation on this framework of value because of one of the features that made our capacity to value metaphysically infinite: because this capacity is unconstrained. The imposition of any limit on the field in which we represent these activities will be a fatal distortion of what is possible in the way of value. Only a network that is potentially unlimited in magnitude and density will guarantee an adequate canvas for representing a world of value created by unconstrained valuers. Veronica's assessment of tea exemplifies one dimension of this need. Her valuing is unconstrained with respect to the magnitude of value she confers on a particular item. What I am suggesting is that even if Veronica is an exceptional valuer, she reflects an important feature of our capacity for valuing: its radical freedom. This feature means we need the same "infinite elbow-room" for representing value as we need for representing objects in space and time.

These reflections give us a slightly deeper explanation for Open-endedness. Open-endedness is true because our framework for representing value must be open-ended. And our framework for representing value must be open-ended because it is a framework for representing the activities of a metaphysically infinite capacity for valuing.

This is a claim about the value of things, but what does it entail about the value of *humanity*? The important point is that the value of humanity is not going to reside anywhere within our "framework" of values for reasons having to do with Superiority. Because our humanity is the condition of the value of things, its value must be at least as great as the value of any of these things. This means it must have infinite value.

Moore suggests that space and time appear mathematically infinite in extension because of the way that our finite cognitive powers interact with the metaphysical infinity of the world. My analogous suggestion is that humanity appears mathematically infinite in value because of the way those same cognitive powers interact with the metaphysical infinitude of our humanity. Our cognitions of value will naturally be oriented in a more or less mathematical framework. But to do justice to our unconstrained power of valuing, this framework must be open-ended in extent. This means that when we then try to orient the value of the power itself within the framework, we find that it has nowhere to fit. It must instead lie *beyond* it, in the way that the first infinite ordinal lies beyond all the natural numbers. We must, that is, represent it as being mathematically infinite.

As I said, this is a more recherché explanation of our first premise, but I hope it might offer a useful account of the deeper reasons behind the surprising claim that the value of persons is infinite.

3. Incomparability and Infinity: Some Historical Arguments

Having laid out a case for the first premise of my target argument, I turn to the second—to the idea that infinite quantities and magnitudes are incomparable. The idea that infinite quantities are incomparable is of a piece with a more general skepticism about our ability to apply mathematical concepts to those quantities. Aristotle is the classic source for this skepticism. To compare two quantities requires our being able to form each into a completed totality, to say that this whole is greater than or equal to that whole. But infinite quantities cannot be formed into completed totalities. This is what distinguishes infinite collections. For however much of the collection we take, there will always be something left over. For example, however many natural numbers I count, there will always be yet more natural numbers; this is what makes the set of natural numbers infinite. When I say that the sets {1, 3, 5} and {2, 4, 6} are the same size, what I mean is that I get to the same place when I count the members of each set. But the natural numbers and the squares are infinite precisely because we can never finish counting them. This means that we can never complete the process—counting—that would ground a comparison of size (*Physics*, III.4–8).

A related argument for the same conclusion relies on a familiar fact known as Galileo's Paradox. Consider the set of natural numbers and the set of square numbers. Both are infinite sets. There is a sense in which the set of natural numbers is larger than the set of square numbers. Every square number is a natural number, while the vast majority of natural numbers are not squares. But there is also a sense in which the sets are the same size. Every square can be mapped onto a unique natural number and every natural number onto a square. So the squares and the naturals can be paired up in a one-to-one relation. We therefore have reason to take the squares to be equal in size to the natural numbers and a reason to take them to be strictly smaller. A natural diagnosis of this result is that the necessary conditions for applying our concepts of greater or equal size are not satisfied for infinite quantities, so comparisons of infinite quantities simply don't make sense.

What are these conditions on size comparison? There seem to be two platitudes. First, one-to-one correspondences entail equality of size. Second, a whole is always larger than its proper parts. (This was one of Euclid's "common notions.") For comparisons of finite quantities these requirements always agree, but for infinite quantities they do not. The natural numbers are in one sense larger than the squares and in another sense equal in size. The machinery, so to speak, we use for comparisons cannot be used in the case of infinite quantities because its conditions are not satisfied.[9]

In the introduction I reported Kant as saying that the infinite is "great beyond comparison." His argument for this claim borrows from both Aristotle and Galileo but involves a transcendental twist. The sort of cognition in which comparisons of size occur will be "mathematical." This means they will employ numerical concepts, which are applied to our experience in the following sort of way. To measure a magnitude—to represent it as being however many units long—we select a "quantum" and successively synthesize copies of it in our imagination until the magnitude is exhausted. Think, very roughly, of covering the length of an ocean liner by stitching together hundreds of buttons, one after another. Mathematical representations of this magnitude depend on this act of imaginative synthesis. One magnitude is larger than another, for example, just in case it takes more copies of the same quantum to cover it in imagination. On this conception, mathematical cognition, including comparison, depends on the success of a particular act of synthesis. But this cognitive machinery breaks down in the infinite case because that synthetic process cannot be completed. When we think about infinite magnitudes mathematically, what we are representing is not a *determinate* magnitude, not a successful synthesis. We are representing an *indefinite* progression of a process of synthesis. Our representation is of an interminable carrying-on rather than a final product. And this is not a suitable object of numerical comparison for the simple reason that it does not constitute a unified object.

Kant's story is a little more complicated than this, but not in a way that negates the basic point. He does think we have a *kind* of grasp of the infinite as a totality (as opposed to the infinite as potential). He says in the *Critique of Judgment*, "Even being able to think [of the infinite] as a whole indicates a faculty of the mind which surpasses every standard of sense . . . [for] to be able to think the given infinite without contradiction requires a faculty in the human mind that is itself supersensible" (5:254). But this "thinking of" is very tenuous. It does not amount to the cognition we have of facts like "there are more dwarves than stooges"—cognition that depends on the successful subsumption of experience under a mathematical concept. It is an "idea of reason": something we can gesture at as the terminus of an unending sequence, but not something we can attribute to an object of cognition. For this reason, the kind of thought we can have of this idea will not support anything like a comparison of size.

4. Incomparability and Infinity: Resistance

The previous section offered some historical arguments for the second premise in our argument. I expect that few readers will be satisfied by them. The reason has to do with the radical shift in thinking about the infinite that took place in the nineteenth century. I can't do justice to all these changes here, but the main points can be neatly summarized. Nowadays most will deny that we can think of infinite collections only as potentials; on the contrary, we can, for example, think of the natural numbers as a set on par with any finite set. The paradoxes of the "actual" infinite unearthed by Aristotle and others are not paradoxes at all but peculiar features of the infinite. Second, most people will happily reject Euclid's "common notion" that a whole must be larger than its proper parts while

192 RETHINKING THE VALUE OF HUMANITY

affirming one-to-one correspondence as the sole criterion of size comparison. This move easily resolves Galileo's Paradox in favor of the claim that the natural numbers and the squares are of the same size. Finally, many will reject Kant's view that mathematical cognition has sensible conditions in favor of a view on which mathematical facts are ascertained by a faculty that operates quite independently of sensory experience.

Accepting these three propositions allows us to turn aside the historical arguments just glossed and open the door to Cantor's paradise. We can insist that there are actually infinite multiplicities, that these multiplicities are of different sizes, and that we can unproblematically compare the size of these multiplicities. In this setting, the claim that the value of persons is infinite does not make comparisons of value impossible. We can satisfy Transcendence and Openendedness by saying that the value of all persons is equal to the first infinite cardinal, what Cantor called $\aleph_0$. This is a value whose "size"—its cardinality—is equal to that of the set of natural numbers. The comparative claim that, for example, two persons have equal value can be true in exactly the same way as the mundane claim that the sets $\{1, 2\}$ and $\{3, 4\}$ are of the same size. If we like, we could even assert *inequalities* in the value of persons. Most persons have value $\aleph_0$, but (we impishly suggest) certain natural aristocrats have value equal to the first uncountable cardinal, $\aleph_1$. Overcome with the zeal of ranking, we might continue by saying that in fact there is a whole hierarchy of personal merit, and the value of each rung in this hierarchy corresponds to a different value: $\aleph_0 < \aleph_1 < \aleph_2 < \ldots$. At the end of this sequence lies $\aleph_\omega$, which is the value of certain world-historical figures like Napoleon or Walt Disney. I am not suggesting that anyone would want to say any of this. The point is that once we accept this picture of the infinite and our thought about it, we have the machinery to make precise, meaningful, and abundant comparisons about things that are infinitely large. And this knocks down the second premise in our opening argument.

5. Restoring Incomparability

I have presented a roughly Kantian case for the two premises in making up our little argument for incomparability. And in the previous section I indicated the point at which I think skepticism about this argument will be most trenchant. I now want to push back against that skepticism. I will not deny any part of the Cantorian landscape just surveyed but instead say that our original argument can be recast in terms perfectly compatible with it.[10]

Open-endedness, as I originally stated it, says that for every finite cardinal κ there could exist a thing whose price is greater than κ. But why make a restriction to finite cardinals? From a pre-Cantorian point of view, this restriction may be justified, since the very idea of infinite price would be incoherent. But if we are going to live in Cantor's paradise, we can't be so squeamish. Here is a simple argument, related to one from before, that we can indeed conceive of things with *infinite* price. The world could be temporally open-ended and valuers could go on reproducing themselves in perpetuity. In this world there are countably infinite valuers. It is also possible that each of these individuals would have an aesthetic experience of finite nonzero value t if they viewed a nice painting. It follows that the extended event whose constituent parts are individual viewings of this painting will have countably infinite value.

What does this liberalization of Transcendence get us? By itself it's no help for our original argument. There could be things whose value is as large as $\aleph_{37}$ and comparisons involving the value of persons would still be tractable. But it raises the question of whether similar reasoning can push the value of things—and with it, via Transcendence, the value of humanity—ever higher up the hierarchy of infinite cardinals, just as our earlier arguments pushed the value of humanity up the hierarchy of finite cardinals.

One simple way to do this is to imagine worlds with ever greater numbers of persons who confer some finite value on things. The problem with this strategy is that for relatively small n, the claim that there could be a world with $\aleph_n$ persons starts to sound incredible. Maybe we can entertain the thought that there are as many valuers as natural numbers, but it's much harder to conceive of a world in which people outnumber the reals. Our other argument proffered in support of Open-endedness—the one involving Veronica accelerating revaluation of tea—depended on the idea that our activities of valuing were open-ended. This approach may be more promising. What we would like are examples of valuing activities that seem to distinguish between *transfinitely* many levels of value. The simplest cases (admittedly quite artificial) will involve individuals who value certain mathematical objects. Here are two:

(i) George is a mathematical aesthete. He believes that certain mathematical structures are beautiful, some elegant, some are dumpy, others sublime. He values them accordingly. George aesthetically values some sets, in part, because they are so *impressive*. One feature of impressiveness is that if S is impressive, then any set strictly larger than S is proportionally more impressive. (So $\{x, y\}$ is twice as impressive as $\{x\}$.) And for this reason, if S is impressive and T is larger than S, then George will value T more than S in proportion to the size of T to the size of S. So described, George's valuing preferences will extend up the same hierarchy as the size of sets.

(ii) The Setters are a people obsessed with mathematical games. The linchpin of their society is a game called Set, with the following structure. A problem is posed whose answer is a set. The larger the set, the harder the Setters think

194 RETHINKING THE VALUE OF HUMANITY

the problem is, and, consequently, the more they value that solution. So if a problem has solution {Harry's cat} or {7}, it is quite easy and no one values that solution very much. A problem whose solution is {Toucan Sam, my left shoe} is a little harder and accordingly valued more. Now imagine that this game is designed so that for every cardinal κ, there is a question whose unique answer has κ members. Like George, the Setters' value attributions would seem to extend up the same hierarchy as the sets.

Both George and the Setters value sets; among those sets they value bigger ones more. This feature of their valuing extends beyond finite sets into the transfinite. If we suppose that these sets have the value they do because of George's and the Setters' valuing activities, then we will need to countenance a *heck of a lot* of different values for sets. If valuers like George and the Setters are possible, then price must extend all the way up the transfinite hierarchy.

This point is significant because it supports a liberalization of Openendedness. Namely this:

Unrestricted open-endedness of price. For every cardinal κ, there could be a thing with value greater than κ.

This version of the principle removes the proviso "finite" from our original version.

Pairing Unrestricted open-endedness with Transcendence has interesting consequences. Suppose that the value of a person is some cardinal κ. By Unrestricted open-endedness, there is a thing more valuable than κ. But by Transcendence *nothing* can be more valuable than a person. So we have a contradiction. For any cardinal whatsoever, the proposition that persons have value κ leads to a contradiction. It would seem to mean that the value of persons must somehow lie *beyond* the hierarchy of cardinals.

Cantor had a name for this exalted status. He called it the "absolutely infinite." Cantor's transfinite mathematics were premised on the notion that we could, *pace* Aristotle, take infinite multiplicities as completed totalities instead of indefinite multiplicities. But Cantor also recognized that there are some multiplicities for which this cannot be done. A simple example is the set of all sets. Now the set of all sets—call it V—must have, like every set, a powerset $\wp(V)$. The powerset of V is a set whose members are the subsets of V. A set is always strictly smaller than its powerset, so V should be smaller than $\wp(V)$. But since V contains all the sets, including itself, $\wp(V)$ must be a subset of V. But a set is at least as big as its subsets. So we have a contradiction: a set of all sets would be both smaller than and at least as big as its powerset. The natural way to assuage this contradiction is to say that there is no set of all sets, and so the "plurality" or "multiplicity" of sets is something else—maybe a "proper class," maybe not an entity at all.

Whatever we say about this plurality, it has no position on the hierarchy of size that Cantor devised, and it is not subject to comparisons of size for more or less the reasons that Aristotle originally gave about the infinite: it cannot be accommodated by our machinery of comparison. Cantor realized this. The absolutely infinite, he says, is a "true infinite" whose "magnitude is not subject to any increase or reduction, and for this reason it must be quantitatively conceived as an absolute maximum." He goes on to talk of the absolutely infinite in terms highly evocative of the metaphysical infinite. The "absolutely infinite" is "realized in the supreme perfection, in the completely independent, extrawordly being, in God."[11]

If examples like George and the Setters are coherent, then the value of humanity is absolutely infinite in something like Cantor's sense. It is an "absolute maximum" and "not subject to any increase or reduction" because the very idea of taking it as a completed totality that we might measure or compare yields the same kind of contradiction as the idea of a set of all sets.

This conclusion is essentially a more extravagant recapitulation of the one drawn two sections ago. The obstacles to comparing infinities suggested by Aristotle, Galileo, and Kant can be re-created in the more permissive climate of Cantor's set theory. Perhaps infinite multiplicities can be formed into totalities and compared in a straightforward way, but if we make some assumptions about what is coherent in the way of valuing, then we should expect the value of persons to transcend *even this* ample scheme.

There is a deeper point here as well. Our cognitive abilities, in particular our mastery of mathematical concepts, makes our ability to represent magnitudes in the world unbounded in a certain sense. Our ability to value things is also unbounded. (This was the deeper rationale for our Open-endedness principles.) Naturally, both of these uses of "unbounded" need to be spelled out, and doing so will occasion disagreement. But if our ability to value things is *at least as unbounded* as our cognitive capacities, then Transcendence forces us to place the value of persons *beyond* whatever framework our cognitive powers employ to represent value. That is, if all quantities we can entertain in cognition are candidates for degrees of valuing a thing, then Transcendence entails that the value of humanity lies *beyond* the realm of cognizable—and so comparable—size. It is hard to spell out the crucial notion of "at least as unbounded" with both exactness and generality, but this relationship between our capacity for valuing and our representational capacity is, I believe, the ultimate reason why the value of persons will be "great beyond all comparison," no matter what our opinions about the infinite are.

196 RETHINKING THE VALUE OF HUMANITY

Why should we accept the claim that our practical ability to value is "at least" as unbounded as our cognitive ability to represent magnitudes? We have already seen Kant's answer. Our rational nature is an absolutely unconditioned and unbounded capacity to confer value on the world. So we must take the framework for conferred value to extend to the very limits of our cognitive capacities. We need all the elbow-room we can get to capture our utterly boundless valuing activities. And we must do this whether those limits are the cozy ones proposed by Aristotle and Kant or the intergalactic ones that Cantor suggests. To think that there is some quantity that can be superseded in *thought* but not in *value* is to see persons as fundamentally limited.

6. The Sublimity of Humanity

The argument I have been considering purports to show that something goes awry when we try to make comparisons with the value of humanity. Comparisons of size, and indeed the broader range of cognitive judgments of which such comparisons are a part, carry certain preconditions, but the value of humanity does not satisfy those conditions. It is "too big" to fit on the apparatus we have for measuring and comparing value. In this final section I want to consider the question of what this argument means for how we ought to think about other persons.

One possible consequence is broadly "antitheory" in the sense that it imperils the possibility that our duties to persons can be codified into a set of consistent, relatively comprehensive, and more or less exceptionless moral rules. But this consequence comes about only in conjunction with two further assumptions:

(a) Much of the explanation of the truth of the principles making up the correct ethical system will ultimately refer to facts about the value of persons. For example, it is because Stump is a person of worth that I have duties of beneficence to him, that I must respect his rights, that I can bind myself to him through promises.

(b) The resolution of many otherwise conflicting moral principles will depend on comparisons involving the grounds of those principles. For example, if I have a prima facie duty against disappointing Stump and a prima facie duty against disappointing a dozen of his confederates, this conflict is resolved by comparing the grounds of those duties—i.e. the value of the persons to whom the duty is directed.

If (a) and (b) are true, then much of ethical theory will depend on comparisons of interpersonal value to resolve prima facie conflicting duties, which are, of course, ubiquitous. So if those comparisons are in fact impossible, then a relatively large part of what we would hope ethical theory would include turns out to be utterly groundless. This is a big "if." Beyond a few primitive forms of consequentialism, it is a perpetual challenge to know whether a particular part of ethical theory is committed to (a) and (b). Doing that would take more attention to detail than I can offer here.[12]

Instead, I want to discuss a more positive consequence of the claim. If the value of humanity is "great beyond all comparison," then how *should* we respond to other persons? What kind of attitude suits creatures with this kind of value? The suggestion I want offer is that the appropriate response is an aesthetic one. The correct response to the incomparable value of a person is to experience that person as sublime. There are hints of this idea in Kant. For Kant, judgments of sublimity have a self-regarding character. To say that Glen Coe is sublime is to say something about the quality of one's own experience. It is to say that viewing the monolith arouses distinctive feelings of humiliation and elevation. The infinite occasions judgments with the same self-regarding character. Despite their surface grammar, they are not fully objective cognitive mathematical judgments like "There are three tigers." They are judgments that implicitly refer to our own cognitive abilities. To say that something is infinite is to say that it exceeds my cognitive capacities—that it is too big to be subsumed under a numerical concept.

This is why the infinite and the sublime are so closely connected. In experiencing Glen Coe as sublime, I am experiencing a "vibration," Kant says, between the painful humiliation of my cognitive capacities and the superiority I feel in my ability to transcend those capacities by pursuing a higher "vocation." To judge that something is infinite is to judge that it is too great for our representational capacities. Hence the humiliation. But to even grasp this idea—the idea of something that transcends those capacities—reflects some superior power in ourselves, a power that Kant associates with a metaphysically infinite power of reason. And this creates a feeling of elevation or superiority.[13]

If persons have infinite value, then it may be appropriate to experience them in this way—as overwhelming our usual ways of representing value in the world. But what exactly would this come to? One facet of the sublime, as I just explained, is the striking down or humiliation of some activity or project connected to the finite parts of our nature. This humiliation involves the revelation that some conceit of this project is an illusion. In Kant's examples, natural wonders may humiliate the understanding's ambition to provide an exhaustive representation of the world. But now consider a different activity, what we could call *pricing*. This activity encompasses all the dispositions to preference and exchange by which things come to have their price. It is predicated on our finite nature because how we value things depends so much on our inclinations and because these practices are codified by mathematical concepts. The infinite value of humanity—be it

198 RETHINKING THE VALUE OF HUMANITY

ours or someone else's—can humiliate us *qua* pricers in the same way that Glen Coe humiliates us *qua* cognizers because it confronts us with the hopelessness of pricing's ambition to orient all value into a common, roughly mathematical framework. This means that the appreciation of a person's worth may involve a certain amount of pain. It may involve the painful realization that the pretensions of comprehensiveness implicit in the activity of pricing are baseless.[14]

The other side of the sublime is a feeling of elevation or superiority. It is easy enough to see why the experience of one's own infinite value would be elevating. The transcendent value that humiliates the ambitions of pricing is, after all, my value, and the frustration of my pricing activities that results from this value will be accompanied by the distinctive pleasure of exercising the "unlimited capacity" that makes this value infinite (5:259). But what about other people? It is not obvious why the transcendence of *your* value should be at all elevating for *me*. Indeed, on first inspection, the most elevating outlook would seem to be a kind of practical solipsism: a view on which I regard myself alone as transcendent of price and everyone else as mere things. Perhaps this outlook is immoral or irrational, but it would make me feel superior. So why would I feel elevated by discovering it is false?

This question is the subject of a famous and famously enigmatic passage from Iris Murdoch ([1959] 1997, 215–216):

> Art and morals are, with certain provisos which I shall mention in a moment, one. Their essence is the same. The essence of both of them is love. Love is the perception of individuals. Love is the extremely difficult realization that something other than oneself is real. Love, and so art and morals, is the discovery of reality. What stuns us into a realization of our supersensible destiny is not, as Kant imagined, the formlessness of nature, but rather its unutterable particularity; and most particular and individual of all natural things is the mind of man. That is incidentally why tragedy is the highest art, because it is most intensely concerned with the most individual thing. Here is the true sense of that exhilaration of freedom which attends art and which has its more rarely achieved counterpart in morals. It is the apprehension of something else, something particular, as existing outside us.

The best thing, Murdoch says, for "stun[ning] us into a realization of our supersensible destiny" is not the "formlessness of nature" but the "unutterable particularity" of "the mind of man." Looking at Glen Coe in solitude is not enough for arousing visceral awareness of my own transcendent value; I need to engage with the particularity of other minds. But why would that be? Murdoch's allusion to the "exhilaration of freedom which attends art" suggests an answer. The "stun" is occasioned by something like the free and imaginative contemplation that characterizes aesthetic experience. If this is right, then Murdoch evidently thinks that the deepest or most acute episodes of this kind of contemplation are in response to the "mind of man."

But why would the mind of man be such an effective inspiration? Murdoch says it is because the mind of man is so "unutterably particular," but I don't find the concept of particularity very helpful. There is a much better explanation for why the mind of man—or, more accurately, humanity—is so apt an object to inspire these imaginative activities: because it is truly, metaphysically infinite. Glen Coe is merely suggestive of infinity. It is big and varied, but it is ultimately a finite amount of earth arranged in a finite number of shapes. And so even if individual intuitions of Glen Coe overwhelm my personal cognitive capacities, I remain convinced that the scene could, in principle, be brought to heel by human cognitive powers. Humanity, on the other hand, *really is* infinite. This means that any finite attempt to come to grips with humanity in the way we come to grips with a work of art—any interpretation, explanation, or prediction—is doomed to failure.

Grasping this fact inspires a two-sided revelation. We recognize the infinitude of the other person in the inadequacy of any finite engagement with their humanity, and we recognize our own infinitude in the indefinite extensibility of that engagement.[15] On my rendering of Murdoch's hypothesis, then, the only way for me to grasp my transcendence is to wrestle with yours. I recognize my infinite nature through the exercise of my capacity to plumb your infinite depths.

We can even capture the final piece of Murdoch's picture if we define love in the right way. "Love is the extremely difficult realization that something other than oneself is real," she says. What does "real" mean? I'm not sure, but why not read it as "metaphysically infinite": love is the realization that something else is *like me* in all those respects that constitute my "true infinity." It is self-sufficient, autonomous, creative, and free.

Recall our question: Why would I feel elevated by the recognition of someone else's transcendence of price? If the thought we find in Murdoch is true, then we have an answer. My transcendence of price becomes viscerally clear to me only as part of an appreciation of another's transcendence of the same. The feeling of superiority over the world of things is possible only through love of another individual; it is, of necessity, a feeling of *shared* superiority.

When this feeling is suitably joined to the complementary feeling of humiliation described above, the result is the feeling of loftiness that we call the sublime. The appropriate response to the infinite value of a person is to feel both pleasure in the superiority you share with that person and humiliation in the inadequacy of your pricing activities to that value. This of course is not to offer any rules or formulae for acting in response to this value. But that is the point. The proper experience of the value of humanity is one of being overwhelmed, of

RETHINKING THE VALUE OF HUMANITY

being wrenched from our workaday practices of valuing, and we should hardly expect a rule to capture this.[16]

Notes

1. Stump's speech seems indebted to Kant's remarks at *Groundwork* 4:434–436. References to Kant use the volume and page number of Kant 1900–.

2. For a different way of setting out this kind of argument see Walden 2020. There I suggest a way of elaborating Kant's compressed argument at *Groundwork* 4:436: "[N]othing has a worth except that which the law determines for it. The legislation itself, however, which determines all worth, must precisely for this reason have a dignity, i.e., an unconditioned, incomparable worth."

3. Also see Kant's claim that my rational nature "infinitely raises my worth" in the *Critique of Practical Reason*, 5:162.

4. This argument has obvious affinity for the "regress on the conditions of value" argument that Kant makes at *Groundwork* 4:428. The principal difference is that I'm interested not in whether humanity has unconditioned or intrinsic value but in an ordering relation—in whether the value of persons is greater than or equal to the value of things whose value depends on their relationship to persons. There is a common objection to Kant's argument that does have apparent force against the principle I call Superiority. The cure for the Red Death is valuable to me. This value is conditioned on my having the Red Death, but this affliction is certainly *not* valuable. My reply to this objection is that my having the Red Death is not a value condition in the sense I specified, but one of the nonnormative facts that explains *why* something else is a value condition. In this case, that something else is my health.

5. This distinction and its enduring role in the history of philosophy is the subject of Moore 2001.

6. I've removed Moore's citations of Kant.

7. I am going to gloss over the fact that Kant says our invisible self is "personality," not "humanity." On the difference and its implications for understanding Kant's claims about value, see Dean 2006.

8. The Categorical Imperative is not such a limitation, but a codification of the form free valuing must take.

9. This is close to Galileo's (1914, 31ff.) own diagnosis.

10. Though I don't pursue the possibility here, there are reasons to resist Cantor outright. See Whittle 2015.

11. *Mitteilungen zur Lehre vom Transfiniten* (1887), quoted and translated in Jané 1995.

12. But see Walden (2020) for a modest attempt along these lines.

13. See *Critique of Judgment*, 5:255.

14. This pain will be closely related to the pain we experience when the moral law "strikes down self-conceit"; see *Critique of Practical Reason*, 5:73.

15. This claim of course bears some similarity to a thesis more closely associated with Fichte and Hegel than with Kant, that I am able to construct, constitute, or posit

myself only through recognition of others. One philosopher who connects this idea with the infinite is Emmanuel Levinas. He says: "To approach the Other in conversation is to welcome his expression, in which at each instant he overflows the idea a thought would carry away from it. It is therefore to receive from the Other beyond the capacity of the I, which means exactly: to have the idea of infinity" (1969, 51). I don't know exactly what this means, but I think I agree.

16. I am grateful to Sarah Buss for discussion and comments on a draft of this chapter and to Alice Phillips Walden for discussion.

References

Aristotle. 1983. *Physics Books III and IV.* Translated by Edward Hussey. Oxford: Oxford University Press. [Cited by book and chapter]

Dean, Richard. 2006. *The Value of Humanity in Kant's Moral Theory.* Oxford: Oxford University Press.

Galileo Galilei. 1914. *Discourses and Mathematical Demonstrations Relating to Two New Sciences.* Translated by Henry Crew and Alfonso de Salvio. New York: Macmillan.

Jané, Ignacio. 1995. "The Role of the Absolute Infinite in Cantor's Conception of Set." *Erkenntnis* 42 (3): 375–402.

Kant, Immanuel. 1900–. *Kants gesammelte Schriften.* 24 vols. Edited by Königlich Preussische Akademie der Wissenschaften zu Berlin, Deutschen Akademie der Wissenschaften zu Berlin, and Akademie der Wissenschaften zu Göttingen. Berlin: De Gruyter.

Levinas, Emmanuel. 1969. *Totality and Infinity.* Translated by Alphonso Lingis. Boston: Kluwer.

Moore, Adrian W. 1988. "Aspects of the Infinite in Kant." *Mind* 97 (386): 205–223.

Moore, Adrian. W. 2001. *The Infinite.* 2nd ed. London: Routledge.

Murdoch, Iris. (1959) 1997. "The Sublime and the Good." In *Existentialists and Mystics,* edited by Peter Conradi, with a foreword by George Steiner, 205–220. New York: Penguin.

Velleman, J. David. 2015. *Beyond Price.* Cambridge, UK: Open Book.

Walden, Kenneth. 2020. "Incomparable Numbers." In *Oxford Studies in Normative Ethics,* vol. 10, edited by Mark Timmons, 106–130. Oxford: Oxford University Press.

Whittle, Bruno. 2015. "On Infinite Size." In *Oxford Studies in Metaphysics,* vol. 9, edited by Karen Bennett and Dean W. Zimmerman, 3–19. Oxford: Oxford University Press.

8
Fichte on the Value of Rational Agency

Michelle Kosch

What role does the idea of the value of humanity play in Fichte's ethics? It seems natural, at least initially, to think it must play a very central role. Fichte saw himself as a Kantian in ethics, and it is, after all, Kant's name that the phrase 'value of humanity' calls first to mind. But this quite natural thought would have to be reconciled with the fact that the phrase 'value of humanity' occurs only once in Fichte's published works, and that its components appear only seldom, and not at all in the ways one might expect (see Section 1).[1] Such a reconciliation would not be impossible: Kant's use of 'humanity' is technical, and Fichte's theory is (like Kant's) one in which rational nature is an obligatory end (Section 2). But to think of Fichte's theory in terms of the value of humanity may in the end be undesirable, since on it the features in virtue of which agents are worthy of moral consideration neither depend nor are guaranteed by membership in the human species (Section 3). So in contexts that do not limit the reference of 'humanity' in the technical sense to human beings in the biological sense, the use of that term is, at best, misleading (Section 4).

1. Texts

The term 'value' appears infrequently in Fichte's ethical writings, and strikingly not at all in the first, foundational division of his main work of ethical theory, the 1798 *System of Ethics*. In fact the term appears only sixteen times in the entire work, and only in the third division, in the sections devoted to the application of the ethical principle. In those occurrences where the value of human beings in particular is at issue (as opposed to the value of goods or types of labor), the context is typically a denial that differential moral regard for individuals is legitimated by their different places in some status hierarchy. These passages express Fichte's commitment to the equal claim to moral consideration of all beings with any claim at all, regardless of their socioeconomic class or caste, their degree of moral virtue, or other differences.[2]

This lack of instances of 'value' in the expected meaning is unsurprising: like Kant's, Fichte's moral theory is not one in which an account of value

Michelle Kosch, *Fichte on the Value of Rational Agency* In: *Rethinking the Value of Humanity*.
Edited by: Sarah Buss and L. Nandi Theunissen, Oxford University Press. © Oxford University Press 2023.
DOI: 10.1093/oso/9780197539361.003.0009

has a foundational role. Foundational, instead, is an account of what rational agents will insofar as they are rational. On Fichte's account, they will certain ends constitutive of rational agency; this is, plausibly, why Fichte prefers talk of ends to talk of values. (The term 'end' and its derivatives occurs over three hundred times in the *System of Ethics*, and occurs throughout the work.) One might legitimately describe those ends as having 'objective value,' but in doing so one would have to bear in mind that the only thing that can mean, in the Fichtean context, is that their pursuit is rationally obligatory. It cannot mean that their value is something independent that grounds the rationality of their pursuit. On this count, though, there is no disagreement with Kant, for whom talk about humanity having 'value' is just a variant of talk about humanity being an 'objective end' or an 'end in itself.'

The term 'humanity' appears only twenty-one times in the *System of Ethics*, and the pattern described above concerning 'value' is repeated: no occurrences at all in the deduction, and all but one occurrence in the sections devoted to application. Fichte uses other terms to refer to moral agents, chiefly 'rational being'; and he never uses 'humanity' as Kant does, to refer to a (special morally relevant) *property* of human beings (a sense of 'humanity' in which it makes sense to talk about humanity '*in* oneself or others'). Nor does he describe humanity as being an object of respect or as possessing a special dignity or as being an objective end or an end in itself. Strikingly, the one occurrence of the term in which it designates, in Kantian fashion, that feature in virtue of which human beings merit moral respect, is within a quotation from Schelling at *SS* IV: 225. In his mature works Fichte uses 'humanity' exclusively as a mass noun to refer to the human species (for instance, to describe humanity's progress over history [as at *SS* IV: 240, 241, 256] or to describe something as good or useful for human beings generally [as at *SS* IV: 176 or VI: 328–329]).[3]

This is also in the end not very surprising, since on Fichte's theory, human beings as such simply have no particular value and are in no sense the end at which moral action aims. That end is the exercise of rational agency; and although there is a meaningful overlap between the set of rational agents and the members of the human species, the overlap is far from complete. This also seems to me to reflect no fundamental disagreement with Kant, who, after all, tells us that what he means by 'humanity,' in the passages in which he describes it as an end in itself, is *rational nature*, and who discusses, explicitly, the possibility of nonhuman finite rational agents no less bound by the moral law than we are (*Groundwork*, AA 4: 408). Still, there is something more radical about Fichte's divorce of rational nature from the biologically human than most interpreters seem to see in Kant.

Before explaining why (Section 3) I will give a brief overview of Fichte's ethical theory (Section 2), because it will be unfamiliar to most readers. (The next section draws heavily on some recent work of mine [Kosch 2014, 2015a, 2017, 2018]. Readers familiar with that work may want to skip it.)

2. Fichte's Ethical Theory

Fichte's theory is a form of constitutivism on which rational agency has a necessary end, and moral obligations are construed as rational obligations to act in ways that further that end. The end is independence (alternatively, self-sufficiency). Independence has a formal and a material aspect.

Formally, independence provides a standard of correctness of *deliberation*. An agent is not deciding (fully formally) rationally unless she is doing so conscientiously in a double sense: letting her own conviction be her guide about what the right thing to do is in the situation (instead of deferring to someone else's opinion), and making sure she has a (genuine) conviction to act on (instead of acting thoughtlessly or impulsively). When an agent performs the action that is dictated by the conviction that issues from the sufficiently energetic application of her reflective capacities in a given situation, and performs it because it is so dictated, she acts independently in this formal sense.[4]

Materially or substantively, independence provides an objective standard of correctness of *actions*: an agent is not acting (fully materially) rationally unless she is taking the best means at her disposal to remove or decrease substantive limitations along one (or more) of the dimensions essential to rational agency. Fichte derives an account of these dimensions in an exercise of transcendental anthropology in the "deduction of principle" sections of the two major works of practical philosophy of the Jena period (the 1796–1797 *Foundations of Natural Right* and the 1798 *System of Ethics*). The idea is to begin from the premise that reflective self-consciousness is possible (a premise Fichte assumes his reader will grant) and to argue for these dimensions of limitation as necessary conditions of self-consciousness.

The conclusion of this set of arguments is that any intellect conscious of itself must be *practical* (a willing, not merely a thinking, being), *embodied* (having real, if finite, external causal powers), and *one among many* such beings (an 'individual'). Duties concerning agents as practical reasoners, as embodied physical causes, and as inhabiting a shared world with other such agents follow from this division. Moral duties are, then, duties to overcome obstacles to the exercise of the practical intellect, to the execution of rationally formed plans, and to the coordination of individual activity in pursuit of these first two ends.[5] (Fichte's normative theory is thus consequentialist in structure,[6] although his account of foundations is Kantian,[7] and although it incorporates an independent formal condition on correct deliberation.[8])

FICHTE ON THE VALUE OF RATIONAL AGENCY 205

A priori principles governing the coordination of the activity of rational agents who are individuals are treated in the *Foundations of Natural Right*. Although Fichte takes some principles governing rational coordination to be a priori, he takes all actual rights to be the products of actual schemes of coordination and so to be entirely conventional. The purpose of such schemes is to allow rational agents who are multiple to 'coexist as free,' by which Fichte means: to exercise their causality in the shared external world without inevitably undermining others' efforts to do the same. To do this, they must divide up the space of *possible* action into non-overlapping individual spheres of *permissible* action and must organize themselves politically so as to guarantee the inviolability of these spheres.

So rational agents need to together develop a structure of rules and roles that order their collective existence, and the result is not only the foundation but also a good part of the edifice of their collective moral life. Although Fichte is a kind of act consequentialist, he believes that virtually everything rational agents accomplish (including what might appear to be solitary pursuits) relies on interpersonal cooperation, and so he also believes that the question of what an individual ought to do in a given situation is almost always settled by the conjunction of the laws they live under and the particular ends and duties that go along with their place in the social division of labor.

For the same reason, he denies that there is a morally sanctioned way of interacting with adults who, for whatever reason, refuse to become or remain members in good standing of some political community. Full moral standing, on his theory, relies on active membership in some such community.

3. The Extent of the Moral Community

The set of beings owed moral consideration is, then, the set of those integrated (or, with caveats I will shortly explain, integratable) into some political community.[9] The problem of identifying (potential) co-citizens is therefore not only politically but also morally extremely important, as Fichte explains in this passage from the *Foundations of Natural Right* (whose context is a discussion of who should be considered potential fellow citizens):

> Kant says: act in such a way that the maxim of your will can be a principle of universal legislation. But who belongs to the kingdom ruled by this legislation, and who is entitled to its protection? I am supposed to treat (*behandeln*) certain beings in such a way that I can will that they treat me in turn according to the same maxim. But I act (*handele*) every day upon animals and inanimate objects without ever seriously raising that question. Someone may say: obviously, only

206 RETHINKING THE VALUE OF HUMANITY

beings capable of the representation of a law, thus rational beings, are at issue. But this only substitutes one indeterminate concept for another, and does not answer my question at all. For how do I know which determinate object is a rational being? (*GN* III: 80–81)

He goes on to ask, in particular, about the status of children, domestic animals, and non-Europeans. He does not ask about women in this context, but his later arguments against according them full legal personhood (*GN* III: 304–312) make them another problematic case.

Fichte's discussion here recalls Bentham's (roughly contemporaneous) remarks about the moral status of entities that are not adult men of European ancestry in the note to chapter 17 of the *Introduction to the Principles of Morals and Legislation*. Both Fichte and Bentham are writing at a time when slavery is still practiced in the Americas and the transatlantic slave trade is still tolerated by the international community, when women have the full legal rights and responsibilities of men nowhere in the world, and when the consensus concerning the moral standing of children and animals is that they lack any. Both see the question of moral standing as a pressing one, given these facts.

For Bentham, the commonality defining morally considerable beings is sentience; so he takes the extent of the set of morally considerable beings to be (relatively) easily fixed. For Fichte the question is more vexed: he takes susceptibility to pleasure and pain to be irrelevant to moral standing (though it may be indirectly relevant to some moral duties), but he has no similarly straightforward criterion to substitute for it.

This might seem strange: has he not, in articulating the theory of agency on which his practical philosophy depends, already provided the relevant criterion? The moral community is made up of those beings who are self-conscious and therefore have the essential features of self-conscious beings (are embodied practical intellects that are individuals). But in the above passage he seems to be claiming that this answer to the question does not suffice.

On reflection we can see that this is true. Part of what it is to say that rational agents are individuals is to say that they lack direct access to one another's mental lives. So to reply that those entitled to the protection of the moral law are the beings who are 'rational' and 'capable of the representation of a law' does not answer the question, in the absence of some behavioral criterion for determining which beings those are. That criterion would then do the actual work of sorting the potential co-citizens from the rest. But delineating such a criterion is far more problematic than delineating a behavioral criterion for sentience, for two reasons.

The first arises from Fichte's view, argued in §§3–4 of the *Foundations of Natural Right*, that a kind of socialization is a necessary condition of reflective self-consciousness. Reflective self-consciousness is the disposition to reflect on one's first-order attitudes and one's own behavior, to form higher-order attitudes, and eventually to adopt principles governing belief and action. So reflective self-consciousness is necessary for rational agency and its attendant capacities. If its existence relies on socialization, so too does rationality, and with it the capacity to represent a law. The socialization required for it is practice in the form of social interaction Fichte calls 'free reciprocal efficacy.' (I argue elsewhere that free reciprocal activity is cooperation, in any of its many forms.)[10] The invitation to such activity Fichte calls a 'summons' or, alternatively, 'upbringing.' So an unsocialized animal, no matter what its intellectual capacities and no matter what its interests, would not become reflectively self-conscious, and its rational potential would never be actualized. If the question Fichte is asking in the above passage is: Who is the appropriate *target* of such socialization (as it plausibly is), the response cannot refer to behavior that is, by hypothesis, impossible prior to such socialization. So the absence of the behavior characteristic of reflectively self-conscious adults cannot indicate the absence of rational potential. (Sentience, by contrast, is not essentially reliant on socialization.)

The second reason for the difficulty of articulating a behavioral criterion is that, on Fichte's view, even achieved reflective self-consciousness cannot display itself as such in the wrong social conditions. That is because the behavior that would display it—free reciprocal efficacy—requires, as its name suggests, another rational agent simultaneously engaged in it. Since recognition of something as a rational being is impossible in the absence of such behavior, two (or more) agents become recognizable to one another as rational beings only if both (or all) engage in free reciprocal efficacy with one another, as Fichte here explains:

> The relation of free beings to one another is therefore necessarily to be understood in the following way, and is posited as being so determined: the knowledge of the one individual by the other is conditioned on the other's treatment of it as free (that is, that the other limit his freedom through the concept of the freedom of the first). This mode of treatment is however conditioned on the action of the first toward the second, this action through the action and through the knowledge of the second, and so on to infinity. The relation of free beings to one another is thus the relation of interaction through intelligence and freedom. Neither can recognize the other if both do not reciprocally recognize one another. And neither can treat the other as a free being if both do not reciprocally treat one another that way. (*GN* III: 44)

The minimal cooperative scheme on Fichte's picture is mutual noninterference: abstaining from physical assault on one another's bodies and dividing the

208 RETHINKING THE VALUE OF HUMANITY

space of possible activity in a way that allows each to pursue some set of activities uninterfered with by the other. The cooperative schemes characteristic of social life are more complex. They include shared language, customs, and norms, which afford ways of displaying rationality even to third parties with whom one is not currently *interacting*. But the availability of these ways does not undercut the condition that Fichte here articulates, and so does not preclude the possibility of a normally socialized adult, able to engage in this sort of behavior but not given the opportunity to engage in it, being thereby rendered unable to present to others as a rational being. A captive in chains, deprived of the ability to act in a way that demonstrates that she grasps the freedom and rationality of her captors, would also be deprived of the opportunity to demonstrate her rationality to them.[11]

These considerations explain why simple appeal to the theory of rational agency cannot answer the question posed in the passage, which we might now rephrase in this way: How can agents living in a world full of items many of which are causally efficacious, which act in a way that is apparently purposive, and which display some intelligence, sort the ones that are potential fellow citizens from the ones that are not? Fichte offers, in the *Foundations*, what look like three different answers to this question.

His reasoning in the second division seems to conclude in the position that nature settles this question for us by giving (potentially) rational agents bodies of a certain sort. There are actually two accounts there, not clearly distinguished.

On the more prominent one (*GN* III: 78–80, 81–82), the form of the body is, in the human case, a kind of natural sign of its rational potential. Human bodies are distinguished from nonhuman animal bodies in lacking an *articulation* that defines a determinate sphere of movement, having instead an articulation that permits 'infinite determinability' (*GN* III: 79).[12] On a second account (only suggested, not explicitly spelled out, at *GN* III: 80–81), we recognize other rational beings by the *similarity* of their bodies to ours. If this were indeed Fichte's view, 'humanity' in the sense of membership in the human species would have real moral significance in his theory. The similarity condition faces problems, of course, insofar as similarity admits of degrees, and the groups about which Fichte is asking are all to some extent similar to, and to some extent dissimilar to, adult European males. But in any event Fichte does not develop the physical similarity criterion, and may not even mean to suggest it in these brief remarks.

Later in the *Foundations* we find a third account, on which we recognize other rational beings by certain features, not of their embodiment, but of their behavior in interaction with us. On this account, it seems that we learn who the potential other rational agents are by *trial and error*. So, for instance, in §43 of the first appendix Fichte writes:

FICHTE ON THE VALUE OF RATIONAL AGENCY 209

> It is a natural drive in human beings to suspect beings outside of themselves of rationality, where this is at all plausible, and to treat objects (for example, animals) as though they had it. The parents will treat their child in the same way, summoning it to free activity; and in this way rationality and freedom will gradually become manifest in it. (*GN* III: 358)

In the Hoijer Nachschrift of the 1798 lectures on logic and metaphysics we find a similar thought. Fichte points out that in early human history people attributed rational agency to inanimate objects like rivers, and he mentions the example of animals in that passage as well (*Gesamtausgabe*, 4,3: 262–264). Clearly the individuals trying to interact in some broadly political way with rivers were not using embodiment as a criterion.

On this third account, there is no nonbehavioral sign of rational potential. What distinguishes (some) humans from (some) nonhuman animals (or inanimate objects) is only the way they respond to our attempts to cooperate with them. This third account is in fact the one foreshadowed in §§3–4 of the deduction; we can see it, for example, in the passage from *GN* III: 44 reproduced above. On it, the answer to the question of who is a rational being is settled only through interaction in which rationality and freedom are, or gradually become, manifest in cooperative behavior. The political community is made up of those who reliably engage in this kind of behavior, and it is to such individuals that the protection of the moral law extends. This is what we should take to be Fichte's considered view, and I will assume it in what follows.

It is clear that it does not entail that moral standing is limited in principle to human beings, nor that it extends to all human beings. Accepting the latter consequence, though it may constitute no departure from the historical Kant, is certainly atypical of contemporary Kantians, who prefer to tie membership in the moral community to rational agency as a potentiality, not only as an actuality. It is thought that it would be a liability of a Kantian picture if it did not allow all human beings, even infants, to be entitled to the full protection of the moral law.[13] But Fichte does not appear to see this as a liability.

He takes rights to accompany active cooperation in a commonwealth: anyone who is not a cooperator is not a rights-bearer in the legal sense (nor, since there are no extralegal rights, in any other sense). So he admits several classes of non-rights-bearing human beings, which we can usefully sort under two general categories. The first consists of those who are not yet, but might become, full citizens with legal responsibilities (children who are still being brought up [*GN* III: 359]; migrants before they have been integrated and assuming they lack the negotiated legal status of the envoys of another state [*GN* III: 383–384]). The second consists of adults who refuse to become or remain part of such a system (hermits, who refuse to enter a commonwealth with those around them and so refuse to have rights [SS IV: 237–238]; criminals, whose actions display their lack of commitment to the cooperative scheme articulated in the law [GN III: 261, 266, 268 et passim]).

Fichte's comments about the status of criminals and children illustrate especially well the connection he sees between an individual's behavior and their claim to be regarded as a rational being. Concerning the former, Fichte reasons as follows: with noncooperators cooperation is impossible; but it is only in cooperation that rationality is displayed; therefore fellow citizens should revise their view of a criminal's rationality. In removing himself from the social contract, the criminal at once forfeits both his political rights and others' recognition of him as a rational being (GN III: 260–261, 384; IV: 279). (Fichte assumes, in drawing this conclusion, that effective mechanisms of enforcement are in place, and that all are able to support themselves within the sphere of activity legally allotted them. Where there is not a system of sanctions sufficient to incentivize compliance in most cases, there is no commonwealth at all; likewise in the case of a system of coordination that would require some to accept starvation or servitude as the price of abiding by the law.)[14]

Children illustrate the same dependency relation in reverse. They lack all political rights, according to Fichte, because they are still in the process of acquiring the capacities and dispositions that will make them reliable cooperators, and their ability to display these is therefore limited (GN III: 359–362). (Fichte explicitly connects their lack of rights to their inability to be the subjects of legal duties: "The child, insofar as it is being brought up, is not at all free, and so not at all a possible subject of rights or duties" [GN III: 359]).

That moral duties concerning rightless individuals are profoundly different from moral duties toward fellow citizens should come as no surprise since, as I have said, most moral duties depend for their concrete determination (and many depend for their very existence) on the rules and roles that order the collective existence of a group of people, and such individuals, ex hypothesi, have no place in such a system.

Moral duties concerning rightless individuals can be sorted under two principles: (1) one should actively try to integrate (or reintegrate) such individuals into the commonwealth, and (2) one should avoid or limit interaction with them unless and until this can be done. So Fichte argues, for instance, that there can be no moral justification for allowing migrants to exist in political limbo: morally, they must be integrated, or, if this is genuinely impossible, deported (GN III: 383–385). Hermits must be avoided if they refuse to be integrated, since there is by hypothesis no rightful way of interacting with them (SS IV: 237–238). The default treatment of criminals is expulsion (or interment, which Fichte regards as a kind of internal exile)—which might be reversed, and full citizenship restored, given sufficient evidence that the individual's cooperation can be relied on in the future.[15] Parents have a moral duty to educate their children, and thereby to make them into rational beings and potential fellow-citizens, while constraining their behavior in extralegal ways for the sake of their own and others' well-being until they reach that point (*SS* IV: 335–341).

The first and second of these moral duties concerning rightless individuals are of course in some tension with one another, insofar as integration is a process of socialization consisting in the very free reciprocal activity that has been suspended, or not yet established, in these cases. Unsurprisingly, different emphasis is placed on the second or the first duty depending on whether it has been suspended or not yet established.

The justification of the second duty (to avoid interaction) is quickly stated: with the person who is not integrated one cannot interact without fear of mutual interference, since his projects, like one's own, will involve parts of the shared physical world, and since by hypothesis neither will know which parts those are (*SS* IV: 237–238).

The justification of the first duty (to educate/integrate) marks another contrast with Kant, at least on standard interpretations. Kant described rational agency as an obligatory end, but contemporary Kantians explain that this does not entail that it is (in virtue of that) something to be created or brought into being, or something to be pursued or promoted in a maximizing way. Korsgaard (1996, 124–125) writes that it "functions in our deliberations negatively—as something that is not to be acted against." This is typical of Kant's interpreters (see also Herman 2007, chaps. 11 and 12). This is usually seen as a positive feature of Kant's theory: taking humanity as one's end does not oblige one to bring more human beings into existence nor to make the ones that do exist more rational than they already are.

Kant did explicitly deny that it is a duty to further the moral or the natural perfection of other adults, and this is usually taken to encompass having as one's (direct) end the improvement of their rational capacities (*Metaphysics of Morals*, AA 6: 385–398). Fichte, by contrast, construes duties of beneficence precisely as duties to further what Kant called the 'natural and moral perfection' of others; and he takes them to include a general moral duty to educate even one's adult peers (*SS* IV: 290–291). It is this general moral duty, "the universal moral duty of every morally good human being to spread morality beyond himself and to promote it everywhere" (*GN* III: 358), that, applied to parents, requires them to cultivate the rational capacities of the children they live with.[16]

So the duty to educate children is an instance of a more general duty to improve actual and to actualize potential rationality, to expand the domain of the rational at the expense of everything outside it. There are two important things to note here, in further contrast with (again, usual understandings of) Kant's view. First, it is ruled out neither by Fichte's texts nor by his principle that there be a duty to produce (more) potentially rational beings. Second, there is no reason to think that the general positive duty to (try to) render the beings that exist more rational is limited to human beings. We have already seen that Fichte takes us to be naturally disposed to behave in an educative manner toward a range of nonhuman objects. The disposition does not direct our efforts exclusively toward human beings. Nor does the account of the duty to cultivate potential rationality offer any resources for limiting that duty to the case of human beings. In fact anything that experience shows to respond appropriately appears to be an object of such duties.

The examples of humans without rights make it clear that for Fichte the community of beings entitled to the protection of the moral law is smaller than the human race. But the account of the identification of potentially rational beings indicates that it might be made larger than the human race as well—how large depending, in part, on human efforts—and the account of the duty to educate seems to entail that we are obliged to make such efforts. There is no reason that I can find, textual or philosophical, for thinking that Fichte would not embrace this result.

Success in such cultivation would bring with it an expansion of the political domain—and with it the set of entities to which the protection of the moral law extends—to encompass everything that shows us through its interaction with us (interaction of the sort described in the quotation from GN III: 44 above) that it is capable of standing in a relation of mutual recognition with us.

4. The Moral Community, Expanded

For someone who accepts the basic Fichtean idea that morality requires continually pushing back limits on rational agency and its exercise, the conclusion that it requires the continual expansion of the moral community will surely seem plausible. In this section I would like to expand on it by considering, in a very preliminary way, two examples of nonhuman agents that might meet Fichte's behavioral criterion for membership in the moral community, one actual and one that is at the moment merely possible: cetaceans and intelligent machines.

Insofar as philosophers have thought about duties concerning nonhuman animals as individuals, they have followed Bentham in focusing on animals *qua* sentient, not *qua* rational or potentially rational,[17] even though it is clear that some nonhuman animals are both highly intelligent and highly social, capable of engaging in voluntary cooperation not only with one another, but also with us.

Whales and dolphins seem to provide the clearest cases. Bottlenose dolphins, to take the most extensively studied example, live (in the wild) in complexly organized, cosmopolitan societies (Connor 2007; Gazda et al. 2005). (They are, among other things, the only nonhuman animals to form higher-order alliances [Connor 2007; Connor, Heithaus, and Barre 2001]).[18] They engage in sophisticated communication (Connor 2007; Marino et al. 2007) and are able to address and to refer to one another by name (Janik and Sayigh 2013; Janik, Sayigh, and Wells 2006). They have culture (Rendell and Whitehead 2001) and use tools (Krützen et al. 2005). Captive dolphins have been shown capable of operating with abstract concepts (including higher-order concepts) and of parsing commands based on their syntactic structure (Herman 2006; Marino et al. 2007). They are capable of joint attention (with both humans and with other dolphins [Pack and Herman 2006]) and of planned joint activity (with other dolphins [Herman 2006]). They also display many aspects of what Fichte would call 'self-consciousness,' including metacognition (Smith et al. 1995), mirror self-recognition (Reiss and Marino 2001), and behavioral self-awareness (Herman 2002, 2006) and self-monitoring (Marino et al. 2007; McCowan et al. 2000).

Like many dolphin species, bottlenose dolphins forage and parent cooperatively and display a wide range of cooperative and altruistic behaviors, not only toward other dolphins but also toward marine mammals of other species.[19] They are known to offer assistance to human beings in distress, as well as to solicit assistance from human beings.[20] Long-term convention-mediated cooperative fishing arrangements involving wild dolphins and human fishermen have been reported in several parts of the world, since antiquity.[21] The last fact is, to my mind, the most interesting. Many domestic animals are able to cooperate with human beings, sometimes in quite sophisticated ways, plausibly because they have been selected for their ability to do so.[22] Few wild animals do this, none (to my knowledge) in a way that displays the flexibility of dolphin-human partnerships.[23]

What can we say about their moral status, from a Fichtean perspective? It seems plausible that they can meet the behavioral criterion for membership in the moral community, indeed that they actually do meet it, insofar as they are actually engaged in cooperative activity with one another and with human beings, both in captivity and in the wild. The limits of the scope and complexity of these interactions seem set not by limits on dolphin intelligence or willingness, nor even by limitations on interspecies communication, but instead by the fact that we and they live in largely non-overlapping physical spaces. We are at most foreign visitors in the sea, and (with rare exceptions)[24] they are not so much as visitors on land. So (certain fishermen aside) we have little use for conventions dividing the space of possible action between us and them. They have more use for these in the somewhat larger area of their interaction with seagoing human beings and as captives in aquaria. But it is an interesting fact that, increasingly, such conventions are being put in place. (Laws in much of the world now prohibit not only hunting dolphins but also fishing with nets in which they can

214 RETHINKING THE VALUE OF HUMANITY

become entangled and drown, and the practice of holding them in captivity for human entertainment is under increasing moral pressure.) So where we do interact with them, increasingly, dolphins are treated less like other animals and more like persons. All of this is what Fichte's theory would predict, and at least part of what it would require.

A second type of candidate, not yet actual but perhaps imminent, are human-level machine intelligences. There is no consensus on how far we are from the development of these intelligences, but the prospect has been the object of increasing attention in recent years, both in the popular press and among professional philosophers. For the most part it has been treated as a danger—an "existential threat" to humanity, in the words of Elon Musk (Gibbs 2017)—because of the assumption that once the human level is reached it will quickly be surpassed by new forms of machine intelligence themselves the product of intelligent machines.[25]

The philosophical literature on this issue is considerably smaller than the animal ethics literature; still, one can discern in it a gap analogous to the one there, namely a relative lack of consideration of what we might owe to such machines, not *qua* sentient but *qua* rational agents in something like the Fichtean sense.[26] This is the case despite the fact that the sort of AIs that would be dangerous to us are, remarkably, typically characterized as rational agents in something very like that sense. This discussion of artificial intelligence from the executive summary of the Global Challenges Foundation's (2015) report *12 Risks That Threaten Human Civilization* is an instructive example:

> AI is the intelligence exhibited by machines or software, and the branch of computer science that develops machines and software with human-level intelligence. The field is often defined as "the study and design of intelligent agents," systems that perceive their environment and act to maximise their chances of success. Such extreme intelligences could not easily be controlled (either by the groups creating them, or by some international regulatory regime), and would probably act to boost their own intelligence and acquire maximal resources for almost all initial AI motivations.
>
> And if these motivations do not detail the survival and value of humanity, the intelligence will be driven to construct a world without humans. This makes extremely intelligent AIs a unique risk, in that extinction is more likely than lesser impacts. On a more positive note, an intelligence of such power could easily combat most other risks in this report, making extremely intelligent AI into a tool of great potential. There is also the possibility of AI-enabled warfare and all the risks of the technologies that AIs would make possible. An interesting version of this scenario is the possible creation of "whole brain emulations": human brains scanned and physically represented in a machine.

This would make the AIs into properly human minds, possibly alleviating a lot of problems.[27]

There are far more philosophically sophisticated discussions of the issues mentioned in this passage (notably Chalmers 2010; Bostrom 2014; see also Bostrom and Yudkowsky 2014), but this one concisely expresses views that are widespread in this literature, and we learn something from how it sets up the problem.

First, notice the description of the constitutive ends of AI *qua* intelligent agent in its first paragraph. Regardless of their more specific ends ("for almost all initial AI motivations"), they will "act to boost their own intelligence" as well to maximize their ability to carry out whatever plans they may form ("to acquire maximal resources"). These appear to be descriptions of the first two components of Fichte's conception of material independence.

As a description of the constitutive end of human agents, Fichte's conception of material independence is often greeted (by philosophers) with skepticism or incredulity. (I have never understood exactly why.) But against that background it is all the more remarkable that an account like his is precisely what is supplied (by other philosophers) when a conception of the generic constitutive end(s) of artificially intelligent agents is called for. Bostrom (2014, chap. 7), for instance, also argues that we can assume that superintelligent machines, whatever else they aim at, will likely aim at self-preservation, protection of goal-integrity, cognitive enhancement, technological progress, and resource acquisition. Omohundro's (2008) list of "basic AI drives" is nearly identical. The content of these lists is strikingly like Fichte's account of the rationally obligatory ends of rational agents—except in one respect.

One end missing from the account in the above passage (as well as from Bostrom 2014 and Omohundro 2008) is the end of coordination with other rational agents. This is because individuality, a constitutive determination of rational agency on Fichte's picture, is not considered to be a constitutive determination of human-(or-higher-)level AI. The existence of a plurality of such agents is not assumed; instead the emergence of a single dominant intelligence able to suppress rivals is taken to be not only a possibility but even the most likely scenario, insofar as, if it does not emerge immediately, it might still emerge at any later point (Bostrom 2014, 216). This is something that could never be true of rational animals, because the way higher animals are produced requires that more than one of them exist. On Fichte's account it is also not something that could be true of reflective agents, because on his account reflective self-consciousness is produced only in the context of social interaction that is cooperative in the way I have described. I will return to that in a moment.

The second thing to notice about the passage above is how its use of the term 'humanity' differs from the Kantian one. The passage does float the suggestion

that some AIs might be appropriately regarded as instances of 'humanity'—
"properly human minds"—though the assumption is that this would be appropriate only if they were digital copies of the mentality of biological humans.[28]
But it is clear, I think, that for both Fichte and Kant (who, after all, explicitly countenanced the possibility of nonhuman rational beings who would nonetheless be bound by the moral law; see *Groundwork* 4: 408), nonreplica artificial intelligences could be members of the moral community because they could exemplify 'humanity' in the technical Kantian sense without being uploaded exemplars of humanity in the biological sense. But this is not the usual assumption in this literature. The result is that a machine intelligence that is not an uploaded human intelligence is typically not considered a potentially morally considerable being, but is instead treated either as a threat to or a tool in the hands of biological human beings.[29]

The threat posed by superhuman AI is conceptualized in a number of ways in the literature on it, not all compatible (in part because the threat itself takes many forms). One aspect of the worry is about the creation of a powerful self-reproducing system that would escape control. But this would not be a fundamentally different kind of threat than the kind posed by any sufficiently robust self-replicating (but unintelligent) machine (or animal), and so not a distinctive sort of threat AI would pose as artificial *intelligence*.

The peculiar sort of threat posed by intelligent beings is their capacity for specifically strategic reasoning: their ability to occupy one's perspective, predict one's rational next move, and plot their own next move accordingly. The assumption of such an ability figures centrally in the worst-case scenarios Bostrom and others describe.

On Fichte's view, the special threat posed by a strategic intelligence and the cooperative possibilities inherent in interaction with a strategic intelligence go hand in hand. His account of the production of reflective self-consciousness assumes that strategic thinking in general has its roots in specifically cooperative interaction, and therefore that the capacity for the former cannot be present without some prior instance of the latter.[30] His amoral rational justification for membership in a commonwealth appeals to the interest any rational agent has in cooperating with such beings—at minimum by finding, and finding a way to enforce, some conventions of mutual noninterference.

Each of these aspects of his view can, of course, be denied.

The plausibility of the first is undermined by evidence that some elements of strategic thinking can emerge among noncooperative social animals.[31] That an AI may be capable of strategic reasoning without being disposed to cooperation (or even capable of cooperation) is certainly an assumption in much of the AI literature (see, e.g., Bostrom 2014, chap. 10). Given how little idea anyone has what form machine intelligence would take, it seems wishful thinking to rule out this possibility.

FICHTE ON THE VALUE OF RATIONAL AGENCY   217

The second, that any rational agent has some (purely self-serving) reason to seek cooperation with other rational agents, is of course true only as a general rule. Fichte admits that it might be prudentially rational for an individual to eschew cooperation with specific others or on specific terms. Given how little we may have to contribute, it is far from clear that even being recognized by potentially cooperative AIs as potential cooperators would suffice to give us a place at any bargaining table. Alternatively, we might be integrated, but on undesirable terms, perhaps as an exploited or neglected underclass (consistent, we can confirm by observation of contemporary societies the world over, with being regarded as part of the moral community by our exploiters or neglecters).

This abundance of bad possible outcomes for biological humans (bad especially for those, like Musk, not already relegated to an exploited or neglected underclass) might explain the popularity of the other path distinguished in the second paragraph of the passage above. This is the path on which AIs are somehow maintained not as genuinely autonomous agents (with whom the prospect of collaborating might arise), but instead as mere tools. Commenting on the European Parliament's resolution to create "an ethical-legal framework for robots" (Leitzén 2017) and in response to the suggestion that robots "as good as human agents" be considered in some respects persons (e.g., as responsible for damage they cause), the chair of Oxford's Digital Ethics Lab has suggested, apparently seriously, that it would be more appropriate to treat them on the model of slaves in Roman law: "As the Romans knew, attributing some kind of legal personality to robots (or slaves) would relieve those who should control them of their responsibilities" (Floridi 2017).

That statement probably requires no comment, but let me just point out that from a Fichtean perspective a dual-status society in which some self-conscious, rational, cooperating members would lack the rights of citizens and with them full moral standing would be both unstable politically[32] and far more problematic morally than human beings' outright replacement with more intelligent, cooperative, powerful artificial rational agents (given certain constraints on how the replacement would be carried out).[33] Indeed it is not clear that he would see any moral cost at all in such a replacement simply per se. This is part of why it seems in the end undesirable, because potentially misleading, to describe Fichte's as an ethical theory in which the 'value of humanity' plays a central role.[34]

Notes

1. The single passage in which the phrase "value of humanity" occurs in Fichte's published work is one in which he explains that the value of humanity consists of its exceptional exemplars, those who have, through great effort, developed their human potential to the highest degree (*Anweisung zum seligen Leben*, V: 426). Clearly, this is

218   RETHINKING THE VALUE OF HUMANITY

far from the usual employment of the phrase in contemporary Kantian ethics. I discuss the components further in Section 1. (Here and throughout, Fichte's works are cited according to the volume and page number of the 1845–1846 and 1834–1835 edition of his collected works and Nachlass, respectively (reprinted as Fichte 1971), except where this is impossible. "SS" in citations refers to *System of Ethics*, "GN" to *Foundations of Natural Right*.)

2. Fichte's target in these passages appears to be theories, like Godwin's, on which certain sorts of people (e.g., Fenelon) are more worthy of moral consideration because of intrinsic properties than other sorts of people (e.g., Fenelon's chambermaid).

3. The only work containing language echoing the Kantian use of 'humanity' is the 1792 *Attempt at a Critique of All Revelation*, in which Fichte follows Kant on a number of other issues as well on which he will, almost immediately after its publication, begin to depart from Kant.

4. See Kosch (2014) for a fuller treatment of conscience in Fichte's theory.

5. See Kosch (2015a, 2018) for a fuller treatment of the substantive condition on moral worth in Fichte's theory.

6. Fichte embraces a maximizing, fully agent-neutral form of consequentialism. See Kosch (2018, chap. 3) for a fuller explanation.

7. One finds this kind of theory structure in Hare (1997) or in Cummiskey (1996), for example. What we have reason to do is cashed out in terms of what it is rational to do, but what it is rational to do involves, in part, acting toward certain ends. So Fichte's theory is teleological in one of the two ways in which that term is used in contemporary ethical theory: its moral principle judges acts correct just in case they promote a specified end. It is non-teleological in the other current sense: it does not derive claims about what one ought to do from independent claims about what is good. It is, to use Cummiskey's language, a normative consequentialism without being a foundational consequentialism.

8. The two criteria of evaluation are independent because an action can be formally correct (that is, conscientiously undertaken) without being, objectively, the action in the circumstances most conducive to the moral end; or an agent may rashly (and so unconscientiously) perform an action that is objectively the correct one in the circumstances. That independence in the formal sense is a constitutive end of rational agency is of course a substantive claim. One might think that, given that he recognizes an objective criterion of right action (viz. material independence), Fichte ought to say that the right way to make decisions is just whatever way turns out to best further that end (and for all we know that might be acting on instinct or on the rules learned in the nursery). But Fichte disagrees, both because he thinks that instincts and rules learned in the nursery often lead us substantively astray and because he thinks we have an independent interest in the rationality, deliberateness, and independence of our procedure in deciding what to do.

9. What I say in this section is an interpretation of Fichte's views during the Jena period. His 1813 lectures on political philosophy (*Die Staatslehre, oder über das Verhältniss des Urstaates zum Vernunftreiche*) seem to me to present a view in some respects irreconcilable with this, and so I have not tried to integrate them here.

FICHTE ON THE VALUE OF RATIONAL AGENCY 219

10. I further explore the connection between cooperative interactions and the possibility of reflective agency in Kosch 2021.

11. Note that the point concerns only the (self-imposed, in this example) epistemic limitations of the captors. Fichte's claim, in the discussion of cosmopolitan right, that there is a moral obligation to allow foreign visitors to "explain themselves" (*GN* III: 384) is an application of this thought. They must be engaged, however briefly, in the free reciprocal efficacy that is the offering and consideration of 'transactions' (which might range from economic or other exchange to application for citizenship). This is equivalent to giving them the opportunity to demonstrate their status as rational beings and potential collaborators. Similar considerations support allowing growing children age-appropriate freedoms (*GN* III: 358–359).

12. Exactly what Fichte has in mind here is difficult to make out, because the actual ground of human flexibility (if by that we mean the ability to suit ourselves to a wide variety of ecological niches) is the malleability of our culture, not that of our bodies.

13. See, e.g., Herman (1996, 61–62), who notes that Kant himself is silent on the question of the moral status of children.

14. I discuss this issue at greater length in Kosch 2017.

15. Fichte's treatment of criminal law is of course more complicated than this, allowing a range of less severe sanctions instituted by common agreement. But the distinctive (and, for my purpose here, important) feature of his view is that punishment is not justified by desert, indeed not justified by anything except its role in deterring future crime. This is permissible (only) because in committing the crime its targets have *already* forfeited the rights to property and bodily inviolability they possessed only *qua* citizens.

16. As one might expect, no duty to educate is grounded in any right of the child to an education (*GN* III: 358) though it may be prescribed by positive law and so correspond to rights of other adult citizens (in which case "it is not a duty owed directly to the child, but to the state" [*GN* III: 360]).

17. Singer (1977) is the most influential modern text. My characterization here applies only to accounts of duties to individual animals. Accounts of duties to species are not typically limited in this way.

18. Several pairs or trios of stably affiliated males will come together into groups of ten to fourteen for the purpose of defending prospective mates or acquiring them from other such groups. Connor (2007) describes what he takes to be third-order alliances as well.

19. See Connor and Norris (1982) for a survey. Examples include supporting sick or injured individuals near the surface and helping beached individuals find their way to safety. For a recent account of a bottlenose dolphin helping humans to rescue a pair of beached pygmy sperm whales, see Lilley (2008).

20. Instances of dolphins helping humans who are drowning or under attack by sharks have been reported since antiquity. For a recent example of a dolphin soliciting human assistance, see Sieczkowski (2013).

21. Pryor et al. (1990) describe a tradition in a Laguna, Brazil, dating to 1847 and cite other sources of accounts of similar cooperation in other parts of the world, going

back to Pliny the Elder. A more recent account of dolphin-human fishing collaboration in Myanmar is Clark (2017). Not surprisingly, the conventions governing such cooperation are different in Myanmar and Brazil.

22. See, e.g., Hearne (1986) for discussion of dogs and horses. Thanks to Sarah Buss for the pointer to Hearne.

23. The other oft-cited example is the honeyguide bird, which leads humans to beehives and then shares the spoils. See Isack and Reyer (1989). Sperm whales may be more cognitively sophisticated, and also more cooperative, even than dolphins, but their behavior has for logistical reasons been less well studied. See Whitehead (2003) for a survey.

24. Like many cetaceans, dolphins sometimes beach. There are even examples of clearly intentional, goal-directed beaching among cetaceans, though I know of no examples involving bottlenose dolphins. In discussing culture among toothed whales, Rendell and Whitehead (2001) discuss a hunting strategy involving intentional beaching in a group of Orcas. Mothers teach offspring to beach on seal breeding grounds in order to hunt the seal pups on land.

25. That there would be an intelligence explosion of this sort, were the human level of intelligence surpassed, can be doubted on a number of grounds, not least (to my thinking) the fact that creating AIs smarter than them would be as dangerous, for any generation of AIs, as creating AIs smarter than us is for us. Since by hypothesis they would be smarter than us, some generation of them could be expected to avoid this danger (assuming it is one). For a discussion of this and other obstacles to an intelligence explosion, see Chalmers (2010).

26. In fact there are few discussions of duties *toward* AIs in this literature at all, as I will explain, but where AIs are taken to be morally considerable, they are usually taken to be considerable just in case they are (and in virtue of being) sentient (cf., e.g., Bostrom 2014, 153–154). Chalmers (2010) is an exception.

27. In the six years that have passed between the first presentation of this paper in 2016 and its final preparation for publication, the literature about the ethical problems posed by AI has grown dramatically. I will not survey most of that literature, but it is worth mentioning that the status of AI as an existential risk to humanity seems to have receded somewhat in the minds of those thinking about it. The 2020 version of the Foundation's *Global Catastrophic Risks* report focuses on already evident problems (such as the political consequences of Facebook policies, the work of companies like Cambridge Analytica, racially biased algorithms, and the like). A survey of the global landscape of AI ethics guidelines (Jobin, Ienca, and Vayena 2019) found transparency (i.e., the ability of human beings to understand why an algorithm gives the results it does) to be the most-cited concern, followed by equity (i.e., the nonintroduction of bias in results). Non-maleficence, the chief concern of people thinking about AI at the time this paper was written, came only third. Of course this change may be explained by the salience of harms already occurring rather than by any change in the assessment of future risks.

28. Notice that the passage concludes with (what looks like) the truly awful inference that in this form, AI would not be (as much of) a threat—notwithstanding the fact that six

of the remaining eleven global catastrophic risks detailed in the report would themselves be the work of biological human beings.

29. Bostrom's (2014, 153–154) discussion of sentient simulations and their treatment ("mind crime") is an exception. See also Chalmers's (2010) description of the destruction of AIs living in a virtual environment as "genocide."

30. I survey the literature in social and evolutionary psychology that supports this thesis in Kosch (2021).

31. Tomasello (2014), for instance, has shown that chimps have a high degree of strategic intelligence in competitive situations, but without having any capacity for cooperation.

32. Where he discusses ancient slavery, in a set of 1813 lectures I have not considered here, Fichte commented that slavery was possible in the ancient world only due to a religious ideology according to which it was divinely ordained (*Die Staatslehre*, IV: 507–508).

33. That the idea of reinstating a system akin to Roman slavery should seem palatable to a twenty-first-century philosopher seems to me on the one hand remarkable, on the other of a piece with the apparently universal toleration of the idea of (indeed, apparent nostalgia for the institution of) slavery in much of this literature. This is true already of the extraordinary Asimov (1950), in which the slave is transformed over the course of the book into a perfectly self-sacrificing maternal figure (remnant of another dual-status system for which these same men have shown even more, and more openly articulated, nostalgia in recent years).

34. I am very grateful to Nandi Theunissen and Sarah Buss for their generous comments on an earlier draft of this paper, and to participants at the first workshop on the value of humanity at Johns Hopkins in 2016 for their feedback on a still earlier version of the paper that I read there.

References

Asimov, Isaac. 1950. *I, Robot*. Garden City, NY: Doubleday.

Bentham, Jeremy. 1907. *An Introduction to the Principles of Morals and Legislation*. Oxford: Clarendon Press.

Bostrom, Nick. 2014. *Superintelligence: Paths, Dangers, Strategies*. Oxford: Oxford University Press.

Bostrom, Nick, and Eliezer Yudkowsky. 2014. "The Ethics of Artificial Intelligence." In *The Cambridge Handbook of Artificial Intelligence*, edited by Keith Frankish and William M. Ramsey, 316–334. Cambridge: Cambridge University Press.

Chalmers, David. 2010. "The Singularity: A Philosophical Analysis." *Journal of Consciousness Studies* 17 (9–10): 7–65.

Clark, Doug. 2017 "In a Fragile Partnership, Dolphins Help Catch Fish in Myanmar." *New York Times*, August 31. https://www.nytimes.com/2017/08/31/world/asia/irrawaddy-dolphins-myanmar-fishing-conservation-cooperation.html.

Connor, Richard C. 2007. "Dolphin Social Intelligence: Complex Alliance Relationships in Bottlenose Dolphins and a Consideration of Selective Environments for Extreme

Brain Size Evolution in Mammals." *Philosophical Transactions of the Royal Society B: Biological Sciences* 362 (1480): 587–602. http://doi.org/10.1098/rstb.2006.1997.

Connor, Richard C., Michael R. Heithaus, and Lynne M. Barre. 2001. "Complex Social Structure, Alliance Stability and Mating Access in a Bottlenose Dolphin 'Super-alliance.'" *Proceedings of the Royal Society B: Biological Sciences* 268 (1464): 263–267. http://doi.org/10.1098/rspb.2000.1357.

Connor, Richard C., and Kenneth S. Norris. 1982. "Are Dolphins Reciprocal Altruists?" *American Naturalist* 119 (3): 358–374. http://www.jstor.org/stable/2460934.

Cummiskey, David. 1996. *Kantian Consequentialism*. Oxford: Oxford University Press.

Fichte, Johann Gottlieb. 1962–2011. *Gesamtausgabe der Bayerischen Akademie der Wissenschaften*. Edited by Reinhard Lauth, Hans Jacob, and Hans Gliwitzky. Stuttgart: Friedrich Frommann.

Fichte, Johann Gottlieb. 1971. *Werke*. 11 vols. Edited by Immanuel H. Fichte. Berlin: de Gruyter. [Cited by volume and page]

Floridi, Luciano 2017. "Roman Law Offers a Better Guide to Robot Rights Than Sci-Fi." *Financial Times*, February 22. https://www.ft.com/content/99d60326-f85d-11e6-bd4e-68d53499ed71.

Gazda, Stefanie K., Richard C. Connor, Robert K. Edgar, and Frank Cox. 2005. "A Division of Labour with Role Specialization in Group-Hunting Bottlenose Dolphins (*Tursiops truncatus*) off Cedar Key, Florida." *Proceedings of the Royal Society B: Biological Sciences* 272 (1559): 135–140. http://doi.org/10.1098/rspb.2004.2937.

Gibbs, Samuel. 2017. "Elon Musk: Regulate AI to Combat 'Existential Threat' before It's Too Late." *The Guardian*, July 17. https://www.theguardian.com/technology/2017/jul/17/elon-musk-regulation-ai-combat-existential-threat-tesla-spacex-ceo.

Global Challenges Foundation. 2015. *12 Risks That Threaten Human Civilization, Executive Summary*. Accessed August 10, 2017. https://globalchallenges.org/iwp-content/uploads/12-Risks-with-infinite-impact-Executive-Summary.pdf.

Global Challenges Foundation. 2020. *Global Catastrophic Risks 2020*. Accessed December 16, 2020. https://globalchallenges.org/wp-content/uploads/Global-Catastrophic-Risks-2020-Annual-Report.pdf.

Hare, Richard M. 1997. "Could Kant Have Been a Utilitarian?" In *Sorting Out Ethics*, 147–165. Oxford: Clarendon Press.

Hearne, Vicki. 1986. *Adam's Task: Calling Animals by Name*. New York: Knopf.

Herman, Barbara. 1997. *The Practice of Moral Judgment*. Cambridge, MA: Harvard University Press.

Herman, Barbara. 2007. *Moral Literacy*. Cambridge, MA: Harvard University Press.

Herman, Louis M. 2002. "Exploring the Cognitive World of the Bottlenosed Dolphin." In *The Cognitive Animal: Empirical and Theoretical Perspectives on Animal Cognition*, edited by Marc Bekoff, Colin Allen, and Gordon M. Burghardt, 275–283. Cambridge, MA: MIT Press.

Herman, Louis. M. 2006. "Intelligence and Rational Behaviour in the Bottlenosed Dolphin." In *Rational Animals?*, edited by Susan Hurley and Matthew Nudds, 429–467. Oxford: Oxford University Press.

Isack, Hussein A., and Heinz-Ulrich Reyer. 1989. "Honeyguides and Honey Gatherers: Interspecific Communication in a Symbiotic Relationship." *Science* 10: 1343–1346.

Janik, Vincent M., and Laela S. Sayigh. 2013. "Communication in Bottlenose Dolphins: 50 Years of Signature Whistle Research." *Journal of Comparative Physiology A* 199 (6): 479–489. https://doi.org/10.1007/s00359-013-0817-7.

Janik, Vincent. M., Laela S. Sayigh, and Randall S. Wells. 2006. "Signature Whistle Shape Conveys Identity Information to Bottlenose Dolphins." *Proceedings of the National Academy of Sciences of the United States of America* 103 (21): 8293–8297. http://doi.org/10.1073/pnas.0509918103.

Jobin, Anna, Marcello Ienca, and Effy Vayena. 2019. "Artificial Intelligence: The Global Landscape of Ethics Guidelines." *Nature Machine Intelligence* 1: 389–399.

Kant, Immanuel. 1900–. *Kants gesammelte Schriften*. 24 vols. Edited by Königlich Preussische Akademie der Wissenschaften zu Berlin, Deutschen Akademie der Wissenschaften zu Berlin, and Akademie der Wissenschaften zu Göttingen. Berlin: De Gruyter.

Kant, Immanuel. 1996. *Practical Philosophy*. Edited and translated by Mary J. Gregor and Allen Wood, with an introduction by Allen Wood. Cambridge: Cambridge University Press. [Cited by volume and page of the Akademie edition]

Korsgaard, Christine. 1996. *Creating the Kingdom of Ends*. Cambridge: Cambridge University Press.

Kosch, Michelle. 2014. "Practical Deliberation and the Voice of Conscience in Fichte's 1798 *System of Ethics*." *Philosophers' Imprint* 14 (30): 1–16.

Kosch, Michelle. 2015a. "Agency and Self-Sufficiency in Fichte's Ethics." *Philosophy and Phenomenological Research* 91 (2): 348–380.

Kosch, M. 2015b. "Fichtean Kantianism in 19th Century Ethics." *Journal of the History of Philosophy* 53 (1): 111–132.

Kosch, Michelle. 2017. "Individuality and Rights in Fichte's Ethics." *Philosophers' Imprint* 17 (12): 1–23.

Kosch, Michelle. 2018. *Fichte's Ethics*. Oxford: Oxford University Press.

Kosch, M. 2021. "Fichte on Summons and Self-Consciousness." *Mind* 130 (517): 215–249.

Krützen, Michael, Janet Mann, Michael R. Heithaus, Richard C. Connor, Lars Bejder, and William B. Sherwin. 2005. "Cultural Transmission of Tool Use in Bottlenose Dolphins." *Proceedings of the National Academy of Sciences of the United States of America* 102 (25): 8939–8943. https://www.pnas.org/doi/10.1073/pnas.0500232102.

Leitzén, Iina. 2017. "Robots and Artificial Intelligence: MEPs Call for EU-Wide Liability Rules." European Parliament Press Room, February 15. http://www.europarl.europa.eu/news/en/press-room/20170210IPR61808/robots-and-artificial-intelligence-meps-call-for-eu-wide-liability-rules.

Lilley, Ray. 2008. "Dolphin Saves Stuck Whales, Guides Them Back to Sea." Associated Press, March 12. http://news.nationalgeographic.com/news/2008/03/080312-AP-dolph-whal.html.

Marino, Lori, Richard C. Connor, R. Ewan Fordyce, Louis M. Herman, Patrick R. Hof, Louis Lefebvre, David Lusseau, Brenda McCowan, Esther A. Nimchinsky, Adam A. Pack, Luke Rendell, Joy S. Reidenberg, Diana Reiss, Mark D. Uhen, Estel Van der Gucht, and Hal Whitehead. 2007. "Cetaceans Have Complex Brains for Complex Cognition." *PLoS Biology* 5 (5): e139. http://doi.org/10.1371/journal.pbio.0050139.

McCowan, Brenda, Lori Marino, Erik Vance, Leah Walke, and Diana Reiss. 2000. "Bubble Ring Play of Bottlenose Dolphins (*Tursiops truncatus*): Implications for Cognition." *Journal of Comparative Psychology* 114 (1): 98–106. http://dx.doi.org/10.1037/0735-7036.114.1.98.

224 RETHINKING THE VALUE OF HUMANITY

Omohundro, Stephen M. 2008. "The Basic AI Drives." *Frontiers in Artificial Intelligence and Applications* 171 (1): 483–492.

Pack, Adam A., and Louis M. Herman. 2006. "Dolphin Social Cognition and Joint Attention: Our Current Understanding." *Aquatic Mammals* 32 (4): 443–460. doi:10.1578/AM.32.4.2006.443

Pallikkathayil, Japa. 2010. "Deriving Morality from Politics: Rethinking the Formula of Humanity." *Ethics* 121 (1): 116–147.

Pryor, Karen W., Jon Lindbergh, Scott Lindbergh, and Raquel Milano. 1990. "A Dolphin-Human Fishing Cooperative in Brazil." *Marine Mammal Science* 6: 77–82.

Reiss, Diana, and Lori Marino. 2001. "Mirror Self-Recognition in the Bottlenose Dolphin: A Case of Cognitive Convergence." *Proceedings of the National Academy of Sciences* 98 (10): 5937–5942.

Rendell, Luke, and Hal Whitehead. 2001 "Culture in Whales and Dolphins." *Behavioral and Brain Sciences* 24 (2): 309–324. doi:10.1017/S0140525X0100396X

Schelling, T. 1958. "The Strategy of Conflict: Prospectus for a Reorientation of Game Theory." *Journal of Conflict Resolution* 2 (3): 203–264.

Sieczkowski, Cavan. 2013. "Divers Rescue Dolphin after It 'Asks' for Help." *Huffington Post,* January 23. http://www.huffingtonpost.com/2013/01/23/dolphin-asks-divers-for-help-caught-in-fishing-line_n_2534674.html.

Singer, Peter. 1977. *Animal Liberation*. New York: Avon Books.

Smith, J. David, Jon I. Schull, Jared Strote, Kelli McGee, Roian Egnor, and Linda Erb. 1995. "The Uncertain Response in the Bottlenose Dolphin (*Tursiops truncatus*)." *Journal of Experimental Psychology: General* 124 (4): 391–408.

Tomasello, Michael. 2014. *A Natural History of Human Thinking*. Cambridge, MA: Harvard University Press.

Tschudin, Alain J.-P. C. 2006. "Belief Attribution Tasks with Dolphins: What Social Minds Can Reveal about Animal Rationality." In *Rational Animals?*, edited by Susan Hurley and Michael Nudds, 413–437. Oxford: Oxford University Press.

Whitehead, Hal. 2003. *Sperm Whales: Social Evolution in the Ocean*. Chicago: University of Chicago Press.

9

Explaining the Value of Human Beings

L. Nandi Theunissen

In these pages, I offer an account of the value of human beings, and therewith, the ground of what is owed to human beings. The account is steeped in the Kantian tradition even as it looks to transcend it. It is steeped in the Kantian tradition insofar as it takes people to be bearers of a value that properly constrains our actions involving others and ourselves. It departs from the Kantian tradition insofar as it proposes that the value of human beings is not absolute but *relational*. The value of human beings is held to be relational in the specific sense that it turns on a propensity to be *good for* something or someone, where *good for* is synonymous with *beneficial*. I take the view that things owe their value to the fact that they are or stand to be beneficial, and that the value of human beings is no exception. More particularly, I develop the perhaps surprising proposal that the value of human beings lies in our capacity to be beneficial for *ourselves*. As valuers, which is to say, as beings who have final ends that give meaning and point to what we do, we are able to lead flourishing lives in the way it is given to human beings to lead them, where the value of a flourishing life is most basically its value for the person whose life it is. In a phrase, we are of value because we can contribute in very particular ways to our flourishing, and we should relate to others and ourselves as such centers of a good life. Even as I respond to likely objections, I will not here defend this as the only or the best approach to the value of humanity. Instead, I devote myself to making a constructive, positive proposal.[1]

In some ways the account proposed here breaks with orthodoxy and is even iconoclastic, but in other ways the project is rather traditional. For I am committed to some idea of *common humanity*—to the idea that independently of race, sexual orientation, class, gender identity, or identification, human beings are owed basic forms of ethical response. By the lights of some working in other reaches of the humanities, this is a quaint and even a naïve starting point. The literary critic Mark Greif (2015, 328) gives voice to the familiar thought that the whole enterprise of thinking through the ground of our ethical significance is misguided.[2] Suffice it to say that I do not share this view. In her introduction to this volume, in the face of nearly twenty essays all grappling with the question of the value of humanity, Sarah Buss speaks to the significance she finds

---

L. Nandi Theunissen, *Explaining the Value of Human Beings* In: *Rethinking the Value of Humanity*.
Edited by: Sarah Buss and L. Nandi Theunissen, Oxford University Press. © Oxford University Press 2023.
DOI: 10.1093/oso/9780197539361.003.0010

226   RETHINKING THE VALUE OF HUMANITY

in our attempts to think and rethink this value. To see the point of this activity, Buss recalls us to the way we are disposed to react to instances of unapologetic expressions of contempt for human beings. At the same time, she notes just how difficult it is to make sense of the value of humanity "*in terms we ourselves can accept.*" I share her belief in the importance and difficulty of deepening our understanding of where we stand on the subject, and that is the first point of inspiration for this essay. Let me now share two more.

In defending a kind of relational theory of the value of humanity, I aim to reclaim the notion of benefit from its strong associations with exchange or market value and to return it to its original sense. Here I note the etymology of "beneficial," with *bene*, meaning "good" or "well," and with *ficus*, from *facere*, meaning "making" or "doing," so that the beneficial is the *well-doing*. This way of thinking about the good is taken for granted in classical philosophical works. There it is not a lowly form of value that stands in contrast to something high like the distinctively moral good. As I see it, devaluing well-doing is part of Kant's legacy, and it is a legacy I wish to interrupt—this is my second point of inspiration.

They say that every book, or as here, essay, is a symptom—a symptom in the psychoanalytic sense; that is certainly true of this work. In this project I give a prominent place to the relation we stand to bear to ourselves; that is, I give a prominent place to the self. The idea that our relation to ourselves could be of ethical significance struck me with the force of revelation when I first encountered it as a student of philosophy. As if by reflex, I had shared the assumption of many contemporary moral philosophers that the ethical has to do with *others* and what we owe to *them*. This is not the case in ancient ethics, and it is not the case in Kant, where we find the fine idea of duties to self. The revelation for me was that how we tend to our own lives, or in a Socratic idiom, how we care for our souls, may actually be at the heart of ethics and of our capacity to relate well and meaningfully with others. This is a live concern for me, and it is at the center of the present undertaking.

1. The Good

The topic of the value of human beings comes up in first-order discussions of how we should relate to others, and it is at stake in metaethical treatments of the normative and its ground.[3] Certainly, to think well about the first kind of question we must take a stand on a host of foundational questions, and it is with these that I begin. It is a first premise of this essay that value or the good, terms I am using interchangeably, is the ground of practical reason. Actions and temporally extended activities properly find their point in view of what is interesting, attractive, pleasant, enriching, excellent (and so on), and these are specific dimensions of the good.[4] I expand on this starting point in what follows, taking a stand on *good for* as the primary evaluative notion, and sharing my reasons for giving up on the notion of absolute value. Discussion of these questions is necessarily programmatic in a piece of this length,[5] but it prepares the ground for the treatment of the value of human beings in the remainder of the essay.

Rather than assert a basic conceptual division between the right and the good, or between the moral and the nonmoral good in such a way that the two represent distinctly different sources of normative concern, I begin with a good-centered monism[6] in which the good (and its contrary) is the ground of all practical concern.[7] Here I draw inspiration from the Greeks. As it happens, Henry Sidgwick (1907, bk. 1, chap. 9) puts the point I would make here very well when he says:

> What mainly marks off ancient ethical controversy from modern is their use of a generic notion instead of a specific one in expressing the common moral judgments on actions. Virtue, or right action, was commonly regarded among the Greeks as only a species of the good; and so, on this view of what the basic moral input is, the first question that offered itself when they were trying to systematise conduct, was: What is the relation of this species of good to the rest of the genus? This was the question that the Greek thinkers argued about, from first to last.

What Sidgwick is saying here is that when the ancients are thinking about the thing to do in the circumstances, the analogue of our notion of obligation or right action, they are thinking of it as an aspect of the good. As I would put the point, the key concepts in classical ethics are virtue and the beneficial, and the guiding question is how to understand the relationship between them. My thinking in this area is shaped by two great philosophers: Judith Jarvis Thomson (1997) and Philippa Foot (2001). Both make use of a schema for thinking about the relationship between virtue and the beneficial that goes something like this. Virtues are ways of doing and being that are necessary because and insofar as some human good hangs on them.[8] On this way of setting things up, virtuous actions and states of motivation are good because and insofar as they protect, facilitate, produce, or realize a good for human beings. Key among "the ways of being good" are *being a good k*—being a good action or being a good person— and *being good for someone*—for example, being good for human beings. Both concepts play important roles in our life and thought, and on this view, *good for* is prior or fundamental.[9]

According to the view that I endorse, the value of whatever is of value is ultimately a function of its actual or possible contribution to the good for someone or for their life. For the simple reason that *we* are the beings whose subject ethics is, ethics pays special attention to the good for human beings.[10] As I read it, this is the program announced in the first sentence of the *Nicomachean Ethics,* where Aristotle tells us that all individual and collective human activity is undertaken for the sake of living well, something we should have clearly in our sights so that we can know what truly to direct ourselves toward.[11] This is also the conception of the good that is at stake in countless Platonic dialogues. The good benefits and the bad harms—for Plato's Socrates, these are conceptual truths.[12] I myself make the point, not as a claim about what good *means*, but as a claim about what good *is*. The good is essentially such as to change or alter something or someone in a positive way. The good is essentially *affecting*, not in the sense that it relates to states of feeling or emotion (though it may), but in the sense that it exerts an influence or has an effect. To my mind, this way of thinking about the good is borne out in a host of ordinary, evaluative explanations: of a nourishing meal, of a conversation with a friend, and of the vocation around which we structure a life.[13] The examples bring out that there is more than one way in which something can be good for us. As the point has long been made, some things are good for us by conducing to other things that are good for us, while others are good for us more directly or in their own right.[14] If there is something to be learned from discussions of the distinctions in goodness, in my view it is that we can properly distinguish between instrumental, noninstrumental, and final value as species of the good for human beings.[15] (This is a point I will come back to.)

In contemporary discussions, the claim that good is good for tends to come up in a critical context.[16] It is asserted against the idea—call it the idea of "nonrelational value"—that some things are good whether or not they are or can be good for anyone.[17] This idea of nonrelational value shows itself differently in different traditions in ethics. In Kant the idea appears as absolute value, while in G. E. Moore it appears as good simpliciter. Often, if the idea is trashed, it is trashed because it is thought mysterious, so that critique of value as a monadic property goes together with critique of metaphysical realism. I am not myself worried about spookiness, or mystery. And whatever concerns one has about Kant's invocation of absolute value, it cannot be that it is a form of value that exists independently of practical agents. A relational theory of value dispenses with commitments that some people find extravagant, but as we will see, there is no denying that it collects others. What motivates my critique is not a concern with theoretical parsimony, but a supposition that value does not work the way Moore thinks it does, or the way Kant sees the value of the good will as working: as being what it is independently of what it does or can do (see 4:394).[18] What I find difficult to understand is the idea of something's being good independently of any propensity to affect, change, or alter the state of something in a positive way. That is because I see that propensity as the very essence of value.

In a clear sense, I am not offering a positive argument for a relational theory of value. Instead, I am taking the idea that value is relational—and again, I am using

EXPLAINING THE VALUE OF HUMAN BEINGS   229

this phrase in the sense that good is good for—as a hypothesis. I have offered lines of thought that are intended to show that the hypothesis is well-taken (it is the classical conception of value that has lately found its way into contemporary discussions; it is motivated by a range of ordinary evaluative explanations), while recognizing that this does not constitute a full defense. My strategy is instead to see whether the hypothesis can cope with a hard case: what can it say about the value of human beings? If it can account for the value of human beings, then we have defended a relational conception of value against a potential objection, and in that way, we have provided further support for it as a starting point for investigation.[19] But of course, it must ultimately be substantiated in other ways too.

What can we say to those who profess a failure to understand this way of thinking about value? For people certainly so profess. Indeed, some have told me they have no idea what I am talking about when I talk about the beneficial. It is unlikely that there is a single rejoinder. Accordingly, one must work on several fronts, responding to a range of questions:

(A) *When something is said to be "good for someone," is that the same as saying that someone is possessing something good (simpliciter), or that something good (simpliciter) is occurring in their lives?* No. That way of construing the locution dates back to Moore (1903, sec. 59), and it amounts to a rejection of the very idea of relational value in the relevant sense. When something is said to be good for a person, it is not that the thing that is good simpliciter has taken up residence in their life or mind, so that "for" signifies a relation of possession or location.

(B) *What, then, does the "for" in "good for" indicate?* As others have argued, the "for" signifies a *relation* of suitability or fit between something and someone. "Good for" picks out a genuinely dyadic form of value in the sense that value *consists* in this relation of fit or suitability.[20] As I put the emphasis, value is relational because it is instantiated in processes of positive change, alteration, or transformation.[21] (I expand on this below.)

(C) *Is "good for" synonymous with instrumental value?* No. Something can be instrumentally or noninstrumentally good for people. For example, engaging with culture and the arts can be good for someone because it gives them something to talk about at a dinner party, or engaging can be good for them by being enriching, edifying, illuminating in its own right.

(D) *Does the relation* being good for *admit of analysis, or is it a primitive?* The relation can be elucidated; for example, I have said that it is essentially affecting, and I would add that it is an irreducibly evaluative relation.[22] But apart from this, I am inclined to say that it is a primitive. We can say that what is good for human beings is advantageous, beneficial, fitting, salubrious, enriching, and suitable, and we can say that what is good for

230 RETHINKING THE VALUE OF HUMANITY

human beings promotes their flourishing, but these are ways of saying the same thing.

(E) *Is the relation* being good for *essentially attitude-dependent, or can it hold in an attitude-independent way?* While our attitudes can bear on the relation's obtaining, so that whether someone would enjoy an activity is relevant to its standing to be good for them, as will become evident, I endorse a realist view according to which there are attitude-independent facts of the matter about the good for human beings.

(F) *In virtue of what do these facts obtain?* I take the view that they obtain in virtue of the character of the relata.

(G) *Can we give a compelling, philosophical account of what is good for human beings?* Unlike Kant, I take the good for human beings to be a proper object of philosophical investigation, and I will give the outline of a valuing-based account below.

(H) *Should we see good for as a unified phenomenon, one that pertains to human beings, but also to other animals, plants, and artifacts?* I regard "benefit" as an evaluative term with richly descriptive implications that have to do with what contributes to and promotes a being's flourishing.[23] I am inclined to see it as having primary application to living beings (though I think we can speak of what is beneficial for artifacts in a secondary or extended sense), and I think we do well to situate the human good in the broader context of the good for living things generally.

(I) *Can a "good for" theorist give a compelling analysis of hard cases apart from human beings? How should such a theorist account for perfectionist values (works of art or cultural and scientific achievements)? How about right action or virtue? How should such a theorist account for the fact that it is proper for the vicious to be punished though it is bad for them?* I have lately written about the first two cases, answering, as I hope, in the affirmative (see Theunissen 2021, Forthcoming). I think we do well to probe the conception of punishment that is at stake in a doctrine of desert. I am rather dubious about Kant's claim that everyone, including the wrongdoers themselves, would agree that it is appropriate and "morally good" for someone to be thrashed for being a nuisance and provoking others (5:61). The ensuing discussion bears on this point.

What one says in response to these questions bears in deep ways on a host of foundational issues—about naturalism, about realism, about the nature of human beings, about whether happiness is a respectable object of study, and so on. My account of the value of humanity certainly has implications for these topics, and it brings me to the heart of many controversies in metaethics. Rather than engage directly in these controversies here, I want to turn to my positive

EXPLAINING THE VALUE OF HUMAN BEINGS   231

account. In making a case for this account, I will implicitly be offering considerations in support of the metaethical commitments that are most congenial to it.

2. From the Good for Human Beings to the Value of Human Beings

So far, I have given my reasons for taking seriously the hypothesis that good is good for, and for thinking that the good for human beings is a primary object of study for ethics. How do we get from a discussion of the good for human beings to that of the value of human beings? To formulate a related question, why would a relational theory of value of the kind proposed treat people as bearers of value at all? Here some stage-setting is in order. In particular, I need to recall a key line of argument from signature discussions of the value of humanity.

According to a prominent line of argument, one that is often put forward by kantians or people who see themselves as marshaling lines of thought from Kant (henceforth, "the kantians"), what is good for human beings matters because we matter.[24] To put this point somewhat differently, what is good for us is positively significant only because we are bearers of value. The argument starts from a perfectly sound assumption about instrumental value—about what is *instrumentally* good for something or someone. The assumption is that what conduces to something bad (or devoid of value) is not positively significant; it is not a form of instrumental value at all. That it would help the white nationalist cause is no reason at all to spread misinformation about the results of the election. Spreading misinformation is certainly *conducive* to white nationalism, but spreading misinformation is not instrumentally *valuable*, because white nationalism is not good—it is pernicious in the extreme. The point may be put by saying that if x is instrumentally good for y, and x is reason-giving, then y must be of value (see Raz 2001, 145–146; Conee 1982).[25]

The kantians propose to extend this point about dependence from instrumental to *noninstrumental* value. They contend that what is noninstrumentally good for people—engaging with cultural or intellectual pursuits is a common example—is of value and positively practically significant only if *we* are of value. In this way, a datum about the value of human beings is taken to fall out of the structure of evaluative explanation—of the explanation of the value of other valuable things. For proponents of this style of argument—David Velleman, Joseph Raz—the form of value that is in question when we are talking about human beings, the beings who lie at the end of a chain of dependence of goods, is nonrelational. Indeed, they contend that the value of human beings must be nonrelational on pain of infinite regress. If human beings were not valuable in a nonrelational way, then none of the prior nodes in the chain of dependence of goods would be valuable. Just as the *instrumental* good for human beings would lack evaluative significance without the *noninstrumental* good for human beings, so the *noninstrumental* good for human beings would lack evaluative significance without the *value simpliciter* of human beings (without our being of value independently of being actually or possibly good for something).

In previous work (Theunissen 2018; 2020, chap. 3) I contest this latter claim: the claim that human beings must be valuable in a nonrelational way for what is good for us to be of value. I develop the suggestion that our value may yet be relational—such that we are of value because we are or can be good for something or someone. Ultimately, I opt for a kind of reflexive explanation: we are of value because we are able to bear a relevant relation to ourselves, the relation of being good for ourselves. I conclude that a datum about our value *does* fall out of the structure of evaluative explanation—we must be of value for what is good for us to be significant. Against the kantians, however, I contend that our value can be of the same sort as the value of the prior nodes. That is, I argue that it is perfectly possible for our value to be relational. And with the way apparently cleared, I go on to develop a relational view of the value of human beings.

As Kenny Walden (2021) has put it to me, while I dispute the ultimate conclusion of the kantians, I concede rather a lot to their way of setting things up. And I am now inclined to take a different, and less concessive, line. In short, I no longer think that a datum about our value falls out of the structure of evaluative explanation. Here I recall the distinctions I drew earlier between instrumental, noninstrumental, and final value. Instrumental value depends for its evaluative significance on noninstrumental value—on things that are good for us in their own right or for their own sake. Noninstrumental value is sometimes thought to depend for its significance on final value understood as the most complete good in the sense that other things are pursued for its sake though it is not pursued for the sake of anything (in the standard case, a well-lived life). Whether noninstrumental value depends on final value in this sense is somewhat controversial, but it is a familiar Aristotelian claim. What seems mistaken to me now is that noninstrumental value, or final value, depends for its evaluative significance on the value of the person for whom it is noninstrumentally or finally good.

Let me illustrate this point with noninstrumental value. To recall, when something is noninstrumentally good for someone, it is directly good for someone, or good for someone in its own right. To go back to the earlier example, engaging with culture and the arts is good for us independently of whether it makes us interesting conversationalists—though that may be a welcome ramification. It is good for us in its own right in the sense that it necessarily involves the use of our imaginative, emotional, and intellectual powers, powers the exercise of which is a constituent of our good. The value *is* the alteration or transformation in the person that is marked when we say she is enriched, nourished, enlivened, moved, uplifted, consoled (etc.) by the work. The relevant form of value is a *re-lation*, in a simple case, a dyad, between an object, a state, or an activity, and a person. Rather than being derived from something that is independently valuable, the value of what is noninstrumentally good for someone is explained by the valuable *relation* itself. To return to the example, engaging with works of art can be noninstrumentally good for us—it can be by itself enriching for us—and that (suitably filled out) is a complete explanation of its value. At least, we do not need to invoke our being of value to explain the value of the work or the value of engaging with it. The value *is* the enlargement of imagination, consciousness, understanding and so on, that is a function of appropriate engagement.[26] While there is a clear sense in which what is instrumentally valuable depends on something independently good, there is no comparable structure of dependence in the noninstrumental case.[27] As I see it, the mistake made by the kantians is to assume that different evaluative concepts have analogous structures of dependence.

One might respond to this argument by reasserting the comparison in something like the following way. Just as what conduces to something that does no good is not instrumentally valuable, so what is directly beneficial for a person may not be good. Here a distinction between the nonmoral and the moral good looks ready to assert itself. It may be proffered that what enriches the sinner may be good for them but morally bad (because undeserved). Or it may be said that while taking pleasure in another's suffering may be good for the one who takes it, so taking pleasure is not ultimately practically significant because it is not morally good.

I submit that what drives the thought here is a degraded conception of the beneficial—the sort of conception that is at stake in a view according to which what is good for someone is to carry out their plans (of which taking pleasure in another's enslavement could be an example).[28] Foot (2001, 94) claims that it strains ordinary English to say that something like that *benefits* a person, and she evidently hears the etymology of well-doing or well-making in talk of the beneficial. Regardless of whether we share the linguistic intuition, I find it quite surprising to think that, absent some special explanation, enjoying seeing another oppressed is good for the one who enjoys it. But the supposition that ill-will and its kin tend to be bad for human beings and, contrariwise, that compassion and the like tend to be good for us, is of course a familiar object of moral skepticism, and it is denied by people who hold certain attitude-constitutive accounts of the beneficial.[29] Thus it emerges that my argument depends on a substantive conception of the good for human beings, one that is not ethically neutral. I will say something to motivate an ethical conception of the beneficial in the next section. As I will express it, living well for human beings involves participation in satisfying interpersonal relationships, engagement in meaningful work, enjoyment of significant forms of culture (etc.), activities that all presuppose the

234 RETHINKING THE VALUE OF HUMANITY

agent appreciating and caring about what she does in the right way. Here I must simply acknowledge that this is a juncture at which the proposal assumes theoretical burdens of its own. I reject a regress argument for nonrelational value. More than this, I contend that a conclusion about our status as valuable does *not* fall out of the structure of evaluative explanation. But in dispensing with these commitments, I am taking on a view of the good for human beings that is *ethically* ambitious.

I have argued that we do not need to be bearers of value for other things to be of value. If something is noninstrumentally good for us, it does not follow that we are of value. And yet, I *do* think that human beings are bearers of value. Here is how I now think we can account for this fact. When philosophers talk about the property of being good or valuable, they are talking about a property possession of which makes something reason-giving. And what property is that?[30] If one takes the view that the good is the beneficial, then good is a relational property. It is the property of being such as to conduce, indirectly or directly, to human life and its flourishing—or more generally, to the good of all forms of life. Being capably or actually beneficial is what makes something practically significant. And now my point is that human beings bear this relation to other things and to themselves. That is, we instantiate the property of being valuable because we are such that we are or can be beneficial for something or someone. As I will now explain, human beings instantiate the property in an interesting and special way. We are not just patients—beings for whom things are good—we are also agents, or as I will put the emphasis, *valuers*: beings whose valuing is crucial for our own good.[31]

3. On Valuing and Living Well for Human Beings

I have so far given my grounds for developing the view that human beings are of value because we are or can be good for something. If the reader is generous enough to grant my starting point, she will now naturally wonder who or what we are supposed to be good for. A reasonable suggestion is that we are or can be good for *one another*.[32] We are instrumentally good for others when we enable, support, or facilitate things that are directly good for them, and we are noninstrumentally good for others when we are part of their good by forming suitable relationships with them as family, neighbors, friends, colleagues, and so on. The proposal has much to recommend it in light of the deeply interdependent nature of the good for human beings—and indeed all forms of life—a point about which there seems to me terrible confusion in our political world. And yet, I can't help hearing a Kantian objection to the effect that a proposal of this kind would make the value of a person dependent on their role, or potential role, in *another's* life in ways that are at odds with how human beings should be treated: as ends in ourselves. I take the point of the Kantian injunction to be that we should recognize value in others independently of their role in our or another's life.[33] As I will adapt it, we should recognize and relate to people always as centers of a life to which they bear a special relation. These are my grounds for developing the suggestion, anticipated above, that the value of human beings is more basically explained in terms of the relation we stand to bear to *ourselves*, a relation of being good for ourselves. As "center of a life" implies, if the unusual phrase "good for ourselves" is to have a sense, it should be taken to mean good for our *lives*. And this brings me to the question of what is involved in living well for human beings.

When Aristotle announced the good human life as the orienting subject for ethics, he began with considerations about what people in fact seek.[34] John Stuart Mill took a related approach, even as his formulations got him into trouble. To express a core Aristotelian idea in a contemporary idiom, people *value* things with a view to living well. We human beings value things in the sense that we have ends, things we mean to bring about or realize by way of our actions. Some of these ends are more architectonic than others in the sense that they play a more unifying or structuring role in our lives. If we have the study of philosophy as a more final end, then it shapes our actions here and now, for example, our decision to attend a conference on a Sunday morning rather than to lounge in bed. It was Aristotle's view that, while there are constraints on the kinds of end that will promote or constitute living well for us, and constraints on the character of our engagement with them (more on this below), human beings are not wrong to value things with a view to living well. It is by engaging appropriately with objects and activities of value—meaningful relationships, forms of work, intellectual and cultural pursuits—that we live well as human beings. The deeper explanation is that it is through valuing that human beings put characteristic agential, cognitive, and emotional powers to work, where putting powers to work in the right way is the schema for the good of whatever can do well or do badly. This is broadly the approach to the good for human beings that I find plausible. Human beings live well by valuing in characteristic ways, and I like the Aristotelian formulation in terms of final ends because it captures the sense in which some of what we value is more defining for us insofar as it plays a structuring role in our activities over time.

Putting this together with what has been said, I am proposing that the value of human beings turns on valuing, for valuing constitutes living well and in that way being "good for ourselves."[35] That the value of human beings in one way or another lies in valuing, or better, in a capacity to value, is an oft-made proposal. While I reject the suggestion that it is Kant's own approach, it is the approach to the value of humanity taken by the kantians of Section 2, and many others besides. These proposals differ according to their accounts of what it is to value something, and they differ according to their proffered explanations for why the capacity to value grounds our value. For some, valuing makes us inventors of value. For others, valuing allows us to pay homage to things that are good in themselves. For still others, being a valuer means that we meet the criteria for bearing the distinctive value that persons are traditionally thought to have. I accept the common supposition that people are of value because we have the capacity to value.[36] But I offer a distinctive explanation for why valuing makes a person valuable. The explanation is that the capacity to value is of value because its exercise is valuable, where its exercise is valuable because it constitutes a person's flourishing, and a person's flourishing is its value for the person whose flourishing it is.

So much for my proposal. Earlier I said that I am committed to an ethical conception of the good for human beings, and I need to offer some support for that claim now. I need to offer some support for that claim now because without an ethically significant account of the good for human beings, I will be stuck with a view according to which the value of human beings could turn on a capacity to value in harmful ways (for this will be said to satisfy the relevant explanans). That ethical virtue is a dimension of living well for human beings is of course a familiar claim of ancient ethics, or at least, a familiar locus of argument and counterargument in which the questions are difficult in part because they are both conceptual and empirical. I have thrown in my lot with a view according to which what is good for human beings is to engage in activities that are characteristic of the kind of being we are. This style of proposal is familiarly put to work to generate an ethical conception of the good for human beings as follows.[37] Characteristic activities of a living being are constitutive of its good, or at least a key determinant thereof. If rational activity is characteristic of human beings, and if a dimension of rationality is what we antecedently recognize as responsiveness to the dictates of ethical virtue, then it follows that being just, temperate, beneficent, courageous and wise is good for human beings. Activity in conformity with the virtues is good for human beings.

This is a venerable form of argument, and it is also a fraught one; it has the air of convenient, or hopeful, stipulation. When a version is given early on in Plato's *Republic*, there is express concern that Socrates has done no more than play with words. Short of providing a full account of our moral psychology, what is needed to begin to respond to this concern is to bear out or substantiate the argument in light of what we know of ourselves and one another. That is, we need to be shown how forms of ethical behavior and motivation facilitate or constitute what we can pretheoretically recognize as good for human beings. The dimension of virtue that is often asked about in this context is justice, a virtue that concerns fair dealings with others. When Socrates is given the task of showing that justice is advantageous to the one who is just, he is asked to show that what is advantageous is really *being*, as opposed to merely *seeming*, just. Accordingly, Socrates is asked to show how the *inner* dimensions of justice, the underlying attitudes and motivations of a just person, could be for their good; the task is to show that fairness of *mind* is good for the one who is so. Of course, Plato sought to answer that question by giving a full theory of the human soul. But he also sought to bear out that theory by offering portraits of people whose lack of justice, whose lack of fairness of *mind*, was in one way or another crippling for them. This is the work of substantiation, and it is the kind of work that is helpful here.[38]

So let me offer an example. Think of the friend or family member who habitually gets in touch when they need something and not otherwise. Perhaps they lack support in their life and things are hard. They make routine inquiries about one's health and happiness, but one knows from the *way* they ask, or from experience over time, that the interest is not fully meant. They know enough about the outward form of relationships to make a show of concern, but they do so, narrowly, with a view to gain. It is natural to wish that this sort of person would *really* take an interest. Why is that? Certainly, being genuinely interested in others would make them better as people. No doubt, being better in this way would make our relationship with them better *for us*. But my sense is that, particularly when we care about the person in question, we wish they would really take an interest because it would be better *for them*. To be without the motivations and affections that are constitutive of genuine concern for others is to be deprived of the pleasure of intimacy or friendship itself, something we can easily recognize as good for human beings. In that case, having the underlying attitudes and feelings of the just person is good for the one who is so because it is part of what constitutes a good whose status as beneficial can be understood in pre-philosophical ways.

In the spirit of using something *better known to us* to clarify something that is less well understood, I have offered a homely example that is meant to help us to see how having certain sorts of affective and motivational orientations toward others is good for the person who is oriented in this way. Justice is often taken to be a hard case, but I have clearly said nothing about how the point generalizes to other dimensions of virtue. Evidently, I have given no more than the outline of a response to the worry that bad or misguided valuation *eo ipso* grounds our value because it satisfies the explanation offered here for why valuing makes us valuable in terms of a well-lived human life. Here I will simply add that people who in fact value badly do not thereby relinquish the capacity to value in the right sorts of ways, so they are not being excluded from the purview of my account.[39]

238 RETHINKING THE VALUE OF HUMANITY

4. The Reasons We Have

I have offered an account of the value of human beings. On my account, human beings are of value in virtue of a capacity to value where that is understood in terms of having final ends. This capacity makes us valuable because its exercise makes us good for ourselves in the sense that it makes us able to live well, where a well-lived life is (minimally) its value for the person whose life it is. The explanation of our value is, as I put it earlier, in a way reflexive: human beings are of value because we bear the relation, being good for, to *ourselves*. I have just offered some reason to think that responsiveness to ethical virtue is a dimension of the good for human beings. In what remains of this essay, allow me to bear out the implications of my account for what is *owed* to human beings—for the forms of ethical behavior to which our value gives rise.

First, I must respond to a basic challenge to the account's standing to generate forms of ethical behavior at all. It is a Moorean complaint about relational value that, to the extent it has a distinctive relational character, it has a limited normative significance.[40] If something is good for one person, then it is clear enough how it is reason-giving for them, but not clear how it is reason-giving for others. The problem arises for me in a special way. If I am proposing that a person is of value because she is good for herself in the sense that I have made out, then how can others have reasons in regard to her? An account of the value of human beings was supposed to ground core forms of ethical behavior owed to one another. Precisely by dint of its relationality, the account looks poised to fail. I appear to be stuck, as David Sussman put it to me, with rational egoism, or as I have put it elsewhere, a kind of solipsism.[41]

In short, my solution to this problem lies in my realist approach to the good for human beings. According to the approach, what is good for human beings is to devote ourselves to meaningful work, relationships, cultural and intellectual activity, in characteristic ways. This is good for us because it makes use of capacities or powers it is good for human beings to have and exercise. To show how this helps with the problem of the generality of the reasons to which we give rise, I need to recall a distinction that is sometimes drawn between impersonal and personal forms of relational value.

In Thomas Nagel's (1989, chaps. 8 and 9) influential discussion, some of the things that are good for us are evaluatively and practically significant in a general way. For Nagel, pleasure and pain are like this. When we think about pleasure and pain, our understanding of their value and disvalue properly detaches in thought from the particular perspective of the person whose pains and pleasures they are. For Nagel that means that pleasure and pain license reasons of a general form—reasons that do not include essential reference to the person whose pains or pleasures are in question. Anyone has reason to want a person's pain to stop or their pleasure to continue. He extends these impersonal values for human beings from simple pleasure and pain to the basic resources of life, and to my mind it is here that his point becomes more obviously compelling. I have reason to want you to have shelter and enough to eat and drink, no matter who you are and no matter what relation you bear to me. I have reason to want you to have access to opportunities and, he adds, to freedom. That these are good for you does not require me to enter into your peculiar subjectivity. They are *human* goods and in that way such that they have general practical import.

Naturally, Sussman's critique will apply to Nagel's observations about pains, pleasures, and the basic resources of life. Rather than defend Nagel's position, I simply want to emphasize what his argument implies about my own account of the value of humanity.[42] I am accepting Nagel's basic point that if we can properly appreciate something as a general form of the human good, then it is practically relevant to all of us. Indeed, I propose to extend this point. In doing so, I depart from an influential aspect of his account. I have so far spoken of Nagel's treatment of impersonal values for human beings, values that have general practical significance in the sense that they are reason-giving for all human beings (or all human agents). But he thinks that not all relational goods are in this way impersonal. Some relational goods have practical relevance only for the agent for whom they are good. His much discussed example of a personal good is someone's end of climbing Mount Kilimanjaro (Nagel 1989, 167). This is a form of value that does not detach relevantly speaking from the evaluative perspective of the person who has that end, and it is in that sense merely *personal*. In my view this is a mistaken characterization. Climbing mountains may not be something we ourselves do— it may not be one of our final ends. But we can surely recognize it as a form of the human good. Climbing Mount Kilimanjaro is an activity that involves the skillful navigation of difficult terrain. It is an activity people undertake in communities, or on their own, so that it involves relations of trust with others, or feats of self-reliance. It requires knowledge of a particular environment, its climate, animals, and species of plant. It holds opportunities for engaging with another culture, language, and so on. It is the kind of thing one needs to train for over time. In these and other ways, it is a very good candidate for a suitable final end. If the pursuit of final ends is the primary way human beings can affect the quality of their lives, as I have urged that it is, its value for an agent perfectly well detaches from their peculiar perspective. A person's end of climbing Mount Kilimanjaro should be counted as an impersonal form of relational value, and it should be counted as something that generates reasons for others.[43]

Though I disagree with Nagel's treatment of the example of climbing Mount Kilimanjaro, the point I am making turns, as it does in his original discussion, on questions of impersonality or objectivity. To repeat, if we can properly appreciate something as a general form of the human good, then it is practically relevant to

240 RETHINKING THE VALUE OF HUMANITY

all of us. I am claiming that the goods that bear on our status as valuable are like this. That is, I am claiming that the final ends that ground our value are intelligible as impersonal goods.

If Nagel's basic point is right, a relational account of the kind given here has normative credentials. What forms of ethical response are licensed by the account? According to the good-centered monism of the kind developed here, the value of what is of value shows us the reasons we have. I join with others in thinking that our basic reason in response to whatever is of value is to protect it so that it can serve or function as the valuable thing it is.[44] I have taken the view that the value of people, our function if you like, is to live flourishing lives. So I am proposing that we have reason to protect other people's capacity to value and, therewith, to live well. More than this, since doing its work as the valuable thing it is requires not just non-malfeasance but, more positively, support or furtherance, I am proposing that we have reason to support others in their exercise of this capacity. Obviously, we cannot support the ends of all people. I share Kant's view that we fulfill our standing responsibility to others by coming up with a coherent plan of action. Perhaps we choose a vocation where we are activists, or we are a head of a household who provides for children and grandparents. There are many possibilities. In these capacities we have reason to help others find out what makes sense for them to value with a view to their life as a whole, and to support them in valuing those things. Here we do not seek to make judgments about which final ends are better (simpliciter) than others. Instead, we aim to help people judge for themselves what is better for them, and to support them in pursuing those things.[45] In this way, a relational theory of the value of human beings of the kind proposed captures basic forms of ethical behavior.

Notes

1. In this essay, I draw from but go beyond lines of argument developed in *The Value of Humanity* (Theunissen 2020). Richard Kraut, Rory O'Connell, Kevin Powell, Andrea Sangiovanni, David Sussman, and Kenneth Walden have responded to *The Value of Humanity* with thought-provoking questions and a good many inform my treatment here. I am grateful to Sarah Buss for exceedingly constructive and generous feedback on an earlier draft, and to Robert Audi for the same. I am also grateful for spirited and helpful conversation about relational value with Tom Hurka and David Hunter at the 2022 Reason, Action, and Mind Speaker Series (virtual) at Ryerson University, and to audience members at the 2022 Central APA in Chicago.

2. I discuss Greif's remarks in Theunissen 2020, 133.

3. Making the value of humanity a topic for metaethics is one of Christine Korsgaard's key innovations and legacies in ethics.

4. Joseph Raz is a prominent contemporary defender of this style of approach, and my thinking owes much to his work. My formulation deliberately recalls Raz 1999a, 30.

5. I explore them at greater length in other forums. See Theunissen 2018, 2020, forthcoming, 2022.

6. I take the helpfully descriptive phrase "good-centered monism" from Kraut 2022, 265. In this and the following section, I respond to questions Richard raised for my approach here and in his contribution to an Author Meets Critics session on *The Value of Humanity* at the Central APA meeting in February 2021. If I hear him right, many are likely to be questions he has at some point asked of himself. It will be apparent that some of the ideas advanced here share much with Kraut 2007, 2011.

7. One of H. A. Prichard's (1912) objectives in his classic "Does Moral Philosophy Rest on a Mistake?" was to defend the view that concepts of obligation or right action, moral goodness, and virtue each plays important and irreducible roles in our life and thought. According to Prichard, attempts to explain right action in terms of the good strain our intuitions. For when we ask ourselves why we feel we ought to pay our debts or tell the truth, our thought is not that by doing so we would be producing something good (25). John Rawls (1999, 21) is part of this legacy in insisting on a basic division between the right and the good, and of course Rawls's treatment is roundly influential. Rawls is inheriting less from Prichard than from Kant, whose discussion of two senses of good, the moral and the nonmoral, in the second *Critique* (5:58–5:63) is naturally paired with Rawls (1999, chap. 1, secs. 5, 6) on the right and the good. In rejecting evaluative explanations of right action, Prichard and Rawls set themselves against consequentialism, and for understandable reasons, it is quite common to push against good-centered or teleological approaches in ethics by attacking this prominent, modern representative. Scanlon (1998, chap. 1) is a notable spokesman here. As will become clear, I look to nonconsequentialist teleological traditions in ethics.

8. Foot (2001) credits Elizabeth Anscombe (1969) with the central idea, and in Anscombe's example, keeping our promises is a virtue because human beings need to bind one another by word and not force in the cooperative activities that are given to us as dependent, social beings. In Foot's (2001, chap. 7) example, kindness and compassion are virtues because every one of us needs help in facing the losses and difficulties that are inevitable for us.

9. The expression "ways of being good" is Thomson's, and it recalls a line from Aristotle to the effect that the good is said in many ways (1096a24). In examples that bear her signature, Thomson (1997, 276) offers being good for use in making cheesecake, being good as Hamlet, being good to look at, and being good with children. One has the impression that she enjoys playing up the range, and to that extent she is naturally read in conversation with Von Wright (1963). But as Thomson (1997, 289) recognizes, and Aristotle with her, we do not here have to do with mere "happenstance clutter," and I share her view that *good for* is in the end basic. I explore and defend this position in Theunissen (forthcoming).

10. Compare Raz (1986, 194) on humanism.

11. This is a central point of emphasis in the reading offered by Vogt 2017, chap. 5, sec. 2.

242 RETHINKING THE VALUE OF HUMANITY

12. See, for example, *Republic* 379b; *Apology* 41c; *Meno* 77–78b; *Euthydemos* 280b–282; *Protagoras* 333d–334a.

13. Richard Kraut has suggested to me that the best strategy that is available to a good for theorist is one that appeals, not to questions of explanation and metaphysics, but to ethics. His point is that the way of being good to which we should assign the largest role in our practical reasoning is that in which something is noninstrumentally beneficial. I do not myself draw a distinction between ethics and metaphysics of the kind Richard recommends. That is because I think we should be reasoning practically in accordance with things as they are.

14. Plato introduces related distinctions in Book 2 of the *Republic* at 357, and Aristotle in Book 7 of *Nicomachean Ethics* at 1097a.

15. Discussion of these distinctions begins with Korsgaard 1983.

16. This is the case in Kraut 2011; Korsgaard 2013.

17. "Relational" and "nonrelational" are terms of art and I use them in a proprietary sense, the sense that is at stake in an important early discussion by Railton 1986.

18. References are to the volume and page number of the Preussische Akademie edition.

19. I am grateful to Felix Koch for discussion of the status of my argument.

20. As Connie Rosati (2008, 329) has made the point, "The relational complex, *X is good for P,* does not include the monadic property *good* at all. Instead, it includes the relational property *is good for P*: it has X and P as relata and *is good for* as a dyadic relation. So the logical form of X is good for P is not: (*X is good*) *for P*, but rather, *xGp* (using 'G' to express the relation *is good for*)." See also Kraut 2007, 87; Raz 2004, 273–274.

21. As Hurka (2021, 810) has observed, the claim that value is relational may mean one of two things. It may mean that the ground of the proposed value is relational, i.e. that the properties that make for the value are relational properties, or it may mean that good for value itself, *qua* value, is relational, i.e. that the value the ground makes for involves a relation. He is right that relational value theorists are not always clear about this difference (though see Theunissen 2020, 28–33). In making the proposal that value is essentially affecting, I am claiming that good for value itself, *qua* value, is relational.

22. Hurka (2021) is right to see that the relation is irreducibly evaluative for the relational value theorist. However, Hurka takes this to preclude its being understood naturalistically (809). In correspondence, David Hunter told me that he is enough of an Anscombean to be suspicious of the proposed distinction between the natural and the evaluative. I could not have said it better. Though I can't discuss it here, this point bears on Hurka's treatment of the value of health (e.g., at 807). Separately, that the relation is irreducibly evaluative means that "good for" as it is used by relational theorists is something of a technical term. Sundry uses (e.g., "guns are good for killing") are not targets of the analysis. Hurka discusses related questions at 805–809.

23. Here I follow Kraut 2007, 131.

24. The argument is defended by Raz 1999b, 273–302; Raz 2001, 145–158; Velleman 1999, 2008. A distinct version of the argument is given by Korsgaard (1983, 177–184; 1986, 190–197). I do not discuss Korsgaard's version of the argument here, but see Theunissen (2020, 139–142). "Kantians" is something of a misnomer for proponents

EXPLAINING THE VALUE OF HUMAN BEINGS 243

of the argument because it is not an argument that Kant himself makes (and I will register this by writing "kantian" with a small k). In saying this, I broadly follow Timmermann 2006.

25. The point is implicit in Velleman (2008, 192). I note that Kant's own treatment of instrumental value is somewhat different. For Kant, an outcome does not need to be good for it to be true that what conduces to it is instrumentally valuable, just as an end does not need to be valuable for it to be the case that we are rationally enjoined to take the relevant means. According to Kant, there are two distinctly different forms of value (the moral and the nonmoral), just as there are two distinctly different kinds of rational imperative (the moral and the instrumental). Where Kant's treatment aligns with that of the kantians is in supposing that the *normativity* of what is instrumentally good for someone is constrained by its moral permissibility or impermissibility. As we might rephrase Kant's position, where someone has an immoral end, taking measures to facilitate it, while "good for" them, will not give decisive reasons for action because the normativity of morality trumps that of the nonmoral good. For Kant's treatment of the nonmoral good, see 5:58–5:63 and 4:414. For Kant's treatment of the instrumental should, see 4:414–4:417. As I indicate below, and argue more fully in Theunissen (forthcoming), I think Kant (and Rawls following him) works with an inadequate or degraded conception of "good for."

26. That engaging with works of art can be noninstrumentally good for us is not controversial. That its standing to be noninstrumentally good for us is a *complete explanation* (suitably filled out) of its value is considerably more so. Some people take the view that a work of art must be good simpliciter for it to be good for us, and this claim is sometimes generalized to whatever is noninstrumentally good for us. The thought is that whatever is good for us is so because it is good. This raises a nice challenge for a relational theory of value (it is one I take up in Theunissen 2022), but it is not a challenge that concerns us here. The present argument concerns the question of whether we need to posit the value of human beings to make sense of the value of engaging with art (or whatever is taken to be noninstrumentally good for us).

27. As I noted earlier, there is a view according to which when we say that something is "noninstrumentally good for someone," we mean that there is a relation of possession to something that is good (simpliciter). So understood, when something is noninstrumentally good for someone, there is a form of dependence on something that is (in that sense) independently good. But that is to give up on the notion of noninstrumental value that is at stake for relational value theorists, and for the kantians. The kantians are not denying, as the Mooreans are apt to deny, that relational value of the relevant kind makes sense, or that it is genuinely different from the nonrelational good.

28. The conception of benefit and the example are due to Rawls 1999, 27–28. For discussion, see Kraut 2007, 21–24. Rawls's account is close to Kant's (and avowedly drawn from him; see 5:58–5:63).

29. Thomson's (1997, 294–298) is another example.

30. My formulation deliberately recalls that of Thomson 2008, 14–17. Interestingly, Thomson rejects the answer to this question that is proposed here on grounds that

being good for is a trivial property that everything has. To my mind, her view is encouraged by the examples she uses, examples such as being good for use in making cheesecake. In Theunissen (2020, 6–8), I contend that the examples, amusing as they are, are misleading.

31. I have urged that we do not need to posit our value to explain the value of what is noninstrumentally good for us. What are the implications of this position for the good for other forms of life? I am prepared to accept that the noninstrumental good for any living being is practically relevant for us. Questions about how the practical relevance of the good for human beings compares with that of other creatures requires fuller treatment than I can give it here. In arguing that relational value theorists face difficulties in making well-being comparisons, Hurka (2021, 820) urges, "If one act will promote A's well-being while another will promote B's, we can only determine which act is right by determining which outcome is in some sense better. But this can't be a relativized sense of 'better.'" In making this argument, Hurka adduces a contentious (consequentialist) premise. I may appropriately prioritize A's well-being because A is my sister, and I need be under no illusion that her flourishing objectively matters more than that of a stranger. I would extend the point to interspecies comparisons. I do not find it obvious that human well-being objectively matters more than the well-being of other animals. (Here I am in agreement with Korsgaard 2018, 5). Though I cannot argue for it here, I think we do well to probe the presuppositions of lifeboat scenarios that appear to force this conclusion. We should also remember that anyone who cares for companion animals or devotes their life to protecting the habitat of a given species is acting in a perfectly reasonable way, though the same resources could go to human beings in need. As Karl Schafer suggested to me, it is also open to me to allow that the character of the reasons to which human beings give rise is affected by the fact that we, as valuers, can contribute to our flourishing in the distinctive way I go on to describe. In his contribution to this volume (sec. 4), Andrea Sangiovanni develops the thought that since human beings, and other sentient beings, have a perspective on their own flourishing, a perspective from which their own flourishing matters to them, then unlike plants which lack such a perspective, their flourishing matters in its own right and for its own sake. I think he is right to emphasize the fact that perspective makes a normative difference, and I share his view that we should not mark this difference in terms of the possession of distinct kinds of value. I have learned much from his insightful discussion.

32. A proposal that I cannot here consider is that we are good for other valuable things. This proposal is thoughtfully developed by Buss (2012), and I offer a response in Theunissen 2018, 354–356.

33. Here I follow Raz 1999b, 294.

34. Vogt (2017, chap. 2) develops this point at length, describing Aristotle as taking an agential perspective on the good.

35. Or rather, the activity of valuing is what agents contribute to their own flourishing, where this leaves open that circumstances may affect it in a way that does not bear on their worth.

36. Drawing on the work of Samuel Scheffler (2010), I elsewhere develop an account of what it is to value. According to the account, to value is to have a final end, where having a final end involves believing that one's end is worthwhile; it involves treating the end as practically significant in relevant contexts; it involves being guided by the end in long-range deliberation and being vulnerable to a range of emotions regarding the success or failure of one's end (Theunissen 2020, chap. 4). The account helps to make the proposal developed here more determinate because it takes a stand on the more particular attitudes and dispositions that ground our value. For recent treatment of valuing and well-being (which differs in its metaethical orientation from my own), see Tiberius 2018. See also Raibley 2013.
37. Here I appeal to the function argument of *Nicomachean Ethics* 1.7.
38. This is the line explicitly taken by Kraut (2018, 6–11) and by Foot (2001, chap 7). See Sangiovanni's discussion of this question in sec. 3 of this volume. I take up these questions at greater length in Theunissen (forthcoming).
39. I discuss questions about the scope of my account in Theunissen 2020, chap. 1.
40. The objection is forcefully developed by Regan 2004.
41. I am grateful to David for raising thoughtful questions of my account at the above-mentioned Author Meets Critics session at the Central APA meeting, 2021. I discuss these questions about normativity in Theunissen 2020, chap 5.
42. In what follows, I make a weaker argument than the argument I make in Theunissen 2020. I am grateful to Andrea Sangiovanni and to Sarah Buss for discussion.
43. I have drawn several sentences in this paragraph from Theunissen 2020, 123.
44. In Raz's (2001, 158, *passim*) terminology, these are reasons of respect.
45. Here I am closely following Theunissen 2020, 129–130.

References

Anscombe, G. E. M. 1969. "On Promising and Its Justice." *Critica* 3 (7–8): 61–83.
Aristotle. 2011. *Nicomachean Ethics*. Translation, introduction, and commentary by Sarah Broadie and Christopher Rowe. Oxford: Oxford University Press. [Cited by book, chapter, and Bekker number]
Buss, Sarah. 2012. "The Value of Humanity." *Journal of Philosophy* CIX: 341–377.
Conee, Earl. 1982. "Instrumental Value without Intrinsic Value?" *Philosophia* 11: 345–359.
Foot, Philippa. 2001. *Natural Goodness*. Oxford: Oxford University Press.
Greif, Mark. 2015. *The Age of the Crisis of Man*. Princeton, NJ: Princeton University Press.
Hurka, Tom. 2021. "Against 'Good For'/'Well-Being,' for 'Simply Good.'" *Philosophical Quarterly* 71 (4): 803–822.
Kant, Immanuel. 1900–. *Kants gesammelte Schriften*. 24 vols. Edited by Königlich Preussische Akademie der Wissenschaften zu Berlin, Deutschen Akademie der Wissenschaften zu Berlin, and Akademie der Wissenschaften zu Göttingen. Berlin: De Gruyter.
Kant, Immanuel. 1996a. *The Critique of Practical Reason*. In *Practical Philosophy*, translated and edited by Mary J. Gregor. Cambridge: Cambridge University Press. [Cited by volume and page of the Akademie edition]

246 RETHINKING THE VALUE OF HUMANITY

Kant, Immanuel. 1996b. *Groundwork of the Metaphysics of Morals*. In *Practical Philosophy*, translated and edited by Mary J. Gregor. Cambridge: Cambridge University Press. [Cited by volume and page of the Akademie edition]

Korsgaard, Christine. 1983. "The Two Distinctions in Goodness." *Philosophical Review* 92 (2): 169–195.

Korsgaard, Christine. 1986. "Kant's Formula of Humanity." *Kant-Studien* 77 (1–4): 183–202.

Korsgaard, Christine. 1997. "The Normativity of Instrumental Reason." In *Ethics and Practical Reason*, edited by Garrett Cullity and Berys Gaut, 215–254. Oxford: Clarendon Press.

Korsgaard, Christine. 2013. "The Relational Nature of the Good." In *Oxford Studies in Metaethics*, edited by Russ Schaffer Landau, vol. 8, 1–26. Oxford: Oxford University Press.

Korsgaard, Christine. 2018. *Fellow Creatures*. Oxford: Oxford University Press.

Kraut, Richard. 2007. *What Is Good and Why*. Cambridge: Cambridge University Press.

Kraut, Richard. 2011. *Against Absolute Goodness*. Oxford: Oxford University Press.

Kraut, Richard. 2018. *The Quality of Life: Aristotle Revisited*. Oxford: Oxford University Press.

Kraut, Richard. 2022. Review of *The Value of Humanity*, by L. Nandi Theunissen. *Mind* 131 (521): 259–267.

Moore, George E. 1903. *Principia Ethica*. Cambridge: Cambridge University Press.

Nagel, Thomas. 1986. *The View from Nowhere*. Oxford: Oxford University Press.

Plato. 1997. *Complete Works*. Edited and with an introduction and notes by John M. Cooper. Indianapolis, IN: Hackett. [Cited by Stephanus number]

Prichard, Harold A. 1912. "Does Moral Philosophy Rest on a Mistake?" *Mind* 21 (81): 21–37.

Raibley, Jason. 2013. "Values, Agency, and Welfare." *Philosophical Topics* 41 (1): 187–214.

Railton, Peter. 1986. "Moral Realism." *Philosophical Review* 95 (2): 163–207.

Rawls, John. 1999. *A Theory of Justice*. Rev. ed. Cambridge, MA: Harvard University Press.

Raz, Joseph. 1986. *The Morality of Freedom*. Oxford: Clarendon Press.

Raz, Joseph. 1999a. "Agency, Reason, and the Good." In *Engaging Reason: On the Theory of Value and Action*, 22–45. Oxford: Oxford University Press.

Raz, Joseph. 1999b. "The Amoralist." In *Engaging Reason: On the Theory of Value and Action*, 273–302. Oxford: Oxford University Press.

Raz, Joseph. 2001. "Respecting People." In *Value, Respect, and Attachment*, 124–175. Cambridge: Cambridge University Press.

Regan, Donald. 2004. "Why Am I My Brother's Keeper?" In *Reason and Value: Themes from the Moral Philosophy of Joseph Raz*, edited by R. Jay Wallace, Philip Pettit, Samuel Scheffler, and Michael Smith, 202–230. Oxford: Oxford University Press.

Rosati, Connie. 2008. "Objectivism and Relational Good." *Social Philosophy and Policy Foundation* 25: 314–349.

Scanlon, Thomas. M. 1998. *What We Owe to Each Other*. Cambridge, MA: Harvard University Press.

Scheffler, Samuel. 2010. "Valuing." In *Equality and Tradition: Questions of Value in Moral and Political Theory*, 15–40. Oxford: Oxford University Press.

Sidgwick, Henry. 1907. *The Methods of Ethics*. London: Macmillan.

Theunissen, L. Nandi. 2018. "Must We Be Just Plain Good? On Regress Arguments for the Value of Humanity." *Ethics* 128 (2): 346–372.

Theunissen, L. Nandi. 2020. *The Value of Humanity*. Oxford: Oxford University Press.

Theunissen, L. Nandi. Forthcoming. "Realism about the Good for Human Beings: On Virtue and the Beneficial." In *The Oxford Handbook of Moral Realism*, edited by Paul Bloomfield and David Copp. Oxford: Oxford University Press.

Theunissen, L. Nandi. 2022. "The New Mooreans." Unpublished manuscript.

Thomson, Judith Jarvis. 1997. "The Right and the Good." *Journal of Philosophy* 94 (6): 273–298.

Thomson, Judith Jarvis. 2008. *Normativity*. The Paul Carus Lectures. Chicago: Carus.

Tiberius, Valerie. 2018. *Well-Being as Value-Fulfilment: How We Can Each Help Each Other to Live Well*. Oxford: Oxford University Press.

Timmermann, Jens. 2006. "Value without Regress: Kant's 'Formula of Humanity' Revisited." *European Journal of Philosophy* 14 (1): 69–93.

Velleman, David. 1999. "A Right to Self-Termination." *Ethics* 109 (3): 606–628.

Velleman, David. 2008. "Beyond Price." *Ethics* 118 (1): 191–212.

Vogt, Katja Maria. 2017. *Desiring the Good: Ancient Proposals and Contemporary Theory*. Oxford: Oxford University Press.

Von Wright, Georg. H. 1963. *The Varieties of Goodness*. New York: Humanities Press.

Walden, Kenneth. 2021. Review of *The Value of Humanity*, by L. Nandi Theunissen. *Ethics* 131 (4): 808–812.

10

Are We of Equal Moral Worth?

Andrea Sangiovanni

One of the most enduring and widely accepted ideas of the modern era is that human beings have an unconditional, intrinsic, and absolute worth—a dignity—that raises them up in the order of nature and that is possessed equally by each one of us. By 'unconditional,' I mean that the worth is not conditioned on what we have done, who we are, what is good for anyone or anything, or what we value. By 'intrinsic,' I mean that the worth is grounded in the intrinsic properties of human beings. Rarity is an extrinsic property; shape is an intrinsic one. Being a friend, or cousin, is an extrinsic property; being a person capable of reasoning is an intrinsic one. And by 'absolute,' I mean that the worth is nonrelational; i.e., the worth is a kind of goodness *simpliciter* rather than goodness of a kind, goodness relative to a point of view, instrumental goodness, or goodness-for.

This dignity sets limits to what others may, with justification, do to us. It also explains why we are owed a respect as persons that is independent of who we are, what we have done, or what we value. And yet the idea is notoriously difficult to defend. In virtue of what are we equal in worth? The most common strategy is to point to a natural property (or set of properties) that is possessed, and possessed equally, by all and only human beings. Prominent candidates include our capacity to produce and accumulate knowledge across generations, or to choose in accordance with reasons (or, more narrowly, to act in accordance with morality), or to love. There are three main problems with this strategy. The first is that the degree to which human beings possess these properties varies from person to person. But if the properties vary, then shouldn't the worth vary along with them? A popular strategy of response posits a threshold above which variation doesn't matter. As long as, for example, one has a sufficiently realized capacity to act in accordance with morality, then variation in that capacity above the threshold doesn't matter. This leads to the second problem: Why should there be such a sharp cut-off in worth between individuals that possess moral capacities to degree n (just above the threshold) and those who possess it to degree $n - 1$? And: If the scalar property underlying the threshold-based property matters below the threshold, then why should it suddenly cease to matter above it? The third problem is that it is difficult to explain why possession of these properties should make their bearers especially worthy. The argument, in its classic form,

---

Andrea Sangiovanni, *Are We of Equal Moral Worth?* In: *Rethinking the Value of Humanity.*
Edited by: Sarah Buss and L. Nandi Theunissen, Oxford University Press. © Oxford University Press 2023.
DOI: 10.1093/oso/9780197539361.003.0011

is *not* that these capacities are good *for* their bearers or for others. (I return to this possibility below.) The possession of the properties is meant to make their bearers *nonrelationally* good, or good *simpliciter*, and good in a way that imposes a set of moral duties to be treated a certain way both by others and by the bearer toward herself. But why? Why should mere possession of a capacity (rather than its exercise) bestow a worth that deserves respect?

In this paper, I will not explore the range of possible attempts to overcome these problems.[1] Rather, let us begin by assuming they all fail. What follows? Must we accept—like Nietzsche—that there is a rank order of human types, with those exhibiting the highest forms of, say, creative and vigorous excellence at the top? Must we accept the idea that those lower in the order must defer and serve those who are higher? No. The right conclusion to draw is that we should *not* abandon the commitment to moral equality but rather the idea that moral equality requires appeal to moral worth, or dignity. We should, that is, abandon the search for absolute-unconditional-intrinsic-good-making natural properties possessed to an equal extent by each one of us. But then what do we say about our commitment to the claim that we are, in some basic sense, one another's equals? Can we still vindicate it without reliance on some account of the equal worth of humanity?

We can make progress in answering this question by asking a different one first: What role does appeal to the idea of moral equality play in our social and political life? It seems clear that it has played a crucial role in the following major developments of the modern era: the democratic revolutions of the eighteenth century, the revolutions of 1848, the abolition of slavery, the patchwork expansion of the franchise across all liberal democracies, labor movements (especially those associated with socialism), the development of human rights in the wake of the Second World War, decolonization in the 1960s, civil rights and women's liberation, the wave of democratizations in the 1980s and 1990s (including the end of apartheid in South Africa), and recent social movements such as Occupy, MeToo, and Black Lives Matter. In each of these cases, the focus of concern has been on the wrongfulness of *treating as inferior*. The role played by calls for equality has been, then, to undermine the structures that serve to enable the oppression of the 'inferior' by the 'superior'. Paradigmatic instances of such wrongful treatment include caste societies; slavery, sexual harassment and assault, segregation and apartheid, political persecution and exclusion, invidious forms of discrimination, demeaning forms of paternalism, concentration and death camps, and genocide. Each involves one or more of the following modes of treating as inferior: *stigmatization, infantilization, objectification, instrumentalization, marginalization*, and *dehumanization*.[2]

In view of this account of the role played by moral equality, the puzzle can now be restated. Our question becomes: When and why is treating someone as an

250 RETHINKING THE VALUE OF HUMANITY

inferior a violation of this person's status as a moral equal, and wrongful for that reason? In seeking an answer to this question, we set aside attempts to ground moral equality in equal moral worth. Instead, we ground our commitment to moral equality in an independent account of harm that, in turn, explains why treating as inferior is wrong. Note that treating as inferior is not always wrong. Hierarchies in power, esteem, and status are an enduring part of all human societies.[3] All human societies contain differences in social status, power, and esteem related to the performance of roles and the possession of resources. Some will be ranked higher than others, and this ranking will affect—whether consciously or unconsciously—their relations with those lower (and those higher) in position. Relations between superiors and inferiors within any formal hierarchy will also always be marked by asymmetry. Military officers, for example, have powers and privileges of control and office that privates do not. This will shape not only their formal interactions but informal ones as well. The same is true of any large organization. Thus, there will always be, in any human society, some who treat others as inferior. But, crucially, not all such forms of treating others as inferior are wrong.

We want to resist the answer: Treating as inferior is wrong in one or more of the relevant senses (from now on, I will drop "in one or more of the relevant senses") when and because it is incompatible with the equal worth bestowed on us by our equal possession of a set of distinctive psychological capacities. Instead, I have argued at length elsewhere that treating as inferior is wrong when and because it constitutes an attack on another's capacity to develop and maintain an integral sense of self (Sangiovanni 2017). It is wrong, that is, when and because of the threat it poses to a constitutive aspect of a person's flourishing—namely their capacity to integrate their choices, values, pursuits, and relationships into a narrative whole in which they see themselves reflected—rather than because it fails to properly recognize a person as equally, unconditionally, intrinsically, and absolutely valuable.

I will not repeat the argument here. Rather, I will extend the argument in two directions. In the first, I will develop the idea that treating as inferior is wrong, when it is wrong, because it is a form of harm. Dignity-based views hold that treating as inferior is a misrecognition of another's worth even if it does not count as an injury to a person's flourishing; the account I defend denies this. But in what sense is treating as inferior harmful? And what do we say about cases in which someone's capacity to develop and maintain an integral sense of self is not, in fact, undermined? What role does the idea of a (potentially unsuccessful) *attack* on another's integrity play? And finally, in what sense, if any, is treating as inferior bad not only for the victim but also for the perpetrator?

Second, I will expand the response to an important objection: even if I am right that treating as inferior is wrong as a distinctive kind of harm, don't I still need to assume that humanity has unconditional, intrinsic, and absolute value in order to explain why human flourishing matters in the first place? Which beings' flourishing matters, and why? In answering this objection, I will take up a powerful recent account, namely Nandi Theunissen's (2020) *The Value of Humanity*.

1.

The best way to test a harm-based account of the wrongfulness of treating as inferior, and so also an account of the grounds of moral equality, is to work through examples that seem to involve *harmless* violations of equal moral status. To focus ideas, I will discuss cases involving invidious racial discrimination, which represent paradigms of an inferiorizing societal practice.

Before turning in Section 2 to cases that might strike one, at first glance, as harmless, I begin with cases of uncontroversially harmful discrimination, but where we need to do some work in isolating the kind of harm at stake. Racial discrimination is harmful, it is often said, when and because it arbitrarily denies opportunities afforded to others on the basis of false empirical beliefs or racial animus regarding members of the racial minority. But it is harmful even when there is neither differential denial of opportunity nor false empirical beliefs about or racial animus toward members of the race in question. For an example of the former, consider *Palmer v. Johnston*, a case decided in the United States in 1971.[4] In 1962, the mayor of Jackson, Mississippi, following federal desegregation legislation, decided to close down five public swimming pools (four of which had been white-only and one of which was Black-only). The mayor closed down the pools to avoid desegregating them: "We will do all right this year at the swimming pools but if these [civil rights] agitators keep up their pressure, we would have five colored swimming pools because we are not going to have any intermingling."[5] The mayor feared that desegregating the pools would lead them to become de facto all-Black because whites would no longer want to swim in them—and further believed that all-Black pools were not worth maintaining, while all-white ones were. This case is relevant because the freedom at stake, namely swimming, is relatively trivial; the opportunities available to Blacks in Jackson—in this case opportunities to swim in public pools—were diminished to exactly the same extent as whites, and we might easily imagine that there were no further downstream effects on equality of socioeconomic opportunity more broadly considered. The closing of the pools is undoubtedly an act of morally wrongful discrimination. But why? And in what sense, if any, is it harmful?

For an example of wrongful discrimination that does not involve false empirical beliefs or racial animus, consider so-called reaction qualifications.[6] Suppose the owner of a city restaurant has a policy of turning away Blacks, not because of any racial hatred or beliefs in the inferiority of Blacks but because he believes *correctly* that his discriminatory policy will make his business more profitable. In this variation of our example, we would still judge the policy to be wrongful. Supposing, moreover, that the policy has no effects on the overall distribution of equality of opportunity, since there are many other restaurants close by, makes no difference to our assessment of its wrongness. Again, why? In what sense, if any, is it harmful?

The distinctive wrong in both these cases does not lie either in the mental attitudes of the actors (consider reaction qualifications) or the causal consequences for distributions of socioeconomic opportunity (as we have seen in both cases, those consequences were negligible). It lies in the *social meanings* of the policies, where a social meaning refers to the beliefs, desires, emotions, commitments, or dispositions expressed by a policy or action.[7] Interpreting social meanings always requires reference to the wider social, political, and cultural background in which a policy or action occurs. In the first case, the policy sends a stigmatizing message to the Black community, tied to white fears of swimming with and undressing in a shared space with Blacks. In the second, it sends a message of indifference and quiet acquiescence to the racist attitudes of the larger population.

Such stigmatizing messages harm when and because they undermine the psychological bases of self-respect. But what is self-respect, and why is it important?[8] As the Court in *Brown v. Board of Education* famously held:

> To separate [Black children] from others of similar age and qualifications solely because of their race generates a feeling of inferiority as to their status in the community that may affect their hearts and minds in a way unlikely ever to be undone.[9]

Feelings of inferiority undermine the sense that one's projects, commitments, and pursuits ought to matter to others. We are, ultimately, sociable beings who have a central interest in social recognition. We each develop a sense of self in dialogue and interaction with others similarly engaged. We are constantly involved in the presentation of a self to a world of other selves. But our capacity to develop and maintain an integral sense of self will not endure—unless we possess unusual strength and resilience (on which more below)—without receiving a some positive echo in the societies of which we are a part. It is for these reasons that rigid, systematically imposed, and negatively tainted identities attack our sense of ourselves *as* self-presenters, as beings who need some degree of control over the terms in which we appear to others in public.[10] As Frantz Fanon (1952, 88) writes:

> And already I am being dissected under white eyes, the only real eyes. I am *fixed*. . . . I am laid bare. I feel, I see in those white faces that it is not a new man who has come in, but a new kind of man, a new genus. Why, it's a Negro! . . . Shame. Shame and self-contempt. Nausea. When people like me, they tell me it is in spite of my color. When they dislike me, they point out that it is not because of my color. Either way, I am locked into the infernal circle.

Such stigmatization is, in turn, deepened and reinforced when the imposed identity denies wholesale the very interiority and capacity for self-presentation on which, paradoxically, the attack depends. The stigmatization then becomes dehumanization—the treatment of another "like an animal." A good example here is the image of the Black man as a hypersexualized and dangerous brute that governs the social background of public bathing in *Palmer*.[11] And, as the Fanon passage highlights, stigmatization has a further predictable effect on our ability to maintain and develop an integral sense of self. The attitudes that express and reinforce the stigma are often echoed in our own self-conception, and so infect the way we interact with others, both intimately and publicly.[12] At the extreme, such stigmatized identities, when fully internalized, undermine our ability to access and realize the most important goods in a human life, such as intimacy and the successful pursuit of our final ends.[13]

It is important to distinguish the account I have given from conventional Kantian understandings of self-respect. On conventional views, one has self-respect when one's relationships both to oneself and to others reflect a sense of one's own absolute, unconditional, and intrinsic worth as a person. One must respect oneself, then, just as one respects others and for the same reason: one must recognize the worth of one's capacity for autonomous choice, and hence act in accordance with only those maxims that are compatible with the laws governing the exercise of that capacity. One must not commit suicide, thereby destroying the life that is at the root of that capacity, or take drugs that destroy one's cognitive abilities, or let others act in ways that deny one's absolute, unconditional, and intrinsic worth. One also has a duty to do what is reasonable to develop the capacity, and its associated talents, through education and training.

Again, my aim here is not to argue directly against this view. Rather, I assume that it cannot be defended. And I ask: Can anything else replace it? In addressing this question, it is worth noting, first, that someone could still have self-respect without believing that they have a special kind of worth, let alone a worth that is due to their possession of a capacity for autonomous choice. They might simply act in a way that is consistent (across many different situations) with the requirements of self-respect without being motivated by the thought that this is required by the worth of their psychological capacities; they might, for example,

254 RETHINKING THE VALUE OF HUMANITY

just be the kind of person who does not surrender easily, takes pride in their achievements, works hard to develop their talents, and demands respect from others. There might be many factors that explain why they have the dispositions they do.

On my view, acting in ways that are consistent with what we have called the requirements of self-respect is good, undoubtedly, but good insofar as and because it is good *for* the person who acts in this way. A person who acts in accordance with the requirements of self-respect lives a more flourishing life, all else equal, than one who doesn't. Self-respect is, in turn, the natural byproduct of someone who acts from an integral sense of self. When someone is capable of integrating their values, pursuits, commitments, and relationships into a narrative whole with which they identify, this is in part because they believe that their projects matter and are worth pursuing. A sense that their projects and relationships don't matter, or are failing in systematic ways, can lead to a loss of integrity, as one struggles to make failure and a sense of worthlessness meaningful. And the loss of integrity often comes with a disposition to let oneself go, or to let oneself be degraded or humiliated by others, or to punish or sabotage oneself in basic and irreversible ways. An attack on one's integrity—as I described above in the case of discrimination—is then also an attack on the psychological bases for self-respect. But this is wrong not as a failure to recognize and appreciate the worth of someone's capacity for autonomous choice, but as an attack on one of the constituents of a flourishing life. Note that, on my view, there is then no *duty* to act in accordance with the requirements of self-respect; there is no duty, for example, to develop one's talents, or to govern oneself with a proper pride in their achievements, or to resist being humiliated; no duty to oneself not to act in a servile way, or not to commit suicide.[14] It is good if one does act in accordance with the standards of self-respect, but only because we then live more flourishing lives than we otherwise would have. Suicide is, on this view, a tragedy rather than a moral wrong.[15]

2.

So far, we have characterized the wrongfulness of two kinds of discrimination, neither of which involved the denial of opportunities afforded to others, the involvement of false empirical beliefs, or animus. I have argued that, even in these cases, the wrongfulness of discrimination is impossible to understand without appeal to its harmfulness, and specifically to the way in which it constitutes an attack on the capacity to develop and maintain an integral sense of self, and hence on one of the key psychological bases of self-respect. We are now in a position to address two important challenges to such a harm-based view of discrimination.

ARE WE OF EQUAL MORAL WORTH?   255

Similar examples, of course, could be reproduced for all of the other modes of inferiorization I have mentioned, but it helps to have a concrete instance of inferiorization in mind to assess the force of the objections.

The first challenge is the following. Suppose the target of a particular act of, say, discriminatory exclusion (or, in other contexts, a particular act of dehumanization, instrumentalization, and so on) is resilient and steadfast. Being subject to such inferiorizing treatment does not beat them down, or undermine the integrity of their sense of self, or cause them to interiorize a negative and tainted self-image.[16] Rather, being subject to discrimination strengthens their resolve, stokes their sense of pride, and pushes them into action against the injustice. Their life no longer, let us add, lacks the purpose it once did. The discrimination has caused their life to flourish in ways it otherwise wouldn't have. As a result, it seems unreasonable to argue that there is any, even *pro tanto*, harm, and certainly no harm of the kind I have described. Similar examples can be given for all cases of inferiorizing treatment that we discussed above. Does this kind of case provide a counterexample to the account I have given of the wrongness of treating as inferior? Note that dignity-based views have a ready answer, since they do not rely on any concept of flourishing or well-being to establish the wrongfulness of inferiorizing treatment.

It might seem tempting to argue that the discrimination is still a form of harm, but of harm to the *group* of which this person is a member. But even if we could explain how a harm to a group isn't merely an aggregate of the harms to its members, the counterexample would still retain its force. This is because we want to preserve the judgment that the discriminatory act wrongs the *target* (namely, our resilient protester) rather than just the judgment that the act harms the group of which the target is a member. We want an explanation that accounts for the fractured *moral nexus* between the discriminator and the target. If my account can't provide the required explanation, then it fails.

We can concede that the act does not harm the target but argue that its wrongfulness must still be explained in terms of the *attack* on the target, which is wrongful because of the harm it *would* or *might have* done.[17] What matters is its nature as an attack. Consider an analogy. When the burglar shoots the gun that he doesn't realize is jammed, he fails to kill or harm the homeowner, who is, we may add, still sleeping in his bed. The act is wrong, we say, as an *attempted* murder. And attempted murder is wrong because it *threatens* to harm.[18] The wrongfulness of the completed act, as Gideon Yaffe has written in an important article on attempts, *transfers* to the attempt.[19] Harm, then, is in the driver's seat in explaining *both* the completed act and the attempt: our objection to the attempt is an objection to the harm that the act would or might have caused. Note further that such attempts are wrong even if the type of gun used has a high failure rate. It is the same with the discriminatory act in question, which is wrong as an attempt

256 RETHINKING THE VALUE OF HUMANITY

on the integrity and self-respect of the target, even if it fails, and even if discriminatory acts have a high failure rate, i.e., they often fail in harming their targets.

One might think that the discriminators in our examples could argue that they didn't *intend* to harm since all they intended to do was to *exclude*, and so, because an attempt requires intent, they did not attempt to harm at all. In defense of this claim, couldn't they argue that they would, indeed, be happier if it turned out there was no harm from their exclusion (recall, in particular, the shopkeeper who just wants to keep his business going)? This defense is no better than the defense offered by the smuggler who has been paid to carry what he believes to be cocaine across the border but who argues that he didn't intend to smuggle *cocaine*, since he would have been happier had it turned out not to be cocaine but a harmless white powder. As Yaffe argues, the smuggler is committed to smuggling for two reasons. First, he is committed because it would make no rational sense for him to reconsider his intention upon finding out that the powder really is cocaine, given his belief that the white powder is, in fact, cocaine. Second, he is committed because he cannot complain about the way the world turned out— given that he believes the powder is cocaine—when the white powder really turns out to be cocaine. Analogously, the mayor and shopkeeper in our examples cannot rationally reconsider their intention to exclude—given their awareness of racism and its associated practices and effects—when they find out their exclusion, in fact, would harm in all the ways mentioned. And the mayor and shopkeeper cannot complain about the way the world turned out—given their awareness of racism and its associated practices and effects—when they find out that their respective exclusions harm in all the ways mentioned. How could they not have been aware, we say, of the harms that racism does? (How can someone not be aware that when they pull the trigger the gun kills?)[20] Hence, in excluding, they cannot but be understood as *trying* to harm—even if they fail, as in our example of the resilient protester.

It should now be clear how one can respond to a second counterexample. Imagine a racist landlord turns away a couple because they are Black.[21] But suppose that the couple does not know that they have been turned away for this reason. And also imagine that they could have permissibly been turned away because they had pets (which the landlord had never bothered to inquire about). Here again there seems to be no harm, and yet we surely want to say that turning away the couple because they are Black is wrong. A dignity-based view has a ready answer: the landlord fails, in his deliberations, to recognize the equal moral worth of the couple. But an account like the one I have been defending also has a ready answer. Recall that, even if we assume that the victim was asleep, the burglar's pointing the gun and pulling the trigger still count as a wrongful attempt. And so it is, I want to argue, with the landlord: in turning away the couple because they are Black, he cannot but be understood as aiming to harm them, both by aiming to deny them an opportunity they would have otherwise had (even if they would not, in fact, have had that opportunity) and by aiming to support and maintain a broader societal practice—sustained, in part, by myriad actions of the same general kind—that attacks the couple in all the ways mentioned. It is relevant here that, had the landlord known about the pets and been merely relieved that he could turn away the couple as a result, the turning away would not have been, on my view, objectionable. Turning away because of race and turning away because of pets describe the same behavior, but they have two very different social meanings, even if the meanings remain hidden (cf. Davidson 2001; Anscombe 1963). This strikes me as the right conclusion: a person who has racist beliefs or desires is criticizable, but the mere having of a belief or a desire is not a wronging of another, any more than the burglar's desires or beliefs regarding the death of the houseowner make it an attempted murder. Mere thoughts cannot be crimes.[22]

3.

I have argued that treating as inferior is wrong, when it is wrong, because it involves either harm or the threat of harm. Thus far, we have focused on harm and threatened harm to the *targets* of inferiorizing acts. But attacking another's capacity to develop and maintain an integral sense of self is also, I now want to argue, harmful to the *attacker*. A life that involves such attacks is, all else equal, less flourishing than one that doesn't. I conclude with an important asymmetry. If I am right, then, while the cruelty implicit in wrongful acts of inferiorization is *necessarily* bad for the perpetrator, such acts are only *contingently* bad for the target. As we have seen, targets can escape the harm threatened by wrongful inferiorization (recall the resilient and steadfast protester). I will argue that the perpetrator, on the other hand, cannot avoid the disfigurement that cruelty leaves in the shape of their life.

Something can be good for someone without being *useful*. This is often missed. The mistake can arise as a result of reasoning in the following way. Knives are good for cutting, flour for baking, arrows for shooting, food for growing. Whenever something is good for something else, this must then be because it contributes to it, and if it contributes to it, then it is a means to it, and hence useful. It makes no sense to say, then, that something can be *noninstrumentally* good *for* something or someone. When we say that friendship is good *for* us we must mean that it is good because of its effects on flourishing or well-being or happiness. On this picture, friendship contributes to well-being as a means to an end, and so instrumentally. This doesn't imply that people must value it instrumentally[23] (they might correctly value it as an end rather than as a means to an

258 RETHINKING THE VALUE OF HUMANITY

end), but it does imply that it derives its value from its instrumental contribution to well-being.

The mistake is that something can contribute to flourishing without being a *means to* flourishing. It can simply be constitutive of flourishing. Water is good for a plant because it is useful: without it, a plant cannot flourish. But the vigor and growth of the plant is good for it not in the sense that it instrumentally contributes to its flourishing. Rather, its vigor and growth make their contribution constitutively: they are what its flourishing consists in.

We can say the same for goods like love, pleasure, knowledge that reflects one's interests and passions, the appreciation of beauty, and health.[24] Each of these is good for us (when they are good for us),[25] not instrumentally but constitutively. The presence of them does not lead to something else, namely our flourishing. Rather, our flourishing just consists in a certain arrangement of the goods of which it is made, just as something's being a sculpture just consists in a certain arrangement of the lump of clay of which it is made. Not all things that are good for us are good in this way. Many things are good for us (when they are good for us) as means to the realization of things that are noninstrumentally good for us: water, shelter, leisure, attractiveness, intelligence, and so on. Note further that something can be noninstrumentally good for us because of its effects. This will be true for many activities that are noninstrumentally good for us, such as reading a good novel. In that case, reading the novel might cause a deeper reflection on our most important relationships, trigger a diffuse feeling of at-homeness in the world, shock us into a sense of the absurdity of our own self-regard, or make us feel the pain of loss, grief, and alienation. Each of these further states is part of the overall experience of reading the book. But the value of reading the book is not to be understood as deriving from its instrumental use in attaining these states, which are the ultimate, noninstrumental repository of value. (That would be true on only the narrowest kind of mental state hedonism.) Reading the book engages all our senses, imagination, and understanding. The connected effects and experiences of this engagement, then, make their contribution to our flourishing constitutively, just as the vigor and growth of a plant.[26]

So far, we have focused on things that are noninstrumentally good for us. And so does most of philosophical writing on the topic. But experiences, relationships, pursuits, and activities can also be noninstrumentally *bad* for us. There is an obvious sense in which some things can be *instrumentally* bad for us. This would be the case if and when they prevent the realization of something noninstrumentally good. Dehydration and unemployment are examples: each of these is bad for us insofar as and because it prevents our being in a state of good health in the first case, and prevents us, among other things, from being able to provide for our family and experience the sense of accomplishment attained by valuable work in the second.

ARE WE OF EQUAL MORAL WORTH? 259

Experiences, relationships, pursuits, and activities can, however, also be *noninstrumentally* bad for us. Such things are not bad for us merely because they prevent something noninstrumentally good; they are also bad for us in their own right. They are constitutive of what Richard Kraut (2007, 148–168) calls 'unflourishing.' Pain or nausea, for example, aren't merely bad for us because they prevent us from experiencing pleasure; rather, they are like the withering or etiolation of a plant. Permanent cognitive impairment provides another example. While such things may prevent us from realizing things that are noninstrumentally good for us, they are *also* states of unflourishing *as such*. Their contribution to unflourishing is direct rather than indirect. It is important that they are bad for us not merely because we dislike them. Our dislike is, after all, a reaction to what pain or nausea feels like, not the other way around. It gets things backwards to say that they are bad for us merely because we dislike them.

One might think that, because their contribution to our flourishing is direct, there is no way for things like pain or even cognitive impairment to be noninstrumentally *good* for us. But this is false. We are self-reflective, sociable, and purposive beings for whom meaning and structure are important. This makes our flourishing very different from that of a plant. Our attitudes toward our own capacities, experiences, relationships, pursuits, or activities can, as a result, affect whether they are noninstrumentally good for us. For example, pain might *not* be noninstrumentally bad for us—might not be an instance of unflourishing—if that pain is perceived as a meaningful part of a larger activity, such as childbirth. (Or consider deafness for many in the deaf community.) Here desire can play a part in making something that would otherwise be bad, good, but the desire is just one element. As sociable and meaning-creating beings, many of the things that are noninstrumentally good for us become so only as a result of their overall role in our life. We might say that noninstrumental goods are, then, only *conditionally* good.[27] This is true even in cases where someone finds no more enjoyment, say, in their chosen profession as a sculptor, and desires to quit. It may still be true that sculpting is noninstrumentally good for them, even though they have lost touch with why or how. This would be the case once we put in focus their overall values and aspirations, their past works and current relationships, and place them within a larger context or narrative. The fulfillment of desires isn't all there is to human flourishing.

So far we have focused on states, activities, and capacities, but relationships can also be noninstrumentally good and bad for us. Relationships of love and affection are, in normal circumstances, noninstrumentally good for us. They are good for us when and because they are complex developments of our powers of empathy, concern, sociability, understanding, cooperation, and imagination. Love, among other things, is the development of a power to learn about and from others with whom we share a common world. The knowledge of ourselves and others we attain is not, however, propositional but experiential. Love involves a knowing *how* rather than a knowing *that*. We learn, as it were, *how* to be ourselves and how it is to be another rather than learn a series of true propositions *about* ourselves or another. And it involves knowledge acquired *with* another, over time, and through a shared life. We learn together, as a result of a shared history of mutual exploration, regard, and activity. As a development of our fundamental powers—some of which, like sociability and empathy, are essentially relational—love is therefore a constitutive element of a flourishing life rather than just an instrument for obtaining one.

On the other hand, relationships of strife—like war, class or ethnic struggle, or enmity—are, in normal circumstances, bad for us. This is not only because they lead to, say, death or suffering. They are also noninstrumentally bad for us. Of course, conflict will also be part of even the best of relationships of love and friendship. The existence of such conflict is not necessarily to be regretted (although sometimes it should be). It can be an essential part of the experiences and relations described above; conflict can be, as it were, productive. In contrast, the kind of strife I am referring to is constitutive of the relationship itself. Such relationships are not noninstrumentally bad for us solely because of the stress, fear, anxiety, and so on that characterize them. They are not bad for us, that is, solely because of the way they feel. (Tecall that negative emotions, like grief or pain, can be good for us depending on their role in our lives.) They are bad for us, I want to argue, because they represent a destruction or inversion of the sociability that is at the root of so many of the most important goods in a human life (cf. Seneca 2010, "Anger"). Strife requires us to shut others out, to shut down our ability to project ourselves imaginatively into another's place and seek a reconciliation with that perspective. It is also associated with the disfigurement of our emotional lives. The infliction of pain and suffering on others is not easy. It is no surprise it often comes with numbness; it often also closes down the possibility of both self-knowledge and knowledge of others. This is not, of course, to deny that good things can come out of what is noninstrumentally bad for us, like good poetry out of war. Or to deny that it is possible to derive meaningfulness from strife. But there will still be loss; these further goods might compensate, but the harm is still there. We may, by contrast, compare the pain, for example, of childbirth, or the grief felt at the death of a loved one. All else equal, strife makes one's life worse; grief at the death of a loved one or pain in childbirth need not.

But surely, it may be objected, we can imagine someone who *thrives* on the infliction of pain and suffering on others, or who actively seeks out relationships grounded in conflict or strife as final ends for their life. I think it is revealing that it is difficult to imagine such individuals without imagining they are ill or disabled in some way. The psychopath, for example, lacks the capacity to feel empathy or to regulate their violent impulses; it is unlikely, as a result, that they will be able to have relationships with others characterized by love or intimacy. They will be lonely and disaffected, often rudderless. Psychopathy, that is, is noninstrumentally bad for the person who suffers from it. But what about someone who *compartmentalizes*: whose life is characterized by relations of strife and conflict in one domain but not in other parts of their life? Examples might include a soldier or a leader of the workers' movement. In these cases, however, it will not be true that either *thrives* from the strife *as such*. The conflict is a necessary, but unwelcome, means to a bigger end. Given all their other commitments, pursuits, plans, and so on, it is not as if either the member of the military will be less flourishing if there is no one to kill or maim, or if class struggle ceases. Indeed, what makes the struggle meaningful to the leader is its role in *ending* class oppression, just as what makes war meaningful to the soldier is the prospect of *returning* to a better peace. Again, there may be derivative benefits that come from class struggle or war—the sense of solidarity with fellow workers or soldiers, the meaning that belonging to a movement or fight against injustice provides, and so on. And of course there can be instrumental benefits from war and class struggle itself. But these derivative and instrumental benefits do not make class struggle *as such* or the killing involved in war noninstrumentally good for anyone. Unlike grief at the death of a loved one or pain in childbirth, relationships founded on strife and conflict cannot, then, be noninstrumentally good for us.

It is also important to distinguish strife as I have characterized it and the conflict that is part of *competition*. Competition, as in games or sport, is different precisely insofar as it does not involve the attempt to maim or destroy another's life. Competitive games, for example, are characterized by a larger spirit of cooperation that provides the background to the regimented and circumscribed conflict that is intrinsic to the game. This background cooperation—the compliance with the game's rules, the spirit of rivalry, the limited nature of the conflict, and so on—is essential to its nature as a *game*. The same background applies to other forms of competition, such as in political elections or the market. Conflict in each of these cases is disciplined and limited by rules whose aim is to stabilize and reproduce a broader cooperation. The kind of strife I have focused on lacks such a cooperative background. War, ethnic or racial violence, persecution, torture, and so on—while they may be structured by rules with which all parties comply—lack the cooperative aim of games, politics, markets, and sport.

It should now be clear why attacking another's capacity to maintain and develop an integral sense of self through one or more of the inferiorizing practices we identified above is noninstrumentally bad for the attacker. The cruelty of such attacks disfigures the life of the attacker. It is an inversion or destruction of the sociability and empathy that underlies the realization of the most important goods in a human life. A person therefore makes a mistake if they think that

262 RETHINKING THE VALUE OF HUMANITY

participating in, for example, racist practices makes their life better as a consequence of, let us imagine, the feeling of domination and superiority that comes with it. If I am right, then the life of the attacker is made worse *directly* rather than merely *indirectly*. Even if there are other compensating goods in their life, or other derivative benefits from participation in racism, their life is still blighted by the harm they threaten. The life of the target, on the other hand, is not made worse in the same way. While their integrity is attacked, it is not necessarily undermined. Resistance and resilience can make one's own life, and the lives of others, better.[28]

4.

In this section, I want to address an additional objection. Even if I am right that treating as inferior is wrong as a distinctive kind of harm, don't I still need to assume that humanity has unconditional, intrinsic, and absolute value in order to explain why human flourishing matters in the first place? The objection is most forcefully put via an argument by David Velleman.

The argument has this shape. Some things are of value because they are good for something or someone else (stairs, for example, are good for climbing, friendship is good for human beings). But, if X is good in virtue of being good *for* Y, then we must presuppose that Y is good. But if Y is good, then it must either be good for something else, Z, or good-in-itself (rather than good for anything else). Because the chain cannot go on forever, and because the goodness of means derives from the ends to which they aim, there must be some things that are good-in-themselves without being good-for-anything; these things are intrinsically or absolutely or nonrelationally good; they are good *simpliciter*. Applied to persons, we can say that if something, say, friendship or appreciating an artwork, is good because it is good for *someone* then *they* must either be good *simpliciter* or good for something or someone else. Eventually the chain must come to an end, and it seems plausible that it should come to an end with the person themselves. According to Velleman (1999, 613):

> [V]alue *for* a person stands to value *in* the person roughly as the value of means stands to that of the end: in each case, the former merits concern only on the basis of concern for the latter. And conditional values cannot be weighed against the unconditional values on which they depend. The value of means to an end cannot overshadow or be overshadowed by the value of the end, because it already is only a shadow of that value, in the sense of being dependent upon it. Similarly, the value of what's good for a person is only a shadow of the value inhering in the person, and cannot overshadow or be overshadowed by it.

ARE WE OF EQUAL MORAL WORTH? 263

Therefore, the person themselves—*qua* being with a capacity for autonomous choice—must have value independently of whatever is good for them (and hence independently of their interests), the person's value must be incommensurable with the value of what is good for them (and hence their interests), and the person's value must be of higher value than what is good for them (and hence whatever is in their interest). In virtue of their capacity for autonomous choice, persons, then, are absolutely, unconditionally, and intrinsically good, and so good *simpliciter*.

There are several places where the reasoning has been questioned.[29] I want to deny that if something is good for Y, then Y must possess a distinct kind of value—nonrelational, unconditional, and intrinsic value. Our flourishing (along with other sentient animals) might matter in a way that, say, a plant's flourishing doesn't *not* because we possess a distinct and higher kind of value that makes our flourishing more worthy of attention, but simply because we meet a condition that explains why our flourishing matters morally. An analogy: possessing a ticket is a condition required for entry to the show, not a condition of our worthiness to attend. As I argue in *Humanity*, our flourishing matters in its own right and for its own sake because we possess a perspective from which it matters what happens to us. We (along with all other sentient beings) are, that is, *evaluative* beings: we react with conscious aversion, attraction (and sometimes indifference) to how the world affects us. The fact that something promotes the flourishing of a being with a subjective perspective explains why we have (final) reasons to promote, protect, and so on, the things that are good for beings of this kind.[30] We do not need to say, in turn, that subjectivity gives such reasons because it bestows a higher worth on its bearer; rather, we say that subjectivity provides reasons because and insofar as it affects the kind of flourishing that is available to us. As I will argue in more detail below, our flourishing has, that is, relational, conditional, and extrinsic value (given by its relation to our subjectivity), but so does our subjectivity (given by its relation to our flourishing). Our subjectively experienced flourishing can, then, function as the needed regress-stopper: that a walk with a friend is good for Y gives us moral reasons not to interfere because Y is a being with a subjective perspective on the world, not because Y possesses a higher, nonrelational, unconditional, or intrinsic worth.

What do we gain? First, there are many reasons to resist ending the regress with something whose goodness is nonrelational (or, equivalently, absolute). Some doubt the very concept of nonrelational goodness, the idea that something can just be good (period), rather than a good member of a kind or good for someone or something (Geach 1956; Thomson 2008). Others grant the coherence of the concept, but believe that such a property either doesn't exist, or, even if it did, fails to provide us with reasons to do anything (Kraut 2011). Others still have more substantive worries: the problem with nonrelational goodness is that it seems hard to explain why it ought to be of practical concern for us and from our point of view. "When something is of value," what we mean is that it "contribute[s] . . . to the quality of the life of human beings (or, more broadly, of beings)" (Theunissen 2020, p. 8). Pointing to our practical concerns makes it intelligible *why* and *in virtue of what* something has value. The problem with making the value of human (and other sentient) beings *nonrelational*, on this picture, is that it seems to require a kind of value of a very different sort, entirely disconnected from our (or anyone's) practical concerns. Nonrelational goodness seems, we might say, altogether too other-worldly.

Second, ending the regress with the relational value of subjectively experienced flourishing rather allows us to distinguish *having value* from *having worth*. On the Vellemanian regress, it is appropriate to refer to the regress-stopper as having a *worth*, or dignity, because the ultimate, nonrelational value—possessed by our capacity for autonomous choice—is of a *higher* order compared with the value of everything else. As I mentioned in the introduction, this leads to worries about whether variation in the underlying capacity should lead to differences in worth. On the view I am defending, subjectively experienced flourishing has a distinct kind of relational value that is neither higher nor lower than the value of other things. It is not as if beings that possess such a point of view ought to be treated in a certain way because such a point of view puts them higher in the order of nature. The difference in relational value between a being with a subjective point of view and one without is *categorial* rather than *ordinal*. Value here just correlates with reasons to promote, protect, respect, not with higher (or lower) worth.

Third, and closely related, ending the regress in this way allows us to distinguish between *basic* and *equal* moral status. *Basic* moral status only tells us that a being's flourishing matters in its own right and for its own sake. Arguing that a being has *equal* moral status requires a further stretch of argument. *Basic* moral status, that is, is not sufficient for *equal* moral status. There is no comparative judgment in the idea of basic moral status, no conclusion implied about how its flourishing ought to be compared to the flourishing of other beings with a similar standing. It also doesn't tell us when and why it is wrong to treat another as inferior. Standards for basic moral status are, to draw an analogy, like eligibility conditions for office (such as, for example, being at least thirty-five years of age is a qualifying condition for election as US president). The qualifying conditions get one in the game; they do not fully determine what makes for a good President, or who will be elected. Suppose, then, that a being has a richer or deeper evaluative response to the world around it. On the view defended, this does not imply that it deserves greater consideration, or that it is more worthy as a result. But it also does not imply that the depth and richness of its experience is morally *irrelevant*.[31] What kind of moral consideration it deserves needs further

ARE WE OF EQUAL MORAL WORTH? 265

argument, which ought to be sensitive to, among other things, the kinds of evaluative response open to it.[32]

One might worry that, if there are moral constraints that arise from a being's
having *basic* moral status, then shouldn't the constraints apply *equally* to everyone who has this status? And if they do, then isn't that all that is required for
establishing a being's equal moral status? Couldn't we just stop there? As I argue
elsewhere, the sense here of a constraint applying *equally* to all beings that have
a certain status is purely formal. It means something like "Treat all who have this
status in accordance with the constraints, unless there is reason to treat them differently" (Sangiovanni 2017, chap. 1; see also Westen 1982; Raz 1986, chap. 9).
This is not sufficient for moral equality, since it is not sufficient to block even
the most heinous forms of invidious discrimination. The most egregious racist,
for example, could hold that there are *some* constraints that apply equally to all
beings, whether Black or White, but deny that these constraints bar prohibiting
miscegenation or denying civil and political rights to Blacks. For moral equality,
we need, that is, an account that gives us something more than the set of rights
and duties that attach to us as evaluatively laden, conscious beings. We need
something that explains why treating as inferior in the ways we have identified is
wrong. That further stretch of argument, on my account, is provided by the harm
(and threat of harm) of attacking the integrity of another's sense of self.

I have argued that the flourishing of beings with a subjective point of view
matters in its own right and for its own sake. For some, this may sound like it
concedes too much to Velleman (and other Kantians). To say that "having a subjective point of view on the world" has special reason-giving weight is just to
say that it has value. But its reason-giving force as a value, some might object,
doesn't seem relational. I have not argued, for example, that "having a subjective point of view" gives us special reasons because it is *beneficial to* the beings
that possess it. I also haven't argued, relatedly, for the voluntarist thesis that our
flourishing matters when and because we value it. Rather, we (along with other
sentient beings) have a basic moral status in virtue of the fact that we have a perspective on the world from which things matter to us, whether negatively or positively, not in virtue of the fact that our flourishing is the (contingent) object of
our valuing. The flourishing of someone who has ceased valuing their life still
ought to matter to us precisely because they have a subjective point of view from
which their despair, as it were, makes sense.[33] Isn't the value of our subjectivity,
then, non-relational?

No. Recall that I said above that subjectivity has relational value in virtue of
its relation to our flourishing. Nandi Theunissen has offered an ingenious solution that we can appeal to in defending this claim. According to Theunissen,
we can end the Vellemanian regress not with a monadic, nonrelational bearer
of value, but with a dyadic, relational one. On her view, we can say that a being

266 RETHINKING THE VALUE OF HUMANITY

matters because its flourishing matters from its point of view, but we can *also* say that its (subjective) capacity to value matters because it contributes to that being's flourishing. The relation at the end of the regress is, that is, self-reflexive, but still relational. We can unpack the account in our terms in the following way. The capacity for conscious intentional action, for responding to the world in evaluatively-laden ways, makes beings of this kind, *valuing* beings. These are beings for whom their life and how it is going is, as Theunissen writes, an *issue* for them and from their point of view (cf. plants, who do not have such a point of view). This is the first half of the circle: these beings matter because how their life is going matters from their point of view. (This is where we left things above and in *Humanity*.) But the fact that they are valuing beings also gives them the capacity to make their lives go well (or badly), and determines, in part, *what it is* for their life to go well or badly (recall the examples we have already discussed about how to determine what counts as noninstrumentally good and bad for human beings). This is the second half of the circle: the (subjective) capacity for valuing matters because it determines, in part, whether and how a being flourishes.[34] At the end of the regress, then, is a mutual relation between ourselves, understood as (subjectively) valuing beings, and our flourishing, each of which is important for, and because, of the other.

Taking stock, this solution allows us to say that both *basic* and *equal* moral status are relational all the way down. Both basic and equal moral status are grounded in facts about what contributes to (and threatens) a good or flourishing life, rather than in facts about the nonrelational worth or dignity of a being, independently of their flourishing. With respect to equality and inequality, what matters is the effect of treating as inferior on the quality of the lives of self-conscious, sociable beings like us, rather than the inherent and equal worthiness of a capacity to act in accordance with reason.

I end with a response to the following important objection. We may wonder whether this argument shows, at best, that a being's flourishing matters for itself as a valuing being, and its having the capacity to value contributes to its flourishing. What it doesn't show is why *any other being* has reason to give this fact about one's relation to oneself any special standing in their deliberation. I want to highlight two possible responses to this worry. One, adopted by Theunissen, is to point to a conceptual truth about value. On this view, (1) the concept of being "of value" is the concept of being such as to make something practically relevant or reason-giving for human beings; (2) being good for human beings is the relation that explains why something is of value when it is; (3) when a person leads a flourishing life she instantiates something that is good for human beings; therefore, (4) every human being has reason to value what is good for another, and hence their flourishing (see Theunissen 2020, 123–124 and her chapter in this volume, sec. 4). The trouble with this argument is that the conclusion at (4) looks to be assured only if we build it into the concept of value at (1), such that to be "of value" is for something to be reason-giving for *every* human being. This leaves it open for an opponent to argue that, conceptually, it is surely possible for something to be of value for one person, and hence reason-giving for that person, without also being of value, or reason-giving, for others. Unless we show, substantively, that the agent-relative reason to take my own flourishing to matter also generates a co-occurring agent-neutral reason for *every* person to take my flourishing to matter, we haven't really answered the objection.[35]

Another response, for which I argue at greater length elsewhere, is simply to say that the fact that flourishing is good for another as a valuing being (and we can add, in line with Theunissen, *also* that its capacity for valuing is good for its flourishing) is a *basic* (agent-neutral) reason to give another's evaluatively laden flourishing a special moral standing in our deliberation (Sangiovanni 2017, 67–71). By "basic" here we mean that its status as a reason isn't grounded or derived from any other reasons. Indeed, the very recognition of the reason as basic seems essential to having a moral point of view in the first place. In this light, the objection, then, really amounts to the question: Why be moral? If that is right, then we face Prichard's dilemma: any answer to the question must either give further moral reasons to be moral, and so presuppose what it is meant to show, or to give nonmoral reasons, in which case it provides the wrong kind of reason. But this is not the only thing we can say in response.

We can also provide *evidence* that the basic reason is genuine by showing the way it contributes to and fits into a good life. We show, that is, that a person who recognizes the basic reason lives a (noninstrumentally) better life as a result of this recognition than someone who doesn't. This is because a recognition of this fact as a reason underlies and makes possible some of the most important goods in a human life, such as friendship and love. It is worth repeating that this is not itself the reason to treat another's flourishing as mattering—that reason, recall, is the fact that another has an evaluatively laden conscious perspective. Rather, the argument seeks to show that a recognition of this basic reason is also good for us—it seeks to show, as we might say, that there is congruence between the right and the good. By showing that the recognition of the reason as basic contributes to the good, we thereby strengthen the reflective equilibrium that supports our judgment that the reason is genuine.

Notes

1. I discuss Kantian (and some Christian) attempts to resolve these problems—including some by Korsgaard, Darwall, Forst, Velleman, and George—in Sangiovanni 2017, chap. 1.

268 RETHINKING THE VALUE OF HUMANITY

2. I discuss these modes of inferiorization at greater length in Sangiovanni 2017, chap. 2; here I also add marginalization. Note that I use definitions of each of these modes that are unmoralized; i.e., I allow that there can be permissible forms of stigmatization, etc. The task is then to explain when and why each of these modes of treating as inferior is wrong.

3. This is a staple of any text on social stratification in sociology.

4. *Palmer v. Thompson,* 403 U.S. 217 (1971), §87.

5. *Palmer v. Thompson,* §87.

6. On reaction qualifications, see Alexander 1992; Arneson 2006.

7. I say much more about what a social meaning is, and why it matters in Sangiovanni 2017, chap. 3. See also Hellman 2008; Eidelson 2015. For critique, see Lippert-Rasmussen 2013.

8. In Sangiovanni (2017), I did not discuss self-respect. Here I show how self-respect can be given a nondignitarian formulation. See also Schemmel 2019; Moody-Adams 1995; Dillon 1997.

9. *Brown v. Board of Education,* 347 U.S. 483 (1954), 494.

10. Cf. Goffman (1956), on which I draw. And see also Velleman 2003.

11. For a lucid account of the racial politics of community swimming pools in the United States, see Wiltse 2007.

12. See, e.g., the powerful account of the wrongness of racial inequality, and its roots in stigma, in Loury 2009, chap. 2. See also Fanon 1952, esp. chap. 5, "L'expérience vécue du Noir" (or "the lived experience of blackness," translated in the English edition, somewhat misleadingly, as "The Fact of Blackness") and Baldwin 2013. See also Haslanger (2012, 65): "A good objectifier will, when the need arises—that is, when the object lacks the desired properties—exercise his power to make the object have the properties he desires."

13. On the importance and usefulness of final ends, see Frankfurt 1999, chap. 7.

14. This doesn't, strictly speaking, follow from adopting a harm-based account, but it is compatible with such an account in a way that a Kantian view is not.

15. I leave aside cases in which suicides might represent wrongs to *others.* We are here focused on duties to self.

16. In Sangiovanni (2017), I discussed a similar counterexample by referring to Zora Neale Hurston's Janie Crawford from *Their Eyes Were Watching God.* Here I expand on that discussion.

17. As I discuss in Sangiovanni (2017, chap. 3), even if the agent lacks an intention, the fact that an action undermined another's capacity to develop and maintain an integral sense of self can also be wrong when the action is negligent or reckless, as in cases of systematic indifference. The indifference sends a demeaning message, and is wrong for that reason. In the following, I focus on intentional attacks.

18. On the connection between threat and attempt, see Westen 2008. Note that it is still attempted murder even if we assume that the probability that the gun will go off is zero.

19. Yaffe 2014.

ARE WE OF EQUAL MORAL WORTH? 269

20. Suppose they really were ignorant about the way racial exclusion harms, and suppose further that they were not culpable in their ignorance. In this case, they would have an excuse, just as someone who puts arsenic in your tea thinking it is sugar has an excuse (in the case in which the person turns out in any case to be immune to the effects of arsenic), and just as the smuggler who nonculpably believes they are carrying talcum is excused (in the case in which the drug dealers are mistaken about the cocaine they falsely believe they are getting the smuggler to carry for them).

21. The example is from Scanlon 1998, 73.

22. I here give a different response than the one I gave in Sangiovanni (2017), which argued that the turning away was harmful in the same sense as an unknown betrayal is harmful. The response I give here can be used also to answer similar counterexamples in Slavny and Parr 2015.

23. For this distinction, see Korsgaard 1996.

24. I do not argue here for a substantive account of human flourishing as an account of well-being, which would take us too far afield. For such accounts, see Foot 2001; Kraut 2007; Thompson 2008. Other accounts of well-being, such as ideal-desire theories, are compatible with everything I say in this paper.

25. All of these goods, that is, can sometimes be bad for us, depending on what else is true of our lives. Pleasure can sometimes be bad for us, just as love can. But when the conditions are right, each of these things makes their contribution to our flourishing constitutively. So, we might say, their value for us is conditional but constitutive. I say more about this below.

26. For this point, see Raz (2001, 147–148) and the very helpful discussion in Theunissen 2020, 42–43.

27. Are there things that are *unconditionally* good for us? This is one of the questions Plato asks in the *Meno* and answers with wisdom.

28. Cf. the master/slave dialectic in Hegel.

29. See also Conee (1982) and Kraut (2011, 35–37) for the idea that the end of this chain need not result in something *good*; it could just as well result in something that is *neither* good *nor* bad.

30. See also Sher 2014, Ch. 1 and Regan 1985.

31. The dignitarian, on the other hand, believes that the argument establishing a being's basic status also serves to establish its equal status. This is why the dignitarian usually argues that, above some threshold, the worth-grounding psychological capacities *cease to matter* for determining what kind of consideration a being is due. From this it follows that all beings above the threshold are due *equal* consideration. On the view I defend, this inference isn't warranted. We need further argument to establish whether (and in what way) we should treat beings with basic moral status as equals. I also suggest, as I mentioned earlier, that using the idea of worth to elucidate what treating as equals requires is bound to produce skepticism. Again, the fact that being thirty-five years of age is an eligibility criterion for office does not imply that *being older* is the only appropriate standard for selecting among candidates for President; neither does not imply that it is the most important or salient consideration in selecting someone for President.

32. For example, its degree of psychological connectedness might matter in determining what kinds of harms it is liable to, and so what kinds of harms ought to enter, morally, into our deliberations regarding whether, say, it permissible to kill it. See, e.g., McMahan 2002, on the relevance of time-limited interests. On this kind of view, a higher degree of psychological connectedness modifies the kinds of harms a being is liable to rather than makes it more worthy.

33. Cf. Korsgaard 2004. And see Langton 2007 for a response wondering, among other things, what to say about someone who has ceased valuing their own life or how it is going. The point here is that, even for this person, how their life is going is an issue for them as an evaluative creature. Indeed, there is no other way to make sense of their *rejection* of their own life as mattering.

34. This account is developed in discussion, among others, with Buss 2012, who argues that human beings are of value because of their (rational) capacity to appreciate the value of things that are good *simpliciter*. On this kind of account, human beings have noninstrumental value because they are good for things of value, rather than the other way around. Theunissen, I think correctly, argues that this can't be right: works of art, for example, are valuable because and insofar as they are good for us, given the role of making and enjoying art in our lives. To argue that human beings are valuable because and insofar as they act as instruments for the appreciation of works of art makes human beings oddly fungible.

35. At 122–124, Theunissen (2020) denies that it is conceptually possible for something to count as a reason for an agent (because it is good for them), but not generate reasons for others not to interfere, to respect, to promote, and so on. This is because, if something is good for an agent, it must be good in virtue of quite general features about her as a human being. Something is good for an agent, then, only if it is, ultimately, an instance of the human good. Let us accept this for the sake of argument. She then goes on to claim that, insofar as an agent's pursuits, etc. are instances of the human good, they must therefore generate reasons for *everyone*. But there are problems here, I think, since the slide from good for me (qua human good) and reason-generating for everyone is too quick: we need some further argument why everyone has reason to promote the human good, and hence this person's pursuits as instances of that good. Furthermore, as Theunissen herself notes, the kinds of reasons something of value creates will vary according to the kind of thing it is and one's relation to it. So, conceptually, it is (I think) fully possible for something to be good for me as an instance of the human good, but not to generate (even *pro tanto*) reasons for others not to promote, interfere, and so on. The reasons not to interfere, if there are any, need to come not from a conceptual claim about relational value as flowing from general features of the human good, but from a substantive argument about why my particular pursuit—or my particular realization of the human good—generates reasons for others of distinctive kinds. I don't deny, of course, that there may very well be such reasons for others not to interfere, etc., as there certainly are in the case of climbing Mount Kilimanjaro; what I deny is that such reasons flow from a conceptual truth about relational value. (And, conversely, note also we could have reasons not to interfere even if no one's good is promoted, in cases, that is, where what I am doing is *bad* for me and good for

no one else). I thank Maria Alvarez, David Owens, and Nandi Theunissen for helpful discussion.

References

Alexander, Lawrence. 1992. "What Makes Wrongful Discrimination Wrong? Biases, Preferences, Stereotypes, and Proxies." *University of Pennsylvania Law Review* 194: 149–219.

Anscombe, Gertrude E. M. 1963. *Intention*. Oxford: Basil Blackwell.

Arneson, Richard. 2006. "What Is Wrongful Discrimination." *San Diego Law Review* 43: 775–808.

Baldwin, James. 2013. *The Fire Next Time* New York: Vintage.

Buss, Sarah. 2012. "The Value of Humanity." *Journal of Philosophy* 109: 341–377.

Conee, Earl. 1982. "Instrumental Value without Intrinsic Value?" *Philosophia* 11: 345–359.

Davidson, Donald. 2001. *Essays on Actions and Events*. 2nd ed. Oxford: Oxford University Press.

Dillon, Robin. 1997. "Self-Respect: Moral, Emotional, Political." *Ethics* 107: 226–249.

Eidelson, Benjamin. 2015. *Discrimination and Disrespect*. Oxford: Oxford University Press.

Fanon, Frantz. 1952. *Black Skin, White Masks*. New York: Grove Press.

Foot, Philippa. 2001. *Natural Goodness*. Oxford: Clarendon Press.

Frankfurt, Harry. 1999. *Necessity, Volition, and Love*. Cambridge: Cambridge University Press.

Geach, Peter. 1956. "Good and Evil." *Analysis* 17: 33–42.

Goffman, Erving. 1956. *The Presentation of Self in Everyday Life*. Edinburgh: University of Edinburgh, Social Sciences Research Centre.

Haslanger, Sally. 2012. "On Being Objective and Being Objectified." In *Resisting Reality: Social Construction and Social Critique*, 35–83. Oxford: Oxford University Press.

Hellman, Deborah. 2008. *When Is Discrimination Wrong?* Cambridge, MA: Harvard University Press.

Korsgaard, Christine. 1996. "Two Distinctions in Goodness." In *Creating the Kingdom of Ends*, 246–275. Cambridge: Cambridge University Press.

Korsgaard, Christine. 2004. *The Sources of Normativity*. Cambridge, UK: Cambridge University Press.

Kraut, Richard. 2007, *What Is Good and Why*. Cambridge, MA: Harvard University Press.

Kraut, Richard. 2011. *Against Absolute Goodness*. Oxford: Oxford University Press.

Langton, Rae. "Objective and Unconditioned Value." *Philosophical Review* 116: 157–185.

Lippert-Rasmussen, Kasper. 2013. *Born Free and Equal?* Oxford: Oxford University Press.

Loury, Glenn. 2009. *The Anatomy of Racial Inequality*. Cambridge, MA: Harvard University Press.

McMahan, Jeff. 2002. *The Ethics of Killing*. Oxford: Oxford University Press.

Moody-Adams, Michelle, ed. 1995. *The Social Basis of Self-Respect*. London: Routledge.

Raz, Joseph. 1986. *The Morality of Freedom*. Oxford: Clarendon Press.

Raz, Joseph. 2001. *Value, Respect, and Attachment*. Cambridge: Cambridge University Press.

Regan, Donald. 1985. *The Case for Animal Rights*. Berkeley: University of California Press.

Sangiovanni, Andrea. 2017. *Humanity without Dignity: Moral Equality, Respect, and Human Rights*. Cambridge, MA: Harvard University Press.

272 RETHINKING THE VALUE OF HUMANITY

Scanlon, Thomas. 1998. *What We Owe to Each Other*. Cambridge, MA: Harvard University Press.

Schemmel, Christian. 2019. "Real Self-Respect and Its Social Bases." *Canadian Journal of Philosophy* 49: 628–651.

Seneca. 2010. *Anger, Mercy, Revenge*. Translated by Robert Kaster and Martha Nussbaum. Chicago: University of Chicago Press.

Sher, George. 2014. *Equality for Inegalitarians*. Cambridge: Cambridge University Press.

Slavny, Adam, and Tom Parr. 2015. "Harmless Discrimination." *Legal Theory* 21: 100–114.

Theunissen, L. Nandi. 2020. *The Value of Humanity*. Oxford: Oxford University Press.

Thompson, Michael. 2008. *Life and Action*. Cambridge, MA: Harvard University Press.

Thomson, Judith J. 2008. *Normativity*. Chicago: Open Court.

Velleman, David. 1999. "A Right of Self-Termination?" *Ethics* 109: 606–628.

Velleman, David. 2003. "Narrative Explanation." *Philosophical Review* 112: 1–25.

Westen, Peter. 1982. "The Empty Idea of Equality." *Harvard Law Review* 95: 537–596.

Westen, Peter. 2008. "Impossibility Attempts: A Speculative Thesis." *Ohio State Journal of Criminal Law* 5: 523–565.

Wiltse, Jeff. 2007. *Contested Waters: A Social History of Swimming Pools in America*. Chapel Hill: University of North Carolina Press.

Yaffe, Gideon. 2014. "Criminal Attempts." *Yale Law Journal* 124: 95–154.

11
The Normative Significance of Humanity

Peter Railton

Introduction

The stakes would appear to be high in discussing the normative significance of humanity. It is a natural thought that the value of much of what we do, and the ways in which we view ourselves and one another, presuppose something fundamental about the value of humanity itself. At the same time, the notion of the value of humanity seems nebulous—even, to some, empty within a secular worldview. What idea of humanity is being called upon? What kind of value might be at issue? Or should we instead be speaking of some other form of significance, importance, or standing? Significance for what, to whom, or in-itself? And how, if at all, would answers to these questions bear on the practice of moral life or politics? In what follows, I will try to avoid begging some of these important questions by asking in the first instance about the *normative significance* of humanity—whether in the end this is best understood as a matter of *value* would need to be shown.

There is, of course, an important Kantian tradition in philosophy in which the idea of humanity as an end-in-itself, or bearer or source of value, figures centrally. In the argument of the *Groundwork* leading up to the third formulation of the categorical imperative, Kant writes:

> [S]uppose there were something the *existence of which in itself* has an absolute worth, something which as *an end in itself* could be a ground of a possible categorical imperative, that is, of a practical law.
>
> Now I say that the human being and in general every rational being *exists* as an end in itself, *not merely as a means* to be used by this or that will at its discretion. . . . [T]heir nature already marks them out as a[n] end in itself . . . and without [this] nothing of *absolute worth* would be found anywhere. (*G* 4:428)

Even within the Kantian or neo-Kantian tradition, however, debate continues over what *humanity* might be, what normative significance it might have, and what justificatory or explanatory role it is being asked to play.[1]

Peter Railton, *The Normative Significance of Humanity* In: *Rethinking the Value of Humanity.*
Edited by: Sarah Buss and L. Nandi Theunissen, Oxford University Press. © Oxford University Press 2023.
DOI: 10.1093/oso/9780197539361.003.0012

So I will begin by taking up preparatory questions about the nature of humanity and then look at some possible connections with normative significance. I hope to find a way of approaching questions about the normative significance of humanity that is responsive to many of the underlying concerns that have animated debates over these questions, while also promising to permit some progress in reaching answers and connecting these debates with issues in moral and political practice. After briefly examining a few issues about the nature of humanity, I will move on to consider an influential contemporary Kantian approach to these issues. Next, I will contrast this approach with an alternative that I think—without scholarly credentials!—can also be found in Kant's writings. I proceed in this Kant-inspired way partly in an effort to remain in contact with existing debates, and partly because I think that the view I will be attributing to Kant makes a fairly plausible case for understanding the nature of humanity and its potential normative significance. At the end I will add a few remarks about how this Kant-inspired approach might be made yet more plausible.

I realize that any attempt to formulate these issues will be controversial, and is bound to appear to some who are deeply concerned with the question of the normative significance of humanity as tendentious or simply missing the point. Therefore I will make no claim to have located the proprietary question, or the philosophically favored approach to it. Perhaps, by going some distance in exploring an unorthodox but still Kant-inspired approach, I can find a path that those traveling other avenues would be glad to know about.

The Nature of Humanity

Capacities and Collections

To begin, we face the question of the nature of *humanity*. A first thing to notice is that 'humanity' is used both for a trait or set of characteristics that agents, attitudes, or actions can possess to a greater or lesser *degree*, and also for a collection of beings of a distinctive *kind*. Kant, for example, distinguished *Humanität*, the trait or set of characteristics, from *Menscheit* or *Menschlichkeit*, the collection of beings.[2] For clarity, when it seems important to make the distinction, let's use 'humanity' (small "h") for the trait or characteristics, and 'Humanity' (capital "H") for the collection of beings. In settings where the distinction is less important or unclear, we will follow most writings and default to 'humanity' (small "h").

What is the relation of Humanity to humanity? It certainly doesn't seem that all of those usually grouped together as Humanity possess humanity—at least, not fully. We might try saying that Humanity is comprised of those beings with a *capacity* for humanity, whether or not this is well developed. Yet this runs afoul of

THE NORMATIVE SIGNIFICANCE OF HUMANITY   275

a familiar list of cases—people in terminal comas, people suffering very serious brain damage or developmental disorders, and so on—where this capacity may be absent.[3] So it probably is more accurate to think of Humanity as a *generic*—a collection of creatures who *typically*, though not always, possess a capacity for humanity, and do so in virtue of characteristic rather than accidental features (e.g., "Horses are quadrupeds" vs. "Horses were used in farming"; "Humans have a sense of self" vs. "Humans engage in farming"). 'Humanity' in this sense is distinct from what we will call 'humankind' or 'human beings,' that is, members of the subspecies *Homo sapiens sapiens*. Even if *Homo sapiens sapiens* alone on this planet generically possess a capacity for humanity, it would be a contingent result of evolution that this is so, not something that would exclude from Humanity whatever other kinds of creatures might somewhere exist who generically possess a capacity for humanity. This is important: if Humanity or humanity were essentially linked to species membership, this would significantly limit its normative significance.

Let's focus, then, on questions about what this capacity might be.

A Contemporary Kantian Approach

Recent debates about humanity and its potential normative significance have been much influenced by a branch of the Kantian tradition according to which humanity as a concept in practical philosophy is the concept of a distinctive power of free choice among ends.[4] Animals, by contrast, are said to be creatures of instinct, such that natural law completely determines their dispositions to behave. Thus they could have no such freedom, and so the presence of this freedom enables us to distinguish humanity from animality:

> The capacity to set oneself an end—any end whatsoever—is what characterizes humanity (as distinguished from animality). (*MM* 6:392)

However interesting such freedom might be, if it were merely a subject's arbitrary ability to pick her goals, how would it give normative significance or unconditional value to humanity as the power of choice? And how could humanity serve as a foundation for the categorical imperative, which by its nature is a "constraint" upon the will independent of subjective ends?

One answer can be found in the nature of *choice*. Making a choice is distinct from arbitrarily picking, since choices are made for some reason—the agent sees something in the choice that could answer the question "Why choose *this* rather than *that*?" If choice is therefore by its nature *reason-based*—whether or not we think the reasons are good ones—then already bound up in humanity's

276 RETHINKING THE VALUE OF HUMANITY

distinctive power of choice is the fact that humans are reason-seeking creatures and select options for the sake of reasons or ends. Mere picking sets oneself no end.[5] Thus the distinctive capacity of humanity isn't unconstrained, arbitrary picking, but something more like "the capacity to set oneself an end *through reason*" (cf. Martin 2006, 105). Reason's constraints upon the will therefore would be part of this power of choice, not something that would need to be added for the sake of some end external to exercise of choice itself. Thus, when fully spelled out, a conception of humanity as "the capacity to set oneself an end" would seem to provide a direct explanation of how humanity could be both a source of freedom and a source of constraint upon the will.

How does this constraint become categorical and objective, if it derives from the exercise of *will*? It can be categorical because allowing the exercise of one's will through reason to regulate one's action, independently of any external end that this might achieve, is in effect giving to one's rational will a kind of nonderivative (i.e., original), unconditional practical normative authority. On this account, Kant sees this kind of authority as treating one's rational will, one's humanity, as if it were an "end in itself," independently of any object it might take. Since this argument would make no appeal to anything peculiar to oneself as a rational chooser, it could identify a ground that is objective as well as subjective—what grounds the "authorization" of action in one's own case could be seen as the same ground for all humans:

> The human being necessarily represents his own existence in this way; so far it is thus a *subjective* principle of human actions. But every other rational being also represents his existence in this way consequent on just the same rational ground that also holds for me; thus it is at the same time an *objective* principle from which, as a supreme practical ground, it must be possible to derive all laws of the will. The practical imperative will therefore be the following: *So act that you use humanity, whether in your own person or in the person of any other, always at the same time as an end, never merely as a means.* (G 4:429)

While Kant might speak of humanity as something "*the existence of which in itself* has an absolute worth," suggesting a realist conception of value, the argument just made concerns how we must *regard* ourselves and others, and how we must *treat* humanity. And that is compatible with one form of "constructivism" about value, in which no antecedent, self-standing "intrinsic value" is posited—not even a "value of humanity." *Value* need not be reified as a "thing," a feature of the universe in itself, which humanity helps us discover and respond to aptly. Instead, *valuing* is an activity belonging to us as rational choosers, possessing the "objectivity," not of self-subsisting objects, but of a requirement of pure practical reason. Even the nonderivative, unconditional authorization we give to our own and others' rational will to "set ends" for us is not a hostage to external fortune—its ground would be that we *necessarily* value ourselves and others as ends-in-themselves in this way, and this is not dependent upon any fact in a putative realm of *things*-in-themselves.

Clearly, there are many steps to be spelled out and justified more fully if this argument is to work, but perhaps this brief sketch gives us an idea of how the normative significance of humanity might be very great indeed: the humanity we take ourselves to possess, understood as the capacity to "set ends through reason" for ourselves, affords a "supreme practical ground" from which we can "derive all the laws of the will."

An Alternative Kantian Approach

I wonder, however, whether this understanding of the Kantian approach to "the value of humanity" can be complete. And seeing what it might be missing—and that Kant himself saw was missing, I will argue—might help us get a clearer understanding of what the normative significance of humanity might be.

Let's return to the idea of a "capacity to set oneself an end—any end whatsoever," and the attempt to elaborate this as a "capacity to set oneself an end through reason." Kant repeatedly distinguishes between "humanity" (*Menscheit*), on the one hand, and "rational beings" (*vernünftige Wesen*), on the other, and yet this distinction plays no role in the argument just given. A rational being as such has the capacity "to set itself an end through reason" and necessarily sees itself and every other rational being as "*exist[ing]* as an end in itself, not merely as a means to be used by this or that will at its discretion" (*G* 4:428), just as the argument above requires. And Kant believes that the human being is a member of the realm of rational beings. So, if the imputed normative significance of humanity or its power of choice belongs equally well to all rational beings, and does so in virtue of their nature, then it would seem that belonging to the general type *rational being*, rather than belonging to the subtype *human being*, is the true locus of normative significance. "Humanity" would be only of taxonomic interest.

But "humanity" is of special normative significance precisely in virtue of how human beings *differ* from rational beings as such—a difference that accounts for the very possibility of morality and duty. Kant's remark:

> The capacity to set oneself an end—any end whatsoever—is what characterizes humanity (as distinguished from animality) (*MM* 6:392)

occurs in the context of a discussion of whether humanity has a duty of self-improvement. Animals, he notes, could have no such duty because their behavior

278 RETHINKING THE VALUE OF HUMANITY

is governed entirely by natural law—the "instincts" that are implanted in them by nature—so they can face no question "What ends shall I set myself? Should these include self-improvement?" However, purely rational beings could also have no such duty, not simply because they need no improvement but because they, too, *act from their nature—rational nature*. So there is no duty for them, no *ought* or *obligation*, since it does not belong to their nature to be capable of setting themselves "any end whatsoever." Humans, by contrast, *can* set themselves "any end whatsoever" and thus cannot simply *act from their nature*, since they have no ends "by nature." Whatever ends they act upon depend upon their use of a *will*. If they do *constrain* their ends "through reason," this will have been done by their personal exercise of will, not by their nature. And if they fail to do so, they will not qualify as rational, but they will still qualify as human—indeed, nothing could be more human.

Humans thus cannot foist upon "human nature" the task of answering the question "What ends shall I set myself?"—whatever the "empiricist" ethicists might preach to the contrary. Kant writes:

> The very *concept of duty* is already the concept of a *necessitation* (constraint) of free choice through the law. This constraint may be an *external constraint* or a *self-constraint*. The moral *imperative* makes this constraint known through the categorical nature of its pronouncement (the unconditional ought). Such constraint therefore does not apply to rational beings as such (there could be *holy* ones) but rather to *human beings*, rational *natural* beings, who are unholy enough that pleasure can induce them to break the moral law, even though they recognize its authority. (*MM* 6:379)

The need for personally imposed constraint upon a will that by its nature could set "any end whatsoever" is at once humanity's greatest burden and humanity's potential escape route from "animality" toward human "dignity." Such dignity can be achieved because we can exercise our will to impose this form of rational self-constraint, but when we do it will not be because our humanity is a "nature" that is the *cause* of our choice, but because humanity will be the *end* we freely set ourselves. Even though we inherited a nature that is "unholy enough" to fail to "set ends through reason," the freedom that is part of that nature is a *capacity* to choose that gives us the opportunity to "cultivate" humanity as an end, thereby showing ourselves to be "worthy" of it:

> Hence there is also bound up with the end of humanity in our own person the rational will, and so the duty, to make ourselves worthy of humanity by culture in general, by procuring and promoting the *capacity* to . . . cultivate the crude

predispositions of his nature, by which the animal is first raised into the human being. (*MM* 6:392)

A human being is indeed unholy enough but the *humanity* in his person must be holy to him. (*CPrR* 5:87)

As Kant argued in the *Groundwork* (*G* 4:394–395), nature did not set any particular end for humans, not even their own happiness. But the very open-endedness of the "power of appetition," combined with the ability to constrain its exercise by self-imposed principles, makes humans the only beings for whom their nature is not their destiny. Humans can make themselves into the only *moral* beings on earth or in heaven, and can work together to create the only moral communities nature will ever see (*MM* 6:216). These are *continuing* tasks, accomplished by human agency rather than by human nature—if humans are to be moral beings living in moral communities, this will have to be sustained anew each day.

Humanity's intermediate and indeterminate position between the "unholy" animal and the "holy" purely rational being thus makes distinctively human lives a struggle within oneself and with one another. That is, agents are not most fully human—their lives are not most expressive of humanity—if they are purely rational. As Kant notes, an agent can show his humanity, and his character as a *moral being*, in the fact that *breaking* the moral law is for him *also* a struggle:

[I]f a human being looks at himself objectively (under the aspect of *humanity* in his own person) . . . he finds that *as a moral being* he is also holy enough to break the inner law *reluctantly* . . . feel[ing] an opposition to breaking it and an abhorrence of himself. (*MM* 6:380n)

Of course, the action of breaking the moral law does not itself have moral worth, but it is the action of a *moral being* when it is painful and self-degrading to perform, however much benefit it confers. Describing the "proper moral condition" of mankind and the nature of virtue, Kant invokes just this kind of continuing struggle:

[H]is proper moral condition, in which he can always be, is *virtue*, that is, moral disposition *in conflict*, and not *holiness* in the supposed *possession* of complete *purity* of dispositions of the will. (*CPrR* 5:84)

Not every form of inner conflict constitutes virtue or manifests dignity—an agent feeling torn between two powerful inclinations toward self-gratification does not, for example. But struggle can be the source of dignity and virtue when it is a struggle for a worthy end, humanity as an end-in-itself, in the face of inclination. Indeed, this struggle can be "sublime" in the sense that it shows a part

280 RETHINKING THE VALUE OF HUMANITY

of nature trying to overcome and exceed nature—"It can be nothing less than what elevates a human being above himself (as a part of the sensible world), what connects him with an order of things that only the understanding can think" (*CPrR* 5:86), becoming for the first time a *person*.

> This idea of personality, awaken[s] respect by setting before our eyes the sublimity of our nature (in its vocation) ...

We humans cannot, however relax into this appreciation of our sublime nature, since that nature is a *vocation*, not a fact—our very appreciation of it gives us awareness that we constantly face the challenge of failing to live up to this vocation's demands. This passage continues:

> ... while at the same time showing us the lack of accord of our conduct with respect to it and thus striking down self-conceit, is natural even to the most common human reason and is easily observed. (*CPrR* 5:87)

Each of us, then, must struggle to "[maintain] humanity in its proper dignity in his own person" (*CPrR* 5:88).

This picture of humanity as characterized by struggle is a great equalizer, comprehensible "even to the most common human reason." None of us is "gifted" by nature with a nature that holds a moral course whatever temptations may arise—indeed, a "nature" of this kind would supplant rather than perfect our moral being. The powerful and wealthy face the temptations of power and wealth, the weak and poor face the temptations of weakness and poverty. What they all share is the struggle of a fully human life. And there is no greater dignity in struggling with the temptations of wealth than struggling with the temptations of poverty—as Kant remarks, each of us, however superior we might think ourselves to be, can find our respect awakened and "self-conceit" struck down by observing a humble individual who, at great expense to himself, holds to a principle of honesty under conditions where he could surely escape with a lie, and where we recognize that we ourselves would seek the convenient way out.

It is, after all, a remarkable thing that there has burst out within the natural world creatures who impose laws upon themselves, laws they know can require them to act against their own interests. Humans can possess and even cultivate "that wonderful capacity in us which we call conscience"—a "prosecutor within" that cannot be "reduce[d] to silence," however much we might try to do so (*CPrR* 5:98). This Kant-inspired picture of humanity is not yet complete, however. Humanity is a power to "set oneself ends" and act accordingly. But choice and action—"setting an end" in the sense of making that end *practical* rather than merely notional—requires *motivation*. Pure practical reason can tell us whether

THE NORMATIVE SIGNIFICANCE OF HUMANITY   281

the maxim of a given action would pass the test of the categorical imperative, but it is not itself a source of human motivation to act. However sublime our thoughts, we thus will not achieve our vocation without entering into the causal world and making things happen. The good will, for example, must not be "a mere wish, but . . . the summoning of all means insofar as they are in our control" (*G* 4:394). Inclination is, of course, a source of motivation, but Kant held that all inclinations, properly so-called, are self-centered (*CPrR* 5:73). So there must be an internal source of motivation apart from inclination yet also belonging to the causal world.

Now "the will, as the power of desire, is one of the many causes in the world" (*CJ* 6:172). Practical reason alone cannot be the source of these desires, since practical reason can exist in a pure form without needing any causal force to operate on behalf of following the laws of reason. "Unholy" beings like us certainly do need such force, and so humanity must possess certain "predispositions" to be motivated, and these must be of a kind that enables the will to deploy causal power to resist inclination, while at the same time providing an *interest* in the moral law as an end that creates the positive *incentive* needed for moral action (*CPrR* 5:78). These predispositions belong to us, then, not as rational beings but as human beings. Moreover, these dispositions must be *antecedent* to acting from duty, since they are presupposed by any practical susceptibility on the part of humanity to the concept of duty:

> There are certain moral endowments such that anyone lacking them could have no duty to acquire them.—They are *moral feeling, conscience, love* of one's neighbor, and *respect* for oneself (self-esteem). There is no obligation to have these because they lie at the basis of morality, as *subjective* conditions of receptiveness to the concept of duty, not as objective conditions of morality. All of them are natural predispositions (*praedispositio*) for being affected by concepts of duty, antecedent predispositions on the side of *feeling*. (*MM* 6:399)

Each of these predispositions has a role to play in moral agency. "*Conscience*," a feeling directed toward the agent himself, "holds the human being's duty before him" by supplying an active *concern* that his actions not violate the moral law or treat others as mere means (*MM* 6:400). "*Love* of one's neighbor" is "a matter of *feeling*" antecedent to willing, since "I cannot love because I *will* to, still less because I *ought* to." Such love directs the agent's interest outward, providing a *positive* interest in taking the ends of others as our own, and while we cannot will it dutifully into existence, we can, by exercising our capacity for fellow feeling, help induce it in ourselves: "*[D]o good* to your fellow human beings, and your beneficence will produce love of them in you" (*MM* 6:401–402). "*Respect*" is also "a feeling of a special kind" motivating agents positively to take others as ends and

282 RETHINKING THE VALUE OF HUMANITY

negatively to resist contrary inclinations, such that failure to act respectfully is damaging to "*self-esteem*," as a feeling "unavoidably force[d]" within them (*MM* 6:402). And, finally, the "moral feeling" is a desire the *content* of which is that one's actions be in accord with the moral law, making such accord with the law a positive *incentive*, not merely a constraint (*MM* 6:399). Taken together, these predispositions supply humanity with the motivational wherewithal to be *alive* to duty and capable of acting for the sake of the moral law *as such*, or for humanity as an *end in itself*, even in the face of contrary inclinations:

> No human being is entirely without moral feeling, for were he completely lacking in receptivity to it he would be morally dead; and if (to speak in medical terms) the moral vital force could no longer excite this feeling, then humanity would dissolve (by chemical laws, as it were) into mere animality. (*MM* 6:400)

Importantly for our purposes here, if we add these "antecedent predispositions on the side of feeling" to the capacity to freely set ourselves ends, we arrive at a Kantian conception of humanity that looks rather more like our familiar notion of humanity than the austere notion of a practically rational being as such—a type of being that we can now see as *more than* human (in the sense that humans are only imperfectly practical rational beings) but also as *less than* human (since moral feeling, conscience, love of one's neighbor, and respect for oneself are not part of, or derivable from, practical reason alone). Humanity, we normally say, involves an intrinsic, motivating interest in the good of others and a sense of respect for oneself and others that prohibits certain kinds of inhumane behavior, along with an active feeling of responsibility and accountability for one's actions and a positive motivation to live up to ideals of beneficence and respect even in the face of self-interest.[6]

We arrive, then, at a more substantive, conflictive, social, and also familiar picture of humanity than the capacity to "set oneself ends through reason," which is a capacity equally possessed by purely rational beings who never know such struggle or need such moral feelings for themselves, or for one another.[7]

The Normative Significance of Humanity

We now have one answer to the question of the normative significance of humanity: humanity is the locus of morality, insofar as morality is to be found at all.

This is, moreover, an answer that helps us make sense of what Kant writes about humanity (*Humanitat*) and Humanity (*Menschheit*) in the *Critique of Judgment*:

> [H]umanity [*Humanitat*] means both the universal *feeling of sympathy*, and
> the ability to engage universally in very intimate *communication*. When these
> two qualities are combined, they constitute sociability that befits humanity
> [*Menschheit*] and distinguishes it from the limitation of animals. (*CJ* 6:355)

This would be a surprising comment if we took humanity to be the power to
set oneself ends through reason, but it makes good sense given what we have
said above. A *universal* feeling of sympathy and a *universal* aspiration for inti-
mate communication aren't mere sentiments of sociality, but can be what Kant
calls "affect of the VIGOROUS KIND (i.e., which makes us conscious that we have
forces to overcome any resistance)"—for example, in seeking to understand
others, to appreciate their situation, and to communicate with them, despite our
differences. These, he writes, are not "maudlin" or "fanciful" sentiments or "in-
sipid moral precepts," but active grounds for seeking community with others on
terms of mutual recognition and respect, taking up the struggle to be sensitive
"to the stern precept of duty" and to refuse to resign "respect for the dignity of
humanity in our own person and for human rights" (*CJ* 6:273).[8]

Such sentiments are requisites for a distinctive kind of sociability where we
can meet one another not as members of this or that class, caste, religion, family,
or country, or as "legalists" looking to advance our own interests while allowing
that others do the same, but rather as free agents on a "cosmopolitan" plane.
Such cosmopolitan agents seek universal mutual *understanding* without prejudice, mutual constraint based on the recognition of one another's *rights* and not
merely our own prudence, and *collaboration* in developing our human capacities
and social powers through culture—a kind of sociability that "befits" humanity,
or is "worthy" of it, but does not come automatically from it. Its laws, unlike the
laws of animal sociality, will have to come from ourselves. Kant continues the
passage just cited:

> There were peoples during one age whose strong urge to have sociability *under*
> *laws*, through which a people becomes a lasting commonwealth, wrestled with
> the great problems that surround the difficult task of combining freedom (and
> hence also equality) with some constraint (a constraint based more on respect
> and submission from duty than on fear). (*CJ* 6:355)

Here Kant gives an imagined history, but it is a story of a continuing, shared
struggle of a recognizably human kind.

This Kant-inspired conception of humanity, and of its normative significance,
seems to me not only more familiar but also in closer accord with a fundamental,
though badly incomplete political project of Kant's era and our own: overcoming
the rule of caste and the ideologies of inequality, and working together toward

284 RETHINKING THE VALUE OF HUMANITY

equal realization of "human rights" and creating the "liberty, equality, and fraternity" of humankind.

At least one Kant interpreter, Allen Wood, locates one origin of Kant's early interest in "humanity" as an organizing concept in his practical philosophy in an incident in which Kant was caught short by his own caste prejudice and ideology of inequality. Wood (1999, xvii) cites a passage from Kant's early writing:

> There was a time when I believed that [thirst for knowledge] constituted the honor of humanity, and I despised the people, who know nothing. Rousseau set me right about this. This binding prejudice disappeared. I learned to honor humanity, and I would find myself more useless than the common laborer if I did not believe that this attitude of mine can give worth to all others in establishing the rights of humanity. (*AK* 20:44)

More than two centuries after Kant read Rousseau's *Social Contract* and *Emile*, we are vividly aware that the idea that all humankind possesses an equal claim—an equal right—to consideration that is independent of birth, ethnicity, class, gender, sexual orientation, or ability, has still not struck home in many parts of the world, and may be increasingly at risk even in those parts of the world where it has been most honored in word, if not always in deed. In this sense, it is quite true that the stakes in discussing the nature and normative significance of humanity are high.

Value and Standing

I have not here tried to enter into the question whether this Kant-inspired approach to the nature of humanity and its normative significance is the most plausible approach to take, all things considered. As suggested at the outset, there are multiple conceptions of humanity and multiple justificatory and explanatory purposes to which they are put—perhaps a diversity of approaches might be the best way to make philosophical progress on these large issues.

I have framed this exploration in terms of question of the normative significance of humanity rather than the value of humanity since answers to that question might take the form of an attempt to justify or explain the *moral standing* of humankind, rather than mankind's *value*. Here's something Kantians and Utilitarians agree on: morality requires that each human individual have equal standing and receive equal consideration. That is already a very substantive claim when viewed from the standpoint of human history, since millennia have passed during which some humans laid claim to be *entitled* to differential moral consideration on the basis of their "nobility", or religion, or ethnicity, or gender,

THE NORMATIVE SIGNIFICANCE OF HUMANITY   285

and often successfully enforced such unequal standing. For example, prevailing ideologies held that some members of humanity were "naturally fit" to govern others, who in turn were "naturally fit" to obey. Such notions have hardly disappeared from the face of the earth, and it seems to me still an urgent task for philosophy to articulate a conception of humanity that could explain or justify equal standing and equal consideration.

One kind of explanation or justification that, while common, faces serious problems, is the idea that human beings have, in virtue of their humanity, an absolute, infinite worth that rules out any comparisons of relative standing amongst themselves, and places them incomparably above other, less-than-fully-human creatures.

Problems arise when we begin to consider the standing of nonhuman animals, often the contrast class for discussions of humanity and its special value. Is there a defensible theory of value that would assign a human being incomparably greater worth than any other animal? All manner of characteristics have been cited as marking off humankind as categorically distinct from the rest of the animal realm, and as justifying the incomparable value of humans: capacity to reason, capacity to value, capacity for autonomous agency, capacity for a sense of self or mutual responsibility, capacity for language and abstract concepts, capacity for the moral sentiments, and more. My skepticism that any of these will really hold up has only grown as we learn more about the brains, minds, and social relations of nonhuman animals. Early in his discussion of the labor process in *Capital,* Marx ([1887] 1954, vol. 1, chap. 7, sec. 1) wrote:

> We presuppose labour in a form that stamps it as exclusively human. A spider conducts operations that resemble those of a weaver, and a bee puts to shame many an architect in the construction of her cells. But what distinguishes the worst architect from the best of bees is this, that the architect raises his structure in imagination before he erects it in reality. At the end of every labour-process, we get a result that already existed in the imagination of the labourer at its commencement.

There is now very good evidence that intelligent animals—I have no idea about bees—form abstract representations of their environment and possible trajectories through it, explore and evaluate multiple trajectories before taking them, and are capable of working backward from a desired destination to an effective path for reaching it (Moser, Kropff, and Moser 2008; Redish 2014). Intelligent animals are not, as Kant and many others thought, creatures of instinct and inclination—they learn representations of values and probabilities and select actions on the basis of comparing expected values (Lak, Stauffer, and Schultz 2014). They form complex social relationships and display a variety of social emotions (Clay and de Waal 2013; Watanabe and Kosaki 2017). And they use compositional signals to communicate information via an iterative syntax (Ouattara, Lemasson, and Zuberbuhler 2009; ten Cate and Okanoya 2012). When will we stop trying to find some feature of human beings, as such, to place humans on a level of infinite or absolute value in relation to our thoughtful, planful, caring, and playful animal relatives? And these are only the *actually, currently existing* nonhuman animals. We need look no further into the realm of possibility than to stare backward in time to see that there were gradations of humanity before there were modern humans. So if we can bring ourselves to abandon this bit of human vanity, then perhaps we can also give up the idea of looking to credit ourselves with infinite absolute value in comparison with other living creatures. Instead, we could become serious about the different kinds of finite, relational value that can be had in lives, whosoever lives they might be, and however these might be realized.

Relational value—not to be confused with relative value or relativistic value—is the kind that depends upon the obtaining of a kind of relationship. Neither element of the relation need have intrinsic or absolute value. Some examples are the theories of value that draw upon relations of "interest" or "valuing" that relate subjects, on the one hand, to objects, actions, or outcomes that in some sense "match," "fulfill," or "realize" this interest or value, on the other. Relational theories of value can be found in twentieth-century figures like John Dewey (1939), C. I. Lewis (1962), and R. B. Perry (1926), the contemporary descendants of whom include the various forms of desire- or preference-satisfaction theories (Sobel 2017). According to such theories, the ground fact that gives rise to, or constitutes, value is the relation of something *mattering* to a being of a kind for which something *can* matter.[9]

Consider aesthetic appreciation. For beings of a certain kind, with certain sensory, cognitive, and affective capacities, a focused sensorily mediated engagement with objects or activities of certain kinds can produce cognitive experiences that enlarge understanding and affective experiences that are for these beings deeply moving or rewarding. To understand how this conjunction could constitute the realization of aesthetic value we need not additionally see beings of this kind, on the one hand, or objects and activities of these kinds, on the other, as possessing "absolute" aesthetic value. Indeed, we might on reflection find that we cannot make sense of an idea of aesthetic value entirely divorced from the capacities of any possible appreciators. Or consider evidential value. For beings of a certain kind, with certain sensory and cognitive capacities, and occupying a certain information state, encountering a particular fact will have evidential value. But do we see this value having its source or ground in either the cognizer or the fact considered *in themselves*? No fact could be "absolute" evidence—evidence with no relation to any cognitive capacity or body of propositions or beliefs. If we deny absolute aesthetic value or absolute evidence, must we be *relativists* about it? No. That encounters between certain subjects and certain objects have aesthetic or evidential value can be an *invariant* relation in the sense that whether it holds between a gen subject and object does not depend upon the perspective from which one views this relation, or whether this encounter would have aesthetic or evidential value for oneself. Relational theories of value are also distinct from various antirealist or irrealist theories of value, such as recent versions of "constructivism" or "projectivism." For example, that a particular fact is evidence for a proposition in a given epistemic context can be an objective matter, independent of whether we or anyone *judges* or *takes* it to be evidence.

The independence of relational value from *judgments* of value is of special importance when we think about value in the realm of nonhuman animals. Rats might never deploy fully-articulated evaluative concepts, but observant veterinarians working with affective neuroscientists and behavioral psychologists can learn that laboratory rats are listless and stressed when left entirely on their own in a Plexiglas shoebox with nothing but woodchips for company. Add some form of activity or a companion, and rats perk up. This is reasonable evidence for thinking that activity and companionship are part of what makes life go well for rats—part of what "matches" their interests or "realizes" what matters to them (Boissy et al. 2007). Humans cannot plausibly hold the view that, because rats cannot "judge" certain things to be good or "take them as ends through reason," nothing can be good or bad for them. And I'm not sure how one could justify the claim that no amount of what matters to nonhuman animals could possibly outweigh even the slightest loss to what matters for human animals. Thus I cannot think that the normative significance of humanity depends upon finding an absolute value peculiar to humans that would place humanity on a plane incomparably above all nonhuman animals. Indeed, I would be inclined to say the opposite. The remarkable capacities in virtue of which humanity makes morality possible (and acquires its distinctive normative significance) are all the more remarkable (and normatively significant) because the cosmopolitan vision they afford us enables us to see not only beyond the confines of our self, or family, or religion, or nation, but also beyond the confines of our species.

Equally, it seems to me that the normative significance of humanity does not depend upon finding an "infinite" value in humans or humanity. Practical reasoning would break down in cases where it is badly needed if we were to try to regulate deliberation and decision-making by "infinite" values. No decision about the allocation of goods is free from questions about how much benefit vs. how much burden will result, or how benefits and burdens will be distributed. Such deliberation can honor the principles of the *equal moral standing, equal consideration*, and *equal rights*, even while noticing that more (relational) value is realized, for example, when a scarce anticancer drug is given to those who have cancer rather than those who do not, or, among those with cancer, to those for

288   RETHINKING THE VALUE OF HUMANITY

whom it is most likely to work. We do not thereby imply that cancer victims have a special value or rights that those without cancer do not have. Instead, we arrive at this distribution *because* we are according the goods or harms experienced by all individuals the same consideration, including an equal right to have their health needs taken into account.

The picture developed here of a world of relational value in which humanity has the normative significance of making morality possible—including moral recognition of nonhuman animals, with the result of generating respect for their needs and interests—might seem less exciting than finding in humanity an absolute, infinite, or incomparable value. But this less exciting answer to questions about the normative significance of humanity might help us avoid the philosopher's temptation to "identify upward"—to look to that which is rational in us as that which is most truly human. I've tried to suggest that, even for someone as drawn to reason as Kant, humanity is as much to be found in our social, feeling nature and in the moral struggle that constitutes a fully human life.[10]

Notes

1. In keeping with current usage, I take the term 'normative significance' to cover such diverse *forms* of significance as value, rights, requirements, and standing. For example, not all interpreters agree that the *value* of humanity is what figures centrally in Kant's moral theory. See Nyholm (2013) for a summary of the debate and an argument that it is taking humanity *as an end-in-itself* that is central in Kant.
2. Cf. *CJ* 6:355; *CPrR* 5:72, 5:86. For a compendium of uses, see Eisler 1930. A caveat: Martin (2006, 100) warns that "Kant's use of 'humanity' is not completely consistent throughout his writings, and all of the passages where this term occurs are subject to a range of competitively compelling interpretations." And this could well be the case. However, not so deeply versed in Kant, I seem to find a clear continuity in what he intends by 'humanity' from the *Groundwork* through to the *Metaphysics of Morals*.
3. There also is the question of whether collective agents like groups with the capacity to deliberate and act in ways embodying humanity—perhaps even to a greater degree than most individuals—should count as belonging to Humanity in their own right. I'll pass over this by confining our attention to (a vague notion of) "creatures." And I'll ignore the problem of saying what 'capacity' might mean. Does any living creature—a cat, say—that might, through some complex intervention, acquire humanity have a "capacity" for it?
4. We see versions of this view in the works of Christine Korsgaard (1986, 2003) and Allen Wood (1998, 1999).
5. Doesn't picking have the end of making *some* selection rather than leave things at a standstill for want of a reason to make one choice rather than another? One can *choose* to *merely pick* for just this reason, but then the end lies with that choice, not the

picking itself. But one needn't have any such reason in order to pick one thing rather than another.

6. A glance at the *OED* reveals that the term "humanity" from its earliest days has had a close connection with a capacity to be moved by a concern for others for their own sake, a sensitivity to what they feel or undergo, a large-hearted kindness and tolerance, mercy, and protection of the most vulnerable.

7. By contrast, Martin (2006, 100) remarks that "it is commonly assumed" that the terms "rational beings," "rational nature," "human beings," and "humanity" "pick out the same thing."

8. It might be worth noting that Kant's idea of humanity here is closely related to his notion of an aesthetic community, in which we seek to approach beauty without prejudice, giving to all fellow humans the standing to exercise their sensibilities and to make and share judgments and objects or experiences of beauty. Similar ideas figure in the Frankfurt School's notion of nondistortive communication (Habermas 1990). From the standpoint of evolutionary theory, it might well be the human capacity to cooperate and collaborate in large communities of nonrelated individuals that most distinguishes *Homo sapiens* from other social animals, though it should be added that there is nothing *species-specific* in Kant's notion of humanity as discussed here.

9. Relational theories of value are sometimes said to be theories of "good-for," but relations can ground value in ways beyond the benefit or well-being of the individuals involved. Friendship and knowledge, for example, might produce various welfare benefits to friends and knowers, but the value of friendship or knowledge—why and how they matter—is not reducible to the benefits they may provide.

10. I would like to thank the editors of this volume for their exceptionally helpful comments and criticisms—and their patience. Christine Korsgaard, Sven Nyholm, and Allen Wood have at various times been generous in helping me to see multiple dimensions of Kant's thinking.

References

Works of Immanuel Kant

AK—Gesammelte Schrigten. Edited by the Königlichen Preußischen (later Deutschen) Akademie der Wissenschaften. Berlin: Georg Reimer/Walter De Gruyter, 1900–.

CJ—Critique of Judgment. Translated by W. S. Pluhar. Foreword by Mary J. Gregor. Indianapolis, IN: Hackett, 1987. [Cited by volume and page in AK.]

CPrR—Critique of Practical Reason. Edited and translated by Mary J. Gregor. Cambridge: Cambridge University Press, 1996. [Cited by volume and page in AK.]

G—Groundwork of the Metaphysics of Morals. Edited and translated by Mary J. Gregor. Cambridge: Cambridge University Press, 1996. [Cited by volume and page in AK.]

MM—Metaphysics of Morals. Edited and translated by Mary J. Gregor. Cambridge: Cambridge University Press, 1996. [Cited by volume and page in AK.]

290 RETHINKING THE VALUE OF HUMANITY

Other Works

Boissy, Alain, Gerhard Manteuffel, Margit Bak Jensen, Randi Oppenrmann Moe, Berry Spruijt, Linda J. Keeling, Christoph Winckler, Bjorn Forkman, Ivan Dimitrov, Jan Langbein, Morten Bakken, Isabelle Veissier, and Arnaud Aubert. 2007. "Assessment of Positive Emotions in Animals to Improve Their Welfare." *Physiology & Behavior* 92: 375–397.

Clay, Zanna, and Frans B. M. de Waal. 2013. "Bonobos Respond to Distress in Others: Consolation across the Age Spectrum." *PLOS One* 8: e55206.

Dewey, John. 1939. *Theory of Valuation*. Chicago: University of Chicago University Press.

Eisler, Rudolf. 1930. *Kant-Lexikon: Nachschlagewerk zu Kants sämtlichen Schriften, Briefen und handschriftlichen Nachlaß*. Berlin: Mittler & Sohn. https://www.textlog.de/rudolf-eisler.html.

Habermas, Jurgen. 1990. "Discourse Ethics: Notes on a Program of Philosophical Justification." In *Moral Consciousness and Communicative Action*, translated by Christian Lenhardt and Shierry W. Nicholsen, 43–115. Cambridge, MA: MIT Press.

Korsgaard, Christine. 1986. "Kant's Formula of Humanity." *Kant-Studien* 77: 183–202.

Korsgaard, Christine. 2003. "The Dependence of Value on Humanity." In *The Practice of Value*, edited and with an introduction by R. Jay Wallace, 63–85. Oxford: Oxford University Press.

Lak, Armin, William R. Stauffer, and Wolfram Schultz. 2014. "Dopamine Prediction Responses Integrate Subjective Value from Different Reward Dimensions." *Proceedings of the National Academy of Science* 111: 2343–2348.

Lewis, C. I. 1962. *An Analysis of Knowledge and Valuation*. La Salle, IL: Open Court.

Martin, Adrienne M. 2006. "How to Argue for the Value of Humanity." *Pacific Philosophical Quarterly* 87: 96–125.

Marx, Karl. (1887) 1954. *Capital*. Vol. 1. Edited by Friedrich Engels. Moscow: Progress Publishers.

Moser, Edward I., Emilio Kropff, and May-Britt Moser. 2008. "Place Cells, Grid Cells, and the Brain's Spatial Representation System." *Annual Review of Neuroscience* 31: 69–89.

Nyholm, Sven. 2014 "On Kant's Idea of Humanity as an End-in-Itself." *European Journal of Philosophy* 24: 358–374.

Ouattara, Karim, Alban Lemasson, and Klaus Zuberbuhler. 2009. "Campbell's Monkeys Concatenate Vocalizations into Context-Specific Call Sequences." *Proceedings of the National Academy of Science,* 106: 22026–22031.

Perry, R. B. 1926. *General Theory of Value*. New York: Longmans, Green.

Redish, A. David. 2014. "Vicarious Trial and Error." *Nature Reviews Neuroscience* 17: 147–159.

Sobel, David. 2017. *From Valuing to Value: A Defense of Subjectivism*. Oxford: Oxford University Press.

ten Cate, Carel, and Kazuo Okanoya. 2012. "Revisiting the Syntactic Abilities of Non-Human Animals: Natural Vocalizations and Artificial Grammar Learning." *Philosophical Transactions of the Royal Society, B*, 367: 1984–1994.

Watanabe, S. and Kosaki S. 2017. "Evolutionary Origin of Empathy and Inequality Aversion." In *Evolution of the Brain, Cognition, and Emotion in Vertebrates*, edited by Watanabe, S., M.A. Hoffman, and T. Shimizu, 273–299. Tokyo: Springer Japan.

Wood, Allen. 1998. "Humanity as an End in Itself." In *Kant's Groundwork of the Metaphysics of Morals: Critical Essays*, edited by Paul Guyer, 165–188. Lanham, MD: Rowman & Littlefield.

Wood, Allen. 1999. *Kant's Ethical Theory*. Cambridge: Cambridge University Press.

12

Finding the Humean Value in Humean Humanity

Don Garrett

> Nature has given all animals a like prejudice in favour of their off-spring. As soon as the helpless infant sees the light, though in every other eye it appears a despicable and a miserable creature, it is regarded by its fond parent with the utmost affection, and is pre-ferred to every other object, however perfect and accomplished. The passion alone, arising from the original structure and formation of human nature, bestows a value on the most insignificant object.
>
> —David Hume, "The Sceptic"

Immanuel Kant thematized the value of humanity—that is, the value to be found in human beings. Both a moral rationalist and a moral antinaturalist,[1] he held that this value is a fundamentally *moral* value that is both *grounded in* and *recognized by* the rationality of human beings as noumenally free agents outside of nature. His moral antirationalist and moral naturalist predecessor David Hume, despite writing a lengthy *Treatise of Human Nature*, did not explicitly discuss "the value of humanity" as such. Yet his evident commitments to moral antira-tionalism and moral naturalism in no way put the topic off-limits to him, and he says enough about both humanity and value in his various writings for us to determine what he could and likely would have said about it. My limited aim in this essay is simply to show specifically what that could and would have been. I will not try to defend the views about the value of humanity that I develop on Hume's behalf, although I think there are some good reasons to find those views appealing, at least in broad outline—especially in comparison with Kant's.

I will begin by explaining Hume's answers to three preliminary but essential questions:

What is "humanity"?
What is the source of value?
How is "real" value determined?

Don Garrett, *Finding the Humean Value in Humean Humanity* In: *Rethinking the Value of Humanity.*
Edited by: Sarah Buss and L. Nandi Theunissen, Oxford University Press. © Oxford University Press 2023.
DOI: 10.1093/oso/9780197539361.003.0013

292 RETHINKING THE VALUE OF HUMANITY

I will then analyze how Hume would answer two central questions directly related to Kant's concerns:

How does humanity have value?
What are the roles of rationality and sensibility in the value of humanity?

Finally, on the basis of the answers to these questions, I will explore Hume's likely answers to four important related questions about the value of humanity:

Is value unique to humanity?
Does every human being have value?
Does humanity as a species have value?
How much value does humanity have?

1. "Humanity" and the Basis of Value

What Is "Humanity"?

Hume occasionally uses the term 'humanity' for possession of the nature that grounds membership in the human species. Thus, he writes that Alexander the Great was convinced that he was not a god by his liability to "sleep and love," while Alexander's servants would have found in his other "numberless weaknesses . . . still more convincing proofs of his humanity" (RPAS 18: 120). Hume also sometimes uses the term for human beings themselves taken collectively as a species, which he more often calls "mankind," "human kind," or "the human species." Thus, he describes the "priests of all religions" as being, by the "character of their profession . . . elevated above humanity" (NC 6: 199). Most often, however, he uses the term 'humanity' for a particular mental quality that he describes as "concern for others" (EPM 5.46) or "fellow-feeling with others" (EPM 5.19n). Its possession as a persistent character trait he frequently declares to be a virtue (e.g., THN 3.3.3.4; EPM 3.8, 5.44), and he attributes its expressions to the operations of one or more psychological "principles of humanity"—present to at least some extent in all normal human beings—that serve, in turn, to produce "sentiments of humanity."

Not surprisingly given his interests, Hume often discusses "humanity" in this third sense especially as it is directed toward human beings in particular, but he is clear that it may also be directed toward other "sensible creatures"[2]—that is, beings having feeling and sensation, including "beasts" or "mere animals." (This agrees, of course, with related contemporary meanings of the terms 'humane' and 'humanity'.) For example, Hume remarks that "we should be bound, by the laws of humanity, to give gentle usage [to] a species of creatures, intermingled with men, which, though rational, were possessed of such inferior strength, both of body and mind, that they were incapable of all resistance" (EPM 3.18). Kant's question about "the value of humanity" concerns Hume's less frequent first and second senses of the term 'humanity', and I will therefore use the term chiefly in those senses in what follows. As we will see, however, "humanity" in his third sense is highly relevant to his answer to Kant's question as well.

Although Hume typically uses the term 'animals' in a way that excludes human beings, that is not because he sees a vast discontinuity between animals and human beings as kinds of sensible creatures. On the contrary, he observes that the extensive similarities between animal and human bodies authorize very strong analogical inferences from the causal operations of the former to those of the latter, and he endorses the making of similar analogical inferences concerning the minds of animals and human beings as a crucial methodological element in his psychological investigation of human nature (THN 2.1.12.1). For this reason, he devotes entire sections of the *Treatise* to "the reason of animals" (THN 1.3.16; EHU 9), "the pride and humility of animals" (THN 2.1.12), and "the love and hatred of animals" (THN 2.2.12; by this latter phrase he means the love and hatred felt *by* animals).

Comparing the reason of animals with that of human beings, he credits humankind with greater "force of reflection [and] penetration" (THN 2.2.12.1), and he praises the range, intricacy, and generality of their reasoning, along with their capacity for correcting errors (DM 5: 82). Nevertheless, he explains the differences in reasoning ability between animals and humans by citing the same general considerations that also explain why some human beings reason better than others (EHU 9.5n20). Comparing the pride and humility of animals with that of human beings, he remarks that "animals have little or no sense of virtue or vice; they quickly lose sight of the relations of blood [i.e., kinship]; and are incapable of right and property" (THN 2.1.12.5). These limitations also apply to the possible causes of love and hatred on the part of animals. Yet if these passions have a wider range of possible causes in human beings, the operations by which the passions are produced, and the further passions that they stimulate, are fundamentally the same.

Hume grants that both the bodies and the minds of all sensible creatures, whether animals or human beings, exhibit "adaptation of means to ends" in the interactions of their parts (THN 14.2.1; EHU 5.21; DNR 12.2–3: 214–215), but this does not imply, in his view, that they are the products of a purposeful designer, let alone one concerned with either their happiness or their virtue (DNR 11.16: 212). Furthermore, in his view, all of the operations of both the bodies and the minds of all sensible creatures fall equally within the scope of explanation by

294 RETHINKING THE VALUE OF HUMANITY

natural, deterministic causal laws (THN 1.3.12.5, 2.3.1; EHU 8.13–15). Finally, he argues in his essay "Of the Immortality of the Soul" that the available evidence supports the conclusion that the minds of all species of sensible creatures are alike mortal, ceasing to exist with the death of the particular bodies on which they depend (IS §§30–37: 596–597). Thus, the continuity among species of sensible creatures precludes for Hume any special status for human beings with respect to three central topics of Kant's metaphysics: God, freedom, and immortality.

What Is the Source of Value?

Hume emphasizes in *An Enquiry concerning the Principles of Morals* that not all ends can be merely instrumental:

> It is impossible there can be a progress *in infinitum*; and that one thing can always be a reason why another is desired. Something must be desirable on its own account. (EPM Appendix 1.19)

His immediate examples in this passage are pleasure and the absence of pain, but he recognizes many other ultimate ends as well. Indeed, he immediately goes on to remark that "virtue is an end, and desirable on its own account, without fee and reward" (EPM Appendix 1.20). And later in the same work, he emphasizes that many of the things that give us pleasure do so only because we first desire them on their own account. These things include the "good" or happiness of friends and other loved ones, for love regularly engenders "benevolence," which is "a desire of the happiness of the person belov'd" (THN 2.2.9.3). As he remarks, "I feel a pleasure in doing good to my friend because I love him; but do not love him for the sake of that pleasure" (DM 10: 85–86).

Crucially, Hume asserts, that which is "desirable on its own account" is so entirely "because of its immediate accord or agreement with human *sentiment and affection*" (EPM Appendix 1.19, emphasis added). Thus, while the faculty of reason can play a role in determining what is instrumentally desirable as a means to an ultimate end, it cannot determine those ultimate ends themselves:

> It appears evident, that the *ultimate ends* of human actions can never, in any case, be accounted for by *reason*, but recommend themselves *entirely to the sentiments and affections* of mankind, without any dependence on the intellectual faculties. (EPM Appendix 1.18, emphasis added)

In his essay "The Sceptic," Hume asserts a parallel doctrine expressed explicitly in terms of *value*, using the term 'passion' in place of 'affection':

FINDING HUMEAN VALUE IN HUMEAN HUMANITY   295

The value of every object can be *determined* only by the sentiment or passion of every individual. (Sc 35: 172, emphasis added)[3]

In a similar passage from the same essay (and returning to the term 'affection'), he elaborates:

> If we can depend upon any principle, which we learn from philosophy, this, I think, may be considered as certain and undoubted, that there is *nothing, in itself, valuable or despicable, desirable or hateful, beautiful or deformed*; but that these attributes *arise from* the particular constitution and fabric of human *sentiment and affection*. (Sc 8: 162, emphasis added)

In writing that "there is nothing in itself" having these attributes, he is not, of course, rejecting his own doctrine that some ends or values are ultimate ("desired on their own account") rather than instrumental; rather, he is emphasizing that these values are metaphysically (as well as epistemologically) "determined by" something outside the valuable objects themselves—namely, sentiment or passion/affection.

Although Hume uses 'passion' and 'affection' as synonyms for one another, it is important to recognize that neither term is synonymous for him with 'sentiment'. Rather, in writing of "sentiment *and* affection" and "sentiment *or* passion," he employs a distinction that he explains at the outset of *Treatise* Book 2 ("Of the Passions") between two different kinds of feelings, both of which fall within his broader category of "impressions of reflection" (as distinguished from "impressions of sensation"):[4]

> The reflective impressions may be divided into two kinds, *viz.* the *calm* and the *violent*. Of the first kind is the sense of beauty and deformity in action, composition, and external objects. Of the second are the passions of love and hatred, grief and joy, pride and humility. This division is far from being exact. The raptures of poetry and music frequently rise to the greatest height; while those other impressions, properly call'd *passions*, may decay into so soft an emotion, as to become, in a manner, imperceptible. But as in general the passions are more violent than the emotions arising from beauty and deformity, these impressions have been commonly distinguish'd from each other. (THN 2.1.1.3, italics in original)

Impressions of reflection of the first and *typically* calmer types Hume calls "sentiments,"[5] and he attributes them to a faculty that he calls "taste." Impressions of reflection of the second and *typically* more violent types—those "properly called passions" (or, equivalently, "affections")—he attributes to a

296 RETHINKING THE VALUE OF HUMANITY

faculty he calls simply "the passions."[6] The examples he gives in this introductory passage are meant to be illustrative rather than exhaustive. Thus, later in Book 2, he goes on to introduce what he calls the "moral sentiments" of *moral approbation* and *moral disapprobation* (also called "sentiments of virtue or vice") which he treats as analogous to the aesthetic sentiments of beauty and deformity. (Indeed, the analogy is so strong that he sometimes refers to virtue as "moral beauty.") These moral sentiments play a central role in Book 3 ("Of Morals"). Similarly, throughout Book 2 itself Hume introduces and discusses a wide range of further passions (such as *hope* and *fear*, *benevolence* and *anger*). Among the passions, however, those most directly relevant to the determination of value are *desire and aversion* (see also Sc 8: 162, 14: 164–165, 34: 171), *love and hatred*, and *pride and humility*.

Each of these pairs of contrasting sentiments or passions evidently determines its own particular kind of value and disvalue. Thus, when Hume refers in the passage previously quoted to the attributes of being "*valuable or despicable, desirable or hateful, beautiful or deformed*," the first pair of attributes constitutes the genus of value and disvalue itself; the second constitutes one important *kind* of value and disvalue that is determined by a particular pair of *passions* (desire and aversion); and the third constitutes one important *kind* of value and disvalue that is determined by a particular pair of *sentiments* (the aesthetic sentiments of beauty and deformity). Yet although the various species of value are distinct, there are nonetheless complex relations among them. For example, whatever traits engender *love* in others can also engender *pride* in oneself. And whatever is originally valued through any other passion or sentiment typically becomes in the process an object of desire as well, and is hence valued also as *desirable*.

That Hume means to employ his distinction between sentiments and passions not only in the *Treatise* but also in "The Sceptic" is shown by the fact that he invokes the distinction in the latter work in order to explain the mind's tendency to "project" (as philosophers would now say) aesthetic and moral sentiments, but *not* passions such as desire, onto the object valued:

> Who is not sensible, that power, and glory, and vengeance, are not desirable of themselves, but derive all their value from the structure of human *passions*, which begets a desire towards such particular pursuits? But with regard to beauty, *either natural or moral*, the case is commonly supposed to be different. The agreeable quality is thought to lie in the object, not in the *sentiment*; and that merely because the *sentiment is not so turbulent and violent* as to distinguish itself, in an evident manner, from the perception of the object. (Sc 15: 165, emphasis added)

FINDING HUMEAN VALUE IN HUMEAN HUMANITY   297

Nonetheless, as we have seen, he holds that "philosophy" can teach us that passion-based values and sentiment-based values are ultimately on a par with respect to their both being determined by feeling.

How Is "Real" Value Determined?

Hume readily acknowledges that the same objects or circumstances may elicit different sentiments or passions in different species of sensible creatures, just as the same objects can elicit different bodily sensations in them. Thus, in introducing a discussion of beauty as leading to love, he writes:

> What seems the most delicious food to one animal, appears loathsome to another: What affects the feeling of one with delight, produces uneasiness in another. This is confessedly the case with regard to all the bodily senses: But if we examine the matter more accurately, we shall find, that the same observation holds even where the mind concurs with the body, and mingles its sentiment with the exterior appetite. (Sc 8: 162)

Hume also emphasizes, throughout his writings and in many different contexts, that a similar variability in response may be observed among different human beings or even within the same human being at different times. Some of these responses, he indicates, are better than others. Thus, in "The Sceptic," he implies that the most complete and useful passion-based evaluations are those that result from a comprehensive rather than a limited view:

> We may observe, that the passion, in pronouncing its verdict [of value], considers not the object simply, as it is in itself, but surveys it with all the circumstances, which attend it. . . . Here, therefore, a *philosopher* may step in, and suggest *particular views, and considerations, and circumstances,* which otherwise would have escaped us; and by that means, he may either moderate or excite any particular passion. (Sc 35: 172, emphasis added)

In the *Treatise,* Hume goes further, noting that undesirable things are sometimes *mistakenly* desired through error, and that desirable things sometimes *fail* to be desired through ignorance (THN 3.1.1.12). Accordingly, he distinguishes *accurate* from *inaccurate* passion-based evaluations:

> It has been observ'd, in treating of the passions, that men are mightily govern'd by the imagination, and proportion their affections more to the light, under which any object appears to them, than to its *real and intrinsic value.* . . . Every

8 RETHINKING THE VALUE OF HUMANITY

thing, that is contiguous to us commonly operates with more force than any object, that lies in a more distant and obscure light. (THN 3.2.7.2, emphasis added)

In writing here of a thing's "real and intrinsic value," Hume means neither its
value "on its own account" (that is, its *ultimate* value as opposed to its *instrumental* value) nor any purported value "in itself" (that is, independent of all
determination by feeling). Rather, he evidently means to invoke a thing's *true*
or *proper* degree of value, as something that *would* be felt after compensating
in some way for limitations of perspective or capacity.

Hume can employ such a distinction because he holds that, in order
to determine the true or proper range of a concept derived from feeling,
human beings often "correct" for differences in felt response that result from
differences in perspective or personal endowments by applying an agreed-
upon "standard" of judgment. This occurs not only when the feelings in question are "reflective impressions" but also when they are sensations of "the
bodily senses." For example, he writes in his essay "Of the Standard of Taste":

> The appearance of objects in day-light to the eye of a man in health, is
> denominated their true and real colour, even while colour is allowed to be
> merely a phantasm of the senses. (ST 12: 234).

Here, the standard for *color*—a quality that, in Hume's view, depends on the mind
much as desirability does—consists of a chosen perspective ("in day-light") and
set of endowments ("in health").

Correction by appeal to a standard is even more prominent for Hume
in the case of sentiments than it is in the case of passions. For example,
the essay "Of the Standard of Taste" is aimed precisely at discovering the
"standard" by which to fix the "real beauty or deformity" (ST 7: 129–130) of
"actions, compositions, and external objects." This "true standard of taste
and beauty," he argues, lies in "the joint verdict of" individuals possessed of
"strong sense, united to delicate sentiment, improved by practice, perfected
by comparison, and cleared of all prejudice" (ST 23: 241). Notably, the first
four items on this list are personal endowments, while the fifth is a kind of
mental perspective.

Similarly, in the *Treatise* Hume describes in some detail the process of arriving
at correct judgments of vice and virtue through "correcting" the sentiments of
what he calls "the moral sense," and he compares that process directly to the correction of aesthetic sentiments from what he calls "the sense of beauty," as well
as to the cases of other qualities discerned through other senses, including the
external senses:[7]

FINDING HUMEAN VALUE IN HUMEAN HUMANITY 299

Our situation, with regard both to persons and things, is in continual fluctuation; and a man, that lies at a distance from us, may, in a little time, become a familiar acquaintance. Besides, every particular man has a peculiar position with regard to others; and 'tis impossible we cou'd ever converse together on any reasonable terms, were each of us to consider characters and persons, only as they appear from his peculiar point of view. In order, therefore, to prevent those continual *contradictions*, and arrive at a more *stable* judgment of things, we fix on some *steady* and *general* points of view; and always, in our thoughts, place ourselves in them, whatever may be our present situation. In like manner, external beauty is determin'd merely by pleasure; and 'tis evident, a beautiful countenance cannot give so much pleasure, when seen at the distance of twenty paces, as when it is brought nearer us. We say not, however, that it appears to us less beautiful: Because we know what effect it will have in such a position, and by that reflection we correct its momentary appearance.

... Such corrections [as those of moral sentiments] are common with regard to all the senses; and indeed 'twere impossible we cou'd ever make use of language, or communicate our sentiments to one another, did we not correct the momentary appearances of things, and overlook our present situation. (THN 3.1.1.15–16)

The standard of judgment for virtue and vice involves for Hume, at a minimum, sympathetically taking up the "point of view" of those who are most closely affected by the traits under consideration while in possession of causal knowledge of the effects of those mental traits on their possessors and others (THN 3.3.1.16). Although I cannot develop the point here, Hume also treats the distinctively epistemic values of "probability" and "evidence" as being derived from feeling—namely, the "force and vivacity" of ideas, which he also calls "the sentiment of belief"—that must be "corrected" for individual perspectives (for details, see Garrett 2015, chaps. 4–6).

It is important to emphasize two points about all regulative standards of judgment for feeling-based concepts as Hume conceives them. First, they arise through a natural process of social convergence in the development of the relevant concepts ("abstract ideas"; THN 1.1.7) themselves; the process is not a matter of recognizing an antecedently "right" standard that is already given *a priori*. Second, when the term that signifies a concept governed by such a standard comes to carry or express approval of whatever falls under the concept—as happens with the value concepts of beauty and virtue, but not with color concepts—*this* feature of the concept, too, has a natural psychological explanation that is not a matter of recognizing norms given *a priori*. Hume describes this further expressive function of a term as its "being taken in a good

300 RETHINKING THE VALUE OF HUMANITY

sense" (EPM 1.10; ST 23.3–7: 227–229; for further explication of both of these points, see Garrett 2015, chaps. 4–5).

Yet despite their importance, no standard of judgment, no matter how fully specified, can resolve or adjudicate every disparity in felt response. Hence, Hume allows for a limited amount of what may be called *subject relativity* about value, in which something can be said to have a real value quality *for* one individual but not *for* another, or at least not to the same degree. For example, although he regards being "in society" with others as desirable for all human beings regardless of their personal differences, he also writes, concerning "value for an object," that

> the catching of flies, like Domitian, if it give more pleasure, is preferable to [i.e., more desirable than] the hunting of wild beasts, like William Rufus, or conquering of kingdoms, like Alexander. (Sc 34: 171)

Similarly, he suggests that the passion of "natural affection" gives offspring more value *for* their own parents than for others (Sc 10: 162–163).

In comparison to passion-based values, sentiment-based values are evidently more resistant to simple relativization for Hume: "there is something approaching principles in mental taste; and critics can reason and dispute more plausibly than cooks or perfumers" (Sc 11: 163). Perhaps human beings resist relativization for sentiment-based value concepts because of the human tendency to "project" sentiments but not passions onto their causes. In any case, sentiment-based values tend, for Hume, to exhibit the somewhat different phenomenon of *blameless diversity*, in which divergent value attributions that are equally in accordance with the relevant standard of judgment are simply considered to be equally proper for all. For example, although Hume holds that the works of Milton are unquestionably more beautiful than the works of Ogilby (ST 8: 230–231), even for those who lack the capacity to feel this value for themselves, he also emphasizes that, in comparing the aesthetic merit of genres or styles of writing, judgments may differ blamelessly from person to person depending on age, station, and temperament without any party's being wrong (ST 28: 243–244).

In the sentiment-based moral domain—concerning what he calls "the value of virtue" (Sc 28: 169)—Hume finds a higher proportion of evaluative judgments that are simply right or wrong than in the aesthetic domain. Yet there still remains at least some blameless diversity in morals as well, especially about the *degree* of value in particular virtues that may be in tension with one another. In addition, he recognizes some moral evaluations—for example, concerning rules of property or sexual modesty and deportment—that are not relative to individuals but may still be relative to entire societies.[8]

2. Human Value, Rationality, and Sensibility

How Does Humanity Have Value?

Human beings *determine* value through both passions and sentiments, according to Hume, and they *possess* both passion-based and sentiment-based value as well. Of course, many kinds of entities—qualities, events, and things—are *desirable*, so it should not be surprising that human beings are often desirable as well. He mentions at least three ways in which they are *distinctively* desirable, however. First, human beings are desirable as cooperators in society:

> 'Tis by society alone [a human being] is able to supply his defects, and raise himself up to an equality with his fellow-creatures [i.e., animals], and even acquire a superiority above them. . . . By the conjunction of forces, our power is augmented: By the partition of employments, our ability encreases: And by mutual succour we are less expos'd to fortune and accidents. 'Tis by this additional *force*, *ability*, and *security*, that society becomes advantageous. (THN 3.2.2.3)

Second, they are desirable as company:

> Company is naturally so rejoicing, as presenting the liveliest of all objects, *viz.* a rational and thinking Being like ourselves, who communicates to us all the actions of his mind; makes us privy to his inmost sentiments and affections; and lets us see, in the very instant of their production, all the emotions, which are caus'd by any object. (THN 2.2.4.4)

In addition, of course, they are also sometimes desirable as objects of what Hume calls "the appetite for generation," which contributes, on his account, to the complex passion of "affection betwixt the sexes" (THN 2.2.11; see also Sc 9: 162).

Moreover, while many kinds of things are desirable, it is only sensible creatures—notably including human beings—that, according to Hume, can be *lovable* (or "lovely," in a now-obsolete sense that he sometimes employs). Unlike many of his contemporaries, however, he does not regard human beings as valuable through being loved or lovable by *God*, for

> [a]ll the *sentiments* of the human mind, gratitude, resentment, love, friendship, approbation, blame, pity, emulation, envy, have a plain reference to the state and situation of man, and are calculated for preserving the existence, and promoting the activity of such a being in such circumstances. It seems therefore unreasonable to transfer such sentiments to a supreme existence, or to suppose

302 RETHINKING THE VALUE OF HUMANITY

him actuated by them; and the phenomena, besides, of the universe will not support us in such a theory. (DNR 3.13: 56)[9]

Nor, Hume asserts, do human beings find one another lovable simply for being human beings:

> In general, it may be affirm'd, that there is no such passion in human minds, as the love of mankind, merely as such, independent of personal qualities, of services, or of relation to ourself. 'Tis true, there is no human, and indeed no sensible, creature, whose happiness or misery does not, in some measure, affect us, when brought near to us, and represented in lively colours: But this proceeds merely from sympathy, and is no proof of such an universal affection to mankind, since this concern extends itself beyond our own species. An affection betwixt the sexes is a passion evidently implanted in human nature; and this passion not only appears in its peculiar symptoms, but also in inflaming every other principle of affection, and raising a stronger love from beauty, wit, kindness, than what wou'd otherwise flow from them. Were there an universal love among all human creatures, it wou'd appear after the same manner. Any degree of a good quality wou'd cause a stronger affection than the same degree of a bad quality wou'd cause hatred; contrary to what we find by experience. (THN 3.2.1.12)

Yet, as this passage also indicates, there are a wide variety of ways by which love of individual human beings *can* be engendered, including personal qualities (such as beauty, wit, and kindness), performance of services, and standing in particular relations. Indeed, on Hume's account, *any* quality of a person, or of something closely related to that person, can, if it causes pleasure in another person, be a cause of the second person's loving the first (THN 2.2.1). He denies only that humanity, in the sense of having the nature that grounds membership in the human species, is by itself one of these qualities.

As Hume emphasizes, his denial of any "love of mankind, merely as such" is entirely compatible with the recognition that *sympathy*—a mental operation in which one's belief about the mental state of another sensible creature that is recognized as resembling oneself becomes enlivened to the point where one comes to share the mental state itself (THN 2.1.11.1–17)—can make one *share* in the pleasures and pains of any or all human beings. Indeed, the operation of sympathy—a causal "principle of humanity," in the sense of producing concern for others—naturally makes many states of affairs that would otherwise be desirable only *for* single individuals also desirable for all those who do or can sympathize with them. In addition, it renders the *happiness and well-being* of others desirable and hence valuable, even if it does not lead to those others *themselves*

FINDING HUMEAN VALUE IN HUMEAN HUMANITY 303

being valued in the way that love for them would. Moreover, Hume asserts that the operation of sympathy *alone* can, when especially strong, sometimes lead to love for the individuals with whom one sympathizes, as can an enduring conjunction of interests more generally (THN 2.2.9). Finally, he maintains that the operation of sympathy is, in nearly all cases, a necessary causal condition for the production of moral sentiments, and hence also for the determination of sentiment-based moral value (THN 3.3.1.10, 3.3.5.11).

According to Hume, the same pleasure-giving qualities that produce *love* when they are found in others typically also produce *pride* when they are found in oneself. In this case, too, they serve as objects of passion-based value, and the felt recognition of this value through pride can *itself* be approved by sentiment as *morally* valuable. Thus, he writes:

> But tho' an over-weaning conceit of our own merit be vicious and disagreeable, nothing can be more *laudable* [as a virtue], than *to have a value for ourselves*, where we *really have qualities that are valuable*. (THN 3.3.2.8, emphasis added)

In fact, although a good deal of the Humean value in human beings is passion-based, an especially significant share of it is, for him, sentiment-based. In the aesthetic domain, human beings who are themselves beautiful will have noninstrumental sentiment-based aesthetic value—as well as passion-based desirability, lovability, and prideworthiness on that account—and those who create or contribute to the beauty of compositions, actions, or external objects will have instrumental aesthetic value. In the important moral domain, human beings who are themselves virtuous will have noninstrumental sentiment-based moral value—as well as passion-based desirability, lovability, and prideworthiness—and those who create or contribute to the virtue of other individuals will have instrumental moral value.

Among the many specific virtues that Hume mentions are kindness, benevolence, cheerfulness, friendship, loyalty, generosity, courage, industry, prudence, justice (i.e., respect for property), fidelity (i.e., promise-keeping), allegiance (i.e., obedience to civil law), cleanliness, wit, wisdom, good sense, and—as noted previously—humanity in the sense of concern for others. He argues in both the *Treatise* and *An Enquiry concerning the Principles of Morals* that every virtue is a mental trait that is useful and/or agreeable to its possessor and/or others. In consequence, it is often a *sentiment*-based moral virtue, in his view, *to value through one's passions* something—such as the well-being of one's children, or even success in business and commerce—that is not *itself* the object of moral sentiments in the way that virtues are. It is therefore important to distinguish clearly between things that strictly speaking *have moral value* for Hume—such as (on its own account) the possession of virtues and (instrumentally) the inculcation of

304   RETHINKING THE VALUE OF HUMANITY

virtues—and things that are *morally worthy of consideration* in the sense that it is *of moral value to desire or otherwise value* them.

Among the many things that it can be of moral value to value, in Hume's view, is *acting with a regard to moral value* itself. Thus, being *dutiful*—that is, being motivated by the second-order desire to perform those acts that other virtuous individuals are motivated to perform by their virtuous first-order desires—consists, on his account, precisely in valuing actions because it is typically of moral value to value them. But although a person's dutifulness is generally useful to others, and thereby a virtue, it is nevertheless for Hume—in sharp contrast to motivation by duty for Kant—something of a second-best virtue, for we feel a greater degree of moral approval for those who are motivated by an original first-order virtuous motive (THN 3.2.1.4–8).[10]

What Are the Roles of Rationality and Sensibility in the Value of Humanity?

According to Kant, human beings have moral value in virtue of their capacity to freely give employment to a faculty of practical reason that is capable of setting and pursuing ends, and they are morally worthy objects of consideration precisely because they possess such a faculty of reason. Having this faculty requires, in his view, existing outside of, as well as within, the order of nature. As Hume understands reason, in contrast, it is the fully natural faculty for making inferences—either demonstrative or probable, but itself yielding only belief or assurance—that are causally determined like all other events in nature. Reason for him is never "practical" in the sense of choosing ultimate ends; it can at most ascertain the causally most effective means to achieving ultimate ends set by the passions and thereby contribute causally to the production of desires for those means (THN 2.3.3).

Nevertheless, rationality—that is, having reason—plays an important role for Hume in the determination of value by human beings. For although he denies that reason is *sufficient* for determining value, reason is *necessary* to the determination of many kinds of value, in his view, because it is essential to making causal inferences and discovering causal relations. Accordingly, it is always necessary for the determination of merely instrumental value. However, it is also necessary for any love or pride engendered by particular personal qualities, services, or relations that must be discovered through causal reasoning. Furthermore, it is necessary to the engendering of love through sympathy, since he maintains that we can come to hold a belief about the mental state of another sensible creature only through causal reasoning. In many cases, he holds, recognizing the beauty of an object requires causal knowledge of its utility, so that one can sympathize with

FINDING HUMEAN VALUE IN HUMEAN HUMANITY   305

the pleasure of imagined users (THN 2.1.8.2). Similarly, he holds that reasoning about the causal consequences of mental qualities is in all or nearly all cases necessary for the production of moral sentiments (EPM Appendix 1). In both passion-based and sentiment-based value, reasoning will often also be necessary in order to apply a relevant standard of judgment—involving how things *would* appear from a certain perspective and with certain endowments—for fixing the "real and intrinsic" value of things in the face of variable circumstances.

Although things may have some kinds of value—including desirability and beauty—without themselves possessing rationality, many of the most important kinds of value possessed by human beings often or always require it. For example, rationality is essential to the desirability of human beings as cooperators in society and as company, and to many of the qualities, services, or relations that make them lovable or prideworthy. Because the operation of sympathy depends, according to Hume, on appreciating similarities between oneself and the object of one's sympathy, shared rationality can make it easier to love another individual as a result of sympathy. The exercise of reason is also necessary for the production of many beautiful actions, compositions, and objects.

In the moral domain, as we have seen, wisdom and good sense—which require reasoning well—are themselves virtues according to Hume, and the use of reason is essential to having and exercising most other virtues as well. In particular, it is essential to the possession of what Hume calls the "artificial virtues"—such as justice, fidelity to promises, and allegiance to government—that depend on the existence of human "artifice and convention" and require an appreciation of the causal consequences of jointly following a mutually agreed course of action (THN 3.1.1–2; EPM 3–4). Even most of what he calls the "natural virtues," such as humanity in the sense of concern for others, could hardly be exercised without reasoning about the likely consequences of one's actions. Finally, in addition to the crucial roles played by rationality in the possession of moral value, rationality also contributes to *being morally worthy of consideration*, both through its capacity to involve its possessors in morally significant relations and through its capacity—as an aspect of resemblance that also causes other aspects of resemblance—to engage or enhance the sympathy of others.

Yet as important as rationality is to human value, sensibility—that is, the capacity for feeling and sensation—is in many ways even more important. For it is ultimately through sensibility, as manifested in passions and sentiments, that human beings determine values, even if reason is typically required in a subsidiary role to help produce those feelings or to regulate their results. Furthermore, although things may have some kinds of value—including desirability and beauty—without themselves possessing sensibility, many of the most important kinds of value possessed by human beings do require it. Only beings with sensibility—sensible creatures—can be desired as cooperators or company, or

306 RETHINKING THE VALUE OF HUMANITY

be objects of love or pride, on Hume's account, and hence only they can have the kinds of value that are determined by those passions. Sensibility is essential to all or nearly all processes of human artistic creation as well. In the crucial moral domain, only beings capable of feeling passions can be motivated to act, according to Hume, and only beings capable of being motivated to act can have virtues. Moreover, only sensible creatures can be objects of sympathy, and, because of the central role of sympathy in producing moral sentiments, all sensible creatures with feelings resembling those of human beings are thereby in principle *morally worthy of consideration.* Indeed, the connection between sympathy and moral sentiment is close enough that nothing can be morally worthy of consideration for Hume *unless* it either is or is somehow related to a being with sensibility.

Kant, as a moral rationalist and moral antinaturalist, holds that the value of humanity is fundamentally moral value that is both grounded in and recognized by the rationality, not the sensibility, of human beings as noumenally free agents outside of nature. In contrast, Hume the moral antirationalist and moral naturalist holds that humanity, as a part of nature, has many kinds of value—including moral value—that are metaphysically and epistemologically determined by sentiment or passion, as assisted by reason, and which typically also depend for their possession on having both reason and sensibility.

3. Further Questions about Humanity and Value

Is Value Unique to Humanity?

As we have observed, Hume does not ascribe any feelings to God or a deity, but he emphatically declares that animals have passions. These include desires for pleasure and the avoidance of pain for themselves, but also desires for the pleasure and the avoidance of pain for other sensible creatures, for "'tis evident, that *sympathy,* or the communication of passions, takes place among animals, no less than among men" (THN 2.2.12.6). The passions of animals also include, as we have seen, love, hatred, pride, and humility. Animals do not employ socially agreed-upon standards of judgment to correct their initial passionate responses, but they certainly have the passions by which human beings determine values, and they might therefore be regarded as themselves determining values—at least values that are relative to themselves—in a rudimentary way. Hume maintains that animals also have sentiments of beauty, which are among their sources of pride:

The very port and gait of a swan, or turkey, or peacock show the high idea he has entertain'd of himself, and his contempt of all others. This is the more remarkable, that in the two last species of animals, the pride always *attends the beauty*, and is discover'd in the male only. (THN 2.1.12.4, emphasis added)

But while they respond to and appreciate beauty, he asserts that "animals have little or no sense of virtue or vice" (THN 2.1.12.5)—that is, they have few or no moral sentiments.

Whatever he would say about the extent of animals' *determination* of value, however, Hume must allow that animals *possess* passion-based value. They are desirable not only by one another but also by human beings, and they are also lovable not only by one another but also by human beings. After remarking that "a dog naturally loves a man above his own species," he adds that the dog "very commonly meets with a return of affection" (THN 2.2.12.2). Animals also have sentiment-based value through their own beauty, which is at least sometimes appreciated both by themselves and by human beings (THN 2.1.8.2).

Less clear is whether animals also possess moral value through having *virtues* in Hume's view. His discussions of moral evaluation are focused entirely on human beings, and there are certainly many virtues that animals do not possess. These include, but are not limited to, the artificial virtues such as justice, fidelity to promises, and allegiance, all of which require participation in a convention. Yet he also writes:

A virtuous horse we can conceive; because, from our own feeling, we can conceive virtue; and this we may unite to the figure and shape of a horse, which is an animal familiar to us. (EHU 2.5)

This implies at least that it is not *impossible* for a horse to be virtuous, and the characterization of virtues as "mental qualities" does not itself preclude animals from having virtues. Humean virtue does not require any kind of free will that animals might lack (EHU 8.23), and his just-mentioned view that animals "have little or no sense of virtue or vice"—that is, largely lack the moral sentiments by which to *discern* virtue and vice—does not entail that they could not *have* any virtues or vices discernible by human beings. Indeed, he specifically mentions both that "animals are found susceptible of kindness" (EPM Appendix 2 §8) and that they have natural affection for their offspring. Both of these traits are virtues, at least when found in human beings.

On the other hand, Hume uses "a virtuous horse" alongside "a golden mountain" as an example of a complex idea created by the imagination; this perhaps

308 RETHINKING THE VALUE OF HUMANITY

suggests that no *actual* horses of our acquaintance are virtuous, or at least not notably virtuous. He explains that we produce the idea of a virtuous horse by combining ideas of virtuous mental qualities familiar to us from human beings with, in his phrase, "the figure and shape"—and so not necessarily the actual mental characteristics—of a horse.[11] Furthermore, he typically describes virtues as mental qualities that are useful or agreeable "to the *person* himself or to others" (emphasis added), and he generally treats the term 'person' as restricted to human beings, even although he also sometimes treats it as equivalent to 'mind' or 'self' (THN 1.4.6).

Whether or not animals possess any strictly moral value through their virtues, however, it is clear that for Hume they are *morally worthy of consideration* by human beings. As we have seen, it is an element of the virtue of humanity to be concerned for the well-being of sensible creatures generally, including animals. It is perhaps partly for this reason that he describes morality itself as having "a reference to mankind *and our fellow-creatures* (EPM 5.44, emphasis added). Nor is this broad scope of moral consideration surprising: as we have seen, almost all moral sentiments are the result of sympathy, on his view, and the operation of sympathy extends in principle to all sensible creatures.

Does Every Human Being Have Value?

Because all functioning human beings have both passions and sentiments of taste, in Hume's view, it is reasonable to conclude that he regards all human beings as capable of *determining* both passion-based and sentiment-based values to at least some extent, even though severe cognitive disabilities might prevent some from applying socially agreed-upon standards of judgment. It is also reasonable to conclude that Hume would regard every functioning human being as *possessing* at least some value. First, nearly all human beings have at least some passion-based desirability, if only as company or partners in cooperation. In addition, he recognizes that sympathy renders the *happiness and well-being* of every human being (if not those human beings themselves) desirable to every other, at least in principle. Furthermore, although he recognizes no "love of mankind as such," it is reasonable to think that every human being has at least some lovable (and prideworthy) traits, and even strong sympathy or a long-term coincidence of interests alone can be a source of lovability. At least many human beings are beautiful and/or capable of producing beauty, and all or nearly all human beings will have at least some strictly moral value through the possession of at least some virtues. Finally, because the trait of humanity as concern for others is a virtue, all human beings will be *morally worthy of consideration* in the sense that it will be of moral value *to* value them and their well-being.

Does Humanity as a Species Have Value?

Humanity considered collectively presumably has at least the accumulated value of its individual members. It may also have additional value, however, through the desires of its members for the continuation of the species. For Hume observes "that men are every where concern'd about what may happen after their death" (THN 1.3.9.13), and it seems undeniable that most human beings desire, and thereby determine it to be valuable, that the human species should continue to exist and flourish, with its distinctive nature, into the future. This desire is surely heightened by the recognition that the annihilation of humankind would bring to an end even the possibility of the determination of those many values that only human beings with their distinctive nature can determine and of the possession of those values that only human beings with their distinctive nature can possess. Furthermore, given the satisfaction that human beings would take in the continuing existence and flourishing of the human species, it seems that the mental trait of being concerned for that existence and flourishing would itself be a moral virtue, with the consequence that the human species and its future is morally worthy of consideration. Satisfaction taken in the existence and flourishing of other species would render them morally worthy of consideration as well.

How Much Value Does Humanity Have?

Humanity possesses such positive Humean values as desirability, lovability, prideworthiness, beauty, and virtue. However, it also possesses such negative Humean values—disvalues—as despicability, odiousness, shamefulness, deformity, and vice. In his essay "Of the Dignity or Meanness of Human Nature," Hume takes up the question of *how highly* humanity should be valued overall. His answer—again a strikingly un-Kantian one—is that an evaluation of degree of this kind depends largely on the scale we employ, and that this, in turn, depends in the present case on the other natures with which we compare human nature:

> That there is a natural difference between merit and demerit, virtue and vice, wisdom and folly, no reasonable man will deny: Yet is it evident, that in affixing the term, which denotes either our approbation or blame, we are commonly more influenced by comparison than by any fixed unalterable standard in the nature of things. In like manner, quantity, and extension, and

310 RETHINKING THE VALUE OF HUMANITY

bulk, are by every one acknowledged to be real things: But when we call any animal *great* or *little*, we always form a secret comparison between that animal and others of the same species; and it is that comparison which regulates our judgment concerning its greatness. A dog and a horse may be of the very same size, while the one is admired for the greatness of its bulk, and the other for the smallness. When I am present, therefore, at any dispute, I always consider with myself, whether it be a question of comparison or not that is the subject of the controversy; and if it be, whether the disputants compare the same objects together, or talk of things that are widely different. (DM 4: 81–82, italics in original)

When compared with animals, Hume claims, humanity does very well in terms of value. Without even mentioning the question of whether animals are entirely incapable of virtue, he emphasizes the much greater wisdom of human beings, whose "thoughts are not limited by any narrow bounds, either of place or of time" (DM 5: 82). The comparison of human beings with imagined superior beings, however, is much less favorable:

Among the other excellencies of man, this is one, that he can form an idea of perfections much beyond what he has experience of in himself; and is not limited in his conception of wisdom and virtue. He can easily exalt his notions and conceive a degree of knowledge, which, when compared to his own, will make the latter appear very contemptible, and will cause the difference between that and the sagacity of animals, in a manner, to disappear and vanish. (DM 6: 83)

Among the most common objects of comparison for human beings, Hume declares, are other human beings. In this case, it is not surprising that a very high degree of either wisdom or virtue will be unusual, from the very conditions of the comparison:

It is also usual to *compare* one man with another; and finding very few whom we can call *wise* or *virtuous*, we are apt to entertain a contemptible notion of our species in general. That we may be sensible of the fallacy of this way of reasoning, we may observe, that the honourable appellations of wise and virtuous, are not annexed to any particular degree of those qualities of *wisdom* and *virtue*; but arise altogether from the comparison we make between one man and another. When we find a man, who arrives at such a pitch of wisdom as is very uncommon, we pronounce him a wise man: So that to say, there are few wise men in the world, is really to say nothing; since it is only by their scarcity, that they merit that appellation. (DM 7: 83, italics in original)

Finally, however, we can also compare humanity as it actually is with humanity as it has been represented to be. In this case, Hume argues, humanity compares favorably from a moral point of view with the portrayal of it made by "those philosophers [presumably including Hobbes and Mandeville], that have insisted so much on the selfishness of man" and who have thereby been "led astray" to greatly exaggerate human vice (DM 10: 85). For the motives of love, benevolence, and humanity are in fact very strong in human nature, and the fact that human beings often seek to benefit one another is not always the result of an underlying selfishness but is often instead the natural consequence of the presence of those intrinsically unselfish motives. For Hume, it is in large part through the prevalence of humanity (as a principle of concern for others) within humanity (as human nature) that the members of humanity (as a species) find value in one another.[12]

Notes

1. By "moral rationalism," I mean the thesis that morality, at least in outline, can be discerned by reason alone. By "moral naturalism," I mean the thesis that morality does not require or depend on anything that would be outside of nature, such as (for example) one or more deities, actions or events not determined by and explicable through natural laws, or explanatorily basic normative properties. By "moral antirationalism" and "moral antinaturalism," I mean, respectively, the denials of these theses.
2. For Hume's use of the term 'sensible creature,' see THN 2.1.12.9, 3.2.1.12, 3.3.1.25; EHU 11.17 and 12.7; DNR 11.5: 205 and 11.14: 212.
3. "The Sceptic" was first published in 1742 as part of the second volume of Hume's *Essays, Moral and Political*. It is the last and longest of four essays—the others are "The Epicurean," "The Stoic," and "The Platonist" (all included in EMPL)—that Hume describes in a footnote to the first as aiming to "deliver the sentiments of sects, that naturally form themselves in the world, and entertain different ideas of human life and happiness" (Ep 1n: 138). Although "The Sceptic" was thus written to express a particular point of view, there are several good reasons to think that it contains no claims that Hume would deny. These include its final and adjudicatory position in the series, the fact that it does not contradict any of his other published writings, and the fact that Hume elsewhere identifies himself as a "sceptic." For an excellent account of the essay and its relation to the others in the series, see Heydt 2007.
4. For the distinction between impression of reflection and impressions of sensation, see THN 1.1.3.1.
5. Occasionally, however, he also uses the term 'sentiment' (and even the term 'sensation') for any kind of feeling. One such example may be Sc 14: 164–165. Among the feelings to which he applies the term 'sentiment' in *An Enquiry concerning Human*

Understanding (EHU 5) is the feeling of force and vivacity in ideas that, in his view, constitutes belief.

6. This distinction between "sentiments" and "passions"—which Hume applies to *types of impressions* on the basis of the *most frequent* degree of calmness or violence found within each type—should not be confused with his later distinction (already hinted at in the quoted passage) between "calm passions" and "violent passions." This later distinction applies not to impression-types but rather, *within* the category of passions, to *individual passion-tokens* on the basis of their *actual* degree of calmness or violence during their datable occurrence (THN 2.3.4.8–10).

7. In addition to a moral sense and a sense of beauty, Hume also refers to a sense by which "wit" is discerned (THN 3.3.4.11) through sentiment (EPM 8.3), suggesting that what we would call "humor" is another sentiment-based value. However, I will not pursue the point here.

8. For more on this topic, see EPM "A Dialogue," and also Garrett 2015, chap. 8, § 5.

9. Hume gives this remark to the character Demea (who is evidently using the term 'sentiment' broadly and nontechnically here, for feelings of any kind) rather than to his own spokesman, Philo. However, Philo does not dispute Demea's claim, and he later argues in his own right that it is improbable on the available evidence that the cause or causes of order in the universe have either benevolence (which love naturally engenders, at least in human beings) or rectitude (i.e., concern for virtue) (DNR 11.16: 212).

10. Hume emphasizes, for example, that those who care for their children out of natural affection are more virtuous than those who do so only out of a sense of duty (THN 3.2.1.5–8). The contrast with Kant, who regards duty as the only praiseworthy motive and employs the same example, could not be more striking.

11. As Hume would be aware, the *Iliad* mentions two immortal horses of Achilles, both of whom stood motionless on the field of battle and wept when Patroclus was killed. Hera later granted one of them the power of speech. Nandi Theunissen reminded me of this example.

12. I thank Nandi Theunissen, Sarah Buss, and the participants in the Johns Hopkins University conference The Value of Humanity for many helpful questions, comments, and suggestions.

References

Works of David Hume

DM "Of the Dignity or Meanness of Human Nature." In EMPL, Part I, Essay XI, 80–86. [Citations are by paragraph number followed by page numbers]

DNR *Dialogues concerning Natural Religion and Other Writings*. Edited by Dorothy Coleman. Cambridge: Cambridge University Press, 2007. [Citations are by part and paragraph number, followed by marginal page number. Marginal page numbers refer to the long-standard edition of *Dialogues concerning Human Understanding*. Edited by Norman Kemp Smith (Indianapolis, IN: Bobbs-Merrill, 1947)]

EHU *An Enquiry concerning Human Understanding*. Edited by Tom L. Beauchamp. Oxford: Clarendon Press, 2000. [Citations are by section and paragraph number]

EMPL *Essays Moral, Political, and Literary*, revised ed. Edited by Eugene F. Miller. Indianapolis, IN: Liberty *Classics*, 1987.

Ep "The Epicurean." In EMPL, Part I, Essay XV, 138–45. [Citations are by paragraph number followed by page number]

EPM *An Enquiry concerning the Principles of Morals*. Edited by Tom L. Beauchamp. Oxford: Clarendon Press, 1998. [Citations are by section and paragraph number]

IS "Of the Immortality of the Soul." In EMPL, Essays Withdrawn and Unpublished, Essay X, 590–598. [Citations are by paragraph number followed by page number]

NC "Of National Characters." In EMPL, Part I, Essay XXI, 197–215. [Citations are by paragraph number followed by page number]

RPAS "Of the Rise and Progress of the Arts and Sciences." In EMPL, Part I, Essay XIV, 111–137. [Citations are by paragraph number followed by page number]

Sc "The Sceptic." In EMPL, Part I, Essay XVIII, 159–180. [Citations are by paragraph number followed by page number]

ST "Of the Standard of Taste." In EMPL, Part II, Essay XII, 226–249. [Citations are by paragraph number followed by page number]

THN *A Treatise of Human Nature*. Edited by David Fate Norton and Mary Norton. Oxford: Clarendon Press, 2007. [Citations are by book, part, section, and paragraph number]

Secondary Literature

Garrett, Don 2015. *Hume*. New York: Routledge.

Heydt, Colin 2007. "Relations of Literary Form and Philosophical Purpose in Hume's Four Essays on Happiness." *Hume Studies* 33 (1): 3–19.

13
Other People

Kieran Setiya

Do you believe in love at first sight? Maybe you do and maybe you don't. Perhaps you will refuse to say, complaining that the question is obscure. I sympathize with that response. In a way, it is the subject of this essay, though I hope to show that there is more at stake. I begin with the prediction that, whatever you make of love at first sight, you do not believe in "love at definite description." You may know on general grounds that there is a shortest spy, but you cannot love the shortest spy if you have not met them and know nothing more about them.[1] You could, I suppose, become invested in the prospects of the shortest spy, whoever that is, preferring outcomes that will benefit them to ones that benefit other people, striving to ensure that the shortest spy survives and flourishes. But this would not be love, and absent further context, it would not be rational.

There may be descriptions that do suffice for love, like "the woman who saved my life" or "the brother I never knew." Special concern for individuals so described may be intelligible. Likewise, perhaps, if the description evokes, in richly textured detail, an attractive human being. Personal acquaintance may not be required for love. But the mere fact that one has a description that identifies an individual, as in "the shortest spy," is not enough.

"Personal acquaintance," here, is a placeholder for the relation to another human being that justifies love at first sight, if there is any such thing; it is the minimal cognitive contact that makes sense of love. This chapter explores the nature of this relation and its place in moral philosophy. As I will argue, personal acquaintance plays a role not just in love but in concern for individuals, as such.

Section 1 is about the connections between personal acquaintance, love, and moral standing. It maps some puzzling features of personal acquaintance that set parameters for any attempt to comprehend it. The task is to account for the ethical significance of this relation. In Section 2, we find a similar structure in concern for others of the sort that is morally required. This structure comes out in recent treatments of contractualism, aggregation, and the trolley problem. Section 3 turns to the work of Emmanuel Levinas as a source of insight into personal acquaintance, tracing the difficulties with his view and the prospects for revision. We are left with a question not just about love but about the basis of human values and the value of human life.

Kieran Setiya, *Other People* In: *Rethinking the Value of Humanity*. Edited by: Sarah Buss and L. Nandi Theunissen, Oxford University Press. © Oxford University Press 2023. DOI: 10.1093/oso/9780197539361.003.0014

1.

In "Love and the Value of a Life," I argued that it is rational for any one of us to love any other human being, whatever their merits, without the need for any past relationship (Setiya 2014, §1). In rejecting the need for virtues or common histories as grounds for love, I agree with David Velleman. Like Velleman, I believe that the subjects of full moral standing, who deserve respect, coincide with those it is rational to love in the distinctive way that we love other people. In his formulation: "[R]espect and love [are] the required minimum and optional maximum responses to one and the same value" (Velleman 1999, 366). By "full moral standing," I mean the kind of significance shared by human beings but not by other animals, at least not the sort we encounter on Earth. Our interests count for more than theirs, and we have rights against each other they do not possess. (We will return to this assumption at the end.)

I differ from Velleman on three counts. First, I do not share his Kantian conception of the basis of moral standing, on which it turns on our rational nature. In my view, human beings who lack reason, or the potential for it, are morally equal to us. Second, I am less resistant than Velleman to the idea that, in its primary forms, love involves a disproportionate concern for the interests of the beloved, concern that goes beyond what is required by moral standing.[2] While there are different varieties of love—erotic, parental, and so on—this is a defining feature of the sort of love that interests me. Finally, while I doubt the need for past relationships as reasons for love, I do not deny that friendship, parenthood, and other relationships provide such reasons.[3]

The permissive view of love is no doubt controversial. My arguments for it turn on the rationality of love in the face of radical change, retrograde amnesia (in which you forget your past relationship), and skeptical delusion (as when you learn that you came into existence an hour ago and that the "memories" of your relationship are false).[4] I won't repeat those arguments here, but I will make two observations. First, although it is natural to illustrate the view by appeal to love at first sight, this is potentially misleading. The sort of love involved is not essentially romantic. We could point instead to the love I might instantly feel for an infant abandoned on my doorstep, knowing right away that I would take care of the child even at considerable cost. Second, love need not be as deep or devoted as romantic or parental love, and it need not involve a strong desire for interaction. Think of my attitude to old friends who I have not seen and may not have thought about for years. I still love them in a meaningful way: if they were in need, I would do much more for them than I would for an arbitrary stranger.

Our topic is not the plausibility of the permissive view but a question neglected by its advocates, about love at definite description.[5] Even on the most liberal conception of love, on which it does not turn on particular merits or

316 RETHINKING THE VALUE OF HUMANITY

past relationships, you cannot love the shortest spy if that description is all you have. What is possible, and rational, is love at first sight. So the position must be qualified. It is rational to love any human being with whom you are personally acquainted, not any human being, full stop. But then we have to ask: What is personal acquaintance, and how does it justify love?

Both the interest and the enigma of personal acquaintance come into focus if I am right about the implications of the permissive view. The most dramatic consequence speaks to the moral significance of numbers. Consider a case in which you can save the lives of three strangers drowning over to the left or a single stranger, M, who is drowning on the right.[6] The circumstance is otherwise unexceptional. You have no special obligation to any given stranger, and their survival would have no unusual consequences, good or ill. On the view that I defend, it would be rational for you to love M, even though you have never met before: this would be love at first sight. I argue further that, in loving M, it is rational to give more weight to her needs than to those of other people. Acting on this concern, it would be rational to save her life instead of saving three. It follows that you could rationally decide to save a single drowning stranger when you could save more. We thus arrive at a version of John Taurek's (1977) startling claim that, in cases of this kind, the numbers do not count; at least, they are not rationally decisive.

I don't expect this thumbnail sketch to be convincing; more argument is required.[7] But it shows how doubts about aggregation flow from the permissive view of love, assuming love can involve a disproportionate concern for someone's needs. Now for the puzzle. When I first drew these connections, I did not stress the role of personal acquaintance. What is arguably rational is to save M at the cost of three lives when you are confronted with M herself: when you look into her eyes and respond with love. That claim is contentious enough. I do not think it would be rational to save the person on the right when you know them only by that description. In what we may call the "anonymous" case, you have no contact with the drowning strangers. You are merely told what is happening and must decide where to send the rescue mission. It is irrational to give priority to the needs of one in the anonymous case. You are not in a position to love the person on the right. That takes personal acquaintance.

The nature of personal acquaintance matters, on the permissive view of love, not just because it makes love rational but because it makes a difference to questions of life and death. This brings out a pivotal constraint on how we conceive the relation of personal acquaintance. When you stand in this relation to M, it is rational to save her life, moved by the urgency of her needs, instead of the lives of the other three. When you lack this relation to M, when you know her only as "the one who is drowning on the right," it is irrational to save her life. Personal acquaintance is ethically significant. At the same time, it is utterly minimal, requiring no history of interaction, as we know from love at first sight. What can this relation be?

We may turn for help to philosophical discussions of "knowing who": to be personally acquainted with M is to know who she is. But accounts of "knowing who" in the philosophy of language only compound the mystery. On the minimal view, you know who someone is when you know an answer to the question "Who is. . . ?" The answer need not even be a definite description. David Braun (2006, 24) begins his essay in defense of this conception with the sentence "Hong Oak Yun is a person who is over three inches tall," adding boldly, "[N]ow you know who Hong Oak Yun is." In whatever sense, if any, this is true, it is not one that matters to moral philosophy or makes love rational.

On a more orthodox view, to know who someone is to know a contextually relevant answer to the question "Who is. . . ?" that takes the form of a definite description.[8] But this does not amount to progress. At best, it frames our problem: Which answers to the question "Who is. . . ?" are ethically relevant? What do you need to know about someone in order to be personally acquainted with them, and why does it matter? In fact, the situation is worse. In love at first sight, you know very little about the person you love apart from their relation to you. Knowing that they are the person with these properties is like knowing that they are the shortest spy. It does not count as knowing who they are in an ethically relevant sense. The most plausible candidates for a description that matters, morally speaking, will be ones that cite your relationship to them. Why not then conclude that this relation matters, not the further relation involved in knowing about it? The appeal to "knowing who" is a distraction.

It is perhaps more promising to invoke objectual knowledge, as in "knowing M." We can know people, places, and things, as well as knowing who, where, and what. When you know someone, it makes sense to love them, even if you don't know much about them. But I doubt that the expression "knowing M" will bear much weight. Unlike personal acquaintance, knowing someone comes by degree: you can know them better or worse.[9] How well you need to know M in order to count as "knowing M" varies by context. Where does personal acquaintance fall? We might identify personal acquaintance with knowing M to the minimal degree that counts as "knowing M." But even this is doubtful. Knowing M is usually thought to be reciprocal: you can't know M unless M knows you (see Lauer 2014; Benton 2017). Personal acquaintance is not like that. You can love someone who doesn't know you exist. Given its contextual flexibility, "knowing M" might be used to refer to personal acquaintance. But this does not illuminate our topic.

Hoping for insight, we may turn instead to the concepts with which we think of others. Personal acquaintance involves the possession of a concept that essentially denotes a particular individual, as in "rigid designation." Is the problem with "loving" the shortest spy or the person who is drowning on the right that their identity is not involved in one's response? They are picked out by properties they could lack. According to Philip Pettit (1997, 158–159), "when an agent displays a commitment to a beloved by acting out of love, the reason that moves the agent has to be rigidly individualized in favour of the beloved. It has to be a reason in which the beloved figures as an essential component." But again, this is not the point. Love at definite description remains irrational, or impossible, when the description is rigidified. It makes no sense to love the actual shortest spy or the person who is actually drowning on the right, picked out in those terms. Nor does the shift to naming change this. Being told that the shortest spy is Ortcutt, or the drowning woman, Pat, is not sufficient to justify love.

The argument so far is that personal acquaintance is a mystery. It does not correspond to "knowing who" or objectual knowledge or rigidified description. And yet it is ethically significant. It is personal acquaintance that explains why it is rational to love someone you have only just met but irrational, perhaps impossible, to love "the shortest spy." It justifies saving one stranger when you could save three; its absence explains why it would be wrong to do so in the anonymous case. Before we try to untangle the mystery of personal acquaintance, I will suggest that it runs deeper. For personal acquaintance is sufficient, all by itself, to justify love. Nothing further is required.

How could personal acquaintance fail to justify love? The idea would have to be that rational love depends not just on personal acquaintance, but on beliefs about the object of love. On the permissive view of love, these cannot be beliefs about their specific merits or about your past relationship. Nor can we plausibly appeal to beliefs about the relation of personal acquaintance. As before, it is the relation that counts, not knowledge of it. Must you believe that the object of love is a "person" in the philosophers' sense, a rational subject? No: you can love human beings who lack reason or the potential for it. Must you believe that the object of love is another human being? I am doubtful. While it may be irrational to love a goat in the way that you love another person, as in the play by Edward Albee (2003), I don't believe that love depends on conjectured species or form of life. That the man across the room is a human being, not a rational Martian, is too theoretical a ground for love at first sight. Finally, we can ask if you must believe that the object of love has full moral standing. There is a sense in which you treat them as if they do, but you need not have beliefs about how they should be treated in order to be rational in loving them.

In principle, there might be other beliefs that justify love, other properties to which we must appeal. There is room for a disjunctive view, on which various beliefs will do. It is not easy to exhaust the options. But if we already know that personal acquaintance matters, that it is morally significant, why keep looking? Why not conclude instead that, given its ethical weight, personal acquaintance is sufficient to justify love, all by itself.[10] As its name suggests, personal acquaintance is a relation we can bear only to those it is rational to love in the way that we love other people, only to those who have full moral standing. You cannot be personally acquainted with a goat, though you might believe you are. It is not a belief about someone that makes them available for love but the relation of personal acquaintance. In Wittgenstein's (1953, 178) words: "My attitude to him is an attitude towards a soul. I am not of the *opinion* that he has a soul."

If this is right, personal acquaintance is ethically significant in two ways. First, because its absence in the anonymous case explains why you cannot save one instead of three; its presence explains why you can. Second, because it is a relation we can have only to those with full moral standing. Each mode of significance constrains what personal acquaintance can be.

2.

Do these issues pertain only to curious views about the nature and justification of love? I don't believe they do. Personal acquaintance plays a tacit but essential role in recent debates about contractualism and social risk.[11]

The puzzle for contractualists comes out in the following cases, described by Johann Frick (2015). In Mass Vaccination (Known Victims), a million children face certain death unless they are treated with a vaccine, administered to all. Vaccine A prevents the fatal illness but will leave the children with a paralyzed limb. Vaccine B prevents the disease without paralysis but "because of a known particularity in their genotype, [it] is certain to be completely ineffective for 1,000 identified children" (183). These children will die. For contractualists, an act is permissible only if it can be justified to each of those affected, in that it is licensed by a principle none of them could reasonably reject. We are not allowed to aggregate claims. Thus, in Mass Vaccination (Known Victims), we compare the harm of losing one's life to the harm of a paralyzed limb. Since no one can be asked to bear the former in order to save someone from the latter, we must choose Vaccine A.

Now consider Mass Vaccination (Unknown Victims). Here a million children face certain death unless they are treated with a vaccine. Vaccine A is available, but there is also Vaccine C, which prevents the fatal disease without paralysis in 99.9% of cases; in 0.1% of cases, it is utterly ineffective. (The probabilities here are epistemic; they reflect our evidence in making the decision.) The challenge for contractualism is to distinguish the second case from the first, given that the outcome of choosing Vaccine C is virtually certain to involve the death of at least one child, and very likely to involve the death of about 1,000.[12] According to Frick (2015, 185):

320 RETHINKING THE VALUE OF HUMANITY

> [In] real life, we often impose social risks that closely resemble that of choosing [Vaccine C] in Mass Vaccination (Unknown Victims). Thus, it is commonly deemed morally unproblematic to systematically inoculate young children against certain serious but nonfatal childhood diseases where there is a remote chance of fatal side effects from the inoculation itself.

Can contractualists explain why it is permissible to impose this kind of social risk while maintaining that it is impermissible to do so when the victims are identified in advance?

Frick's (2015, 187–188) solution takes the form of "ex ante contractualism," according to which we should evaluate Mass Vaccination (Unknown Victims) not by considering how individuals fare in the possible outcomes but by considering how our policies affect their prospects now. The claim is that Vaccine C improves the ex ante prospects of each individual child, by our evidential lights. It gives them a 99.9% chance of perfect health with a 0.1% chance of failure, which is arguably better than the assurance of paralysis with Vaccine A. That is how a policy of using Vaccine C can be justified to all. (If you believe that the imposition of a 0.1% chance of death on a given individual cannot be justified as the alternative to paralysis, reduce the risk until you agree. The general point remains.)

Ex ante contractualists thus permit the imposition of social risk while resisting the imposition of harms when the victims are known, or knowable, in advance.[13] It is important to stress that the dividing factor is not the chanciness of Vaccine C or the possibility that no one dies. It is about identification. Consider a third case, Mass Vaccination (Unknown but Definite Victims), which is just like Mass Vaccination (Known Victims) except that there is no way to guess who has the distinctive genotype. Vaccine A prevents the fatal illness but leaves each child with a paralyzed limb. Vaccine B prevents the disease without paralysis except for 1,000 unidentified children. For the ex ante contractualist, this case is like Mass Vaccination (Unknown Victims): Vaccine B improves the prospects of each child, by our evidential lights. No individual should object to our choosing Vaccine B even though, as in Mass Vaccination (Known Victims), 1,000 children are sure to die.[14]

Some will resist this verdict, assimilating victims who are definite but unknown to those who are known in advance. They will need to square their resistance with a plausible view of social risk. Why refuse to employ Vaccine B in Mass Vaccination (Unknown but Definite Victims) when it improves the prospects of each individual as much as Vaccine C? Imagine administering the vaccine to each child in succession. On our evidence, it is preferable to administer Vaccine B rather than Vaccine A, just as it was preferable to go with Vaccine C in Mass Vaccination (Unknown Victims). Shouldn't we choose Vaccine B? But if we should do it for each child, we should do it for all.[15] I won't pursue this reasoning here. I want instead to trace the implications of ex ante contractualism, drawing out an ethical idea that turns on personal acquaintance. In doing so, I will assume, for the sake of argument, that Frick's analysis is right.

The basic question for ex ante contractualists is what distinguishes Mass Vaccination (Known Victims) from Mass Vaccination (Unknown but Definite Victims), given that the objective probabilities of the various outcomes are the same. The terminology tells us that the difference is whether the victims are identified or known. But what exactly does that mean? It had better not suffice for a victim to be identified that we can pick them out by definite description. After all, we could "identify" the unknown victims by some irrelevant feature, like height: "the shortest child who has the gene"; "the second shortest child who has the gene"; and so on. We know that these children will not be saved by Vaccine B in Mass Vaccination (Unknown but Definite Victims). If that makes them "known victims," the alleged distinction will collapse. Suppose instead that we are given a list of names: these are the children who have the distinctive gene. We have no other way to determine who they are. Again, this is not enough. We knew all along that the children had names; knowing what they are is not sufficient to identify them, not in the sense that matters here. In contrast, I would urge, personal acquaintance must suffice for a victim to be identified or known, to transform the circumstance into Mass Vaccination (Known Victims), and so preclude the use of Vaccine B. What guides the ex ante contractualist is the idea of "personal concern": a concern for others directed at them as individuals, made possible, and rational, by personal acquaintance.

This leaves some difficult questions. Presumably, it is not required that we in fact identify the victims or that we know who they are. For the ex ante contractualist, the question is what personal concern would motivate if we were personally acquainted with those involved, given what we know, or what is knowable, about them (again, see Frick 2015, 191–193). In Mass Vaccination (Known Victims), concern of this kind does not speak with a single voice; for those who have the gene, it favors Vaccine A; for those who do not, Vaccine B. Where the victims are unknown, personal concern is arguably unanimous: it favors Vaccine B on behalf of each. That is why it is permissible to choose Vaccine B.

The idea, then, is not that you should be more concerned with personal acquaintances than anyone else, or that it is rational to give their interests greater weight. The idea is that, when you aim to justify a policy to each of those affected, their prospects on your evidence will depend on how you pick them out. In Mass Vaccination (Unknown but Definite Victims), the prospects of the shortest child with the gene are very bad if she is given Vaccine B. But if you meet a random child, her prospects on your evidence look better with Vaccine B than Vaccine A. For the ex ante contractualist, the first way of picking children out, by definite description, is irrelevant: that is not how you should think of individuals when you ask whether a policy can be justified to each. In contrast, the second way of picking children out, by personal acquaintance, is morally apt.

Whatever you make of contractualism as a theory of right and wrong, the idea of personal concern, concern that is mediated by personal acquaintance, is ethically compelling. It is like love, as described in Section 1, except that it is not disproportionate, and like respect but unlike love, it is a response to others we are required to have. It is a form of impartial concern for individuals that personal acquaintance demands. Arguably, such concern is akin to love in that its justification does not turn on further beliefs about the object of concern. Personal acquaintance is again significant in two ways. First, because it justifies a kind of concern that has ethical weight in decisions that benefit others, a weight that is not shared by concern for the person, whoever it is, that meets a given description. Second, because it is a relation we can have only to those with full moral standing. Each mode of significance constrains what personal acquaintance can be.

I have argued that ex ante contractualists share the puzzle of personal acquaintance: the task of explaining its character in a way that meets these ethical constraints. But the idea of personal concern appears elsewhere. Perhaps the most self-conscious invocation of personal concern in recent moral philosophy is due to Caspar Hare (2016, §3). Hare begins with the standard Footbridge case, introduced by Judith Thomson (1976): you can push a button to drop one person from a bridge into the path of a speeding trolley that will otherwise kill five. Most believe that doing so would be wrong. Hare contrasts the original case with what we can call "Opaque Footbridge": six acquaintances are caught up in the trolley case, five on the track, one on the bridge, but you do not and cannot know where in particular they are. As Hare contends, there is a powerful argument that concern for each of those involved counts in favor of pushing the button. If we give them alphabetical names, we can see that, by your lights, pushing the button will improve A's prospects from a 5/6 chance of death to just 1/6. It is true that pushing the button will change the potential cause of death, from being hit by a runaway trolley to falling from a bridge as a result of your intervention. But from A's perspective, why care? Why should it matter whether you die on the tracks or falling from a bridge to save the five? The upshot is that, in Opaque Footbridge, concern for A alone, not weighing her interests against those of others or aggregating claims, should lead you to push the button. The same is true of concern for B, C, and all the rest. Benevolence speaks with a single voice.

As Hare (2016, 466) insists, this argument does not apply in the original Footbridge case. Again, suppose you know the six involved, from A to F. If you know that F is on the bridge, concern for each is not unanimous. There is no way to argue that you ought to push the button without comparing or combining claims. Benevolent concern is simply divided. Concern for F speaks against

OTHER PEOPLE 323

pushing the button; concern for the others speak in favor. This conflict cannot be ignored.

Hare gives further arguments, but we need not go into them.[16] Nor need we accept his conclusion that, in Opaque Footbridge, you ought to push the button.[17] What matters is that, regardless of this conclusion, Hare's argument taps an ethical idea that has real force. He seems right to insist that in Opaque Footbridge, concern for the interests of those involved speaks unanimously for pushing the button. If there is a moral objection to doing so, it does not flow from benevolent concern but from a different and potentially conflicting source: a respect for rights that is not grounded in and may diverge from people's interests.

As with ex ante contractualism, this reasoning appeals to personal concern: concern for individuals that rests on personal acquaintance. We can see this by asking what explains the contrast between Footbridge and Opaque Footbridge. The answer is that, in Opaque Footbridge, you do not know who will die if you push the button, whereas in Footbridge, you do: the victim is identified or known. As before, it had better not suffice for identification that you locate someone by description, since you can "identify" the victim in Opaque Footbridge as "the one who is on the bridge." If that makes them an identified victim, the contrast we are tracking disappears. Nor do names suffice. The verdict of benevolence does not change when you are told that the person on the bridge is Jim—unless you know Jim in some other way.

In what meaningful sense, then, do you know who the victim is in Footbridge but not in its opaque counterpart?[18] Confronted with this question, Hare contends that the sort of "knowing who" that makes a difference is knowing facts about what matters in the lives of those involved, about their friends and families, hobbies and careers. What blocks the argument for pushing the button is the plurality of values realized by these diverse activities: values that are incommensurable (Hare 2016, §6). But this cannot be the right account. It would not affect the ethics of Footbridge if the people involved were perfect duplicates of one another, identical sextuplets who lead identical, solitary lives. Nor would it matter if they were people you just met, about whom you know nothing at all. What counts is personal acquaintance, not biographical knowledge. In Footbridge, personal concern for the one who is on the bridge restrains you from pushing the button. In Opaque Footbridge, personal concern—concern for individuals that turns on personal acquaintance—speaks in favor. Concern for the person on the bridge, described as such, can be ignored.

Again, the moral of the story is that personal concern has ethical weight. It is not that you should be more concerned with personal acquaintances than anyone else, or that it is rational to give their interests greater weight. The idea is rather that concern mediated by personal acquaintance has an ethical significance that is not shared by concern for the person, whoever it is, that meets a given description.

324 RETHINKING THE VALUE OF HUMANITY

When you care about people's interests, their prospects, given your evidence, depend on how you pick them out. In Opaque Footbridge, the prospects of the person on the bridge are bleak if you push the button. But the prospects of A to F, picked out by personal acquaintance, all improve. It is the second fact that counts. Concern for F has ethical weight that concern for the person on the bridge, whoever it is, does not. In order to make sense of this, to see the contrast between Footbridge and Opaque Footbridge, we must appeal to a form of concern that attaches to individuals not by name or description but by personal acquaintance. Such concern resembles love, except that it is not disproportionate and is not merely rational but required. It is tempting to add, once more, that the justification for personal concern does not depend upon beliefs about its object: personal acquaintance is enough. It is a relation we can have only to those with full moral standing.

There are thus three routes to the puzzle of personal acquaintance. It follows from the permissive view of love, from ex ante contractualism, and from Hare's appeal to concern for others in Opaque Footbridge, that personal acquaintance justifies a kind of concern that makes a difference.[19] My hope is that, even if you doubt the premise of each argument, you can feel the pull of personal concern as an ethical idea. Nonaggregative, distributed concern for individuals with whom one is personally acquainted: this makes moral sense. Concern that is mediated by definite descriptions or the secondhand use of names does not. An account of personal acquaintance should explain why.

3.

The idea of personal concern is easy to misconceive. To repeat what was said before, the suggestion is not that you should give priority to those with whom you are personally acquainted over those with whom you are not. In the versions of Footbridge above, we assumed for simplicity that you were personally acquainted with all of those involved. The argument was that concern mediated by personal acquaintance has an ethical significance that is not shared by concern for the person, whoever it is, that meets a given description. Concern for F counts against your pushing the button in Footbridge: it has ethical weight. In Opaque Footbridge, concern for the person on the bridge, described as such, does not. It is left open what this means for cases in which you are not personally acquainted with some or all of those involved. For instance, it does not follow that, if you are personally acquainted with the people on the track and you know where they are, but you are not acquainted with the person on the bridge, you should push the button, saving your acquaintances by killing a stranger. More plausibly, you should act as if you were personally acquainted with everyone, but have no additional knowledge about their locations.

The crucial fact is that when you weigh the effects of your actions on the prospects of individuals, it matters how you pick them out, and thus how your concern is directed toward them. F's prospects may differ from the prospects of the person on the bridge, going by your evidence, even though, unbeknownst to you, F is the person on the bridge. Which way of picking people out is morally relevant? It is the one involved in personal concern, which runs through personal acquaintance, not concern for the person on the bridge, as such.

We can spell this out in terms of thoughts sustained by personal acquaintance. The relation of personal acquaintance plays a role in determining the object of one's attitude that is elsewhere played by definite descriptions or the secondhand use of names. It is a mode of presentation deployed in thoughts—as for instance, beliefs about the prospects of a given individual—that interact with personal concern. In Fregean terms, personal acquaintance is the basis of distinctive singular concepts; alternatively, it is a guise under which we can think of others. On the Fregean view, we can say that propositions that involve such concepts—that this act will harm F, in particular—count as a reasons in a way that merely descriptive propositions—for instance, that it will harm the person on the bridge— do not. We know that there are reasons of the first kind in Opaque Footbridge, but we don't know what they are. That is why this case is morally different from Footbridge.[20] Similarly, it is personal-acquaintance-based thoughts that justify love at first sight and that are absent in relation to the shortest spy.

These clarifications help us to say what personal acquaintance is: it is a cognitive relation that individuates its object, sustaining reference. This relation is the minimal cognitive contact that justifies love and it is the basis for personal concern. But our account so far is structural. It is about the role that personal acquaintance plays. Can we give a positive account of the relation that plays this role?

In the work of Emmanuel Levinas, spanning four decades of the mid-twentieth century, we find what I think is a profound phenomenology of personal acquaintance.[21] Levinas comes back again and again to the face of the other as an ethical address. This theme is central to his most well-known book, *Totality and Infinity* (1961). But his argument is sketched in "Freedom and Command," published in 1953:

> The being that expresses itself, that faces me, says *no* to me by this very expression. This *no* is not merely formal, but it is not the *no* of a hostile force or a threat; it is the impossibility of killing him who presents that face; it is the possibility of encountering a being through an interdiction. The face is the fact that a being affects us not in the indicative, but in the imperative, and is thus outside all categories. . . . The metaphysical relationship, the relationship with the exterior, is only possible as an ethical relationship. (Levinas [1953] 1998, 21)

326   RETHINKING THE VALUE OF HUMANITY

Levinas is as much concerned with justice ("That shalt not kill") as with benevolence, though he connects the two:

> From the start, the encounter with the Other is my responsibility for him. That is the responsibility for my neighbor, which is, no doubt, the harsh name for what we call love of one's neighbor; love without Eros, charity, love in which the ethical aspect dominates the passionate aspect, love without concupiscence. (Levinas [1982b] 1998, 103)

Levinas insists on the particularity of our relation to the other, its distributed, nonaggregative character, in ways that resonate with personal concern.

> I must judge, where before I was to assume responsibilities. Here is the birth of the theoretical; here the concern for justice is born, which is the basis of the theoretical. But it is always starting out from the Face, from the responsibility for the other that justice appears, which calls for judgment and comparison, a comparison of what is in principle incomparable, for every being is unique; every other is unique. (Levinas [1982b] 1998, 104)[22]

For Levinas, our relation to the other is always already ethical: it affects us in the imperative, not the indicative. He does not try to justify this relation or explain its basis in other terms. To many philosophers, this will seem like an abdication of responsibility. What grounds the ethical phenomena Levinas describes? What cognitive relation justifies love at first sight and mediates personal concern, a form of concern that structures ethical thought? Since the ethical supervenes on the nonethical, there must be an answer to this question.[23] Isn't that where personal acquaintance comes in? As I read him, however, Levinas does not believe that the gap can be filled.[24] I think he is right to see a difficulty here. It is hard to say what personal acquaintance is in terms that are both extensionally adequate and account for its ethical role.

In Section 1, we considered and dismissed some simple views: personal acquaintance is not "knowing who" or objectual knowledge or rigidified description. We did not draw an obvious connection, between personal acquaintance and "acquaintance" as a term of art in the philosophy of mind. For Russell (1910–1911) and others, acquaintance with particulars is what makes them available as direct objects of thought.

Russell's views about this topic evolved over time, and they are subject to interpretive dispute, but in his early phase, he seems to have believed that we are acquainted only with sense data, universals, and the self. That idea has not fared well, and many are now skeptical of any role for acquaintance as a condition of "singular thought."[25] For those who are sympathetic to the idea, the paradigm of acquaintance is perceptual contact of the sort that sustains demonstrative reference.[26] This looks promising at first. Perceptual contact is present in love at first sight and the case in which you see the drowning M; it is absent when you think of the shortest spy or the person who is drowning on the right. Perhaps the singular concepts involved in personal concern and the reasons to which it responds are concepts that were formed on the basis of perception.

The problem is that it is not clear why perceptual contact, past or present, should have the ethical significance that personal acquaintance does. Why should seeing someone, or having seen them in the past, make it rational to give priority to their needs, to save their life at the cost of three? Why should we organize our concern for individuals by perceptual acquaintance, not description? There are extensional problems, too. If you are looking at someone but take them to be a statue, you are not personally acquainted with them, though you are in a position to engage in acquaintance-based thought: that looks like a statue to me.

Personal acquaintance may involve perceptual contact, but perceptual contact is not enough. What can we add to it in order to explain why personal acquaintance matters? One idea is to look at the facts to which we gain perceptual access. Personal acquaintance might involve perceptual contact of a kind that affords perceptual knowledge of properties that matter, morally speaking. For instance, it might allow for knowledge of mental states. When we are personally acquainted with someone, the suggestion runs, we can perceive their joy and suffering, weal and woe. Whether or not that is true, however, it is doubly unpromising. First, it gets the extension wrong. If we can perceive human suffering, why not the suffering of nonhuman animals, who lack moral standing of the sort at issue here? Second, it is hard to see why the perception of suffering, or its possibility, should matter more than knowledge of human suffering acquired by other means. Why would the suffering of someone perceptually given to me count for more than the suffering of the person on the bridge? The second problem applies to variations of this approach that turn on perceptual access to specifically human qualities, to perception of the face or mind or body that brings it under concepts specific to human life. Views of this kind fare better extensionally, but they do not explain the moral weight of personal acquaintance. If it is simply a matter of how we know about the other, why should personal acquaintance matter in the ways it does? For Levinas, "[the] encounter with the face is not an act of seeing; it is not perceptual or judgmental" (Morgan 2007, 75; see also 92).

What goes missing in the turn to perceptual knowledge is the practical dimension of personal acquaintance. One way to fill this deficit is to the stress the role of perceptual contact as a basis for human interaction. Personal acquaintance matters, on this more Kantian approach, because it allows us to act and reason together. For Christine Korsgaard (1993, 298), "the violation of a deontological constraint *always* involves an agent and a victim, and thus . . . deontological

328 RETHINKING THE VALUE OF HUMANITY

reasons are always shared reasons. They cannot be the personal property of individual agents. Instead, they supervene on the relationships of people who interact with one another. They are intersubjective reasons." That might explain why personal acquaintance counts. It is in the spirit of Stephen Darwall's (2006) invocation of the "second-person standpoint," the point of view from which we make claims on one another, holding each other accountable, you and I.

Is personal acquaintance reciprocal recognition or the nexus of rational wills? I don't believe it is. The proposal could take various forms, but they share two basic flaws. The more mundane objection is again extensional. Human beings with whom we cannot interact as agents have full moral standing. They are rational objects of love and personal concern. This is true even when they lack the potential to achieve the relevant forms of reciprocity. I don't know how to prove that infants with irreparable cognitive disabilities and people in persistent vegetative states are morally equal to us, and I do not think the implications of this fact are clear, but I am quite sure that it is true.[27]

The less mundane objection is phenomenological. Though Darwall cites both Levinas and Martin Buber ([1923] 1970) as precedents for the second-person standpoint, their views are not the same.[28] Buber appeals to the reciprocity of the "I-Thou" relation. Levinas emphatically does not.

> [The] relationship with the other is not symmetrical, it is not at all as in Martin Buber. When I say *Thou* to an *I*, to a me, according to Buber I would always have that me before me as the one who says Thou to me. Consequently, there would be a reciprocal relationship. According to my analysis, on the other hand, in the relation to the Face, it is asymmetry that is affirmed: at the outset I hardly care what the other is with respect to me, that is his own business; for me, he is above all the one I am responsible for. (Levinas [1982b] 1998, 105)

> One of the themes of *Totality and Infinity* . . . is that the intersubjective relationship is a non-symmetrical relationship. In this sense, I am responsible for the other without waiting for reciprocity, were I to die for it. Reciprocity is *his* affair. (Levinas [1982a] 1985, 98; see also Morgan 2007, 62)

On this point, I think Levinas is right. The phenomenology of personal acquaintance is not mutual or interactive: the demand for personal concern is unilateral. It is about what I owe to you, not what we owe to one another.[29] This ethical reality is obscured by the Kantian focus on the second person. We should not conflate attention to relational phenomena in ethics—not just personal concern but the relational or bipolar notion of wronging an individual—with appeal to reciprocal recognition.[30] The second person matters, but it is not essential to "directed duty."

OTHER PEOPLE 329

Though it is impossible to survey every option, I hope you can begin to see how hard it is to describe the nature of personal acquaintance itself: to identify a psychological relation we can bear only to those with full moral standing, a relation that justifies love and necessitates personal concern. It is no accident that Levinas does not describe the basis of the ethical relation; he is not being willfully obscure. There is an echo of Wittgenstein (1953, §217) in his refusal: "If I have exhausted the justifications I have reached bedrock, and my spade is turned." Cora Diamond (1991, 55) takes a similar view of membership in the moral community:

> The sense of mystery surrounding our lives, the feeling of solidarity in mysterious origin and uncertain fate: this binds us to each other, and the binding meant includes the dead and the unborn, and those who bear on their faces "a look of blank idiocy," those who lack all power of speech, those behind whose vacant eyes there lurks "a soul in mute eclipse." I am not arguing that we have a moral obligation to feel a sense of solidarity with all other human beings because of some natural or supernatural property or group of properties which we all have, contingently or necessarily. I am arguing, though, that there is no need to find such a ground.

Levinas in fact goes further. My relation to the other is ethical through and through: it lacks any rational-psychological ground. Nor can its content be expressed in words. This relation is presupposed by communicative speech, which is a condition of language and so of rational thought. (Like many philosophers, Levinas sees a distinction in kind between our mental lives and the "nonconceptual" psychology of nonlinguistic animals.) If thought depends on language, which depends in turn on our ethical relation to the other, this relation is a precondition of openness to the world: "the order of meaning, which seems to me primary, is precisely what comes to us from the interhuman relationship, so that the Face, with all its meaningfulness as brought out by analysis, is the beginning of intelligibility" (Levinas [1982b] 1998, 103). Since the relation is prelinguistic, and thus preconceptual, we cannot express with concepts how it represents the other. The ethics of the face, of love and personal concern, is the transcendental origin of thought, as such.[31]

This is the argument of *Totality and Infinity*, in brief.[32] It is transcendental in two ways. First, the ethical relation is transcendental in that it cannot be conceptualized: it is fundamentally inexpressible. Second, the argument is transcendental in a Kantian sense: it aims to undermine a skeptical threat by showing how the skeptic's position assumes or implies the very thing she purports to doubt. In this case, the moral skeptic cannot think conceptually without relying on a public language that depends in turn on her ethical acknowledgment of the

330 RETHINKING THE VALUE OF HUMANITY

other. For Levinas ([1961] 1969, 198), "[to] kill is not to dominate but to annihilate; it is to renounce comprehension absolutely."

I have sketched this argument not because I accept it but to give a more adequate view of Levinas on the ethical roots of metaphysics, and to explain how the ineluctably ethical character of personal acquaintance or the face might bear on moral philosophy. Those are topics to pursue elsewhere. I want to return, instead, to the supervenience of the ethical: the pressure to insist that the justification of love and personal concern derives from a relation to the other we can specify in other terms. As we have seen, it is difficult to meet this pressure, to give a psychological account of personal acquaintance, of the relation that makes love rational and calls for personal concern. Must we concede that, in this respect, morality is groundless?

Perhaps there is another way. Suppose, to begin with, that love and personal concern are natural kinds, emotions that play particular, distinctive roles in human life. Suppose, further, that they are regulated by a relation, R, that can be specified in psychological terms. And adopt the conjecture that R is personal acquaintance. Human beings feel love or personal concern for those with whom they are personally acquainted, not those who are known to them merely by name or by minimal description, like "the one on the right" or "the shortest spy." We should treat this as a generic proposition, a claim about what is characteristic of us that allows for exceptional cases, in which our emotions are misdirected. The psychological relation we are targeting is one by which they are naturally regulated, though the regulation may be imperfect. Suppose, finally, that the psychological relation thus described is one that relates human beings only to those with full moral standing: presumably, in the first instance, other human beings. We cannot be personally acquainted with inanimate objects or with nonhuman animals of the sort we encounter on Earth.

The discussion so far has asked, in effect, why relation R would justify love and necessitate personal concern. It treats our hypothesized emotions as if they were in need of external vindication, holding human nature up to a normative standard independent of us. Could that be a mistake? What if we insist that human nature, and the facts of human life, play a constitutive role in ethics, pursuing a line of thought that descends from Aristotle (see Foot 2001; Thompson 2013)? That a human response is rational or justified is not independent of the fact that this response, or affirmation of this response, is functional for us, where the standards of functioning derive from the natural history of human life. We need not read the virtues directly or naïvely from the book of human nature in order to accept some measure of constitutive dependence. In fact, we had better not, unless we believe that human beings are by nature perfectly good. The devil is in the details.[33] But the approach has interest, in part because it is the only way we have seen, thus far, to reconcile the ethics of personal acquaintance with its psychological grounds. On this view, personal acquaintance matters not because it ought to play a certain role in human life, by standards independent of human life, but because of the role it characteristically plays: it is the relation that underlies both love and personal concern. For the neo-Aristotelian, this fact about human life has ethical significance. Personal concern is called for, and love is justified, whenever they are humanly possible.

There is more to say in defense of these ideas. Because I don't know how to say it, I want to end, instead, by placing the puzzle of personal acquaintance in a wider context of reflection on human values. At the beginning of Section 1, I assumed without argument that human beings have an ethical significance that is not shared by other terrestrial animals. Our interests count for more than theirs, and we have rights against each other they do not possess. Positions of this sort have acquired a very bad name. Don't they reflect an odious "speciesism"?[34] It helps to emphasize their relational character: they are about the significance we have for one another, not about the significance of human beings in some absolute sense, as though we should matter more to rational Martians than they do to themselves. But even with this proviso, the basic challenge remains. How is such "humanism" (as I prefer) morally better than racism or sexism, attributing ethical significance to brute biological difference?[35] This question, which casts doubt on the distinctive value of humanity, has less force if human nature is involved in the foundations of ethics. If human beings by nature respond to one another in distinctive ways, as with love or personal concern, and this fact plays a constitutive role in how it is rational to respond, humanism might be true. By contrast, there is no credible theory of ethics on which its foundations appeal to race or sex, nor is there reason to believe that human beings are by nature racist or sexist in ways that might support an Aristotelian defense of such repugnant views.[36] There is, if not a direct argument from humanism to Aristotelian ethics, at least an affiliation between the two.[37]

The ethics of personal acquaintance amplifies and complicates this connection. It is, to begin with, another instance of moral thinking that is difficult to sustain if we deny a constitutive role in ethics to the facts of human life. Perhaps we should not hope to sustain these thoughts, but if we do, we will be led, through Levinas, to Aristotle. At the same time, personal acquaintance puts constraints on the nature of moral standing: it has to mesh with human psychology in ways hypothesized above.

This points to a final question, often raised as an objection to humanism: What about rational Martians? Don't members of other rational species count for us in the same way other humans do? The standard response, which I accept, is that humanism does not imply otherwise. What it suggests is not that rational Martians lack full moral standing but that, if they have it, the ground on which they do so is quite different from the ground that applies to you or me. Whether

332 RETHINKING THE VALUE OF HUMANITY

we should care about the members of another rational species, what rights they have against us: these are open questions. The answers turn on how they relate to one another and to us. (Bernard Williams [2006, 149–152] makes this vivid by imagining rational predators who come from outer space.)

The idea of personal acquaintance introduces something new. For there is nothing in the psychology of love or personal concern that prevents us from being personally acquainted with nonhuman beings. One thing we learn from unimaginative science fiction, in which the aliens are mostly humanoid, is that love across species boundaries makes sense. The same is true of personal concern. If it is rational to love the members of another rational species, their moral standing should not be in doubt. The ethics of personal acquaintance is not humanist in giving special weight to specifically human life. It is humanist in treating every human being as a moral equal and, in its Aristotelian form, in giving special weight to human values, values that may be cosmically cosmopolitan.

We have traveled far along a speculative path. Let us go back to the start. I have argued that personal acquaintance plays a crucial role in the permissive view of love, and in the idea of personal concern that is brought into focus by ex ante contractualism and Opaque Footbridge. If we want to make sense of these phenomena, we need an ethics of personal acquaintance. But it is hard to say what personal acquaintance is in terms that would explain why it justifies love and calls for personal concern. We have considered an approach that has some promise, one that draws on Aristotle, echoing Levinas without his quietism. Personal acquaintance is a cognitive relation whose significance for us can be explained by giving an essential role in ethics to the facts of human life. If this is wrong, we are left with a serious, unsolved puzzle. Can we make sense of love at first sight, and of concern for individuals, as such?[38]

Notes

1. The example derives from Kaplan 1968, 192–193.
2. Compare Velleman 1999, 353; Setiya 2014, 252–254.
3. Setiya 2014, 258–262, responding to Kolodny 2003.
4. I develop these themes in Setiya 2014, 254–261.
5. The neglect is partial: I appeal to "singular thought" at several points (Setiya 2014, 260n21, 265–266). Velleman (2008, 269–270) has urged that emotions such as love depend on "acquaintance-based thought," though he does not develop the point and it is in tension with his earlier remarks about the attachment of adopted children to birth parents they have never met (see 263–264).
6. The case derives from Anscombe 1967, 17.
7. I provide at least some of it in Setiya 2014.
8. This is a drastic simplification of the theory proposed in Boër and Lycan 1986.

9. On knowing someone well, see Talbert 2015.

10. A case of particular interest is self-love. Surely this does not depend on the belief that you are a person or a human being or have moral standing. Nor, as I have argued elsewhere (Setiya 2015), does it rest on beliefs about who you are. Instead, it turns on personal acquaintance with yourself.

11. Contributions include Scanlon 1998, 208–209; Reibetanz 1998; Ashford 2003; Lenman 2008; Fried 2012; James 2012; Dougherty 2013; Kumar 2015; Frick 2015; Horton 2017.

12. The likelihood is > 0.99 that 1,000 children ± 100 will die (Frick 2015, 183n14).

13. On the extension from known to knowable victims, see Frick 2015, 191–193. I return to this below.

14. Unfortunately, Frick does not discuss this case, but he considers a variant of Mass Vaccination (Known Victims) in which the genetic test is very costly, and concludes, on ex ante contractualist lines, that it is permissible to choose Vaccine B; see Frick 2015, 193–194.

15. For a similar argument, see Horton 2017, 69–70.

16. His strategy is to decompose your action into six, each of which affects only one individual, improving their prospects without affecting anyone else. For details, see Hare 2016, §4.

17. I object to it in Setiya 2020.

18. A question raised about a similar case by Elizabeth Harman (2015, 870), in her review of Hare 2013. For related discussion, see Mahtani 2017.

19. As I argue in Setiya (2020), there is a fourth route, too, through the nature of respect for rights.

20. I develop this contrast in Setiya 2020.

21. I am no expert on Levinas, but I have been inspired by his writings. Michael Morgan's (2007) *Discovering Levinas* is an invaluable guide; I have also been helped by Perpich 2008.

22. On the particularity of ethics in Levinas, see Morgan 2007, 61, 79–80.

23. I discuss supervenience in Setiya 2012, 8–11.

24. Here I follow Morgan (2007, 46–50); see also Perpich 2008, 51–54, 74–75, 115–117.

25. For a recent critique, see Hawthorne and Manley (2012, chap. 3). On the relation between Russellian acquaintance and knowledge of other people, see Kremer 2015.

26. See, for instance, Dickie 2015, chap. 4.

27. I defend this view in Setiya 2018.

28. On Levinas, see Darwall (2006, 21–22n44); on Buber, see Darwall (2006, 39–40).

29. Levinas ([1982b] 1998, 106, 109) finds a deeper asymmetry in the ethical relation: "If there were only two of us in the world, there wouldn't be any problem: it is the other who goes before me. . . . The only absolute value is the human possibility of giving the other priority over oneself." I don't think this is right, either in substance (one is not required to give the other priority over oneself) or in form. Since the ethical relation is reflexive, it cannot involve the priority of an other. We are personally acquainted with ourselves.

334 RETHINKING THE VALUE OF HUMANITY

30. This distortion affects even those who resist the Kantian line. In a broadly Aristotelian approach to bipolarity, Michael Thompson (2004, 348, 367–372) assumes that "relations of right" are fundamentally reciprocal: in the paradigm case, they are recognized on both sides, though there may be marginal occasions in which the party who is wronged is unable to recognize the obligation of the other. If I understand him, Levinas would question this assumption.

31. "Preexisting the disclosure of being in general taken as basis of knowledge and as meaning of being is the relation with the existent that expresses himself; preexisting the plane of ontology is the ethical plane" (Levinas [1961] 1965, 201).

32. See, especially, Levinas (1961) 1965, 72–81, 194–219. The argument is explored by Morgan (2007, 52–55) and Perpich (2008, 132–135, 140–149). An early version appears in Levinas (1953) 1998, 18.

33. If we focus on practical rationality, the simplest view identifies this trait with the proper functioning of our psychology with respect to practical thought. I find it more plausible to begin with ethical judgment as a capacity that regulates human life; practical rationality is what this form of judgment tracks when it is functioning well. I defend this sort of view, under the heading of "Natural Externalism," in Setiya 2012, chap. 4.

34. The term was coined by Peter Singer (1975, 6).

35. This challenge is central to Singer's (1975) argument; for a more recent discussion, see McMahan 2005, §3.

36. I defend this claim in Setiya 2012, 142–158.

37. I pursue this connection in Setiya 2018.

38. For discussion of this material, I am grateful to Gregory Antill, Marcia Baron, Anastasia Berg, Ian Blecher, Paul Boswell, Matt Boyle, Jason Bridges, Sarah Buss, Alex Byrne, Imogen Dickie, Jimmy Doyle, Kyla Ebels-Duggan, Camil Golub, Marah Gubar, Matthias Haase, Caspar Hare, Samia Hesni, Abby Jaques, A. J. Julius, Irad Kimhi, Andy Koppelman, Michael Kremer, Ben Laurence, Jonathan Lear, Michael Morgan, Anselm Müller, Sasha Newton, Ryan Preston-Roedder, Tamar Schapiro, Paul Schofield, Will Small, Jack Spencer, David Sussman, Daniel Telech, Nandi Theunissen, Quinn White, Stephen White, and Steve Yablo, and to audiences at Brown University, the Normativity Research Group in Montreal, Northwestern University, the University of Chicago, Brandeis University, the University of Arizona, and MIT. Special thanks to Jennifer Lockhart for generous, constructive comments on an earlier draft.

References

Albee, Edward. 2003. *The Goat, or Who Is Sylvia?* London: Penguin.

Anscombe, Gertrude E. M. 1967. "Who Is Wronged?" *Oxford Review* 5: 16–17.

Ashford, Elizabeth. 2003. "The Demandingness of Scanlon's Contractualism." *Ethics* 113: 273–302.

Benton, Matthew. 2017. "Epistemology Personalized." *Philosophical Quarterly* 67: 813–834.

Boër, Steven E., and William G. Lycan. 1986. *Knowing Who.* Cambridge, MA: MIT Press.

OTHER PEOPLE 335

Braun, David. 2006. "Now You Know Who Hong Oak Yun Is." *Philosophical Issues* 16: 24–42.

Buber, Martin. (1923) 1970. *I and Thou*. Translated by W. Kaufmann. New York: Touchstone.

Darwall, Stephen. 2006. *The Second-Person Standpoint*. Cambridge, MA: Harvard University Press.

Diamond, Cora. 1991. "The Importance of Being Human." In *Human Beings*, edited by David Cockburn, 35–62. Cambridge: Cambridge University Press.

Dickie, Imogen. 2015. *Fixing Reference*. Oxford: Oxford University Press.

Dougherty, Tom. 2013. "Aggregation, Beneficence, and Chance." *Journal of Ethics and Social Philosophy* 7: 1–19.

Foot, Philippa. 2001. *Natural Goodness*. Oxford: Oxford University Press.

Frick, Johann. 2015. "Contractualism and Social Risk." *Philosophy and Public Affairs* 43: 175–223.

Fried, Barbara. 2012. "Can Contractualism Save Us from Aggregation?" *Journal of Ethics* 16: 39–66.

Hare, Caspar. 2013. *The Limits of Kindness*. Oxford: Oxford University Press.

Hare, Caspar. 2016. "Should We Wish Well to All?" *Philosophical Review* 125: 451–472.

Harman, Elizabeth. 2015. "Review: Caspar Hare, *The Limits of Kindness*." *Ethics* 125: 868–872.

Hawthorne, John, and David Manley. 2012. *The Reference Book*. Oxford: Oxford University Press.

Horton, Joe. 2017. "Aggregation, Complaints, and Risk." *Philosophy and Public Affairs* 45: 54–81.

James, Aaron. 2012. "Contractualism's (Not So) Slippery Slope." *Legal Theory* 18: 263–292.

Kaplan, David. 1968. "Quantifying In." *Synthese* 19: 178–214.

Kolodny, Niko. 2003. "Love as Valuing a Relationship." *Philosophical Review* 112: 135–189.

Korsgaard, Christine. 1993. "The Reasons We Can Share." In her *Creating the Kingdom of Ends*, 275–310. Cambridge: Cambridge University Press.

Kremer, Michael. 2015. "Russell on Acquaintance, Analysis, and Knowledge of Persons." In *Acquaintance, Knowledge, and Logic*, edited by Donovan Wishon and Bernard Linsky, 129–152. Stanford, CA: CSLI.

Kumar, Rahul. 2015. "Risking and Wronging." *Philosophy and Public Affairs* 43: 27–49.

Lauer, David. 2014. "What Is It to Know Someone?" *Philosophical Topics* 42: 321–344.

Lenman, James. 2008. "Contractualism and Risk Imposition." *Politics, Philosophy, and Economics* 7: 99–122.

Levinas, Emmanuel. (1953) 1998. "Freedom and Command." In *Collected Philosophical Papers*, translated by Alphonso Lingis, 15–23. Pittsburgh, PA: Duquesne University Press,.

Levinas, Emmanuel (1961) 1969. *Totality and Infinity*. Translated by Alphonso Lingis. Pittsburgh, PA: Duquesne University Press.

Levinas, E. (1982a) 1985. *Ethics and Infinity: Conversations with Philippe Nemo*. Translated by Richard A. Cohen. Pittsburgh, PA: Duquesne University Press.

Levinas, Emmanuel (1982b) 1998. "Philosophy, Justice, and Love." In *Entre Nous: On Thinking-of-the-Other*, translated by Michael B. Smith and Barbara Harshav, 103–121. New York: Columbia University Press.

Mahtani, Anna. 2017. "The Ex Ante Pareto Principle." *Journal of Philosophy* 114: 303–323.

McMahan, Jeff. 2005. "Our Fellow Creatures." *Journal of Ethics* 9: 353–380.

Morgan, Michael. 2007. *Discovering Levinas*. Cambridge: Cambridge University Press.

Perpich, Diane. 2008. *The Ethics of Emmanuel Levinas*. Stanford, CA: Stanford University Press.

Pettit, Philip. 1997. "Love and Its Place in Moral Discourse." In *Love Analyzed*, edited by Roger E. Lamb, 153–163. Boulder, CO: Westview Press.

Reibetanz, Sophia. 1998. "Contractualism and Aggregation." *Ethics* 108: 296–311.

Russell, Bertrand. 1910–1911. "Knowledge by Acquaintance and Knowledge by Description." *Proceedings of the Aristotelian Society* 11: 101–128.

Scanlon, Thomas M. 1998. *What We Owe to Each Other*. Cambridge, MA: Harvard University Press.

Setiya, Kieran. 2012. *Knowing Right from Wrong*. Oxford: Oxford University Press.

Setiya, Kieran. 2014. "Love and the Value of a Life." *Philosophical Review* 123: 251–280.

Setiya, Kieran. 2015. "Selfish Reasons." *Ergo* 2: 445–472.

Setiya, Kieran. 2018. "Humanism." *Journal of the American Philosophical Association* 4: 452–470.

Setiya, Kieran. 2020. "Ignorance, Beneficence, and Rights." *Journal of Moral Philosophy* 17: 56–74.

Singer, Peter. 1975. *Animal Liberation*. New York: Random House.

Talbert, Bonnie. 2015. "Knowing Other People: A Second-Person Framework." *Ratio* 28: 190–206.

Taurek, John. 1977. "Should the Numbers Count?" *Philosophy and Public Affairs* 6: 293–316.

Thompson, Michael. 2004. "What Is It to Wrong Someone?" In *Reason and Value*, edited by R. Jay Wallace, Philip Pettit, Samuel Scheffler, and Michael Smith, 333–384. Oxford: Oxford University Press.

Thompson, Michael. 2013. "Forms of Nature: 'First,' 'Second,' 'Living,' 'Rational,' and 'Phronetic.'" In *Freiheit Stuttgarter Hegel-Kongress 2011*, edited by Gunnar Hindrichs and Axel Honneth, 701–735. Frankfurt: Klostermann.

Thomson, Judith J. 1976. "Killing, Letting Die, and the Trolley Problem." *The Monist* 59: 204–217.

Velleman, J. David. 1999. "Love as a Moral Emotion." *Ethics* 109: 338–374.

Velleman, J. David. 2008. "Persons in Prospect." *Philosophy and Public Affairs* 36: 221–288.

Williams, B. 2006. "The Human Prejudice." In *Philosophy as a Humanistic Discipline*, edited by A. W. Moore, 135–152. Princeton, NJ: Princeton University Press.

Wittgenstein, Ludwig. 1953. *Philosophical Investigations*. Translated by Gertrude E. M. Anscombe. Oxford: Basil Blackwell.

14

Learning from Love: Reasoning, Respect, and the Value of a Person

Kyla Ebels-Duggan

> We mourn the death of #TimothyCaughman, a fellow human being murdered for being Black.
>
> —The King Center, public Facebook post

At a climactic moment in *The Sources of Normativity* Christine Korsgaard (1996b, 123) declares, "It follows from this argument that human beings are valuable. Enlightenment morality is true." Here, she purports to accomplish what many take to be the defining aim of moral philosophy. If you think that what philosophers do is to try to construct non-question-begging, valid arguments for their positions, then it seems a moral philosopher would have to aim to reason to moral convictions. Korsgaard's argument comes closer to accomplishing this ambitious aim than any other of which I am aware.

But I want to consider whether we can argue to moral convictions at all, whether anything would count as the sort of vindication of morality's authority that this conception of moral philosophy seeks. I agree that human beings are valuable. In fact I think that each of us has the sort of value beyond price that Kant calls *dignity*. And I agree that what Korsgaard calls "enlightenment morality," an overriding requirement to treat each person in accord with this value, is authoritative for us. We have sufficient reason for affirming these things and acting from these convictions and failing to do so would be wrong. But I don't think that we can arrive at the attitudes constituting these commitments just through argument or reasoning. Moreover, the idea that we can, and the attendant thought that we have a rational obligation to try, carries certain moral dangers. I will argue that this way of thinking of the warrant for our moral commitments is itself in tension with these commitments.

On my view, then, we have sufficient reasons for, but cannot reason to, central moral commitments. But if we cannot reason to our moral commitments, cannot vindicate them with philosophical argument, what does it mean to have reasons for them, and what could make it the case that we do? I will argue that

Kyla Ebels-Duggan, *Learning from Love: Reasoning, Respect, and the Value of a Person* In: *Rethinking the Value of Humanity*. Edited by: Sarah Buss and L. Nandi Theunissen, Oxford University Press. © Oxford University Press 2023. DOI: 10.1093/oso/9780197539361.003.0015

338 RETHINKING THE VALUE OF HUMANITY

we can make progress on these questions by thinking about love. Contemporary moral philosophers often treat interpersonal love as in presumptive conflict with a distinctively moral attitude or outlook. The tension arises insofar as morality demands impartial regard for everyone, while love requires partiality toward those whom we love. Considered this way the philosophical task becomes either protecting the moral demand against the encroachments of personal attachment or protecting the integrity of interpersonal relationships against the demands of an impersonal moral law.[1] But important ethical traditions have always placed love at the very center of the moral life. The biblical tradition, for example, presents love of God and of one's neighbor as the most fundamental moral demand, the summary of the law.[2] Here I join a small but growing group of contemporary moral philosophers who endorse a view in this spirit.[3]

I will argue that three sorts of experiences can reveal to us the value of other human beings, the value to which morality responds: love for particular individuals; singular respect, an experience structurally similar to love; and witness of the love of others. In Section 1, I argue that our experience of love gives us insight into the value of individuals. It discloses the content of the concept of *the value of humanity*, a concept that figures centrally in Kantian moral theory and more generally in any ethical view that recognizes the incommensurable value of each person.[4] In Section 2, I argue that this value cannot be reduced to any set of properties, whether natural or nonnatural. In Sections 3–5, I argue that three experiences—love, singular respect, and the witness of the love of others—can provide grounds for attributing value to others, grounds that reasoning alone could not deliver. I conclude with some reflections on the implications of all of this for the practice of moral philosophy.

1. Learning from Love: The Value of Humanity

Korsgaard's argument concludes: *human beings are valuable*. Let's restate this as *each person has infinite and irreplaceable value* and call that claim *the moral conclusion*. The moral conclusion can also take the form of an intention—what Kant would call a maxim or principle of action—to treat everyone in accord with this value, or as this value demands. Affirmation of the moral conclusion in both of these forms is at least partially constitutive of a robust moral commitment.

But to comprehend what we affirm or commit to when we take up these attitudes, and so be in a position to draw the moral conclusion, we need an understanding of the value that human beings have. To put it in cognitive terms, we need to be in possession of the concept of what Kant calls *the value of humanity* or *dignity,* value beyond price (4:434–436).[5] In this section, I argue that loving an individual provides a route to apprehending the value that we are here trying to name. Love is not an attitude to which we can reason, yet it is a contentful attitude, not merely a passive state. Its content includes ascribing value to the beloved and taking this value to be both nonfungible and independent of one's own attitudes toward the beloved. Value of that kind is what the moral conclusion ascribes to all.

Judgments ascribing color concepts to objects provide a helpful analogy to the moral conclusion here. We can make, and can reason to, such judgments about objects that we do not see and have not seen. But we can understand these judgments only if we have prior perceptual experience that puts us in a position to use the color concepts that figure in them. In Frank Jackson's (1986) famous case, Mary, the color scientist who has lived only in a black and white room, needs to see red before she knows what red looks like or what redness is.[6] No amount of descriptive information that could be available by mere report could put her in full possession of the color concept.[7] My suggestion is that the concept of the value of humanity is like redness in this way, and that loving an individual can play a role analogous to seeing red things. We can *sincerely judge* of a person that she has dignity without loving her, and can sincerely judge that everyone has dignity without loving each of them, and we can act from these judgments. But we can grasp the content of these judgments, and so take up the distinctively moral attitude, only if we appreciate the value of some particular individuals. Interpersonal love is our normal route to this appreciation.

The analogy with seeing color holds insofar as loving someone constitutively involves experiencing him as valuable. When you love someone you regard him as having great and irreplaceable worth, a value that Kant rightly says cannot be reduced to price. Our ascription of this value to those we love is made searingly clear in experiences of loss, the grief of departure and especially of death (cf. Gaita 1991; Brewer 2018). Here we experience viscerally what we try to say about a person when we say that he has infinite and irreplaceable value. But it is not only these negative moments that reveal the value in question. If we pay attention—or in those moments of grace in which our attention is arrested—we can find ourselves overwhelmed by the value of the individual person in front of us.[8] Anyone who has experienced love knows what this is like, and reflection on such experiences gives us a grasp on what we mean by talk of the infinite and irreplaceable worth of a person.

But loving a person is not just a matter of experiencing her *as if* she has this value. It involves something much more like an endorsement of this idea. Such endorsement need not be explicit, of course. Love doesn't require formulating the thought: *this person is of infinite and irreplaceable worth.* (Perhaps only a philosopher would think such a thought.) But regarding the experience of the beloved's value as misleading or illusory, or thinking that her worth could be expressed as a price or exchange value, would be in tension with loving her.[9] That is to say,

340   RETHINKING THE VALUE OF HUMANITY

there is a rational incompatibility between loving a person and denying that that person has nonfungible worth. We may sometimes have grounds for attributing to a person both love for another and a denial of his incomparable worth, just as we can have grounds to attribute a pair of contradictory beliefs to someone. But in both of these cases, holding this combination of attitudes amounts to a serious rational failing on the part of the agent, one that borders on unintelligibility: the agent should take each attitude in the pair to be a decisive consideration against the other.

Love cannot simply be assimilated to belief or to judgment. Unlike beliefs, love cannot be acquired through testimony or drawn as the conclusion of explicit reasoning (cf. Ebels-Duggan 2019).[10] Yet the rational incompatibility between love and judgments about the value of the beloved shows that love is also not just a passive experience or a matter of things appearing to you in a certain way, but an attitude that involves a commitment to the idea that the beloved is incomparably valuable. In this way, love differs from seeing color and shares something with belief. You can—without any rational failing—see something as blue while simultaneously judging that the experience is illusory. You cannot rationally believe that it is blue while judging that your belief is wrong. Unlike perception, belief contains a built-in concern about the possibility of a difference between appearance and reality, and love is like belief in this way.[11]

* * *

So far I have claimed that to love someone involves experiencing him as having great and nonfungible value and is not compatible with regarding this experience as illusory. Next I argue that love is also incompatible with the idea that the value of the person you love depends on your attitudes toward him or the relationship in which you stand to him. In this way loving a person involves thinking of his value as objective and in important ways unconditional.

To bring this out, I'm going to follow Kant's strategy in *Groundwork I*, contrasting a variety of attitudes that I might express in treating you well. Kant is interested in isolating a distinctively moral attitude, but his approach can also help us identify the attitude that is distinctive of interpersonal love. It's no accident that a parallel strategy works in both of these cases if I am right in thinking that both attitudes are responses to, or apprehensions of, the value of humanity.

Kant begins with the case of the honest merchant, who treats another as he deserves only because doing so serves the merchant's self-interest, in particular business interests that are independent of any interests he might have in standing in a morally decent relationship with his customers. Kant says that, though the merchant's actions accord with duty, they lack moral worth. The actions are permissible, even required of him, but in so acting he expresses

LEARNING FROM LOVE   341

no distinctively moral attitude toward his customers. Similarly, action motivated by narrow self-interest would also fail to express love. Regarding the reasons that you have to treat someone well as wholly conditioned on prior, independent interests of your own would be incompatible with valuing her as you must in order to love her.[12]

Suppose that, instead, I treat you well because it *pleases me* to do so. The reasons on which I act in this case are not conditioned on some independent interest of mine, but they are conditioned on my own preferences: I enjoy or take pleasure in interactions that contribute to your well-being or the advancement of your interests. I like playing the role of benefactor. Kant's Sympathetic Person, whom he describes as one who "without any other motive of vanity or self-interest [finds] an inner satisfaction in spreading joy and can take delight in the satisfaction of others so far as it is [his] own work," can be understood in this way (4:398–399).[13] We may think that there is something more admirable here than in the first case, but taking your interests seriously because it's something that I enjoy doing still fails as an expression of a distinctively moral attitude. By the same token, I cannot love you well while at the same time thinking of the actions that I take with respect to you as worth doing only because I happen to enjoy them (cf. Lockhart 2017). The problem here is that your value or standing as a distinct individual with authority to make claims on my action is playing no role at all.

Suppose, then, that I treat you as you deserve to be treated just because I like *you*. My positive regard makes me willing to sacrifice for you and to treat you well even in instances in which I don't feel like or enjoy doing so. That sets this case apart from the second one. Moreover, there's plausibly a response to your own value here. But if my actions are to express love, I can't regard the reasons that I have to treat you well as merely a function of my own responses to you. If I combine my liking of you with the view that, were I not fond of you, you would have no claim on me, this would provide grounds for rejecting my claim that I love you. This is the thought that T. M. Scanlon (1998, 164–165) elicits when he points out that there would be something disconcerting about a friend who would steal a kidney for you. Such willingness indicates that your friend regards the kidneys of those who are not his friends as available for his use. And this, in turn, suggests that he would also be willing to steal your kidney were you not his friend. But regarding your standing to claim control over your own body as conditioned on his preferences in this way is incompatible with the regard one should have for a friend.

This point does need to be made with some care: loving someone is compatible with thinking that contingent preferences figure in why you love *that* person rather than some other person. Friendships or romantic partnerships might, perfectly appropriately, depend in part on brute preferences of that

342 RETHINKING THE VALUE OF HUMANITY

kind. Other sorts of relationships may depend importantly on contingent facts. Love for one's own children seems to be like that. I can love my child while acknowledging that this one *just happens* to be mine, and that, had things happened differently, I would have some other child, whom I would love just as much. But the question I have in view concerns not the comparison between loving one person and loving some other one, but rather whether *love,* and the profound appreciation and valuing of a person that it involves, is an appropriate, justified, or rationally warranted response to the person in question.[14] I am claiming that it is internal to love to ascribe to the beloved a value that makes it so. By contrast with, say, a taste for chocolate, love cannot be regarded from the inside as merely the expression of some preference of the lover. I can think that under different circumstances I would have loved another child just as much, but I cannot think that the justification or rational warrant of my love for this child depends only on what I happen to like or enjoy.

In contrast to all of these cases, then, acting *out of love for you* requires thinking of you as having a value to which I would have to respond regardless of whether I like you, enjoy doing things for you, or find it in my interest to do so. Such value is independent of the lover, and so one to which anyone must respond.[15] Love commits us to the idea that the object of love is of value, and this value is more than agent-relative. This is not to say that loving you commits me to thinking that anyone must *love* you. But I cannot both love you and regard your value as depending solely on me. In loving you, I take your value to be objective, in the sense that it is not conditioned by my particular attitudes and response, and so provides reasons to which anyone must respond. We may think of love as the most preferential of interpersonal attitudes. Nevertheless, it involves responsiveness to a value that we must regard as independent of our preferences.

David Velleman (2006, 374) evocatively claims that *love is a moral education.* In this section I have tried to explain why this might be so. In order to take up the moral attitude, we need some way of marshaling the conceptual resources involved in attributing dignity to each person. My suggestion is that we can find these resources in love. To love someone is to experience that person as valuable and is not rationally compatible with denying his value. Moreover, the value that we cannot deny has at least these two features: it is nonfungible; it cannot be bought or sold for any price.[16] And it is unconditioned by our own attitudes or reactions toward the person. I claim that it is this same value, the value of humanity or dignity—objective value beyond price—that the moral conclusion attributes and to which moral commitment responds.[17]

2. Understanding the Value of Humanity: Against the Property View

I have spoken of *the value of humanity*, used the phrase "great and irreplaceable worth," and also suggested that the value in question is what Kant names *dignity* and contrasts with price. But I find all of this language inadequate to name or talk about the value that a person has. Philosophers have made other attempts as well. Talk of the *humanity, personhood, individuality, preciousness*, or *sacredness* of the person, of the *soul, the person herself*, or her *real self*, or—among Kantians—her *rational nature* or *noumenal self* can all be understood as attempts to refer to this value, but none seems quite up to the task.[18] While it would be interesting to reflect on the distinctive shortcomings of each, I think it is no accident that all fail. The problem here is not merely that we haven't yet hit upon the right term. Instead, the problem—at least one problem—is that any such term can sound as if it is trying to name some part or property of a person, the sort of thing that could be described, understood, and so considered apart from an experience such as love, and could provide the necessary and sufficient condition for something—someone—to be the intelligible object of love.[19] But this way of understanding a person's value is doomed to fail.

Humanity might suggest—at least to those not steeped in Kant's writing— membership in a biological species. *Personhood, individuality*, or *rational nature* might be thought to pick out some set of capacities, for reasoning or for valuing or setting ends, and to invite further inquiry about what these capacities may be. It is less tempting to understand the *soul* or *noumenal self* in naturalistic terms, but if we are willing to admit such entities into our ontology, it is then tempting to think of them on a descriptive model, as naming some immaterial part that a being could have or fail to have, a sort of glowing ball inside her (cf. Korsgaard 2008, 132–135). Even the phrase "the value of the person" can sound as if refers to some such part or entity. But when we talk about a person's value or dignity, it's not some feature or property of her, but rather *her*, her self, the very one that can be loved, that we are trying to talk about.[20]

If we try to think of value as a part or property of a person, we seem to have only two choices. On the one hand, we can think of it as naming some set of ordinary natural properties.[21] But to think that a person has value beyond price is not the same as believing that she possesses any such set of properties. All such beliefs face the seemingly unbridgeable gap between the descriptive and the normative that Moore (1993, 66–69) identified in his famous open question argument. Someone might agree that a being has the relevant properties, yet refuse—explicitly or just in practice—to regard her as valuable. Such a person may be making a serious, morally significant error, but we cannot expose this

344 RETHINKING THE VALUE OF HUMANITY

error merely by analyzing the concepts that she uses or bringing to light internal tensions in her commitments. She may be fully cognizant of what these natural properties amount to without this making her error manifest to her (cf. Korsgaard 2008; Scanlon 1998, 95–100; Brewer 2009, chap. 5; Buss 1999). Even so, her attitudes do not seem to contradict one another.[22]

The alternative version of the property view would treat terms like *dignity* as attempts to name the value itself, a nonnatural thing or property of a sui generis metaphysical kind, the glowing ball to which I referred above. I am very doubtful that we can make sense of this idea. But even supposing we could, attributing such a property to others does not seem to capture what we are doing when we value them. Becoming convinced that no such property exists, or even that no such property could exist, would not lead a clear-thinking person to doubt or revise her values or ethical outlook.[23] And conversely, it's not clear that value conceived on this glowing ball model could play the relevant role in our ethical thought, even if we posit its existence. Insofar as we think of value itself as an object to which our terms could refer, or a property that figures in a complete description of the world, the problems that plague the attempt to reduce value to empirical descriptive facts rearise: if value were just part of the world, even a special, mysterious metaphysical part, we should want to know why it makes sense to be specially guided by this part.[24] This way of thinking of the value of a person opens a question that should not be open; it treats as intelligible a question that is not so.

The sort of question that we settle when we ascribe value to a thing is not a question about what objects there are or what properties these objects have. It is, instead, a broadly practical or ethical question about what should guide our actions, ethical thought, and attitudes: a question about what it makes sense to care about and orient ourselves toward, and so how we have reason to live our lives. We sometimes use the terms canvassed at the beginning of this section in a different way, one that is closer to the mark. We speak of a person's humanity, or invoke the fact that someone is "a fellow human being," as the chapter epigraph does. What is said here is not an attempt to clarify, as if it were in doubt, that Timothy Caughman is a member of a biological species or has some capacity or property that someone might have been thinking that he lacked. Nor is it the assertion of a metaphysical thesis. It is, rather, an attempt to make salient that this person is an individual, someone who shares with us and those we love the value in question. His characterization here as a "fellow human being" does not pick out or refer to a property that gives us independent purchase on that value or serve as even the beginning of an account of the necessary and sufficient conditions for having it.[25] Rather this phrase, in this context, depends for its sense on our prior grasp of this value, without which it cannot do the evocative, and so the ethical, work for which it was intended. In speaking about this value we are urging the appropriateness of certain responses, here responses that register the enormity of the tragedy of a person's violent death, while also trying to elicit those responses. If you love or have loved someone, then you have in that experience a touchstone that allows you to apprehend what it means for someone to be a fellow human being in this sense.

So I take the felt inadequacy of the terms to count in favor of, rather than presenting a problem for, the view that I am advocating. It is a symptom of the fact that our grasp on the sort of value that human beings have, our understanding of what we mean when we talk about human dignity, *has to be* informed by experience of individuals who bear this value. Any attempt at ways of talking about the value of a person divorced from such experience will fall flat. Having tried to say something about why any terms may seem inadequate, I will continue to use both "dignity" and "the value of humanity" as interchangeable placeholders for that kind of value that human beings have.

3. Addressing Skeptical Challenges to Love

So far I have argued that loving a person involves ascribing to her the incomparable and unconditional value that Kant calls *dignity*, and that this ascription cannot be reduced to any set of beliefs about her properties, whether natural or nonnatural. But so far this is just a claim about what love *is*. I've not addressed the question of whether we are right to regard other people in this way, whether the ascription of value constitutive of love could be rationally grounded, warranted, or justified. In this section, I turn to justificatory questions and consider skeptical challenges to or doubts about the rational warrant of interpersonal love.[26]

I argue that we have sufficient reasons *for* interpersonal love, though we cannot reason *to* it or fully articulate the reasons for it in the form of an argument. In fact, I will argue for the stronger claim that love is rationally incompatible with thinking that its warrant depends on being in possession of some argument for it. This makes interpersonal love an important counterexample to a powerful philosophical ideal of critical thought, an ideal on which we should seek arguments to vindicate all of our commitments. The best way to make sense of all of this is to think of love as direct appreciation of the beloved, and so of his value, in something like the way that many philosophers think perception is direct awareness of the empirical world. In the next two sections I will argue that two other sorts of experience, singular respect and witness of the love of others, can also disclose this value to us. We cannot arrive at a robust moral outlook absent some such experience.

I've already argued that love involves the endorsement of some content; it is not a mere taste, brute preference, or disposition to act. This is sufficient to establish that love can intelligibly be subjected to justificatory questions and so is the sort of attitude for which we can have reasons. Asking about the justifying reasons for love is not the sort of category mistake that asking for justifying reasons for a headache would be. Here is another way to think of it: love is an activity, something that you can be *doing*. Indeed many people take loving other individuals to be among the most important things that they do. So—as with anything you do—it is possible to ask after not just a causal story about how it is that you came to be in the bodily state of doing it, but also the reasons *why* you do it, and whether these reasons are sufficient.[27]

A skeptic doubts that this query can be satisfactorily answered. That is, he doubts that there are reasons sufficient to warrant interpersonal love. As above, I don't mean that he questions whether it makes sense to pursue some particular kind of *relationship* with a given person. That sort of question has a familiar home in, for instance, earnest conversations between friends who doubt the wisdom of one another's romantic pursuits. Rather, the skeptic questions the value that your love affirms: whether a person is rightly regarded as having value of the kind that we attribute to her when we love her, and so is a fitting object of love at all (again, cf. Helm 2021). Focusing on romantic cases can be misleading here. The content and the import of the question of interest is clearer if we imagine it addressed to a parent concerning her love for her child.[28] In contrast to the romantic case, it is easier to hear the justificatory challenge here as addressing the value of the child, whether she is worth loving, rather than targeting the wisdom of the relationship or offering the thought that a different individual might be a better candidate for a partner in it.

I've claimed that such skeptical challenges concerning the value of the beloved are not nonsense, in the sense that they lack intelligibility or that we have no idea what they could mean. We understand what it is to raise the justificatory question about love, and what it would be to conclude that this question has no satisfactory answer. But I now want to suggest that the skeptic's question is nevertheless meaningless in a different, but crucial, sense: *the question cannot be taken wholly seriously from within the perspective of the love that it seeks to challenge.* The idea that all of our commitments, and most especially our normative commitments, should be subjected to critical scrutiny, and the stronger idea that we should maintain only those that we are able to justify on reflection, is often presented as a guiding philosophical ideal, even as constitutive of doing philosophy. But I claim there is no stance or attitude that would count from the point of view of, for example, a parent as appropriate, yet genuine, critical consideration of the question whether her child is, in truth, valuable in a way that makes her worth loving.

The philosophical literature contains actual instances of skepticism about the value of certain human beings. We see it, for example, with respect to those subject to a range of serious disabilities, especially cognitive disabilities.[29] If the parent of such a person takes it that a philosopher means to present for serious consideration the idea that her child lacks the value that makes love appropriate, what response should that parent have? Situated as they are in the philosophical discourse, these skeptical questions seem to demand answers in the form of an argument, a set of premises leading to the conclusion that the skeptic has called into doubt. Such an argument could be offered as an answer to the skeptic, and could also serve to settle, or resettle, one's own mind if one has been gripped by doubt or has otherwise entered into the skeptical standpoint. I am claiming that no appealing philosophical ideal could demand, or even recommend, that the parents who love these children seriously engage such questions and seek such arguments in defense of their love (cf. Hopwood 2016).

One problem with the suggestion that they should is that argument cannot possibly yield love, or any sort of grasp of the value that we appreciate in love. Seeking arguments is often a sensible, responsible approach when responding to justificatory challenges to your beliefs or intentions. If you call a belief or intention into question, and then reason your way back to it, you will have established it on a firm rational footing, a paradigm of philosophical success. But though a line of reasoning can conclude with a belief or intention, no line of reasoning could conclude with the attitude of love. No one could be moved to share your love by any deduction, nor could any such deduction reestablish love that has been subjected to genuine doubt. In a similar way, we cannot reason our way to aesthetic appreciation of works of art or literature: The attitude in question requires appreciative experience of its object, and so cannot be reached by inference. Just so, loving someone involves encountering, experiencing, and appreciating her value directly. If one were to treat this value as an object of intellectual curiosity, and begin to speculate about it, distancing oneself from a full affirmation of the value by inhabiting the skeptical question, no answer to that question—at least none that takes the form of an argument—would be capable of closing this gap.[30]

A parent who did somehow manage to take up this speculative stance about the value of her child would, thereby, falter in her love for that child. The ideal of critical thought tells you to distance yourself from your commitments and attempt to articulate the reasons for them. But a loving parent cannot suspend or step back from this commitment and then see whether she can work her way back to it through objective consideration of the reasons. Whether their child has value is not a question on which parents should sincerely speculate and so not one that they could argue over in good faith. Love thus provides an important counterexample to this purported philosophical ideal that normative commitments should be subject to critical thought and reasoning.

348 RETHINKING THE VALUE OF HUMANITY

I have claimed that, on the one hand, you cannot reason to love or present an argument for it that would move someone who was genuinely skeptical of its justification. But, on the other hand, love is an intelligible attitude, with content subject to justificatory query and normative standards. The best way to make sense of both of these claims together is to think that what justifies, warrants, or makes sense of love for an individual is that it amounts to direct appreciation of the value of the beloved. Again it may help to compare with knowledge gained through perception. On at least some views, perception involves direct awareness of the material world, and beliefs about the world can be warranted by this awareness rather than by any inference or argument. Argument or reasoning cannot substitute for such awareness as a ground for belief, at least not in a totally general way.[31] On the view that I am defending, love for a person is also best conceived as a way of being in touch with reality, here the reality of that person's value, or, again, the reality of the person herself.[32] That a person has such value is sufficient to justify loving him, and it follows that it can never be a mistake to love a fellow human being.[33]

Both the sufficiency of a person's humanity to justify love for him and the impossibility of reasoning to the attitude of love are apparent in the case of parents seeking to adopt a child. Such parents stand ready to love their child, whoever that child is and without regard to any particular qualities that he has or appeal to any prior relationship that they have with him. Nor is this attitude any sort of error or mistake. The expectant parents would not do better to withhold commitment to their child until they see whether they got a sufficiently good one, one whose qualities or properties make him worthy of love. The fact that he is a child, a bearer of humanity or fellow human being, is enough. On the other hand, though these expectant parents know perfectly well in advance of meeting the child that this will be true of him, and so know that he will be worthy of love, they do not and cannot love *him* until they encounter and come to know him. They cannot use their knowledge that he will be a bearer of humanity as a premise in an argument that concludes with love for him, but can develop this love only through direct experience of him as an individual.

In this section I've argued that there is no skeptical or critical stance that one can take on love that is not itself in tension with love. Further, if one did successfully distance oneself from one's love in this way, there would be no route back to it through argument. And finally, the best sense that we can make of this is to think that what does provide warrant for love is the value of the person that we appreciate in loving her. This last suggestion, that the value that you appreciate in love also provides the justifying grounds for love, may have an air of circularity. It would be circular if it were meant as an argument in support of love that was supposed to answer the skeptic, or that might guide a lover who has taken the skeptic's question seriously, and suspended her love, back to her commitment.

LEARNING FROM LOVE 349

But my point has been that no such argument can be given, none should be attempted, and none is intended here. We do not show that loves meets its justificatory standard via some inference from the fact that the beloved is valuable. Rather, love is warranted because it is a direct appreciation of the beloved herself.

4. Singular Respect

The singular attitude of love takes a particular individual as its object, ascribing value beyond price to *her*. What I have called the moral conclusion is the more general judgment that *all* have dignity, or the intention to treat *everyone* as such. Unlike love, a judgment or intention can stand as the conclusion of an argument or explicit line of reasoning. If you appreciate the value of your beloved, and you recognize that there is no relevant difference between her and others, then you can, in principle, use these two commitments to construct an argument for the moral conclusion:

P1: My beloved has nonfungible and unconditional value.
P2: There is no relevant difference between my beloved and all others.
C: Everyone has nonfungible and unconditional value.

Nevertheless, there remain many sorts of failures of moral commitment, failures to occupy a moral outlook, that reasoning cannot address. Straightaway we might notice that the first premise of this argument refers to the value of a person as disclosed in love. I have been arguing that no line of reasoning would be capable of bringing us to appreciate this value.

Moreover, reasoning alone cannot settle disagreements or doubts about the boundaries of the moral community, about who has dignity or is a bearer of the value of humanity. Disagreements about these boundaries could present as resistance to the second premise.[34] Or someone might accept the second premise, and reason sincerely to the moral conclusion, and yet limit its scope in unwarranted ways. Those who believe that all of the animals fall under the protection of the moral law attribute this sort of error to those who limit membership in the moral community to human beings. Some philosophers argue that certain positions in the philosophy of disability do the same. Arguably, many instances of racial, gender, and other sorts of bias manifest this error. Call this collection of issues *the boundary problem*.

Reasoning can address some limited versions of the boundary problem. In the simplest kind of case, failure to apply the moral principle appropriately arises from false beliefs about those who do not register as having dignity. If such beliefs are the sole obstacle, reasoning that convinces someone to change them would thereby correct the moral failures. But, as I argued above, one might make no such descriptive errors, yet still fail to grasp or appreciate that the members of some group have, or that each one taken individually has, dignity.[35] One can even fail in this way while offering explicit endorsement of the claim that those in question have dignity. It is hard to sort out exactly what is going on with these attitudes, yet we human beings do seem to be tragically susceptible to this sort of failure, especially at the limits of social categories including nationality, gender, race, class, and physical or cognitive abilities.[36]

A person cannot be argued out of, or reason herself out of, this sort of error. Since it does not rest on any mistaken belief, no reasoning to a better belief can correct it. A possible alternative is singular recognition of the value of the individual in question, or of a member of the disfavored group of people. Call this attitude toward another *singular respect*. In contrast to the generalized respect expressed by the moral conclusion, singular respect is an immediate response to a particular individual. It involves an experience of being *struck by* the value of someone's humanity.[37] One could reach for many examples here. Cora Diamond (1978, 477) invokes George Orwell's account of being unable to shoot an enemy soldier whom he saw trying to hold up his trousers while running. Orwell's appreciation of the man's humanity in that moment is singular respect. (Though the example suggests that it is not dignity, as we normally understand it, that calls forth the attitude in question. In fact, vulnerability—and our sense of this vulnerability as shared—is probably more effective.)

Such recognition of value—while not identical with love—shares much in common with it. Like love, singular respect has content but outstrips any belief about or intention concerning a person and cannot be the conclusion of an argument.[38] Just as we cannot reason to love, we cannot reason to this sort of recognition of another's humanity. No more can we reason to a moral outlook that constitutively includes such recognition.[39] But, like love, singular respect is an intelligible, contentful attitude. Affirmation of the great and irreplaceable value of another person, and the claims that this value makes on others, is part of this content.

Raimond Gaita claims that the ascription of value to others characteristic of moral regard is especially clear in the experience of remorse. We might think that, as the grief of loss stands to love, so remorse stands to singular respect: the first element of each pair is a negative experience of the appreciation of the value of the individual characteristic of the second. Gaita (1991, xiv) defines remorse as "[a] pained, bewildered relisation of what it means . . . to wrong someone." Given the ineliminably first-personal character of remorse, I think that he ought rather to say that it is a realization that *I* have done wrong to a particular person, and of the significance of this. Gaita presents a scenario in which you are responsible for the death of a vagabond who was loved by no one. He is impressed with

LEARNING FROM LOVE   351

the fact that it is not only possible, but fully intelligible, to experience remorse over such a death. We might go further still, and suggest that failure to respond with remorse in such a situation would be a moral failure. Since the victim leaves no survivors, remorse cannot be a reaction of concern for them and their suffering. It can only be a way of registering, of experiencing, the violated value of the dead man, who was, after all, a fellow human being.

Singular respect is a reaction to or experience of a particular individual, while the generalized respect embodied in the moral conclusion figures in a belief about or intention toward everyone. In distinguishing them, I don't mean to privilege the former. Though respect as a response to individuals is an important part of a full moral outlook, we cannot get by morally on our susceptibility to being struck by the humanity of our fellows one by one. The generalized judgment or commitment to a principle of respect is also necessary for a complete and robust moral commitment. The person who displays *only* the singular reaction is too much like Kant's Sympathetic Helper and shares his moral weaknesses. His moral commitment is not exactly conditional. He does not and would not think *I will help you only because your plight happens to move me.* But neither is his willingness to help exactly independent of his own responses. By hypothesis he also does not think *I will help you because you deserve help, whatever my feelings may be.* Moral philosophy should not abandon those sorts of thoughts.

Moreover, though I've been arguing that we cannot understand, and so cannot adopt, the moral conclusion without some singular experience of the value of an individual, acting from the moral conclusion is sufficient for full moral regard in some contexts. We do not always need the phenomena of the appreciation of the value of individuals before our minds to count as acting out of moral regard for them. For some purposes, a sincere and informed conviction that others are entitled to respect for their rights, and an effective intention to act accordingly, is all we need. This may be true when we act in legislative or administrative roles that require the making or enforcing of general rules. But there are also important examples in our navigation of our ordinary lives. We need not be in the grip of the experience of singular respect, overwhelmed with the full humanity of each of our fellow human beings, at each moment or in each encounter with them. Indeed, it is difficult to see how anyone could live that way, though perhaps it is a mark of a certain sort of saint.

I have been explaining why even sincere endorsement of the moral conclusion could yet fail to be enough to embody a full moral outlook or robust moral commitment.[40] Full moral commitment requires not merely judging that others have dignity, but *regarding them* that way, as fellow human beings, as "one of us." Perhaps to some ears *regarding* someone as having infinite value sounds *less* demanding than *actually believing* this about them. But my point is that one can affirm this belief sincerely—one isn't lying or mistaken about

352 RETHINKING THE VALUE OF HUMANITY

one's convictions—yet fail to internalize it. To resist this failure, and so regard someone as valuable, is the more demanding standard.[41] If we fail to have this response, then we have moral work to do, and this is work that no argument can accomplish.

So far we have that there is a morally significant attitude of singular respect that shares many of the features of love. It is a contentful attitude, an appreciation of the value of another, but not the sort that could be the conclusion of an argument; we cannot reason to it. I've suggested that singular respect can bridge a possible gap between our commitment to a general moral conclusion and its application to particular interactions with our fellow human beings.

5. Witnessing the Love of Others

I turn now to a third way in which sincere endorsement of the moral conclusion can fall short of a complete moral outlook due to failures in application that reasoning cannot address, and a third resource for bridging the gap. The kind of case I am interested in here contrasts with the category that I've just been discussing in that it involves clear-eyed denial that certain beings are persons, bearers of dignity or the value of humanity. It also differs from the first kind of case, in which failure to attribute dignity stems from a mistaken belief about the properties of individuals or groups of people. Here I am concerned with disagreement about moral status that outstrips disagreement about empirical facts. The controversy or doubt in these cases is not about what certain beings are like, but about whether we should take them to have dignity, given what they are like. This last category is thus especially significant in that it directly concerns skeptical questions about the justification for certain moral attitudes. These are intelligible questions that not only can, but actually do, figure in philosophical discourse.

Philosophers have made various attempts to draw the boundaries around who matters morally, citing, for example, sentience, susceptibility to pain, self-awareness, and certain cognitive and emotional capacities as purported bright lines between those who have dignity and those who do not. None of these commands universal assent, so we face a question about how to arbitrate these disagreements and settle our own views about them.

Love or singular respect can begin to address these questions, but only with respect to those individuals of whom we have direct experience of these kinds and those we regard as sufficiently like them. Where we lack such experience, it's tempting to switch gears and regard disagreements over controversial cases as ideally settled through consideration of the arguments for and against the various positions. But the claims of Section 2 raise doubts about the idea that this strategy could settle questions about who has dignity. Such procedures of reasoning would either depend upon or reveal the necessary and sufficient conditions for being a bearer of the value of humanity. But I argued above that the value of humanity cannot be defined in terms of properties that we could understand independent of our experience of the value of individuals. Judgments about whether some quality or capacity matters morally are better regarded as expressions of particular moral convictions than as independent premises through which we could arrive at moral conviction or arbitrate disagreements among them.[42]

In several discussions Gaita offers an alternative resource for arbitration. He urges that seeing someone as an intelligible object of *someone's* love rationally commits you to taking a moral attitude toward her. You must regard such a person as a fellow human being (cf. Setiya 2014, 263). There is a familiar phenomenon in the neighborhood here. We often set victims of violence or tragedy in the context of relationships with those who love them in an attempt to make their unspeakable value salient. We say, *she is someone's daughter; he is someone's son.*[43] Imagining another person as the object of someone's love in this way heightens awareness of the victim as having the sort of value that we find in those we love, a value—I have argued—to which no one could reasonably be indifferent. We cannot regard others' love as warranted while denying the dignity of the person in question.

Gaita describes at least two kinds of cases in which someone not antecedently viewed as having value that would give him full moral standing comes to appear as "one of us" when seen in the light of another's love for him. First, he relates his encounter with a nun whose treatment of patients suffering from profound mental disability manifests not merely consideration or respect but love for them, love such as we can have only for a fellow human being (Gaita 2000, 17ff.). In the second, he considers the love of an expectant mother for, as he sometimes puts it, "that which she carries in her pregnancy," and the way in which witnessing such love might change a person's thinking about the significance of abortion (Gaita 1991, 161).[44] The claim is not that the love of the nun, or of the mother, *confers* value on those they love. It is, rather, that when we witness this love and see it as intelligible—if we do—we thereby see the object of that love as meriting moral regard, as a fellow human being or bearer of the value of humanity.

That the love appears intelligible is important. If the nun loved a rock or a gerbil with the profound love that Gaita describes, this would not lead us to think of the rock or gerbil as having the sort of value that makes it one of us, but rather to question the sanity of the nun. Witnessing her love for her patients could, in principle, have the same effect: one might find her response to them unintelligible. Gaita's testimony is that he did not find it so. Her love appeared apt to him, and in seeing that love as making sense, he came to understand the patients as having a value he had not previously attributed to them. That is why he says that the nun's love *revealed* their value to him.

354 RETHINKING THE VALUE OF HUMANITY

So, the *intelligibility* in the seeing-as-intelligible matters. But so, too, the *seeing as* matters. Gaita's examples treat two instances sometimes characterized as "marginal cases" of moral status, cases implicated in philosophers' disagreements over which qualities matter morally. Philosophers standardly approach these disagreements by seeking arguments to settle the question of whether to attribute full humanity to those in question. Gaita's appeal to witness is not an attempt to provide such an argument, but rather a rejection of the idea that argument is the right tool for addressing that sort of question. He appeals to what we see, not how we reason. He suggests that it is possible to see not merely that someone loves, but that that love makes sense. Rather than *argue* that the love of the nun or the expectant mother is intelligible, he prompts us to reflect on the implications of seeing it that way, as he does and as we might. He suggests that, as we cannot seriously doubt the intelligibility of our own love in ordinary cases, he was not able seriously to doubt that the nun's love was warranted. Seeing her love revealed the value of the patients to him with "certainty."

Finding love of some individual intelligible in this way provides reason to reject a claim that she and those like her lack the value that I have been calling dignity. The rational grounds here are given in what you see, witness, or recognize, and we should expect them to outstrip any argumentative formulation that would be communicable to someone who did not see it that way. Depending, as it does, on morally significant experience, this approach may still be powerless to convince those with whom you disagree. But it can help you settle for yourself what to think about such disagreements or to parry their potential skeptical effects on your own thinking. My suggestion is that, though distinct from reasoning, Gaita's approach provides a perfectly rational way to do so.

6. On the Task of Moral Philosophy

I have argued that, while we can reason to the moral conclusion if we have the right conceptual materials, there are certain obstacles to adopting and occupying a moral outlook that reasoning cannot overcome and likewise certain skeptical challenges that it cannot address. In this sense, we cannot reason to moral commitment, just as we cannot reason to love. So, just as we cannot fully vindicate love in argument, neither can we fully vindicate moral commitment this way.

My argument has important implications for the way that we should regard moral skepticism, and so for the practice of moral philosophy. It demonstrates that it can be inappropriate to *speculate* about the justification of moral commitment in something like the same way that it would be inappropriate for a parent to speculate about the justification of his love for his child. A certain way of taking skeptical challenges seriously, distancing oneself from one's own recognition of others' dignity in a way that allows one genuinely to doubt it, and then seeking arguments back to an affirmation of this value, is itself incompatible with moral respect, just as a similar disinterested inquiry would be incompatible with interpersonal love. Both speculative undertakings are affronts to the value affirmed in the attitudes that they seek to justify.

At the beginning I said that this sort of speculative inquiry about moral value and the authority of moral requirements is often regarded as the central or even characteristic task of moral philosophy. But if what I've gone on to say is right, then there are certain questions of moral significance that it is possible for us to frame, but that we have moral reason not to engage. Bernard Williams (1973, 92–93) recognizes this in his defense of preserving a moral category of the *unthinkable* against the relentlessly calculative attitude of the utilitarian. The methodology that we see in a certain sort of case-driven moral philosophy, paradigmatically exemplified by Trolley Problems, errs insofar as it fails to allow the possibility of this category. It describes cases that, taken seriously, could only be regarded as overwhelming tragedies and presumes that we will, and that we should, set aside the reactions appropriate to tragedy and consider these cases in a dispassionate administrative mode.

Moral philosophers then face a choice about how to understand our undertaking. We can characterize moral philosophy by specifying its *tools or methods*, the methods of dispassionate inquiry, and the construction, consideration, and critique of arguments. Or we can characterize moral philosophy as inquiry into a particular set of questions. But if we try to specify both methods and questions, we must recognize the possibility of a mismatch between them. The methods of argument construction may not be well-suited to questions that have been regarded as fundamental to, even defining of, moral philosophy, questions like: Why should we be moral? Are there ways that it is impermissible to treat anyone? Are all human beings equally valuable? How valuable are they? Why are they valuable?

The danger here is similar to the danger of relying on the methods of argument to see if it makes sense to affirm the value of your child. The methods of philosophy force us into a speculative mode not suited to the address of these questions, one in which we doubt, or at least play at doubting, convictions that should not be subject to doubt. To speculate about these questions, to entertain doubt about the value of some human beings, and to proceed as if commitment to the idea that each one has infinite and irreplaceable worth requires argumentative backing before it can be responsibly affirmed, is already to take up an attitude toward at least some individuals that is incompatible with the attitude of moral respect owed to them.

I have claimed that we cannot argue to an outlook that comprises moral commitment, which entails that there is no such thing as an argument in response to

356 RETHINKING THE VALUE OF HUMANITY

certain moral skeptics. Convincing the moral skeptic, and so also settling certain of our own moral doubts, is not really a task for moral philosophy. This is the paper's negative thesis. I have also described three positive relationships in which love stands to moral commitment. First, the nature of the value to which moral commitment responds is something that we can, and normally do, learn about in the experience of love. Second, moral commitment requires susceptibility to singular respect for individuals, an attitude that shares structural features with love. Third, both the experience and the witness of love can give us insight into the boundaries of the moral community. In sum, my positive claim is that love can provide resources for establishing warranted moral commitment that reasoning alone lacks.

I have not argued that reasoning about moral questions can do no ethical work. Indeed, I take this essay itself to be an exercise in moral philosophy that aims to do some such work. In arguing for the limits of the standard tools of philosophy, their impotence in the face of certain morally significant questions, I hope to have used these same tools to quiet another kind of moral anxiety. Once in the grip of certain skeptical doubts, it can seem that only an argument could rescue you. I have urged, argued really, that accepting this limit would be to place too much faith in argument, and that trusting instead in your morally significant experience can be entirely appropriate and rationally warranted. You can be rationally permitted to trust this experience even if you are unable to communicate its import to others who do not share it. Similarly, patience with and charity toward those who cannot articulate the full import of their own experience to us is a rational and moral demand.[45] That a certain overestimation of the power and importance of argument can obscure these permissions and demands is itself a morally significant conclusion of philosophical argument.[46]

Notes

1. The latter has been the more popular position. See, e.g., Railton 1984; Williams 1981; Wolf 1982; Scheffler 1994; Frankfurt 1988. Certain Kantians might be read as engaged in the former. See, e.g., Herman 1993a, 1993b, 1993c; Baron 1995.
2. See, e.g., Leviticus 19, Matthew 5, Matthew 22, Galatians 5.
3. Iris Murdoch (1970b) is a central figure here. Her approach to moral philosophy is driven by the idea that *any adequate moral philosophy would put love at its center*: "Love is a central concept in morals" (2); "the central concept of morality is 'the individual' as knowable by love" (29); "Will not *act lovingly* translate *act perfectly,* whereas *act rationally* will not?" (90). Contemporary writers who endorse and attempt to work out a view of this kind include Velleman 2006; Setiya 2014; Gaita 1991, 2000. For a development of the case that Murdoch's loving attention is the same as Kantian motivation by duty, see Bagnoli 2003.

LEARNING FROM LOVE 357

4. See Rawls (1971) on the separateness of persons and Ebels-Duggan forthcoming-b.

5. What I am really after here is what Rawls calls a conception: a thick, contentful notion of value, not a mere normative placeholder. See Rawls (1971) on the concept/conception distinction.

6. Jackson (1986) is most concerned with phenomenal properties that cannot be reduced to physical descriptive properties, and not with how we learn the content of the concepts.

7. In one sense Jackson's Mary can make or reason to judgments that make use of the concept of red even though she lacks this sort of full possession of the concept. She is a scientist with detailed knowledge of the science of color. She knows that, e.g., ripe sour cherries have the physical properties that make them appear red. So she can judge that *cherries will appear red to those who have normal color vision* or even *cherries are red.* She can reason that if this thing is a ripe cherry, then *this thing is red.* All this is to say that she can achieve reference with the color concept. But if phenomenal qualities, what red looks like or what it is like to see red, figure in the concept, then she does not herself understand—arguably does not herself know—to what this important concept in the judgment refers. And if that is right, then she does not really understand what it is that she is judging. So perhaps it is too strong to say, as I do above, that we could not be in a position to *make* the judgment, to form the attitude, that each person has dignity. It may be better to say that we cannot understand this judgment, and so cannot apply it in practice.

8. The language of attention is from Murdoch 1970a. The idea of arrested attention is from Velleman 2006.

9. Of course, just as one may regard a person as a means without regarding him as a *mere* means, one may think that there is some aspect of a person's worth that can be expressed as price without thinking that his value can be fully expressed or captured as price. Both regarding a person as a means, and setting a price on him—or at least on some use of his skills or stretch of his time—seem to be going on when you hire someone to do some task.

10. Sharing some things with belief and others with perception may be a feature love shares with a wider class of attitudes, such as emotions, though I doubt that it is satisfactory to classify love as an emotion. For discussion of the ways in which emotions have been construed as judgments, on the one hand, and perceptions, on the other, see Scarantino and de Sousa, 2018.

11. Thanks to Sarah Buss for suggesting this last formulation of the view.

12. Cf. Aristotle's discussion of friendships of utility in *Nicomachean Ethics* VIII. For commentary, see Cooper 1980.

13. For more detail, see Korsgaard's introduction to that volume and see Korsgaard's introduction to Kant 1998; Ebels-Duggan 2011.

14. Compare the distinction in Helm (2021) between two different justificatory queries about love, distinguished by the alternatives against which they ask for justification: What, if anything, justifies my loving rather than not loving this particular person? What, if anything, justifies my coming to love this particular person rather than someone else?

358 RETHINKING THE VALUE OF HUMANITY

15. This is an argument that we may actually make to people we love who are prone to underestimate their own worth or are averse to asserting their rights. I might point out to such a person that *I* love him, and use this—along with an implicit suggestion that I am not wrong to love him—to attempt to make salient to him that *anyone* should respect him. I am trying to get him to see his own worth in the light of my love for him.

    We see a similar thought in Gaita's (1991, 50) discussion of remorse in *Good and Evil*: "[T]he nature of what he suffers in remorse because he murdered his friend is such that it is conditioned by the fact that he should suffer it if he murdered an anonymous tramp. And that is to say, it is fundamental to his understanding of friendship that *it be bound by moral constraints which are what they are precisely because the evil of murdering a friend is the evil of murdering another human being*." Here Gaita argues that a person's response to having profoundly wronged a person whom he loves internally involves a commitment to the idea that the value or standing of that person is independent of his love.

16. Compare what Setiya (2014) says about the "picture" of the value of a life that is involved in his conception of love, and the implications of this picture for the ways in which others create reasons for us (see esp. 275–276).

17. Here, I intend "objective" to contrast with "conditional," not immediately with "subjective," and don't mean to commit to a metaphysical view that posits absolute value as a sort of entity in the world. Subjective value is standardly taken to be a function of the attitudes or perspectives of particular agents, and so also conditional in the sense that matters to me here. But Korsgaard argues that unconditional or absolute value is best interpreted as intersubjective, that which can or should be valued from all points of view. She appeals to a version of Kant's argument for the Formula of Humanity to claim that all people, and later all nonhuman animals as well, have value of this kind (see Korsgaard 1996a; 2018, chaps. 2 and 8). Cf. Theunissen (2020), who argues that valuing agents are valuable because we are valuable to, or good for, ourselves. While I'm not entirely satisfied with either of these arguments, neither do I take anything that I say here to exclude them.

18. For example, Setiya (2014, 262) criticizes Velleman (2006) for relying on the term "rational nature" and explains why he prefers "humanity." Gaita (1991, 2000) both uses and criticizes the use of "preciousness." Elsewhere he uses "individuality," which I prefer, though it has problems of its own. He also tries "humanity," while seeking to distinguish it from the term that picks out the biological species. Gaita strongly resists the Kantian language of "dignity," claiming that it could only be taken as a parody. Diamond (1978) relies on "fellow human being," and more broadly "fellow creature," which she also regards as importantly distinct from biological concepts.

19. Many discussions of so-called marginal cases of moral status presume that there must be some such capacity or property and attempt to characterize it. See, e.g., Singer 1975; Regan 1983; Harman 1999. Resistance to this way of approaching ethical questions about nonhuman animals is one of Cora Diamond's central themes. See, especially, Diamond 1978, 1988, 1991. See also Korsgaard (2018, 79–93) for a discussion of the argument from marginal cases.

20. For this reason I think that it is an error to classify Velleman's (2006) view about the reasons for love as a quality theory, as Kolodny (2003) does. Cf. Gaita's (1991) reasons for distinguishing between appreciating someone's individuality and treating him as a representative of humanity.

21. Here, compare *the property view* about what grounds or gives reason for interpersonal love. For some representative examples, see Badhwar 1987; Delaney 1996. *The relationship view* (Kolodny 2003; Scheffler 1997) is usually presented as the leading alternative. The position that I am advocating rejects both of these.

22. Valuing a person and attributing to him some set of descriptive properties can come apart in either direction. We can fail to regard someone as having the value in question in a way that cannot be corrected simply by learning new facts about him. Such failure seems constitutive of many misogynist or racist attitudes. Conversely, the love of parents for profoundly disabled children embodies ascription of the value in question, and this love can occur absent some or all of the candidate descriptive properties. These two sorts of cases show that attributing value cannot be identified with the attribution of a set of empirical properties. I will return to each below.

23. Thus I find a Mackie-style (1977) error theory to be a nonstarter. It is possible that there is nothing worth valuing or caring about, but this couldn't be true simply because analysis of the idea of value shows that it requires us to posit an odd metaphysical entity that the world lacks.

24. Here, I follow Korsgaard 2008. Cf. Korsgaard 2018, chap. 2.

25. "Not to know what it is to look at another human being with such recognition or with its denial, not to know how that differs from what is possible with animals, is not to have as fully as one might and as one should the concept of a human being. . . . To have the concept of a human being is to know how thoughts and deeds and happenings, and how happenings are met, give shape to a human story. . . . What it is to grasp the biological concept is nothing like what it is to grasp the concept of a human being" (Diamond 1988, 265; cf. Diamond 1978, 1991).

26. The strategy here to some extent parallels Buss 1999.

27. Many philosophers are tempted by the idea that love could not be the sort of thing for which there are reasons. Harry Frankfurt is the most prominent contemporary defender of this view (see, e.g., Frankfurt 2004). I think that the attraction of this view can be explained by two things: (1) the plausibility of the idea that preferences, brute attraction, or taste can play an indispensable role in justifying particular relationships, and (2) the idea that we could not fully state the reasons for love in a way that would allow us to reason to it. But one can agree with both of these, while resisting the claim that love itself is not subject to a justificatory query.

28. In Ebels-Duggan (2008) I argue that it is distorting to treat the parent-child relationship as primary, and that loving relationships between equally situated adults provide a better paradigm. I still think that those *relationships* provide an important paradigm, an ideal case that ought to shape our thinking about the parent-child relationship, among others. Nevertheless, for reasons explained above, focus on the parent-child case is helpful for thinking about love as such.

29. I have in mind here, e.g., Singer 2011, 2016; McMahan 2002, esp. 230.

30. Diamond (2003, esp. 11–12), develops a similar thought, that neither skeptical questions nor any attempt to answer them in argument is the right way to approach a person. Here she is discussing Cavell 2002.

31. On perception, see Crane and French, 2017, esp. sec. 3.

32. Especially in light of the perceptual metaphor, one might worry that the idea that love is warranted because it puts us in touch with the "reality" of another's value forces us to regard value as a part or property of the person in the way that I rejected in the previous section. But there is no need to restrict our notion of reality to the set of physical facts, or of these plus more mysterious metaphysical facts that are construed on the model of physical ones. Instead of beginning from some theoretical view about what can count as real and trying to shoehorn what we learn from love into it, we begin with the sort of experience we have in love, and use this to make sense of our talk of the value of a person. We can understand the important thing that we say when we say that Timothy Caughman is a fellow human being. There is nothing substandard about this reality.

Compare here Nagel's (1970) idea that we are each one among others, *equally real*. The sort of argument that he makes in *The Possibility of Altruism* is more closely related to the attitude of singular respect that I describe below than to that of love. But both of these are responses to, ways of coming to understand, the value of a person. It is also worth comparing Rawls's (1971) appeal to the separateness of persons. And compare Diamond (2003) on the unthinkability, splendor, and horror of our separateness from one another. Diamond is, in part, responding to Cavell 1979.

33. Cf. the argument of Setiya (2014), against Kolodny (2003), that you need not bear a special relationship to a person in order to reasonably care specially about him. Kolodny objects against any view that appeals to qualities or properties of the beloved as the reasons for loving her, on grounds that if these were the reasons, the lover should be happy with any substitute who has the same properties. He then argues that appeal to our rational nature or humanity as the reason grounding love is subject to a particularly acute version of this worry. For, on this view, the lover should be happy to substitute her beloved for *anyone*. The problem with this argument is that Kolodny treats the value of humanity as a fungible value, an instance of price. But the whole point of saying that persons have dignity rather than price is that their value is *not* exchange value. Each person has it, but it does not follow that we'd be happy to substitute one for another. To love a person, to appreciate the sort of value she has, is to be aware of it as *not* substitutable.

34. The burden of proof lies with those who would reject this premise: a skeptical challenger must state, and defend the moral relevance of, some particular difference. The argument of Section 1 bars appeal to the fact that some people, but not others, are loved by her. Any alternatives can be intelligibly doubted or challenged and face assessment on their merits. Many such claims are nonstarters. For example, the moral conclusion is far more plausible than the idea that moral worth varies by nationality. Even if one were to fail to persuade an adversary who holds the latter view, her resistance would put no rational pressure on one's own moral commitments.

LEARNING FROM LOVE 361

Korsgaard (1996b) relies on this burden-of-proof argument when she makes the generalizing move from *my own* value to that of anyone with humanity. She imagines the futility of an agent trying to resist generalization by saying "I am *me*, after all" (43). Yet elsewhere (e.g., 10ff.) she seemingly allows the skeptic to rely on the mere intelligibility of the challenge that he presses.

35. Compare Gaita (2000) on racism. Gaita contrasts the slaveholder's profound moral error about the significance of a woman he enslaves with an error based on purported empirical differences. The slaveholder does not posit any such differences, nor even feel rational pressure to do so. He simple fails to see the woman in question as a human being. The slaveholder cannot demonstrate that he is correct in regarding her as other than "one of us," yet neither could it be demonstrated to him that he is wrong about this. If it could be so demonstrated to him, then he would only be making a "mistake."

36. One thing that might be lacking is an understanding of others as having a complex internal emotional life, not unlike our own. Cf. Gaita 2000, esp. 57--73. To have not merely practically efficacious judgment about how I must treat others but the visceral appreciation of the value that grounds or warrants this treatment seems to importantly involve this appreciation. Again, this may be part of what Nagel (1970) had in mind in referring to others as "equally real."

37. Also relevant here is the role of both photography and narrative essay in journalism, and the way that these can make us think differently about tragedies by eliciting awareness of the value of singular individuals swept up in them.

38. Compare what Setiya calls "personal concern" in his essay in this volume.

39. Cf. Gaita's (2000, 19) claim that no philosophical theory can capture or relate what the nun's love reveals.

40. Gaita (1991, 144) holds that Kant cannot account for this because of the deep division he draws between *duty* and *inclination*: "[T]he Kantian division between inclination and duty excludes sorrow for [the victim's] death as *internal* to the moral response to his murder. His death is internal only to the description of the deed as one which falls under the moral law."

I develop a similar criticism of Kant in (Ebels-Duggan forthcoming-a), arguing that Kantian moral psychology threatens to treat a division between states to which we can reason, on the one hand, and mere sensibility or brute, arational inclination, on the other, as exhaustive. This taxonomy requires supplementation by a third category: responses that cannot be reasoned to and yet are intelligible. On this issue it is instructive to compare the attempt of Bagnoli (2003) to capture Murdoch's case, mentioned above, in Kantian terms. Bagnoli rightly holds that in order to do so we would have to capture the mother-in-law's change in view in terms of a change in her *maxims*. Bagnoli thinks this can be done, and sketches a strategy of execution. I'm not convinced that her account succeeds in capturing the change.

41. Pointing out and trying to correct for the failure of this sort of regard is, for example, one of the aims of the Black Lives Matter movement. Some of the resistance to this movement might be understood as arising from failure to distinguish between *believing* that the lives of Black people matter just as much as those of white people, and regarding individual Black persons in this way. Those who take themselves to

362 RETHINKING THE VALUE OF HUMANITY

have the relevant belief resist the idea that they could be legitimate targets of the criticism that they do not think that Black Lives Matter. But the movement demands something that goes beyond belief: understanding, recognition, and regard for humanity as well as the practical and political consequences that would follow on that.

42. Cf. Setiya's (2014, 258) point that mentioning certain properties is more like an expression than a justification of love.

43. This sort of appeal is in order insofar as it aims to make salient the infinite and irreplaceable worth of these individuals by making us think of them as intelligible objects of love. It becomes problematic insofar as it suggests that their value depends on or is conditioned by their relationship to others. It seems not accidental that victims who are female or members of disempowered racial or cultural groups are more often talked about in this way, though that could be subject to either explanation. On the one hand, people are, in general, less likely to take the suffering of these people seriously as relevantly like their own or that of those they love, so there is work to be done in making their dignity salient. On the other hand, such appeals can suggest or presume a primarily male and/or white audience in a way that perpetuates rather than undermines the idea that these victims are individuals, bearers of humanity in their own right.

44. The unwieldy formulation is Gaita's attempt, in my view as successful as any could be, to avoid begging questions in the description of the phenomenon, as calling that which the expectant mother loves either "her unborn child" or "the fetus" might be thought to do. The phrasing can be heard as a tender description of something rightly loved, or as achieving reference by a definite description that mentions no morally salient properties or status. But part of Gaita's point, as I elaborate below, is that we do not and cannot see the phenomenon in an ethically neutral way. We see the love as intelligible or as not.

45. Both self-trust and the demand for interpretive charity seem to me especially important for politically and socially disempowered people and groups of people, whose experiences may be less widely shared or are underrepresented in widely available art, media, and culture.

46. I worked on this paper over a long enough period of time, presented versions of it in enough places, and talked about the issues it addresses with enough people, to feel that it is hard to know where to begin, and where to leave off, in acknowledging the many debts that I have incurred. I am grateful for wonderful discussions at Northwestern University's Practical Workshop, the Other Minds/Other Wills Workshop at the University of Chicago, the Wheaton Political Theory Workshop, the UK Kant Society conference at St. Andrews University, the Society of Christian Philosophers meeting at Asbury University, the Arizona Workshop in Normative Ethics, the Boston University Workshop in Late Modern Philosophy, the University of Wisconsin–Madison, the Rice Workshop in Humanistic Ethics, the Conference on Kant and Confucianism at Sungkyungkwan University, Brown University, and the North American Kant Society Meeting at the APA in January 2020. I am grateful for conversations with Lucy Allais, Mark Alznauer, Matthew Boyle, Sarah Buss, Brad Cokelet, Ryan Davis, Bennett Eckert, Heidi Giannini, Richard Kimberly Heck, P. J. Ivanhoe, Christine Korsgaard,

Benjamin Lipscomb, Jennifer Lockhart, José Medina, Richard Moran, Oded Na'amen, Bernard Reginster, Carole Rovane, Kieran Setiya, Karen Stohr, David Sussman, Julie Tannenbaum, Aleksy Taresenko-Struc, Nandi Theunissen, Stephen White, Susan Wolf, and Vida Yao. And I am especially grateful to the students in my spring 2019 graduate seminar: Juan Andres Abugattas, Henry Andrews, John Beverly, Hansen Breitling, Bennett Eckert, Christiana Eltsiste, Regina Hurley, Nate Lauffer, Hao Liang, Mauricio Maluff Masi, and Spencer Paulson. Despite this long list, I am certain that I have neglected to mention others who deserve acknowledgment.

References

Aristotle. 1998. *The Nicomachean Ethics.* Translated by William D. Ross, John L. Ackrill, and James O. Urmson. Oxford World's Classics. Oxford: Oxford University Press. [Cited by book]

Badhwar, Neera Kapur. 1987. "Friends as Ends in Themselves." *Philosophy and Phenomenological Research* 48 (1): 1–23.

Bagnoli, Carla. 2003. "Respect and Loving Attention." *Canadian Journal of Philosophy* 33 (4): 483–516.

Baron, Marcia. 1995. *Kantian Ethics Almost without Apology.* Ithaca, NY: Cornell University Press.

Brewer, Talbot. 2009. *The Retrieval of Ethics.* Oxford: Oxford University Press.

Brewer, Talbot. 2018. "Acknowledging Others." *Oxford Studies in Normative Ethics* 8: 9–31.

Buss, Sarah. 1999. "Respect for Persons." *Canadian Journal of Philosophy* 29 (4): 517–540.

Cavell, Stanley. 1979. *The Claim of Reason: Wittgenstein, Skepticism, Morality and Tragedy.* Oxford: Clarendon Press.

Cavell, Stanley. 2002. "Knowing and Acknolwledging." In *Must We Mean What We Say?,* 220–245. Cambridge: Cambridge University Press.

Cooper, John. 1980. "Aristotle on Friendship." In *Essays on Aristotle's Ethics,* edited by Amélie Oksenberg Rorty, 301–340. Berkeley: University of California Press.

Crane, Tim, and French, Craig. "The Problem of Perception," *The Stanford Encyclopedia of Philosophy (Spring 2017 Edition),* Edward N. Zalta (ed.), https://plato.stanford.edu/archives/spr2017/entries/perception-problem/.

Delaney, Neil. 1996. "Love and Loving Commitment: Articulating a Modern Ideal." *American Philosophical Quarterly* 33 (4): 339–356.

Diamond, Cora. 1978. "Eating Meat and Eating People." *Journal of the Royal Institute of Philosophy* 53: 157–175.

Diamond, Cora. 1988. "Losing Your Concepts." *Ethics* 98: 255–277.

Diamond, Cora. 1991. "The Importance of Being Human." *Royal Institute of Philosophy Supplement* 29: 35–62.

Diamond, Cora. 2003. "The Difficulty of Reality and the Difficulty of Philosophy." *Partial Answers: Journal of Literature and the History of Ideas* 1 (2): 1–26.

Ebels-Duggan, Kyla. 2008. "Against Beneficence: A Normative Account of Love." *Ethics* 119 (1): 142–170.

Ebels-Duggan, Kyla. 2011. "Kantian Ethics." In *The Continuum Companion to Ethics,* edited by Christian Miller, 168–189. New York: Continuum.

364 RETHINKING THE VALUE OF HUMANITY

Ebels-Duggan, Kyla. 2019. "Love and Agency." In *Routledge Handbook of Love*, edited by Adrienne Martin, 300–312. New York: Routledge.

Ebels-Duggan, Kyla. Forthcoming-a. "Bad Debt: The Kantian Inheritance of Humean Desire." In *Kantian Freedom,* edited by Dai Heide and Evan Tiffany. New York: Oxford University Press.

Ebels-Duggan, Kyla. Forthcoming-b. "On Dignity and Consequences." In *The Norton Introduction to Ethics*, edited by Elizabeth Harman and Alex Guererro. New York: Norton.

Frankfurt, Harry. 1988. *The Importance of What We Care About: Philosophical Essays*. Cambridge: Cambridge University Press.

Frankfurt, Harry. 2004. *The Reasons of Love*. Princeton, NJ: Princeton University Press.

Gaita, Raimond. 1991. *Good and Evil: An Absolute Conception*. New York: Routledge.

Gaita, Raymond. 2000. *A Common Humanity*. New York: Routledge.

Harman, Elizabeth. 1999. "Creation Ethics: The Moral Status of Early Fetuses and the Ethics of Abortion." *Philosophy and Public Affairs* 28 (4): 310–324.

Helm, Bennett. "Love," *The Stanford Encyclopedia of Philosophy (Fall 2021 Edition)*, Edward N. Zalta (ed.), https://plato.stanford.edu/archives/fall2021/entries/love/.

Herman, Barbara. 1993a. "Integrity and Impartiality." In *The Practice of Moral Judgment*, 23–44. Cambridge, MA: Harvard University Press.

Herman, Barbara. 1993b. "On the Value of Acting from the Motive of Duty." In *The Practice of Moral Judgment*, 1–22. Cambridge, MA: Harvard University Press.

Herman, Barbara. 1993c. "The Practice of Moral Judgment." In *The Practice of Moral Judgment*, 73–93. Cambridge, MA: Harvard University Press.

Hopwood, Mark. 2016. "'Terrible Purity': Peter Singer, Harriet McBryde Johnson, and the Moral Significance of the Particular." *Journal of the American Philosophical Association* 2 (4): 637–655.

Jackson, Frank. 1986. "What Mary Didn't Know." *Journal of Philosophy* 83 (5): 291–295.

Kant, Immanuel. 1900–. *Kants gesammelte Schriften*. 24 vols. Edited by Königlich Preussische Akademie der Wissenschaften zu Berlin, Deutschen Akademie der Wissenschaften zu Berlin, and Akademie der Wissenschaften zu Göttingen. Berlin: De Gruyter.

Kant, Immanuel. 1998. *Groundwork of the Metaphysics of Morals*. Translated by Mary J. Gregor. Cambridge: Cambridge University Press. [Cited by volume and page of the Akademie edition]

Kolodny, Niko. 2003. "Love as Valuing a Relationship." *Philosophical Review* 112 (2): 135–189.

Korsgaard, Christine M. 1996a. "The Reasons We Can Share." In *Creating the Kingdom of Ends*, 275–310. Cambridge: Cambridge University Press.

Korsgaard, Christine M. 1996b. *The Sources of Normativity*. Cambridge: Cambridge University Press.

Korsgaard, Christine M. 2008. "Realism and Constructivism in Twentieth-Century Moral Philosophy." In *The Constitution of Agency*, 302–326. Oxford: Oxford University Press.

Korsgaard, Christine M. 2018. *Fellow Creatures*. Oxford: Oxford University Press.

Lockhart, Jennifer. 2017. "Moral Worth and Moral Hobbies." *Ergo* 4 (21): 611–636.

Mackie, J. L. 1977. *Ethics: Inventing Right and Wrong*. London: Penguin.

McMahan, Jeff. 2002. *The Ethics of Killing*. Oxford: Oxford University Press.

Moore, G. E. 1993. *Principia Ethica*. Revised ed. Cambridge: Cambridge University Press.

Murdoch, Iris. 1970a. "The Idea of Perfection." In *Sovereignty of the Good*, 1–44. New York: Routledge and Kegan Paul.

Murdoch, Iris. 1970b. *The Sovereignty of Good*. New York: Routledge and Kegan Paul.

Nagel, Thomas. 1970. *The Possibility of Altruism*. Oxford: Clarendon Press.

Railton, Peter. 1984. "Alienation, Consequentialism, and the Demands of Morality." *Philosophy and Public Affairs* 12 (2): 134–171.

Rawls, John. 1971. *A Theory of Justice*. Cambridge, MA: Harvard University Press.

Regan, Tom. 1983. *The Case for Animal Rights*. Berkeley: University of California Press.

Scanlon, Thomas. 1998. *What We Owe to Each Other*. Cambridge, MA: Harvard University Press.

Scarantino, Andrea, and de Sousa, Ronald. "Emotion," *The Stanford Encyclopedia of Philosophy (Winter 2018 Edition)*, Edward N. Zalta (ed.), https://plato.stanford.edu/archives/win2018/entries/emotion/.

Scheffler, Samuel. 1994. *The Rejection of Consequentialism: A Philosophical Investigation of the Considerations Underlying Rival Moral Conceptions*. Revised ed. Oxford: Clarendon.

Scheffler, Samuel. 1997. "Relationships and Responsibilities." *Philosophy and Public Affairs* 23 (3): 189–209.

Setiya, Kieran. 2014. "Love and the Value of a Life." *Philosophical Review* 123 (3): 251–280.

Singer, Peter. 1975. *Animal Liberation*. New York: Harper Collins.

Singer, Peter. 2011. *Practical Ethics*. 3rd ed. Cambridge: Cambridge Univeristy Press.

Singer, Peter. 2016. "Twenty Questions." *Journal of Practical Ethics* 4 (2): 67–78.

Theunissen, Nandi. 2020. *The Value of Humanity*. Oxford: Oxford University Press.

Velleman, David. 2006. "Love as a Moral Emotion." In *Self to Self*, 86–136. New York: Cambridge University Press.

Williams, Bernard. 1973. "A Critique of Utilitarianism." In *Utilitarianism: For and Against*, edited by J. J. C. Smart and Bernard Williams, 77–150. Cambridge: Cambridge University Press.

Williams, Bernard. 1981. "Persons, Character, and Morality." In *Moral Luck*, 1–19. Cambridge: Cambridge University Press.

Wolf, Susan. 1982. "Moral Saints." *Journal of Philosophy* 79 (8): 419–439.

15

The Invention of Value and the Value
of Humanity

Elijah Millgram

Persons are ends in themselves, we are often told; we owe each of them respect, not in virtue of anything they have done or their particular merits, but due to the value that inheres in any human being. And here is a reasonably representative sample of how philosophers nowadays characterize the value of humanity. We "will generally agree," Joseph Raz (1999, 274–275) tells us, "that whatever else people having value in themselves, or being ends in themselves, means it means that, other things being equal, their interests should count." He continues, "Many will say that an essential element of the idea that people have value in themselves is that they must be respected" (275). Perhaps less apparent than the content of the evaluation is a default conception of its status: the value of humanity is presumed by most philosophers to be a metaphysical fact. That is, first, humanity *is* valuable, in the very special way that we are said to have in mind (it is a *fact*); second, the value, whatever it comes to, is already, permanently, and absolutely there, written as it were into the nature of the world itself, or of what it is to be a person or human being (that is, the fact is, on a widely shared, albeit problematic conception of metaphysics, *metaphysical*).

From the medium distance, this sort of moral doctrine can look like wishful thinking striking a philosophical pose. Such postures are rarely a satisfactory basis for getting through life, and a useful corrective would be engaging a philosopher for whom it is a ground rule that such putative evaluative facts, etched into the fabric of the universe, are on the face of them some sort of pretense. And so here I am going to try distilling a handful of connected problems and ideas out of Friedrich Nietzsche's most famous book, *Thus Spoke Zarathustra*.[1]

Let me quickly preempt a pending misunderstanding. To someone like Nietzsche, reconstructing our values out of our readily available emotions, prescriptions to ourselves, or briefly, any of the usual suspects in the repertoire of metaethical noncognitivism would be making what is actually much the *same* mistake as the purveyor of imaginary facts. As that observation might suggest, Nietzsche's philosophizing was driven, in large part, by a metaethical innovation, one that we have not yet assimilated. (That of course is how we would now put

Elijah Millgram, *The Invention of Value and the Value of Humanity* In: *Rethinking the Value of Humanity.*
Edited by: Sarah Buss and L. Nandi Theunissen, Oxford University Press. © Oxford University Press 2023.
DOI: 10.1093/oso/9780197539361.003.0016

it; metaethics, conceived as a distinct subject matter, crystallized only after his death.) And it was also motivated by a substantive concern, that humanity, he thought, was well on its way to being entirely valueless. That catastrophic outcome can yet be forestalled, because values—and here is that metaethical step—are *invented*; that is, as a matter of fact, they always have been invented, whether we have been aware of it or not, and from here on out, they are *to be* invented.

1.

To preview where we'll be going, here is how those two ideas—the metaethical innovation and the substantive concern—are connected. Because values have hitherto been invented, generally in a completely unselfaware manner, without any of the knowledge or thoughtfulness that would allow for intelligently crafted values serving the needs of their clients, and, often perversely, in the service of an ongoing, deeply bitter, and self-destructive form of resentment, they have for the most part not been serving us well. For one thing, values have almost always been presented (and enforced) as one-size-fits-all requirements, but because values guide their users and shape their personalities, and because different people need different kinds of guidance and molding, different customers require different values. And thus the task of what Nietzsche called "philosophers of the future" will be to invent values.[2] These values are to be idiosyncratic, temporary, deeply novel and will promote, not exactly the welfare, but what Nietzsche thought of as the true interests of those who produce and are to be guided by them.[3]

Inventing values is, Nietzsche took it, our best shot at staving off nihilism: that almost-completed process of humanity's becoming entirely worthless. We have to make humanity valuable ourselves, and this is how. If we are to be fully mobilized and intelligently guided in this enterprise, it will be by a particular invented value, specifically the metavalue of inventing values—which Nietzsche takes to be his own invention. In *Zarathustra*, we will see, the metavalue is personified as the notorious Overman.

In that book, Nietzsche is especially attending to an obstacle that his program must overcome if it is to fulfill its promise, and I want to make sure that we have it clearly in view, in its full generality. To that end, I will introduce values, as Nietzsche thinks of them, and show how his conception disallows a working assumption that was built into both of the main competing wings of twentieth-century metaethics—roughly, that what you bring to bear in your assessments is available up front, *already*. I will also argue that values, again as Nietzsche thinks of them, require ongoing monitoring, intervention, and regulation. The upshot will be that we have to address the challenge of imbuing humanity—*ourselves*—with value in a way that goes very much against the grain: what comes naturally

368   RETHINKING THE VALUE OF HUMANITY

is to relax into supposing that some value or other (even some Nietzschean construct, such as the Overman) can be treated as given and as a fixed point of reference.

In that connection, by way of providing some (terse) guidance for *Zarathustra*'s readers, I will sketch how the book is meant to exhibit that trap. If Nietzsche's metavalue is seen through the lens of older metaethics, adopting it is all too likely to short-circuit rather than promote the self-aware invention of one after another after another of the values, tailored to the needs and exigencies of their creators and users, that Nietzsche is encouraging us to fabricate.

2.

But first, an unavoidable preliminary. I am very aware that Nietzsche's texts function as a sort of literary Rorschach inkblot, not only for casual and philosophically untrained readers but for all but a very small handful of the professional Nietzsche scholars. I am going to be simply laying out, without textual argument, what I take his ideas to be; nevertheless, I claim to be not merely free-associating as I stare at the inkblot but telling you what Nietzsche was thinking—with a handful of important qualifications. I do promise to provide the requisitely argued reading of the texts elsewhere, but if you do not feel comfortable accepting that historical claim as is, please consider the philosophical moves on their own merits and defer issues of attribution to another occasion.

However, I can't proceed any further without putting those qualifications on the table. Without further ado, here they are, and since they are consequences of Nietzsche's ideas, I submit them without argument as well.

Our interpretative practice involves ascribing beliefs and other propositional attitudes, as well as strategies and the like, to the author of the text we are explaining.[4] When we ascribe a position or stance to a text or its author, we announce what he full-fledgedly believes, or intends us to conclude, or whatever—rather than what he doesn't believe but nonetheless somehow finds himself thinking, or doesn't really want but still seems to be pursuing. Intuitively, the distinction, familiar to many academic philosophers from the work of Harry Frankfurt and others, is that between a claim you will stand behind, and something that you said but which you then disavow ("I didn't really mean it"), or again, between an action you have chosen and executed deliberately, and the activities that you admit you were involved in but which, as we say, just kind of happened. By way of a shorthand, I'll say that we're distinguishing the *superlative attribution* (of attitudes and actions) from their *mere attribution*.

The mainstream view is that superlative attribution is supported by the stable and coherent organization of a personality, and Nietzsche (although the

THE INVENTION OF VALUE   369

qualification I'm introducing applies here, too) concurs.[5] However, Nietzsche presents himself, throughout his later writings, as not having the organized personality that would allow there to be anything that he *really* thinks—*really* believes or wants or intends—and he goes to great lengths to exhibit his views as attitudes that he is in a position to honestly disown, as on a par with blurts, with thoughts he can't help entertaining but won't endorse, and with other happenings in his mental life that aren't fully *his*.

It's not feasible, in a brief exposition, to keep reminding the reader of this issue. But when I tell you that Nietzsche believes or concludes or intends this or that, recall throughout that you are meant to take it with an appropriately sized grain of salt.

Next, in his successive books, Nietzsche presents one after another 'perspective'; each of these—embodied in the personality of one of his books' very different implicit authors—is, to a first approximation, a conceptual scheme, system of evaluative standards, and sense of salience. Accordingly, the ideas, arguments, assessments, and so on appear and reappear, differently inflected on each occasion by the perspective on display, and here is a quick example, just to give you a feel for it. The pressing sense that humanity is not merely well nigh valueless but dismaying is the content given to that central Nietzschean concept, *nihilism*, in *Zarathustra*; there are other writings in which that term labels a more elaborate version of the urge that cats seem to experience when they are about to die—to crawl into a quiet place where they can let things wind down. (In due course, we'll be able to say why the concept is firmed up into these rather different forms.) So in his later works, there is, for a second reason, no straight answer to what Nietzsche thinks; it comes out one way in one perspective, and another way in another.

Here is a stopgap description of the relation between those perspectives and what is apprehended or expressed through or in them (quick, not entirely accurate, but like those perspectival observations, meant to be acceptable for the moment). Leaning on Aristotle's contrast between form and matter, we can say that the matter—ideas, demands, concepts, doctrines, and the like that recur in one after another of Nietzsche's writings—is differently shaped up, or "enformed," by the conceptual schemes, idioms, and hang-ups depicted as aspects of the various authorial personalities. Here I'll mostly be talking my way through the matter—those ideas and the connections among them—in a way that, as much as I can manage, sets to one side the framing of those elaborately represented perspectives, though I do want to acknowledge the dangers of proceeding this way: especially, the ease with which one comes to suppose that there must be an already present, formless version of those ideas, etc. Because I will be focusing on the concerns of *Thus Spoke Zarathustra*, at appropriate points I will take time out to explain features of the perspective of the fictional author of that work and to say what we are supposed to learn from it.

370 RETHINKING THE VALUE OF HUMANITY

Finally, in my exposition I am going to take very much the sort of liberties that Peter Strawson allowed himself when explaining Kant. That is, the exercise is not, as the New Age community used to put it, to "channel" Nietzsche—to open one's mouth and have the voice of the dead philosopher emerge from it—but to recast the ideas in a contemporary intellectual vocabulary. After all, if we are to benefit philosophically from an engagement with a historical figure, we will want thoughts that *we* can entertain and perhaps adopt, rather than antiquated ideas that only someone raised during the nineteenth century could treat as live.

3.

I'll be using Nietzsche's own term "value," despite the disadvantages of doing so. (These days, it comes with a great deal of baggage that is likely to get in the way of recognizing Nietzsche's innovations for what they are.)[6] First, by way of getting the notion in our sights, I'll provide a sample value or two, with commentary; the emphasis will be on the values' different scopes and modes of introduction. Then I'll explain why we can't simply define the concept on Nietzsche's behalf. And then I'll highlight the features that will primarily figure into his arguments: to anticipate, Nietzsche's values function both as standards, and as ideals.

The typical trajectory of dominant values in older societies, as they emerged in the distant past, was to be laid down by, perhaps, a rude chieftain. Such values served to reinforce differences between groups and to focus collective efforts on urgent, often military needs; Zarathustra informs us that excellence in archery was such a value for the ancient Persians (Z I.15/4:74–75). Norbert Elias (2000) has documented the evolution of another such value in our own society: etiquette or manners, which radiated outward from the inner circles of courtly aristocracy, and had as its primary function distinguishing the members of court (and after that, of social circles closer to the court) from lower-class outsiders.[7] The coverage of values of this type tends to be restricted to the society that produces them; not that other values are even acknowledged, but outsiders are dismissed as barbarians, infidels, and "lesser breeds without the law": who cares what *they* value? However, within the society, the value is presumed to be relevant to everyone, although not necessarily in the same way; medieval peasants were not expected to behave like courtiers, but they *were* expected to defer to them.

Once values have been established, they take on a life of their own and escape the control of the founding figures; as Zarathustra quaintly puts it, the current of a people carries them irresistibly along (Z II.12/4:146–147). Nietzsche argues that values are interpreted and enforced ever more rigorously—out of the need to exert ever more control over oneself, but his reasons for insisting we have that need won't detain us here—and over time, that pressure characteristically

THE INVENTION OF VALUE 371

transforms a value into something qualitatively very different from what it had been at the outset. Both content and function can shift dramatically; under the former heading, in the case of manners, come the turn of the twentieth century, the directives given by medieval etiquette guides—about such matters as how to spit or clean one's teeth at table, or how to relieve oneself in public, or to whom one may display one's private parts—had themselves become unmentionable.

If Elias is reading the history correctly, the escalation of the demands of politeness played a central role in reshaping the personalities of Europeans, from the top of the social scale to, eventually, its very bottom. At the outset of the process, manners served to mark a class whose behavior was not just freewheeling but exhibited a scarcely imaginable lack of impulse control; think of road rage being the day-to-day norm for personal interaction. At our stage of the process, manners are part of a technique for producing rigidly controlled personalities; road rage is an anomaly, and that, Elias holds, is in large part due to this sort of training. When values take on a life of their own, they eventually end up dropping their original function, typically replacing it with what is easy to describe as that function's very opposite; indeed, by the end of the nineteenth century, European upper classes had come to regard their code of etiquette as binding and to be enforced on all social classes indiscriminately. Nietzsche's label for such transformations is "self-overcoming," and we'll see more of the phenomenon shortly; a characteristic aspect of the trajectory of a value, it will be needed to pin down Nietzsche's Overman.

At least as of the advent of Christianity, we also see values purporting to have *universal* coverage, that is, to apply indifferently, not just within a given society but to absolutely everybody; eighteenth-century instances might be toleration and enlightenment. Nietzsche sometimes seems to describe such values as fabricated by conspiracies of priests, and sometimes presents them as the products of impersonal sociological processes.[8] Famously, he claims that our own moral values originated as weapons of class warfare in the ancient world, and it's not too soon to notice that, in introducing those values, the early Christians were trying to make *themselves* valuable in a way that had not been possible before.

Notice that values—which figure as the standards, ideals, and forms of assessment that function to guide people's lives—have almost never been chosen on the basis of real scientific, historical, and cultural knowledge of their effects on their users. Neither those ignorant tribal leaders nor those priests had any idea what they were doing when they came down from one or another Mount Sinai with their alternate lists of commandments.[9] Only now (that is, only by the nineteenth century) are we finally equipped to do a better job of it.

Last for now, let's consider a couple of relatively low-key illustrations of the sorts of values that Nietzsche wants us to start inventing. (As most readers will be aware, Nietzsche's own discussion is anything but low-key, and in due course

372 RETHINKING THE VALUE OF HUMANITY

we'll have to ask why.) First, artists frequently attempt to develop a distinctive personal style, one that anchors and constrains their work in progress, that serves as a target or benchmark, and which can be refined over the course of a career. In these cases, although the style can be instantly recognized (think of Francis Bacon or Lucien Freud), and although the artist can be held to it and called out for lapses, it may not be realistically possible to fully spell out the demands that it makes on him. Notice that such an artist might well not want the value to be broadly adopted; on the contrary, it is supposed to be deployed *only* by him. Notice also that such values are often meant to be temporary; artists will adopt and abandon them, and when they are as famous as, say, Picasso, those occasions bracket what come to be called their "periods." And notice that, frequently enough, the styles are *crafted*; values are sometimes, we observed in passing, created inadvertently and unintentionally by social processes, but here, values are being invented, in the word's full-throated and paradigmatic sense.

Values can be conjured up not merely for one's own personal use but nonetheless without an accompanying demand that everyone—or even some antecedently specified class of people—adopt and adhere to them. Sticking with the example, a group of artists may adopt a shared set of guidelines, objectives, and stylistic constraints without insisting that everyone, or even all artists, join their school. Georges Perec lived up to the aspirations of the Oulipo group by writing a novel that managed not to use the letter "e," without taking the imposition of this sort of artificial constraint on one's literary productions to be binding on authors outside the group.

If you are an analytic philosopher, I can appropriate our own relatively recent past as a second illustration. When Bertrand Russell and G. E. Moore founded our intellectual tradition, they were inventing a value in very much the way that Nietzsche conceived of doing so, and one that was neither meant only for their own personal use nor to bind anyone and everyone. They laid down novel standards meant to govern the new way of philosophizing, and under this heading, Russell's ([1905] 1973) enormously influential paper, "On Denoting," was taught to generations of students more as a model (of the new practice, conceptual analysis) than for its content proper. Russell and Moore formulated aspirations to a new understanding of clarity, one that was only fully metabolized into practice come the high-water mark of analytic philosophy, around the 1970s.[10] (Compare what Moore *says* about clarity with the flailing muddiness of his own writing; as always, the new skills could become a deftly exhibited second nature only in the founders' academic grand- and great-grandchildren.) And over the past fifty years, we have witnessed a process that, we have already noted, Nietzsche thinks of as an almost inevitable phase of the history of a value. Here, its self-overcoming played out through the increasing mastery and control of analytical rigor being turned on and used to undercut the theoretical underpinnings of the characteristic methodologies and style of the analytic movement.[11]

THE INVENTION OF VALUE   373

I have been introducing the Nietzschean notion without giving anything like an explicit definition of it, because once we have accepted, however tentatively, Nietzsche's understanding of values as something that you invent, we have to be willing to postpone the attempt to say what values *are*. I acknowledge that this is a big ask, especially given the way the exposition will proceed, for readers who are trained to distinguish values (which are out there) from valuings (which are something we do), and especially given the multiplicity of ways values are going to be turning up in the ensuing discussion: as embodied in rituals or institutions, as inventions and also as means for handling inventions, and so on. We will shortly see Nietzsche himself wrestling with this issue; for now, taking seriously our own experience with inventions, we are not usually in a position to say what a given invention *is* until long after it has taken root.

The internet (or rather, the ARPAnet, its original core), to help ourselves to a vivid and large-scale example, was originally designed to allow researchers at one location to use custom-built computers at other locations; it was promoted to its military sponsors as a battlefield management tool; at the outset, what we now think of as email was considered and dismissed, as an application that no one would ever use. A decade or two into its existence, the scientists most closely involved in its development enthused about it as a technology that would deepen and extend political democracy. Even today, we are probably not in a position to say what the internet is; it certainly was never what the engineers who built it thought, and it is starting to look like the invention that broke democracy.[12] If values are inventions, and we are now inventing the practice of treating them that way explicitly, we should not expect to know what individual values amount to, what values are as a category, or what inventing them will turn out to be, until we are much, much farther into the ongoing practice of inventing values that Nietzsche was trying so hard to launch. Philosophers are trained to explain their terms; if one is talking about values, one owes one's audience a definition. But if we are thinking about inventions, we will have to suppress that training.

Even if we cannot say what values are in retrospect going to turn out to have been, we can identify two aspects that Nietzsche's values wear, and which figure into his own arguments. First, they provide standards, which are invoked in the course of assessments or evaluations. And second, they function as ideals, which here means that they morph over the course of their life spans, becoming ever more demanding; it is a very important feature of values as Nietzsche understands them that their contents change over time, and eventually these transformations are far reaching (even before we take into account the phenomenon I have now flagged twice, that of self-overcoming). For instance, priesthoods often adopt a value that they characterize as purity, and Nietzsche emphasizes the way that, early on, there is not much more to it than, perhaps, ritual ablutions and such; in due course, purity can come to be understood spiritually and to involve, say, the

374 RETHINKING THE VALUE OF HUMANITY

ruthless regimention of one's motivations (GM I.6/5:264–265); purity (and here is the self-overcoming) may end up requiring one to ignore precisely the initially demanded bodily cleanliness.

To be sure, values can also involve or set goals; however, because Nietzsche has unfamiliar views about how goals or ends figure into our cognitive economy (see especially GS 360/3:607–608), I am going to navigate the exposition away from that dimension of value.

4.

With that introduction to Nietzsche's notion of a value in hand, let's turn to his nihilism, as it appears in *Thus Spoke Zarathustra*. Here is its protagonist complaining about the current state of humanity's value:

> Naked I had once seen both, the greatest man and the smallest man: all-too-similar to each other, even the greatest all-too-human. All-too-small, the greatest!—that was my disgust with man. And the eternal recurrence even of the smallest—that was my disgust with existence. (Z III.13.2/4:274–275)

We'll provide context for that remark about the Eternal Return shortly, but first let's see Zarathustra recounting a vision elsewhere:

> A young shepherd I saw, writhing, gagging, in spasms, his face distorted, and a heavy black snake hung out of his mouth. Had I ever seen so much nausea and pale dread on one face? (Z III.2.2/4:201–202)

He is returning to an image that has earlier been glossed for his readers:

> The bite on which I gagged the most . . . [was] my question: What? does life *require* even the rabble? . . . [M]y nausea gnawed hungrily at my life. (Z II.6/4:125, restoring Nietzsche's emphasis of *nöthig*)

Nietzsche's nihilism (in the perspective displayed in *Zarathustra*, at any rate) does not, as commentators frequently enough take it to be, consist in the stance that values are not real: that they are not supernatural objects floating above the visible universe (a denial Nietzsche took almost for granted), together with the presumed consequence (hastily and incorrectly imputed to him) that evaluations, of whatever sort, can be shrugged off. After all, Zarathustra's revulsion, directed specifically toward his fellow man, is driven by an evaluation, roughly, that two millennia of Christian and Christian-inspired striving for a kind of herd-animal human has produced a species that is as dishearteningly unimpressive as it is possible to be. Here he is, in the book's preface, attempting to shock an audience out of its complacency:

> The earth has become small, and on it hops the last man, who makes everything small.... "We have invented happiness," say the last men, and they blink. (Z P.5/ 4:19)

The complaint is not confined to *Zarathustra*; just for instance, Nietzsche characterizes the proper object of pity in *Beyond Good and Evil* as follows: "[W]e see how *man* makes himself smaller.... Well-being as you understand it ... soon makes man ridiculous and contemptible" (BGE 225/5:160–161). Having tried so determinedly to make itself valueless, we should not be surprised to see that humanity has succeeded. Also unsurprisingly, given the mendacity that Nietzsche takes to have permeated the enterprise, precisely the undistinguished element of humanity—the merely being *just anyone*—is trumpeted as that very special value inhering in each and every last human being and the proper object of Kantian respect.

Now, the nihilism has somewhat more content than that deeply felt disappointment in his contemporaries, and here I need to correct—once again, very quickly, and very dogmatically—a widely accepted reading of Nietzsche's doctrine of the Eternal Return. On that reading, we are asked to imagine the history of the world repeating itself, without any changes at all, endlessly; our willingness to affirm that endless repetition is a litmus test for whether, on balance, we accept the world as a whole, the bad along with the good, because we can see the bad to be a necessary precondition for the greater good. On one popular version of the familiar reading, it is the Overman who will redeem humanity's depressing present; we accept even a world containing our contemptible contemporaries, because they are an indispensible run-up to the Overman.[13]

The passages we have just seen make it quite clear that the alleged solution to Nietzsche's problem is actually the problem itself. That solution, again, is purported to be that the valueless parts of the world are required by the much more valuable ones, but that life *requires* the *canaille*—Nietzsche's French might be colloquially rendered as "trash"—is what Nietzsche simply cannot stand and what prompted his most viscerally felt response.

5.

What are we to make of Nietzsche's dismissive and miserable assessment of his fellow man? Any evaluation invokes values; this one must do so; but which ones?

376 RETHINKING THE VALUE OF HUMANITY

The prevalent and culturally available values, which we can presume to be our own, and which Nietzsche rejects? Or other values that he has invented and is purporting to lay down as the law? If the former, how can his assessment be the upshot? (Aren't those the very values that have shaped us into what we are?) In any case, where does *he* get off applying them? And if the latter, why should *we* care about the assessment?

If Nietzsche thinks we have to take his evaluation seriously nonetheless, mustn't he be taking the values which he invokes to be the *real* ones? Moreover, if we are inventing values, don't we have to assess those inventions in order to decide whether to adopt or abandon them, and won't that evaluation have to be conducted by deploying values that are *there already*? And so surely Nietzsche is committed to a metaethically familiar position after all: "moral realism," the view that values are (very special, no doubt) facts—unchangeable facts—out there in the world.

This cluster of reactions is, to a professional philosopher, almost inevitable, but I am going to put it to one side. Instead of addressing the issue directly, here are remarks meant to postpone it.

As the complaint I have just sketched indeed suggests, Nietzsche does mean to be introducing a new, very-big-picture evaluative contrast, one intended to replace the older contrast used for assessing people, that between 'good' and 'evil.' "Impressive vs. unimpressive" might be a natural and low-key way to put it, and when he is talking this way, Nietzsche sometimes says "noble"; but of course this does not tell us much, if we don't yet know what it takes to be impressive.[14]

Still, as far as the content of his evaluation goes, while Nietzsche is being over-dramatic, I can see, as we say it nowadays, where he is coming from. For instance, and to keep it close to home, when I travel the diaspora of analytic philosophy, I find myself visiting departments that feel themselves to be the outposts of a distant empire. When they strive for professional respectability and even ambition, they understand that to mean, not working on the philosophical problems *they* have and whose terms *they* set, but on what other people, in the faraway capitals of that empire, who don't know what the philosophers in the outposts are thinking about, have set as the philosophical problems, along with the terms in which those problems are to be treated. That willingness, to let one's intellectual agenda be controlled by people who can't so much as be bothered to pay attention to what one is doing or concerned with, produces undistinguished results and unimpressive philosophy; it is a depressing sight, and I can render that judgment without needing to bring distinctively Christian or Nietzschean values to bear.[15]

And I, too, wonder: in order for there to be philosophical agenda setting, the sort of value creation that gives rise, sometimes, to remarkable or bold or refined philosophizing, do there *have* to be those vast hinterlands of would-be philosophers, allowing their own minds to be made up for them by strangers?

THE INVENTION OF VALUE 377

Thus in part because I am inclined to let Nietzsche have his much more extreme version of my own response, I am willing to waive, for the moment, the metaethical complaint with which we started off the section. But in addition and more importantly, that complaint has built into it the assumption that the standards which you use to assess something must be prior to it: they are *there already*. Now, when it comes to inventions, the assumption is unrealistic and does not square with our own experience of the invention-saturated world in which we live. Returning to our examples, we are developing our views as to how to size up the internet only as we come to see the (formerly entirely unforeseeable) impacts it has on our lives; we are far from being done revising the evaluative tools we will be using for this task. Again, analytic philosophy started out as a relentlessly ahistorical tradition; as it broadened and became capable of appropriating one after another figure within the traditional philosophical canon, it became necessary to find ways of assessing analytic history of philosophy—to figure out what we should reasonably want from it, to determine when and how it is successful, when poorly done, and so on. The values governing those assessments are inevitably subsequent to the appearance of plausibly serious analytic treatments of the past: to the groundbreaking work of, say, Gregory Vlastos, who showed us how to extract argumentation from Plato, or of Peter Strawson, who rehabilitated Kant. With any luck, once we surmount the challenges involved in a successful analytic reading of Nietzsche, that will further adjust the standards we use to assess the history of philosophy, to accommodate writings that don't lend themselves to more familiar sorts of reconstruction.

Let me take as one more quick illustration an assessment of some of our own recently invented assessment tools. Law schools on the American model are a relatively recent social innovation. Because potential students need to evaluate prospective law schools, a news magazine, *US News and World Report*, has invented a way of ranking them, intended for that purpose. It's clear enough that such a device could have been worked up only after law schools had been part of the educational landscape for quite some time; without that experience, the inventors of the new evaluation techniques would not have known what to watch out for. Now that *USNWR* rankings have been in circulation for a while, we are starting to see the first attempts to assess *them*; as before, it is clear that the contours of those evaluations can be firmed up only well after the invention— those rankings—that they assess.[16] It is unreasonable to insist that *USNWR* rankings were laid up in the heaven of Plato's Forms, before law schools ever appeared on the scene; likewise, the values we develop to assess those rankings and others like them cannot have preceded their objects. And in general, assessment tools work because they are designed for the types of thing they are applied to, which entails that they must normally appear *later*.[17] In a world of invention, what values do is proliferate, and the moral realists' notion that our evaluations

378 RETHINKING THE VALUE OF HUMANITY

bottom out in values that have always been there is, and this is a point to which we'll return, back to front.[18]

For about the last hundred years, the default alternative to the view that values are already present facts has been the suggestion that our evaluations express attitudes: maybe emotions, maybe commitments, but there are many variants on the noncognitivist stance. So notice, now, that it is just as unrealistic to think that we already had attitudes, lurking so to speak within our psychological reservoirs, that would underwrite serviceable assessments of law schools or law school rankings, or contributions to analytic philosophy, or the internet or the work of a deeply creative artist with his own signature style, before the objects of assessment actually appeared. Despite their radically different self-presentations, moral realism and noncognitivism make the *same* mistake, that of thinking that you can be evaluatively prepared, ahead of time, for whatever innovation is coming down the pike. You can't, and that is why values have to be *invented*.[19]

6.

If Nietzsche is unsatisfied with humanity as we have it, we should anticipate a two-pronged remedy: on the one hand, we no doubt will see a program for altering the objects of evaluation, that is, the people; on the other, we will en-counter revisionism about values, where the standards we have been trying for so long to live down to are replaced by standards to which we can live up. In fact, in Nietzsche's vision, the improvements in people and in the standards to be applied to them are not merely tailored to one another, but the very same improvements. It is precisely by inventing novel values that people can become more impressive, and more impressive by the lights of the very values that they invent.

Recall that values function both as standards and as ideals: over time, the demands involved in a value are ratcheted up, sometimes from very simple beginnings, into ever more demanding aspirations. As that happens, and as the people who allow themselves to be governed by a value respond to its ever more demanding standards, it will not be surprising to find them becoming more and more impressive. If people invent values suited to them, to which they then am-bitiously try to live up, we can expect them to be still more impressive than if they merely accept the demands made by values they inherit. And if they have also adopted the metavalue of the invention of values, we can expect humanity overall to become gradually more impressive, in part because the value allows us to see humanity as living up to it, and in part because human beings are be-coming more impressive by striving to live up to it. All of that is plausible enough.

Or is it? Adopting newly invented values, and allowing them to shape one's be-havior and personality, cannot be enough; after all, Nietzsche is rebelling against

Christian values, invented long ago, and which have over time, he holds, made those who live by their ever more exacting demands impressively *un*impressive. So new values might be badly chosen. Moreover, because the contents of values develop over time, and because they might develop in more than one direction, an apparently promising value might nevertheless become corrupted, and even be turned into almost its very opposite. Nietzsche attentively followed the so-called Higher Criticism, that is, the emerging secular Bible scholarship of his day. (He seems to have been especially influenced by Julius Wellhausen and David Strauss, and their respective treatments of the Old and New Testaments.)[20] The theoretical common denominator of that movement was the doctrine that, as religions are institutionalized, the values of their founders are inverted, to make them suit the needs and sensibilities of, precisely, an institution.[21] That is, if you are an ecclesiastical bureaucrat, trying to get your new cathedral paid for, "Consider the lilies of the field" is not the attitude you need your congregants to have.[22] Thus Nietzsche was very concerned by the prospect that this sort of process would subvert the kinds of values he was proposing. For a pastor tending to his flock, "Invent your very own values" will be the last thing he wants them to have as their motto; large doses of idiosyncratic evaluative novelty are not normally compatible with institutional self-perpetuation.

We are in a position to make the diagnosis somewhat more contoured than Nietzsche himself left it: it is not just the effect of the self-interest of a class of priests, as Enlightenment ideology had it, or even of the need to keep membership up, as when the early Church found it necessary to prohibit suicide. As we are by now aware, institutions need institutionally usable values, which means, first and foremost, that they have to be legible and they have to be commensurable. That is, the institution has to be able to tell, more or less procedurally, whether its standard is being met, the ideal approached, and so on, if it is to track compliance. And the value has to support routinized decisions within the institution.[23] Neither requirement is compatible with genuine inventiveness, deep and thoroughgoing personalization, or the delicacy and nuance you would hope a guiding light that you could take fully seriously would exhibit.

If I am reading it right, a large part of the agenda of *Thus Spoke Zarathustra* is to pose this problem and show just how philosophically challenging it is. We can work our way into it via an expository route that is somewhat different than Nietzsche's own.

If a value functions as, *inter alia*, an ideal, as its content changes, it might change in an unsatisfactory or even perverse fashion. So in order to monitor and intervene in the process, one needs ways of assessing values; that is, one needs a metavalue, say, the value of inventing values.[24] Let's pause on the question of whether we should take the Overman to be a personification or icon of that metavalue.

380 RETHINKING THE VALUE OF HUMANITY

We have already registered Nietzsche's notion of self-overcoming, and in the section "On Old and New Tablets" we're told that Zarathustra "picked up the word 'overman' . . . and that man is something that must be overcome"; that is, we are being told that the Overman is what man will overcome himself into (Z III.12.3/4:248). Elsewhere, in "On the Thousand and One Goals" (Z I.15/4:74–76), Nietzsche's character announces that "'man' . . . means: the esteemer"—that is, as the section makes clear, the creature that creates and applies values. Putting the pieces together, the Overman is an icon for the outcome of the process of self-overcoming that valuing generally is traversing. Bearing in mind the program we have been sketching, where values were formerly laid down in a clumsy and un-self-aware manner and were meant to cover everyone indifferently, from here on out they can be crafted to serve the idiosyncratic needs of individuals. That is, the Overman is a literary presentation of the metavalue we have been considering—in which case, we had better get back to asking ourselves why Nietzsche would present it as though he were prophesying a secular Messiah.

With the metavalue in place, we can deliberate about whether to give the way a particular value is developing a thumbs up. Recall those *USNWR* rankings: do they tend to make law schools into places that promote the thoughtful, intelligent invention and articulation of values and standards and their embodiment in the law? Or do they instead push all of that to one side, in favor of a laser-like focus on LSAT scores, placement statistics, and selectivity metrics?

But of course, the metavalue is a value; the contents of values develop over time; thus the metavalue might itself be progressively articulated in, putting it crudely, a right way or a wrong way. We will shortly return to "On the Thousand and One Goals," where we see Zarathustra preaching the need for "one yoke for the thousand necks," that is, for a single system of values that will one day direct *everybody*. He evidently has the Overman in mind, and I want to suggest that this is intended as an illustration of the effects of institutionalization, and not as Nietzsche's own recommendation: it represents a likely perversion of the value he hopes you will adopt. If we need to discriminate versions of a value that Nietzsche endorses from perverse versions of it that he would reject, then we need not only the metavalue but a way of telling whether it is developing satisfactorily. Do we need a meta-metavalue? Nietzsche's Eternal Return might seem to serve: we can ask whether applying the metavalue, and the first-order values it serves to regulate, puts you in a position to assent to living your whole life, with all of history as its backstory, just as was, all over again. That would no doubt be a very interesting proposal, but Zarathustra makes a point of reminding Nietzsche's readers that even that meta-metavalue can *also* be firmed up badly:

> Verily, I also do not like those who consider everything good and this world the best. Such men I call omni-satisfied. . . . I honor the recalcitrant choosy tongues

and stomachs, which have learned to say "I" and "yes" and "no." . . . Always to bray Yea-Yuh ["I-a," that is, a phonetic rendering of "Yes" in German]—that only the ass has learned, and whoever is of his spirit. (Z III.11.2/4:243–244)

If your affirmation is merely indiscriminate, you are an ass, and so we must further discriminate among the ways we might affirm our past and accept our fellow human beings.

Although Nietzsche does not put the problem quite this way, it looks like the invention of value involves us in a vicious regress. Surely, what will have to terminate that regress is some value that is *already* there—no doubt, readers familiar with Nietzsche will expect, will to power—and in that case, whatever we think of that bottom-line value itself, there is less to the metaethical innovation with which we started than meets the eye.

7.

Let's step back and place Nietzsche's worries about the institutionalization of values as a special case of what we can now see to be a more general problem.

Allow that values are, *inter alia*, assessment tools. Allow that assessment tools are, by and large, only effective when they are tailored to the things that are to be assessed. And allow, finally, that we live in a world where invention and novelty are the norm: new devices, social arrangements, and, yes, even new standards are regularly introduced. You can't know what these will be—what they will be *like*—in advance. It follows that, even if we don't buy Nietzsche's own reasons for thinking that values are always pushing their envelopes, a value that is not an ephemeral throwaway will *have* to evolve over time, in more or less the way ideals do, to accommodate those regular doses of novelty.

And values had better not be ephemeral throwaways. Not only do they function as ideals; they function as standards. Like other tools, standards work well only after being debugged in actual use and only when their users have become well practiced in applying them. Moreover, and this is very much Nietzsche's own concern, when a new value is first announced, unless its dictates can be paraphrased via already available values, there is just not that much to them. Surely the interesting case of value introduction is the one that does not lend itself to, as we philosophers say it, the reduction of the new value to older values. But what you cannot say up front normally takes a great deal of time and effort to put into place, as indeed our illustrations make clear. I'll remind us of just one of them: by around 1975 we had come to have quite elaborate, extremely nuanced, if also controversial and largely tacit standards for what counts as good philosophical work in our tradition. (Perhaps these have eroded in the meantime.)

382 RETHINKING THE VALUE OF HUMANITY

At the outset of analytic philosophy, there were not enough in the way of shared standards to underwrite such judgments; those could come about only over time.

Exercising control over the emerging content of an assessment tool requires further assessment tools. But no assessment tool is exempt. The temptation is to act as though one or another value *was* exempt: as though, say, the Overman or the will to power or for that matter the value of humanity, as conceived by Kantians, could terminate the regress. But we can now see that the regress does not terminate.

Philosophers are trained to treat nonterminating regresses as "vicious" because they presume that there must be something there already to (in this case) anchor and fix the upshots of the sequence of evaluations. But that is, by Nietzsche's lights, an inexcusable surrender. The open-ended regress consists, rather, in developing further standards and ideals as they are called for, and developing each of them further as *that* is called for; that is, the regress is virtuous, in that it amounts to ever-improving evaluative sophistication, called forth by the need for further increments of it.[25]

8.

Can Nietzsche's program for retrieving the value of humanity—or perhaps for finally getting us to be valuable for the very first time—actually anchor that value as we understand it today? Surely the sanctity of life is one of its most important aspects; if that sanctity is supposed to have been invented, and if inventions are optional and can be superseded, are we to conclude that, perhaps, one day murder and even genocide will be just fine (again)?[26]

Although we do not want to underestimate the degree to which Nietzsche is willing to controvert our sensibilities, moral and otherwise, inasmuch as his values are taken to be inventions, some compare-and-contrast with another lower-key invention may deescalate the issue, and let's take light bulbs. It is important to recall that we got along without either light bulbs or a version of the value of humanity that could underwrite the sanctity of life until remarkably recently. Nevertheless, light bulbs have become indispensible; no longer a luxury, they are presupposed by and threaded into our architecture and interior design, our transportation systems, and our very schedules: we are not about to go back to bedtime at dusk and reading by candlelight. For practical purposes, they are completely nonoptional; light bulbs are here to stay, and if the value of humanity and, as part of it, the sanctity of life become as systematically integrated into our practices and institutions, what more could we ask for, as far as its permanence and stability go?

It *is* the indispensibility that does the work. Suppose that somehow it looked like everyone was going to give up on light bulbs and return to the now-literal

THE INVENTION OF VALUE 383

Dark Ages. Would it help for desperate philosophers to insist, in the manner of those moral realists, that light bulbs have always existed or that they are somehow a distinctive and foundational component of reality? If a future society collectively determines that they have no further use for light bulbs, such pronouncements are not going to keep them from moving on. In real life, moral realism makes no more of a difference than metaphysical realism about light bulbs.

If the value of humanity proves indispensible, however, should it matter that we do think of it as an invention rather than a very peculiar eternal fact? Playing out that compare-and-contrast a bit further, light bulbs are indispensible, all right, but because we understand them to be an invention, we treat them as *re*inventable. As I write this, incandescent bulbs are in the process of being replaced by LEDs. Halogens made possible a vastly expanded range of applications in comparison with early Edison-era bulbs. And briefly, over time, technical innovation has dramatically altered what light bulbs are and are for. Nietzsche's metaethics analogously allows the value of humanity (once we actually do achieve it!) to be both indispensible and amenable to reinvention.

What would it be like to reinvent the value of humanity? Nietzsche conveniently provides a small-scale illustration, and one that seems already to have gotten a good deal of uptake. To accept *Freitod*—"free death," Nietzsche's neologism, but now an ordinary German word—is to adjust one's vision of the sanctity of life, away from an older conception that, for theological reasons, prohibited suicide. Building into one's respect for life the option of choosing its closure point, and so the ability to opt out of a degrading old age, reconceives what it is for human life to be sacred (Z I:21/4:93–96; see also TI IX.36/6:134).

9.

The sensitive reader is no doubt thinking that Nietzsche would himself be quite impatient with this way of writing about him; leaving to one side the issue of whether it's sufficiently histrionic, it addresses itself to a philosophical conversation that is by his lights deeply misguided. But recall that my exposition has been Strawsonian—that is, I mean to be recasting Nietzsche's thoughts in a contemporary intellectual idiom—and that my generalization of Nietzsche's worry was developed in that spirit. Let's return to the instance of it that preoccupies him in *Zarathustra*. God is dead; that is, the responsibility for evaluation and judgment can't be fobbed off on anything else, not a deity, not a metaphysical substitute for a deity (such as the moral realists' version of values), and not internal attitudes that you happen to have and can't help having. *You're* responsible, not exactly all the way *down*—because that turn of phrase suggests a bedrock where evaluation

384   RETHINKING THE VALUE OF HUMANITY

stops—but all the way *out*. (Not that you can meet that responsibility by simply deciding on one thing or another, as some of the existentialists of the previous century perhaps thought; there is much more to getting an invention, of a value or anything else, to come together than announcing it.)

One can succumb to the ever-present temptation to foist that responsibility onto something that is already there, even when one is committed to the very value of inventing values; Nietzsche's Overman is Exhibit A. It's observed often enough that Nietzsche hardly tells his readers anything about the Overman, and you'll recall that we had to put together the pieces that let us identify its role in Nietzsche's intellectual not-exactly-system for ourselves. Nietzsche's early uptake was largely one after another very crude distortion of the concept by one after another very clumsy imagination, the English rendering, "Overman," being an attempt on the part of mid-last-century scholarship to distance itself from the more egregious of these. "Superman," the earlier translation, for most of us has come to name a muscle-bound, flying do-gooder in a cape and tights, but it also used to refer to those blond, blue-eyed members of a master race who went into the business of running concentration camps; and then there were the undergraduates, fictionalized in Hitchcock's (1948) *Rope*, who having read too much Nietzsche too quickly, murdered a fellow college student to prove to themselves that they were above the moral law (Baatz 2009). The inevitable thinness of a newly introduced value lends itself to these sorts of appropriations, but notice that each of them solidified the outlines of the new value into something that was taken to be already there, already valuable, all on its own—that is, the very opposite of what the value as introduced had promoted.[27]

Until this point in time (for Nietzsche, the nineteenth century, but it is not as though there has been progress on this front since), the only routinized technique for developing the content of a new value into a robust and effective guide to assessment has been institutionalization. Paradigmatically, this is managed by something on the order of a church, but for readers of this essay universities are probably a more familiar example: think of how different academic disciplines train up generation after generation of students into shared conceptions of acceptable methodology, of standards for assessing contributions to one's field, for determining what is shoddy work, what a compelling argument, and so on. But Nietzsche accepted the view of the Higher Criticism, that such institutions have a track record of inverting the values that they were constructed to sustain. Returning to one of our own examples, recall that at its founding, analytic philosophy was a violent rejection of metaphysics generally, and in particular of the holism that characterized the metaphysics of British Idealism. Remarkably, a century down the road, analytic metaphysics is considered not just a respectable subfield of the discipline but one of its more prestigious branches; central to its methodology today are appeals to reflective equilibrium, to the 'web of belief,'

THE INVENTION OF VALUE   385

and to cost-benefit trade-offs between theoretical components, which together amount to a revival of that formerly repudiated holism.

Recapitulating our problem, recall that we owe an account of Nietzsche's allegorizing his signature metavalue, as well as of the overdramatic tone of the composition. If I am right, *Thus Spoke Zarathustra* is advanced as an elaborate display of the challenge to Nietzsche's program that we have been sketching. Modeled on the Higher Critics' accounts of Holy Scripture, it casts Zarathustra as a prophet; the Overman is announced in the all-too-familiar register of the prophesied Messiah and becomes, not the reminder that you have the difficult task of inventing values for yourself to guide you in your own life, but instead the bottom-line, already-given value, where assessment stops, and which (rather, *who*) will lift the final burden of evaluation from your shoulders. The Overman, that "yoke for the thousand necks," is relegated to a distant future, for which not just you but future generations are to be sacrificed; as Albert Camus (1971, 70) complained, "[I]n his theory of superhumanity . . . [Nietzsche] replace[d] the Beyond by the Later On." We are told at the outset of the book that we are about to see the downfall of its protagonist.[28] We can now see that downfall to be metaethical; in large part it is a matter of Zarathustra's followers—and Nietzsche's readers—doggedly misconstruing his metaethical innovation as the announcement of yet one more value of the metaethically familiar kind.

As in the Higher Critics' reading of both Old and New Testaments, the perversion of the founders' doctrines is superimposed on a text in which the original doctrines are still discernible, and indeed, we also see Nietzsche's prophet encouraging inventors of values in the here and now, reminding them how socially alienating the process is, how distant it is from the brouhaha of the public square, but nonetheless how very important it is (Z I.1/4:29–31; II.18/4:166–171; I.22/ 4:97–102). But along with those Nietzschean ideas, the text models the way they are almost bound to be undercut. For instance, the over-the-top, florid prose and even more florid verse parodies the attempt of religious rhetoric to cut short their adherents' autonomous evaluations; the tactical consideration being imputed to the implicit author is that, with sufficiently exaggerated posturing, the priest's audience will simply accept—rather than autonomously assess—what they are told. We can see that the Overman-as-Messiah is not going to redeem humanity because it will not make humanity valuable; there is scarcely anything less inspiring than the vision of Nietzschean masses worshiping their future God-substitute.[29]

In *Zarathustra*, Nietzsche poses his problem and does not lay out his proposed solution to it. So here I won't try to reconstruct the response that, if I am seeing his intellectual development correctly, occupied him for the remainder of his working life. But we can say something about what *kind* of response it would have to be. Where old-school metaethicists see a regress of assessments—a new value, a metavalue that is needed to control the development of the new value,

386   RETHINKING THE VALUE OF HUMANITY

a meta-metavalue to do the same to the metavalue, and so on—as requiring an intangible and magical solution, Nietzsche's response will be, precisely, tangible and very, very hands-on. To get a sense of what that comes to, let's go back to one of our illustrations, in which *USNWR* rankings are used to assess law schools, with unfortunate consequences; it will do no good to insist that, in some invisible world behind this one, there are *real* values and that they disagree with those rankings. (Law school administrators will shrug their shoulders; what are they supposed to *do*?) A tangible, hands-on response, as opposed to a dose of meta-ethical insistence, will involve thinking through a way of assessing those rankings that can be brought to bear in the working lives of academic administrators, prospective students, and government officials, and will allow them to shift the incentive structures that law schools now face. This is only a promissory note, and to be sure a large one, but Nietzsche's very innovative solution to the concrete version of the problem that he took himself to face personally was every bit as tangible as *that*.

Suffice it for the moment that we have laid out for our own consideration the program of improving the value of humanity by encouraging and embarking on the invention of value, that we appreciate the substantive problem of regulating and managing values that we introduce, and that we understand how difficult it is to avoid lapsing into the pretense that some value, already out there or in here, will remove the need to decide for ourselves what matters and what is important. Suffice it that we realize that the concrete cost of that lapse is to make ourselves individually, and humanity as a whole, of lesser value. And suffice it that we have been brought face to face with Nietzsche's challenge to metaethics as we have it, on which it almost always turns out to be a theoretical superstructure for just that last sort of evasion of responsibility.[30]

Notes

1. I will refer to *Thus Spoke Zarathustra* by Z, part, section number, and subsection, with P indicating "Zarathustra's Prologue"; while Nietzsche himself did not assign numbers to the sections, Kaufmann's table of contents, at Nietzsche (1954, 112–114), is widely available and will spare you counting them off. Where possible, I also give book and section for works other than *Zarathustra*, following the usual conventions, with BGE for *Beyond Good and Evil*, TI for *Twilight of the Idols*, AC for *The Antichrist*, GM for *On The Genealogy of Morals*, and GS for *The Gay Science*. Citations in this format are followed by volume and page of the *Kritische Studienausgabe* (1988); thus, the first quotation in the final paragraph of this note is to part 2, section 16 of *Thus Spoke Zarathustra*, to be found at vol. 4, p. 162 of the most widely available critical edition of Nietzsche's works. Unless otherwise noted, I will be using Walter Kaufmann's translations (1954, 1974, 2000), because he is better than anyone else in the Nietzsche

business at matching certain aspects of English to German style: Kaufmann's renderings reproduce the literary failings of Nietzsche's German remarkably well.

In such discussions, respect is standardly distinguished from esteem, as per, e.g., Neuhouser 2008, 62–63. However, since Nietzsche thought the distinction as intended perverse, "respect" will be used here in the broader, ordinary sense. For one account of why the written-into-the-world conception of metaphysics is problematic, see Millgram 2018.

When philosophers today make it out that people are, as one way of saying it goes, ends in themselves, that often includes a further commitment, to the bottom-line equality of human beings. Readers will not be surprised to hear that Nietzsche does not share this view: "men are *not* equal: thus speaks justice" (Z II.16/4:162, and similar remarks at II.7/4:130, TI IX:48/6:150; compare AC 43/6:217 on "the poison of the doctrine of '*equal* rights for all,'" or AC 57/6:244: "The source of wrong is never unequal rights but the claim of '*equal*' rights" [restoring Nietzsche's emphases]). Here I will leave to one side Nietzsche's view that the value of humanity, when it has any, is unevenly distributed.

2. 'Thus': because "philosophers of the future" is a designation for those who do; see BGE 42–43, 211–212/5:59–60, 145ff.

3. Here we can mark a complicated question on Nietzsche's behalf: to what extent can our interests be independent of our values? Readers familiar with his ideas will immediately think of will to power as what adopting a set of values promotes or diminishes, but this is not the place to try to explain that concept and the way it can be substantively shaped by the values one has.

4. Nehamas (1981) is an attempt to account for the practice, in a way that is meant to avoid the so-called intentional fallacy, and which has shaped the reading of Nehamas (1985)—one of the better discussions of Nietzsche's work.

5. See Millgram (2015, chap. 10) for an overview of a recent and well-worked-out position of this sort, with pointers to earlier work, and BGE 19/5:31–34 for one Nietzschean variant.

6. Baggage is fine, but we have the *wrong* baggage: a series of moves triggered by J. L. Mackie's (1977) well-known complaint that values are 'queer.' The helpful background, which is at this point unavailable to most English-speaking readers, is the way that the neo-Kantian tradition, in particular its Southwest School, shaped the notion, and the work that it did for them. Although the following essay was not one that Nietzsche could have read, a reader confined to English can get a decent impression of how values were discussed from Windelband 2015.

7. That the illustration is apt is not an accident; Elias had embarked on the project of finding out what, as a matter of historical fact rather than genealogical speculation, had made Europeans into Nietzsche's "tame domestic animals" (GM II.6/5:301).

8. In Section 2, I explained that Nietzsche's texts are, to now borrow Bernard Williams's (2006) way of saying it, booby-trapped so as to preempt the straightforward attribution of philosophical positions, authorial intentions, and the like, and this is an occasion to provide an illustration.

388   RETHINKING THE VALUE OF HUMANITY

In the *Genealogy*, Nietzsche claims that we tend to misrepresent a great many phenomena to ourselves as the operation of a prior or underlying cause, where that cause is merely the phenomenon imagined as present for a second time: we distinguish between the lightning and the flash it causes, but there is just one lightning flash. William James (1987, 1216–1217) remarks on the tendency as well: living through the 1906 San Francisco earthquake, and understanding very well that "earthquake is simply the collective *name* of all the cracks and shakings and disturbances that happen," he nonetheless felt that "*the* earthquake was the *cause* of the disturbances." We likewise distinguish between the force and its effects, and—importantly—the person and the actions we imagine him to stand behind and produce. That is, just as we "redouble" or "reduplicate" the lightning (we have no conception of the lightning behind the flash, except as yet another flash), the person is similarly copied over, as his own soul. This is a metaphysical mistake (there's no such substratum), but Nietzsche suggests further that it's also motivated self-deception: distinguishing the person from his actions allows the resentful and injured to blame others for their actions. After all, since you are not simply the sum of your actions, you could have done things other than you did.

In the immediately following section (the so-called "Tour of the Workshop," that is, the workshop "where ideals are fabricated"), ideals (the effects) are distinguished from their cause: the men of *ressentiment*, probably a conspiracy of priests, who are being graphically blamed. The juxtaposition of the two sections amounts to announcing that we are to take Nietzsche's own presentation as motivated self-deception of the sort he has just described: what seems to be a conspiracy of priests can only be an impersonal sociological process, which is being "redoubled" in the manner of the lightning and its flash, or a person and his soul (GM I.13–14/5:278–283). That is, Nietzsche is both staking out a position, in this case about the origins of morality, and disavowing it on the spot; the upshot for our purposes is that it would be misguided, here, to apply the usual ways of ascribing positions to philosophical texts.

9. Though Nietzsche seems at points to exempt the authors of certain Hindi legal texts (e.g., TI VII.3/6:100–101; AC 57/6:241–244).

10. If you are not trained as an analytic philosopher, this is not the place to try to say just what the understanding was, but here is something that will give you the flavor of it. I was recently having a conversation (with a philosopher who will remain unnamed) in which I marveled that there are texts in our canon that seem to support endless interpretation: after more than two millennia, a student working on Plato or Aristotle can still reasonably expect to find something new to say about them. My interlocutor took that to be decisive evidence of unclear writing.

11. For a history which emphasizes this aspect of the development of the analytic tradition, see Nevo 2009.

12. For the early history, see Abbate 1999.

13. Anderson (2009) labels this the "Compensation Model" of Nietzschean redemption; for typical discussions of the topic, see Danto (1965) 1980, 212; Clark 1991, chap. 8; or Nehamas 1985, chap. 5.

THE INVENTION OF VALUE 389

14. That latter value term is advanced in part 9 of *Beyond Good and Evil*, titled "What Is Noble." Elsewhere, however, Nietzsche claims that the basic value words "good" and "bad" (and their translations in various languages) start out as self-descriptions by a politically dominant class (GM I.5/5:262–263); perhaps more recent examples of the phenomenon that Nietzsche is describing would include "urbane" (i.e., urban, used by city dwellers) and "redneck" (a derogatory epithet used by city dwellers to describe the rural poor). Nietzsche further explains that such terms—like, in this case, "noble"—take their content from the self-conception of the class that originated them. Thus without knowing what that self-conception is, we don't know what evaluation the term expresses.

    In other writings, he works very hard at introducing a contrast between will to power and decadence, but with our focus on *Zarathustra*, it won't serve us well to attempt to recover that here.

15. With that in mind, let's take a first stab at articulating Nietzsche's concern, that the *canaille* are perhaps required for, say, the Overman. If they were, then when you worked up values that would allow you to assess the Overman, and which enabled you to affirm him, wouldn't your values have to allow you—or even compel you—to affirm the *canaille*? But then, what kinds of values would they *be*? Wouldn't there be something *wrong* with them—and so, with *you*?

16. Espeland and Sauder 2016; the focus of their discussion is effects of the rankings on the law schools themselves.

17. 'In general': although it is a good rule of thumb that tools (and values, as a special case) have to be designed for the items to which they are going to be applied, there are of course cases when a tool is serendipitously effective.

    At this point in such discussions, I have noticed that academically trained philosophers (but hardly anyone else) find themselves insisting that apparently novel evaluations *must* be applying already-available values (or sometimes, already-available desires), and they start casting around for eternal values that might be at work in the case at hand; it is almost a reflex. Since Nietzsche means to be contesting precisely this point, it's important to disarm the reflex (as well as the related reflex, of attempting to assimilate the moves he is making to one or another back and forth in familiar literatures). By and large, here I am going to have to delegate the task of disarming to the reader, but I can help out with a couple very terse suggestions.

    First, values are rarely produced in an evaluative vacuum; on the contrary, rather as Harold Bloom's "strong poets" have thoroughly digested the predecessors they proceed to remake, those who most impressively displace older values have thoroughly internalized the values they are displacing beforehand. In this respect, values are typical of invention generally; when Silicon Valley produces a new device or application, that is possible only because of all those *other* devices or applications that were already produced, many of which the new invention will actually incorporate. That does not vitiate its status as an *invention*; in our own vocabulary, when a new invention depends on previous inventions, it is not thereby *reduced* to them.

    And second, if you are an academic reader, imagine someone adopting that posture, not toward standards and evaluations, but a paper you are working on. Imagine

390 RETHINKING THE VALUE OF HUMANITY

him insisting that you must have had a complete, albeit tacit, conception of the paper as you sat down to write it, and that your experience of working out those thoughts, and arriving at something new to say, was some sort of illusion. He can say all the same things our philosophers are inclined to say about values, and in this case I am quite sure you are not about to let him get away with it.

18. Nietzsche is of course not alone in rejecting the notion that evaluations have to bottom out in something that is already there. For instance, Beauvoir (2018) argues that "seriousness"—her label for roughly that attitude—is a personal and ethical failing. Or again, John Dewey (1984) complains about utilitarianism that it "holds down value to objects *antecedently* enjoyed"; as in earlier pragmatists, what our conception of something comes to is a matter of how it (eventually) pans out—of what it leads us to—and so Dewey tells us that "to declare something satis*factory* is . . . in effect, a judgment that the thing 'will do' . . . it contemplates a future in which the thing . . . *will* do . . . a consequence the thing will actively institute; it will *do*" (206–208). Or yet again, Schroeter and Schroeter (2009), adapting moves made in the discussion of natural-kind terms launched by Hilary Putnam, suggest that the meaning of evaluative terms is a matter of "coordinated improvisation." But this is not the place to compare and contrast the different attempts to let go of that widely shared metaethical assumption.

19. At this point, some professionally knowledgeable readers will leap to classify Nietzsche as a constructivist, and we can ask ourselves what that would get right and what it would get wrong.

The notion of constructivism dates to the 1980s and initially was a very crisp intellectual tool; it has in the last while unfortunately come to be used much more loosely. (For an anthology that will give you a sense of more recent usage, see Bagnoli 2013.) I'll remind readers what the original and very useful sense of the term was, and stick to that.

Rawls (1989) introduced an alternative to the realist-or-noncognitivist mainstream of previous metaethics: a moral or practical status could be the output of a procedure, in something like the way that who wins a game of chess is the result of playing it out. A 'construction procedure,' so understood, has to be definite enough so that it settles the result—if you play out the game of chess, following the rules, it's clear who won the game—or, if you want to go by what the results of executing the procedure *would* be, definite enough so that there is a clear answer to *that* question (not the case in a chess game).

In certain respects, Nietzsche's values have the look and feel of the statuses produced in this way: they are neither eternally present superfacts nor reflections of our attitudes, but introduced by us, to guide our future activities. But Nietzsche was not a constructivist: values are invented, and there is no procedure for inventing things.

20. We still have Nietzsche's marked-up copy of Wellhausen (1883), and he discusses Strauss (1892) as a book that he engaged closely early on (AC 28/6:199).

21. The imprint of the Higher Criticism appears at many points in Nietzsche's work. For instance, we are told that "the *proprium* of all great, and especially sectarian veneration [is that] it blots out the original . . . features. . . of the venerated being. . . . When the first [Christian] community needed a judging, quarreling, angry, malignantly

sophistical theologian, . . . it put into [Jesus's] mouth, without any hesitation, those wholly unevangelical concepts which now it cannot do without" (AC 31/6:202–203; compare AC 37/6:208–209).

22. Compare Renan's (1955, 197) biography of Jesus, with which Nietzsche was familiar and which echoes some of the doctrines of the Higher Critics: "[T]his exaggerated taste for poverty could not be very lasting. It was one of those Utopian elements which always mingle in the origin of great movements, and which time rectifies."

23. On the legibility requirement, see Scott (1998, chap. 1) and Porter (1995). On commensurability, see D'Agostino 2003.

24. We could well have qualms at this point: surely the best inventions do not come from inventors who are motivated primarily by an enthusiasm for invention itself; perhaps this is a self-effacing value? I take the reservation seriously, but I don't know that there's a yes-or-no answer to the question; surely the effects of applying such a value will depend on how it, in turn, develops.

25. Nietzsche's way of seeing things shares some of its approach with Buss (n.d.); that any normative claim is to be underwritten with, *inter alia*, a further normative claim, seems to be common ground. However, I'm unclear whether Buss thinks of those underwriting claims as antecedently in place; on Nietzsche's way of thinking, we have been emphasizing, they come along later on.

26. I'm grateful to Harry Bloomfield for pressing me on this. Relatedly, for reminders that people have not always had the view that the value of humanity involves the equality of its members, see Elias (2000, 175); since we noticed Nietzsche being willing to dismiss it, should we worry that this commitment is liable to evaporate as well?

27. If a newly introduced value is inevitably thin, at any rate when it is not reducible to already available values, is it even, at that point, a value at all? This is a problem that deserves genuine consideration, even if we are not in a position to resolve it cleanly: recall that just as we knew what cars amounted to only long after they were first invented, we will know what it takes to be an idiosyncratic Nietzschean value— or even a value, plain and simple—only far down the road, in retrospect. However, suppose we tentatively take Moore's Open Question as characteristically applicable to values: that is, for any given value, ____, and any description of a state of affairs that is suitably independent of that value, we can ask, "The description holds, but is ___ _ present in it?" and have that make sense. Recall that priestly value of purity, whose earliest version was a list of ritual ablutions; you might well wonder whether, *then*, the question, "He has performed his ablutions, but is he *pure*?" did make sense.

28. Z P.1, 10/4:12, 28; see also II.2/4:109; III.12.12/4:255; "downfall" amends Kaufmann's poorly chosen "going under" as a rendering of *Untergang*.

29. Returning to the question of why nihilism presents differently in *Zarathustra* and in Nietzsche's other later writings: to a heroic prophet, idolized by his followers as himself the value that provides one's reason for living, the problem of nihilism must seem external to him, a feature of the humanity he observes. In Nietzsche's other authorial perspectives, all of which are in one way or another marked by, and the products of,

392 RETHINKING THE VALUE OF HUMANITY

the two-thousand-year-long history of attempts to make people ever less impressive, nihilism will be experienced much more personally, as a problem within *themselves*.

30. I'm grateful to Dani Attas, Teresa Burke, David Enoch, Svantje Guinebert, Hillel Millgram, Henry Richardson, Aubrey Spivey, Dar Triffonres, and Verena Wagner for helpful discussion; to Chrisoula Andreou, Sarah Buss, C. Thi Nguyen, and Nandi Theunissen for comments on drafts; to the Hebrew University for support through a Lady Davis Fellowship; and to the University of Utah's Philosophy Department for a Sterling M. McMurrin Esteemed Faculty Award.

References

Abbate, Janet. 1999. *Inventing the Internet.* Cambridge, MA: MIT Press.

Anderson, Lanier. 2009. "Nietzsche on Redemption and Transfiguration." In *The Re-Enchantment of the World*, edited by Joshua Landy and Michael Saler, 225–258. Stanford, CA: Stanford University Press.

Baatz, Simon. 2009. *For the Thrill of It: Leopold, Loeb, and the Murder That Shocked Jazz Age Chicago.* New York: Harper Perennial.

Bagnoli, Carla, ed. 2013. *Constructivism in Ethics.* Cambridge: Cambridge University Press.

Beauvoir, Simone. 2018. *The Ethics of Ambiguity.* Translated by Bernard Frechtman. New York: Open Road.

Buss, Sarah. n.d. "Against the Quest for the Source of Normativity." Unpublished manuscript.

Camus, Albert. 1971. *The Rebel.* Translated by Anthony Bower. New York: Penguin.

Clark, Maudemarie. 1991. *Nietzsche on Truth and Philosophy.* Cambridge: Cambridge University Press.

D'Agostino, Fred. 2003. *Incommensurability and Commensuration.* Aldershot: Ashgate.

Danto, Arthur. (1965) 1980. *Nietzsche as Philosopher.* New York: Columbia University Press.

Dewey, John. 1984. *The Quest for Certainty.* Carbondale: Southern Illinois University Press.

Elias, Norbert. 2000. *The Civilizing Process.* Revised ed. Translated by Edmund Jephcott. Malden, MA: Blackwell.

Espeland, Wendy N., and Michael Sauder. 2016. *Engines of Anxiety.* New York: Russell Sage Foundation.

Hitchcock, Alfred, dir. 1948. *Rope.* Burbank, CA: Warner Bros. Pictures.

James, William. 1987. "On Some Mental Effects of the Earthquake." In *William James: Writings 1902–1910*, edited by Bruce Kuklick, 1215–1222. New York: Library of America.

Mackie, John L. 1977. *Ethics: Inventing Right and Wrong.* New York: Penguin.

Millgram, Elijah. 2015. *The Great Endarkenment.* Oxford: Oxford University Press.

Millgram, Elijah. 2018. "Hypophilosophy." *Social Philosophy and Policy* 35 (2): 138–157.

Nehamas, Alexander. 1981. "The Postulated Author: Critical Monism as a Regulative Ideal." *Critical Inquiry* 8: 133–149.

Nehamas, Alexander. 1985. *Nietzsche: Life as Literature.* Cambridge, MA: Harvard University Press.

THE INVENTION OF VALUE   393

Neuhouser, Frederick. 2008. *Rousseau's Theodicy of Self-Love*. Oxford: Oxford University Press.

Nevo, Yanni. 2009. *Izmel she-Kahah*. Tel Aviv: Resling.

Nietzsche, Friedrich. 1954. *The Portable Nietzsche*. Edited and translated by Walter Kaufmann. New York: Penguin Books.

Nietzsche, Friedrich. 1974. *The Gay Science*. Translated by Walter Kaufmann. New York: Vintage Books/Random House.

Nietzsche, Friedrich. 1988. *Sämtliche Werke: Kritische Studienausgabe*. Edited by Giorgio Colli and Mazzino Montinari. 15 vols. Berlin: Deutscher Taschenbuch Verlag/de Gruyter.

Nietzsche, Friedrich. 2000. *Basic Writings of Nietzsche*. Edited and translated by Walter Kaufmann. Introduction by Peter Gay. New York: Modern Library/Random House.

Porter, Theodore. 1995. *Trust in Numbers*. Princeton, NJ: Princeton University Press.

Rawls, John. 1989. "Themes in Kant's Moral Philosophy." In *Kant's Transcendental Deductions*, edited by Eckhart Förster, 81–113. Stanford, CA: Stanford University Press.

Raz, Joseph. 1999. *Engaging Reason*. Oxford: Oxford University Press.

Renan, Ernest. 1955. *The Life of Jesus*. Introduction by John H. Holmes. New York: Modern Library.

Russell, Bertrand. (1905) 1973. "On Denoting." In *Essays in Analysis*, edited by Douglas Lackey, 103–119. New York: George Braziller.

Schroeter, Laura, and François Schroeter. 2009. "A Third Way in Metaethics." *Noûs* 43 (1): 1–30.

Scott, James. 1998. *Seeing Like a State*. New Haven, CT: Yale University Press.

Strauss, David F. 1892. *The Life of Jesus Critically Examined*. 2nd ed. Translated by George Eliot. New York: Macmillan.

Wellhausen, Julius. 1883. *Prolegomena zur Geschichte Israels*. Berlin: G. Reimer.

Williams, Bernard. 2006. "Nietzsche's Minimalist Moral Psychology." In *The Sense of the Past*, edited by Miles Burnyeat, 299–310. Princeton, NJ: Princeton University Press.

Windelband, Wilhelm. 2015. "History and Natural Science." In *The Neo-Kantian Reader*, edited by Sebastian Luft, 287–298. London: Routledge.

16
The Human Foundations of Our Political Ideals: An Essay on Gandhi's Political Radicalism

Akeel Bilgrami

Introduction

I would like, in this essay, to explore the value of humanity, not in response to questions about the nature of human dignity and respect, nor even in response to questions about what sets human subjects apart from all else, but rather in response to the subtle reductions or, better, diminishments, that political developments of the modern period have visited upon the very idea of human beings.

Two preliminary qualifications and one preliminary methodological admission, before I begin. First, these initial disavowals imply no denial of the centrality of notions of dignity and intrinsic respect-worthiness in characterizing the human nor any denial that human beings are, indeed, set apart in some important sense from all else (though how to elaborate what that sense is in a way that avoids familiar invidious forms of anthropocentric humanism remains an important and delicate philosophical issue). In fact, the points and argument I present in the paper will, no doubt, presuppose the importance of human dignity and some of the capacities and properties that (as far as we know) only human beings possess. It's just that these ideas are not driving my diagnosis of what is diminished by some tendencies of modern liberal politics.

Second, I have, in what I said a moment ago, quite deliberately added to "reductions" the improved term "diminishments" because I don't really have in mind the strict sorts of programmatic conceptual exercises that philosophers are prone to—the idea that some concept can be exhaustively understood, without any remainder, in terms of another. I mean something more informal, best described, as I said, as the *diminishing* of a concept, the concept of human beings, by developments in politics and political economy.

The methodological admission I must make is that in speaking of various developments in "liberalism," I am not primarily concerned with a particular

Akeel Bilgrami, *The Human Foundations of Our Political Ideals: An Essay on Gandhi's Political Radicalism* In: *Rethinking the Value of Humanity*. Edited by: Sarah Buss and L. Nandi Theunissen, Oxford University Press.
© Oxford University Press 2023. DOI: 10.1093/oso/9780197539361.003.0017

philosophical theory. Rather, I will be speaking to the theoretical assumptions which inform the dominant tendencies of the modern period of liberal politics and political economy as they surface over a few centuries in societies and states in Europe after the Westphalian peace, and then—through the agencies of settler colonialism—spread to North America, the Antipodes, and so on. A reader might well think that this or that point or criticism I present should be addressing some idea in, say, Kant or Rawls or Sen in order to be fully convincing. But that would be to miss the point of how I am proceeding. So, too, would any responses that appeal to highly idealized accounts of liberalism. A longer work elaborating on large methodological issues is needed to show exactly why that is so. There is nothing to do but to acknowledge at the outset that this essay cannot possibly be that work.

It is not as if I will myself entirely eschew idealization in the responses I present to the kind of impasse for liberalism that I identify in this paper. But the reconfigured ideals I do offer emerge not from a self-standing liberal philosophical theory but from an argument that tries to keep faith with the developments that emerge in a history of liberal political and economic formations and in the intellectual history that seeks to rationally consolidate them.

This methodological caution in some respects echoes, for political philosophy, Bernard Williams's (1985) attitude to ethics as a philosophical discipline, insisting on its historical contexts and sticking close to those contexts when seeking to make philosophical points and arguments. But it is also made inevitable by the fact that I will be constructing my argument from very nonstandard intellectual sources and resources, which in substantial measure owe their theoretical ground to historical context.

For some years now, I have been writing on Gandhi's moral and political philosophy, expounding the ways in which he departs from the familiar moral doctrines owing to Kant on the one hand and to utilitarianism on the other, and even more explicitly and avowedly departs from the broad liberal perspectives that have dominated political philosophy and theory in (what Gandhi himself often described as) "the modern West." The present paper is not a scholarly paper on Gandhi. It is intended rather to construct an argument on the basis of some ideas and commitments that were central to his thought on matters that fall within a wide range of interests (history, politics, political economy, philosophy, intellectual history). The argument itself, in the explicit form and vocabulary in which I construct it, obviously cannot be expected to be found in Gandhi's writing. How could it? Gandhi, though a remarkable philosopher, was not a salaried philosopher. He was not in the business of constructing detailed arguments. This having been said, the conclusions I reach on the basis of the argument I develop will not only draw on conceptual ingredients in Gandhi's philosophy, they will be entirely in keeping with the detail of Gandhi's thought on these matters.

396 RETHINKING THE VALUE OF HUMANITY

In fact, I can say with conviction that they reflect Gandhi's views in every important detail, even if the mode of articulation is not always his. In effect, then, the discussion that follows expresses my respect for a major philosopher in just the way, for instance, that two centuries of commentary have shown respect for Kant without mimicking his particular philosophical style of argument nor even his particular philosophical vocabulary.

Gandhi's humanism has been widely recorded and admired, so it is natural to think of his ideas as particularly worth presenting in a volume such as this. But I want to focus on a very *specific* dimension of his thinking. First, I focus on his diagnosis of the ways in which theoretical developments around liberal politics and political economy have steered liberalism's own ideals into deeply troubling tensions. Second, I focus on his positive proposal to the effect that these ideals might be reconfigured more satisfactorily by stressing another ideal that is more directly tied to human beings' relations to each other and the world they inhabit. It is not in his very *general* and straightforwardly humanist pronouncements that Gandhi's profoundest understanding of the value of humanity lies; rather, it emerges more obliquely, in this way, through his criticisms and reconfiguration of the liberal ideals of his country's colonizers.

To put it in the simplest and the most radical terms that he himself sometimes used, Gandhi simply did not share what was perhaps the deepest commitment of the political Enlightenment—that what was bad in human beings could be made better by good politics: by making human beings over into an abstract form of being called "citizens." All the codifications and constitutions that gradually emerged in the liberal nation-building exercises after the Westphalian peace are founded on this commitment about which Gandhi expressed a constant skepticism. For him, lofty though it was to make citizenship central to our political understanding, it amounted in some indirect fashion to a diminishment of the very idea of humanity. For him the most fundamental goal of politics did not start or rest with the idea of a citizen and the codes and ideals which constituted it. The goal was to realize a more agelessly human ideal.

To put it in these flamboyantly radical and omnibus terms, however, hides the details of a very complex argument. It is this argument I want to unearth.

1. Gandhi's Radicalism

Before I present a few of the ideas from which this argument is drawn and reconstruct the extended argument itself, here are a few preliminary stage-setting remarks to explain why I think this argument is important for anyone interested in Gandhi today.

HUMAN FOUNDATIONS OF OUR POLITICAL IDEALS 397

There is a great and natural tendency to think that his most widely read and controversial work, *Hind Swaraj*,[1] represents the reactionary Gandhi (2009) who opposed modernity, a position from which he slowly backpedaled over the next few decades, as he allowed the experience of the long anticolonial struggle he led to educate him toward more progressive ideas and ideals. As I said, this is a *natural* reading of Gandhi, but it is not a reading that shows much sympathy for or comprehension of his deepest intellectual and political motives. It is a reading which, from the very outset, rules out the possibility that one might interpret his antimodernism *itself* as progressive.

It might seem that there is something startling, something almost paradoxical about using the word "progressive" as I just have. After all, the whole point of the contrast between reactionary and progressive derives from an ideal of progress in which the past is overcome in modernity, so that to hearken back to it is reaction, while to embrace it is to be progressive. How, then, can a stance of antimodernity be said to be progressive without paradox?

This seeming paradox is amicably resolved if we replace all occurrences of the word "progressive" in what I have said so far with the word "radical." I don't mean "radical" in the very general sense of the vehement repudiation of conventional thinking (even Fascism is radical in that highly general sense). I mean rather "radical" in the quite usual specific sense that left-wing commentary evokes in describing its own conceptions of politics (though it too often assimilates this characterization with what is "modernist" and "progressive," thus ruling out at the outset, as I said, that there may be radical possibilities in the opposition to modernity).[2] To put it in a word, I am asking: Is there a left-wing or radical Gandhi *in* the antimodern Gandhi? And I am casting doubt on the more natural but unsympathetic reading which asserts that there is a left-wing or radical Gandhi *despite* the antimodern Gandhi.

One way to pursue the question I have just posed about the radical possibilities *in* Gandhi's antimodernism is to find continuities between Gandhi's opposition to features of European (or what he sometimes called "Western") modernity and the opposition in the *early* modern period by radicals in Europe to what they *presciently foresaw* as the alarming direction in which *their* incipient modernity was heading. I am referring here to dissenters in the land of his colonial masters such as the Diggers, some of the more radical among the Levellers, and a variety of other radical sects, memorably studied by Christopher Hill (1972). Their alarm turned out to be entirely justified. But their voices were the dissenting voices of a radical opposition in the seventeenth century that lost out in history. If Gandhi, in *Hind Swaraj*, was, in some core sense, expressing a counterpart alarm almost three centuries later—an alarm about an incipient modernity in India heading in the lamentable direction that the early dissenters had foreseen, a direction being imposed on it by its colonizers—then a plausible way to press on with this

398 RETHINKING THE VALUE OF HUMANITY

dialectic is to read *Hind Swaraj* as being written under the shrewd perception by its author that, in 1909, when he wrote it, India was at just the crossroads that Europe was at in early modernity.

What I am proposing, therefore, is a genealogical grounding of Gandhi's radicalism in the radicalism of an earlier period in the land of his colonial masters. In so doing, I will be arguing that what seems antimodern in his thought would not seem so if we kept this dialectic firmly in our sights.

In general, the fact that the elements with affinities to the radical dissenting ideas voiced in the *early* modern period should appear to us as *antimodern* is due to a confluence of two closely related factors. It is due, first, to our tendency to think of the path from early to late modernity as a teleological inevitability. It is due, second and consequently, to our late tendency to either entirely overlook the substantial presence of the dissenting voices of the earlier period or to obscure their significance. These two factors conspire to make it seem as if any assertion of some of the radical ideas to be found in early modern dissenting traditions at a date as late as, for instance, 1909, necessarily occupies a stubbornly reactionary position—something they would not seem to do if we viewed the teleology as noncompulsory, as Gandhi certainly did, and if we kept fully in our view of the past the power and pregnant possibilities of those dissenting ideas.

I've spoken of Gandhi's radicalism so far only by way of distancing his political philosophy from the taint of reactionary antimodernism. But I have yet to say anything about how his radicalism is deeply tied to ideas about the value of humanity, ideas that are, in a key respect, quite of a piece with Marx. To bring this out, I will now begin to reconstruct Gandhi's extended argument against liberal formulations of our political ideals. I will show how Gandhi contrasts the value of human beings with the value of citizen subjects—championing the former over the latter.

2. Some Philosophical and Political Claims in Gandhi

Let me begin by briefly listing the *four* broad philosophical claims and commitments in Gandhi's thinking which are essential to this argument and which I will invoke at various stages of my argument.

1. First, Gandhi took ethics to be a primarily *perceptual* discipline. On his view, the world, the *perceptible* world we inhabit, makes normative demands on us to which our practical agency responds.

Such a view has in recent years been attributed by John McDowell to Aristotle, and McDowell (1979, 1998) himself has developed it along very interesting lines.

But that is a high philosophical location for it. The view may be found in popular religion in virtually every part of the world.

In Gandhi's own thinking it derived partly from the Bhakti influences on his thought and partly from his own repudiation of the great centrality that modern science had come to have in the worldview he associated with the modern West.[3] In line with a great deal of popular religion, including popular Christianity, Gandhi believed that the world we inhabit (including nature and even our own bodies) is sacralized by the presence of divinity and thus shot through with normative properties that are not reducible to those studied by natural and social science. Thus, for instance, a storm was not just a meteorological phenomenon; it was a "threat" to a fisherman living on the coastline. The body was not just composed of limbs and torso, flesh and bone; it was also a site of emotions and meanings which needed to be in equilibrium. The social conditions of the peasantry cannot be captured in exclusively clinical terms—for instance, in terms of the calorie counts of their diet; there is also an irreducible description of them in the evaluative vocabulary of "malnutrion," "need," and "suffering." In a word, matter is not mere matter but shot through with values, whose ultimate source is divine.

It was this sacralization of nature that began to be unsettled in the seventeenth century in a process often described as "disenchantment"; this was a result not so much of the rise of modern science itself as of the centrality that natural science had begun to be given by the institutions around natural science that first emerged in the second half of the seventeenth century (such as, for instance, initially the Royal Society in England), institutions that slowly formed lasting alliances both with *High* (not popular) *Christianity* (Anglicanism in England) and with *commercial* interests. This alliance of interests developed a worldview according to which the very idea of nature was equated (without remainder) with "that which the natural sciences study" and eventually with the idea of natural resources. Since the natural sciences do not study value or the sacred, value and sacral properties were, by this equation, evacuated from matter and nature.[4] The divine was given only a providential place *outside* the universe (a clock winder, in Newton's metaphor), and with increasing secularization, all values were thought to be derived from human states of mind, desires, and moral sentiments (to use Hume's and Adam Smith's terminology). Eventually, the very idea of nature was transformed into the idea of natural resources; nature came to be regarded as something from which we could take with impunity because its value was exclusively a function of our needs and desires.

Gandhi was explicitly opposed to this understanding of nature and matter. Because of his deep commitment to a sacralized world, both natural and social, he saw our states of mind and motivation not as the source of value but rather as responses to the value in the world we inhabit (including the value in/of our

400 RETHINKING THE VALUE OF HUMANITY

own bodies and in/of nature itself). To return to the example I gave earlier, the phenomenon on the horizon is not simply a meteorological phenomenon to be studied and predicted in scientific terms; it is also a threat, something that natural science does not and cannot study but which prompts our *practical* agency.[5] Thus the perceptible world, including nature, consists of threats as much as it consists of H_2O, condensation, etc. For Gandhi, practical agency and the entire discipline of ethics was thus a perceptual response to the world around us that makes normative demands on us, over and above the demands gratified by scientific explanation and prediction.

It is not as if Gandhi, in claiming the primacy of perception, denied that there is ethical deliberation. Rather he thought that deliberation is a secondary sophistication; it occurs either when we have *conflicting perceptions* of what the value-laden layout of the world demands of our practical agency or when we find that our initial or instinctive agentive responses to those perceived normative demands are not adequate. It is only then that the usual deliberative cogitations of ranking and weighing and self-critical reflection are made necessary.

2. A second philosophical claim concerns what is conspicuously *missing* in Gandhi's philosophical outlook. It is remarkable that though he thought long and hard about the nature of politics, the ideals of liberty and equality, as they were theoretically developed in the political Enlightenment, were not central in his understanding of the polity. In this, though he never deployed the analytical category "bourgeois" in his writings, he was aligned with Marx, who, as is well known, dismissed both liberty and equality as bourgeois ideals.[6]

3. To the extent that Gandhi wrote about liberty at all, his conception of individual liberty was that it was a form of *self-governance* or what he often called *swaraj*.[7] Individual liberty, for him, consists of each one of us making decisions that shape our material and spiritual lives. For Gandhi democracies are substantially (as opposed to merely formally) in place only when individual liberty, understood as self-governance, does in fact translate into our shaping the world to be in accord with these decisions.

4. Gandhi thought that alienation was an increasing problem in modern societies, and that a chief goal of politics should be to overcome this alienation. The problem, more specifically, was an increasing attitude of *detachment* in our relations to each other and the world—where the opposite of detachment is not attachment so much as engagement.[8] Gandhi often expressed what he had in mind by such detachment by asking the question: How is it that we have transformed our conception of the world from a place to live in to a place to master and control? Realizing that this was too general and remote a way of expressing the notion of alienation, he asked, more particularly: How is it that we have transformed the concept of nature into the concept of natural

HUMAN FOUNDATIONS OF OUR POLITICAL IDEALS   401

resources? How is it that we have transformed the concept of people into the concept of populations? How is it that we have transformed the concept of knowledges to live by into the concept of expertise to rule by? And even, and this is startling for us who have been brought up on liberal doctrine: How is it that we have transformed the concept of human beings into the concept of citizens? Gandhi tries to show that all these transformations are really, at bottom, the same transformation, in that they all reflect an increasing alienation and disengagement in our outlook on the world—in our understanding of nature, human subjects, and human knowledge. Here, too, he traced the problem to the increasing centrality that science came to have in the mentalities that have shaped the "modern West."

Though he was not a socialist, like Marx he thought that this disengagement of modernity owed much to capitalist economic formations that began to take hold at about the time that science became central to people's worldview. It is striking, then, that for all their large and well-known differences, in stressing alienation and not stressing liberty and equality, Gandhi was Marx's intellectual partner.

With these four claims in place, I'll proceed now to the promised philosophical argument. This argument will show how to *integrate* these seemingly miscellaneous Gandhian claims.

3. Early Modernity and Political Rationality

In India, many people have recently protested against the government's promotion of corporate projects via an "eminent domain" form of dispossession of the poor peasantry (and agricultural laborers) in various parts of the countryside as well as of the foresters from the extensive commons which they inhabited and which was their only source of sustenance. Against this protest, even so humane an economist as Amartya Sen (2010) declared in an article in the Kolkata *Telegraph* that, just as England went through pain in order to create such vital urban centers as London and Manchester, so too, India will have to go through pain in order to create its own Londons and Manchesters.

In making that remark, Sen was not just expressing a considered view that is widely held among economists and social scientists; he was also revealing an assumption widely shared by the lay intelligentsia—that the social and economic developments that happened in Europe must happen everywhere else in the world, including its erstwhile colonies. What underlies this assumption?

It may seem, at first sight, that the assumption reflects a commitment to some sort of "iron laws" of history and political economy, whereby what happened in Europe in the early modern period *will* happen everywhere else. A certain rigid

402 RETHINKING THE VALUE OF HUMANITY

stagial (sometimes called "stadial") reading of Marx suggests that he believed in laws of this sort. That is a vexed interpretative issue in the study of Marx. But liberal political doctrine, which provides the framework within which Sen writes, does not endorse any such historical determinism. Rather, with his stress on normative notions of rationality, Sen is making a more prescriptive assumption: what happened in Europe in the early modern period must happen elsewhere because what happened in Europe was *rational*.[9]

Let us explore this appeal to rationality. In the early modern period one particular social theory defended the rationality of the very incipient forms of capitalism that can be located in the privatization of land out of the commons. At the core of this theory was a form of contractualism that can be traced to John Locke.

As is well known, the point of social contract theory, whether in Lockean or some other form, is to establish that in an originary prepolitical condition described as a "state of nature" (or an "original position"), when people *freely consent* to being constrained by certain principles or arrangements, they are thereby transformed into citizens, and the state of nature into a polity. And consenting to live according to these principles or arrangements is rational if, and only if, the result is that these people will, in the main, be *better off*.

In the contractualist strand I am concerned with, the canonical scenario has it that were someone in a state of nature to come upon a stretch of land in the commons and fence it and register it at an elementary form of bureau set up for this kind of registry, then the land would become *his*.[10] Suppose then that this is done by some of the people, and they each keep faith with the general rational requirement mentioned above—that no one is made worse off and at least some are made better off than they were in the state of nature. Suppose, too, that they clarify this requirement by adding the following crucial clause: "If those who had done this were then to hire others, who had not, at wages which enable these others to live better, then the arrangement would be justified since they too would be better off than they were in the state of nature."

Such was the explicit argument of the Lockean model of the social contract (roughly an argument from Pareto-improvement), which went on to became the cornerstone for certain political principles and arrangements that came to be incorporated into a liberalism in which free speech (except for atheists, heretics, Catholics, etc.), private property, and wage labor were seen as progressive advances justified by the mutual advantage for *all* concerned (or, in the limiting case, the advantage for some and no resulting *dis*advantage for anyone else).

When one asks the question "What in the historical context was motivating the articulation of such a contractualist theory?," the answer is that the theory philosophically consolidated the system of enclosures which had been maintained by brute force for many decades. It justified this system and the laws that supported it as a system of moral rights.

Part 8 of volume 1 of Marx's ([1867] 1990) *Capital* presented in detail the nature of such primitive accumulation in general, and in chapter 27 he presented, in particular, the predatory nature of the form it took with the enclosures in England. This critique in Marx was presciently anticipated in the widespread protest against the enclosures among some of the radical groups during the English Revolution. These protests predate Locke, but they can be understood as preemptively challenging Locke's claim that such departures from the state of nature would be universally endorsed. A dissenting radical voice like Gerard Winstanley's, the remarkable leader of the Diggers, could be heard as anachronistically saying to Locke (anachronistically in the dual sense that they predated him and that the vocabulary was not available to them), "The entire contractualist scenario as you have presented it generates an *opportunity cost.* An opportunity cost is the cost of an avoided benefit paid for making a certain choice. That avoided benefit is the collective cultivation of the commons that is prevented by the choice to privatize the land in your initial step in the scenario. Once the step is taken, it is true, as you say, that those who were hired for wages are better off than they were in *the state of nature.* But they are not better off than they *would have been* if the land had not been privatized in the first place and if there was a collective cultivation of the commons instead."

The criticism, based on a relatively simple counterfactual, appeals to a quite different notion of consent from the one Locke assumes. In Locke, a contractor has implicitly consented to a principle or policy if he is, as a result, made better off than he was (or at any rate, not worse off) in the state of nature; whereas for Winstanley, someone has implicitly consented to living in a condition that differs from the state of nature if (and only if) this condition was the best alternative to the state of nature. Since, according to Winstanley, the institution of private property is not as desirable as the condition of collective cultivation, we cannot be assumed to have rationally consented to the institution of private property. Otherwise put, the consent Locke imagines on the part of those who are hired to work for wages is coerced by a condition they could not avoid: their nonpossession of the land in the face of others' possession of it. In short, the Lockean contractualist tradition presents a *coerced* implicit consent fraudulently as a *freely chosen* implicit consent.

I said earlier that a great deal of social theory presented the developments in political economy in the early modern period as advances in political *rationality*; it is the rationality of these developments which was invoked to justify later claims that the rest of the world, including Europe's erstwhile colonized lands, would have to adopt these political and economic arrangements if they were going to "progress." But, if I am right, the supposition that the historical developments in England were "rational" depends on two assumptions about the rationality of consenting to these developments: (1) consenting would make one

404 RETHINKING THE VALUE OF HUMANITY

better off, and (2) the consent would be freely given. If the criticism implicit in Winstanley's dissenting stances is correct, *these two conditions cannot be satisfied jointly here*. According to Winstanley's counterfactual notion of consent, the first requirement has not been met, and if you simply reject the counterfactual notion of consent, you have no reason to assume that the consent to which you appeal was freely given (by the nonpossessors of land).

This argument seems to leave Lockean social theorists without their premise, to say nothing of their conclusion. But it would be too quick and premature to leave the counterargument here. Locke, in the early modern period, only *began* an argument that I have been countering on behalf of the radical dissenters. His argument has been updated and fortified by more recent theoretical developments within the framework of liberal political thought. The riposte to Locke that I put in the mouth of the preemptive dissenting voices in early modern England made counterfactual use of the ideal of a *collective cultivation of the commons*. But liberal theory more recently has deployed further conceptual resources to try to undermine this ideal. So let me now very briefly address one central strand of such resources. This will allow me also to come to my Gandhian themes of alienation and human subjectivity.

4. More Recent Updating of Political Rationality

Perhaps the most standard strategy for defending liberal theory is by way of appeal to the so-called tragedy of the commons. Following Garret Hardin, the idea, very roughly put, is to raise an intractable problem for any ideal of cooperative life, such as collective cultivation of the commons. The intractable problem is supposed to be that, given human psychology, individuals are rationally required to behave in ways that undermine the collective; they are required to not cooperate in the ways necessary to sustain the collective. The cooperation necessary for the collective ideal requires each commoner to pay a certain cost. (Sometimes—in fact oftentimes—this cost takes the form of restraint, since often overuse or overcultivation is the problem.) If each individual commoner pays the cost, of course everyone gains. But each individual commoner will have to consider that if he does not cooperate (i.e., does not pay the cost), the gains are immediate, whereas the gains from cooperation are long term; moreover, the gains from noncooperation are all for himself, whereas the gains from paying the cost are spread over the whole group. Above all—and this is really the crucial and clinching consideration—he is never sure that if he pays the cost, others will do so, too. Since one is in the epistemic dark about whether others are contributing the bit demanded of them in the collective cultivation, one constantly fears that one's contribution will be wasted if others don't do their bit.[11]

HUMAN FOUNDATIONS OF OUR POLITICAL IDEALS   405

On such an understanding of the collective ideal—which is pervasive in many liberal frameworks—some individual commoner who decides not to cooperate is always at an advantage since the gains of noncooperation will be immediate and all for himself and completely assured, whereas the gains from cooperating are long term, dispersed over the whole group, and, above all, *always uncertain*. Noncooperation for him, as an individual, would thus be rational. But the commons cannot survive if each individual does this individually rational thing. It is doomed. Thus the tragedy. So privatization is a better bet.

It is often said in critical response to this liberal argument that the tragedy of the commons idea can be developed not in the direction of providing a rational basis for privatization but rather to argue for regulating the commons and its collective use by monitoring, policing, and punishing noncooperation. Elinor Ostrom's (1990) fine analytical and extensive empirical study, for instance, presents the principles for such regulation after a scrutiny of various commons and their governance on four continents.[12] Now, who can be opposed to such regulation? It is obviously a good thing. There is no gainsaying that. *But* this critical reinterpretation of the argument of the tragedy of the commons does not address its fundamental assumptions. Indeed, *the idea of policing and regulation is vulnerable to attack from the same kind of thinking, the same considerations that lead to the tragedy of the commons.* It just happens one level up. Even if we ignore the well-known difficulties of detecting many nonobvious forms of noncooperation, we can ask *why anyone should cooperate with policing and detection and punishment* if he can get away with *not* cooperating—by offering bribes, for instance, or making mafia-style threats against those who detect and police or those who cooperate with the policing and detecting (witnesses, for example), or by loopholing the laws and regulations to make noncooperation legal after all. These are familiar and pervasive phenomena in a wide range of societies, with the last of these strategies most operative in societies (not to mention institutions such as international credit agencies, trade organizations, etc.) that congratulate themselves on being free of the more blatant forms of political corruption exemplified by bribes and threats. Though we should obviously support regulation, it may thus be worth probing whether there is something more deeply problematic in the appeal to the tragedy of the commons—something that can't be rectified by solutions like regulation and policing.

Short of a more fundamental critique, it may rightly be said that Locke, anticipating these later arguments (against the very idea of the cooperation needed for the collective cultivation of the commons and anticipating also the vulnerability to similar arguments of the idea of the cooperation needed to sustain a system of regulating the commons), was correct to see his version of the implicit consent of *all* contractors (possessors *and* nonpossessors of land) as rational, and *even freely given*. After all, there appears to be no other alternative to the tragedy of

406 RETHINKING THE VALUE OF HUMANITY

the commons. It is just such a fundamental critique that I want to offer here.[13] Appealing to the four Gandhian philosophical claims listed in Section 2, I want to show how Gandhi sheds light on what is wrong with the whole way of thinking that underlies the argument of the tragedy of the commons and thereby hints at alternative conceptions of our political ideals. But first I need to add a second, very central line of development in liberal doctrine concerning the ideals of liberty and equality.

5. The Political Ideals of the Enlightenment

It is a large and familiar curiosity that liberal doctrine, as soon as it articulated its two great ideals of liberty and equality, went on over the next two centuries to theoretically develop them in a way that put them in indissoluble tension with one another. The Cold War debate over the relevant importance of each ideal is only the crudest and most publicly familiar symptom of this perverse development. The tension was charted in far more sophisticated theoretical work for well over a century before the Cold War. What generated the tension? In essence it was produced by certain features of liberty. There are a number of such features, but let me mention just two.

The most well-known and well-studied feature is that the possession of property bestows a particular form of liberty on its possessors (something justified by arguments such as the one I just presented from the social contract and fortified by tragedy-of-the-commons arguments). This put liberty structurally at odds with equality in ways that are so widely studied that I need hardly say anything more about it here. Marx was only the most powerful and systematic critic of liberty, so construed.

Another feature is what I will call "the incentivization of talent," also pervasive in liberal ways of thought and taken for granted by virtually everyone within its orbit, and not necessarily only theorists and intellectuals. Talent was initially distinguished from the capacity for labor; while labor was evenly distributed among people, talent was not. With the entrenchment of highly individualized notions of individual liberty (a locution which may seem to contain an element of redundancy, but which, as I shall try to explain later, does not), the idea of desert—of the right to reap the praise and reward for the productions of one's talent[14]— became central to the notion of liberty itself. If one did not allow praise and reward for the productions of talent, one would, it was thought, be praising and rewarding the zeitgeist. This would be to demote the individual to nothing more than a symptom of the zeitgeist in embodied human form.[15] And this would be incompatible with the right of self-governance. So, too, it would be a violation of this basic right if one were to prevent *others* from enjoying these productions *at their most (incentivized) excellent* if desert, the reaping of the rewards of talent, was not in place as an individual right. And all this generated inequalities in ways that are too obvious to elaborate.

The features that shape the interaction between the two chief ideals of liberal doctrine are so entrenched in defining those ideals that policies proposed within liberal societies to get rid of them altogether would not merely be disallowed; they would be viewed as an egalitarian affront. Indeed, this attitude is now so embedded in these ideals that there is no way to make them compatible without substantially revising the very *meanings* of the terms "liberty" and "equality" as they have come to be theoretically elaborated and politically implemented in liberal democratic societies. The tension, in a sense, defines them, so much so that they have come to be seen as standing in a *built-in trade-off relation*, whereby an increase in the one is bound to be achievable only at the cost of a diminishing of the other.

Now, except in shallow taxonomical exercises, meanings inherited by long-standing doctrinal formulations and institutional application cannot be changed stipulatively. If new meanings are to be nonarbitrary, the terms or concepts to be transformed have to emerge (organically, as it were) from revised theory. How might this be done? Gandhi's ideas give a hint about one direction in which one might proceed.

6. The Gandhian Ideal of the Unalienated Life

As I read Gandhi, it is on account of the irresolvable tension between them in our inherited understanding that we must remove the ideals of liberty and equality from center stage, where liberalism has put them. In their place we are to envisage a more basic and *human* ideal, an ideal that speaks more directly and foundationally to the human subject without the mediations of the liberal polity: the ideal of an *unalienated life*. This ideal can be found in traditions outside of liberalism, whether in Marx or, as with Gandhi, in a wide range of popular religions that have been agelessly present in a plurality of social worlds. Having introduced this ideal, it is Gandhi's proposal that we usher liberty and equality back in (through the backdoor, as it were), *not* as central, but *now as nesting within* the more basic ideal. As I will bring out below, in Gandhi's view, it is in this way that liberty and equality are no longer necessarily in a trade-off tension with each other. It wouldn't be misleading to suggest here that Gandhi's strategy, at least in broad outline, is Kuhnian. "Liberty" and "equality" in this new setting change their meanings, much like the meaning of "mass" was said to have done in its migration from the framework of Newtonian mechanics to the framework of Einsten's physics. And so the view that emerges is not an "improvement" on the liberal account; rather it "changes the subject."

408 RETHINKING THE VALUE OF HUMANITY

What is this ideal of an unalienated life? As a starting point, think of it as characterized by the sense of belonging that was made possible by the social frameworks of a period prior to modernity. All major political and social philosophers—Marx and Hegel and Rousseau are only the most prominent; more recently there is Sartre as well—have tended to agree that whatever the defects of societies prior to modernity, alienation was not among them. Alienation is a malaise of modernity. But the point remains that, as is well known and widely acknowledged by the very same philosophers, the unalienated life of those earlier times was marred by oppressive defects in those societies. (To say "feudal" to describe that oppression would be merely to use a *vastly* summarizing and somewhat misleading category that we have all been brought up with.)

It is precisely those defects that the sloganized ideals of liberalism, liberty and equality, were intended to address. We have seen, however, that the methodological and theoretical framework within which those two concepts were developed made it impossible to so much as conceive how they could be jointly implemented. This suggests that we focus, first, on the ideal of unalienatedness, and on how it might be realized outside oppressive structures. If, in the elaboration of the answer to this question, liberty and equality come to be of a piece with the idea of an unnalienated life, this is because they will now, as concepts, be importantly different from the mutually incompatible concepts they were when at the center of liberal theorizing. This, at any rate, is a possibility we find in Gandhi. He offers us a transformed notion of liberty and equality by offering us *a transformed notion of the unalienated life*. It is a holistically triangular transformation: we overcome a certain conceptual-historical dialectic and in doing so *together and at once transform all* three *concepts* that feature in the dialectic.

The transformation of these concepts starts with liberty. Gandhi finds no place for the highly individualized notion of liberty that is conceptually tied to private property and the incentivization of talent. If one were to find a way of thinking of liberty in nonindividualist terms it would be quite of a piece with the ideal of an unalienated life that Gandhi thought central to politics. I want to stress here that in saying this, I attribute to Gandhi *no interest whatever in the idea of collective liberty*. Indeed, there is much evidence in his writing that any such idea would be anathema.[16] It was individual liberty that was his only concern and for which he was seeking a reconfiguration along lines that were not individualistic, a project that in no way struck him as paradoxical.

For Gandhi, as I anticipated in Section 2, the notion of individual liberty is constitutively tied to the idea of self-governance: the power to make the decisions that shape the material and spiritual aspects of our lives. This being so, in order to transform the notion of liberty in the way we have just seen is required, we would have to envisage each individual as approaching these decisions nonindividualistically. This seemingly paradoxical suggestion can be

HUMAN FOUNDATIONS OF OUR POLITICAL IDEALS 409

presented in two stages. (I want to register as a caveat right away that the first stage is misleading as an attribution to Gandhi since it looks like an ethical position that criticizes self-interest rather than what it is in Gandhi: an epistemological position based on his metaethical assumption about the nature of values that I mentioned in Section 2. I'll get to that more authentically Gandhian position in the second stage.)

In the first stage, one might say that what is required is that an individual make these decisions not primarily with her own interests in mind but with a concern for the interests of the group or collective as well. Simple examples, such as the following, can illustrate how this requirement is met: I am to decide on how to vote on a recruitment for my philosophy department. I must be motivated in my decisions (voting decisions, say) to favor someone who is good for the department, even if there are others whom I would prefer from my own personal point of view, whose presence would be better for me, given my own individual interests. It is worth pointing out that, even though, in this first stage, the proposal looks like an utterly familiar critique of self-interest, in the Gandhian dialectic within which I am making the proposal, it is a critique of self-interest that is in the service of *a reconstruction of a notion of liberty*. When we note that, it is not just a familiar and platitudinous proposal but a distinctive and unusual one.

In the second stage, its distinctiveness gets another dimension. The perceptualist metaethics briefly sketched in Section 2 comes into focus, and there is no overt reference to self-interest. If the exercise of our individual liberty in self-governance is to make decisions that seek to shape our material and spiritual lives, then, when an individual makes decisions of this sort, she responds to the *perceptually given* normative demands that the *world* (both the natural and the social world) presents to her. This, in turn, means that self-governing decisions require us to *see* the world right, to see correctly what its normative demands are, and to respond to those demands. The point is, in a sense, quite literally phenomenological. *And what it is for each individual to see the world right is to be understood, in a way I explain at length a little later, in terms of the idea of an unalienated life. In a world without alienated relations between individuals, each individual's perceptual orientation toward the world is such that the individualistic perspective on it is not primary.*

There is nothing paradoxical about this idea of an individual seeing the world from a nonindividualistic or larger point of view than her own. It is constantly and everywhere present. Consider how, when one is driving a car on the road (as opposed to, say, when one is walking on the road), one orients oneself perceptually to the demands of the world ahead not from the point of view of *one's own individual body* (as one does when one is walking on the road) but from the point of view of something larger than one's individual body, from the point of view of the *whole car*. This is, of course, only a *bodily* example of an expanded perceptual

410 RETHINKING THE VALUE OF HUMANITY

orientation. I am presenting it *only* as an example to remove the seeming element of paradox in the general idea of an individual's perceptual perspective on the world being nonindividualistic, that is to say, taking in, in one's perceptions, the properties of the world from a point of view larger than one's own. Obviously, what Gandhi is seeking is a *social*, not just bodily, expansion of the individual's perceptual orientation on the world's value properties. It goes without saying that that will be a more complex expansion.

We get a better glimpse of such a socially expanded perceptual phenomenology of acting upon the world's demands on one, if we consider more standard examples in the philosophical literature, such as the individual player of an instrument in an orchestra perceiving (hearing) the normative demands on her from a larger point of view than her own, or a player in a soccer game perceiving the normative demands on her from a larger point of view than her own. The example of an individual faculty member seeing the world from the department's perspective, rather than his own, was similarly intended to be an example of this general sort.[17]

I repeat here what I said at the outset in Section 2, that Gandhi's perceptualist view of value and ethics was not denying that inquiry and deliberation may well be needed in ethical and political matters. But at the end of it, once the verdicts of the inquiry and deliberation are in, it makes us *see* the world and its normative demands on us differently.[18] And in this second stage of the point I am making about the decisions that go into the exercise of liberty as self-governance, one is not seeing the world aright unless the *basic* orientation one has on it is the orientation of the larger collective (whether an orchestra, a soccer team, or a philosophy department, or an even larger social group whose governance is at stake). I emphasized the word "basic" in the previous sentence and I will return to it a little later when comparing the idea of such moral perception in an unalienated set of human relations with Wittgenstein's idea of a "basic (intentional) action." The reason I present all this as a second stage in elaborating the transformed notion of liberty as self-governance is that assimilating this notion to the ideal of unalienatedness reflects not so much a moralist's critique of self-interestedness as an authoritative experience, according to a credible *epistemology* of morals. This will become clearer when we consider some of the further implications of the idea of nonalienation.

The upshot of making the exercise of liberty be shaped and constituted in this way by an ideal of an unalienated life is intended by Gandhi to yield a form of liberty that is not at odds with the notion of equality. If the very exercise of liberty requires one to make the decisions that go into self-governance by responding to the world's normative demands on one from a point of view larger than one's own (a point of view that comes to be naturally adopted when one's relations with others are unalienated, from the point of view of the group, then—on such a

HUMAN FOUNDATIONS OF OUR POLITICAL IDEALS   411

conception of liberty—equality is not something *extra or further* to be navigated in terms of a trade-off with liberty; the removal of this trade-off relationship between the two concepts, rather, is *built into* the exercise of *liberty* itself, when liberty is so understood.[19] The point is not that liberty, so conceived, will actually deliver equality within the group. The point rather is that it is no longer defined in such a way that it needs to be in trade-off relations with equality. That is all that was being sought in the promised triangular conceptual reconfiguration of our ideals.[20]

My reading of Gandhi had proposed a triangular transformation of all three notions—liberty, equality, and the unalienated life—together and at once, so as to be able to finesse a seemingly irresolvable tension that existed between the ideals of liberty and equality and thereby, in turn, to repudiate a path of defense and fortification of Lockean ideas about the rationality of certain political and economic arrangements that Sen, in the remark I cited, had assumed to be inevitable for Indian society. That path of defense and fortification appealed to considerations that go into what is called "the tragedy of the commons," considerations that are driven, among other things, chiefly by certain qualms or anxiety that is summoned in each commoner, if he is rational. It is these considerations that are addressed by the transformations I have sought. In particular, if the notion of liberty is transformed by nesting it within the ideal of unalienatedness, not only does it lose its trade-off relations with equality, but, given this reconfiguration, it is now *not even so much as possible to raise the considerations that led to the tragedy of the commons.*

The idea is this: in an unalienated society, the commoner cannot make sense of the driving anxiety and qualms, the question "Would my efforts and contributions to the collective cultivation (or restraint from overcultivation) be wasted if others don't also contribute?" For Gandhi, *this question is itself a symptom of alienation.* Or to put it differently, for Gandhi, a central element in the very idea of being unalienated is that *this question does not occur to one.* When each unalienated person, in exercising liberty and making his self-governing decisions, sees the world's normative demands aright, in the way Gandhi proposes, this anxiety is *preempted.* The point, once again, is epistemological rather than moral. It is not as if there is something morally wrong about raising the question (a morally distasteful anxiety prompted by one's self-interest). Rather, in an unalienated group or society, the question *does not compute* for the individual commoner.

To be unalienated, then, is to be free of a certain malaise. But that malaise gets a rather philosophical formulation in Gandhi. It is an epistemological and phenomenological lapse. Thus our avoidance of the path which leads to the tragedy of the commons (something that owes to the fact that we stand in unalienated relations with others) requires no particular gallantry of us. To be in unalienated social relations with others is not to have sympathy for or feel fraternity[21] with others nor

412 RETHINKING THE VALUE OF HUMANITY

to show solidarity or be altruistic toward others rather than being self-interested, good though it is to have and do all those things. Rather, it is to be *free of a way of thought* in which—when we make the decisions we make in governing ourselves as individuals in the exercise of our liberty—we do not really find it wrong but cannot even find it *so much as intelligible* to have the qualm that leads to the tragedy of the commons. To be free of that form of thinking is the other side of a fitting phenomenology of value. On this conception of nonalienation, to *see* the world and its value properties aright and to overcome alienation are not two things but one.

To explain why this is so, permit me the indulgence of a personal anecdote. It concerns an experience with my father in my preteen youth that I recounted in an earlier essay on Gandhi (Bilgrami 2001).[22] He would sometimes ask that I go for walks with him in the early morning on the beach near our home in Bombay. One day, while walking, we came across a wallet with some rupees sticking out of it. My father stopped me and said somewhat dramatically, "Akeel, why shouldn't we take this?" And I said sheepishly, though honestly, "I think we should take it." He looked irritated and said, "Why do you think we should take it?" And I replied, what is surely a classic response, "Because if we don't take it, somebody else will." I expected a denunciation, but his irritation passed and he said, "If we don't take it, nobody else will." I thought then that this remark had no logic to it at all. Only decades later, when I was thinking of questions of alienation, did I realize that his assumption reflected an unalienated framework of thinking.

The "nobody else will" in my father's response cannot be expressive of unalienatedness if it is interpreted as a prediction of what others will do. When we predict what others will do, we relate to them from a disengaged perspective. That is the perspective that pervades alienated social relations. In fact, it is only when we view others from this perspective that we are prompted to ask the question that drives the tragedy of the commons: "What if I paid the cost of cooperation and others didn't?" From a detached perspective, what my father said might seem like naïve optimism about what others will do. But the assumption that others will not take the wallet if we don't is *not* made from that detached point of view. It is an assumption of a quite different sort, more in the spirit of "Let's see ourselves this way," an assumption that is unselfconsciously expressive of our unalienatedness, of our being engaged with others and the world, rather than assessing, in a detached mode, the prospects of how they will behave. My father was suggesting, in other words, that my ground for giving my response to his initial question is a reflection of just the kind of falling short of the ideal of unalienatedness as I am claiming is reflected in the question that is supposed to occur to the rational commoner in a certain conception of social and political rationality that drives the considerations that lead to the tragedy of the commons.

To return to the perceptual understanding of our normative responses, if each commoner in exercising his liberty or self-governance is *seeing* the world's

HUMAN FOUNDATIONS OF OUR POLITICAL IDEALS   413

normative demands right, seeing these demands from the nonindividualistic perspective, a perspective larger than her own, the question that leads eventually to the tragedy (Should I contribute the costs of cooperation if others don't?) is simply preempted. Or, to approach it from the other side and invoke the analogy I gave earlier, to ask that question in the social context of a commoner's contribution to the collective cultivation of the commons is analogous (in the bodily context I mentioned earlier) to seeing the road ahead from the point of view of your own body rather than from the point of view of the car. The tragedy of the commons is, then, like the tragedy of a car crash, something you land in when you have an alienated (motor-unworthy) perspective on the world.[23] And what will help preempt the tragedy is a conceptual shift that radically alters which of our political ideals is central, placing the unalienated life center stage.

The point, it is important to stress, is not that there is an independent *argument* for conceptualizing self-governance or liberty in a way that helps preempt the tragedy. The point, rather, is that, given that this way of seeing is available to us, one of our reasons to embrace it is that doing so preempts the tragedy. Once one has internalized the ideal of unalienatedness, one no longer sees liberty as in a trade-off tension with equality; once one has made this conceptual shift, one is no longer capable of endorsing the way of thinking that generates the tragedy of the commons. From this new perspective, the tragedy of the commons takes the wrong things to be the *basic* actions of an individual's participation in *social* life.

The idea of a "basic action" comes from Wittgenstein, who, after presenting a celebrated example, concluded that a *basic* intentional action is something one does without there being anything else one does *in order to* do it. Wittgenstein asked (I am modifying the example slightly for my purposes): "What is the difference between my, say, waving to a friend and my moving my arm?" He had in mind to criticize philosophers who say that the intentional act of waving to a friend, say, is accomplished by doing something else, for instance, willing to move certain muscles in one's arm. It (the intentional act, the waving) cannot be conceptually broken down into other, more basic exercises of agency. It cannot be seen as emerging as a result of *accretions upon something more basic*. The *waving* is basic.

Wittgenstein was concerned with the idea of a basic action because he was interested in an individual's intentionality. And I am asking, on behalf of Gandhi, might there be an extension of this idea of a basic action that characterizes an individual's sociality, something that each individual engages in, in the exercise of her self-governance or liberty? Such an extension, again, would depend on the right phenomenology of value, that is, of seeing aright the normative demands on our agency made by the value properties we perceive in the world. For Gandhi, in an unalienated social world, an individual sees the world aright in just this way. This is the social version of the phenomenology of driving a car. The

414   RETHINKING THE VALUE OF HUMANITY

crucial point is this. When an individual's liberty-constituting or self-governing decisions and actions are a result of this moral phenomenology, the idea of the social does not emerge via some accretions to a more basic form of thinking, the form of thinking, for instance, that goes into generating the anxiety (What if I did my bit and others did not?) that underlies the argument for the tragedy of the commons. The very idea of such a tragedy is intelligible only on the assumption that an individual's relation to the social is *built up via accretions attaching to this more basic form of thinking*. As I said, for Gandhi, in an unalienated life and society, the question "What if I did my bit and others didn't?" would simply not compute. It would be, if Wittgenstein is right, as unintelligible as the question "What if I moved my arm and it wasn't a waving?" Nothing short of establishing that sort of incoherence captures the ideal of an unalienated life.

There is a point of striking importance and relevance to be made just here that reveals the unusual nature of the ideal of an unalienated life and how and why it relates to the theme of this book. I have said that it is an ideal reflected in a human subject seeing aright the normative demands made by the values we perceive in the world and responding suitably with her agency. And I have suggested that, as such, it preempts the kind of thinking that underlies the argument that leads to conclusions about the tragedy of the commons. That thinking, therefore, is a mentality that surfaces when we have fallen away from this ideal of unalienatedness. And I have suggested that that falling away is akin to the phenomenon of misconceiving the nature of individual intentionality by locating what is basic in human action at the wrong place. It might be objected that this analogy is not quite right since I am talking of an *ideal* (of an unalienated life), whereas the idea of a basic action that makes for individual intentionality in Wittgenstein is *not an ideal*. This objection is misguided. Wittgenstein is indeed summoning an ideal when he speaks of "a basic action." And it is a point of striking interest and importance that the philosophical nature of the ideal of an unalienated life, as Gandhi understood it, is quite akin to the sort of ideal that Wittgenstein had in mind when he wrote of the idea of basic actions that lie at the heart of individual intentionality.

In what sense might it be apt to say that Wittgenstein had an ideal in mind? Ideals, by their nature, are such that one can fall short or afoul of them. Though there are different sorts of ideals, as we will see in a moment, this is a minimal requirement of *all* ideals. That is what made it appropriate to say, as I just did, that it is when we fall short of or fall away from the ideal of unalienatedness that we indulge in the thinking that underlies the argument that leads to the conclusion of the tragedy of the commons. So we must now ask: What similar falling short or falling away is appropriate to invoke for Wittgenstein's point about basic actions and individual intentionality?

HUMAN FOUNDATIONS OF OUR POLITICAL IDEALS   415

Consider the example we have given, of my waving to a friend. Imagine that I have become estranged from my friend and am now seeking to show her goodwill so as to indicate that the estrangement is a thing of the past. But the estrangement has caused a sort of mental shrinkage from the normal bonhomie that we would display to one another. I am self-conscious now, given the recent estrangement. I am seeking to come out from under the shadow of the estrangement, but it has left this mark, this shrinkage in me. As a result I can't quite find my way to the usual unselfconscious nonchalance that accompanies my greeting of her in such acts as waving when we meet. So I can't quite wave with the same jaunty naturalness; it's more deliberately mobilized, more like, "*Let me just move my arm* with a kind of vigor and exertion and *hope that it conveys my goodwill.*" When there is such shrinkage that I am trying to describe, the waving is not the basic action; it is my moving of my arm that is basic. Examples such as this can be multiplied to indicate why Wittgenstein did indeed have an ideal in mind. There are "forms of life" in which an ideal is enacted, but we can, for one or other reason, abstract away from that form of life, and when that happens, the basic action seems to be something short of the usual enactments, and we can at best hope that these actions will go on to achieve the effect that is usually (when the ideal *is* being lived up to) built into the enactments in the form of life as it is ideally being lived.

It is in just this sense that we can fall short of the ideal of an unalienated life when we ask the anxious question: What if I did my bit and others did not? It is in just this sense again that I would say the thing that disappointed my father: if we don't take it, somebody else will. The mentality present in individual sociality is just like the mentality present in individual intentionality, living up to ideals embedded in "forms of life" from which we can shrink when the ideal is not working. But this raises a pair of parallel questions that are revealing: Why does the idea of a basic action, as Wittgenstein understood it, not wear on its sleeve its status as an ideal? Why did it seem natural to pose a prima facie objection in which it was declared that his idea of a basic action was not an ideal (unlike unalienatedness), requiring me to make the special effort to bring out why it was indeed an ideal, as I did in the previous paragraph? The other question is: Why does Gandhi think that the ideal of an unalienated life is quite distinct, a more human ideal, than what we standardly conceive as ideals—liberty and equality, as they surface in the liberal tradition, for instance—and which Gandhi did not think of as possessing the same fundamental centrality as the ideal of the unalienated life?

I think the key to answering both questions lies in a common property of what both Wittgenstein and Gandhi have in mind by an ideal. For both, *when the ideal they have in mind is working, it does not seem to be an ideal.* It does not come off as an ideal. It appears as an ideal only when we fall short of it, as in the shrinkage

416 RETHINKING THE VALUE OF HUMANITY

I mentioned or as in my remark to my father or in the qualm that leads in the argument we are considering to the tragedy of the commons, What if I cooperated and others did not? That it does not come off as an ideal when it is working is more obvious in the case of Wittgenstein since, as we saw, it did seem like a real question to raise whether Wittgenstein was really summoning an ideal when he spoke of basic actions. But I think it is just so in the case of unalienatedness too. My father was essentially saying that in an unalienated society, his remark "If we don't take it, nobody else will" would not need to be said. What his remark expressed was the unselfconscious attitudes we have when we are unalienated. He had to say it only when confronted with a young man's expression of an alienated point of view. And in saying it, my father was, in effect, saying that what we would do –by not taking the wallet—is exemplary but not in a supererogatory or optional sense, rather in a representative sense, representative of our humanity, representative of being human (or, as Marx would have put it, representative of us in our "species being"). He was urging us to see ourselves as what we fundamentally are, where this just is what we are when we have internalized the ideal of unalienatedness.

It is for this reason that Gandhi thought that the ideal of unalienatedness stood apart from such values as liberty and equality as they were articulated in liberal theory. It is not something we can insert into a code or constitution; it stood deeper beneath and lay behind these more explicit ideals like liberty and equality that are constantly encoded and enshrined in policy and law, and if we transformed these other ideals to be more of a piece with unalienatedness, they too might have a quite different significance. They would now not come off as a kind of social engineering. And so, one might say that what I've tried to do in this elaborate dialectic presenting how Gandhi reconfigured our political ideals is to show how the pursuit of liberty and equality may be seen less as a form of social engineering and more as reflective of an ideal that reveals the value of humanity.

Quite apart from this dialectic and argument, speaking more generally, it is not even so much that Gandhi had an antipathy to the whole discursive field of constitutions and codes and principles and laws upon which liberal democratic citizenship is constructed. When he expressed an indifference to them, he was only suggesting that they have no self-standing point. If they have a point, it is to raise us or restore us to what we have fallen away from: the shared nondiscursive understandings that are present in the *habits* of a democratic *way of life*.[24]

7. Politics and the Unalienated Life

The term "alienation" has surfaced in a wide range of modern philosophical discussions, and the overcoming of alienation—the ideal of an unalienated

HUMAN FOUNDATIONS OF OUR POLITICAL IDEALS 417

life—has surfaced in doctrines foregrounding a wide range of ideas, from ideas about political economy, as in Marx's ideal of a classless society, to far more personal visions that stress ideas of authenticity, as in the work of Sartre in the long early existentialist phase of his intellectual career, or ideas of "integrity," as in the work of Bernard Williams.[25] In the argument of this paper, the ideal of an unalienated life has surfaced in a very specific dialectic with a very specific role, namely, that of preempting the very possibility of a certain question (What if I paid the cost of social cooperation and others did not?) arising in the mentalities of human subjects. The dialectic within which this ideal emerged started with claims I first attributed (anachronistically, as I said) to early modern radical dissenting voices and which, I said, were redeemed centuries later in ideas I tried to unearth in Gandhi's moral and political philosophy.

Returning to what I said in Section 1, I have tried, by this dialectic, to reinterpret some of the elements of Gandhi's so-called antimodernism and tie them to early modern radicalism. But this tie would be loose and incomplete if I didn't say something, as I conclude this paper, to address a skeptical objection that is bound to be raised. According to this objection, though the radicalism of the early modern period may have been possible for politics in a past time, by the time Gandhi was writing, political economies had advanced in directions that reduced such possibilities to nostalgic illusions.

Before I address this objection, I can't resist reminding those who complacently sneer at what they regard as weak-minded nostalgia that the most creative efforts of the Renaissance were similarly dismissed by the medieval scholastics as a nostalgia for a bygone classical age. The fact is that the complacence is often *not innocent*. What people choose to be complacent about and what they therefore choose to dismiss (as nostalgic) is rather selective, and the selectivity is driven by ideological considerations. Charges of nostalgia are a cousin of what we might call the "It's too late" phenomenon. If something is too late to reverse, it is nostalgic to wish to reverse it. "It's too late to return to 1967 borders in Israel; there have been far too many settlements over the decades" is just one among any number of complacencies one can cite regarding present conditions. But notice that no one ever said during the decades-long Cold War "It's too late; the Soviet Union is here to stay, and in a large part of the world, private capital is simply a thing of the past. It would be nostalgic to aspire to return to it there." Instead they put unrelenting pressure (even the pressure of untold violence in Southeast Asia and Latin America) on any socialist experiment, whatever its faults, decade after decade, till virtually every such experiment fell apart. Thus qualms about nostalgia, of what is and isn't too late, not only reflect an unwarranted complacency; this complacency often reflects ideological commitments one need not endorse.

418 RETHINKING THE VALUE OF HUMANITY

Concerns about motives aside, how shall we assess the charge of nostalgia itself? More specifically, should Gandhi's ideal of an unalienated life be dismissed as a nostalgic hankering for a premodern social outlook?

Gandhi's stubborn refusal to be dissuaded by all such dismissals of his position is based, I think, on a surely correct claim on his part that not just the prospect of but the *reality* of unalienatedness is everywhere available, not in some outlook of the remote past but in the *quotidian present*. I emphasize both "quotidian" and "present" quite deliberately. We can present his view here by introducing the familiar idea of a "frame." Human subjects often find themselves thinking in two different frames, which are sealed off from each other. We may have thoughts (or responses to the world) that, were they in the same frame, would be sensed as contradictory, though given the separate frames, we do not experience them this way. Let me give you the simplest and crudest of examples, a personal example, to illustrate this. It is not an example that has anything to do with alienation and unalienatedness, only an example to bring out what is meant by "frame." My mother-in-law was a conservative Republican. On one of her visits, I had to pick her up from the airport in New York and drive her home. On the route from the airport to my home on the Upper West Side near Columbia University, one has to traverse the slums in Harlem. My mother-in-law, driving past the homeless poverty of the denizens of Harlem, was genuinely upset by what she saw. More than once she repeated with heartfelt compassion, "This is simply terrible. Something has to be done about the conditions of people living like this." This pleased me. We arrived home. Over drinks I asked her, "Your response to what you saw in Harlem was wonderful. So, do you think there should be public expenditure to improve the conditions you just saw?" She looked at me with horror. "Are you mad? Absolutely not!"

As I said, this is the simplest of examples of two thoughts, each in a different, insulated frame. In one frame, she expressed real humanity. It was the quotidian frame of a subject responding directly to the normative demands she perceived in the world around her. In the other frame, her response was quite inconsistent with the other response.[26] Except that it was not inconsistent *within her psychology*, because these two frames were sealed off from one another, and from the subjective point of view consistency and inconsistency appear, as such, only within a frame, not across frames.

This example does not, of course, illustrate the theme of alienation and unalienatedness. It was only intended to convey the general idea of a subject thinking in two frames. But the simple and obvious point it makes about frames applies quite obviously to that theme. The plain fact is that each one of us goes in and out of being alienated, and the notion of a frame is a good way to account for this. What made Gandhi impervious to charges of nostalgia about his ideal of an unalienated life is that he was convinced that there are many quotidian

HUMAN FOUNDATIONS OF OUR POLITICAL IDEALS   419

contexts in the present, not just in a bygone past, in which we are completely *un*alienated. One sign of unalienatedness, we have seen, consists in the fact that it does not occur to one to ask "What if I paid the cost of cooperation and others did not?" There are many contexts, for instance in everyday ashram life, as Gandhi described it, in which such a question would never occur to one. Or we might say, it would never occur to a father (or most fathers) to ask such a question of his daughter: What if I cooperated and she didn't? In those contexts, if we invoke the idea of a frame, the mentality of human subjects may be said to be within an unalienated frame. Yet, in the very same people, there are frames, again frequently shaped by the sort of education provided by the zeitgeist of capitalist modernity that Gandhi repudiated, where that question does surface and drives one's thinking and behavior. Again, one has no awareness that one is being inconsistent because each response is in a distinct, insulated frame.

The vital point for Gandhi was that the frame within which responses are unalienated is possessed by subjects of society *here and now*, not just subjects in societies of a past to which he was nostalgically appealing. He thought that one task of a humane politics is to remove the boundaries between these frames, creating a unified frame, so that people first come to realize their inconsistencies. A further aim, once this is done, is to publicly educate people into the importance of *scaling up* the sorts of response that were expressed in the quotidian frame, bringing them to bear on the domain where social principles and policies are devised and articulated. For Marx, this sort of humane politics was to be found in the solidarities that the proletariat forged in their revolutionary struggles. For Gandhi, it was to be an extension of the outlooks forged in ashram life and in the pluralist practices of popular religion, all of which he brought to bear in a variety of movements he led and mobilized during India's long freedom struggle. Though his radicalism differed from Marx's in many important respects, it shared the basic insight that the unalienated life is the most fundamental ideal that expresses the value of humanity and, therefore, our other more familiar and more discursively prominent political ideals gain a quite different meaning when they are made to nest within it.[27]

Notes

1. Apart from his autobiography, which is perhaps more widely read by nonscholars, this is Gandhi's other considerable book. There are, however, an enormous number of essays, letters, speeches, memos, and a wide scattering of other writings (now collected in about a hundred volumes) some of which carry his most interesting and insightful ideas.
2. In what follows I shall restrict my use of the word "radical" to this particular meaning.

420 RETHINKING THE VALUE OF HUMANITY

3. It's important to emphasize that Gandhi was made anxious not by science itself (he would think it impertinent, for instance, that someone like him should have anything to say about Newton's laws) but by a certain dominance that science came to have in the culture of the "modern West," eventually shaping the mentality of people and shaping attitudes about the social and the political, including ideas of governance, in particular.

4. We (I count myself as falling within this plural) might think that the value element can be divorced from the sacral element here, though this was not, of course, Gandhi's own view. For the purposes of the argument I am constructing, the sacral is not going to play any essential role and so, in this respect, I am abstracting away from an aspect of Gandhi's thought, while retaining an (abstracted version of) his opposition to a kind of scientism or what analytic philosophers would call a "scientific naturalism."

5. Of course, whether someone perceives a threat may depend on her desires and goals, but that does not cancel the fact that she perceives threats in the world—no more than the fact that scientific discoveries depend on the beliefs of scientists cancels the fact that these scientists are perceiving phenomena in the world. The point here is only that seeing threats and other value (or, as in this case, disvalue) properties prompt our *practical* agency rather than the disengaged perspective of the agency by which we explain and predict.

6. Marx (2000) is just one prominent location of this dismissal.

7. The term *swaraj*, as is well-known, is deployed by Gandhi to mean "individual self-governance" and also as a description of his own idea of anti-imperialism, that is, of the self-governing independence of his country from British rule. But in this latter deployment too, Gandhi does not restrict it to anti-imperialism in the narrow sense of getting rid of colonial governance. For him *swaraj* and anti-imperialism consist also in refusing a colonial conceptual legacy, that is, refusing to adopt a mimicry of the conceptual outlooks of India's colonizers, and more generally of Europe and of "the West."

8. In fact, he often wrote against attachment in ways thoroughly familiar from long-standing ascetic traditions in different religious traditions.

9. In a familiar tradition owing initially to Hegel, these two motivations perhaps cannot be kept entirely apart since—in this tradition—History itself is tracking Reason. But for the purposes of interpreting Sen and many others who would make his assumption, I will proceed as if these motivations are quite distinct.

10. Obviously, any other personal pronoun here would be anachronistic.

11. I am stressing this epistemic anxiety more than other considerations that drive the so-called dominance argument because Gandhi's ideas, which I will present below, spoke most directly to this consideration.

12. The work is particularly interesting because it seeks to expound *non*centralized forms of governance in which some of the alternative mentality I am gesturing at with the concept of "unalienatedness" might even potentially be exemplified, thus *combining* regulation with the deeper goal that Gandhi sought. See also Ostrom's (2010) Nobel Prize acceptance speech. These are all issues well worth exploring in detail.

HUMAN FOUNDATIONS OF OUR POLITICAL IDEALS 421

13. Seeking such a fundamental critique that rejects a whole way of thinking—rather than accepts it and imposes regulatory constraints on its seeming fallout—in the matter of the commons is, in my view, just a special case of seeking deeper solutions to the problems that I raise for liberalism in the next section than are provided by the familiar aspiration to develop social democratic constraints within a liberal framework. These constraints are usually seen to soften the impact of Sen's remark that I began with, constraints which Sen himself is well-known to have put forward as softening its impact. The idea that one could accept liberalism's conception of its own ideals and get past the problems that arise for them that I raise below by putting such constraints is precisely to seek a regulatory and constraining solution to those problems, avoiding the more fundamental critique. I obviously cannot in the present paper elaborate and develop this generalization to social democratic constraints on capital of what I am saying here about the particular case of regulatory constraints on noncooperation among commoners. At its most general and simple, of course, the point is one that Gandhi himself often invoked in a remark of Einstein's, "We cannot solve our problems within the thinking that we used when we created them," but its particular application to the inefficacies of social democracy in constraining and regulating in any *abiding* way the tendencies of capital, remains a large and basic issue for another occasion.

14. Note that I am not here distinguishing what someone deserves from what she is entitled to.

15. If we take a very long view of human history, and rely on such historical record (and the absences in that record) as we have, for most of it, it was indeed largely the zeitgeist that was praised for the excellence of its productions; it is a relatively recent phenomenon that individuals began to get the praise and reap rewards for their talent's output. Even when individuals began to be recognized, it was often the exception, not the rule. This is certainly true of what is recoverable from the historical record, whereby we marvel at the remarkable quality and quantity of, say, "Ancient Greek pottery" without really even being able to name particular potters.

16. It should be obvious that his anti-imperialism, that is to say his campaigns seeking freedom from colonial rule for his country, ought not to be confused with any theoretical aspiration to "collective freedom." Quite possibly some collectivist ideals of liberty were theoretically the basis of what drove some developments in the Jacobin aftermath of the French Revolution, but those were never the theoretical ground that Gandhi was exploring. His anti-imperialism, thus, cannot be equated with the idea of collective liberty just because it was a *whole country* whose liberation from colonial rule was being sought. That would be a numbingly gross conflation.

17. Something like Rousseau's idea of the general will gives us the most articulated idea of an individual seeing the world from an expanded point of view, and, in fact, it is quite plausibly arguable that his term "will" should not distract us from the fact that what is being argued for is an outcome that captures a political *truth*, a *cognitive* achievement, just as in Gandhi. (The only way to understand Rousseau's otherwise monstrous-seeming attitude toward minority political opinions is if one sees his contractualist vision as finding those opinions to be a cognitive failure, i.e., as failing to perceive the

422 RETHINKING THE VALUE OF HUMANITY

world right, as being akin, say, to the flat-earther today.) In a telling passage in a long letter to his brother, Gandhi makes it clear how much ethics is for him a matter of cognitive inquiry, not a matter of will but a matter of "getting it right." He writes, in a letter to Lakshmidas Gandhi in April 1907, "Formerly, there was no difference of opinion or misunderstanding between us, hence you had affection for me. Now you have turned away from me because my views have changed, as I have said. Since you consider this change has been for the worse, I can quite understand that some of my answers will not be acceptable to you. But as the change in my ideas is due to my pursuit of truth, I am quite helpless" (Gandhi 1999, 6: 430–435).

18. As I hope is clear, I am not intending to review the deliberative steps that would support this perception. My aim is simply to present, in a way I hope will seem attractive and plausible, an alternative conception of the relation among individuals and their perspectives.

19. The idea of "seeing things from a larger point of view than one's own" in one's exercise of self-governance will be different (and more or less complicated) depending on what the issues at stake are. Since I am entirely focused on the issue of liberty's or self-governance's relations of tension with material inequality, an individual's seeing things from a larger point of view than her own may not involve taking in a range of things that would be involved when another issue, say, involving ethnic or religious difference rather than difference in material well-offness, is at stake.

20. Obviously, all sorts of other conditions, including institutional arrangements, will be needed to actually deliver equality. Gandhi's own views, focused on the predominantly agrarian economy of Indian society, stressed decentralized political governance and a vision of productive forces modeled on farming cooperatives and cottage industries, providing work for all the local populations of each region. Unlike, for instance, Marx, there was no overt stress on abolition of private property or on a classless society. It is not as if Gandhi was committed to private property (he, in fact, sometimes wrote against it), but he wrote instead of trusteeships as the primary distributive mechanism, where the gratuitous wealth remaining after meeting the basic needs of those who possessed it would be deposited for the uplift of those whose basic needs remained unfulfilled; since he did not base his understanding of society on the concept of class, the idea of a classless society was orthogonal to his vision.

Gandhi also did not think of these institutions as *determining* our political ideals. There was no echo of the claim, sometimes attributed to Marx, that an unalienated society could be achieved only when private property and class distinctions were abolished. His view is much more akin to those remarks in Marx which envisage the working-class solidarities that emerge in the class struggle itself as the first instance of a notion of community that was unalienated. (For Marx this was the "modern" rather than the "primordial" notion of community.) The best way to describe how he saw the relation between the institutions of local governance, cooperatives, trusteeships, etc. on the one hand, and the ideal of unalienatedness (as well as of liberty and equality, no longer in tension with one another), on the other, is that they were "of a piece." They promoted each other in a mutual relation. He often said when elaborating his ideas of cooperatives, ashrams, trusteeships, that they be understood as exemplifying the conviction that "nobody is well-off, if somebody is very badly off." Obviously, the notion of well-off here has a double meaning. Even the "well-off" (in one sense) are not "well-off" (in another sense) if there are others who are very badly off by the lights of well-offness in the former sense. Being unalienated is precisely the latter sense of well-off. That is the kind of well-offness lacking in even the well-off (in the former sense) when there are others who are badly off (in that sense). In some ways this is a shrewd conceptual moral-psychological insight. It is often asked by philosophers as a challenge to be met: Why should the well-off be concerned about the badly off? How can we motivate in them a concern for the badly off? And the answer seems to be precisely to stress as a motivation the second sense of being well-off that they lack—because they are, precisely, alienated.

21. It is worth observing and underlining here that this is precisely the reason why Gandhi does not do the simpler and more natural thing of appealing to the third ideal in a familiar sloganized trio, the ideal of "fraternity," to reconfigure the other two ideals of the trio, "liberty" and "equality." He chooses instead to appeal to the ideal of "the unalienated life" as the more basic thing to focus on in bringing about this reconfiguration.

22. In that essay I mentioned this anecdote to elaborate how Gandhi intended to generate an ethics of "exemplarity" rather than of "principle" and of "imperative" as, he claimed, is pervasively to be found in what he called the ethical tradition of the "modern West." In the present essay I am trying to dig deeper and find in the anecdote a way of elaborating the ideal of an unalienated life.

23. The analogy here being that you do the "rational" thing of noncooperating that leads to the tragedy, just as you try to steer the car into narrower spaces than it will go, if you *see* the normative demands on you of the world (of the road ahead) from the point of view of your individual body rather than from the larger point of view of the car.

24. In Ostrom (1990) there is a particularly interesting effort to expound *non*centralized forms of governance of the commons. In such governance, the alternative mentality I am gesturing at with the concept of "unalienatedness" might even potentially be exemplified, thus *combining* regulation with the deeper goal that Gandhi sought.

25. The locus classicus in Marx is Marx and Engels 1988. Sartre's discussion of alienation is scattered in works too numerous to mention, though an obvious and widely read essay in which it is pervasively present is "Existentialism Is a Humanism" in Kaufmann 1956. For Williams, see his "Integrity" in Williams and Smart 1973.

26. Of course, it is quite possible that there are cases when people who had responses like hers have clearly worked out *alternatives* to public expenditure (views about charitable donations providing the funds, say, or even some version of standard "trickledown" theories), but she was not such a person. And she is by no means unique in this. It is quite common for people to just imbibe a dogma in the air—"Public expenditure is a bad thing"—without having any alternatives, while also responding in quotidian contexts with sympathy to what they see in the world around them. I confess that, in giving this example of what I am saying is an inconsistency, I am assuming (it is indeed a conviction of mine) that there is no alternative to public expenditure to address the issues that she wanted to see addressed. If a reader does not share my assumption,

424 RETHINKING THE VALUE OF HUMANITY

I leave it to him to construct his own example of inconsistencies going unnoticed by a subject because of the two inconsistent thoughts being in distinct insulated frames. I merely turned to a simple case with anecdotal verity that was at hand.

27. My grateful thanks to Sarah Buss and Nandi Theunissen for their acute and generous comments on a draft of this paper, which have helped to improve it.

References

Bilgrami, Akeel. 2001. "Gandhi's Integrity: The Philosophy behind the Politics." *Raritan Review* 21 (2): 79–93.

Gandhi, Mahatma.1999. *The Collected Works of Mahatma Gandhi*. 98 vols. New Delhi: Publications Division, Government of India.

Gandhi, Mahatma. 2009. *Hind Swaraj*. Centennial ed. Edited by Anthony Parel. Cambridge: Cambridge University Press.

Hill, Christopher. 1972. *The World Turned Upside Down*. London: Penguin Books.

Kaufmann, Walter, ed. 1956. *Existentialism from Dostoevsky to Sartre*. Translated and with introduction and prefaces by Walter Kaufmann. New York: Meridan Books.

Marx, Karl. (1867) 1990. *Capital*. Vol. 1. Translated by Ben Fowkes. Introduction by Ernest Mandel. London: Penguin Books.

Marx, Karl. 2000. "On the Jewish Question." In *Karl Marx: Selected Writings*, edited by David McLellan, 2nd ed, 46–70. Oxford: Oxford University Press.

Marx, Karl, and Frederick Engels. 1988. *Economic and Philosophical Manuscripts of 1844, and the Communist Manifesto*. Translated by Martin Milligan. New York: Prometheus Books.

McDowell, John. 1979. "Virtue and Reason." *The Monist* 62 (3): 331–350.

McDowell, John. 1998. *Mind, Value, and Reality*. Cambridge, MA: Harvard University Press.

Ostrom, Elinor. 1990. *Governing the Commons*. Cambridge: Cambridge University Press.

Ostrom, Elinor. 2010. "Beyond Markets and States: Polycentric Governance of Complex Economic Systems." *American Economic Review* 100: 641–672.

Sen, Amartya. 2010. "Prohibiting the Use of Agricultural Land for Industry Is Ultimately Self-Defeating." *The Telegraph* (Kolkata), July 23.

Williams, Bernard. 1985. *Ethics and the Limits of Philosophy*. Cambridge, MA: Harvard University Press.

Williams, Bernard, and John J. C. Smart. 1973. *Utilitarianism: For and Against*. Cambridge: Cambridge University Press.

Index

Endnote numbers are indicated by 'n' after the page numbers.

abortion, 39, 353
absolute value, 227
  dignity as, 248
  as intersubjective value, 358 n17
  Kant, Immanuel, 48, 153, 154, 228, 273, 276
  nonrelational value, 228
  value of humanity as, 153, 154, 273, 276, 285,
    286, 287, 288, 366
  See also relational value
absolute worth. *See* absolute value
accountability, 11
  animals, 32
  being rational and being accountable, 6
  Grotius, Hugo, 10, 140, 143–4, 145–6
  moral power and, 131–2
  moral responsibility as accountability, 137
  moral status and, 32, 34, 35, 38
  mutual accountability, 43 n39, 143–4,
    145, 147
  as obligation imposed by God, 11
  Pufendorf, Samuel, 10, 11, 131–2, 135–8,
    146, 147 n7
  second-personal nature of, 137
  types of, 7, 149 n20
aesthetics
  aesthetic community and humanity, 289 n8
  aesthetic sentiments, 296, 298, 300, 306–7
  aesthetic value, 286–7, 303
  See also beauty; works of art
AI (artificial intelligence)
  enslaving of, 217
  ethical problems posed by, 220 n27
  as "existential threat" to humanity, 214, 216,
    220 n25, 220 n27
  Fichte, Johann Gottlieb, 14, 214, 215–17
  Global Challenges Foundation (2015) *12*
    Risks That Threaten Human Civilization,
    214–16, 220–1 n28
  Global Challenges Foundation (2020) *Global*
    Catastrophic Risks; 220 n27
  as mere tool, 217
  strategic reasoning, 216
Albee, Edward, 318

Alexander the Great, 83, 292
alienation, 408
  Gandhi, Mahatma on, 400–1, 404, 411, 416
  Gandhi, Mahatma: unalienated life ideal,
    20–1, 407–16
  politics and the unalienated life, 416–19
Allison, Henry E., 176 n17, 177 n29
Althusser, Louis Pierre, 88 n6
Amery, Jean, 4
analytic philosophy, 372, 376, 377, 378, 381–2,
  384, 420 n4
  analytic metaphysics, 384–5
ancient Greece, 7–8, 48–72
  equality, 3, 49, 62–5
  ethics, 48, 127, 226, 227
  fellow feeling, 7, 9, 17, 57
  good/the good, 50, 128, 227
  humanity, 2, 55–8
  human rights and, 66, 71–2 n39
  humans as rational beings, 7–8
  kinship with the divine/ideal of becoming
    like god, 8, 57–60, 61–2
  monetary value, 50, 51, 54
  rationality, 7–8, 56, 61–2
  slavery, 69 n15
  value, 1, 49–55
  value of humanity, 7–8, 48–9, 50–5, 57–62,
    65–7, 69 n15
  vice, 49, 51, 68 n9
  virtue, 50, 51, 227
  worthiness (*axiôma*), 50
  See also Aristotle;
    Plato; Sophists; Stoics
Anderson, Lanier, 388 n13
angels, 39
animal rights, 7
  "all animals are equal" 38
  dolphins, 213–14
  Fichte, Johann Gottlieb, 213–14
  Spinoza, Baruch, 78
animals (nonhuman)
  accountability of, 32
  aesthetic sentiments, 306–7

426 INDEX

animals (nonhuman) (*cont.*)
  animals/human beings distinction, 41 n19,
    74, 75, 78–9, 97, 110, 116–17, 208, 209,
    275, 277–9, 283, 285, 286, 289 n8, 293
  apes, 6, 39, 40, 45 n54
  asocial/social animal, 25
  cetaceans, 45 n54, 212, 220 n24
  concernworthiness, 26–8, 38, 39, 44 n49
  conscious animals, 43 n42, 44 n49
  consent, 36
  different treatments of different types of
    animals, 25, 26
  dolphins, 6, 39, 212–14, 219–20 nn18–21,
    220 nn23–4
  domestic animals, 25, 32, 116–17, 213
  higher animals, 26, 34, 38
  inference by, 33
  intelligent animals, 285–6
  intelligibility, 35–6, 37
  judgment-involving attitudes, 6, 33, 37
  love, 307
  lower animals, 26
  moral sentiments, 307
  moral status of, 6, 7, 14, 24–5, 38, 40, 213, 285
  moral status and entitlement against
    violence, 26
  passions, 306
  psychological capacities, 25, 26
  rationality, 78, 87, 293
  rats, 287
  recognitionworthy animals, 36–7, 39, 43 n42,
    44–5 n50
  relational value, 287
  respectworthy animals, 39
  responsiveness of, 6, 33, 34, 307
  social cooperation, 213–14, 219–20 nn18–23
  souls of, 75
  strategic reasoning, 216, 221 n31
  training of, 38
  virtues, 293, 307–8, 312 n11
  wild animals, 32, 61, 213
Anscombe, Gertrude Elizabeth Margaret, 127,
  241 n8, 242 n22
anti-humanism, 75, 88 n6
  Spinoza, Baruch, 76–7, 87–8
Antipater, 68 n8
Antiphon, 63–4, 65, 71 n37
Aquinas, 127
Aristotle, 19, 369
  axia, 51
  comparative value, 51–2, 54, 68 n9
  ethics as perceptual discipline, 398
  friendship, 52, 53–4, 57

good life, 228, 235
good/the good, 59–60, 241 n9, 244 n34
human capacity to form a "community in law
  and agreement" 53–4, 68 n11, 69 n14
human nature, degrees of, 8, 60
humans/animals/plants distinction, 55–
  6, 69 n17
infinity/the infinite, 189–90, 191, 194,
  195, 196
justice, 52–4, 57
kinship with the divine, 59–60, 71 n34
personal acquaintance, 330, 331, 332
philosophical contemplation as highest good
  for human beings, 59–60
slavery, 8, 10, 53, 54, 60, 64, 98, 99, 100, 102,
  106, 113, 114, 115
soul, 59, 60
value, 51–2
value of humanity, 52–5, 60, 61
virtue, 17, 51, 60
women, 8, 53, 60
Aristotle: works by
  Ethics, 59–60
  Metaphysics, 59
  Nicomachean Ethics, 8, 51–2, 54–5, 59,
    63, 228
  On the Soul, 55–6
  Physics, 190
  Politics, 53, 56, 60, 64, 99
Asimov, Isaac, 221 n33
atheism, 87
Augustine, 5
Aulus Gellius, 55, 57
Auschwitz, 4

Bader, Ralf M., 5, 7, 11–12, 16, 153–80
Bagnoli, Carla, 361 n40
Barbeyrac, Jean, 127, 140–1, 142
beauty, 258
  aesthetic community and, 289 n8
  Hume, David, 295, 296, 297, 298, 299, 302,
    303, 304–5, 306–7, 308, 309
  See also aesthetics
Beauvoir, Simone, 390 n18
beliefs
  animals, 32, 33
  discrimination and, 251–2, 254, 257
  love and, 318, 340, 343, 349
  power structures and, 4
  value of humanity and moral beliefs, 5
Bentham, Jeremy, 206, 212
Bett, Richard, 7–8, 48–73
Bierling, Friedrich Wilhelm, 114

Bilgrami, Akeel, 20–1, 394–424
Black, Max, 89 n8, 89 n9
Black Lives Matter movement, 249, 361–2 n41
blame, 137, 148 n10, 388 n8
  "communicative blame" 137
Bostrom, Nick, 215, 216, 221 n29
Boxel, Hugo, 76
Braun, David, 317
brute condition, 253
  brute animals, 97, 110, 114, 115
  brute force, 136, 402
  brute pleasure, 34, 43 n38
  brute preferences, 341, 345, 359 n27
Buber, Martin, 328
Burge, Tyler, 28–9
Burnett, Thomas (of Kemney), 113
Buss, Sarah, 1–23, 67 n2, 87, 225–6, 270 n34,
  391 n25

Camus, Albert, 385
Cantor, Georg, 192, 193, 196
  "absolutely infinite" 13, 194–5
capacity
  critical reason as capacity to evaluate the
    force of reasons, 38
  distinction between capacity for judgment
    and to reason critically and reflectively, 6–7
  human capacity to form a "community in law
    and agreement" 53–4, 68 n11, 69 n14
  humanity as capacity to "set ends through
    reason" 277
  improving rational capacities, 13, 14, 211–12
  judgment capacity, 26, 33–4, 38
  moral status and human capacities, 7
  natural capacities and differences in, 6
  nature of humanity: capacities and
    collections, 274–5, 287, 288 n3
  potential for becoming rational, 114–16
  reasoning capacity grounds a special
    status, 11–12
  respectworthiness of human beings
    as grounded in their capacities for
    reasoning, 24
  sentience as capacity for sensation, 41 n11
  valuing, capacity for, 15, 187–9, 195–6, 236,
    266, 270 n34
Carlisle, Clare, 84, 85
Carmichael, Gershom, 99–100, 118 n3
Cato, 51
Caughman, Timothy, 337, 344, 360 n32
Cavendish, Margaret, 101, 119 n11
charity, 111, 112, 326, 356, 362 n45
  See also love

children
  age-appropriate freedoms, 219 n11
  moral status of, 206, 210
  right to education, 219 n16
  See also parents and children
Christianity, 115, 371
  Catholicism, 3
  High/popular Christianity
    (Anglicanism), 399
  Higher Criticism, 379, 384, 385, 390–
    1 nn21–2
  Nietzsche, Friedrich and, 374–5, 378–9, 384,
    385, 390–1 nn21–2
Chrysippus of Soli, 62
Cicero, 55, 56, 60, 61, 70 n24
civil rights, 29, 91 n27, 249, 251
Cold War, 406, 417
colonialism
  Diggers, 397, 403
  Gandhi, Mahatma on, 396, 397, 420 n7, 421 n16
  Levellers, 397
community
  aesthetic community and humanity, 289 n8
  Fichte: moral community, 205–17
  human capacity to form a "community in law
    and agreement" 53–4, 68 n11, 69 n14
  moral community, 329, 349, 356
concern, 69 n14
  equality and, 38
  human beings as subjects of ethical concern,
    48, 69 n14
  moral status: concernworthiness, 26–8, 30–1,
    34–5, 38
  obligatory objects of, 24
  practical concern, 24, 264
  See also personal acquaintance
conscience
  Kant, Immanuel, 280, 281, 282
  moral conscience, 30
  Pufendorf, Samuel, 135–8
consciousness
  conscious animals, 43 n42, 44 n49
  emotions as conscious states, 43–4 n42
  Fichte, Johann Gottlieb: self-consciousness,
    204, 206–7, 213, 215, 216
  Kant, Immanuel, 74
  moral status and, 24, 27–8, 31, 39
  reflective self-consciousness, 204, 206–7,
    215, 216
  self-consciousness, 22 n6, 74, 75, 77, 89 n8,
    204, 213
  unity of consciousness, 74
  "universal reason"/"conscience" 127–8

428 INDEX

consent
  consensuality and equality, 30
  consensual relationships and moral status,
    29–30, 31, 35, 38
  moral power of consent, 134
  nonpersons, 36
consequentialism, 128, 197, 204, 205, 241 n7
  Fichte, Johann Gottlieb, 204, 205, 218 n6
  Kantian consequentialism, 175 n15
  normative consequentialism, 218 n7
constitutivism, 19, 204
constructivism, 276, 287, 390 n19
contempt, 1, 226, 307
  self-contempt, 253
Cooper, John, 71–2 n39
cosmopolitanism, 61, 283, 287, 332
  cosmopolitan right, 219 n11
Crisp, Roger, 68 n11
critical reason, 37, 38, 41 n19
  as capacity to evaluate the force of reasons, 38
  Kant, Immanuel, 28–30
  moral significance of, 29
  See also rationality; reason/reasons
Cummiskey, David, 175 n15, 218 n7

Darwall, Stephen, 10–11, 127–52, 328
  Second-Person Standpoint, The, 137, 138
death, 66, 94 n67, 350–1, 399
death penalty, 3, 5
  Leibniz, Gottfried Wilhelm, 121 n40, 122 n49
  Locke, John, 9, 107
dehumanization, 3, 16, 69 n13, 253
democracy, 249, 373, 400, 416, 421
  liberal democracy, 407, 416
  social democracy and capital, 421 n13
Descartes, René, 5, 75, 89–90 n13
Dewey, John, 286, 390 n18
Diamond, Cora, 22 n9, 329, 358 n18, 358 n19,
    359 n25, 360 n32
  singular respect, 350
dignity, 5, 28, 394
  absolute value, 248
  accountability, 146
  axiological readings of, 153, 154, 156, 157,
    174, 176–7 n27
  as bestowed by society, 4
  consensual relationships, 29
  deflationary readings of, 154, 175 n4
  deontological readings of, 154, 159, 174
  as deontological status, 154, 155, 159, 162–74
  dignitas, 83
  dignity/price distinction, 132, 167, 181
  doctrine of the dignity of persons, 10, 128

domain of universalization, 174
ends-in-themselves and, 154, 174
equal social status, 29
as extrinsic value, 105
Grotius, Hugo, 128, 141, 146–7, 148 n16
Hobbes, Thomas, 105, 129
honor and gloria, 83
incomparable value of, 181
inferiorizing treatment: dignity-based views,
    250, 255, 256
as instrumental value, 105
as intrinsic value, 248
love and, 337, 338, 339, 342, 343, 344, 345,
    349–50, 351, 352–3, 354, 355, 357 n7, 360
    n33, 362 n43
as modern idea, 128
natural dignity, 129
natural law, 128, 146
as noninstrumental worthiness, 83, 93 n54
respect, 19, 128, 146, 174, 248
second-personal nature of, 129, 137, 139, 146
slavery and, 29
"sociability" 129, 146
Spinoza, Baruch, 77, 82–6, 93 n54
treatment of persons and, 128
as value, 154–61
See also Grotius, Hugo; Kant on dignity
    and humanity; price/price value;
    Pufendorf, Samuel
Dilthey, Wilhelm, 89 n10
Diogenes of Babylon, 68 n8
Diogenes Laertius, 50, 56, 61, 66, 67 n2
discrimination and marginalization, 16, 35, 38,
    249, 268 n2
  See also inferiorizing treatment; racism
Douglass, Frederick, 68–9 n13
duties, 196
  duties to persons and the infinite, 196–7
  duties to the self, 166–7, 226, 253, 254
  duty of self-improvement, 277–9
  Kant, Immanuel, 16, 278, 281, 283, 312 n10
  normative significance of humanity: duty
    concept, 16, 278, 281, 283
  perfect/imperfect duties, 140, 153, 156–8, 174
  See also obligations

early modern philosophy, 9–11, 97
  denial of human special moral status, 8
  slavery, 9–10
Ebels-Duggan, Kyla, 18, 19, 21, 337–65
Einstein, Albert, 421 n13
Elias, Norbert, 370, 371, 387 n7,
    391 n26

INDEX 429

end-in-itself
   definition, 172, 176 n20, 178 n41
   Fichte, Johann Gottlieb: rationality as
      obligatory end, 203, 204, 211, 215
   humanity as objective end, 156, 203
   Kant, Immanuel, 16, 158–61, 162, 164, 168–9,
      170–4, 176 nn25–6, 177 nn29–30
   Kant, Immanuel: humanity as end-in-it-self,
      12, 153, 155, 156, 168, 174, 203, 211, 273,
      276, 279
   negative nature of, 173, 174
   as objective end, 173
   persons are ends in themselves, 366
   respect for, 173, 174
   sources of ends, 172–3
   types of, 168
   well-being of others as end in itself, 10
   See also ends; mere means
ends
   Fichte, Johann Gottlieb, 203
   final end, 225, 235, 238, 239–40, 245 n36,
      253, 260
   humanity as capacity to "set ends through
      reason" 277
   humanity and freedom of choice among
      ends, 275, 278, 280
   relative end, 171, 172–4, 178 n43
   See also end-in-itself
entitlement, 54
   against being harmed, 26
   against being harmed for
      entertainment, 41 n8
   against unjust discrimination or
      subordination, 29
   to autonomy, 30
   to just treatment, 69 n14
   to moral education, 30
   to recognition, 35
Epictetus, 60–1, 62
Epicureans, 66, 68 n11
Epicurus, 66
equality, 15–16, 284
   "all animals are equal" 38
   ancient Greece, 3, 49, 62–5
   basic/equal moral status distinction, 264–5,
      269 n31
   consensuality and equality, 30
   equal social status, 25, 29–30
   Fichte, Johann Gottlieb, 202
   Gandhi: liberty, equality, and unalienated life,
      408–11, 416, 422 n19, 423 n21
   Gandhi: liberty, equality and the value of
      humanity, 20, 416

harmless violations of equal moral status, 251
Hobbes, Thomas, 102–3
liberalism and, 400, 406–7, 408, 415
Locke, John, 105–6
moral equality, 13, 38, 249–50, 251, 265, 315
morality, 284
moral status and, 25, 29–30, 31, 35, 37, 38
normative dimension of human equality, 103
normative significance of humanity,
   284, 287–8
Plato, 63, 64, 65
Pufendorf: equal dignity, 129–30, 132, 146
Pufendorf: "equality of right" 130, 132, 133,
   134, 135, 138, 140, 146
right to equality, 97–8
self-interest and, 29
Sophists, 8, 64, 65
Spinoza, Baruch, 80–1
See also inequality; inferiorizing treatment
Erasmus, 89 n8
ethics, 5
   ancient Greece, 48, 127, 226, 227
   modern ethical philosophy, 127–8
   as perceptual discipline, 398–400, 410, 412
   See also metaethics
Euclid: "common notions" 190, 191–2
evidential value, 286–7
evolutionary theory, 289 n8
extrinsic value, 105, 108

Fanon, Frantz, 252–3
Felden, Johann von, 115
fellow feeling
   ancient Greece, 7, 9, 17, 57
   as "basis" of the value of humanity, 17
   "fellow human being" 344–5, 348, 351, 353,
      360 n32
   Hume, David, 17, 292, 308
   Spinoza, Baruch, 9, 14
Fichte, Johann Gottlieb, 11, 13–14
   AI (artificial intelligence), 14, 214, 215–17
   animal rights, 213–14
   animals/humans distinction, 208, 209
   cetaceans/dolphins, 212–14, 219–20 nn18–
      21, 220 nn23–4
   consequentialism, 204, 205, 218 n6
   divorce of rational nature from the
      biologically human, 203, 207, 209–10, 212
   ends, 203
   equality, 202
   ethical theory, 204–5
   Fichte/Kant comparison, 13, 202–3,
      209, 211–12

430 INDEX

Fichte, Johann Gottlieb (*cont.*)
  humanity, 203, 208, 216
  improving rational capacities, 13, 14, 211–12
  independence/self-sufficiency of rational
    agents, 13, 204, 215, 218 n8
  infinity/the infinite, 200 n15
  Kant and, 13, 202, 204, 205, 218 n3
  moral community, 205–12
  moral community expansion, 212–17
  moral obligations, 13, 204, 206, 210–12
  moral status, 209
  punishment for criminals, 210–11, 219 n15
  rationality as obligatory end of rational
    agents, 203, 204, 211, 215
  rights, 209–11
  self-consciousness, 204, 206–7, 213, 215, 216
  social cooperation, 13, 205, 207–8, 209, 213–
    14, 216–17, 219 n11, 219–20 nn18–23
  social recognition, 16, 207, 212
  value, 202–3
  value of humanity, 202, 203, 217–18 n1
  women, 206
Fichte, Johann Gottlieb: works by
  1798 lectures, 209
  1813 lectures on political philosophy, 218 n9
  Attempt at a Critique of All Revelation, 218 n3
  Foundations of Natural Right, 204, 205–6,
    207, 208–9
  System of Ethics, 202, 203, 204
Filmer, Robert, 101, 105
final value, 228, 232
Florentinus, 139, 145
Floridi, Luciano, 217
Foot, Philippa, 227, 233, 241 n8
Foucault, Michel, 88 n6
Frankfurt, Harry, 359 n27, 368
freedom. *See* liberty
Frick, Johann, 319–21, 333 n14
Fricker, Miranda, 137
friendship, 267
  Aristotle, 52, 53–4, 57
  impossibility of friendship with animals,
    80, 91 n31
  inequality, 52
  Spinoza, Baruch, 78, 80–2, 87, 91 n32
  well-being and, 257–8
Fyge, Sarah, 101

Gaita, Raimond, 358 n18, 359 n20, 361 n35,
  361 n40
  love and moral status, 353–4, 358 n15,
    362 n44
  remorse, 350–1

Galileo's Paradox, 190, 192, 195
Gandhi, Lakshmidas, 422 n17
Gandhi, Mahatma, 20–1, 395, 419 n1
  alienation, 400–1, 404, 411, 416
  anti-imperialism, 420 n7, 421 n16
  antimodernism, 397–8, 417, 419
  citizens/citizenship, 396, 416
  colonialism, 396, 397, 420 n7, 421 n16
  equality (liberalism), 400, 406–7, 408, 415
  ethics as perceptual discipline, 398–400,
    410, 412
  Hind Swaraj, 397–8
  human beings vs citizens, 398, 401
  humanism, 390
  India, 397–8, 401, 419, 422 n20
  individual liberty, 20, 400, 406, 408–
    10, 412–13
  liberalism, critique of, 20, 395, 396, 404, 406–
    7, 408, 415, 416
  liberty (liberalism), 400, 406–7, 408, 415
  liberty/equality incompatibility (liberalism),
    20, 406–7
  liberty, equality, and unalienated life, 408–11,
    416, 422 n19, 423 n21
  liberty, equality and the value of humanity,
    20, 416
  Marx and, 398, 400, 401, 402, 403, 406,
    407, 419
  "modern West" 395, 399, 401, 420 n3,
    423 n22
  political Enlightenment, 396, 400, 406–7
  political rationality: early modernity, 401–4
  political rationality: updating, 404–6
  politics and the unalienated life, 416–19
  radicalism of, 396–8, 417, 419
  sacralized nature/world, 399–400, 420 n4
  science, 399–400, 401, 420 n3
  self-governance (*swaraj*), 20, 400, 408–9, 410,
    412–13, 420 n7, 422 n19
  self-interest, 409, 411, 412
  unalienated life ideal, 20–1, 407–16
  value of humanity, 21, 396, 398, 416, 419
Garrett, Don, 11, 15, 17, 19, 291–313
Garthoff, Jon, 6–7, 10, 24–47
Glück, Louise, 74
God
  accountability as obligation imposed by God, 11
  death of, 383
  essence of, 93 n60, 94 n68
  God's love, 81–2, 92 n43, 301–2
  human beings as created "in God's Image" 75
  human beings as God's property, 9, 106, 107,
    120 n23

INDEX 431

humanity as "God's race" 75
human special moral status and, 8
intellectual perfection, 94 n68
legitimacy of God's commands, 11
love of God, 338
as master of human beings, 121 n40
moral/physical entities and, 130–1, 132
Pufendorf, Samuel: sociability and God's
    moral power, 130–3, 135, 139, 146
rights over human beings, 98, 108, 117,
    121 n40
Spinoza, Baruch, 81–2, 92 nn38–43, 94 n68
Spinoza, Baruch: "being-in-God" 9, 85,
    87, 93 n63
See also gods/the divine
gods/the divine, 39, 56
ancient Greece: kinship with the divine/ideal
    of becoming like god, 8, 57–60, 61–2
Aristotle, 59–60, 71 n34
humanity: middle rank between the divine
    and nature, 75
Plato, 8, 57–9
Stoics, 8, 61–2
See also God
good for something/someone, 15, 262, 264
benefit/well-doing (*bene, ficus/facere*), 226,
    233, 234
degraded conception of the beneficial, 233,
    243 n25
ethical conception of the beneficial, 233–4,
    236–7, 238–40
from the good for human beings to the value
    of human beings, 231–4
good for as *beneficial*, 225, 227, 228, 229
human flourishing, 15, 225, 230, 234
instrumental value, 229, 231, 232, 234, 243
    n25, 257–8
Kant, Immanuel, 243 n25
noninstrumental value, 229, 231–3, 234, 243
    nn26–7, 244 n31, 257, 258, 259
normativity, 238, 240, 243 n25, 244 n31
as a primitive, 229–30
realist approach, 238
reasons we have, 238–40, 266–7, 270 n35
relational theory of value, 225, 227–31, 234,
    242 nn21–2
relational value of humanity, 225–6, 229, 232–4
value of humanity: being beneficial for
    ourselves, 15, 225, 234, 235, 238
value of humanity: being good for one
    another, 234
valuers: being beneficial for themselves, 15,
    94 n70, 234

valuing and living well for human beings,
    233, 234–7, 238, 244 n35, 266–7
See also good simpliciter; good/the good;
    relational value
good life, 15
Aristotle, 228, 235
as value of humanity, 240
valuing and living well for human beings,
    233, 234–7, 238, 244 n35, 266–7
See also human flourishing
good simpliciter, 14–15, 229, 232, 243 n27, 249,
    270 n34
dignity, 248
"good for itself" 94 n70, 228, 262
persons as good simpliciter, 262–3
See also good for something/someone
good/the good, 15
ancient Greece, 50, 128, 227
Aristotle, 59–60, 241 n9, 244 n34
as beneficial, 48
benefit/well-doing (*bene, ficus/facere*),
    226, 233
classification of goods, 67 n2
"good-centered monism" 227, 240, 241 n6
instrumental, noninstrumental, final value,
    228, 229
kalon (the intrinsically good or fine), 128
nonrelational value, 228
Plato, 228
prudential/impartial good, 128
relational theory, 226–31
right/good distinction, 241 n7
Spinoza, Baruch, 86, 94 n68
Stoics, 49, 67 n5
unconditionally good, 12, 153, 154, 158, 178
    n37, 269 n27
virtue and the beneficial, 227
Greif, Mark, 225
Grotius, Hugo, 127
accountability, 10, 140, 143–4, 145–6
dignity, 128, 141, 146–7, 148 n16
equality of right, 141–4, 145, 146
equal sociability as "the fountain of
    right" 138–9
ius and sociable relations, meanings
    of, 139–41
liberty, 142
modern moral philosophy, 127
natural law, 128, 141, 143, 144
obligations, 140, 141, 143
On the Law of Prize and Booty, 141, 142, 143
Pufendorf/Grotius comparison, 138–9, 145, 146
punishment for violation of dignity, 143, 149 n19

432 INDEX

Grotius, Hugo (*cont.*)
  respect, 138
  Rights of War and Peace, 99, 100, 139, 140–1,
    143, 144, 145–6, 148 n14
  rights theory, 139–41, 142–3, 146
  second-personal standpoint, 139
  slavery, 99, 100
  "sociability" 129, 141, 146
  "sociability . . . is the fountain of right" 140,
    143, 144–6
Guyer, Paul, 178 n40

Hadot, Pierre, 61
happiness, 176 n20
  eudaimonia, 50
  as good-maker, 175 n8
  Kant, Immanuel, 155, 156, 158–9, 176 n18
  Leibniz, Gottfried Wilhelm, 10, 112, 113,
    114–15, 116, 122 n47
  of slaves, 10, 112, 113
  value and, 50, 67 n4
  See also well-being
Harcourt, Bernard, 3
Hardin, Garret, 404
Hare, Caspar, 322–3, 324
Hare, Richard M., 218 n7
harms, 15–16
  causing harms, 26–7
  self-interest, 16
  See also inferiorizing treatment
Haslanger, Sally, 268 n12
hatred, 1, 296, 302
  animals, hatred felt by, 293, 306
  racial hatred, 252
Hegel, Georg Wilhelm Friedrich, 408, 420 n9
  infinity/the infinite, 200 n15
  Lectures on the History of Philosophy, 87
  'principle of subjective freedom' 72 n39
  punishment as right of the transgressor, 38
  self-consciousness, 22 n6
  Spinoza and, 87–8
Heidegger, Martin, 88–9 n6
Helm, Bennett, 357 n14
Hesiod, 63
Hill, Christopher, 397
Hobbes, Thomas, 10, 16, 311
  absolute power of governments, 101–2, 103
  De cive, 102, 103
  dignity, 105, 129
  domination, 102, 104, 119 n15
  Elements of Law, 102
  equality, 102–3
  "foole" 144, 149 n22

Hobbes/Locke comparison, 10, 98, 107,
  108, 117–18
intrinsic human value, 103, 105, 117, 119 n20
Leviathan, 101, 102, 103, 104, 105
liberty, 102–3, 149 n17
moral rights, 119 n20
natural law, 103, 119 nn13–14
price value, 9
Pufendorf and, 129, 147 n10
rejection of the 'Highest Good' notion,
  86, 93 n61
"right of nature" 129
right to kill other human beings, 102–3
self-preservation and peace among human
  beings, 9, 102, 103
slavery, 9, 98, 100, 101–5, 117
social contract, 101, 103–4, 119 n13
state of war, 103
Hohfeld, Wesley Newcomb, 129, 142
Homer: *Iliad*, 312 n11
Huber, Ulrik, 99
human flourishing, 16, 21
  basic/equal moral status, 266
  capacity to value and, 266, 267
  competition, 261
  conflict/strife and, 260–1
  constitutively good for us, 258, 269 n25
  ending the regress, 263–4, 266
  essential condition of, 16, 20
  good for something/someone, 15, 225,
    230, 234
  inferiorizing treatment and, 16, 250, 253, 254,
    255, 257, 266
  instrumentally/noninstrumentally bad for
    us, 258–9
  integral sense of self and, 254, 261
  love and, 260
  relational, conditional, and extrinsic value
    of, 263
  relationships as noninstrumentally good/bad
    for us, 259–62
  self-respect, 254
  Spinoza, Baruch, 77
  subjectivity and, 263–4, 265–6, 267
  supporting others in their exercise of, 240
  unflourishing, 259
  value of, 15, 225
  as value of humanity, 240
  valuers, 244 n31, 266, 267, 270 n33
  See also good life
humanism
  Gandhi, Mahatma, 390
  Heidegger, Martin, 89 n6

INDEX 433

Kant, Immanuel, 74, 89 n8
modern philosophy, 74–5
nature vs. humanity gulf, 76, 89 nn9–10
notion of, 75–6
philosophical humanism, 76, 89 n8
Renaissance humanism, 89 n8
special status of humanity, 76, 77, 86
humanity
ancient Greece, 2, 55–8
Being, 88–9 n6
common features of, 55–7
common humanity, 1, 2, 3, 21 n2, 225
diminishing of the concept by politics and
political economy developments, 394, 396
as end-in-itself, 153
as feeble and limited, 71 n34
Fichte, Johann Gottlieb, 203, 208, 216
freedom of choice among ends, 275, 278, 280
human beings, 4–5, 7–8, 15
humanitas, 55, 57
'Humanity'/'humanity' 274–5, 282–3
Hume, David, 292–4
language as feature of, 56–7, 88 n6, 285
middle rank between the divine and
nature, 75
OED (Oxford English Dictionary), 289 n6
philanthrôpia, 57
rational beings, 6, 56, 61
special status of, 58, 59, 76, 77, 97, 109, 110,
117, 394
See also Kant on dignity and humanity; value
of humanity
human rights, 3, 91 n27, 249
ancient Greece and, 66, 71–2 n39
claim rights, 9, 129, 142, 149 n20
culture of, 21 n2
values and, 3
See also civil rights; moral rights; natural
rights; rights
Hume, David, 11, 17, 19
aesthetic sentiments, 296, 298, 300, 306–7
animals, 293, 306–8
beauty, 295, 296, 297, 298, 299, 302, 303, 304–
5, 306–7, 308, 309
deploying stolen property for the general
good, 144–5, 149 n23
desirability, 298, 303, 305, 308, 309
fellow feeling, 17, 292, 308
how does humanity have value? 301–4
is value unique to humanity? 306–8
judgment, 298, 299–300, 305, 306, 308, 310
Kant and, 11, 17, 291, 293, 294, 304, 306,
312 n10

love, 294, 297, 301–3, 304, 311
moral antirationalism, 291, 306
moral naturalism, 291, 306
moral sentiments, 17, 296, 299, 303, 305, 306,
307, 308
moral value, 291, 303–4, 305, 306,
307, 308–9
passion-based values, 17, 297–8, 300, 301,
303, 305, 307, 308
rationality, role in the value of humanity, 17,
294, 304–5, 306
"real" value, determination of, 297–300, 305
sensibility/sentience, 17, 292, 306
sensibility, role in the value of humanity, 17,
294, 305–6
"sensible knave" 144, 149 n22
sentiment, 295
sentiment-based values, 297, 299, 300, 301,
303, 305, 307, 308, 312 n7
sentiment/passion distinction, 295–
6, 312 n6
special value of humanity, 309
subject relativity about value, 300
sympathy, 17, 302–3, 304, 305–6, 308
value, source of, 294–7
value of every human being, 308–9
value of humanity, 291, 306, 309–11
vice, 296, 298–9, 307, 309, 311
virtue, 17, 296, 298–9, 300, 303–4, 305, 307–
8, 310
what is "humanity"? 292–4
Hume, David: works by
*Dialogues concerning Natural Religion and
Other Writings*, 301–2
*Enquiry concerning Human Understanding,
An*, 307, 311–12 n5
*Enquiry concerning the Principles of
Morals, An*, 292, 293, 294, 299–300, 303,
307, 308
Essays Moral, Political, and Literary, 311 n3
"Of the Dignity or Meanness of Human
Nature" 293, 294, 309–11
"Of the Immortality of the Soul" 294
"Of National Characters" 292
"Of the Rise and Progress of the Arts and
Sciences" 292
"Of the Standard of Taste" 298
"Sceptic, The" 291, 294–5, 296, 297, 300, 311
n3, 311 n5
Treatise of Human Nature, 291, 293, 294, 295,
296, 297–9, 301–4, 306–7, 309
Hunter, David, 242 n22
Hurka, Tom, 242 nn21–2, 244 n31

434 INDEX

ideology, 3, 75, 417
incomparability
  dignity, incomparable value of, 181
  Kant, Immanuel, 182
  value comparisons involving persons are
    impossible, 182–3
  value comparisons involving persons are
    inapt, 181–2
  value of persons as incomparable, 181–2,
    196, 285
  See also infinity/the infinite
inequality, 1, 284–5
  Aristotle: comparative value, 51–2, 54, 68 n9
  Aristotle: inequality in friendship and love, 52
  hierarchies in power, esteem, and status,
    250, 285
  Kant, Immanuel: caste and inequality, 283–4
  Nietzsche, Friedrich: moral inequality of
    human beings, 249, 387 n1
  as permissible, 250
  wrongful treatment, 249
  See also equality; inferiorizing treatment
inferiorizing treatment, 16, 249–50
  dehumanization, 16, 249, 253
  dignity-based views, 250, 255, 256
  harm-based view of discrimination, 254–7
  as harmful, 250–2, 254, 257
  as harmful to the attacker/perpetrator, 250,
    257, 261–2
  human flourishing and, 16, 250, 253, 254,
    255, 257, 266
  indifference, 268 n17
  infantilization, 16, 249
  instrumentalization, 16, 249, 255
  integral sense of self and, 16, 250, 252, 253,
    254, 268 n17
  intentional attacks, 256
  marginalization, 16, 249, 268 n2
  objectification, 16, 249
  as permissible, 250
  racial discrimination, 251–3, 254–7
  reaction qualifications, 251–2
  resistance and resilience, 252, 255, 257, 262
  self-presentation, 252–3
  self-respect, 252, 253–4, 256, 268 n8
  social recognition, 252
  stigmatization, 16, 249, 252, 253
  threat and attempt, 255–6, 268 n18
  as violation of the person's status as moral
    equal, 250
  wrongfulness of, 250, 251, 254, 255, 257, 262,
    265, 268 n2
  See also inequality

infinity/the infinite
  "absolutely infinite" 13, 194–5
  Aristotle, 189–90, 191, 194, 195, 196
  Cantor, Georg, 13, 192, 193, 194–5, 196
  capacity for valuing as metaphysically
    infinite, 187–9, 195–6
  duties to persons and, 196–7
  engaging with the other's infinity, 199, 200–
    1 n15
  Fichte, Johann Gottlieb, 200 n15
  Galileo's Paradox, 190, 192, 195
  Hegel, Georg Wilhelm Friedrich, 200 n15
  incomparability, 182, 192–6, 285
  incomparability and infinity: historical
    arguments, 189–91, 195
  incomparability and infinity: resistance, 191–2
  infinite value, 12, 14, 19
  infinity and the sublime, 197
  Kant on dignity and humanity, 182, 200 n3
  Kant on the infinite, 186–8, 190–1, 192, 195,
    196, 200 n3
  Kant on the sublime, 197, 279–80
  Levinas, Emmanuel, 201 n15
  love as metaphysically infinite, 199
  mathematically infinite, 186–7, 189
  metaphysically infinite, 186–9
  open-ended framework for representing
    value, 13, 183, 184–6, 187, 189, 192–3, 194
  persons as metaphysically infinite, 187,
    197, 199
  pricing, 197–8
  rational nature as metaphysically infinite,
    187–8, 196, 197, 199
  sublimity of humanity, 196–200
  Transcendence, 183, 184, 192, 193, 194, 195,
    198, 199
  transfinite levels of value, 193–4
  value of persons as infinite, 285, 286, 287,
    288, 338, 339
  value of persons as infinite: mathematical
    demonstration, 183–6
  value of persons as infinite: philosophical
    explanation, 186–9, 195
  valuers, 13, 189, 193
  See also incomparability
instrumental value, 66
  dignity, 105
  good for something/someone, 229, 231, 232,
    234, 243 n25, 257–8
  human value, 105, 270 n34
  Kant, Immanuel, 243 n25
  See also intrinsic value;
    noninstrumental value

INDEX

intelligibility, 329, 346, 354
  moral status and, 32, 34, 35–6, 37, 38, 44 n47
intrinsic value, 97, 98, 158, 168, 276, 286
  dignity, 248
  Hobbes, Thomas, 103, 105, 117, 119 n20
  Leibniz, Gottfried Wilhelm, 10, 98, 109,
    112, 117
  Locke, John, 108, 117
  See also instrumental value
invention of value, 20, 367, 386
  examples of, 370–2, 373, 377–8, 380, 381–2,
    384–5, 386
  institutions and, 379, 381, 384
  metaethical innovation, 366, 367, 377, 381,
    385, 386
  metavalue of value innovation, 20, 367, 368,
    378, 379–81, 385–6
  moral realism, 376, 378, 383
  new inventions depend on previous
    inventions, 377–8, 384, 389–90 nn17–18
  Nietzsche, Friedrich, 366–7, 370–3, 376,
    378–86, 390 n19
  noncognitivism, 366, 378
  open-ended regress, 382
  "philosophers of the future" 367
  respect, 387 n1
  sanctity of life, 382–3
  self-aware invention, 368
  universal coverage of values, 371
  value, 370, 373, 376
  value of humanity and, 367–8, 374–6, 382–
    3, 386
  valuers, 236
  values: ongoing monitoring, intervention,
    and regulation, 367, 379
  values as standards and as ideals, 370, 371,
    373, 378, 381
  See also Nietzsche, Friedrich; valuers; valuing
Irwin, Terence, 68 n11, 68 n12
Isocrates, 56

Jackson, Frank, 339, 357 nn6–7
James, William, 388 n8
Jorati, Julia, 9–10, 14, 97–126
judgment, 334 n33
  animals: judgment-involving attitudes,
    6, 33, 37
  as capacity to infer, 33
  as capacity to respond to reasons, 38
  conscience and, 135–6
  freedom and, 44 n43
  Hume, David, 298, 299–300, 305, 306,
    308, 310

intermediate moral status and judgment
  capacity, 26, 33–4, 38
  mental states involving judgment, 33
  as most primitive locus of reasons-
    response, 43 n37
  Pufendorf, Samuel, 135–6, 148 n10
justice
  Antiphon, 65
  Aristotle, 52–4, 57
  commutative/distributive justice, 111
  divine justice, 111
  injustice, 3, 4
  Leibniz, Gottfried Wilhelm, 109, 111, 116
  Plato, 63
  Plato on injustice, 48–9, 58

Kant, Immanuel
  absolute value, 48, 153, 154, 228, 273
  animals/human beings distinction, 74, 78,
    275, 277–9, 283
  axiological theory, 153
  common humanity, 21 n2
  conditions for being a bearer of value, 12
  conscience, 280, 281, 282
  consciousness, 74
  consequentialism, 175 n15
  critical reason, 28–30
  deceiving or coercing persons, arguments
    against, 37
  duty concept, 16, 278, 281, 283, 312 n10
  Fichte and, 13, 202–3, 204, 205, 209, 211–
    12, 218 n3
  "good for" 243 n25
  good will, 12, 154–5, 158–9, 228, 281
  happiness, 155, 156, 158–9, 176 n18
  humanism, 74, 89 n8
  Hume and, 11, 17, 291, 293, 294, 304, 306,
    312 n10
  infinity/the infinite, 186–8, 190–1, 192, 195,
    196, 200 n3
  instrumental reasoning, 165, 171, 173, 177
    n28, 177 n31, 178 n43
  instrumental value, 243 n25
  love, 281, 282
  moral feeling, 281, 282
  morality, 10, 17, 40 n3, 144, 156, 166, 169–70,
    174 n1, 176 n18, 281, 291
  moral rationalism, 8, 10, 291, 306
  moral status, 24, 25, 28–9
  pure practical reason, 155, 156, 163, 164, 165,
    169, 170, 177 n31, 280–1
  pure reason, 21, 170, 172, 173
  rationality, 11–12, 74, 187–8, 196, 203, 211

436 INDEX

Kant, Immanuel (*cont.*)
  regress argument, 158–9, 176 n21, 200 n4
  self-legislation, 41 n21
  'status of humanity' 154, 162
  sublimity, 197, 279–80
  Sympathetic Person, 341, 351
  theory of value, 155–8
  well-doing, 226
  See also Kant on categorical imperative; Kant on dignity and humanity
Kant, Immanuel: works by
  Amphiboly, 172
  Anthropology from a Pragmatic Point of View, 74, 90 n22
  Critique of Judgment, 191, 281, 282–3
  Critique of Practical Reason, 155, 156, 187–8, 200 n3, 279, 280, 281
  Feyerabend lectures, 159, 161, 167
  Gesammelte Schrigten, 284
  Groundwork, 40 n1, 161, 175 n12, 177 n32, 200 n1, 273, 276, 277, 279, 280, 288 n2, 340
  Groundwork II, 37, 169, 170, 175 n12, 176 n26
  Groundwork II (4:428), 74, 153, 159–60, 168, 200 n4, 273, 277
  Groundwork II (4:436), 170, 171, 173, 200 n2
  Groundwork III, 169–70, 174 n1
  Metaphysics of Morals, 40 n1, 147 n4, 164–5, 211, 275, 277, 278–9, 281–2, 288 n2
  Metaphysik Mrongovius, 178 n34
  Religion within the Boundaries of Mere Reason, 40 n1, 177 n30
Kant on categorical imperative
  domain of universalization, 162–4, 166–7, 169
  end-in-itself, 168
  ground of the categorical imperative, 168–70
  humanity, formula of, 153, 170
  humanity as the ground of the categorical imperative, 153, 170, 174, 275–6
  perfect/imperfect duties, 156
  rational beings, 166
  second formulation of the categorical imperative, 6, 153, 157
  third formulation of the categorical imperative, 273
  variants of, 170–1
  See also Kant, Immanuel; Kant on dignity and humanity
Kant on dignity and humanity, 10, 12, 24, 28, 42 n25, 74, 128, 153, 200 n3, 284, 338
  absolute value of humanity, 153, 154, 273, 276
  aesthetic community and humanity, 289 n8
  capacity to act on maxims, 164–5

caste and inequality, 283–4
dignity as deontological status, 155, 159, 162–74
dignity and the good will, 166–7
dignity and price, 132, 153, 167–8, 182, 337, 338, 339, 343
duties to the self, 166–7
end-in-itself, 16, 158–61, 162, 164, 168–9, 170–4, 176 nn25–6, 177 nn29–30
form and matter, 170–2
freedom of choice among ends, 275, 278, 280
ground of the categorical imperative, 168–70
human being as moral being, 279
humanity, argument for, 158–61
humanity, conception of, 24, 28–9, 41 n17, 153, 203
humanity, never to be used as mere means, 153, 157, 174
humanity as end-in-it-self, 12, 153, 155, 156, 168, 174, 203, 211, 273, 276, 279
humanity and good will, 154–5
humanity as ground of the categorical imperative, 153, 170, 174, 275–6
"humanity" (*Menscheit*)/"rational beings" (*vernünftige Wesen*) distinction, 277
humanity as objective end, 156, 203
inviolability, 157, 175 n15
mere means, 166, 167–8, 276
moral value, 291, 304, 306
objects of practical reason, 155–6
perfect/imperfect duties, 153, 156–8, 174
priority of the right over the good, 153, 156
relative ends, 171, 172–4, 178 n43
respect for humanity, 21, 153, 156, 157–8, 162, 168, 170, 173, 281–2, 283
self-constraint and struggle, 16, 278, 279–80
self-respect/self-esteem, 253, 281, 282
universalization domain/"maxims" 12, 162–4, 166–7, 169, 170–2, 173, 174, 177 n28, 338
value of humanity, 5, 153–4, 156, 157–8, 162
value of humanity as moral value, 291, 304, 306
values: promoted/respected, 157–8, 168, 175 n16
virtue, 279
See also Kant, Immanuel; Kant on categorical imperative; normative significance of humanity
Kerstein, Samuel, 161, 166, 176 n17, 178 n37
Kolodny, Niko, 360 n33
Korsgaard, Christine M., 40 n6, 41 n11, 44 n45, 45 n51, 176 n17, 178 n40, 178 n42, 211, 361 n34
  absolute value as intersubjective value, 358 n17

critical reason, 41 n19
deontological reason, 327–8
enlightenment morality, 337
metaethics, 240 n3
moral conclusion, 338
Sources of Normativity, The, 337
Kosch, Michelle, 13–14, 202–24
Kraut, Richard, 241 n6, 242 n13, 245 n38, 259

Langton, Rae, 270 n33
Leibniz, Gottfried Wilhelm, 109
  animals/human beings distinction, 74, 75,
    110, 116–17
  animals' souls, 75
  City of God, 110, 114
  death penalty, 121 n40, 122 n49
  God as master of human beings, 121 n40
  happiness, 10, 112, 113, 114–15, 116, 122 n47
  humans as God's race, 92 n49
  human value, 110, 117
  intrinsic human value, 10, 98, 109, 112, 117
  justice, 109, 111, 116
  love/disinterested love, 10, 109, 111–12
  moral obligations, 109, 110, 111, 112, 117
  moral rights, 110, 111, 113, 114
  natural law, 111
  ownership, 112, 121 n41
  policy proposal for Louis XIV, 110, 113
  rationality, 10, 109, 110–11, 113–17
  slavery, 10, 98, 100, 101, 109–17, 120 n33,
    122 n48
  Spinoza and, 90 n17
  theology, 115, 122 n48
  virtue, 10, 114–15, 116, 122 n47
Leibniz, Gottfried Wilhelm: works by, 109
  Codex Juris Gentium Diplomaticus, 121 n40
  Definitionum Juris Specimen, 121 n43
  Discours de métaphysique, 75, 90 n17, 92 n49
  "Diviso Societatum" 115
  New Essays on Human Understanding, 115–16
  New Method, 121 n40
  "On the Common Notion of Justice" 109,
    110, 112, 113, 117, 121 n40
Leitzén, Iina, 217
Levinas, Emmanuel
  Ethics and Infinity, 333 n29
  "Freedom and Command" 325
  infinity, 201 n15
  personal acquaintance, 18, 19, 314, 325–30,
    332, 333 n29, 334 n31
  Totality and Infinity, 325, 328, 329–30,
    334 n31
Lewis, C. I., 286

liberalism
  equality, 400, 406, 407, 408, 415
  Gandhi's critique of, 20, 395, 396, 404, 406–7,
    408, 415, 416
  liberal philosophers, 21 n2
  liberal politics and political economy, 395
  liberty, 400, 406–7, 408, 415
  Locke as "father of liberalism" 105, 120 n30
  social democracy and capital, 421 n13
  tragedy of the commons, 404–6, 411–14, 416
liberty (freedom)
  children: age-appropriate freedoms, 219 n11
  collective liberty, 408, 421 n16
  Gandhi: individual liberty, 20, 400, 406, 408–
    10, 412–13
  Gandhi: liberty, equality, and unalienated life,
    408–11, 416, 422 n19, 423 n21
  Gandhi: liberty, equality and the value of
    humanity, 20, 416
  Grotius, Hugo, 142
  Hobbes, Thomas, 102–3, 149 n17
  inalienable freedom of rational beings, 112
  liberalism and, 400, 406–7, 408, 415
  liberty/claim right distinction, 129
  Locke, John, 105–6, 107, 117
  natural liberty, 103, 129, 142, 149 n17
  'principle of subjective freedom' 72 n39
  right to freedom, 9, 10, 97–8, 113, 116, 117
Locke, John
  death penalty, 9, 107
  equality, 105–6
  "father of liberalism" 105, 120 n30
  freedom, 105–6, 107, 117
  God's rights over human beings, 98, 108, 117,
    121 n40
  Hobbes/Locke comparison, 10, 98, 107,
    108, 117–18
  human beings as God's property, 9, 106, 107,
    120 n23
  intrinsic human value, 108, 117
  moral rights, 108
  natural rights, 98, 105–6, 108
  obligations, 106, 107
  slavery, 9, 10, 98, 100, 101, 105–8, 117, 118 n3
  slave trade, 10, 107–8
  social contract, 402, 403, 404, 405
  state of war, 107
  Two Treatises of Government, 105–7, 108,
    113, 149 n19
love, 19, 267
  Aristotle: inequality in love, 52
  beliefs and, 318, 340, 343, 349
  charity, 111, 112, 326, 356, 362 n45

438 INDEX

love (*cont.*)
    content of, 339, 345
    definition, 198, 199, 259
    dignity, 337, 338, 339, 342, 343, 344, 345,
       349–50, 351, 352–3, 354, 355, 357 n7, 360
       n33, 362 n43
    emotion and, 357 n10
    as essence of art and morals, 198
    "fellow human being" 344–5, 348, 351, 353,
       360 n32
    God's love, 81–2, 92 n43, 301–2
    human flourishing and, 260
    Hume, David, 294, 297, 301–3, 304, 311
    interpersonal love, 338, 339, 340, 345, 346,
       355, 359 n21
    Kant, Immanuel, 281, 282
    knowledge of ourselves, 259–60
    Leibniz, Gottfried Wilhelm: disinterested
       love, 10, 109, 111–12
    love at definite description, 314, 315, 318
    love at first sight, 314, 315–17, 318, 325, 326,
       327, 332
    love of God, 338
    love of one's neighbor, 281, 282, 338
    as metaphysically infinite, 199
    moral commitments, 337, 342, 351, 354,
       355–6, 360 n34
    moral conclusion, 338–9, 342, 349, 350, 351,
       352, 354, 360 n34
    as moral education, 342
    morality and, 18, 198, 338
    moral philosophy and, 338, 354–6, 356 n3
    moral status and, 353–4, 358 n15, 362 n44
    Murdoch, Iris, 198–9, 356 n3
    as noninstrumentally good for us, 259
    parental love, 19, 300, 312 n10, 315, 342, 346,
       347, 348, 353–4, 359 n22, 359 n28, 362 n44
    permissive view of, 315, 316, 318, 324, 332
    personal acquaintance and, 18, 19, 314, 315,
       322, 325, 330–2
    personal acquaintance, love and moral
       standing, 18, 314, 315–19, 331
    property view, 338, 343–5, 360 n32
    romantic love, 315, 341–2, 346
    self-interested love, 112, 175 n7
    self-love/self-esteem, 84–5, 127, 333 n10
    singular respect, 338, 345, 349–52, 356
    skeptical challenges/moral skepticism, 345–
       9, 354–5, 356, 360 n34
    unconditional value and, 340, 345, 349
    value of humanity, 338–42, 345
    value of individuals and, 19, 338–40, 342,
       345, 348–9, 356, 358 n15

witnessing the love of others, 338, 345, 352–
    4, 356

McDowell, John, 398
MacIntyre, Alasdair, 21 n1
Mackie, John L., 359 n23, 387 n6
Mandelstam, Nadezhda, 4
Martin, Adrienne M., 276, 288 n2, 289 n7
Marx, Karl, 408
    Capital, 285, 403
    classless society, 417, 422 n20
    Gandhi and, 398, 400, 401, 402, 403, 406,
       407, 419
    liberty and equality, 422–3 n20
    Theses on Feuerbach, 22 n5
Melamed, Yitzhak Y., 5, 8–9, 74–96
mere means, 357 n9
    Kant, Immanuel, 166, 167–8, 276
    Kant, Immanuel: humanity never to be used
       as mere means, 153, 157, 174
    price and usefulness of, 167, 168
    See also end-in-itself
metaethics, 226, 230–1, 240 n3, 409
    metaethical innovation, 366, 367, 377, 381,
       385, 386
    Nietzsche, Friedrich, 366–7, 383, 385, 386
    Rawls, John, 390 n19
MeToo movement, 249
Mill, John Stuart, 235
Millgram, Elijah, 19–20, 366–93
modern philosophy
    humanism, 74–5
    modern ethical philosophy, 127–8
    See also slavery
Moore, Adrian W., 186, 188, 189
Moore, George E., 128, 228, 229, 372
    Open Question, 343, 391 n27
moral commitments, 22 n9, 337, 342, 351, 354,
    355–6, 360 n34
moral conclusion, 338–9, 342, 349, 350, 351,
    352, 354, 360 n34
moral convictions, 337, 353
moral education, 30, 342
morality, 97, 127, 144
    'bourgeois' morality, 4
    enlightenment morality, 337
    equality, 284
    human being as moral being, 279
    humanity as locus of morality, 282
    Hume, David, 308
    Kant, Immanuel, 10, 17, 40 n3, 144, 156, 166,
       169–70, 174 n1, 176 n18, 281, 291
    love and, 18, 198, 338

as mutual accountability, 145
personal acquaintance and, 18, 314, 316–19,
 323–4, 327–8, 330, 331
as reciprocal, 166
moral naturalism, 291, 306, 311 n1
 moral antinaturalism, 291, 306
moral obligations, 13, 15, 27, 34, 127, 138, 143,
 147 n2, 149 n20
 disinterested love as moral obligation, 111–12
 Fichte, Johann Gottlieb, 13, 204, 206, 210–12
 Leibniz, Gottfried Wilhelm, 109, 110, 111,
  112, 117
 parental moral obligation to educate their
  children, 211
 See also obligations
moral personality, 69 n14
moral philosophy
 case-driven moral philosophy, 355
 Grotius, Hugo, 127
 love and, 338, 351, 354–6, 356 n3
 modern moral philosophy, 127–8
 personal acquaintance, 314, 317, 322, 330
 tools/methods, 355, 356
moral rationalism, 311 n1
 Kant, Immanuel, 8, 10, 291, 306
 moral antirationalism, 291, 306
moral realism, 230, 238, 276, 376, 378, 383,
 390 n19
moral responsibility, 30, 34, 38
 as accountability, 137
moral rights, 97, 119 n20, 402
 Leibniz, Gottfried Wilhelm, 110, 111,
  113, 114
 Locke, John, 108
 rationality and, 113–15
moral status, 6–7, 24–45
 accountability, 32, 34, 35, 38
 animals, 6, 7, 14, 24–5, 26, 38, 40, 213, 285
 basic/equal moral status distinction, 264–5,
  269 n31
 children, 206, 210
 comments on concernworthiness and
  respectworthiness, 30–1
 concernworthiness, 26–8, 34–5, 38
 consciousness and, 24, 27–8, 31, 39
 consensual relationships and, 29–30,
  31, 35, 38
 definition, 24
 denial of human special moral status, 8
 equality, 25, 29–30, 31, 35, 37, 38
 Fichte, Johann Gottlieb, 209
 intelligibility, 32, 34, 35–6, 37, 38, 44 n47
 intermediate moral status, 6, 25–6, 38

intermediate moral status and judgment
 capacity, 26, 33–4, 38
Kant, Immanuel, 24, 25, 28–9
life as criterion for, 28, 39
love and moral status, 353–4, 358 n15, 362 n44
marginal cases of, 40 n3, 354, 358 n19
mutual justifiability and, 30, 31, 38
natural capacities and differences in, 6
of nonrational/nonhuman beings, 6, 7, 14,
 24–5, 26, 40 n3
rationality and, 5, 6, 7, 9, 24
recognitionworthiness, 31–5, 38, 40
recognitionworthiness/respectworthiness
 distinction, 35–8
respectworthiness, 28–30, 38, 42 n25
sensation as criterion for, 27, 28, 39, 206
status above respectworthiness, 39
types of, 24–6, 38–40, 41 n16, 42 n25
types of moral status as hierarchy and
 developmental sequence, 31, 34–5, 38–9
moral value, 2, 156, 355
 human special moral value, 5, 7
 Kant, Immanuel, 291, 304, 306
 moral value of humanity, 8, 15, 16, 291,
  304, 306
 rethinking of, 2
 See also dignity; Kant on dignity and
  humanity; Hume, David
Morgan, Michael, 327, 333 n21
Müller, August Friedrich, 176 n25
Murdoch, Iris, 198–9, 356 n3, 357 n8, 361 n40
Musk, Elon, 214, 217

Nagel, Thomas, 41 n13, 238–40, 360 n32, 361 n36
naïveness, 2, 21–2 n2, 225, 412
naturalism, 230
 moral antinaturalism, 291, 306
 moral naturalism, 291, 306, 311 n1
 "scientific naturalism" 420 n4
 Spinoza, Baruch, 77
natural law, 9, 100–1, 103, 311 n1
 dignity, 128, 146
 Grotius, Hugo, 128, 141, 143, 144
 Hobbes, Thomas, 103, 119 nn13–14
 Leibniz, Gottfried Wilhelm, 111
 Pufendorf, Samuel, 129, 131, 132, 134
natural rights, 8, 142
 claim rights, 9, 142, 149 n20
 Hobbes, Thomas, 129
 liberty/claim right distinction, 129
 Locke, John, 98, 105–6, 108
 Pufendorf, Samuel: "equality of right" 130,
  132, 133, 134, 135, 138, 140, 146

440 INDEX

natural rights (*cont.*)
  right to equality, 97–8
  right to freedom, 9, 10, 97–8, 113, 116, 117
  right to kill other human beings, 102–3
  right to punish, 107, 143
  right to self-preservation, 9, 102
  second-personal nature of, 146
  See also Grotius, Hugo
Nehamas, Alexander, 387 n4
neo-Aristotelianism, 331
neo-Kantian tradition, 89 n10, 273, 387 n6
Nicholls, William, 99, 101
Nietzsche, Friedrich, 20, 368–70
  death of God, 383
  Eternal Return, 374, 375, 380
  Freitod ("free death"), 383
  Higher Criticism, 379, 384, 385, 390–1 nn21–2
  "infinite" value of human beings, 19
  metaethics, 366–7, 383, 385, 386
  moral inequality of human beings, 249, 387 n1
  morality, 21 n1
  moral realism, 376
  nihilism, 367, 369, 374–5, 385, 391–2 n29
  Overman, 20, 367, 371, 375, 379–80, 384, 385, 389 n15
  "self-overcoming" 371, 372, 374, 380
  Spinoza and, 77
  value, 370, 373–4, 376, 389 n14
  value of humanity, 367, 374–5, 378, 382, 383
  will to power, 381, 382, 387 n3, 389 n14
  Zarathustra, 370, 374, 380–1, 385
  See also invention of value
Nietzsche, Friedrich: works by, 369
  Antichrist, The, 387 n1, 388 n9, 390–1 n21
  Beyond Good and Evil, 375, 389 n14
  Gay Science, The, 374
  On The Genealogy of Morals, 374, 387 n7, 388 n8, 389 n14
  Thus Spoke Zarathustra, 366, 367–8, 369, 374–5, 379–81, 383, 385, 389 n14, 391 n29
  Twilight of the Idols, 383, 387 n1, 388 n9
nihilism, 367, 369, 374–5, 385, 391–2 n29
  See also Nietzsche, Friedrich
noninstrumental value, 228, 270 n34
  dignity, 83, 93 n54
  final value and, 232
  good for something/someone, 229, 231–3, 234, 243 nn26–7, 244 n31, 257, 258, 259
  noninstrumental goods as *conditionally* good, 259
  relationships as noninstrumentally good/bad for us, 259–62
  See also instrumental value

nonmoral reactive attitudes, 34, 37, 43 n42
nonmoral responsibilities, 34, 37
nonrelational value, 16, 228, 249, 263–4
  regress argument, 231, 234, 263
normative significance of humanity, 16–17, 273–4, 277, 282–4, 287–8
  absolute value of humanity, 273, 276, 285, 286, 287, 288
  duty concept, 16, 278, 281, 283
  duty of self-improvement, 277–9
  equality, 284, 287–8
  human being as moral being, 279
  humanity as capacity to "set ends through reason" 277
  humanity as locus of morality, 282
  humanity as such/rational nature as such: distinction, 16, 277, 281, 282, 288
  'Humanity'/'humanity' 274–5, 282–3
  human sociality, 16, 17, 283, 288
  human sociality: universal sympathy, 16–17, 283
  infinite value of humanity, 285, 286, 287, 288
  Kant, Immanuel, 273, 275, 277, 278–84, 288 n2
  Kant-inspired approach, 274, 277–82, 283–4, 288
  nature of humanity: alternative Kantian approach, 277–82
  nature of humanity: capacities and collections, 274–5, 287, 288 n3
  nature of humanity: contemporary Kantian approach, 275–7
  'normative significance', meaning of the term, 288 n1
  relational value of humanity, 16, 286–8
  value and standing, 284–8
  valuing, 276
normativity, 391 n25
  good for something/someone, 238, 240, 243 n25, 244 n31
  moral entities, normative nature of, 131
  normative consequentialism, 218 n7
  normative dimension of human equality, 103
  power structures and normative facts, 4
  Pufendorf, Samuel, 130, 131
Nozick, R., 157

obligations, 54
  Grotius, Hugo, 140, 141, 143
  Locke, John, 106, 107
  mutual obligation, 132, 134, 139
  Pufendorf, Samuel, 130, 131, 132, 134, 135, 136, 137, 139

INDEX 441

rationality and, 10
sanctions and, 130, 147 n10
self-preservation as obligation, 107
See also duties; moral obligations
Occupy movement, 249
Omohundro, Stephen M., 215
On Deadly Danger (film), 181
O'Neill, Onora, 177 n33, 178 n39, 178 n40
Orwell, George, 350
Ostrom, Elinor, 405, 423 n24

Panaetius of Rhodes, 60, 61, 62
parents and children, 52, 67 n3
   absolute power over children, 104, 105
   adopting a child, 348
   expectant mother, 353–4, 362 n44
   mourning the dead, 66
   parental love, 19, 300, 312 n10, 315, 342, 346,
      347, 348, 353–4, 359 n22, 359 n28, 362 n44
   parental moral obligation to educate their
      children, 211
   subjection of children, 98, 99, 101, 104, 106,
      112, 114, 120 n22
   See also children
people with disabilities, 115, 116, 353, 359 n22
   cognitive disabilities, 308, 328, 347
   newborn malformations, 116
Perry, R. B., 286
personal acquaintance, 18–19, 314
   aggregation, 314, 316, 319
   Aristotle, 330, 331, 332
   as cognitive relation, 332
   contractualism, 18, 314, 319–22, 324, 332
   Footbridge/Opaque Footbridge cases, 322–5, 332
   Levinas, Emmanuel, 18, 19, 314, 325–30, 332,
      333 n29, 334 n31
   love and, 18, 19, 314, 315, 322, 325, 330–2
   love, moral standing and, 18, 314, 315–19, 331
   love, permissive view of, 315, 316, 318,
      324, 332
   love at definite description, 314, 315, 318
   love at first sight, 314, 315–17, 318, 325, 326,
      327, 332
   Mass Vaccination case, 319–21, 333 n14
   moral equality, 332
   morality and, 18, 314, 316–19, 323–4, 327–8,
      330, 331
   moral philosophy, 314, 317, 322, 330
   nature of, 325–30, 332
   nonhuman beings, 331–2
   as perceptual contact, 326–7
   personal (benevolent) concern for others, 18,
      314, 322–5, 328, 330–1, 332

practical dimension of, 327–8
psychological grounds, 329, 330–1
reciprocity, 328, 333 nn29–30
secondhand use of names, 324, 325
Trolley Problem, 18, 314, 322–3
Pettit, Philip, 318
Pico Della Mirandola, Giovanni, 89 n8
Plato
   cave image, 58–9
   equality, 63, 64, 65
   good/the good, 228
   "human being is measure of all things"
      58, 63, 76
   human progress over time, 63
   injustice, 48–9, 58
   justice, 63, 236–7
   kinship with the divine/ideal of becoming
      like god, 8, 57–9
   "learning is recollection" 58, 59
   Platonic Forms, 58–9
   Protagoras, 56, 57, 58, 62–3, 65, 70 n31,
      76, 89 n7
   Socrates, 48, 51, 58, 71 n34, 228, 236–7
   value of humanity, 59, 60, 63, 65
Plato: works by
   Apology, 71 n34
   Crito, 48
   Gorgias, 48
   Meno, 58, 269 n27
   Phaedo, 58
   Phaedrus, 58
   Protagoras, 56, 57, 63, 64, 65, 76
   Republic, 48, 58–9, 236–7
   Theaetetus, 58, 63
Plotinus, 66
Plutarch, 61
political philosophy, 105, 108, 218 n9,
   395, 398
potential. *See* capacity
power
   absolute power of governments, 101–2, 103
   absolute power over children, 104, 105
   absolute power over slaves, 98, 104, 107, 108,
      117, 118
   moral power and use of force, 134
   parental power, 9–10, 104
   power to confer status, 4
   power relations, 4, 16
   power structures, 2, 3, 4
   Pufendorf, Samuel: moral power, 130–4, 135,
      139, 146
   value of humanity and, 2
preference-satisfaction theories, 286

442 INDEX

price/price value
ancient Greece: monetary value, 50, 51, 54
dignity/price distinction, 132, 167, 181
Hobbes, Thomas, 9
Kant, Immanuel: dignity and price, 132, 153,
167–8, 182, 337, 338, 339, 343
pricing infinite value as baseless, 197–8
setting price on a person, 357 n9
Prichard, Harold A., 241 n7, 267
projectivism, 287
psychopathy, 260–1
Pufendorf, Samuel
accountability, 10, 11, 131–2, 135–8,
146, 147 n7
"common life" 129, 131, 132, 137, 138, 146
conscience, 135–8
dignity, 118 n7, 128, 129, 146–7
dignity as grounded on God's moral
power: instability of the idea, 133–5
equal dignity, 129–30, 132, 146
"equality of right" 130, 132, 133, 134, 135,
138, 140, 146
esteem/respect, 132–3, 146
Grotius/Pufendorf comparison, 138–9,
145, 146
Hobbes and, 129, 147 n10
moral effects, 130, 131, 133–4
moral/physical entities, 130–1, 132
moral power, 130, 131, 133–4
natural law, 129, 131, 132, 134
normativity, 130, 131
obligations, 130, 131, 132, 134, 135, 136,
137, 139
"Pufendorf's Point" 137, 138, 146
rights, 130, 134, 135
sanctions, 130, 131, 137, 138, 147–8 n10
second-personal standpoint, 137
shame, 135
slavery, 99, 118 n4
"sociability" 129, 132, 133
sociability and God's moral power, 130–3,
135, 139, 146
Pufendorf, Samuel: works by
De Jure Naturae et Gentium, 131
De Officio, 147 n7
On the Duty of Man and Citizen, 99, 129, 130
On the Law of Nature and Nations, 131–
2, 135–6
Two Books of the Elements of Universal
Jurisprudence, 132, 138
punishment, 230
Fichte: punishment for criminals, 210–11,
219 n15

Grotius: punishment for violation of dignity,
143, 149 n19
Hegel: punishment as the right of the
transgressor, 38
right to punish, 107, 143
See also sanctions
Putnam, Hilary, 390 n18

Rabossi, Eduardo, 21 n2
racism, 38, 80, 108, 110, 262, 265, 331, 361 n35
harm-based view of discrimination, 254–7
racial discrimination, 251–3, 254–7
racial hatred, 252
Railton, Peter, 5, 7, 14, 16–17, 273–90
rationality
ancient Greece, 7–8, 56, 61–2
animals, 78, 87, 293
being rational: being accountable and having
claim to recognition, 6
Descartes, René, 5
Fichte, Johann Gottlieb, 203, 204, 211, 215
humans as rational beings, 7–8
inalienable freedom of rational beings, 112
Kant, Immanuel, 11–12, 74, 187–8, 196, 203, 211
Leibniz, Gottfried Wilhelm, 10, 109, 110–
11, 113–17
limited nature of human rationality, 86
moral rights and, 113–15
moral status and, 5, 6, 7, 9, 24
political rationality, 401–6
potential for becoming rational, 114–16
rational nature as metaphysically infinite,
187–8, 196, 197, 199
Spinoza, Baruch, 9, 78, 86–7, 94 nn67–68
See also reason/reasons
Rawls, John, 44 n44, 138, 178 n39, 243 n28, 395
conception, 357 n5
'construction procedure' 390 n19
"good for" 243 n25
metaethics, 390 n19
moral personality, 69 n14
nonrelational value of humanity, 231–2
persons as "self-originating sources of valid
claims" 128
right/good distinction, 241 n7
'separateness of persons' 42 n27, 360 n32
Raz, Joseph, 231, 241 n4, 242 n24, 366
realism, 230
metaphysical realism, 228
moral realism, 230, 238, 276, 376, 378, 383,
390 n19
reason/reasons
animals: strategic reasoning, 216, 221 n31

authority and reason, 10
capacity to reason grounds a special status, 11–12
deontological reason, 327–8
distinction between capacity for judgment
and to reason critically and reflectively, 6–7
"egoistic reason" 127
Kant, Immanuel: instrumental reasoning,
165, 171, 173, 177 n28, 177 n31, 178 n43
Kant, Immanuel: pure practical reason,
155, 156, 163, 164, 165, 169, 170, 177
n31, 280–1
Kant, Immanuel: pure reason, 21, 170,
172, 173
"universal reason"/"conscience" 127–8
See also critical reason; rationality
recognition, 85, 200–1 n15, 355
entitlement to, 35
mirror self-recognition, 213
moral recognition respect, 128, 129
mutual recognition, 13, 19, 20, 212,
283, 328
recognitionworthiness, 31–5, 38, 40
recognitionworthiness/respectworthiness
distinction, 35–8
social recognition, 16, 207, 212, 252
Regan, Tom, 45 n51
regress argument
ending the regress, 263–4, 266, 381, 382
Kant, Immanuel, 158–9, 176 n21, 200 n4
nonrelational value, 231, 234, 263
open-ended regress, 382
regress-stopper, 263, 264
Vellemanian regress, 264–5
relational value, 14, 16, 286–7, 289 n9
animals, 287
basic/equal moral status as relational, 266
definition, 286
ethical behavior and, 238–40
good for something/someone, 225
impersonal/personal forms of, 238–40
normative significance of humanity and,
16, 286–8
normativity, 238, 240
relational/relative value distinction, 286
relational theory of value, 225, 227–31, 234,
242 nn21–2
relational value of humanity, 16, 225, 226,
229, 232–4, 286–8
subjectively experienced flourishing, 263, 264
subjectivity, 265–6
See also absolute value; good for something/
someone
Renan, Ernest, 391 n22

respect, 1, 14, 19, 366
dignity, 19, 128, 146, 174, 248
as direct apprehension of someone's value as
human being, 19
Grotius, Hugo, 138
Kant, Immanuel: respect for humanity, 21,
153, 156, 157–8, 162, 168, 170, 173, 281–
2, 283
moral status: respectworthiness, 28–31,
38, 42 n25
Pufendorf, Samuel: esteem, 132–3, 146
respect for different point of views, 14
respect for the value of humanity, 21
respectworthiness of human beings
as grounded in their capacities for
reasoning, 24
respectworthiness presupposes
concernworthiness, 31
seeking arguments to affirm someone's
dignity is incompatible with moral
respect, 19
self-respect, 252, 253–4, 256, 268 n8
singular respect, 338, 345, 349–52, 356
Reuchlin, Johann, 89 n8
Rickert, Heinrich, 89 n10
rights, 10, 90–1 n27
cosmopolitan right, 219 n11
Fichte: non-rights-bearing human
beings, 209–11
governments unrestricted rights over their
citizens, 9
Grotius: *ius* and sociable relations, meanings
of, 139–41
perfect/imperfect rights, 140, 148 n14
right theories, 128
usufruct rights, 112–13
'utilitarianism of rights' 157
See also animal rights; civil rights; human
rights; moral rights; natural rights
Roman law, 109, 118 n5, 217, 221 n33
Rorty, Richard, 21 n2, 22 n4
Rosati, Connie, 242 n20
Rousseau, Jean-Jacques, 284, 408,
421–2 n17
rule of law, 42 n24
Russell, Bertrand, 326, 372

sanctions, 210, 219
Pufendorf, Samuel, 130, 131, 137, 138, 147–
8 n10
Sangiovanni, Andrea, 7, 14, 15–16, 244
n31, 248–72
Humanity, 263, 266

444 INDEX

Sartre, Jean-Paul, 88 n6, 408, 417, 423 n25
Scanlon, Thomas M., 42 n29, 241 n7, 341
Schafer, Karl, 244 n31
Scheffler, Samuel, 245 n36
Scholastics, 127, 417
Schroeter, Laura, and François Schroeter, 390 n18
secularism, 75
self-interest, 16, 144, 340–1, 379
  Antiphon, 65, 71 n37
  equal social status and, 29
  Gandhi, Mahatma on, 409, 411, 412
  self-interested love, 112, 175 n7
self/the self, 226
  duties to the self, 166–7, 226, 253, 254
  duty of self-improvement, 277–9
  human flourishing and integral sense of self, 254, 261
  inferiorizing treatment and integral sense of self, 16, 250, 252, 253, 254, 268 n17
  noumenal self, 343
  reflective self-consciousness, 204, 206–7, 215, 216
  self-consciousness, 22 n6, 74, 75, 77, 89 n8, 204, 206–7, 213, 215, 216
  self-love/self-esteem, 84–5, 127, 333 n10
  self-presentation, 252–3
  self-preservation, 9, 102, 103, 119 n14, 129, 215
  self-respect, 252, 253–4, 256, 268 n8
  suicide, 253, 254, 379, 383
Sen, Amartya, 401–2, 411, 420 n9, 421 n13
Seneca, 62, 260
sentience, 207
  as capacity for sensation, 41 n11
  moral status of nonrational animals, 6
  sensation as criterion for moral status, 27, 28, 39, 206
  See also Hume, David
Setiya, Kieran, 18–19, 314–36, 358 n18, 360 n33
  "Love and the Value of a Life" 315
sexism, 38, 331
Sextus Empiricus, 56, 63, 66
Sidgwick, Henry, 127–8, 227
Singer, Peter, 45 n51, 69 n14, 219 n17
  "speciesism" 331
Skorupski, John, 45 n52
slavery
  abolition of, 249
  absolute power over slaves, 98, 104, 107, 108, 117, 118
  AI (artificial intelligence), 217
  ancient Greece, 69 n15

Aristotle, 8, 10, 53, 54, 60, 64, 98, 99, 100, 102, 106, 113, 114, 115
chattel slavery, 10, 97, 98, 99, 105, 107, 108, 109, 118 n4
cruelty, 99
dignity and, 29
early modern Europe, 98–9
Fundamental Constitutions of Carolina, 108
Grotius, Hugo, 99, 100
happiness of slaves, 10, 112, 113
hereditary slavery, 101, 104–5, 107, 108, 109, 120 n29
Hobbes, Thomas, 9, 98, 100, 101–5, 117
legitimate forms of slavery, 98, 107
Leibniz, Gottfried Wilhelm, 10, 98, 100, 101, 109–17, 120 n33, 122 n48
Locke, John, 9, 10, 98, 100, 101, 105–8, 117, 118 n3
modern philosophy, 97, 98, 99–100, 117
natural law, 100–1, 111
natural slavery, 10, 64, 98, 99, 100, 102, 106, 113–14, 115, 118 n6
New World slavery, 107–8, 118 n3
ownership rights over slaves, 9, 98, 99–100, 102, 104–5, 108, 109, 110, 112–13, 116–17, 118, 118 n1, 118 n4, 121 n40
penal slavery, 101
as permissible, 100–1, 107, 110, 113, 115, 118, 122 n48
Pufendorf, Samuel, 99, 118 n4
right to equality, 97–8
right to freedom, 9, 10, 97–8, 113, 116, 117
Roman law, 109, 118 n5, 217, 221 n33
slave trade, 10, 99, 107–8, 206
special status of human beings and intrinsic value, 97, 98
subjection of children and women, 10, 98, 99, 101
value of humanity and, 9–10, 97
voluntary slavery, 100, 107, 108, 109
war and, 9, 100–1, 104, 107, 108, 110, 118 n8, 120 n33
See also Hobbes, Thomas; Leibniz, Gottfried Wilhelm; Locke, John
social contract
  contractualism, 18, 314, 319–22, 324, 332, 402, 403
  Hobbes, Thomas, 101, 103–4, 119 n13
  Locke, John, 402, 403, 404, 405
social relations, 10
  animals: social cooperation, 213–14, 219–20 nn18–23

INDEX 445

consensual relationships and moral status, 29–30, 31, 35, 38
dignity and sociability, 129, 146
Fichte: social cooperation, 13, 205, 207–8, 209, 213–14, 216–17, 219 n11, 219–20 nn18–23
Grotius: sociability, 129, 138–9, 140, 141, 143, 144–6
human sociality, 16, 17, 283, 288
Pufendorf: sociability, 129, 130–3, 135, 139, 146
relationships as noninstrumentally good/bad for us, 259–62
universal sympathy, 16–17, 283
See also community; recognition; relational value
Socrates, 48, 51, 58, 71 n34, 226, 228, 236–7
solipsism, 198, 238
Sophists, 8, 64, 65
Sophocles
Antigone, 64–5, 71 n35
"Ode to Man" 76
Spinoza, Baruch, 8–9, 74–94
acquiescentia (self-esteem), 84–5
"all men share the same common nature" 80–1
animals/human beings distinction, 78–9, 80–1, 91 n30
anthropomorphism, critique of, 76–7, 90 n17
anti-humanism, 76–7, 87–8
"being-in-God" 9, 85, 87, 93 n63
cognition, 84–5, 86
critique of, 87–8, 90 n17
dignity, 77, 82–6, 93 n54
equality, 80–1
fellow feeling, 9, 14
friendship, 78, 80–2, 87, 91 n32
God, 81–2, 92 nn38–43, 94 n68
good/the good, 94 n68
Hegel and, 87–8
'Highest Good' 86
human flourishing, 77
Leibniz and, 90 n17
national honor, 83
naturalism, 77
Nietzsche and, 77
rationality, 9, 78, 86–7, 94 nn67–68
value of humanity, 77, 87, 94 n70
vegetarianism, 78, 79–80
Spinoza, Baruch: works by
Ethics, 77, 78, 79–81, 83, 84–5, 86, 87, 89 n10, 90 nn19–21, 91 nn28–30, 91 n33, 92 n43, 93 n55, 94 n68, 94 n70

Letters, 76, 90 n17
Metaphysical Thoughts, 89–90 n13
Political Treatise, 77, 80
Theological-Political Treatise, 80, 81–2, 86
Treatise on the Emendation of the Intellect, 76, 82–3
Stobaeus, Joannes, 50, 67 n2, 68 n8
Stoics, 67 n2
good things/the good, 49, 67 n5
human capacity to form a "community in law and agreement" 68 n11
humans/animals/plants distinction, 55–6, 69 n17
indifference, 49–50
kinship with the divine, 8, 61–2
"life in agreement" 50, 67 n6
rationality, 61–2
value, 49–50
value of humanity, 50–1, 54, 60–2
virtue, 49, 50, 51, 67 n5
Strauss, David, 379, 390 n20
Strawson, Peter, 43 n42, 44 n45, 137, 370, 377, 383
Suarez, Francisco, 140
subjectivity
absolute value as intersubjective value, 358 n17
human flourishing and, 263–4, 265–6, 267
'principle of subjective freedom' 72 n39
relational value, 265–6
subjective capacity for valuing, 266
subjective value, 358 n17
sublimity
infinity and the sublime, 197
sublimity of humanity, 196–200, 279–80
suicide, 253, 254, 379, 383
Sussman, David, 238, 239
sympathy, 411–12
human sociality: universal sympathy, 16–17, 283
Hume, David, 17, 302–3, 304, 305–6, 308

Taurek, John, 316
terrorism, 66
Theunissen, L. Nandi, 1–2, 3, 14–15, 16, 67 n5, 94 n70, 225–47, 264, 265–7, 270 nn34–5
The Value of Humanity, 240 n1, 251
Thomasius, Christian, 99, 100
Thompson, Michael, 334 n30
Thomson, Judith Jarvis, 227, 241 n9, 243–4 n30, 322
Thucydides, 66

446 INDEX

Timmermann, Jens, 176 n17, 243 n24
Tomasello, Michael, 221 n31
Tuck, Richard, 141–2, 143, 148 n16
Tyrrell, James, 100

unconditional value, 10, 14, 358 n17
    love and unconditional value, 340, 345, 349
    unconditional authorization, 276–7
    unconditionally good, 12, 153, 154, 158, 178
        n37, 269 n27
    unconditional value of human beings, 12,
        248, 250, 253, 262, 263
utilitarianism, 128, 284, 355, 390 n18, 395
    hedonistic utilitarianism, 41 n27
'utilitarianism of rights' 157

Valla, Lorenzo, 89 n8
value
    ancient Greece, 1, 49–55
    apaxia ("disvalue"), 49, 50
    axia, 49, 50, 51, 68 n8
    constructivism, 276
    ethical/nonethical values distinction, 67 n5
    Fichte, Johann Gottlieb, 202–3
    happiness and, 50, 67 n4
    having value/having worth distinction, 264
    Kant, Immanuel: promoted/respected values,
        157–8, 168, 175 n16
    power structures and, 3
    pursuing things that have value, 50, 67 n2
    tên dosin kai timen kath'hauto, 68 n8
    things of value, 67 n2
    usefulness and, 178 n36
    well-being and, 50
    See also invention of value
value of humanity, 1, 21, 48, 87, 343, 366
    absolute value of humanity, 153, 154, 273,
        276, 285, 286, 287, 288, 366
    ancient Greece, 7–8, 48–9, 50–5, 57–62,
        65–7, 69 n15
    challenges in understanding of, 2, 226
    fellow feeling as "basis" of the value of
        humanity, 17
    Fichte, Johann Gottlieb, 202, 203, 217–18 n1
    Gandhi, Mahatma, 21, 396, 398, 416, 419
    human flourishing as value of humanity, 240
    Hume, David, 291, 301–4, 306, 308–11
    infinite value of humanity, 285, 286, 287, 288
    invention of value and, 367–8, 374–6, 382–
        3, 386
    love and, 338–42, 345
    as metaphysical fact, 366
    moral beliefs and, 5

moral value of humanity, 8, 15, 16, 291,
    304, 306
naïveness, 2, 21 n2, 225
Nietzsche, Friedrich, 367, 374–5, 378,
    382, 383
nonrelational value of humanity, 231–2
    privilege and, 2
relational value of humanity, 16, 225, 226,
    229, 232–4, 286–8
rethinking of, 5, 7, 226
Spinoza, Baruch, 77, 87, 94 n70
sublimity of humanity, 196–200
    See also good for something/someone;
        Hume, David; Kant on dignity and
        humanity
valuers, 12–13, 20, 225, 276
    animals as, 94 n70
    being beneficial for themselves, 15, 94 n70, 234
    as condition of the values of things, 12, 17, 189
    human flourishing, 266, 267, 244 n31, 270 n33
    infinite value of, 13, 189, 193
    invention of value, 236
    subjectivity, 266
    See also invention of value; valuing
valuing, 276
    capacity for valuing, 15, 236, 266, 270 n34
    capacity for valuing as metaphysically
        infinite, 187–9, 195–6
    as having a final end, 245 n36
    human flourishing and capacity for valuing,
        266, 267
    misvaluation, 181
    protection of the valued as part of valuing it,
        15, 240
    pure practical reason and, 276
    relational value, 286
    subjective capacity for, 266
    value of the capacity to value, 15, 236
    valuing and living well for human beings, 15,
        233, 234–7, 238, 244 n35, 266–7
    valuing perspectives, 12, 13, 14, 20, 266
    See also incomparability; infinity/the infinite;
        invention of value; valuers
Varner, Gary, 40 n6
Varro, 55
Vasquez, Gabriel, 142
veganism, 44 n47
vegetarianism, 44 n47, 78, 79–80
Velleman, J. David, 42 n27, 358 n18, 359 n20
    love, 315, 332 n5, 342, 359 n20
    moral standing, 315
    nonrelational value of humanity, 231–2
    persons as good simpliciter, 262–3

respect, 315
value comparisons involving persons are inapt, 181–2, 183
Vellemanian regress, 264–5
vice
ancient Greece, 49, 51, 68 n9
Hume, David, 296, 298–9, 307, 309, 311
virtue
ancient Greece, 50, 51, 227
animals, 293, 307–8, 312 n11
Aristotle, 17, 51, 60
"artificial virtues" 305, 307
"great-souledness" 51
Hume, David, 17, 296, 298–9, 300, 303–4, 305, 307–8, 310
Kant, Immanuel: self-constraint and struggle, 16, 278, 279–80
Leibniz, Gottfried Wilhelm, 10, 114–15, 116, 122 n47
"natural virtues," 305
Stoics, 49, 50, 51, 67 n5
Vlastos, Gregory, 377
Vogt, Katja Maria, 241 n11, 244 n34
Von Wright, Georg. H., 241 n9

Walden, Kenneth, 5, 7, 11, 12–13, 14, 16, 20, 181–201, 232
war, 260, 261
English Civil War, 99
just war, 9, 100, 107, 108
slavery and, 9, 100–1, 104, 107, 108, 110, 118 n8, 120 n33
state of war, 103, 107
values as weapons of class warfare, 371
World War II, 75, 249
Welchman, Jennifer, 120 n29

well-being, 10, 24
friendship and, 257–8
value and, 50, 67 n4
See also happiness
Wellhausen, Julius, 379, 390 n20
Williams, Bernard, 22 n9, 355, 387 n8, 395, 417
Williams, Zoe, 66
Wilson, Catherine, 120–1 n35
Windelband, Wilhelm, 89 n10, 387 n6
Winstanley, Gerard, 403–4
Wittgenstein, Ludwig, 319, 329, 410, 413–16
women
Aristotle, 8, 53, 60
Fichte, Johann Gottlieb, 206
moral value as human beings, 8, 361 n35
subjection of, 10, 98, 99, 101, 119 n11
Wood, Allen, 176 n17, 177 n29, 284
works of art, 230, 347
love as essence of art, 198
as noninstrumentally good for us, 232–3, 243 n26
as valuable things, 67 n2, 184, 270 n34
See also aesthetics
worthiness
ancient Greece: *axiôma*, 50
dignity as noninstrumental worthiness, 83, 93 n54
having value/having worth distinction, 264
Wycliffe, John, 3

Xenophanes, 76

Yaffe, Gideon, 255, 256

Zeno of Citium, 62, 70 n24